Horizons, 6th Edition

Joan H. Manley, Stuart Smith, John T. McMinn, Marc A. Prévost

Custom Edition

UBC Department of French, Hispanic and Italian Studies

FREN 101 & 102

1914–2014
Nelson Education celebrates 100 years of Canadian publishing

NELSON / EDUCATION

COPYRIGHT © 2015 by Nelson Education Ltd.

Printed and bound in Canada
3 4 5 18 17 16

For more information contact Nelson Education Ltd., 1120 Birchmount Road, Toronto, Ontario, M1K 5G4. Or you can visit our Internet site at http://www.nelson.com

ISBN-13: 978-0-17-658836-6
ISBN-10: 0-17-658836-1

Consists of Selections from:

Horizons, 6th Edition
Joan H. Manley, Stuart Smith, Marc A. Prévost, John T. McMinn
ISBN 10: 1-285-42828-5, © 2015

Cover Credit:

Nejron Photo/Shutterstock

Brief Contents

CHAPITRE PRÉLIMINAIRE: On commence!.. 2

CHAPITRE 1: À l'université 28

CHAPITRE 2: Après les cours 64

CHAPITRE 3: Un nouvel appartement.. 104

CHAPITRE 4: En famille 140

CHAPITRE 5: Les projets 178

CHAPITRE 6: Les sorties 220

CHAPITRE 7: La vie quotidienne 258

CHAPITRE 8: La bonne cuisine 300

CHAPITRE 9: En vacances.. 340

TABLEAUX DES VERBES 370

VOCABULAIRE FRANÇAIS – ANGLAIS 376

VOCABULAIRE ANGLAIS – FRANÇAIS 395

INDEX 410

TABLE DES MATIÈRES

© Bucchi Francesco/Shutterstock.com

Le monde francophone	Themes and Functions	Vocabulary	Culture
CHAPITRE PRÉLIMINAIRE: On commence! • 2			
Regional Focus: Bienvenue dans le monde francophone! • 4			
COMPÉTENCE 1	**Greeting people**	Les formules de politesse *6* Les salutations familières *8*	
COMPÉTENCE 2	**Counting and describing your week**	Les nombres de zéro à trente *10* Les jours de la semaine *12*	
COMPÉTENCE 3	**Talking about yourself and your schedule**	Un autoportrait *14* L'heure *16*	
COMPÉTENCE 4	**Communicating in class**	En cours *20* Des expressions utiles et l'alphabet *22*	
COMPARAISONS CULTURELLES • 24			**L'heure officielle** *24*
VOCABULAIRE • 26			

Sur la Côte d'Azur	Themes and Functions	Vocabulary
CHAPITRE 1: À l'université · 28		
Regional Focus: La France et ses régions · 30		
COMPÉTENCE 1	**Identifying people and describing appearance**	Les gens à l'université *32*
COMPÉTENCE 2	**Describing personality**	Les personnalités *38*
COMPÉTENCE 3	**Describing the university area**	Le campus et le quartier *44*
COMPÉTENCE 4	**Talking about your studies**	L'université et les cours *50*
LECTURE ET COMPOSITION · 56		
COMPARAISONS CULTURELLES · 58		
RÉSUMÉ DE GRAMMAIRE · 60		
VOCABULAIRE · 62		
CHAPITRE 2: Après les cours · 64		
Regional Focus: Nice · 66		
COMPÉTENCE 1	**Saying what you like to do**	Le temps libre et les loisirs *68*
COMPÉTENCE 2	**Saying how you spend your free time**	Le week-end *74*
COMPÉTENCE 3	**Asking about someone's day**	La journée *82*
COMPÉTENCE 4	**Going to the café**	Au café *88*
LECTURE ET COMPOSITION · 94		
COMPARAISONS CULTURELLES · 96		
RÉSUMÉ DE GRAMMAIRE · 98		
VOCABULAIRE · 100		
Interlude musical · 102		*Je suis* (Amel Bent) *Chantez, chantez* (Amadou Bagayoko and Mariam Doumbia)

	Structures	Culture	Learning Strategies, Readings, Listening Passages, Writing Strategies
			Stratégies et Lecture *36* **Pour mieux lire:** *Using cognates and familiar words to read for the gist* **Lecture:** *Qui est-ce?*
	Les adjectifs et **il est / elle est** + adjectif ou **c'est** + nom *34*		
	Les pronoms sujets, le verbe **être,** la négation et d'autres adjectifs *40* Les questions *42*		
	Le genre, l'article indéfini et l'expression **il y a** *46* **C'est** ou **il est / elle est** et la place de l'adjectif *48*		
	L'article défini *52* **Vidéoreprise:** *Les Stagiaires 54*		
			Pour mieux lire: *Scanning to preview a text 56* **Lecture:** *L'accent grave* **Pour mieux écrire:** *Using and combining what you know 57* **Composition:** *Un autoportrait*
		Les études *58*	
			Stratégies et Compréhension auditive *72* **Pour mieux comprendre:** *Listening for specific information* **Compréhension auditive:** *On sort ensemble?*
	L'infinitif *70*		
	Les verbes en **-er** et les adverbes *76* Quelques verbes à changements orthographiques *80*		
	Les mots interrogatifs *84* Les questions par inversion *86*		
	Les nombres de trente à cent et l'argent *90* **Vidéoreprise:** *Les Stagiaires 92*		
			Pour mieux lire: *Making intelligent guesses 94* **Lecture:** *Aux Trois Obus* **Pour mieux écrire:** *Using logical order and standard phrases 95* **Composition:** *Au café*
		Les cafés en France *96*	

En Amérique	Themes and Functions	Vocabulary
CHAPITRE 3: Un nouvel appartement • 104		
Regional Focus: En Amérique: Le Canada et le Québec • 106		
COMPÉTENCE 1	**Talking about where you live**	Le logement *108*
COMPÉTENCE 2	**Talking about your possessions**	Les effets personnels *114*
COMPÉTENCE 3	**Describing your room**	Les meubles et les couleurs *120*
COMPÉTENCE 4	**Giving your address and phone number**	Des renseignements *126*
LECTURE ET COMPOSITION • 132		
COMPARAISONS CULTURELLES • 134		
RÉSUMÉ DE GRAMMAIRE • 136		
VOCABULAIRE • 138		
CHAPITRE 4: En famille • 140		
Regional Focus: En Amérique: En Louisiane • 142		
COMPÉTENCE 1	**Describing your family**	Ma famille *144*
COMPÉTENCE 2	**Saying where you go in your free time**	Le temps libre *150*
COMPÉTENCE 3	**Saying what you are going to do**	Le week-end prochain *156*
COMPÉTENCE 4	**Planning how to get there**	Les moyens de transport *162*
LECTURE ET COMPOSITION • 168		
COMPARAISONS CULTURELLES • 170		
RÉSUMÉ DE GRAMMAIRE • 172		
VOCABULAIRE • 174		
Interlude musical • 176		*Fille de Ville* (Marie-Élaine Thibert) *Nonc Willie* (Bruce Daigrepont)

Structures	Culture	Learning Strategies, Readings, Listening Passages, Writing Strategies
Les nombres au-dessus de 100 et les nombres ordinaux *110*		**Stratégies et Lecture** *112* **Pour mieux lire:** *Guessing meaning from context* **Lecture:** *Un nouvel appartement*
Le verbe **avoir** *116* Quelques prépositions *118*		
La possession et les adjectifs possessifs **mon, ton** et **son** *122* Les adjectifs possessifs **notre, votre** et **leur** *124*		
Les adjectifs *ce* et **quel** *128* Vidéoreprise: *Les Stagiaires 130*		
		Pour mieux lire: *Previewing content 132* **Lecture:** *Les couleurs et leurs effets sur la nature humaine* **Pour mieux écrire:** *Brainstorming 133* **Composition:** *Un mail*
	Le Québec d'aujourd'hui *134*	
Les expressions avec **avoir** *146*		**Stratégies et Compréhension auditive** *148* **Pour mieux comprendre:** *Asking for clarification* **Compréhension auditive:** *La famille de Robert*
Le verbe **aller**, la préposition **à** et le pronom **y** *152* Le pronom sujet **on** et l'impératif *154*		
Le futur immédiat *158* Les dates *160*		
Les verbes **prendre** et **venir** et les moyens de transport *164* Vidéoreprise: *Les Stagiaires 166*		
		Pour mieux lire: *Using your knowledge of the world 168* **Lecture:** *Deux mots* **Pour mieux écrire:** *Visualizing your topic 169* **Composition:** *Ma famille*
	L'histoire des Cadiens *170*	

À Paris	Themes and Functions	Vocabulary
CHAPITRE 5: Les projets • 178		
Regional Focus: La France • 180		
COMPÉTENCE 1	**Saying what you did**	Le week-end dernier *182*
COMPÉTENCE 2	**Telling where you went**	Je suis parti(e) en voyage *188*
COMPÉTENCE 3	**Discussing the weather and your activities**	Le temps et les projets *194*
COMPÉTENCE 4	**Deciding what to wear and buying clothes**	Les vêtements *200*
LECTURE ET COMPOSITION • 208		
COMPARAISONS CULTURELLES • 210		
RÉSUMÉ DE GRAMMAIRE • 212		
VOCABULAIRE • 214		
Bienvenue en Europe francophone • 216		
CHAPITRE 6: Les sorties • 220		
Regional Focus: Paris • 222		
COMPÉTENCE 1	**Inviting someone to go out**	Les invitations *224*
COMPÉTENCE 2	**Talking about how you spend and used to spend your time**	Aujourd'hui et dans le passé *230*
COMPÉTENCE 3	**Talking about the past**	Une sortie *236*
COMPÉTENCE 4	**Narrating in the past**	Les contes *242*
LECTURE ET COMPOSITION • 248		
COMPARAISONS CULTURELLES • 250		
RÉSUMÉ DE GRAMMAIRE • 252		
VOCABULAIRE • 254		
Interlude musical • 256		*La garde-robe d'Élizabeth* (Amélie-les-crayons) *Premier amour* (Tony Parker/Rickwel)

Structures	Culture	Learning Strategies, Readings, Listening Passages, Writing Strategies
		Stratégies et Lecture *186* **Pour mieux lire:** *Using the sequence of events to make logical guesses* **Lecture:** *Qu'est-ce qu'elle a fait?*
Le passé composé avec **avoir** *184*		
Le passé composé avec **être** *190* Les expressions qui désignent le passé et reprise du passé composé *192*		
Le verbe **faire**, l'expression **ne... rien** et les expressions pour décrire le temps *196* Les expressions avec **faire** *198*		
Les pronoms **le, la, l'** et **les** *202* Vidéoreprise: *Les Stagiaires 206*		
		Pour mieux lire: *Using visuals to make guesses 208* **Lecture:** *Je blogue donc je suis* **Pour mieux écrire:** *Using standard organizing techniques 209* **Composition:** *Un voyage en France*
	Le sport et le temps libre des Français *210*	

Structures	Culture	Learning Strategies, Readings, Listening Passages, Writing Strategies
		Stratégies et Compréhension auditive *228* **Pour mieux comprendre:** *Noting the important information* **Compréhension auditive:** *On va au cinéma?*
Les verbes **vouloir, pouvoir** et **devoir** *226*		
L'imparfait *232* Les verbes **sortir, partir** et **dormir** *234*		
L'imparfait et le passé composé *238* Le passé composé et l'imparfait *240*		
Le passé composé et l'imparfait (reprise) *244* Vidéoreprise: *Les Stagiaires 246*		
		Pour mieux lire: *Using standard formats 248* **Lecture:** *Deux films français* **Pour mieux écrire:** *Using standard formats 249* **Composition:** *Un film à voir*
	Le cinéma: les préférences des Français *250*	

La Normandie	Themes and Functions	Vocabulary
CHAPITRE 7: La vie quotidienne • 258		
Regional Focus: La France et sa diversité • 260		
COMPÉTENCE 1	**Describing your daily routine**	La vie de tous les jours *262*
COMPÉTENCE 2	**Talking about relationships**	La vie sentimentale *270*
COMPÉTENCE 3	**Talking about what you did and used to do**	Les activités d'hier *278*
COMPÉTENCE 4	**Describing traits and characteristics**	Les traits de caractère *284*
LECTURE ET COMPOSITION • 290		
COMPARAISONS CULTURELLES • 294		
RÉSUMÉ DE GRAMMAIRE • 296		
VOCABULAIRE • 298		
CHAPITRE 8: La bonne cuisine • 300		
Regional Focus: La Normandie • 302		
COMPÉTENCE 1	**Ordering at a restaurant**	Au restaurant *304*
COMPÉTENCE 2	**Buying food**	Les courses *314*
COMPÉTENCE 3	**Talking about meals**	Les repas *322*
LECTURE ET COMPOSITION • 330		
COMPARAISONS CULTURELLES • 332		
RÉSUMÉ DE GRAMMAIRE • 334		
VOCABULAIRE • 336		
Interlude musical • 338		*Retomber amoureux* (Chimène Badi) *Pour toi* (Princess Sarah)

Structures	Culture	Learning Strategies, Readings, Listening Passages, Writing Strategies
Les verbes réfléchis au présent *264*		**Stratégies et Lecture** *268* **Pour mieux lire:** *Using word families and watching out for* **faux amis** **Lecture:** *Il n'est jamais trop tard!*
Les verbes réciproques au présent et les verbes réfléchis et réciproques au futur immédiat *272* Les verbes en **-re** *276*		
Les verbes réfléchis et réciproques au passé composé *280* Les verbes réfléchis et réciproques à l'imparfait et reprise de l'usage du passé composé et de l'imparfait *282*		
Les pronoms relatifs **qui, que** et **dont** *286* **Vidéoreprise:** *Les Stagiaires 288*		
		Pour mieux lire: *Recognizing conversational style 290* **Lecture:** *Conte pour enfants de moins de trois ans* **Pour mieux écrire:** *Organizing a paragraph 293* **Composition:** *Le matin chez moi*
	L'amour et le couple *294*	

Structures	Culture	Learning Strategies, Readings, Listening Passages, Writing Strategies
Le partitif *310*		**Stratégies et Compréhension auditive** *312* **Pour mieux comprendre:** *Planning and predicting* **Compréhension auditive:** *Au restaurant*
Les expressions de quantité *318* L'usage des articles *320*		
Le pronom **en** et le verbe **boire** *324* Les verbes en **-ir** *326*		
Vidéoreprise: *Les Stagiaires 328*		
		Pour mieux lire: *Reading a poem 330* **Lecture:** *Déjeuner du matin* **Pour mieux écrire:** *Finding the right word 331* **Composition:** *Une critique gastronomique*
	À table! *332*	

Aux Antilles	Themes and Functions	Vocabulary
CHAPITRE 9: En vacances • 340		
Regional Focus: La France d'outre-mer • 342		
COMPÉTENCE 1	**Talking about vacation**	Les vacances *344*
COMPÉTENCE 2	**Preparing for a trip**	Les préparatifs *350*
COMPÉTENCE 4	**Deciding where to go on a trip**	Un voyage *356*
LECTURE ET COMPOSITION • 362		
COMPARAISONS CULTURELLES • 364		
RÉSUMÉ DE GRAMMAIRE • 366		
VOCABULAIRE • 368		

Structures	Culture	Learning Strategies, Readings, Listening Passages, Writing Strategies
		Stratégies et Lecture *348* **Pour mieux lire:** *Recognizing compound tenses* **Lecture:** *Quelle aventure!*
Le futur *346* Les verbes **dire, lire** et **écrire** *352* Les pronoms compléments d'objet indirect **(lui, leur)** et reprise des pronoms compléments d'objet direct **(le, la, l', les)** *354*		
Les expressions géographiques *358* **Vidéoreprise:** *Les Stagiaires 360*		
		Pour mieux lire: *Understanding words with multiple meanings 362* **Lecture:** *Ma grand-mère m'a appris à ne pas compter sur les yeux des autres pour dormir* **Pour mieux écrire:** *Revising what you write 363* **Composition:** *Un itinéraire*
	La culture créole aux Antilles *364*	

TABLEAUX DES VERBES • 370

VOCABULAIRE
  FRANÇAIS – ANGLAIS • 376

VOCABULAIRE
  ANGLAIS – FRANÇAIS • 395

INDEX • 410

PREFACE

Do you have a gift for languages?

Have you ever heard people say that they know someone who has a gift for languages? What does that mean? Are some people born with a special ability to learn languages? How do you know if you have a gift for languages? If you understood the sentence you just read, then you have a gift for languages. After all, you have already learned to speak and understand at least one language well—English. Everybody is born with a natural ability to learn languages, but some individuals seem to learn languages more quickly than others do. This is because, over time, we develop different learning styles.

The process individuals use to learn languages depends a great deal on their personality. As with any other process, such as learning a new computer program or writing a composition for English class, individuals can attain similar results, although they approach the task differently. Some language learners like to plan each step before beginning. Others prefer to jump in as soon as they know enough to get started, and continue from there using a hit-or-miss method. Some language learners like to understand in detail why a language works the way it does before they try to use it, whereas others are ready to try speaking as soon as they know only the most basic rules, making educated guesses about how to express themselves.

Both methods have advantages and disadvantages. Some people become so bogged down in details that they lose sight of their main purpose—communication. Others pay so little attention to details that what they say is unintelligible. No matter what sort of learner you are, the most important part of the language-learning process is to constantly try to use the language to express yourself. Always alternate study of vocabulary and structures with attempts to communicate.

Since you now know that you have a gift for languages, you might think of the following pages as a user's manual that suggests how to use your language-learning capacity to learn French efficiently. Some of the learning techniques will work for you, others may not fit your learning style. Read through the following three sections before beginning your French studies, and refer to them later to develop the language-learning process that works best for you.

- **Goals and expectations:** How much French should you expect to learn in your first year of study and how much time and effort will be required of you?
- **Motivation:** How do you motivate yourself to study and practice the language?
- **Learning techniques:** What are some study tips that will facilitate learning French?

GOALS AND EXPECTATIONS
Who can learn a language?

Many people believe that, as an adult, you cannot learn a language as well as you might have when you were a child. It is true that children are good language learners, but there is no reason why adults cannot learn to speak a language with near-native fluency. Children learn languages well because they can adapt very easily and they do it willingly. Being able to adapt is very important in language learning. Children are not afraid to try something new, and they are not easily embarrassed if things do not turn out as they expect. Adults, on the other hand, are often afraid of doing something wrong or looking ridiculous. Don't be afraid to experiment, using what you already know to guess at how to express yourself in French. It does no harm if you try to say something and you do not get the expected response. Just try again.

By the time people become adults, they generally learn by analyzing, rather than by doing. They have also grown so accustomed to their own way of doing things that they are reluctant to change. Similarly, adult language learners often feel that the way English works is the natural way. They try to force the language they are learning into the same mold. In fact, languages work in a variety of ways, all equally natural. Learn to accept that the French way of doing things is just as natural and valid as the English way.

Another difference in the way that children and adults learn languages is that children spend a lot more time focused on what they are doing. When children learn languages, they spend almost every hour they are awake for several years doing nothing but learning the language. Learning to communicate is their principal objective in life. Most adults, on the other hand, spend just a few hours a week studying a new language, and during this time they are often distracted by many other aspects of their lives. In a classroom setting where small children have contact with a foreign language for just a few hours per week, children do not learn better than adults. In fact, adults have several advantages over children, such as their ability to organize and their longer attention spans. Your ability to develop fluency in French depends mainly on three things: the amount of time you spend with the language, how focused you are, and how willing you are to try to communicate using it.

How well will you speak after a year?

Those of you who are new to foreign language study probably have a variety of ideas about what you will be doing in this course. People who become frustrated in foreign language study generally do so because they start off with the wrong expectations. Some people begin a foreign language course with a negative attitude, thinking that it is impossible to really learn a language without going to a country where it is spoken. Although it is indeed usually easier to learn French in a French-speaking region, you can learn to speak French very fluently here as well. Once again, it is a question of spending time with the language, while focusing on how to communicate with it.

There are also some students who begin foreign language classes with expectations that are too high, thinking that they will begin speaking French with complete fluency nearly overnight. Learning a language takes time. Even after two years of concentrated study, it is reasonable to have achieved only basic fluency. If you set a goal for yourself to have everyday conversation skills after your second year of study, and if you work hard toward this goal, you will be able to function in most everyday conversation settings; however, you will still frequently have to look for words, you will probably still speak in short simple sentences, and you will often have to use circumlocution to get your meaning across. In *Horizons,* you will learn how to function in the most common situations in which you are likely to find yourself in a francophone region. To illustrate how much you will learn during the first few weeks of study, take out a sheet of paper, and list, in English, the first eight questions you would probably ask in the following situation: Before the first day of class, you sit down next to a student you have never seen before and you begin to chat.

In this situation, students generally ask questions like the following:

- How are you doing?
- What's your name?
- What are you studying?
- Where are you from?
- Where do you live? / Do you live on campus?
- Do you like it there?
- Do you work? Where?
- When are you graduating?

This is the extent of the conversation that you have with many people you will meet, and you will be able to do this in French after only a few weeks.

How much time and effort must you invest to be a successful language learner?

There are three Ps involved in learning a language: patience, practice, and persistence. We have already said that success in learning a foreign language depends on how much time you spend studying and practicing it. You might wonder how time-consuming French class will be. The amount of time required depends on your study skills and attention span. However, nobody can be successful without devoting many hours to studying and using the language. Generally, to make steady progress at the rate that material is presented in most college or university classes, you should expect to spend two to three hours on the language outside of class, for every hour that you are in class.

What is involved in learning to express yourself in another language?

Students studying a foreign language for the first time may have false expectations about what is involved in learning to speak another language. Many people think that you just substitute a French word for the equivalent word in English. Most of the time, you cannot translate word for word from one language to another. For example, if a French speaker substituted the equivalent English word for each French word in the following sentence, it would create a very unusual sentence.

Nous ne l'avons pas encore fait.
We not it have not still done.

You might be able to figure out that this sentence means, "We haven't done it yet," but sometimes translating word for word can give a completely wrong meaning. For example, if you translate the following sentence word for word, you would think that it has the first meaning that follows it, whereas it really has the second. This is because the indirect object pronoun **vous *([to] you)*** precedes the verb in French.

Je voudrais vous parler demain, s'il vous plaît.
I would like you to speak tomorrow, if it you pleases.
I would like to speak to you tomorrow, please.

You probably noticed in this last example that one word in English may be translated by several words in French and vice versa (**voudrais** = *would like,* **vous** = *to you,* **parler** = *to speak,* **s'il vous plaît** = *please*).

Differences in languages are not due simply to a lack of one-to-one correspondence between words and structures. Cultural differences also strongly affect how we communicate. Culture and language are so interrelated that it is impossible to learn a language fluently without becoming familiar with the culture(s) where it is spoken. For example, in French, a cultural difference that affects the spoken language is that French society is not as informal as ours. Adults generally do not call each other by their first names, and the words for *sir* and *madam* are used much more frequently than in English. For example, it is normal to say **Bonjour, monsieur** *(Hello, sir),* whereas English speakers say *Hello.*

Cultural differences affect the spoken language and also nonverbal communication. For instance, when the French speak to each other, they generally stand closer than we do. When we are talking to a French-speaker, we may feel that our space is invaded and back away. The French may interpret this as being standoffish. As you can see, learning to communicate in French entails a lot more than substituting French words for English words in a sentence.

Does practice make perfect?

Your goal in learning French should not be to say everything perfectly. If you set this goal for yourself, you will probably be afraid to open your mouth, fearing mistakes. Your goal should be to communicate clearly, but you should expect to make mistakes when speaking. If you make a mistake that impedes communication, those you are speaking to will ask for clarification or repeat what you have said to be sure of what you mean. Listen carefully to how they express themselves, and make adjustments the next time you need to convey a similar message.

Although perfection is not the goal of language learners, practice is vital to success. (Remember the three Ps of language learning: patience, practice, and persistence.) You can learn every vocabulary word and rule in the book, but unless you practice regularly, listening to French and attempting to speak it, you will not learn the language. Practicing a language is just as necessary for success as practicing a sport or a musical instrument. Imagine that you are a football player or pianist. You might know every play in the book, or you might understand music theory completely, but unless you practice, you will never be able to perform. It is important to learn the rules of French, but you must also practice it regularly.

What do you do if foreign languages make you panic?

Most individuals feel nervous when they have to speak to strangers. This is true when you speak your own language, and it's even truer when speaking a foreign language. There is no reason to be nervous, yet fear of looking ridiculous is often difficult to control. It is normal to experience some anxiety in class. If you suffer extreme anxiety in language class—to such a degree that it impedes your ability to concentrate—it is best to recognize that you fear having to perform in class. Go see your instructor and discuss your anxiety. In order to conquer it, you must acknowledge it.

MOTIVATION
How can learning a foreign language help you?

Learning a foreign language should be fun. After all, you will spend a lot of class time chatting with classmates, which most of us find enjoyable. However, learning French takes time and effort. No matter how much you enjoy it, there will be times when you need to motivate yourself to study or practice. You can use motivation techniques for practicing a language similar to those musicians or athletes use to practice an instrument or a sport.

Many musicians and athletes have a personal goal. They imagine themselves playing a great concert at Carnegie Hall or winning a big game, receiving applause and praise. Similarly, each time you start to practice French, imagine yourself speaking French fluently with a beautiful accent. In this mental image, you might be a diplomat, or you might be talking to the waiter at a French restaurant, impressing your friends.

Some people who practice an instrument or a sport do so for personal growth. Many people feel that learning

a new language helps them discover a new side of their personality. By learning to appreciate another culture, you learn to understand your own better. You also come to know yourself better and you broaden your horizons.

Of course, a lot of people are motivated to practice an instrument or a sport because they make their living from it. This is good motivation for learning a language too. In today's international economy, the best jobs are going more and more to those who speak more than one language, and who have an understanding of other cultures. Many jobs in the travel industry, in communications, in government, and in companies dealing in international trade and business require proficiency in another language.

How can you learn to enjoy studying?

As with any accomplishment, learning a foreign language requires a lot of work. You will enjoy it more if you think of it as a hobby or a pastime and as an opportunity to develop a skill. Here are some training techniques that can help you learn a new language.

- Get into a routine. Devote a particular time of day to studying French. It is best to find a time when you are fresh and free of distractions, so you can concentrate on what you are doing. If you study at the same time every day, getting started will become habitual, and you will have won half the battle. Once you are settled working and learning, it becomes fun.
- Make sure that the place where you study is inviting and that you enjoy being there.
- Study frequently for short periods of time, rather than having marathon sessions. After about two hours of study, the ability of the brain to retain information is greatly reduced. You tend to remember what you learn at the beginning of each study session and at the end. What you study in the middle tends to become blurred. To illustrate this, read the following words one time, then turn the page and see how many you remember. dog, house, sofa, cat, rooster, room, telephone, mouse, book, pencil, television. Most people can remember the first word and the last. The longer the list, the harder it is to remember the words in the middle. The same is true with studying. Study smaller "chunks" of material more frequently, and set reasonable goals for yourself. Don't try to learn it all at once.
- Study with a classmate or a friend. It is much easier to practice talking with someone else, and it is easier to spend more time working with the language if you are interacting with another person. Also, by studying with classmates, you will feel more comfortable speaking in front of them, which eliminates some of the embarrassment some adults feel when trying to pronounce foreign words in front of the whole class.
- Play games with the language. It is fun to learn how to say things in a new language. For instance, ask yourself how you would say things you hear on the radio or

television in French. If you do know how to say something in French that you hear, your knowledge will become more certain. If you don't know how to say something in French, that's normal if you are a beginner. When you finally learn the word or expression you were wondering about, you will remember it more easily, because you have already thought about it.

- Surround yourself by French. Rent French movies or watch DVDs of American movies in the French-language track, listen to French music, and search the Web for French websites with recent news or topics that interest you. Websites with a lot of pictures are the best, because the pictures give you clues to the meaning of unfamiliar words. You probably will not understand very much at first in movies and songs, but they will motivate you to learn more. They teach you about cultural differences, and they help give you a sense of good pronunciation.

- Don't let yourself get frustrated. If you are frustrated each time you sit down to study, ask yourself why. First of all, make sure that you are not studying when you are too tired or hungry. Also, make sure that you clearly understand your assignment and its purpose. Learn to distinguish a language-learning problem from a problem understanding instructions. If you are confused about what you are to do or why, see your instructor during office hours or contact another student. (This is another reason to study with a classmate!)

LEARNING TECHNIQUES
How can you spend your study time most efficiently?

Individuals organize material differently as they learn it. Some people learn better by seeing something; others learn better by hearing it. The following are some study tips for how to go about learning French. You may find that some of these methods work for you and others do not. Be creative in practicing your French, using a variety of study techniques.

General study tips

- Learn not to translate word for word. Learn to read and listen to whole sentences at a time.

- Keep a log of your study time in a small spiral notebook. This will help you learn to study more efficiently. Each time you sit down to study new material, write down the time you begin. When you finish, write down the time you stop, and two or three sentences summarizing what you studied. Students often feel frustrated that they spend a lot of time studying, but they do not retain much. By keeping a log, you will know exactly how much time you spend on French. Writing one or two sentences summarizing what you studied helps you check your retention.

- Alternate speaking, listening, reading, and writing activities. By changing tasks frequently, you will be able to study longer without losing your concentration.

Vocabulary-learning techniques

- Use your senses. Pronounce words aloud as you study them. Close your eyes as you pronounce the word and picture the thing or activity represented by nouns or verbs.

- Use flashcards. When possible, draw a simple picture instead of the English word. Also, write a sentence using the word on the card, trying to remember it each time you look at the card. Use different colored inks to help you visualize the meaning of words. For example, when studying colors, write them on the flashcard in that color. When learning food items, write the words for red foods, such as strawberries and tomatoes, in red, the words for green foods in green, etc. Write words that can be associated with shapes, such as tall, short, big, small, round, or square, with letters having similar shapes.

- Learn useful common phrases such as "What time is it?" or "How are you?" as a whole.

- Label household items in French on masking tape.

- Tape lists of vocabulary in places where you spend time doing routine tasks.

- Study vocabulary in manageable "chunks." Each morning, write out a list of 20 new words and carry it in your pocket. A few times during the day, spend two minutes trying to remember the words on the list. Take out the list and review the words you forgot for two minutes. By the end of the day, you will have spent just a few minutes and you will have learned the 20 words.

- Learn 10 useful phrases every day.

- Audio of the end-of-chapter vocabulary words is downloadable from the *Horizons* Premium Website. Download it and play it at home, while you jog, or in your car.

- Make tests for yourself. At the end of a study session, write the English words or phrases on a sheet of paper. Put the sheet of paper away for a few hours. Later, take it out and see how many of the French equivalents of these words or phrases you remember.

- Group words in logical categories. For example, learn words for fruits together, words for animals together, sports-related vocabulary together, etc.

- Make flashcards with antonyms on each side, such as hot/cold, near/far, to go to sleep/to wake up, etc.

- Use related English words to help you remember the French. For example, the French word for *to begin* is **commencer.** Associate it with *to commence.* Be creative in finding associations. For example, the word for *open* is **ouvert.** You can associate it with *overture,* which is the opening part of a musical piece, or an *overt* action, which is one that is done in the open. Write related English words on flashcards.

- Learn to say **"Comment dit-on... ?"** (*"How do you say . . . ?"*) when you do not know a word or phrase.

- Remember that we cannot say everything even in our own language. If you do not know a word, try to think of another way to say what you want. Use circumlocution. For example, if you do not know how to say "to drive," say "to take the car" instead.

Grammar-learning techniques

- Play teacher. Try to guess what your instructor would ask you to do if he or she were giving a quiz the next day.
- Do the *Pour vérifier* self-checks in the margins next to explanations of structures.
- Use color coding to help you remember grammatical information. For example, all nouns in French are categorized either as masculine or feminine, and you must memorize in which category each noun belongs. When you make flashcards, write feminine nouns on pink cards or with pink/red ink and use blue for masculine nouns. Use an eye-catching color on flashcards to indicate points you want to remember, such as irregular plurals or verbs that take **être** in the **passé composé.**
- If you like to use lists to study, organize them so that they help you remember information about words. For example, to remember noun gender, write masculine words in a column on the left and feminine words in a column on the right. If you can visualize where the word is on the list, you can remember its gender.
- Learn to accept ambiguity. Sometimes, as soon as you learn a new rule, you find out that it doesn't always work the way you expect it to.

Pronunciation-learning techniques

- Repeat everything you hear in French under your breath or in your head, even if you have no idea what it means. This will not only help your pronunciation, it will help your listening comprehension and your ability to learn vocabulary. For instance, if you keep repeating an unfamiliar word you hear in your head, when you finally find out what it means, you will remember it very easily.
- Read French words aloud as you study.
- Listen to the audio that goes with the book and the Student Activities Manual several times. It is impossible to concentrate both on meaning and pronunciation the first time you listen to them. Listen to them at least once focusing on pronunciation only.
- Make recordings of yourself and compare them to those of native speakers.
- Exaggerate as you practice at home. Any pronunciation that is not English will seem like exaggeration. Psychologically, it is very difficult to listen to yourself speaking another language. Pretend you are a French actor playing a role as you practice pronunciation.
- Listen to French songs on the Internet. Search for the lyrics and sing along.

Using the Text Audio Recordings and the SAM Audio Recordings

There are two distinct sets of audio programs that go with each chapter of the *Horizons* program: the Text Audio and the SAM Audio. The recordings on the Text Audio correspond to the listening sections marked with an audio icon in the textbook. The SAM Audio corresponds to the listening activities in the Student Activities Manual. The audio that accompanies the text is on the *Horizons* Premium Website. It is also accessible via the *iLrn™ Heinle Learning Center.* This audio allows you to review material covered in class on your own, or to prepare for the next day's class. When using the audio, it is important to make sure that you have accessed the right audio for either the textbook activities or the SAM.

In order to get maximum benefit from the recorded listening activities, approach them with the right attitude. It takes time, patience, and practice to understand French spoken at a normal conversational speed. Do not be surprised if you find it difficult at first. Relax and listen to passages more than once. You will understand a little more each time. Remember that you will not understand everything and that, for some exercises, you are only expected to understand enough to answer specific questions. Read through exercises prior to playing the audio, so that you know what to listen for.

If you find you do not have enough time to process and respond to a question before the next one begins, pause the audio to give yourself more time. Most importantly, be patient and remember that you can always listen again.

Be willing to listen to the audio activities several times. It is important to listen to them at least one separate time, focusing solely on pronunciation. Practice, patience, and persistence pay!

We hope that the preceding suggestions on how to go about learning French will serve you well, helping you to become a successful language learner. Good luck with your French studies, and most of all, enjoy yourself!

HORIZONS ILRN™ HEINLE LEARNING CENTER AND PREMIUM WEBSITE

As a student of French, you have access to a multitude of online resources. They can be accessed at www.cengagebrain.com. Here is what you will find on each one.

Horizons iLrn™ Heinle Learning Center:
Audio-enhanced vocabulary flashcards
Grammar tutorials
Grammar and pronunciation podcasts
Concentration games
Crossword puzzles
Glossary
Web links
Basic tutorial quizzes
Google Earth™ coordinates

Horizons Premium Website:
Text Audio
SAM Audio
Video

ACKNOWLEDGMENTS

We are grateful to a great many people for helping us transform our collective classroom experience into this text. Principal among these are Beth Kramer and Nicole Morinon, for the opportunity to work with Cengage Learning and for their support; Esther Marshall, Isabelle Alouane, Mayanne Wright, Greg Madan, Linda Jurras, Morgen Gallo, Peter Schott, John Farrell, Sev Champeny, native reader and proofreader, Julie Low, photo researcher, and Jenna Gray, PreMediaGlobal project manager. Our thanks also go to: Annick Penant who helped with the culture updates, Myriam Arcangeli, who worked on the review chapter, Jessica Sturm, from Purdue University, who updated the Web quizzes and cultural activities, Lara Finklea who updated the sample lesson plans, and our other freelancers.

We would particularly like to thank our reviewers of the current and previous editions.

Ahmed Bouguarche, *California State University—Northridge*

Alexandra Kuzmich, *Rochester Institute of Technology*

Amy Griffin Sawyer, *Clemson University*

Amy Hubbell, *Kansas State University*

Anna Brichko, *Mission College*

Annabelle Dolidon, *Portland State University*

Anne-Hélène Miller, *East Carolina University*

Anne-Marie Obajtek-Kirkwood, *Drexel University*

Antoinette Sol, *University of Texas—Arlington*

Bonnie Sarnoff, *Limestone College*

Caroline Jumel, *Oakland University*

Catherine Webster, *University of Central Oklahoma*

Cheryl Hansen, *Weber State University*

Christy Frembes, *State University of New York—Oneonta*

Claude Fouillade, *New Mexico State University*

Colleen Sandford, *Suffolk County Community College*

Constance Dickey, *Syracuse University*

Daniel E. Rivas, *Irvine Valley College*

Elaine Ancekewicz, *George Mason University*

Elaine Hayashi, *Oregon State University*

Gabriella Baika, *Auburn University*

Gloria Pastorino, *Fairleigh Dickinson University*

Hervé Corbe, *Youngstown State University*

Jaklin Yermian, *Los Angeles Valley College*

Janet Solberg, *Kalamazoo College*

Janette Funaro, *Johnson County Community College*

Jean-Luc Desalvo, *San José State University*

Jessica Sturm, *Purdue University*

Joan Debrah, *University of Hawaii—Manoa*

Jody Ballah, *University of Cincinnati—Raymond Walters College*

Johanna Needham, *Tacoma Community College*

John Moran, *New York University*

Joseph Price, *Texas Tech University*

Karina Rodegra, *University of Central Florida*

Keith Palka, *Central Michigan University*

Kelle Truby, *University of California—Riverside*

Kindra Santamaria, *Texas Christian University*

Kory Olson, *Richard Stockton College*

Lee Slater, *Old Dominion University*

Lisa Blair, *Shaw University*

Maria Melgarejo, *St. Cloud State University*

Marie Glynn, *Washington State University*

Mark Andrew Hall, *Ithaca College*

Martina Wells, *Chatham College*

Martine Howard, *Camden County College*

Meekyoung Yi, *Northern Virginia Community College*

Mercedes Rooney, *State University of New York—New Paltz*

Meredith Josey, *Western Washington University*

Michael Saclolo, *St. Edward's College*

Monique Manopoulos, *California State University—Hayward*

Monique Zibi, *Lone Star College—Kingwood*

Monty Laycox, *University of Central Missouri*

Nathalie Cornelius, *Bloomsburg University of Pennsylvania*

Nedialka Koleva, *Mesa Community College*

Nikki Kaltenbach, *Purdue University—Westville*

Nina Furry, *University of North Carolina at Chapel Hill*

Pamela Mansfield, *Union County College*

Pamela Park, *Idaho State University*

Patricia Cesario, *Suffolk County Community College*

Patricia Scarampi, *Lake Forest College*

Richard Gray, *Carson-Newman College*

Ruth Caldwell, *Luther College*

Shawn Morrison, *College of Charleston*

Stéphane Natan, *Rider University*

Susan Clay, *Clemson University*

Tamara Lindner, *University of Southwestern Louisiana*

Thierry Torea, *Hobart and William Smith Colleges*

Thomas Buresi, *Southern Polytechnic State University*

Vicki Earnest, *Calhoun Community College*

Vikrant Ahuja, *Mott Community College*

Yvon Joseph, *Suffolk County Community College*

A special thanks to both Jims, Laura, Andrew, Annick, Daniel, and Joel.

Last, but obviously not least, we thank each other for the tolerance, mutual encouragement, and strengthened bonds of friendship such an endeavor requires.

Merci mille fois!

THE *HORIZONS* VIDEO PROGRAM, *LES STAGIAIRES*

Les Stagiaires was written by the *Horizons'* authors to offer students more exposure to the text's vocabulary and grammar in a seamlessly integrated manner. The video, comprising ten episodes, provides learners with further listening practice. Students have the opportunity to learn about and experience French culture in the context of a storyline that involves seven characters and their interactions in a French office environment. The activities in each chapter's ***Vidéoreprise*** section are now designed with pre- and post-viewing activities. In addition, these activities simultaneously review the entire chapter's vocabulary and grammar.

In this video, we meet two interns, Amélie Prévot and Rachid Bennani. They are just starting their summer internships at Technovert, a small green-technology company.

Amélie Prévot

Rachid Bennani

Henri Vieilledent is the founder, owner, and leader of this dynamic and fast-growing company. Coffee and croissants are his daily motivators.

Henri Vieilledent

Camille Dupont

His faithful assistant, Camille Dupont, helps him run the business . . . and keeps his coffee-and-croissant supply abundant.

Céline Diop

One of Vieilledent's weapons in his efforts to make the company flourish and remain competitive is Céline Diop. The confident and driven sales manager also becomes an effective and appreciated mentor to the two young interns.

You might not be able to tell right away, but Matthieu Sauvage is a wiz. His area of expertise? Computers. However, interactions with the staff can sometimes be challenging for him. He can be extremely shy and awkward. When Amélie joins the Technovert staff, will Matthieu finally take a risk and break his painful timidity?

Matthieu Sauvage

Christophe Vieilledent

Finally, Christophe Vieilledent is the company's gofer—though he doesn't go for . . . a lot! The mail delivery and other odd jobs he does around the building do not keep him from indulging in his favorite pastime: reading manga. With a father in high places he is able to keep a low profile . . .

Le monde francophone

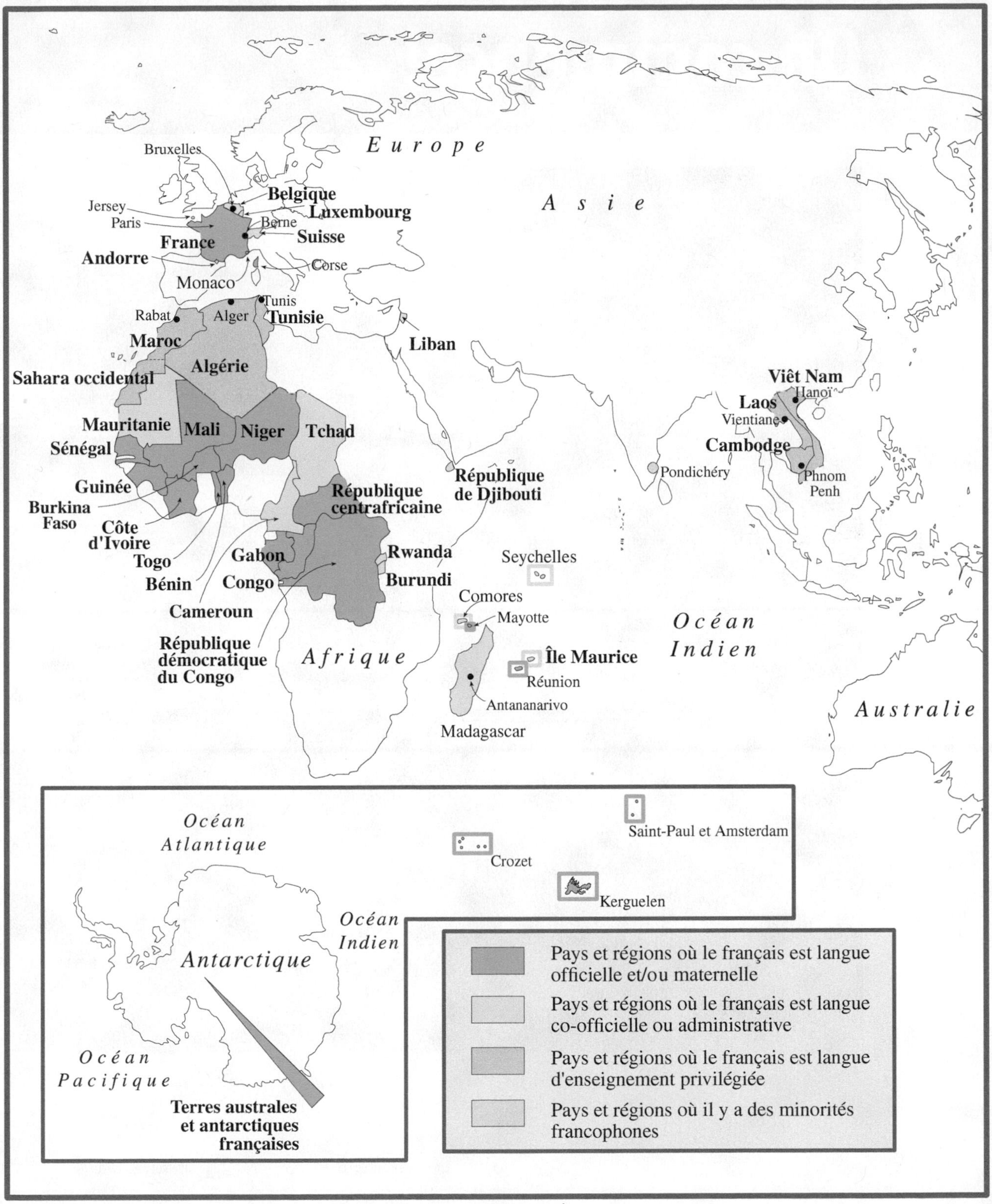

Europe
Asie
Bruxelles
Belgique
Luxembourg
Jersey
Paris
Berne
France
Suisse
Andorre
Corse
Monaco
Tunis
Rabat
Alger
Tunisie
Maroc
Liban
Algérie
Sahara occidental
Viêt Nam
Hanoï
Laos
Vientiane
Mauritanie
Mali
Niger
Tchad
Cambodge
Sénégal
Pondichéry
Phnom Penh
Guinée
République centrafricaine
République de Djibouti
Burkina Faso
Côte d'Ivoire
Togo
Gabon
Rwanda
Seychelles
Bénin
Congo
Burundi
Comores
Cameroun
Mayotte
Océan Indien
République démocratique du Congo
Afrique
Île Maurice
Réunion
Antananarivo
Madagascar
Australie
Océan Atlantique
Saint-Paul et Amsterdam
Crozet
Kerguelen
Océan Indien
Antarctique
Océan Pacifique
Terres australes et antarctiques françaises
Pays et régions où le français est langue officielle et/ou maternelle
Pays et régions où le français est langue co-officielle ou administrative
Pays et régions où le français est langue d'enseignement privilégiée
Pays et régions où il y a des minorités francophones
© Cengage Learning

Le monde francophone
On commence!

iLrn iLrn Heinle Learning Center			Internet web search
www.cengagebrain.com			Pair work
Audio			Group work

2

© Jorge Royan/Alamy

P

COMPÉTENCE

1 Greeting people
Les formules de politesse
Les salutations familières

2 Counting and describing your week
Les nombres de zéro à trente
Les jours de la semaine

3 Talking about yourself and your schedule
Un autoportrait
L'heure

4 Communicating in class
En cours
Des expressions utiles et l'alphabet

Comparaisons culturelles *L'heure officielle*

Vocabulaire

BIENVENUE DANS LE MONDE FRANCOPHONE!

With what do you immediately associate France and French culture – food and wine, film, art, music, literature, fashion . . . ? Did you also know that France is a world leader in agriculture, science, technology, medicine, telecommunications, and aerospace engineering, and is the fifth largest export nation in the world?

Le penseur de Rodin

La fusée Ariane 5

Le TGV

Bienvenue dans le monde francophone! *Welcome to the French-speaking world!*

On parle français au Québec...

et à Tahiti!

iLrn In the **Culture Modules** in the video library, see **The Francophone World.**

Look in the front of the book at the map of the countries and regions where French is spoken. Are you surprised that some of these countries and regions are francophone? Pick one of them and research its history on the Web to find out why people speak French there, and if they speak any other languages.

Did you know that French is spoken throughout the world? Want to discover the world? Discover French – a language you can use right here in North America . . . and across the continents!

Le savez-vous?

What makes French one of the most important global languages? Take this quiz and find out. If you don't know, guess!

1. Look at the map in the front of the book to answer questions **a–i.**

    a. In how many countries is French spoken: about 5, about 25, about 40, or about 100?

    b. In or near which continents does French have a linguistic or cultural influence: Europe and Africa; Europe, Africa, and the Americas; or every continent?

    c. Are most of the francophone countries in Africa located in the north, the south, the east, or the west?

    d. Which province in Canada has the largest number of French speakers: British Columbia, Newfoundland and Labrador, or Quebec?

    e. True or false? French is not spoken in any areas of the South Pacific.

    f. True or false? There is a francophone influence in the USA, particularly in Louisiana and in the northeast.

    g. Where in South America is French spoken?

    h. In which three of these places in the Caribbean is French an important language: the Dominican Republic, Haiti, Guadeloupe, the Virgin Islands, the Bahamas, Martinique, the Cayman Islands?

    i. In which six of these European countries is French spoken: France, Portugal, Belgium, Italy, Andorra, Switzerland, Monaco, Albania, Luxembourg?

2. About how many people in the world speak French as their primary or secondary language: about 100 million, about 270 million, about 550 million?

3. In the USA, how many people speak French at home: close to one million, close to two million?

4. About how many French speakers are there in Canada: 5 million or 11 million?

5. The top two most frequently studied foreign languages worldwide and the only two global languages are _____ and _____.

6. French is an official language of: **a.** the United Nations, **b.** the International Olympic Committee, **c.** UNESCO, **d.** NATO, **e.** the European Union, **f.** all of these

On parle français au *French is spoken in*   **et à** *and in*

Bienvenue dans le monde francophone! | *cinq* **5**

5

Greeting people

LES FORMULES DE POLITESSE

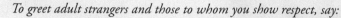

To greet adult strangers and those to whom you show respect, say:

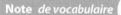
1-2

— Bonjour, madame.
— Bonjour, monsieur. Je suis Hélène Cauvin. Et vous, comment vous appelez-vous?
— Je m'appelle Jean-Luc Bertin.

— Bonsoir, monsieur. **Comment allez-vous?**
— Bonsoir, madame. **Je vais très bien, merci.** Et vous?
— **Assez** bien.

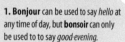
1-3

Et vous? Comment allez-vous?

Je vais très bien. Assez bien. / **Pas mal. / Comme ci comme ça.** Pas très bien.

Notes
1. Boldfaced words are glossed at the bottom of the page. Try to guess their meaning from the context before looking at the glosses.
2. Audio for items accompanied by this symbol 🔊 are accessed online.

PRONONCIATION

Les consonnes muettes et la liaison 🔊
1-4

In French, consonants at the end of words are often silent and **h** is always silent, as it is in some English words such as *hour* and *honest.* The consonants **c, r, f,** and **l** (CaReFuL) are the only consonants that are generally pronounced at the end of a word. However, do not pronounce the final **r** of **monsieur.**

Mar**c**   bonjou**r**   acti**f**   Chanta**l**

— Bonjou**r**, monsieur. Je m'appelle Paul Richar**d**. Et vous, comment vous appelez-vous?
— Je m'appelle Henri Dula**c**. Comment allez-vous?
— Je vais très bien, merci.

If a consonant at the end of a word is followed by a word beginning with a vowel sound (**a, e, i, o, u, y**) or a mute **h,** the final consonant sound is often pronounced and is linked to the beginning of the next word. This linking is called **liaison.** In liaison, a single **s** is pronounced like a **z.**

Comment vous ᶻappelez-vous? Comment ᵗallez-vous?

Comment allez-vous? *How are you?*   **Je vais très bien, merci.** *I'm doing very well, thank you.*   **Assez** *Fairly, Rather*   **Pas mal.** *Not bad(ly).*
Comme ci comme ça. *So-so.*

A **Prononcez bien!** Copy these sentences, crossing out the consonants that should not be pronounced and marking where liaison would occur.

EXEMPLE Comment‿allez-vous, monsieur?

1. Je suis Chantal Hubert.
2. Bonjour, madame. Comment allez-vous?
3. Très bien, monsieur. Comment vous appelez-vous?
4. Je m'appelle Henri Dufour. Et vous?

Now go back and reorder the four sentences to create a logical conversation to read aloud with a partner.

B **Bonjour, monsieur/madame.** Imagine that you are meeting a new French business associate. Read the following conversation with another student, changing the words in italics so that they describe you and your partner.

— Bonjour, *madame.* Comment allez-vous?

— Bonjour, *monsieur.* Je vais *très bien,* merci. Et vous?

— *Assez bien,* merci. Je suis *Jules Alami.* Et vous, comment vous appelez-vous?

— Je m'appelle *Emma Delors.*

C **Que dit-on?** Complete the conversations and act them out with a partner. Expand them and present them to the class.

1.

2.

3.

D **Bonsoir!** Imagine that you are at a formal reception. Go around the room and greet at least three people, exchanging names, and finding out how they are doing. Be sure to shake hands.

LES SALUTATIONS FAMILIÈRES

Note *culturelle*

When people greet one another in France, they usually shake hands or exchange a brief kiss on each cheek called a *bise*. What do people do when they greet each other in your region?

To greet classmates, friends, family members, or children, say:

🔊 1-5

Vocabulaire supplémentaire

Comment t'appelles-tu? / Comment tu t'appelles? *What's your name?* (familiar)

Comment vas-tu? *How are you?* (familiar)

Ciao! *Bye!* (familiar)

Bon week-end! *Have a good weekend!*

Bonne journée! *Have a good day!*

— **Salut**, Pierre. **Ça va?**
— Salut, Juliette. **Ça va.** Et toi, **comment ça va?**
— Pas mal.

— Bonjour, je m'appelle Pauline. Et toi, tu t'appelles comment?
— Moi, je m'appelle Lucas.

🔊 1-6

Here are several ways to say good-bye. Use **À plus!** *and* **Salut!** *only in familiar situations. The other expressions may be used in either formal or familiar situations.*

Au revoir! *Good-bye!*
À tout à l'heure! *See you in a little while!*
À bientôt! *See you soon!*

À demain! *See you tomorrow!*
À plus tard! / À plus! *See you later!*
Salut! *Bye!*

PRONONCIATION

*Les voyelles **a, e, é, i, o** et **u*** 🔊 1-7

ⓘLrn Prononcez bien! See Modules 7–10, 13, 23, and 27.

When you pronounce vowels in English, your tongue or lips move as you say them, so that the position of your mouth is not the same at the end of a vowel as at the beginning. In French, you hold your tongue and mouth firmly in one place while pronouncing vowels. This gives vowels a tenser sound. Practice saying these sounds.

a [a]:	à	ça	va	madame	mal	assez
e [ə]:	je	ne	que	de	demain	devoirs
é [e]:	café	pâté	bébé	été	préféré	répété
i [i]:	quiche	idéal	Paris	machine	six	merci
o [o]:	bientôt	vélo	hôtel	kilo	mots	trop
u [y]:	tu	salut	Luc	super	du	université

The vowel **o** has two pronunciations, [o] or [ɔ], and the vowel **e** has three pronunciations, [ə], [e], or [ɛ]. You will learn more about this in *Chapitre 3*. Final *unaccented* e is not generally pronounced, unless it is the only vowel in a word, as in **je**.

Franc**e̸**   madam**e̸**   appell**e̸**   un**e̸**   Ann**e̸**

Compare these words:

Mari**e** / mari**é**   divorc**e** / divorc**é**   fatigu**e** / fatigu**é**

Salut! *Hi!, Bye!*   **Ça va?** *How's it going?*   **Ça va.** *It's going fine.*   **Comment ça va?** *How's it going?*

🔊 A Prononcez bien! Listen as different people give their name and indicate whether it is the first or second name shown.

1-8

1. Alisa	Élisa	**5.** Élona	Ilona	**9.** Abdel	Abdul
2. Amélie	Émelie	**6.** Albert	Hubert	**10.** Éric	Ulrick
3. Ali	Éli	**7.** Mariel	Muriel	**11.** Nicolas	Nicolo
4. Éliana	Iliana	**8.** Arielle	Urielle	**12.** Mano	Manu

B Dans quelle situation? Read each of these phrases aloud and say whether you would be more likely to hear it in situation **A** or **B**.

A. **B.**

© Moodboard/Getty Images © kali9/iStockphoto.com

1. Bonjour, madame.
2. Salut, Thomas.
3. Très bien, merci. Et vous?
4. Tu t'appelles comment?

5. À plus!
6. Comment allez-vous?
7. Ça va. Et toi?
8. Comment vous appelez-vous?

Now give a logical response to each of the items above.

C On dit... What would you say in French . . .

1. to greet your professor during the day? in the evening?
2. to ask your professor's name? to tell him/her your name?
3. to ask your professor how he/she is doing?
4. to say that you are doing very well? fairly well? not badly? not very well?
5. to greet a classmate? to ask a classmate's name?
6. to ask a friend how it's going? to tell him/her that it's going well?
7. to say good-bye to someone? to say that you will see him/her tomorrow? soon? later today?

👥 D Que disent-ils? Imagine that you and a classmate are meeting for the first time in class. Prepare a brief conversation with a partner in which you greet each other, exchange names, ask and say how it is going, and say good-bye. Shake hands or exchange **bises**.

© Cengage Learning

Now redo the conversation as strangers meeting at a formal conference.

iLrn 🌐 You can find a list of the new words from this ***Compétence*** on page 26 and access the audio online.

COMPÉTENCE 2

Counting and describing your week

LES NOMBRES DE ZÉRO À TRENTE

Note *culturelle*

The French manner of counting on one's fingers is with palms facing in and starting with the thumb rather than the index finger. Ask your classmates how they count on their fingers. Are there any variations by nationality or regional origin?

Comptez de zéro à trente, **s'il vous plaît!**

0 zéro		
1 un	**11** onze	**21** vingt et un
2 deux	**12** douze	**22** vingt-deux
3 trois	**13** treize	**23** vingt-trois
4 quatre	**14** quatorze	**24** vingt-quatre
5 cinq	**15** quinze	**25** vingt-cinq
6 six	**16** seize	**26** vingt-six
7 sept	**17** dix-sept	**27** vingt-sept
8 huit	**18** dix-huit	**28** vingt-huit
9 neuf	**19** dix-neuf	**29** vingt-neuf
10 dix	**20** vingt	**30** trente

2 + 2 = 4   **Combien** font deux et deux?
Deux et deux font quatre.

10 − 3 = 7   Combien font dix moins trois?
Dix moins trois font sept.

PRONONCIATION

Les nombres et les voyelles nasales   1-9   **Gilrm** Prononcez bien! See Modules 11, 32, 35, 36, 37, and 38.

Although final consonants are generally silent in French, they are pronounced in the following numbers when counting. In **sept,** the **p** is silent, but the final **t** is pronounced. The final **x** in **six** and **dix** is pronounced like the *s* in *so*.

cinq   six   se**p**t   huit   neuf   dix

Many numbers also contain nasal vowels. In French, when a vowel is followed by the letter **m** or **n** in the same syllable, the **m** or **n** is silent and the vowel is nasal. Use the words below as models of how to pronounce each of the nasal sounds. The letter combinations that are grouped together are all pronounced alike.

[ɑ̃]:	**an / am**	blanc	anglais	dimanche	chambre
	en / em	trente	comment	ensemble	embêtant
[ɛ̃]:	**in / im**	cinq	quinze	vingt	important
	un / um	un	lundi	brun	parfum
	ain / aim	demain	américain	mexicain	faim
[ɔ̃]:	**on / om**	onze	bonjour	non	nom
[jɛ̃]:	**ien**	bien	combien	canadien	rien
[wɛ̃]:	**oin**	moins	loin	coin	soin

Comptez *Count*   **de** *from*   **à** *to*   **s'il vous plaît** *please*   **Combien** *How much, How many*

🔊 1-10 **A** **Prononcez bien!** How are the italicized letters in the following French-English cognates pronounced? Sort the words under the appropriate columns. Then listen and repeat, comparing the pronunciation of these words with their English cognates.

*im*bécile	*em*blème	*jun*gle	*im*pact	*am*bition	*bun*galow	*com*plice
*ins*titut	*en*semble	refr*ain*	*an*thologie	s*ain*t	*am*phibien	b*om*be
*an*droïde	*con*cert	*com*bat	bar*on*	*em*ployé	*en*cyclopédie	acti*on*

[ɛ̃] as in **un, cinq**:	[ɑ̃] as in **trente**:	[ɔ̃] as in **onze**:

👥 **B** **C'est logique!** Complete each list with the logical numbers. Practice reading them aloud with a partner.

1. ☐1☐ ☐3☐ ☐5☐ ☐ ☐9☐ ☐11☐ ☐ ☐15☐☐17☐ ☐
2. ☐2☐ ☐4☐ ☐ ☐8☐ ☐10☐ ☐ ☐14☐ ☐ ☐18☐☐20☐
3. ☐0☐ ☐5☐ ☐10☐ ☐ ☐20☐ ☐ ☐30☐

4. ☐20☐☐19☐☐18☐ ☐ ☐16☐☐15☐ ☐
5. ☐10☐☐11☐☐12☐ ☐ ☐14☐☐15☐ ☐
6. ☐11☐☐13☐☐15☐ ☐ ☐19☐☐21☐☐23☐☐25☐ ☐

C **Combien font...?**

1. 2 + 3 =
2. 1 + 3 =
3. 14 + 16 =

4. 18 + 12 =
5. 15 + 11 =
6. 13 – 5 =

7. 17 – 11 =
8. 30 – 13 =
9. 21 – 6 =

D **En taxi.** You've taken a taxi in a francophone country. Tell the driver the address of your destination.

EXEMPLE 28, avenue des Champs-Élysées
Vingt-huit avenue des Champs-Élysées, s'il vous plaît.

1. 27, boulevard Diderot
2. 11, rue Petit
3. 16, place Saint-Denis
4. 25, rue Bonaparte

5. 15, rue Sébastopol
6. 12, rue Garibaldi
7. 30, boulevard Gabriel
8. 7, rue du Temple

© lotsostock/Shutterstock.com

🔊 1-11 **E** **Comparaisons culturelles.** There are about 270 million French speakers in the world, of which 65 million live in France. Here are the ten countries with the largest number of French speakers after France. You will hear the number of speakers. Fill in the missing numbers.

1. la République démocratique du Congo: ___ millions
2. l'Algérie: ___ millions
3. la Côte d'Ivoire: ___ millions
4. le Canada: ___ millions
5. le Maroc: ___ millions

6. le Cameroun: ___ millions
7. la Tunisie: ___ millions
8. la Belgique: ___ millions
9. la Roumanie: ___ millions
10. le Sénégal: ___ millions

LES JOURS DE LA SEMAINE

Note *culturelle*

The first day of the week on French calendars is *lundi,* not *dimanche.* Do you think this would make it more convenient for planning your weekend?

To ask and tell the day of the week, say:

— **C'est quel jour, aujourd'hui?**
— C'est lundi.

lundi	mardi	mercredi	jeudi	vendredi	samedi	dimanche
(17)	18	19	20	21	22	23
24	25	26	27	28	29	30

© Cengage Learning

Vocabulaire supplémentaire

pendant la semaine *during the week*
sauf *except*

Do not translate the word **on** *to say that you do something* **on** *a certain day. To say that you do something* **every** *Monday (or another day), use* **le** *with the day of the week.*

Je travaille **lundi.**   *I work on Monday.* (this coming Monday)

Je travaille **le lundi.**   *I work on Mondays.* (every Monday)

To say **from** *what day* **to** *what day you do something every week, use* **du... au...** *Use* **tous les jours** *to say you do something* **every day.**

Je travaille **du** lundi **au** vendredi.   *I work Mondays to Fridays.* (every week)

Je travaille **tous les jours.**   *I work every day.*

Use **le matin, l'après-midi,** *or* **le soir** *to say you do something* **in the morning, in the afternoon,** *or* **in the evening,** *and* **le week-end** *to say* **on the weekend.** *Use* **avant** *to say* **before** *and* **après** *to say* **after.**

Note *de vocabulaire*

1. Days of the week are not capitalized in French.

2. Use **du... au...** to say *from... to...* with days of the week when talking about what one does in general every week, but use **de... à...** instead to talk about what one is doing one particular week. **Je travaille** *du lundi au vendredi.* **Cette** *(This)* **semaine, je travaille** *de lundi à mercredi.*

3. Notice that you use two words, **ne... pas,** to say what someone does *not* do. They are usually placed around the verb in a sentence. You will learn more about this in *Chapitre 1.*

Le matin, je suis **à la maison** avant **le cours de français.**

L'après-midi, **je ne suis pas** à la maison. Je suis **en cours** de français et après, je suis **dans un autre cours.**

Le soir, **je travaille.**

Le week-end, **je ne travaille pas.** Je suis à la maison.

Line art on this page: © Cengage Learning

Les jours de la semaine *The days of the week*   **C'est quel jour, aujourd'hui?** *What day is it today?*   **à la maison** *at home*
le cours de français *French class*   **je ne suis pas** *I am not*   **en cours** *in class*   **dans un autre cours** *in another class*
je travaille *I work*   **je ne travaille pas** *I don't work*

1-12

Two friends are talking about their schedule this semester.
— **Tu es** en cours quels jours **ce semestre**?
— Je suis en cours le lundi, le mercredi et le vendredi.
— Tu travailles **aussi**?
— **Oui,** je travaille le mardi matin, le jeudi matin et le week-end.

A Salut! Say good-bye to a friend and say that you'll see him/her on the indicated day.

EXEMPLE Monday **Au revoir! À lundi!**

1. Sunday
2. Friday
3. Thursday
4. Tuesday
5. Saturday
6. Wednesday

B C'est quel jour? Complete the statements that follow.

1. Aujourd'hui, c'est...
2. Demain, c'est...
3. Après-demain, c'est...
4. Les jours du week-end sont...
5. Avant le week-end, c'est...
6. Après le week-end, c'est...
7. Les jours du cours de français sont...
8. Je suis en cours...
9. Je travaille...
10. Je suis souvent *(often)* à la maison...

C Emploi du temps. A student is talking about her week. Select the option in parentheses that is logical in each sentence.

1. Aujourd'hui, c'est (jeudi, le jeudi) et demain, c'est (vendredi, le vendredi).
2. Ce semestre, je suis en cours tous les jours (du, au) lundi (du, au) jeudi. Je ne suis pas en cours (vendredi, le vendredi).
3. Je suis en cours de français (après-midi, l'après-midi).
4. Ce semestre, je suis à la maison le matin (avant, après) le cours de français et je travaille l'après-midi (avant, après) le cours de français.
5. Ce semestre, je travaille (samedi, le samedi).
6. Ce week-end, je travaille (lundi, dimanche) aussi.

Now go back and change the statements so that each one is true for you. If a statement is already true, read it as it is.

 ## D Et toi? Complete these statements with the appropriate days of the week to describe yourself. Then, circulate through the classroom to try to find two people who completed at least three of the statements the same way you did. Write down their names.

EXEMPLE Je suis en cours **du lundi au vendredi.**
Je suis en cours du lundi au vendredi. Et toi?
Moi aussi, je suis en cours du lundi au vendredi. /
Moi, je suis en cours le mardi et le jeudi.

1. Ce semestre, je suis en cours...
2. Je ne suis pas en cours...
3. Je travaille... (Je ne travaille pas.)
4. Je suis souvent *(often)* à la maison...

À VOUS!

With a partner, read aloud the conversation at the top of the page, paying particular attention to the pronunciation. Then act it out, adapting it to make it true for you. Switch roles and do it again.

You can find a list of the new words from this *Compétence* on page 26 and access the audio online.

Tu es *You are*   **ce semestre** *this semester*   **aussi** *also, too*   **Oui** *Yes*

Talking about yourself and your schedule

UN AUTOPORTRAIT

Note *culturelle*

In France, all students finishing secondary school have studied several years of a foreign language, and many have studied more than one. How does this compare to the situation in your area?

Use these expressions to talk about yourself. Include the ending in parentheses if you are a female.

Je suis...	étudiant(e).
Je ne suis pas...	professeur.
	américain(e).
	canadien(ne).
	de Chicago.
	d'ici.

Note *de grammaire*

1. The words **je**, **ne**, and **de** change to **j'**, **n'**, and **d'** before vowels or a mute **h**. Similarly, **parce que** *(because)* changes to **parce qu'**. This is called elision.
2. Many adjectives in French add an **e** when describing females.

J'habite...	à Toronto.
Je n'habite pas...	**seul(e).**
	avec **un ami / une amie.**
	avec deux amis / deux amies.
	avec ma famille.
	avec **un colocataire / une colocataire.**
	avec **un camarade de chambre / une camarade de chambre.**

Je suis canadienne, de Montréal, mais j'habite à Paris maintenant. Je parle anglais et français.

Je travaille...	**beaucoup.**
Je ne travaille pas...	à l'université.
	pour Apple.

Je parle...	anglais.
Je ne parle pas...	français.
	espagnol.
	beaucoup en cours.

Je pense que le français est...	intéressant.
	assez **facile.**
	un peu difficile.
	super!
	assez cool!

Vocabulaire sans peine!

Vocabulaire sans peine! notes in the margin will help you learn vocabulary quickly by pointing out cognate patterns between English and French. Cognates are words that look similar and have the same meaning in two languages.
1-13
Note these patterns of adjectives indicating where people are from:
-ain = *-an*
américain(e) = *American*
africain(e) = *African*
-ien(ne) = *-ian*
canadien(ne) = *Canadian*
australien(ne) = *Australian*
How would you say these in French?
Mexican
Colombian

In the following conversation, two people meet at a Canadian-American cultural event in Montreal.

— **Vous êtes** canadien?
— Oui, je suis d'ici. Et vous, vous êtes canadienne aussi?
— Non, je suis de Cleveland.
— **Mais** vous parlez très bien français! Vous habitez ici **maintenant**?
— Oui, **parce que** je suis étudiante à l'université. Et vous, vous travaillez ici?
— Non, je suis étudiant aussi.

---

de (d') *from*   **d'ici** *from here*   **J'habite** *I live*   **seul(e)** *alone*   **un ami** *a friend* (male)   **une amie** *a friend* (female)
un colocataire *a housemate* (male)   **une colocataire** *a housemate* (female)   **un camarade de chambre** *a roommate* (male)
une camarade de chambre *a roommate* (female)   **beaucoup** *a lot*   **pour** *for*   **Je parle** *I speak, I talk*   **Je pense que** *I think that*   **facile** *easy*   **un peu** *a little*   **Vous êtes** *You are* (formal)   **Mais** *But*   **maintenant** *now*   **parce que** *because*

A **Moi, je...** Choose the words in parentheses to describe yourself.

1. (Je suis / Je ne suis pas) étudiant(e).
2. (Je suis / Je ne suis pas) de Los Angeles.
3. (Je suis / Je ne suis pas) canadien(ne).
4. (J'habite / Je n'habite pas) à Minneapolis.
5. (J'habite / Je n'habite pas) avec ma famille.
6. (Je travaille / Je ne travaille pas) à l'université.
7. (Je parle / Je ne parle pas) très bien français.

B **Descriptions.** A Canadian student is talking about himself. Change the words in italics as needed to make the paragraph true for you.

Je m'appelle *Chris Jones*. Je suis *canadien* et je suis de *Toronto*. J'habite *avec un colocataire* à *Chapel Hill*. Je suis *étudiant* à *l'université de Caroline du Nord*. Je parle *un peu* français. Je parle *anglais et espagnol*. Je pense que le français est *très facile*.

C **En rond.** Work in groups of three. For each item, say what is true for you and ask the student on your right about himself/herself, using **Et toi?** He/She will complete the item and ask the person to his/her right the same question, who will answer and then ask you. Start each item with a different person.

1. Je m'appelle... Et toi?
2. Je suis... Et toi?
3. Je suis de... Et toi?
4. J'habite à... Et toi?
5. J'habite avec... (J'habite seul[e].) Et toi?
6. Je travaille... (Je ne travaille pas.) Et toi?
7. Je parle... Et toi?
8. Je pense que le français est... Et toi?

D **Et vous?** Imagine that you and your partner have just met at an international professional conference in Denver. Take turns asking and answering these questions.

1. Comment vous appelez-vous?
2. Comment allez-vous?
3. Vous êtes étudiant(e)?
4. Vous travaillez aussi?
5. Vous êtes américain(e)?
6. Vous êtes d'ici?
7. Vous habitez à Denver maintenant?
8. Vous parlez espagnol?

À VOUS!

With a partner, read aloud the conversation on the preceding page, paying particular attention to the pronunciation. Then act it out, adapting it to make it true for you. Afterward, switch roles and do it again.

L'HEURE

Note culturelle

Traditionally, the French workday followed a particular pattern: breakfast in the early morning, work, a two-hour break for lunch, then work in the afternoon and into the evening. Most people went home for lunch to eat and be with their family. As France has become more urban, however, *la journée continue,* or a nine-to-five schedule, has become a way of life. There is a shorter lunch break, and people have lunch at work or in a nearby restaurant, fast-food chain, or café. How does this compare to a typical workday in your area?

Note de vocabulaire

1. Some people use **douze heures** for **midi.**

2. One may also tell time by telling the minutes after the hour, instead of using **et quart, et demie,** and **moins le quart.** For example, one hears **Il est trois heures quinze** or **Il est cinq heures trente.**

3. Use **du matin / de l'après-midi / du soir** only for indicating *A.M.* and *P.M.* when telling time. Use **le matin / l'après-midi / le soir** to say *in the morning / afternoon / evening* in all other cases.

4. Although *at* may be dropped in English, **à** cannot be omitted in French. To ask *(At) What time is French class?,* use **À quelle heure est le cours de français?**

Quelle heure est-il? *What time is it?*

*To tell time **on the hour,** use:*

> **Il est** + *number* + **heure(s).**   **Il est trois heures.**   *It's 3:00.*

*When telling the time, use **une** for **one.** The word **heures** has an **s** except in **une heure.** Don't use **heure** after **midi** and **minuit.***

Il est une heure.   Il est deux heures.   Il est midi.   Il est minuit.

*To tell time **after the hour up to the half hour,** use:*

> **Il est** + *number of hour* + **heure(s)** + *minutes.*   **Il est trois heures cinq.**   *It's 3:05.*

*For **a quarter after,** use **et quart** and for **half after,** use **et demie.** With **midi** and **minuit,** use **et demi** without the final **e.** These are the only times **et** is used in telling time.*

Il est une heure dix.   Il est une heure et quart.   Il est une heure et demie.   Il est midi et demi.   Il est minuit et demi.

*To tell time **until the next hour,** use:*

> **Il est** + *number of next hour* + **heure(s) moins** + *minutes until the hour.*   **Il est six heures moins cinq.**   *It's 5:55.*

*For **a quarter until the hour,** use **moins le quart.** This is the only time **le** is used in telling time.*

Il est deux heures moins vingt-cinq.   Il est deux heures moins vingt.   Il est deux heures moins le quart.

Line art on this page: © Cengage Learning

The following clock is useful in visualizing how time is expressed. With **moins…,** remember to use the number of the *upcoming* hour.

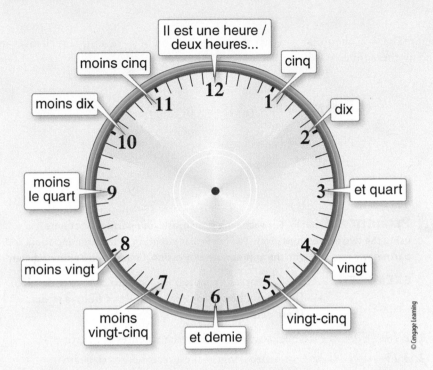

© Cengage Learning

Instead of using **A.M.** *and* **P.M.,** *use the expressions that follow, except with* **midi** *or* **minuit.**

du matin *(after midnight until noon)*	Il est huit heures **du matin.**
de l'après-midi *(after noon until 6 P.M.)*	Il est une heure **de l'après-midi.**
du soir *(6 P.M. until midnight)*	Il est neuf heures **du soir.**

Use **à** *to ask or tell* **at what time** *something takes place.*

Le cours de français est **à quelle heure**?

© Cengage Learning

Le cours de français **commence** à une heure.

Le cours de français **finit** à deux heures et quart.

To say that you do something **from** *a certain time* **to** *another, use* **de… à.**

Le lundi, je suis en cours **de** neuf heures **à** une heure.

(iLrn) 🌐 You can find a list of the new words from this *Compétence* on page 27 and access the audio online.

---

commence *begins*   **finit** *finishes, ends*

PRONONCIATION

L'heure et la liaison
1-14

Notice that there is liaison before the word **heure(s)** and that the pronunciation of some numbers changes in this liaison. Practice pronouncing these times.

Quelle heure est‿il?

Il est deux‿heures. | Il est sept‿heures.
Il est trois‿heures. | Il est huit‿heures.
Il est cinq‿heures. | Il est neuf‿heures.
Il est six‿heures. | Il est dix‿heures.

Il est dix heures moins le quart.

👥 **A Prononcez bien!** For each time shown, ask your partner what time it is, using the two expressions given. Pay particular attention to the pronunciation. Your partner will respond with the appropriate expression. Change roles after each item.

EXEMPLE   *2:00*   Il est deux heures. / Il est deux heures et demie.
— **Il est deux heures ou** *(or)* **il est deux heures et demie?**
— **Il est deux heures.**

1. *2:10*   Il est deux heures dix. / Il est deux heures et quart.
2. *3:15*   Il est trois heures vingt. / Il est trois heures et quart.
3. *4:20*   Il est quatre heures vingt-cinq. / Il est quatre heures vingt.
4. *5:30*   Il est cinq heures et demie. / Il est cinq heures et quart.
5. *6:45*   Il est six heures moins le quart. / Il est sept heures moins le quart.
6. *8:35*   Il est neuf heures moins vingt-cinq. / Il est huit heures moins vingt-cinq.
7. *9:50*   Il est neuf heures moins dix. / Il est dix heures moins dix.
8. *12:00 A.M.* Il est midi. / Il est minuit.

👥 **B Quelle heure est-il?** Take turns asking and telling the time with a partner.

EXEMPLE      — Quelle heure est-il?
— Il est une heure de l'après-midi.

1.  2.   3.   4.

5.  6.  7. 8.

© Cengage Learning

🔊 **C Il est quelle heure?** Write the times you hear. Notice how the word **heure(s)** is abbreviated in French.
1-15

EXEMPLE   VOUS ENTENDEZ *(YOU HEAR):* Il est dix heures et quart.
VOUS ÉCRIVEZ *(YOU WRITE):* **10h15**

D Où êtes-vous? Say whether or not you are usually at the indicated place or with the indicated people at the time given.

EXEMPLE Le lundi à 9h15 du matin, *je suis / je ne suis pas* en cours.
Le lundi à neuf heures et quart du matin, je suis en cours.
Le lundi à neuf heures et quart du matin, je ne suis pas en cours.

1. Le lundi à 7h00 du matin, *je suis / je ne suis pas* à la maison.
2. Le mercredi à 2h30 de l'après-midi, *je suis / je ne suis pas* en cours de français.
3. Le jeudi à 5h20 de l'après-midi, *je suis / je ne suis pas* dans un autre cours.
4. Le vendredi à 10h45 du soir, *je suis / je ne suis pas* avec des amis.
5. Le samedi à minuit, *je suis / je ne suis pas* seul(e).
6. Le dimanche à 7h30 du soir, *je suis / je ne suis pas* avec ma famille.

E Quand? Complete these sentences so that they are true for you the first day of the week you have your French class.

EXEMPLE Je suis à la maison **avant sept heures et demie.**
                                         before   *[time]*

1. Je suis à la maison _____ _____.
                        before   *[time]*
2. Je suis à l'université _____ _____. (J'habite sur *[on]* le campus.)
                          after   *[time]*
3. Le cours de français commence _____ _____.
                                   at   *[time]*
4. Le cours de français finit _____ _____.
                               at   *[time]*
5. Je suis en cours _____ _____ _____ _____.
                     from   *[time]*   *to*   *[time]*
6. Je travaille _____ _____ _____ _____. (Je ne travaille pas.)
                 from   *[time]*   *to*   *[time]*
7. Je suis à la maison _____ _____.
                        after   *[time]*

🎙️ F Mon emploi du temps. On a sheet of paper, make two copies of this schedule, changing it to describe your schedule on one copy and leaving the other one blank. With a partner, take turns describing your schedules. On the blank schedule, fill in your partner's schedule as he/she describes it to you.

EXEMPLE Le lundi, je suis en cours de dix heures à une heure. Je travaille de deux heures à quatre heures. Je suis à la maison après cinq heures. Le mardi...

Communicating in class

EN COURS

Le professeur **dit aux** étudiants:

EN COURS

Ouvrez votre livre à la page 23.

Fermez votre livre.

Écoutez la question.

Répondez à la question.

Allez au tableau.

Écrivez la réponse avec une phrase complète.

Prenez une feuille de papier et un crayon ou un stylo.

Faites l'exercice A à la page 21.

Donnez-moi votre feuille de papier.

À LA MAISON

Lisez la page 17 et **apprenez** les mots de vocabulaire.

Préparez l'examen pour le **prochain** cours.

Faites **les devoirs** dans **le cahier**.

dit aux *says to the*   **Écoutez** *Listen to*   **Faites** *Do*   **Donnez-moi** *Give me*   **Lisez** *Read*   **apprenez** *learn*   **prochain(e)** *next*
les devoirs *the homework*   **le cahier** *the workbook*

PRONONCIATION

iLrn Prononcez bien! See Modules 16 and 31.

🔊
1-16
Les voyelles groupées

Practice the pronunciation of the following vowel combinations. Notice that the combination **eu** has two different sounds, depending on whether it is followed by a pronounced consonant in the same syllable.

- a + u / e + u / o + u

au, eau [o]:	au	aussi	beaucoup	tableau
eu [ø]:	deux	un peu	jeudi	monsieur
eu [œ]:	heure	neuf	professeur	seul(e)
ou [u]:	vous	douze	jour	pour

- a + i / e + i / o + i / u + i

ai [ɛ]:	français	je vais	je sais	vrai
ei [ɛ]:	treize	seize	beige	neige
oi [wa]:	moi	toi	trois	au revoir
ui [ɥi]:	huit	minuit	aujourd'hui	je suis

🔊
1-17
A **Prononcez bien!** Listen and repeat the following cognates, paying attention to the pronunciation of the italicized vowel combinations. Then, go back and say whether the words describe you (Je suis... / Je ne suis pas...). Use the form indicated in parentheses if you are a female.

1. *au*stralien(ne)
2. *au*daci*eux* (*au*daci*eu*se)
3. c*ou*rag*eux* (c*ou*rag*eu*se)
4. c*ou*rt*ois*(e)
5. japon*ai*s(e)
6. millionn*ai*re
7. chin*ois*(e)
8. b*ou*rge*ois*(e)
9. s*ui*sse

B **Comment dit-on...?** Decide which of the words given could be used to make logical commands. Read all of the possibilities aloud.

1. (Allez / Lisez / Écoutez) la phrase.
2. (Faites / Allez / Écrivez) les devoirs.
3. (Comptez / Fermez / Ouvrez) de 0 à 30.
4. (Fermez / Donnez-moi / Allez) le cahier.
5. (Allez / Fermez / Ouvrez) au tableau.
6. (Répondez / Lisez / Apprenez) les mots de vocabulaire.

C **En cours.** In groups, make up commands your instructor might give you by matching items from the two columns. Which group can come up with the most commands?

Lisez...	... le professeur.
Apprenez...	... l'exercice A.
Comptez...	... de 0 à 30.
Écoutez...	... les devoirs.
Prenez...	... une feuille de papier.
Écrivez...	... la phrase.
Faites...	... les mots de vocabulaire.

Vocabulaire sans peine!

Noticing cognate patterns can help you learn new words more quickly. Many adjectives ending in *-ous* in English are similar in French, but end with **-eux (-euse)**.

-eux (-euse) = *-ous*
sérieux (sérieuse) = *serious*
victorieux (victorieuse) = *victorious*

How would you say these in French?
religious
scandalous

DES EXPRESSIONS UTILES ET L'ALPHABET

Note *d'orthographe*

1. The **cédille** occurs only on the letter **c** and causes it to be pronounced /s/ before the vowels **a, o,** and **u.**
2. The accent marks occur only on vowels, and the **accent aigu** only on the vowel **e.**
3. Accents in French do not indicate stress. They are used to indicate a difference in pronunciation (**é** versus **è**), to differentiate two words (**ou** *[or]* versus **où** *[where]*), or for historical reasons.

You will learn about accent marks and the use of the **cédille** in *Chapitre 2.* For now, learn the accents as part of the spelling of a new word.

Note *de vocabulaire*

1. There are several ways to say *You're welcome.*
De rien.
Il n'y a pas de quoi.
Je vous en prie. (formal)
Je t'en prie. (familiar)
2. *Pardon* and *excusez-moi* are not always interchangeable. Generally, use **pardon** to pass through a crowd or get someone's attention. Use **excusez-moi (excuse-moi** [familiar]) if you want to say you're sorry about something you have done or to get someone's attention.

iLrn 🌐 **Prononcez bien!** See Modules **2** and **3.**

When you hear new words, it may be helpful to see how they are spelled. You can ask:

Ça s'écrit comment?	*How is that written?*
Ça s'écrit avec ou sans accent?	*Is that written with or without an accent?*
Ça s'écrit avec un ou deux **s** en français / en anglais?	*Is that written with one or two **s**'s in French / in English?*

a	a	**A**nne	**q**	ku	**Q**uentin
b	bé	**B**runo	**r**	erre	**R**omane
c	cé	**C**aroline	**s**	esse	**S**téphane
d	dé	**D**idier	**t**	té	**T**ristan
e	e	**E**mma	**u**	u	**U**rsula
f	effe	**F**rançoise	**v**	vé	**V**alérie
g	gé	**G**abriel/**G**érard	**w**	double vé	**W**ladimir
h	hache	**H**ugo	**x**	iks	**X**avier
i	i	**I**sabelle	**y**	i grec	**Y**ves
j	ji	**J**ules	**z**	zède	**Z**oé
k	ka	**K**arima			
l	elle	**L**ola	**é** = **e** accent aigu		**ç** = **c** cédille
m	emme	**M**argot	**è** = **e** accent grave		**'** = apostrophe
n	enne	**N**athan	**â** = **a** accent circonflexe		**-** = trait d'union
o	o	**O**livier	**ï** = **i** tréma		**ll** = deux **l**
p	pé	**P**ascal			

You may also need to use these expressions.

Comment? Répétez, s'il vous plaît.	*What? Please repeat.*
— Vous comprenez?	*— Do you understand?*
— Oui, je comprends.	*— Yes, I understand.*
Non, je ne comprends pas.	*No, I don't understand.*
— Comment dit-on *a pen* en français?	*— How does one say **a pen** in French?*
— On dit **un stylo.**	*— One says **un stylo.***
— Qu'est-ce que ça veut dire **votre**?	*— What does **votre** mean?*
— Ça veut dire *your.*	*— It means **your.***
— Je ne sais pas.	*— I don't know.*
— Merci. / Merci bien.	*— Thank you., Thanks.*
— De rien.	*— You're welcome.*
— Pardon. / Excusez-moi.	*— Excuse me.*

🔊 **A** **Des animaux.** Listen as the names of some animals are spelled out and write them down.
1-18

> **EXEMPLE** Vous entendez: A-N-I-M-A-L
> Vous écrivez: **animal**

B Comparaisons culturelles. Working with a group, see how many of the names of these francophone places you can complete within the time limit set by your professor. The team with the most correct names wins. When you are done, take turns spelling out the names of the places.

EXEMPLE <u>Q</u> uébec **Q-U-E accent aigu B-E-C**

1. _____ rance
2. _____ lgérie
3. _____ ôte d'Ivoire

4. _____ ahiti
5. _____ uadeloupe
6. _____ aroc

7. _____ énégal
8. _____ ouisiane
9. _____ elgique

C Les SMS (text messages). Here are some common abbreviations used in French text messages (**les SMS** or **les textos**). First, spell them out, using the French alphabet and numbers. Then, match each one to its equivalent. In some cases, attempting to read the symbols aloud may help you determine the meaning.

| de rien | ciné (cinema) | à demain | je sais | excellent | à plus (tard) |
| | Tu es OK? | bonjour | salut | s'il vous plaît | |

1. A+
2. Je c
3. 2 ri 1
4. a2m1
5. 6né
6. XLnt
7. TOK
8. SLT
9. SVP
10. bjr

D Qu'est-ce que ça veut dire? Comment dit-on...? With a partner, take turns asking and telling what each of the following words or phrases means.

EXEMPLE ouvrez — Qu'est-ce que ça veut dire *ouvrez*?
— Ça veut dire *open*!

| ouvrez | fermez | le prochain cours | les mots | apprenez |
| | faites | un crayon | un stylo | l'examen | lisez |

Now, ask your partner how to say in French each of the following words or phrases. When he/she tells you, ask how it is spelled.

EXEMPLE *open* — Comment dit-on *open* en français?
— On dit *ouvrez*.
— Ça s'écrit comment?
— Ça s'écrit O-U-V-R-E-Z.

| open | please | Thanks! | You're welcome. | the workbook |
| I don't know. | Excuse me. | the homework | the next class |

E Réponses. Look back at the expressions above and below the alphabet on the preceding page. What would you say in the following situations?

1. You understood the question, but you don't know the answer.
2. You want to know how to say *giraffe* in French.
3. You want to know if *giraffe* is written with one *f* or two in French.
4. You want to know what the word **fou** means in English.
5. You need to pass through a group of students.
6. You stepped on someone's foot.

You can find a list of the new words from this *Compétence* on page 27 and access the audio online.

L'HEURE OFFICIELLE

In all schedules and sometimes in conversations, the French use the 24-hour clock rather than the conversational manner of telling time that you have already learned. With the 24-hour clock, you continue counting 13 to 24, instead of beginning with 1 to 12 o'clock again during the P.M. hours. For example, 2:00 A.M. is **deux heures** and 2:00 P.M. is **quatorze heures.** The expressions **du matin, de l'après-midi,** and **du soir** are not used with the 24-hour clock.

When using the 24-hour clock, state the hour and the number of minutes after the hour with a number, instead of using **midi, minuit, et quart, et demie,** or **moins le quart.** You will need the numbers **quarante** *(forty)* and **cinquante** *(fifty).*

How would you express each of these times in conversational time? In official time?

12:30 A.M.	3:45 A.M.	1:20 P.M.
10:40 A.M.	12:15 P.M.	11:55 P.M.

Il est quatorze heures six.

A **Horaire de train.** You are flying into Paris to study for a month at a French language institute in the town of **Le Creusot.** The institute's website lists the following **TGV** trains you can take daily from the **Gare de Lyon** station in Paris to **Le Creusot.** Say what time each train arrives, using official time. The first one has been done as an example.

Paris - Le Creusot TGV	
Départ Paris Gare de Lyon	Arrivée Le Creusot TGV
6h10	7h32
7h30	8h54
13h00	14h27
16h00	17h22
18h00	19h25
20h00	21h22

EXEMPLE   6h10
Le train de six heures dix arrive à sept heures trente-deux.

B **À la télé.** A friend wants to watch these shows on TV5, the international French TV station. Tell him what time each one is on. First use official time, then convert it to conversational time.

EXEMPLE *Monsieur Dictionnaire*
Monsieur Dictionnaire **est à treize heures vingt-huit,** c'est-à-dire *(that is to say)* **à une heure vingt-huit de l'après-midi.**

1. *Des chiffres et des lettres*
2. *Objectif nature*
3. *Chaplin*
4. *Le journal de France 2*
5. *Un livre un jour*
6. *Pauline et François*

Grille des programmes

Mercredi 25 avril

Matin

04:01 UN PRINTEMPS EN MÉDITERRANÉE
04:54 COURTS SÉJOURS
05:00 FLASH INFO
05:02 LE JOURNAL DE RADIO-CANADA
05:29 TV5MONDE LE JOURNAL AFRIQUE
05:42 TÉLÉMATIN
06:30 LE JOURNAL DE LA RTBF
07:00 TV5MONDE LE JOURNAL
07:23 PORTRAITS
07:30 TV5MONDE LE JOURNAL
07:53 ET DIEU CRÉA... LAFLAQUE
08:00 TÉLÉMATIN
08:48 KAAMELOTT
09:00 TV5MONDE LE JOURNAL
09:24 CHACUN SA TERRE
09:30 TV5MONDE LE JOURNAL
09:53 DES HOMMES ET DES BÊTES
10:01 COQUELICOT & CANAPÉ
10:28 UN LIVRE UN JOUR
10:31 L'ÉPICERIE
10:55 UN OBJET, UNE HISTOIRE
11:00 TV5MONDE LE JOURNAL
11:23 L'INVITÉ
11:32 «10»
11:55 FLASH INFO

Après-midi

12:01 VU SUR TERRE
12:54 COURTS SÉJOURS
13:00 LE JOURNAL DE LA RTS
→ 13:28 MONSIEUR DICTIONNAIRE
13:30 FLASH INFO
13:33 TOUT LE MONDE VEUT PRENDRE SA PLACE
→ 14:19 DES CHIFFRES ET DES LETTRES
14:49 PLUS BELLE LA VIE
15:15 TV5MONDE LE JOURNAL
→ 15:25 OBJECTIF NATURE
15:30 T'CHOUPI ET DOUDOU
15:35 PETIT LAPIN BLANC
15:39 PETIT LAPIN BLANC
→ 15:44 CHAPLIN
15:51 LOU!
16:04 STELLINA
16:29 «10»
16:56 MERCI PROFESSEUR!
→ 17:00 LE JOURNAL DE FRANCE 2
→ 17:26 UN LIVRE UN JOUR
17:28 LE POINT
18:29 QUESTIONS POUR UN CHAMPION
19:00 TV5MONDE LE JOURNAL
19:24 LE JOURNAL DE L'ÉCONOMIE
19:30 DES RACINES & DES AILES

Soir

21:30 TV5MONDE LE JOURNAL
→ 22:00 PAULINE ET FRANÇOIS
23:37 HURLEMENT D'UN POISSON
00:00 TV5MONDE LE JOURNAL
00:22 KAAMELOTT
00:35 LA GRANDE LIBRAIRIE
01:36 NEC PLUS ULTRA
02:02 ACOUSTIC
02:30 FLASH INFO
02:34 LE MARQUIS

© Cengage Learning

C **À discuter**

1. Is the 24-hour clock used in your country? In what circumstances?
2. Does using the 24-hour clock make things clearer or less clear to you? Why?

(iLrn Share It!

Visit **www.cengagebrain.com** for additional cultural information and activities.

VOCABULAIRE

COMPÉTENCE 1

Greeting people

GREETING PEOPLE

Bonjour.	*Hello., Good morning.*
Bonsoir.	*Good evening.*
monsieur (M.)	*Mr., sir*
madame (Mme)	*Mrs., madam*
mademoiselle (Mlle)	*Miss*
Comment allez-vous?	*How are you? (formal)*
Je vais très bien.	*I'm doing very well.*
Assez bien.	*Fairly well.*
Comme ci comme ça.	*So-so.*
Pas mal.	*Not bad(ly).*
Pas très bien.	*Not very well.*
Salut!	*Hi!, Bye!*
Comment ça va? / Ça va?	*How's it going? (familiar)*
Ça va.	*It's going fine.*
et	*and*
Et vous?	*And you? (formal)*
Et toi?	*And you? (familiar)*
moi	*me*
merci	*thank you, thanks*

EXCHANGING NAMES

Comment vous appelez-vous?	*What's your name? (formal)*
Tu t'appelles comment?	*What's your name? (familiar)*
Je m'appelle...	*My name is . . .*
Je suis...	*I am, I'm . . .*

SAYING GOOD-BYE

À bientôt.	*See you soon.*
À demain.	*See you tomorrow.*
À plus tard. / À plus.	*See you later.*
À tout à l'heure.	*See you in a little while.*
Au revoir.	*Good-bye.*

COMPÉTENCE 2

Counting and describing your week

COUNTING TO 30

Comptez de... à...	*Count from . . . to . . .*
s'il vous plaît	*please (formal)*
un, deux, trois, quatre,	*one, two, three, four,*
cinq, six, sept, huit,	*five, six, seven, eight,*
neuf, dix, onze, douze,	*nine, ten, eleven, twelve,*
treize, quatorze, quinze,	*thirteen, fourteen, fifteen,*
seize, dix-sept,	*sixteen, seventeen,*
dix-huit, dix-neuf,	*eighteen, nineteen,*
vingt, vingt et un,	*twenty, twenty-one,*
vingt-deux, vingt-trois,	*twenty-two, twenty-three,*
vingt-quatre, vingt-cinq,	*twenty-four, twenty-five,*
vingt-six, vingt-sept,	*twenty-six, twenty-seven,*
vingt-huit, vingt-neuf,	*twenty-eight, twenty-nine,*
trente	*thirty*
Combien font deux et deux?	*How much is two plus two?*
Deux et deux font quatre.	*Two plus two equals four.*
Combien font cinq moins deux?	*How much is five minus two?*
Cinq moins deux font trois.	*Five minus two equals three.*
un nombre	*a number*

TELLING THE DAY OF THE WEEK

les jours de la semaine	*the days of the week*
aujourd'hui	*today*
C'est quel jour, aujourd'hui?	*What day is today?*
C'est...	*It's . . .*
lundi	*Monday*
mardi	*Tuesday*
mercredi	*Wednesday*
jeudi	*Thursday*
vendredi	*Friday*
samedi	*Saturday*
dimanche	*Sunday*

DESCRIBING YOUR SCHEDULE

Tu es...?	*Are you . . . ?*
Je suis / Je ne suis pas...	*I'm / I'm not . . .*
en cours	*in class*
à la maison	*at home*
dans un autre cours	*in another class*
le cours de français	*French class*
Tu travailles?	*Do you work?*
Je travaille...	*I work . . .*
Je ne travaille pas...	*I don't work . . .*
Quels jours... ?	*What days . . . ?*
le lundi	*on Mondays*
le lundi matin	*(on) Monday mornings*
du lundi au vendredi	*from Monday to Friday (every week)*
le matin, l'après-midi, le soir	*in the morning, in the afternoon, in the evening*
la semaine	*the week*
tous les jours	*every day*
le week-end	*weekends / on the weekend*
ce semestre	*this semester*
avant	*before*
après	*after*
aussi	*also, too*

Talking about yourself and your schedule

TALKING ABOUT YOURSELF

un autoportrait	*a self-portrait*
Vous êtes...?	*Are you . . . ?*
Je suis / Je ne suis pas...	*I am / I am not . . .*
américain(e)	*American*
canadien(ne)	*Canadian*
de (d')... (+ city)	*from . . . (+ city)*
d'ici	*from here*
étudiant(e)	*a student*
professeur	*a professor*
Vous habitez...?	*Do you live . . . ?*
J'habite / Je n'habite pas...	*I live / I do not live . . .*
à... (+ city)	*in . . . (+ city)*
avec ma famille	*with my family*
avec un(e) ami(e)	*with a friend*
avec un(e) camarade de chambre	*with a roommate*
avec un(e) colocataire	*with a housemate*
seul(e)	*alone*
Vous parlez...?	*Do you speak . . . ?*
Je parle / Je ne parle pas...	*I speak / I do not speak . . .*
anglais	*English*
espagnol	*Spanish*
français	*French*
beaucoup en cours	*a lot in class*
Je pense que le français est...	*I think that French is . . .*
un peu difficile	*a little difficult / hard*
assez facile	*fairly easy*
intéressant	*interesting*
super	*great*
assez cool	*pretty cool*
Vous travaillez...?	*Do you work . . . ?*
Je travaille...	*I work . . .*
Je ne travaille pas...	*I do not work . . .*
pour...	*for . . .*
à l'université	*at the university*
ici	*here*
maintenant	*now*
mais	*but*
non	*no*
oui	*yes*
parce que	*because*

TELLING TIME

l'heure	*the time*
une heure	*an hour*
Quelle heure est-il?	*What time is it?*
Il est une heure / deux heures	*It's one o'clock / two o'clock*
midi / minuit	*noon / midnight*
et quart / et demi(e)	*a quarter past / half past*
moins le quart	*a quarter till*
À quelle heure?	*At what time?*
à... heure(s)	*at . . . o'clock*
du matin	*A.M., in the morning [when telling time]*
de l'après-midi	*P.M., in the afternoon [when telling time]*
du soir	*P.M., in the evening [when telling time]*
Le cours de français est... de... à...	*French class is . . . from . . . to . . .*
Le cours de français commence à... / finit à...	*French class starts at . . . / finishes at . . .*

Communicating in class

Comment? Répétez, s'il vous plaît.	*What? Please repeat.*
Vous comprenez?	*Do you understand?*
Oui, je comprends. / Non, je ne comprends pas.	*Yes, I understand. / No, I don't understand.*
Comment dit-on... en français / en anglais?	*How does one say . . . in French / in English?*
On dit...	*One says . . .*
Je ne sais pas.	*I don't know.*
Qu'est-ce que ça veut dire?	*What does that mean?*
Ça veut dire...	*That means . . .*
Ça s'écrit comment?	*How is that written?*
Ça s'écrit avec ou sans accent?	*That's written with or without an accent?*
Ça s'écrit...	*That's written . . .*
Merci (bien).	*Thank you., Thanks.*
De rien.	*You're welcome.*
Pardon. / Excusez-moi.	*Excuse me.*
Le professeur dit aux étudiants...	*The professor says to the students . . .*
Ouvrez votre livre à la page 23.	*Open your book to page 23.*
Fermez votre livre.	*Close your book.*
Écoutez la question.	*Listen to the question.*
Répondez à la question.	*Answer the question.*
Allez au tableau.	*Go to the board.*
Écrivez la réponse avec une phrase complète.	*Write the answer with a complete sentence.*
Prenez une feuille de papier et un crayon ou un stylo.	*Take out a piece of paper and a pencil or a pen.*
Faites l'exercice A à la page 21.	*Do exercise A on page 21.*
Donnez-moi votre feuille de papier.	*Give me your piece of paper.*
Lisez la page 17.	*Read page 17.*
Apprenez les mots de vocabulaire.	*Learn the vocabulary words.*
Préparez l'examen pour le prochain cours.	*Prepare for the exam for the next class.*
Faites les devoirs dans le cahier.	*Do the homework in the workbook.*

Pour l'alphabet, voir la page 22.

Sur la Côte d'Azur
À l'université

 iLrn Heinle Learning Center

 www.cengagebrain.com

 Horizons Video: Les Stagiaires

 Audio

Internet web search

 Pair work

 Group work

COMPÉTENCE

1 Identifying people and describing appearance
Les gens à l'université

Identifying and describing people
*Les adjectifs et **il est / elle est** + adjectif ou **c'est** + nom*

Stratégies et Lecture
* • **Pour mieux lire:** *Using cognates and familiar words to read for the gist*
* • **Lecture:** *Qui est-ce?*

2 Describing personality
Les personnalités

Describing people
*Les pronoms sujets, le verbe **être,** la négation et d'autres adjectifs*

Asking what someone is like
Les questions

3 Describing the university area
Le campus et le quartier

Saying what there is
*Le genre, l'article indéfini et l'expression **il y a***

Identifying and describing people and things
***C'est** ou **il est / elle est** et la place de l'adjectif*

4 Talking about your studies
L'université et les cours

Identifying people and things
L'article défini

Vidéoreprise *Les Stagiaires*

Lecture et Composition
* • **Pour mieux lire:** *Scanning to preview a text*
* • **Lecture:** *L'accent grave*
* • **Pour mieux écrire:** *Using and combining what you know*
* • **Composition:** *Un autoportrait*

Comparaisons culturelles *Les études*

Résumé de grammaire

Vocabulaire

© Art Kowalsky/Alamy

LA FRANCE ET SES RÉGIONS

© Cengage Learning

Quelles régions françaises **connaissez-vous**? La Normandie? La Provence? La Champagne? **Voici** des photos de quatre régions pittoresques. **Laquelle voudriez-vous visiter?**

© Hans Georg Elben/Getty Images

La Vallée de la Loire

© D0Photo/Shutterstock.com

La Côte d'Azur

© Irbiss/Shutterstock.com

---

connaissez-vous *do you know*   **Voici** *Here are*   **Laquelle voudriez-vous visiter?** *Which one would you like to visit?*
La Vallée de la Loire *The Loire Valley*   **La Côte d'Azur** *The French Riviera*

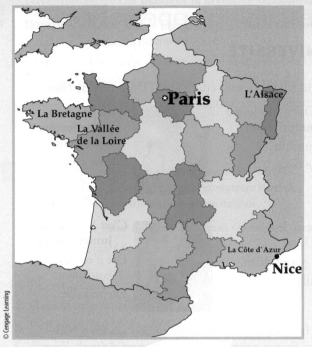

© Cengage Learning

La France (la République française)

🌐 Visit it live on Google Earth!

NOMBRE D'HABITANTS:
65 350 000 (les Français)

CAPITALE: **Paris**

Le savez-vous?

Look at the map and photos and guess which province each sentence below describes. Which would you most like to visit?

la Côte d'Azur	**la Vallée de la Loire**
la Bretagne	**l'Alsace**

1. This region shows both French and German influences in its architecture and culture because it was formerly part of Germany.

2. This area is known for its numerous castles and excellent wine.

3. Named for the color of the sky and water, this region is located along the Mediterranean sea.

4. The stone megaliths and tables reflect the traditions of the ancient people who inhabited this region from 3 000 to 5 000 years before our era.

La Bretagne

🌐 Which are the most famous castles along the Loire? Who set up the megaliths in Carnac (**Bretagne**)? Why is Alsace a mix of French and German culture? Search for information on the Web on any of these topics and share it with the class.

L'Alsace

IDENTIFYING AND DESCRIBING PEOPLE

Les adjectifs et *il est / elle est* + *adjectif ou* *c'est* + *nom*

Adjective forms vary depending on whether they describe a male or a female and whether they describe one person or more than one. The masculine singular form of the adjective is the base form. Add an **e** to change this form to feminine, unless it already ends in an *unaccented* **e.** If it ends in an *accented* **é,** add another **e** to form the feminine. Add an **s** to make an adjective plural, unless it ends in **s** or **x.**

MASCULINE		FEMININE	
SINGULAR	PLURAL	SINGULAR	PLURAL
petit	petit**s**	petit**e**	petit**es**
jeune	jeune**s**	jeune	jeune**s**
marié	marié**s**	marié**e**	marié**es**
français	français	français**e**	français**es**

Gros doubles its final consonant before adding the **e** for the feminine form, as do adjectives ending in **-en,** like canadi**en.**

MASCULINE		FEMININE	
SINGULAR	PLURAL	SINGULAR	PLURAL
gros	gros	gros**se**	gros**ses**
canadien	canadien**s**	canadien**ne**	canadien**nes**

The adjectives **beau, jumeau,** and **vieux** are irregular.

MASCULINE		FEMININE	
SINGULAR	PLURAL	SINGULAR	PLURAL
beau	beaux	belle	belles
jumeau	jumeaux	jumelle	jumelles
vieux	vieux	vieille	vieilles

Notice how to say *he/she/it/this/that is* and *these/those/they are.* When *identifying* people with *nouns,* use **c'est** and **ce sont.** When *describing* people with *adjectives,* use **il est, elle est, ils sont,** and **elles sont.** Use **ils** for a group of males or a mixed group and **elles** for a group of all females.

To *identify* people with *nouns,* use:	To *describe* people with *adjectives,* use:
c'est + *noun* **ce sont**	**il/elle est** + *adjective* **ils/elles sont**
C'est Jean. *It/This/He is Jean.*	**Il est célibataire.** *He is single.*
Ce sont mes amis. *They are my friends.*	**Ils sont français.** *They are French.*

To negate the verb, place **ne (n')** *before* it and **pas** *after* it. **Ne** becomes **n'** before vowel sounds.

Ce n'est pas ma sœur. *She/This isn't my sister.*	**Elles ne sont pas américaines.** *They aren't American.*

✔ Pour vérifier

These self-check questions are provided throughout the book. Read the entire explanation before trying to answer the questions.

1. What is the base form of an adjective? What do you usually do to make it feminine if it ends in **e**? in **é**? another vowel? a consonant?

2. What is the feminine form of **gros**? **canadien**? **beau**? **vieux**?

3. What do you usually do to make an adjective plural? What if it ends in **x** or **s**?

4. What two expressions are used to *identify* who someone is with a *noun*? What are the negative forms of these expressions?

5. When *describing* someone with an *adjective,* how do you say *he is? she is? they are* for a group of all females? *they are* for a group of all males or for a mixed group? What are the negative forms of these expressions?

6. Is there a difference in pronunciation between **espagnol** and **espagnole**? between **petit** and **petite**? Is the final **s** of the plural form of an adjective pronounced?

ⒾLrn Grammar Tutorials

Note *de grammaire*

Also use **il est, elle est, ils sont,** and **elles sont** to state someone's profession (including **étudiant[e]**), nationality, or religion. However, unlike in English, do not include the French equivalent of the word *a.*

Elle est étudiante. *She's a student.*

Il est américain. *He's (an) American.*

Ils sont catholiques. *They're Catholic(s).*

You will learn more about this later in this chapter.

PRONONCIATION

iLrn Prononcez bien! See **Module 22**.

1-20

Il est + *adjectif* / *Elle est* + *adjectif*

Since most final consonants are silent in French, you will not hear or say the final consonant of masculine adjective forms, unless they end in **c, r, f,** or **l**. When the **e** is added to make the feminine form, the consonant is no longer final and is pronounced.

> petit / petite   français / française

When a masculine adjective form ends in a pronounced final consonant, or in **e** or **é,** however, you will hear no difference between the masculine and feminine forms.

> espagnol / espagnole   jeune / jeune   marié / mariée

The final **s** of plurals is not pronounced, nor is a consonant that immediately precedes it, unless it is **c, r, f,** or **l**. The masculine plural forms sound like the masculine singular forms and the feminine plural forms sound like the feminine singular forms. You must pick up the plurality from the context.

> Il est petit. / Ils sont petits.   Elle est petite. / Elles sont petites.

A Prononcez bien! Écoutez les phrases. C'est la phrase **a** pour Gabriel Bellon
1-21 ou la phrase **b** pour Gabrielle Lacoste?

1. **a.** Gabriel est grand.
   b. Gabrielle est grande.
2. **a.** Gabriel n'est pas petit.
   b. Gabrielle n'est pas petite.
3. **a.** Gabriel est français.
   b. Gabrielle est française.
4. **a.** Gabriel n'est pas canadien.
   b. Gabrielle n'est pas canadienne.
5. **a.** Gabriel n'est pas gros.
   b. Gabrielle n'est pas grosse.

a. Gabriel Bellon   **b.** Gabrielle Lacoste

Maintenant, lisez une seule *(a single)* phrase de chaque paire. Votre partenaire va dire si *(is going to say if)* vous dites la phrase **a** ou la phrase **b**.

B Qui est-ce? Comment sont-ils? D'abord *(First)*, utilisez **c'est** ou **ce sont** pour identifier chaque personne. Ensuite *(Then)*, dites si chaque adjectif décrit la personne. Utilisez **il est / il n'est pas, elle est / elle n'est pas, ils sont / ils ne sont pas** ou **elles sont / elles ne sont pas** et la forme correcte de l'adjectif.

EXEMPLE   C'est David. Il n'est pas grand. Il est petit...

David
(grand/petit/
mince/gros/
beau/laid)

1. Léa
(grand/petit/
mince/gros/
beau/laid)

2. David et Jean
(français/
américain/jumeau/
vieux/jeune)

3. Léa et Lisa
(français/
américain/jumeau/
vieux/jeune)

STRATÉGIES ET LECTURE

It may seem overwhelming to read a lengthier text in French at first. However, there are strategies you can use to learn to read more easily. This section is designed to help you learn to apply these strategies.

POUR MIEUX LIRE: Using cognates and familiar words to read for the gist

Cognates are words that look the same or similar in two languages and have the same meaning. Take advantage of cognates to help you read French more easily. There are some patterns in cognates. What three patterns do you see here? What do the last two words in each column mean?

soudainement *suddenly*	obligé *obliged*	hôpital *hospital*
décidément *decidedly*	sauvé *saved*	île *isle, island*
complètement *?*	compliqué *?*	honnête *?*
généralement *?*	décidé *?*	forêt *?*

Recognizing words you have already learned in different forms will also help you read. Use the two familiar phrases on the left to guess the meanings of those on the right.

Comment dit-on *pen* en français? → Qu'est-ce que tu dis?
Je ne sais pas la réponse. → Lisa ne sait pas quoi répondre.

A **Avant de lire.** Can you state the general idea of the following sentences? Do not try to read them word by word; rather, focus on the words that you can understand.

Lisa hésite un moment avant de répondre.
C'est juste à ce moment que Léa arrive.
Léa sauve la pauvre Lisa.
David voit Léa et Lisa et s'exclame: «Je vois double!»

B **Mots apparentés.** Before reading the following text, *Qui est-ce?*, skim through it and list the cognates you see. You should find about twenty.

Lecture: *Qui est-ce?*

🔊
1-22
Lisa Clark is visiting her twin sister, Léa, a student at the University of Nice. As she waits for her sister in front of the **musée des Beaux-Arts,** a young man approaches. Since she does not speak French very well, Lisa is unsure what to say when he speaks to her.

— Salut, Léa! Ça va?

Lisa hésite un moment avant de répondre.

— Non, non... euh, ça va, mais... euh... je regrette... je ne suis pas Léa. Je suis Lisa.

— Qu'est-ce que tu dis, Léa?

Lisa pense: «*He thinks I'm Léa. How do I tell him . . . ?*»

— Non, non, répond Lisa. Vous ne comprenez pas. Je ne suis pas Léa.

— Comment ça, tu n'es pas Léa?

Décidément, ce jeune homme ne comprend rien! Lisa insiste.

— Je ne suis pas Léa. Vous ne comprenez pas! Écoutez! Je ne suis pas Léa! Je ne suis pas étudiante.

— Mais qu'est-ce que tu dis? demande David. Tu es malade? C'est moi, David. Nous sommes dans le même cours de littérature.

Lisa pense: «*I'm never going to get this guy to understand. He's so sure I'm Léa.*»

C'est juste à ce moment que Léa arrive. La pauvre Lisa est sauvée.

— Salut, Lisa! Bonjour, David!

David, très surpris de voir les sœurs jumelles, s'exclame:

— Mais, ce n'est pas possible! Je vois double! Maintenant, je comprends. C'est ta sœur jumelle, Léa.

— Mon pauvre David! Voilà, je te présente ma sœur, Lisa.

— Bonjour, Lisa. Désolé pour la confusion, mais quelle ressemblance!

A **Avez-vous compris?** Qui parle: **David, Lisa** ou **Léa**?

1. Vous ne comprenez pas. Je ne suis pas Léa.

2. Mais nous sommes dans le même cours de littérature.

3. Je ne suis pas étudiante à l'Université de Nice.

4. Je ne parle pas très bien français.

5. Je te présente ma sœur.

B **D'abord...** Which happens first, **a** or **b**?

1. a. David dit bonjour à Lisa.
　b. Lisa arrive au musée des Beaux-Arts.

2. a. David dit: «Bonjour, Léa.»
　b. Lisa pense: «Il ne comprend pas.»

3. a. Lisa hésite à répondre parce qu'elle ne parle pas très bien français.
　b. Lisa répond: «Non, non, vous ne comprenez pas.»

4. a. David comprend que Léa et Lisa sont sœurs jumelles.
　b. Léa arrive.

5. a. David dit: «Désolé *(Sorry)* pour la confusion.»
　b. David comprend la situation.

Describing personality

LES PERSONNALITÉS

Je suis très...   Je suis **plutôt**...   Je suis assez...   Je suis un peu...

Je **ne** suis **pas (du tout)**...

optimiste /
pessimiste
idéaliste / réaliste

intelligent(e) / **bête**
intellectuel(le)

timide / extraverti(e)

**dynamique /
paresseux
(paresseuse)**
sportif (sportive)

intéressant(e) /
**ennuyeux
(ennuyeuse)**
amusant(e) /
marrant(e)

agréable / désagréable
**gentil (gentille) /
méchant(e)
sympathique (sympa) /
antipathique**

What are you like, compared to your best friend?

Je suis **plus** dynamique **que mon meilleur ami (ma meilleure amie).**

Je suis **aussi** sportif (sportive) **que** mon meilleur ami (ma meilleure amie).

Je suis **moins** timide **que** mon meilleur ami (ma meilleure amie).

1-23

Une **nouvelle** amie, Nadia, parle avec David.

NADIA: **Tes amis** et toi, vous êtes étudiants, non?

DAVID: Oui, nous sommes étudiants à l'Université de Nice.

NADIA: Vous êtes plutôt intellectuels, alors?

DAVID: Mes amis sont assez intellectuels, mais moi, **pas tellement.**
Et toi? Tu es étudiante aussi?

NADIA: Non, **les études, ce n'est pas mon truc.**

DAVID: Et le sport? **Tu aimes** le sport?

NADIA: Oui, j'aime bien le tennis, mais je n'aime pas beaucoup **le football.**

Vocabulaire sans peine!

Noticing cognate patterns can help you learn new words more quickly.

-if(-ive) = *-ive*

agressif = *aggressive*

-iste = *-ist(ic)*

matérialiste = *materialistic*

How would you say these words in French?

impulsive   imaginative

conformist   perfectionist

plutôt *rather*   **ne... pas (du tout)** *not (at all)*   **bête** *stupid, dumb*   **dynamique** *active*   **paresseux (paresseuse)** *lazy*
ennuyeux (ennuyeuse) *boring*   **marrant(e)** *funny*   **gentil(le)** *nice*   **méchant(e)** *mean*   **sympathique / sympa** *nice*
antipathique *disagreeable, unpleasant*   **plus... que** *more...than*   **mon meilleur ami (ma meilleure amie)** *my best friend*
aussi... que *as...as*   **moins... que** *less...than*   **nouveau (nouvelle)** *new*   **Tes amis** *Your friends*   **pas tellement** *not so much*
les études *studies, going to school*   **ce n'est pas mon truc** *it's not my thing*   **Tu aimes** *You like*   **le foot(ball)** *soccer*

A **Ils sont comment?** Complétez les phrases.

> **EXEMPLE** Danny DeVito est (plus, moins, aussi) grand que Tom Cruise.
> **Danny DeVito est moins grand que Tom Cruise.**

1. Johnny Depp est (plus, moins, aussi) beau que Jack Black.
2. Jim Carrey est (plus, moins, aussi) marrant que Will Ferrell.
3. Serena Williams est (plus, moins, aussi) sportive que Venus Williams.
4. Scarlett Johansson est (plus, moins, aussi) belle que Jennifer Aniston.
5. Ellen DeGeneres est (plus, moins, aussi) intéressante qu'Oprah Winfrey.
6. Donald Trump est (plus, moins, aussi) désagréable que Kim Kardashian.

B **Comment sont-ils?** Complétez les phrases suivantes pour parler de vous, vos amis et vos professeurs.

MOI

1. *J'aime / Je n'aime pas* le sport.
2. *Je suis / Je ne suis pas* sportif (sportive).
3. Je suis *plutôt extraverti*(e) */ un peu timide.*
4. *Je parle / Je ne parle pas* beaucoup.

MON MEILLEUR AMI / MA MEILLEURE AMIE

7. *Il/Elle aime / Il/Elle n'aime pas* les études.
8. *Il/Elle est / Il/Elle n'est pas* intellectuel(le).
9. *Il/Elle est / Il/Elle n'est pas* très intelligent(e).
10. Il/Elle est *agréable / désagréable.*

MES AMIS ET MOI

5. Nous sommes *dynamiques / paresseux.*
6. *Nous sommes / Nous ne sommes pas* très sympas.

MES PROFS

11. Ils sont *sympas / antipathiques.*
12. *Ils sont / Ils ne sont pas* intelligents.

C **Et vous?** Comment êtes-vous?

← très   plutôt   assez   un peu   ne... pas du tout →

> **EXEMPLE** optimistic
> **Je suis très / plutôt / assez / un peu optimiste.**
> **Je ne suis pas (du tout) optimiste.**

1. idealistic
2. mean
3. lazy
4. intellectual

5. shy
6. boring
7. athletic
8. married

À VOUS!

Avec un(e) partenaire, relisez à haute voix *(aloud)* la conversation entre Nadia et David. Ensuite, adaptez la conversation pour décrire *(to describe)* votre situation.

iLrn You can find a list of the new words from this *Compétence* on page 62 and access the audio online.

DESCRIBING PEOPLE

*Les pronoms sujets, le verbe **être**, la négation et d'autres adjectifs*

Below are the subject pronouns *(I, you, he . . .)* and the forms of the verb **être** *(to be)*.

Use **tu** to say *you* when speaking to a friend, family member, classmate, child, or animal. Use **vous** to say *you* when speaking to any unknown adult, someone to whom you should show respect, or when talking to more than one person.

For **je** and other one-syllable words ending in **e** (ne, que, me, le...), replace the **e** with an apostrophe before a vowel or mute **h.** This is called *elision.*

The word **être** is the infinitive, the verb form you find in the dictionary. This chart shows the conjugation, the forms to use with different subject pronouns.

ÊTRE *(to be)*					
je	suis	*I am*	nous	sommes	*we are*
tu	es	*you are*	vous	êtes	*you are*
il	est	*he is, it is*	ils	sont	*they are*
elle	est	*she is, it is*	elles	sont	*they are*

To negate a conjugated verb, place **ne... pas** around it. Remember to use **n'** before a vowel sound or mute **h.**

ne (n') + verbe + pas		
je **ne** travaille **pas**	je **n'**habite **pas**	je **n'**aime **pas**
je **ne** suis **pas**	tu **n'**es **pas**	il/elle **n'**est **pas**
nous **ne** sommes **pas**	vous **n'**êtes **pas**	ils/elles **ne** sont **pas**

Note the patterns of these common adjective endings.

MASCULINE	FEMININE	MASCULINE		FEMININE	
		SINGULAR	PLURAL	SINGULAR	PLURAL
-eux	-euse(s)	paress**eux**	paress**eux**	paress**euse**	paress**euses**
-en(s)	-enne(s)	canadi**en**	canadi**ens**	canadi**enne**	canadi**ennes**
-if(s)	-ive(s)	sport**if**	sport**ifs**	sport**ive**	sport**ives**
-el(s)	-elle(s)	intellectu**el**	intellectu**els**	intellectu**elle**	intellectu**elles**
-er(s)	-ère(s)	prem**ier**	prem**iers**	prem**ière**	prem**ières**

Gentil doubles the final consonant before adding the **e** for the feminine form (**gentil → gentille**).

The adjectives **beau, nouveau, jumeau,** and **vieux** are irregular, but follow a similar pattern.

MASCULINE		FEMININE	
SINGULAR	PLURAL	SINGULAR	PLURAL
beau	beaux	belle	belles
nouveau	nouveaux	nouvelle	nouvelles
jumeau	jumeaux	jumelle	jumelles
vieux	vieux	vieille	vieilles

✔ *Pour vérifier*

1. Would you use **tu** or **vous** to address a child? two children? a salesclerk? an adult you've just met?

2. How do you say *I* in French? When do words like **je, ne,** and **que** replace the final **e** with an apostrophe (**j', n', qu'**)? What is this called?

3. How do you say *he* in French? *she*? *they* for a group of all females? *they* for a group of all males? *they* for a mixed group?

4. What is an infinitive? How do you say *to be*? What form of **être** do you use with each subject pronoun?

5. What do you place before a conjugated verb to negate it? What do you place after it? What happens to **ne** when it is followed by a vowel sound?

6. What are five irregular patterns of adjective agreement?

7. What is the feminine form of **gentil**? of **beau**? of **nouveau**? of **vieux**?

⌨ **Prononcez bien!** See **Module 20.**

⌨ **Grammar Tutorials**

Note *de grammaire*

With noun subjects or compound subjects, use the verb form that goes with the corresponding subject pronoun.

David is = he is (**il est**) = **David est**
David and I are = we are (**nous sommes**) = **David et moi sommes**
your friends and you = you (plural) are (**vous êtes**) = **tes ami(e)s et toi, vous êtes**
my friends are = they are (**ils/elles sont**) = **mes ami(e)s sont**

🌐 **Sélection musicale.** Search the Web for the song **"Exactement"** by **Vive la fête** to enjoy a musical selection containing these structures.

A **Tu ou vous?** Demandez à ces personnes d'où elles sont *(where they are from)*.

EXEMPLES your classmate: **Tu es d'où?**
your boss: **Vous êtes d'où?**

1. your roommate   **3.** a salesclerk   **5.** your parents
2. your teacher   **4.** two friends   **6.** a new elderly neighbor

B **Quel pronom?** Complétez les phrases avec le bon pronom sujet personnel *(correct subject pronoun):* **je, tu, il, elle, nous, vous, ils, elles.**

1. David est étudiant à l'université, mais _____ n'est pas très intellectuel.
Nadia n'est pas intellectuelle non plus *(either)*. _____ est plutôt sportive!

2. Léa et Lisa ne sont pas paresseuses. _____ sont dynamiques. David et
Jean sont dynamiques aussi, mais _____ sont moins dynamiques que Léa
et Lisa. Mes amis et moi, _____ sommes assez dynamiques aussi. Et tes
amis et toi, _____ êtes dynamiques?

3. David et Léa ne sont pas mariés. _____ sont célibataires. Moi, _____
suis célibataire aussi. Et toi, _____ es célibataire ou marié(e)?

C **Comment sont-ils?** Dites si ces adjectifs décrivent *(describe)* bien ces
personnes. Changez la forme de l'adjectif si nécessaire.

EXEMPLE Léa... beau, laid   **Léa est belle. Elle n'est pas laide.**

Léa...
intellectuel,
gros, paresseux,
dynamique

Léa et Lisa...
américain,
français, gentil,
antipathique,
beau

David et Jean...
laid, beau,
vieux, jeune

Moi, je...
dynamique,
paresseux,
ennuyeux,
sportif

D **Descriptions.** Décrivez ces personnes avec une phrase à l'affirmatif et une
autre phrase au négatif.

EXEMPLE **Moi, je suis (très) optimiste. Je ne suis pas (du tout) pessimiste.**

| moi, je | le professeur de français | les étudiants du cours de français |

très	**plutôt**	**assez**	**un peu**	**ne... pas (du tout)**
dynamique	sportif	paresseux	intellectuel
optimiste	pessimiste	réaliste	idéaliste
gentil	antipathique	sympa	intéressant
intelligent	intéressant	ennuyeux	marrant

| ma famille et moi | mes parents | mes amis et moi |

ASKING WHAT SOMEONE IS LIKE

✔ *Pour vérifier*

1. What are three ways of asking a question that can be answered with **oui** or **non**? What happens to your intonation in each case?

2. What happens to **que** before a vowel sound?

 Prononcez bien! See **Module 21.**

Les questions

There are several ways to ask a question that will be answered *yes* or *no*.

• You can ask a question with rising intonation. A statement normally has falling intonation.

Tu es extravertie?   Tu es sportive?

• You can ask a question by placing **est-ce que** before the subject and the verb and using rising intonation. Note that **que** becomes **qu'** before vowel sounds.

Est-ce que tes amis sont étudiants?   Est-ce qu'ils sont intellectuels?

Est-ce que tu es marié?   Est-ce qu'elle est étudiante?

• If you are presuming that someone will probably answer *yes,* you can use either **n'est-ce pas?** *(right?)* or **non?** at the end of a question with rising intonation.

Il est marié, n'est-ce pas?   Il est marié, non?

🀫🀫🀫 A Personnalités. Recopiez le tableau qui suit *(the chart that follows)* sur une feuille de papier. Posez des questions à d'autres étudiants pour trouver une personne qui correspond à chaque *(each)* adjectif.

EXEMPLES — Mario, est-ce que tu es sportif?
— Non, je ne suis pas sportif.

— Brianna, est-ce que tu es sportive?
— Oui, je suis sportive.

sportif (sportive) *Brianna*	plutôt extraverti(e)	un peu timide
très optimiste	un peu paresseux (paresseuse)	assez intellectuel(le)
marié(e)	idéaliste	très dynamique

Maintenant, présentez un(e) des étudiant(e)s à la classe.

EXEMPLE C'est Brianna. Elle est sportive.

ii B **Encore des questions!** Formez des questions logiques avec le verbe **être** et posez-les à votre partenaire.

> **EXEMPLE** — Est-ce que tu es marié(e)?
> — Oui, je suis marié(e). / Non, je ne suis pas marié(e).

Est-ce que	tu... nous... tes amis... ton meilleur ami / ta meilleure amie...	marié(e)(s) assez intellectuel(le)(s) d'ici en cours à une heure plus extraverti(e)(s) que toi très sportif(s) (sportive[s]) aussi intelligent(e)(s) que toi

C **Et Léa?** Léa répond aux questions d'une nouvelle amie. Utilisez ses réponses pour déterminer quelles questions son amie lui a posées *(her friend asked her)*.

> **EXEMPLE** — **Est-ce que tu es professeur?**
> — Non, je ne suis pas professeur.

1. — _____?
— Oui, je suis étudiante.

2. — _____?
— Oui, je suis plutôt intellectuelle.

3. — _____?
— Oui, les cours sont faciles.

4. — _____?
— Oui, les professeurs sont gentils.

5. — _____?
— Non, Lisa n'est pas étudiante.

6. — _____?
— Oui, elle est sportive.

7. — Et ta sœur et toi? _____
_____?
— Non, nous ne sommes pas canadiennes.

8. — _____?
— Oui, nous sommes américaines.

ii D **Entretien.** Interviewez votre partenaire.

1. Est-ce que tu es américain(e)? Ta famille et toi, vous êtes d'ici?

2. Est-ce que tu es dans un autre cours après le cours de français? Est-ce que les études sont faciles ou difficiles pour toi? Tes amis et toi, est-ce que vous êtes intellectuels? Est-ce que ton meilleur ami (ta meilleure amie) est plus intellectuel(le) ou moins intellectuel(le) que toi? Est-ce qu'il/elle est étudiant(e) aussi?

3. Est-ce que tu aimes le sport? Tu es plutôt sportif (sportive)? Est-ce que tu es très dynamique ou plutôt paresseux (paresseuse)?

© Mike Kemp/Getty Images

Describing the university area

LE CAMPUS ET LE QUARTIER

Qu'est-ce qu'il y a sur votre campus?

Sur le campus, **il y a...**

des salles *(f)* de cours

des bureaux *(m)* pour les professeurs (profs)

un amphithéâtre

une bibliothèque avec Wi-Fi

des résidences *(f)*

un stade
des matchs *(m)* de foot(ball) américain

une librairie

un parking

Dans le quartier universitaire, près de l'université, il y a...

des bâtiments *(m)* modernes

des maisons *(f)*

un parc
des arbres *(m)*

des concerts *(m)* de rock *(m)* de jazz *(m)* de musique *(f)* pop(ulaire) de musique classique

Line art on this page: © Cengage Learning

Qu'est-ce qu'il y a...? *What is there...?* **sur** *on* **il y a** *there is, there are* **un bureau** *an office* **un amphithéâtre** *a lecture hall* **une résidence** *a dormitory* **Dans le quartier universitaire** *In the university neighborhood* **près de** *near* **un bâtiment** *a building*

une boîte de nuit

un théâtre

un cinéma
des films *(m)*
étrangers /
américains

une salle de gym

1-24

Léa parle avec un ami.

RÉMI: Comment est **ton** université, **là-bas** en Californie? Tu aimes le campus?

LÉA: Oui, il est très agréable. Les vieux bâtiments sont très **jolis.**

RÉMI: Qu'est-ce qu'il y a sur le campus?

LÉA: Il y a une grande bibliothèque et beaucoup d'arbres, mais **il n'y a pas assez de** parkings.

RÉMI: Qu'est-ce qu'il y a dans le quartier?

LÉA: Il y a de jolies maisons, des cafés, deux ou trois **bons** restaurants et beaucoup de **mauvais** fast-foods.

Chez nous. Décrivez votre université.

1. Sur le campus, il y a *plus de nouveaux bâtiments / plus de vieux bâtiments.*
2. *Il y a / Il n'y a pas* le Wi-Fi dans tous les *(all the)* bâtiments.
3. *Il y a / Il n'y a pas* assez de résidences sur le campus.
4. *Il y a / Il n'y a pas* beaucoup d'arbres sur le campus.
5. Le restaurant universitaire est un *bon / mauvais* restaurant. *(Il n'y a pas de restaurant sur le campus.)*
6. *Il y a / Il n'y a pas* assez de parkings.
7. Le week-end, il y a souvent *(often) des matchs de football américain / des concerts / des films étrangers / des films américains / ???.*
8. Dans le quartier près de l'université, il y a *des cafés / un joli parc / ???.*
9. *BookPeople / Monster Books / ???* est une bonne librairie dans le quartier.

 À VOUS!

Avec un(e) partenaire, relisez à haute voix la conversation entre Rémi et Léa. Ensuite, adaptez la conversation pour décrire votre université.

(iLrn) You can find a list of the new words from this *Compétence* on page 63 and access the audio online.

étranger (étrangère) *foreign* **ton (ta, tes)** *your* **là(-bas)** *(over) there* **joli(e)** *pretty* **il n'y a pas** *there isn't, there aren't*
assez de *enough* **bon(ne)** *good* **mauvais(e)** *bad*

SAYING WHAT THERE IS

✔ *Pour vérifier*

1. What are the two forms of the word for *a*? When do you use each? How do you say *some*?

2. How do you say *there is*? *there are*? *there isn't*? *there aren't*?

3. In what three circumstances do you use **de (d')** instead of **un, une,** or **des**? What is an exception to replacing **un, une,** or **des** with **de (d')** in a negative sentence?

iLrn Grammar Tutorials

Vocabulaire sans peine!

Nouns ending in **-tion** and **-té** are usually feminine. Notice these cognate patterns.

-tion = *-tion*
une nation = *a nation*
-té = *-ty*
une activité = *an activity*

How would you say these nouns in French?

*a conversation   an administration
a minority   a majority*

Le genre, l'article indéfini et l'expression **il y a**

To say *there is* or *there are* in French, use the expression **il y a (un, une, des…)**. To say *there isn't* or *there aren't*, use **il n'y a pas (de…)**.

All nouns in French have a gender (masculine or feminine). The categorization of most nouns as masculine or feminine cannot be guessed, unless they represent people.

The short word **un** *(a, an),* **une** *(a, an),* or **des** *(some)* before a noun is called the *indefinite article.* Use **un** with masculine singular nouns, **une** with feminine singular nouns, and **des** with all plural nouns.

Always learn a new noun as a unit with the article (**un, une**) in order to remember its gender!

	MASCULINE	FEMININE
SINGULAR	un théâtre	une bibliothèque
PLURAL	des théâtres	des bibliothèques

To make a noun plural, add an **s** to the end of it, unless it ends in **s, x,** or **z.** Nouns that end in **-eau (bureau)** form their plural with an **x (bureaux).**

Un, une, and **des** change to **de (d')** in the following cases.

- After most negated verbs.

  Il y a **un** stade. → Il n'y a **pas de** stade.
  Il y a **une** résidence. → Il n'y a **pas de** résidence.
  Écrivez **des** phrases complètes. → N'écrivez **pas de** phrases complètes.
  Il y a **des** étudiants dans la classe. → Il n'y a **pas d'**étudiants dans la classe.

  But not after the verb **être:**
  C'est **un** bon restaurant. → Ce n'est **pas un** bon restaurant.

- After expressions of quantity, such as **assez, beaucoup,** and **combien.**

  Il y a **un** parking. → Il y a **assez de** parkings.
  Il y a **une** bibliothèque? → Il y a **beaucoup de** bibliothèques.
  Il y a **des** cinémas. → Il y a **combien de** cinémas?

- Directly before a plural adjective.

  Il y a **des bâtiments modernes.** → Il y a **de jolis** bâtiments.

PRONONCIATION

L'article indéfini
1-25

Be careful to pronounce **un** and **une** differently. Use the very tight sound **u** with lips pursed, as in **tu,** to say **une.** To pronounce the **u** sound, position your mouth to pronounce a French **i** with your tongue held high in your mouth. Then, purse your lips. The vowel sound of **un** is nasal. Pronounce the **n** in **un** only when there is **liaison** with a following noun beginning with a vowel sound.

une résidence   **un** bâtiment   **une** amie   **un‿**ami

A **Prononcez bien!** Complétez les questions suivantes sur cette photo avec **un, une** ou **des.** Après, posez les questions à votre partenaire. Faites attention à la prononciation.

1. C'est _____ bibliothèque, _____ petite salle de cours ou _____ grand amphithéâtre?

2. Il y a _____ professeur?

3. Les autres *(others)*, ce sont _____ étudiants ou _____ professeurs?

4. Il y a _____ tableau dans l'amphithéâtre?

© Lisa Klumpp/Getty Images

B **Comparaisons culturelles.** Relisez les *Notes culturelles* aux pages 38 et 44. Sur le campus d'une université française, est-ce qu'il est probable qu'on trouve ces choses *(one finds these things)*?

EXEMPLES un restaurant universitaire des matchs de football
Oui, il y a un restaurant **Non, il n'y a pas de matchs**
universitaire. **de football.**

> **des amphithéâtres** **un stade** **des bureaux de profs**
> **une bibliothèque** **des résidences** **des salles de cours**
> **une boîte de nuit** **des matchs de football américain**

Maintenant, dites s'il y a ces choses *(these things)* sur votre *(your)* campus.

C **Chez nous.** Complétez chaque phrase avec **un, une, des,** ou **de (d').** Ensuite *(Then)*, dites si les deux dernières phrases *(the last two sentences)* de chaque groupe sont vraies ou fausses.

1. C'est _____ restaurant.
Il y a _____ bon restaurant sur notre *(our)* campus.
Il y a _____ bons restaurants dans le quartier.

2. C'est _____ bibliothèque.
Il n'y a pas _____ bibliothèque sur notre campus.
Il y a _____ bibliothèque municipale près d'ici.

3. C'est _____ parking.
Il y a assez _____ parkings sur notre campus.
Il y a _____ parkings payants *(pay)* près d'ici.

4. Ce sont _____ arbres.
Il y a beaucoup _____ arbres sur notre campus.
Il y a _____ parc avec _____ beaux arbres dans le quartier.

© Cengage Learning

IDENTIFYING AND DESCRIBING PEOPLE AND THINGS

C'est ou *il est / elle est* et la place de l'adjectif

All nouns in French are masculine or feminine. There is no neuter. Generally, use **il** or **elle** to say *it* and **ils** or **elles** to say *they* when talking about things, depending on the gender of the noun being referred to.

Le campus? **Il** est beau.   Les parkings? **Ils** sont petits!
La bibliothèque? **Elle** est jolie.   Les résidences? **Elles** sont très vieilles!

Note that **c'est,** as well as **il est / elle est,** can mean *he is / she is / it is,* and **ce sont,** as well as **ils sont / elles sont,** can mean *they are.* These expressions are not interchangeable.

Use **c'est** and **ce sont:**

- with *nouns* to identify or describe.
  C'est David.
  C'est un jeune homme sympathique.
  C'est mon ami.
  C'est le frère de Jean.

Use **il est / elle est** and **ils sont / elles sont:**

- with *adjectives* to describe.
  Il est petit et sympathique.
- with *prepositional phrases* to say such things as where someone or something is or is from.
  Il est de Nice.
  Il est en cours.
- with *nationalities, professions* (including **étudiant[e]**), *and religions* without the indefinite article.
  Il est français.
  Il est étudiant.
  Il est catholique.

In French, most descriptive adjectives are placed *after* the noun they describe.

un campus moderne   une boîte de nuit populaire   des amis sympas

However, these 15 very common adjectives are placed *before* the noun.

beau (belle)	jeune	bon (bonne)	grand(e)	autre
joli(e)	vieux (vieille)	mauvais(e)	petit(e)	même
	nouveau (nouvelle)	gentil(le)	gros(se)	seul(e) *(only)*
				premier (première)

un joli campus   une grande boîte de nuit   de bons amis

The adjectives **beau, nouveau,** and **vieux** have alternate masculine singular forms, **bel, nouvel,** and **vieil,** that are used before nouns beginning with a vowel sound.

MASCULINE SINGULAR (PLUS CONSONANT SOUND)	MASCULINE SINGULAR (PLUS VOWEL SOUND)	FEMININE SINGULAR
un beau quartier	un bel ami	une belle amie
un nouveau quartier	un nouvel ami	une nouvelle amie
un vieux quartier	un vieil ami	une vieille amie

✔ Pour vérifier

1. Do you use **c'est** and **ce sont** or **il est / elle est** and **ils sont / elles sont** with a noun to identify or describe someone or something? with an adjective to describe? with a prepositional phrase to say such things as where someone or something is or is from? with nationalities, professions, and religions without the indefinite article?

2. Are most adjectives placed before or after the noun they describe? Which 15 adjectives are placed before the noun they describe?

3. What are the alternate masculine singular forms of **beau, nouveau,** and **vieux**? When are they used?

Note *de grammaire*

Remember to use **il y a** to say *there is / there are.* Use **c'est / ce sont** and **il est / elle est / ils sont / elles sont** to say *this/that/he/she/it is* and *these/those/they are.*
Sur le campus, **il y a** beaucoup de nouveaux bâtiments. **Ils sont** beaux!
On the campus, **there are** *a lot of new buildings.* **They are** *beautiful!*

Sélection musicale. Search the Web for the song "**Je suis un homme**" by Zazie to enjoy a musical selection containing these structures.

A **Qu'est-ce que c'est?** Identifiez ces personnes et ces choses. Après, décrivez-les avec l'adjectif le plus logique de chaque paire.

EXEMPLES

café
(grand / petit)
(agréable / désagréable)
C'est un café.
Il est petit.
Il est agréable.

étudiantes
(sympa / antipathique)
(intéressant / ennuyeux)
Ce sont des étudiantes.
Elles sont sympas.
Elles sont intéressantes.

1.

homme
(paresseux / dynamique)
(intéressant / ennuyeux)
(beau / laid)
(grand / petit)

2.

étudiants
(gros / mince)
(beau / laid)
(intellectuel / paresseux)
(jeune / vieux)

3.

femme
(paresseux / sportif)
(gros / mince)
(jeune / vieux)
(grand / petit)

4.

maisons
(moderne / vieux)
(joli / laid)
(grand / petit)
(agréable / désagréable)

B **C'est un(e)... / Ce sont des...** Maintenant, identifiez et décrivez chaque personne ou chose de l'exercice précédent. Utilisez le nom et un adjectif logique.

EXEMPLES

café
(grand / petit)
(agréable / désagréable)
C'est un petit café.
C'est un café agréable.

étudiantes
(sympa / antipathique)
(intéressant / ennuyeux)
Ce sont des étudiantes sympas.
Ce sont des étudiantes intéressantes.

C **Léa.** Léa parle de ses études. Complétez chaque phrase par **c'est, ce sont, il est, elle est, ils sont** ou **elles sont**.

1. Le cours de littérature, _____ mon cours préféré. _____ plutôt facile. _____ à huit heures du matin. _____ dans un grand amphithéâtre.

2. Mes profs? _____ intéressants. _____ de bons profs. _____ à l'université tous les jours. _____ intelligents. _____ sympas.

3. Mon meilleur ami, _____ David. _____ d'ici. _____ un bon ami. _____ très marrant. _____ français. _____ le frère de Jean.

D **Compliments.** Écrivez la forme correcte de l'adjectif le plus logique au bon endroit *(in the right position)* dans la phrase pour faire un *compliment*.

EXEMPLE C'est une _____ femme **dynamique.** (paresseux / dynamique)

1. C'est un _____ restaurant _____. (bon / mauvais)

2. Ce sont de/des _____ chiens *(dogs [m])* _____. (méchant / sympathique)

3. C'est un _____ campus _____. (beau / laid)

4. C'est une _____ femme _____. (ennuyeux / intéressant)

5. C'est un _____ homme _____. (laid / beau)

6. C'est une _____ résidence _____. (nouveau / vieux)

7. C'est un _____ amphithéâtre _____ (nouveau / vieux)

Line art on this page: © Cengage Learning

Talking about your studies

L'UNIVERSITÉ ET LES COURS

Vocabulaire sans peine!

Like nouns ending in **-tion** and **-té**, those ending in **-ique** and **-ie** are usually feminine. Notice these cognate patterns.

-ique = *ic(s)*
l'électronique = *electronics*
-ie = *-y*
l'archéologie = *archeology*

How would you say these nouns in French?

*statistics   robotics
anthropology   sociology*

Est-ce que vous aimez l'université?

J'aime beaucoup...	J'aime assez...	Je n'aime pas (du tout)...	Je préfère...
les professeurs	la bibliothèque	les devoirs	**les fêtes**
les étudiants	le labo(ratoire)	les examens	le sport
le campus	de langues	la salle	les matchs
les cours en ligne		d'informatique	de basket

Qu'est-ce que vous étudiez?

J'étudie la philo(sophie).   Je n'étudie pas la littérature.

LES LANGUES *(f)*
l'allemand *(m)*
l'anglais *(m)*
l'espagnol *(m)*
le français

LES SCIENCES HUMAINES *(f)*
l'histoire *(f)*
la psycho(logie)
les sciences po(litiques) *(f)*

LES ARTS *(m)*
le théâtre
la musique
la peinture

LE COMMERCE
la compta(bilité)
le marketing

LES TECHNOLOGIES
l'informatique *(f)*
les mathématiques
(les maths) *(f)*

LES SCIENCES *(f)*
la bio(logie)
la chimie
la physique

© Cengage Learning

J'aime beaucoup le cours de... Il est facile / difficile / intéressant.

1-26

David et Léa parlent de **leurs** études.

DAVID: Qu'est-ce que tu étudies ce semestre?

LÉA: J'étudie le français et la littérature classique. Et toi?

DAVID: J'étudie la philosophie et la littérature classique, comme toi.

LÉA: Comment sont tes cours?

DAVID: J'aime beaucoup le cours de philosophie. Il est très intéressant. Je n'aime pas du tout le cours de littérature, parce que le prof est ennuyeux.

---

une fête *a party*   l'allemand *German*   les sciences politiques *government, political science*   la peinture *painting*
la comptabilité *accounting*   l'informatique *computer science*   la chimie *chemistry*   leur(s) *their*

A **Préférences.** Interviewez votre partenaire sur ses préférences.

EXEMPLE le français / les mathématiques
— **Est-ce que tu préfères le français ou les mathématiques?**
— **Je préfère le français.**

1. les langues étrangères / les arts
2. le français / l'espagnol / l'allemand
3. la musique / le théâtre / la peinture
4. les sciences naturelles / les sciences sociales
5. la chimie / la physique / la biologie
6. l'histoire / les sciences politiques / la psychologie
7. le commerce / les technologies
8. l'informatique / la comptabilité / les mathématiques
9. les cours dans les grands amphithéâtres / dans les petites salles / dans le laboratoire de langues / dans la salle d'informatique / en ligne
10. les examens / les devoirs / les fêtes

B **Opinions.** Faites des comparaisons.

EXEMPLES **Les maths sont plus/moins/aussi faciles que la psychologie.**
La chimie est plus/moins/aussi utile que la biologie.

La cour de la Sorbonne

les maths	facile	la psychologie
la chimie	utile *(useful)*	la biologie
la comptabilité	difficile	le marketing
la philosophie	intéressant	la littérature
les étudiants	sympa	les profs
les matchs de basket	amusant	les matchs de foot

C **Entretien.** Interviewez votre partenaire.

1. Qu'est-ce que tu étudies ce semestre? Comment sont tes cours ce semestre? Comment sont tes profs? Quels cours est-ce que tu préfères? Pourquoi *(Why)*?
2. Tu aimes être en cours le matin, l'après-midi ou le soir? Tu aimes les cours en ligne?
3. Qu'est-ce que tu aimes à l'université? Qu'est-ce que tu n'aimes pas?

À VOUS!

Avec un(e) partenaire, relisez à haute voix la conversation entre David et Léa. Ensuite, adaptez la conversation pour décrire vos cours ce semestre.

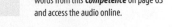 You can find a list of the new words from this *Compétence* on page 63 and access the audio online.

IDENTIFYING PEOPLE AND THINGS

✔ Pour vérifier

1. What are the four forms of the word for *the* in French? When do you use each one?

2. Besides meaning *the,* what are two other uses of the definite article in French?

3. When is the **s** of the plural form **les** pronounced?

L'article défini

The words **le, la, l', les** *(the)* before nouns are called the *definite article*. The form you use depends on the noun's gender and number and whether it starts with a consonant or vowel sound.

	SINGULAR BEFORE CONSONANT SOUND	SINGULAR BEFORE VOWEL SOUND	PLURAL
MASCULINE	**le** livre	**l'**homme	**les** livres, **les** hommes
FEMININE	**la** librairie	**l'**étudiante	**les** librairies, **les** étudiantes

Use the definite article before nouns:

- To specify items, as when using *the* in English.
  Apprenez **les** mots de vocabulaire.   *Learn **the** vocabulary words.*

- To say what you like, dislike, or prefer.
  Je n'aime pas **les** devoirs.   *I don't like homework.*

- To talk about something as a general category or an abstract noun.
  Les langues sont faciles pour moi.   *Languages are easy for me.*

In the last two cases, note that there is no article in English.

 Sélection musicale. Search the Web for the song **"Salut à toi"** by Kiemsa to enjoy a musical selection containing these structures.

PRONONCIATION

La voyelle **e** et l'article défini 🔊 1-27

As you know, a *final* unaccented **e** is usually not pronounced, unless it is the only vowel, as in **le.**

grand**e**   histoir**e**   langu**e**   bibliothèqu**e**   j'aim**e**

Otherwise, an unaccented **e** has three different pronunciations, depending on what follows it.

- In short words like **le** or **je,** or when **e** is followed by a single consonant within a word, pronounce it as in:
  j**e**   n**e**   l**e**   r**e**garde   d**e**voirs

- When, as in **les, e** is followed by an unpronounced consonant at the end of a word, pronounce it as in:
  l**es**   m**es**   parl**ez**   aim**ez**   étudi**ez**

- In words like **elle,** where **e** is followed by two consonants within a word, or by a single pronounced consonant at the end of a word, pronounce it as in:
  int**e**llectuel   b**e**lle   qu**e**l   **e**spagnol   bask**e**t

Since the final **s** of plural nouns is not pronounced, you must pronounce the article correctly to differentiate singular and plural nouns. Listen carefully as you repeat each of the following nouns. Notice the **z** sound of final **s** in liaison.

le livre	la science	l'étudiant	l'étudiante
les livres	les sciences	les ᶻétudiants	les ᶻétudiantes

A Prononcez bien! Listen as David talks about university life. In each sentence, you will hear the singular or plural form of one of the following nouns. Indicate which form you hear by writing the article on your paper.

1. le professeur – les professeurs
2. le cours – les cours
3. l'étudiant – les étudiants
4. le devoir – les devoirs
5. le livre – les livres
6. l'exercice – les exercices
7. le campus – les campus
8. la bibliothèque – les bibliothèques

B Vos cours. Est-ce que vous étudiez les matières suivantes *(following subjects)*?

EXEMPLE Oui, j'étudie la chimie.
Non, je n'étudie pas la chimie.

1.　2.　3.　4.

5.　6.　7.　8.

C Et vous? Complétez les phrases pour parler de vos cours et de votre université.

1. J'étudie...
2. J'aime beaucoup...
3. Je n'aime pas beaucoup...
4. Je comprends bien...
5. Je ne comprends pas bien...
6. Je pense que le cours de... est...

D Entretien. Complétez les questions suivantes avec l'article défini (**le, la, l', les**), l'article indéfini (**un, une, des**) ou **de (d')**. Après, posez ces questions à votre partenaire.

1. Tu aimes _____ sport? Est-ce qu'il y a _____ grand stade sur _____ campus de cette *(this)* université? Est-ce qu'il y a souvent *(often)* _____ matchs de football américain le week-end? Tu préfères _____ foot, _____ football américain ou _____ basket?

2. _____ campus ici est agréable? Il y a _____ vieux bâtiments sur le campus? Il y a _____ bâtiments modernes? Est-ce qu'il y a beaucoup _____ arbres? Il y a assez _____ parkings? Est-ce qu'il y a _____ grande bibliothèque? Est-ce que _____ bibliothèque est moderne?

3. Tu comprends bien _____ français? _____ langues sont faciles ou difficiles pour toi? Tu aimes _____ cours de français? Combien _____ étudiants est-ce qu'il y a dans le cours? Est-ce qu'il y a _____ étudiants étrangers dans _____ cours? _____ cours est difficile? Est-ce qu'il y a _____ examen aujourd'hui?

VIDÉOREPRISE

Les Stagiaires *(The Interns)*

The fourth **Compétence** of each chapter of **Horizons** ends with a **Vidéoreprise** section that reviews the grammar presented in the chapter through activities that revolve around a segment of the **Horizons** video, **Les Stagiaires**. In the video, two students, Rachid Bennani and Amélie Prévot, have just begun an internship at the company Technovert. Before you watch the first episode, do these exercises to review what you have learned in **Chapitre 1** and learn more about the characters that you will see in the video.

See the **Résumé de grammaire** section at the end of each chapter for a review of all the grammar of the chapter.

A   Qui est-ce?   Voici des descriptions des deux stagiaires de la vidéo, Rachid et Amélie. Complétez chaque phrase avec **c'est, il est** ou **elle est.**

____1____ Rachid Bennani.
Sur cette photo, ____2____ au *(at the)* bureau de Technovert.
____3____ un jeune homme sympa.
____4____ intéressant.
____5____ étudiant à l'École de Commerce Extérieur.
____6____ du Maroc *(from Morocco)*.

____7____ Amélie Prévot.
____8____ une femme intelligente.
____9____ française.
____10____ très belle.
____11____ stagiaire à Technovert.
____12____ aussi étudiante.

Maintenant, identifiez un(e) des étudiant(e)s de votre classe et parlez un peu de lui *(him)* ou d'elle.

B   Rachid.   Rachid parle de ses *(his)* études. Complétez les phrases avec la forme correcte du verbe **être.**

EXEMPLE   Je **suis** étudiant à l'École de Commerce Extérieur.

1. Je _____ en cours tous les jours.
2. Les cours _____ faciles pour moi.
3. Mes profs _____ gentils.
4. Mon meilleur ami _____ étudiant.
5. Mes amis et moi, nous _____ assez intellectuels.

 Maintenant, changez les phrases précédentes pour décrire votre situation et posez des questions à votre partenaire basées sur ces phrases.

EXEMPLE   — Je suis étudiant(e) à... Et toi? Est-ce que tu es aussi étudiant(e) à...?
— Oui, je suis aussi étudiant(e) à...

C Descriptions. Amélie parle de ses nouveaux collègues à Technovert. Traduisez *(Translate)* les adjectifs pour compléter les phrases. Faites attention à la forme et à la position de l'adjectif.

EXEMPLE Rachid est un ami *(good)*. **Rachid est un bon ami.**

1. M. Vieilledent, c'est mon chef [*boss*] *(new)*.

C'est un homme *(smart)*.

Ce n'est pas un homme *(young)*.

2. Son fils *(His son)*, Christophe, est un jeune homme *(lazy)*.

Ce n'est pas un homme *(active)*.

Ce n'est pas un homme *(very smart)*.

3. Matthieu, l'informaticien *(computer specialist)*, est un homme *(shy)*.

C'est un homme *(handsome)*.

Matthieu et Rachid sont des collègues *(nice)*.

4. Céline, la directrice du marketing, est une femme *(pretty)*.

Camille, l'assistante de M. Vieilledent, est une femme *(smart)*.

Camille est une amie de Céline *(good)*.

D Mes études. Amélie parle de ses études. Complétez ce qu'elle dit avec **un, une, des, le, la, l', les** ou **de (d')**. Ensuite, adaptez le paragraphe pour décrire vos cours, votre université et le quartier universitaire.

Ce semestre, j'étudie __1__ marketing et __2__ comptabilité. J'aime __3__ université parce qu'il y a __4__ salle d'informatique moderne et il y a aussi __5__ nouveaux laboratoires de langues. __6__ quartier est beau et il y a beaucoup __7__ arbres. Dans le quartier, il y a __8__ cinéma où on passe *(they show)* __9__ films étrangers. J'aime beaucoup __10__ films étrangers.

Access the Video *Les Stagiaires* on iLrn.

▶ **Épisode 1: Comment sont-ils?**

AVANT LA VIDÉO

Dans ce clip, Amélie, Rachid et Camille parlent de certains de leurs *(about some of their)* collègues. Avant de regarder le clip, choisissez *(choose)* les adjectifs à connotation positive: **intelligent, paresseux, nerveux, timide, dynamique.**

APRÈS LA VIDÉO

Regardez le clip et dites *(say)* comment Camille décrit *(describes)*:
• Céline • Christophe • Matthieu

LECTURE ET COMPOSITION

LECTURE

You are going to read a work by Jacques Prévert (1900–1977), one of France's most popular writers of the last century, from his collection **Paroles** (1949). You have learned to use cognates to make reading easier. It can also help you read if you scan a text before reading it in order to anticipate its content.

On peut deviner! Scan the reading *L'accent grave* and answer these questions to prepare yourself for understanding the text.

1. This is clearly a conversation. Who is it between? Where do you think it takes place?
2. What is the student's name? Where have you heard this name before? What was that character famous for saying?

L'accent grave

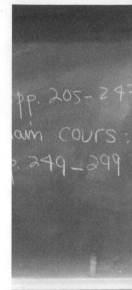

Le professeur Élève Hamlet!

L'élève Hamlet (sursautant) ... Hein... Quoi... Pardon... **Qu'est-ce qui se passe...** Qu'est-ce qu'il y a... Qu'est-ce que c'est?...

Le professeur (mécontent) Vous ne pouvez **pas répondre** «présent» **comme tout le monde?** Pas possible, vous êtes **encore dans les nuages.**

L'élève Hamlet Être ou ne pas être dans les nuages!

Le professeur Suffit. Pas tant de manières. Et conjuguez-moi le verbe être, comme tout le monde, **c'est tout ce que je vous demande.**

L'élève Hamlet To be. . .

Le professeur En Français, s'il vous plaît, comme tout le monde.

L'élève Hamlet Bien, monsieur. *(Il conjugue:)*

Je suis ou je ne suis pas, tu es ou tu n'es pas, il est ou il n'est pas, nous sommes ou nous ne sommes pas...

Le professeur (excessivement mécontent) Mais **c'est vous qui n'y êtes pas,** mon pauvre ami!

L'élève Hamlet C'est exact, monsieur le professeur, Je suis «où» je ne suis pas. Et, **dans le fond,** hein, à la réflexion, être «où» ne pas être, c'est **peut-être** aussi la question.

Jacques Prévert, "L'accent grave" in *Paroles* © Éditions GALLIMARD.
© Fatras / succession Jacques Prévert pour les droits électroniques réservés

un élève *a student, a pupil* **sursautant** *looking up startled* **Hein** *Huh* **Quoi** *What* **Qu'est-ce qui se passe?** *What's going on?* **mécontent** *displeased* **Vous ne pouvez pas répondre...?** *Can't you answer...?* **comme tout le monde** *like everyone* **encore dans les nuages** *still in the clouds* **Suffit.** *Enough.* **Pas tant de manières.** *Don't make such a fuss.* **c'est tout ce que je vous demande** *that's all I'm asking of you* **c'est vous qui n'y êtes pas** *you're the one that's not all there* **dans le fond** *really, basically* **peut-être** *perhaps*

© Generistock/Getty Images

COMPOSITION

Certain strategies can help you learn to write better in a foreign language. When you write, avoid translating. It is very difficult to translate correctly. Use and combine what you already know in French instead. Link sentences with words like **et, mais, alors,** or **parce que** to make your writing flow better.

Organisez-vous. You will be writing a short description of yourself and your studies. First, organize your thoughts by completing these sentences in French.

1. Je m'appelle...
2. Je suis de (d')... et/mais j'habite à...
3. Du point de vue *(view)* physique, je suis...
4. Du point de vue personnalité, je suis...
5. Je suis étudiant(e) à... où j'étudie...
6. Sur le campus, il y a..., mais il n'y a pas...
7. Dans le quartier universitaire, il y a..., mais il n'y a pas...
8. En général, j'aime / je n'aime pas l'université parce que...

Compréhension

1. Dans quel cours sont-ils? À votre avis *(In your opinion)*, les élèves sont très jeunes, assez jeunes ou pas jeunes? Pourquoi *(Why)*?
2. Qu'est-ce que ça veut dire, **ou**? et **où**? Qu'est-ce que ça veut dire **être ou ne pas être**? et **être où ne pas être**?
3. Comment est l'élève Hamlet? attentif ou inattentif? conformiste ou rebelle? bon ou mauvais? intelligent? intellectuel?
4. Comment est le professeur? patient ou impatient? intéressant ou ennuyeux? sympathique ou antipathique?

Un autoportrait

Write a short paragraph introducing yourself. Use the sentences you completed in *Organisez-vous* above to guide you. Remember to use words like **et, mais,** or **parce que** to make your paragraph flow better.

> **EXEMPLE** **Je m'appelle Daniel Reyna. Je suis de San Antonio, mais maintenant j'habite à Austin...**

iLrn Share It!

57

COMPARAISONS CULTURELLES

iLrn In the **Culture Modules** in the video library, see **Universities**.

LES ÉTUDES

How similar **(semblable)** is the French education system to the education system in your area? Read these descriptions of secondary schools and universities in France and compare them to schools in your region, by saying one of the following:

C'est très semblable ici. / C'est assez semblable ici. / C'est très différent ici.

1. The French equivalent of the high school diploma is called **le baccalauréat** or **le bac.** There are three types of **baccalauréat** degrees. The **baccalauréat technologique (bac techno)** mixes general and vocational education and prepares students to continue their professional education at the post-secondary level. The **baccalauréat professionnel (bac pro)** is designed to prepare students

to enter directly into the workplace. The **baccalauréat général (bac général)** prepares students to continue on to higher education. Students who pursue the **baccalauréat général** do so in a chosen category (called **série), la série littéraire (L), la série scientifique (S),** or **la série économique et sociale (ES).**

2. At the end of their secondary studies, French students must pass a series of difficult national exams, also called **le baccalauréat** or **le bac,** covering all the material they have studied, in order to receive the **baccalauréat** degree. Students who do not pass may retest the two subjects in which they did the least well a few weeks later or may retake the last year at the **lycée** and retest all exams.

3. Every student who has received the **bac** is eligible for a nearly free university education. Students only pay the equivalent of a few hundred dollars per year to attend French universities, because the government finances higher education.

4. Students have a large range of choices for continuing their education after the **bac,** as listed in the chart on the next page. However, students are only accepted into certain specialized schools or fields by competitive exams. To be accepted at the most competitive French universities, the **grandes**

écoles, which prepare students for high-level positions in the public and private sectors, students generally take two years of preparatory courses and must pass a highly competitive exam.

Dans une université:	Dans un lycée:
THREE-YEAR DEGREE: une licence	**TWO-YEAR CERTIFICATE:** un BTS (brevet de technicien supérieur)
FIVE-YEAR DEGREE: un master	**TWO YEARS OF PREPARATORY SCHOOL:** les classes préparatoires aux grandes écoles (CPGE)
EIGHT-YEAR DEGREE: un doctorat	
FIVE- TO ELEVEN-YEAR DEGREES: un diplôme de médecine, de chirurgie dentaire ou de pharmacie	**Dans une grande école (GE):**
	THREE- TO FIVE-YEAR DEGREES: un diplôme d'ingénieur, de sciences, d'économie, de commerce, de lettres...
Dans un institut universitaire de technologie (IUT):	**Dans une école spécialisée:**
TWO-YEAR DEGREE: un DUT (diplôme universitaire de technologie)	**TWO- TO FIVE-YEAR DEGREE:** un diplôme d'art
	THREE- TO FIVE-YEAR DEGREES: un diplôme de travail social ou de commerce
TWO-YEAR DEGREE: un DEUST (diplôme d'études universitaires scientifiques et techniques)	**SIX-YEAR DEGREE:** un diplôme d'architecte

5. In France, most older universities do not have campuses. Each **faculté** *(division or school)* has buildings, often older ones, where classes meet, and often each **faculté** is centered in a different area of town. Many of the more modern universities, however, do have a campus that is more similar to universities in the United States and Canada.

© Nico Tondini/Robert Harding World Imagery/Getty Images

Compréhension

1. What is the French equivalent of a "high school diploma"? What do students have to do to earn it? What do you think are the advantages and disadvantages of a system in which students must pass a rigorous cumulative exam in order to receive a secondary education diploma?

2. What are the three types of **baccalauréats?** For students preparing the **baccalauréat général,** in what general fields can they earn their diploma? Would you have liked to pick your "major" while still in high school? What might be the advantages and disadvantages?

3. What options do French students have for continuing their studies after the **lycée**? How do these compare to the options in your area?

4. Who is entitled to a college education? Is it expensive? What are the advantages and disadvantages of making higher education almost free?

5. What are the older French universities like? What is a division, or school, called within a French university?

6. Reread the four *Notes culturelles* from earlier in this chapter. How much of a role do extracurricular activities and sports play in university life? Can students enter directly into courses of their field of study? Where do most students live? How does this compare to your university?

iLrn Share It!

Visit **www.cengagebrain.com** for additional cultural information and activities.

RÉSUMÉ DE GRAMMAIRE

SUBJECT PRONOUNS, THE VERB *ÊTRE* AND *IL Y A*

Je **suis** timide.
Tu **es** étudiant?
Le professeur **est** sympa.
Nous **sommes** d'ici.
Vous **êtes** français?
Ils **sont** en cours.

Conjugate verbs by changing their forms to correspond to each of the subject pronouns. Here is the conjugation of **être**.

ÊTRE *(to be)*					
je	**suis**	*I am*	nous	**sommes**	*we are*
tu	**es**	*you are*	vous	**êtes**	*you are*
il/elle	**est**	*he/she/it is*	ils/elles	**sont**	*they are*

Je **ne** suis **pas** optimiste.
Tu **n'**es **pas** d'ici!

To negate a verb, place **ne** before it and **pas** after. **Ne** becomes **n'** before vowels or a silent **h.**

Il est sympathique.
Il est en cours.
Il est catholique.
Elle est française.
Ils sont étudiants.
C'est un bon ami.
Ce sont mes amis.

Use **il est / elle est** and **ils sont / elles sont** with *adjectives*, to describe people or things, or with *prepositional phrases* to say such things as where someone or something is or is from. Also use them, without the indefinite article, to state professions, nationalities, or religions.

Use **c'est** and **ce sont** instead of **il est / elle est** and **ils sont / elles sont** to say *he/she/it/ this/that is* or *they/these/those are* when identifying or describing someone with *a noun.*

— **Il y a** un examen demain?
— Non, **il n'y a pas** d'examen.

Use **il y a** instead of **être** to say *there is* or *there are.* Its negated form is **il n'y a pas.**

NOUNS AND ARTICLES

Nouns in French are classified as either masculine or feminine. The form of the definite and indefinite articles depends on a noun's gender and whether it is singular or plural.

INDEFINITE ARTICLE *(a, an, some)*		
	SINGULAR	**PLURAL**
MASCULINE	**un** cours, **un** examen	**des** cours, **des** examens
FEMININE	**une** salle, **une** étudiante	**des** salles, **des** étudiantes

Il y a **des** restaurants près d'ici?
Chez Pierre est **un** bon restaurant.
Tu as *(have)* **une** amie américaine?

The indefinite article changes to **de** (**d'** before vowel sounds) . . .

Il **n'**y a **pas de** librairie ici.
(Ce **n'est pas une** librairie.)
Il y a **beaucoup de** devoirs et **d'**examens.
Ce sont **de bons** amis.

- after negated verbs (except after **être**).
- after expressions of quantity like **beaucoup, assez,** or **combien.**
- directly before plural adjectives.

DEFINITE ARTICLE *(the)*		
	SINGULAR	**PLURAL**
MASCULINE	**le** cours, **l'**examen	**les** cours, **les** examens
FEMININE	**la** salle, **l'**étudiante	**les** salles, **les** étudiantes

Où sont **les** étudiants?
Ils sont à **la** bibliothèque.

Le and **la** elide to **l'** before vowel sounds.

Use the definite article to say *the* and . . .

J'aime **la** musique classique.
Les concerts de rock sont amusants.
Je n'aime pas **le** jazz.

- to say what you like or prefer.
- to make generalized statements.

The definite article *never* changes to **de (d').**

ADJECTIVES

Adjectives have masculine and feminine, singular and plural forms, which correspond to the nouns they describe. Add an **e** to the masculine form of most adjectives to form the feminine, unless it already ends in an *unaccented* **e.** Add an **s** to make an adjective plural, unless it already ends in **s, x,** or **z.**

MASCULINE		FEMININE	
SINGULAR	**PLURAL**	**SINGULAR**	**PLURAL**
joli	jolis	jolie	jolies
divorcé	divorcés	divorcée	divorcées
français	français	française	françaises
jeune	jeunes	jeune	jeunes

The following adjective endings have other changes before adding the **e** for the feminine form.

	MASCULINE		FEMININE	
	SINGULAR	**PLURAL**	**SINGULAR**	**PLURAL**
-eux / -euse:	ennuyeux	ennuyeux	ennuyeuse	ennuyeuses
-en / -enne:	canadien	canadiens	canadienne	canadiennes
-if / -ive:	sportif	sportifs	sportive	sportives
-el / -elle:	intellectuel	intellectuels	intellectuelle	intellectuelles
-er / -ère:	étranger	étrangers	étrangère	étrangères

The adjectives **bon (bonne), gros (grosse),** and **gentil (gentille)** double their final consonants.

Adjectives generally are placed *after* nouns they describe. However, the following adjectives go *before* nouns.

beau (belle)	jeune	bon (bonne)	grand(e)	autre
joli(e)	vieux (vieille)	mauvais(e)	petit(e)	même
	nouveau	gentil(le)	gros(se)	seul(e)
	(nouvelle)			premier (première)

The adjectives **beau, nouveau,** and **vieux** have irregular forms. The alternate singular forms **bel, nouvel,** and **vieil** are used before masculine singular nouns beginning with a vowel sound.

MASCULINE		FEMININE	
SINGULAR	**PLURAL**	**SINGULAR**	**PLURAL**
beau (bel)	beaux	belle	belles
nouveau (nouvel)	nouveaux	nouvelle	nouvelles
vieux (vieil)	vieux	vieille	vieilles

QUESTIONS

Questions that are answered with **oui** or **non** have rising intonation. You may just use rising intonation or you may begin the question with **est-ce que,** which elides to **est-ce qu'** before vowel sounds.

If you expect the answer to a question to be **oui,** use **n'est-ce pas?** or **non?** to translate tag questions like *right?, isn't he?, can't you?,* or *won't they?* in English.

Le parc est **joli.** / La maison est **jolie.**

Il est **divorcé.** / Elle est **divorcée.**

Mes amis sont **français.** / Mes amies sont **françaises.**

Il n'est pas **jeune.** / Elle n'est pas **jeune.**

Le film est **ennuyeux.** / La fête est **ennuyeuse.**

Paul est **canadien.** / Marie est **canadienne.**

David est **sportif.** / Lisa est **sportive.**

Ils sont **intellectuels.** / Elles sont **intellectuelles.**

Il est **étranger.** / Elle est **étrangère.**

Il est **bon.** / Elle est **bonne.**

Il est **gros.** / Elle est **grosse.**

Il est **gentil.** / Elle est **gentille.**

C'est un **cours intéressant,** mais il y a beaucoup d'**examens difficiles.**

Sur le campus, il y a beaucoup de **nouveaux bâtiments** et une **grande bibliothèque.**

un **beau** parc / un **bel** homme / une **belle** femme

un **nouveau** film / un **nouvel** ami / une **nouvelle** amie

un **vieux** bâtiment / un **vieil** homme / une **vieille** femme

Le professeur est bon?

Est-ce qu'il est sympa?

Tu étudies le français, **n'est-ce pas?**

Nous sommes dans le même cours, **non?**

VOCABULAIRE

COMPÉTENCE 1

Identifying people and describing appearance

NOMS MASCULINS

mes amis	my friends
un cours de littérature	a literature class
un frère	a brother
les gens	people
un (jeune) homme	a (young) man

NOMS FÉMININS

mes amies	my friends
une (jeune) femme	a (young) woman
la France	France
une semaine	a week
une sœur	a sister
l'université	the university

ADJECTIFS

américain(e)	American
beau (belle)	handsome, beautiful
célibataire	single
divorcé(e)	divorced
fiancé(e)	engaged
français(e)	French
grand(e)	tall, big
gros(se)	fat
jeune	young
jumeau (jumelle)	twin
laid(e)	ugly
marié(e)	married
même	same
mince	thin
petit(e)	short, small
premier (première)	first
vieux (vieille)	old

EXPRESSIONS VERBALES

C'est…	He is / She is / It is / This is / That is …
Ce sont…	They are / These are / Those are …
Ce n'est pas…	He is not / She is not / It is not / This is not / That is not …
Ce ne sont pas…	They are not / These are not / Those are not …
Comment est…?	What is … like?
Il est / Elle est…	He is / She is / It is …
Ils sont / Elles sont…	They are …
Il n'est pas / Elle n'est pas…	He is not / She is not / It is not …
Ils ne sont pas / Elles ne sont pas…	They are not …
Nous sommes…	We are …
(pour) étudier	(in order) to study
(pour) visiter	(in order) to visit
(pour) voir	(in order) to see
rencontrer	to meet (for the first time or by chance), to run into
Tu es…	You are …

DIVERS

à	to, at, in
alors	so, then, therefore
c'est ça	that's right
comme	like, as, for
de	of, from, about
d'où	from where
non?	right?
pendant	during
son / sa / ses	his, her, its

COMPÉTENCE 2

Describing personality

NOMS MASCULINS

tes amis	your friends
le foot(ball)	soccer
mon meilleur ami	my best friend
le sport	sports
le tennis	tennis

NOMS FÉMININS

tes amies	your friends
les études	studies, going to school
ma meilleure amie	my best friend
la personnalité	personality

ADJECTIFS

agréable	pleasant
amusant(e)	fun, amusing
antipathique	disagreeable, unpleasant
bête	stupid, dumb
désagréable	unpleasant
dynamique	active
ennuyeux (ennuyeuse)	boring
extraverti(e)	extroverted, outgoing
gentil (gentille)	nice
idéaliste	idealistic
intellectuel(le)	intellectual
intelligent(e)	intelligent
intéressant(e)	interesting
marrant(e)	funny
méchant(e)	mean
nouveau (nouvelle)	new
optimiste	optimistic
paresseux (paresseuse)	lazy
pessimiste	pessimistic
réaliste	realistic
sportif (sportive)	athletic
sympathique / sympa	nice
timide	timid, shy

EXPRESSIONS VERBALES

être	to be
je suis…	I am …
tu es…	you are …
il est…	he is / it is …
elle est…	she is / it is …
nous sommes…	we are …
vous êtes…	you are …
ils sont…	they are …
elles sont…	they are …
j'aime… / je n'aime pas…	I like … / I don't like …
tu aimes…	you like …

DIVERS

assez	rather
aussi… que	as … as
Ce n'est pas mon truc.	That's not my thing.
Est-ce que…	(particle used in questions)
moins… que	less … than
ne… pas	not
ne… pas du tout	not at all
n'est-ce pas?	right?
pas tellement	not so much
plus… que	more … than
plutôt	rather
un peu	a little

Describing the university area

NOMS MASCULINS

un amphithéâtre	a lecture hall
un arbre	a tree
un bâtiment	a building
un bureau (pl des bureaux)	an office
un café	a café
un campus	a campus
un cinéma	a movie theater
un concert (de jazz, de rock, de musique pop[ulaire], de musique classique)	a (jazz, rock, pop music, classical music) concert
un fast-food	a fast-food restaurant
un film	a movie, a film
un match de foot(ball) américain	a football game
un parc	a park
un parking	a parking lot
un quartier (universitaire)	a (university) neighborhood
un restaurant	a restaurant
un stade	a stadium
un théâtre	a theater (for live performances)
le Wi-Fi	Wi-Fi

NOMS FÉMININS

une bibliothèque	a library
une boîte de nuit	a nightclub
une librairie	a bookstore
une maison	a house
une résidence	a dormitory
une salle de cours	a classroom
une salle de gym	a gym, a fitness club

ADJECTIFS

bon(ne)	good
catholique	Catholic
étranger (étrangère)	foreign
joli(e)	pretty
mauvais(e)	bad
moderne	modern
populaire	popular
seul(e)	only
universitaire	university

EXPRESSIONS VERBALES

Comment est...?	What is . . . like?
Il y a...	There is, There are . . .
Il n'y a pas (de)...	There isn't, There aren't . . .
Qu'est-ce qu'il y a...?	What is there . . . ?

DIVERS

assez (de)	enough (of)
avec Wi-Fi	with Wi-Fi
beaucoup (de)	a lot (of)
combien (de)	how much (of), how many (of)
dans	in
des	some
là(-bas)	(over) there
près de	near
sur	on
ton, ta, tes	your
un(e)	a, an

Talking about your studies

NOMS MASCULINS

l'allemand	German
l'anglais	English
les arts	the arts
le basket	basketball
le commerce	business
un cours en ligne	an online course
les devoirs	homework
l'espagnol	Spanish
un examen	an exam
le français	French
un labo(ratoire) de langues	a language lab
le marketing	marketing
le théâtre	theater, drama

NOMS FÉMININS

la bio(logie)	biology
la chimie	chemistry
la compta(bilité)	accounting
une fête	a party
l'histoire	history
l'informatique	computer science
une langue	a language
la littérature classique	classical literature
les mathématiques (les maths)	mathematics (math)
la musique	music
la peinture	painting
la philo(sophie)	philosophy
la physique	physics
la psycho(logie)	psychology
une salle d'informatique	a computer lab
les sciences (humaines)	the (social) sciences
les sciences po(litiques)	political science, government
les technologies	technical courses, technologies

EXPRESSIONS VERBALES

Comment sont...?	What are . . . like?
Est-ce que vous aimez...?	Do you like . . . ?
J'aime beaucoup / assez...	I like a lot / somewhat . . .
Je n'aime pas (du tout)...	I don't like . . . (at all).
Je préfère...	I prefer . . .
Qu'est-ce que vous étudiez / tu études?	What are you studying?, What do you study?
J'étudie...	I'm studying, I study . . .
Je n'étudie pas...	I'm not studying, I don't study . . .

DIVERS

en ligne	online
le, la, l', les	the
leur(s)	their

Sur la Côte d'Azur
Après les cours

iLrn iLrn Heinle Learning Center		Internet web search
www.cengagebrain.com		Pair work
Horizons Video: Les Stagiaires		Group work
Audio		

© Roman Borodaev/YAY Micro/age fotostock

2

COMPÉTENCE

1 Saying what you like to do
Le temps libre et les loisirs

Saying what you like to do
L'infinitif

Stratégies et Compréhension auditive
- **Pour mieux comprendre:** *Listening for specific information*
- **Compréhension auditive:** *On sort ensemble?*

2 Saying how you spend your free time
Le week-end

Telling what you do, how often, and how well
Les verbes en -er et les adverbes

Telling what you do
Quelques verbes à changements orthographiques

3 Asking about someone's day
La journée

Asking for information
Les mots interrogatifs

Asking questions
Les questions par inversion

4 Going to the café
Au café

Paying the bill
Les nombres de trente à cent et l'argent

Vidéoreprise *Les Stagiaires*

Lecture et Composition
- **Pour mieux lire:** *Making intelligent guesses*
- **Lecture:** *Aux Trois Obus*
- **Pour mieux écrire:** *Using logical order and standard phrases*
- **Composition:** *Au café*

Comparaisons culturelles *Les cafés en France*

Résumé de grammaire

Vocabulaire

Quand vous visitez une nouvelle **ville,** qu'est-ce que vous préférez **faire**? Visiter les sites historiques et les musées? faire du shopping? dîner au restaurant? profiter des festivals? **sortir** en boîte de nuit? **faire une promenade**? admirer la vue panoramique?
À Nice, il est difficile de **choisir**!

La Promenade des Anglais

Le Carnaval de Nice

Le quartier médiéval du Vieux Nice

Quand *When*   **ville** *city*   **faire** *to do*   **sortir** *to go out*   **faire une promenade** *to take a walk*   **choisir** *to choose*

Le marché Saleya

Les ruines romaines du quartier Cimiez

Nice

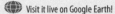 Visit it live on Google Earth!

NOMBRE D'HABITANTS: **345 000 (et son agglomération [metropolitan region]: 950 000) (les Niçois)**

DÉPARTEMENT: **Alpes-Maritimes**

RÉGION: **Provence-Alpes-Côte d'Azur**

Le savez-vous?

Voudriez-vous visiter ou étudier à Nice? Quel endroit (place) ou événement (event) à Nice de la liste ci-dessous (below) correspond à chaque description?

la Promenade des Anglais	**le marché Saleya**
le Carnaval de Nice	**le quartier Cimiez**
le Vieux Nice	

1. Dans ce quartier chic, il y a des ruines romaines, le musée Matisse et un monastère franciscain du XVIe siècle *(from the XVIth century)*. Les jardins *(gardens)* du monastère offrent une vue magnifique de Nice et de la mer Méditerranée.

2. Les touristes et les Niçois visitent cet endroit pour faire des promenades ou du roller *(rollerblading)* ou pour contempler la Baie des Anges dans une des célèbres chaises bleues *(famous blue chairs)*.

3. Cette célébration date de 1294. Aujourd'hui, plus d'un million de personnes participent à cet événement durant deux semaines en février ou mars.

4. Il y a toujours beaucoup d'étudiants dans les restaurants et les boîtes de nuit des rues étroites *(narrow streets)* de ce vieux quartier animé.

5. Les couleurs et le parfum des roses et des autres fleurs de ce marché enchantent les touristes et les Niçois.

Les jardins du monastère franciscain de Cimiez

France is divided into regions and departments. Nice is in the region **Provence-Alpes-Côte d'Azur** and in the department **Alpes-Maritimes**. On the Web, find out what the ten largest cities in France are, and which region and department they are in. Then pick the city you would most like to visit besides Paris and find five interesting facts about it to share with the class.

Le marché *The market*

Saying what you like to do

LE TEMPS LIBRE ET LES LOISIRS

— Qu'est-ce que vous aimez **faire** après les cours?

— J'aime...   — Je n'aime pas...   — Je préfère...

— Qu'est-ce que **vous voudriez** faire aujourd'hui après les cours?

— **Je voudrais...**

SORTIR AVEC DES AMIS

aller au cinéma
(aller) voir un film

aller au café
(aller) **prendre un verre**

aller en boîte (de nuit)
(aller) danser

dîner au restaurant

faire du sport
jouer au tennis / au basket /
au football / au volley

faire de l'exercice
faire du vélo
faire du jogging

RESTER À LA MAISON

lire

bricoler

dormir

inviter des amis à la
maison

parler au téléphone
envoyer des textos *(m)*

jouer de la guitare / **de
la batterie** / du piano

le temps libre *free time*   **un loisir** *a leisure activity, a pastime*   **faire** *to do*   **vous voudriez** *you would like*   **Je voudrais** *I would like*   **sortir** *to go out*   **aller** *to go*   **prendre un verre** *to have a drink*   **faire du vélo** *to ride a bike*   **rester** *to stay, to remain*   **bricoler** *to do handiwork*   **envoyer un texto** *to send a text message*   **de la batterie** *drums*

Vocabulaire supplémentaire

courir *to run*
cuisiner *to cook*
dessiner *to draw*
faire de la muscu(lation) *to do bodybuilding*
faire de l'aérobic / de la gym(nastique)
jardiner *to garden*
marcher *to walk*
nager *to swim*
peindre *to paint*
promener le chien *to walk the dog*
voyager *to travel*

écouter la radio /
de la musique

regarder la télé(vision) /
une vidéo / un DVD
jouer à des jeux vidéo *(m)*

travailler sur l'ordinateur
surfer sur Internet
écrire des mails *(m)*

David invite Léa à sortir.

1-29

DAVID:	Tu es **libre ce soir**? Tu voudrais faire **quelque chose**?
LÉA:	**D'accord.** Où est-ce que tu voudrais aller?
DAVID:	Je ne sais pas. **Ça te dit d'**aller en boîte?
LÉA:	Non, **pas vraiment.** Je préfère aller au cinéma.
DAVID:	Bon, alors **allons** au cinéma! **On va** prendre un verre avant?
LÉA:	**Pourquoi pas? Vers** quelle heure?
DAVID:	Vers sept heures, sept heures et demie... au café La Martinique?
LÉA:	D'accord. Alors, à plus tard.
DAVID:	Salut, Léa. À ce soir!

A **Qu'est-ce que vous aimez faire?** Complétez les phrases.

1. Après les cours, j'aime... Aujourd'hui, après les cours, je voudrais...
2. Le samedi matin, j'aime... Ce samedi matin, je voudrais...
3. Le samedi soir, j'aime... Ce samedi soir, je voudrais...
4. Le dimanche, je préfère... Ce dimanche, je voudrais...
5. À la maison, j'aime... Je n'aime pas du tout...

B **Invitations.** Invitez votre partenaire à faire une des choses suivantes. Ensuite, changez de rôles et faites des projets pour un autre jour.

EXEMPLE demain: jouer au tennis
— **Tu es libre demain? Tu voudrais jouer au tennis avec moi?**
— **Oui, d'accord. / Pas vraiment. Je préfère aller au cinéma.**
— **À quelle heure?**
— **Vers deux heures.**
— **À deux heures? Alors, à demain.**
— **Salut, à demain.**

cet après-midi	jouer au tennis
ce soir	dîner au restaurant
demain après-midi	aller voir un film
demain soir	faire du jogging
vendredi soir	aller prendre un verre
???	???

À VOUS!

Avec un(e) partenaire, relisez à haute voix la conversation entre David et Léa. Ensuite, choisissez une activité et invitez votre partenaire à la faire *(to do it)*.

You can find a list of the new words from this **Compétence** on page 100 and access the audio online.

écrire un mail *to write an e-mail* **libre** *free* **ce soir** *tonight, this evening* **quelque chose** *something* **D'accord** *Okay*
Ça te / vous dit de...? *Do you feel like...?* **pas vraiment** *not really* **allons** *let's go* **On va...?** *How about we go...?*,
Shall we go...? **Pourquoi pas?** *Why not?* **Vers** *About, Around, Toward*

SAYING WHAT YOU LIKE TO DO

✔ Pour vérifier

1. What do you call the basic form of the verb that you find listed in the dictionary?

2. What are the four possible endings for infinitives in French?

3. When you have a sequence of more than one verb in a clause, which one is conjugated? Which ones are in the infinitive?

L'infinitif

To name an activity in French, use the verb in the infinitive. The infinitive is the basic form of the verb that you find listed in the dictionary. French infinitives are single words ending in **-er, -ir, -oir,** or **-re,** like **jouer** *(to play),* **dormir** *(to sleep),* **voir** *(to see),* or **être** *(to be).* In French, whenever there are two or more verbs together in a clause, the first verb is conjugated, but verbs that immediately follow are in the infinitive.

— Qu'est-ce que tu **aimes faire**?
— J'**aime jouer** au football américain.

— Est-ce que tu **voudrais sortir**?
— Non, je **préfère rester** à la maison.

Use **jouer** *au* to talk about playing most sports using balls or pucks. Many other sports use **faire** *du / de la / de l' / des.*

jouer **au** baseball   jouer **au** golf   faire **du** ski   faire **de l'**exercice

Use **jouer** *du / de la / de l' / des* to talk about playing most musical instruments.

jouer **du** piano   jouer **de la** guitare

As with **un, une,** and **des; du, de la,** and **de l'** change to **de (d')** after a negative expression.

— Tu joues **de la** guitare?
— Non, je ne joue pas **de** guitare.

— Tu fais **du** jogging le week-end?
— Non, je ne fais pas **de** jogging.

ⓘ**Lrn** Prononcez bien! See **Module 17.**

PRONONCIATION

La consonne r et l'infinitif 1-30

The consonant **r** is one of the few (CaReFuL) consonants that are often pronounced at the end of words. The final **r** of infinitives ending in **-er,** however, is not pronounced. The **-er** ending is pronounced [e], like the **é** in **café.**

parler   inviter   danser   aller
regarder   jouer   écouter   dîner

The **r** in infinitives ending in **-ir, -oir,** or **-re** is pronounced. To pronounce a French **r,** hold the back of your tongue firmly arched upward in the back of your mouth and pronounce a vocalized English *h* sound in your throat.

Pronounce the **-ir** verb ending as [iR], unless the verb ends in **-oir** [waR].

sortir   dormir   voir

The **e** in the infinitive ending of **-re** verbs is pronounced when this ending is preceded by a consonant, but not when it is preceded by a vowel.

faire   lire   être   prendre

Note *de vocabulaire*

To say you don't like either activity, use **ne... ni... ni...** *(neither... nor...)*: **Je** *n'*aime *ni* lire *ni* surfer sur Internet. To say that you like *both* activities, use **J'aime les deux.**

A **Prononcez bien!** Demandez à votre partenaire quelle activité il/elle préfère. Faites attention à la prononciation de l'infinitif.

EXEMPLE lire / surfer sur Internet
— **Tu préfères lire ou surfer sur Internet?**
— **Je préfère lire.**

1. faire de l'exercice / dormir
2. sortir avec des amis / rester à la maison
3. prendre un verre au café / dîner au restaurant
4. jouer au tennis / regarder un match de tennis à la télé
5. regarder la télé / aller au cinéma
6. être à la maison / être en cours
7. parler à un ami au téléphone / inviter un ami à la maison
8. écrire des mails / envoyer un texto à un ami
9. faire du jogging / faire du vélo

B **Chacun ses goûts.** Est-ce que vous aimez ces activités?

J'aime beaucoup...	Je n'aime pas beaucoup...
J'aime assez...	Je n'aime pas du tout...

EXEMPLE J'aime assez bricoler.

 1.

2.  3. 4.

5.  6. 7.

Line art on this page: © Cengage Learning

C **Entretien.** Interviewez votre partenaire.

1. Qu'est-ce que tu aimes faire après les cours? Qu'est-ce que tu voudrais faire aujourd'hui après les cours?

2. Est-ce que tu aimes rester à la maison le week-end? Qu'est-ce que tu aimes faire le week-end? Qu'est-ce que tu voudrais faire ce week-end?

3. Est-ce que tu aimes travailler sur l'ordinateur? Tu aimes surfer sur Internet? Tu préfères téléphoner, écrire des mails ou envoyer des textos à des amis?

4. Est-ce que tu voudrais aller au cinéma ce week-end? Quel film est-ce que tu voudrais voir? Tu préfères aller voir un film au cinéma ou regarder un film à la maison?

STRATÉGIES ET COMPRÉHENSION AUDITIVE

> **POUR MIEUX COMPRENDRE:** *Listening for specific information*
>
> It takes time and practice to understand a foreign language when you hear it. However, using listening strategies can help you learn to understand spoken French more quickly.
>
> Often, you do not need to comprehend everything you hear. Practice listening for specific details, such as times, places, or prices. Do not worry about understanding every word.

🔊 1-31 **A   Quand?**   Écoutez ces trois scènes. Indiquez le jour et l'heure choisis *(chosen)*.

SCÈNE A: LE JOUR _____
             L'HEURE _____

SCÈNE B: LE JOUR _____
             L'HEURE _____

SCÈNE C: LE JOUR _____
             L'HEURE _____

© Stockbyte/Getty Images

🔊 1-32 **B   Qu'est-ce qu'elles font?**   Léa invite Lisa à sortir. Pour les trois scènes, indiquez ce que Lisa préfère faire.

SCÈNE A: _____   SCÈNE B: _____   SCÈNE C: _____

Compréhension auditive: *On sort ensemble?*

🔊 David, Lisa, and Léa run into two of David's friends. Listen to their conversation.
1-33 Do not try to understand every word. The first time, listen only for the leisure activities they mention. Each time you hear one mentioned, write it down.

A **Vous comprenez?** Écoutez une seconde fois *(time)* la conversation entre David et ses amis et répondez à ces questions.

1. Est-ce que Thomas et Elsa sont des amis de Léa?

2. Faites une liste de trois choses que Thomas et Elsa découvrent *(discover)* au sujet de Léa et de Lisa *(about Léa and Lisa)*.

3. Qu'est-ce que les cinq jeunes gens décident de faire ensemble *(together)*? Qu'est-ce que David, Léa et Lisa voudraient faire après?

B **Tu voudrais sortir?** Invitez votre partenaire à faire les choses suivantes. Utilisez *B. Invitations* à la page 69 comme modèle.

voir un film

jouer au foot

faire du vélo

Compétence 1 | *soixante-treize* **73**

73

COMPÉTENCE 2

Saying how you spend your free time

LE WEEK-END

Comment est-ce que vous aimez **passer** le week-end? Qu'est-ce que **vous faites d'habitude** le samedi? Est-ce que vous passez **la matinée** à la maison?

(presque) toujours	souvent	quelquefois	rarement	ne... jamais
(almost) always	*often*	*sometimes*	*rarely*	*never*

Je reste souvent au lit **jusqu'à** 10 heures.

Le samedi matin, je mange **d'abord** quelque chose.

Quelquefois l'après-midi, je **révise** mes cours (j'étudie).

Le soir, je ne reste presque jamais **chez moi. Je vais** souvent au cinéma.

Est-ce que vous aimez faire du sport? Vous jouez bien au foot? Est-ce que vous aimez faire de la musique? Est-ce que vous jouez bien du piano?

très bien	assez bien	assez mal	très mal
very well	*fairly well*	*fairly badly*	*very badly*

Je nage assez mal.

Je gagne souvent **quand** je joue au hockey. Je joue **mieux** au hockey **qu'**au foot.

Je joue assez bien du piano.

Je chante très bien.

Line art on this page: © Cengage Learning

---

passer *to pass, to spend* (time)   **vous faites** (**faire** *to do, to make*)   **d'habitude** *usually, generally*   **la matinée** *the morning*
jusqu'à *until*   **d'abord** *first*   **réviser** *to review*   **chez moi** *at home, at my house* (**chez...** = *to / at / in / by the house of . . .*)
Je vais (**aller** *to go*)   **Je gagne** (**gagner** *to win*)   **quand** *when*   **mieux (que)** *better (than)*

1-34

Léa et David parlent de leurs activités *(f)* du week-end.

LÉA:	Qu'est-ce que **tu fais** d'habitude le week-end?
DAVID:	Le samedi matin, je reste au lit, le samedi après-midi, je joue au tennis et le soir, j'aime sortir. Et toi?
LÉA:	Le matin, je révise mes cours, l'après-midi, j'aime **faire du shopping** et le soir, moi aussi, j'aime sortir.
DAVID:	Alors, tu es libre samedi soir? Tu voudrais sortir? Il y a un bon film au ciné-club **à la fac**. C'est un classique de Truffaut.
LÉA:	Oui, oui, j'aime bien les vieux films de Truffaut.
DAVID:	Le film commence à huit heures. Je **passe** chez toi vers sept heures?
LÉA:	D'accord! À samedi, alors.

Le temps libre. Complétez ces phrases pour parler de vous.

Vous dansez bien?

© Yuri Arcurs/Shutterstock.com

1. Le samedi matin, je passe *presque toujours / souvent / rarement* la matinée à la maison. *(Je ne passe jamais la matinée à la maison.)*

2. Le samedi matin, je reste au lit jusqu'à *sept heures / dix heures / ???.*

3. D'habitude, le samedi matin, je mange quelque chose *à la maison / dans un fast-food / au café / ???. (Je ne mange pas le samedi matin.)*

4. Comme *(As)* exercice, je préfère *faire du sport / faire du jogging / nager / ???. (Je n'aime pas faire d'exercice.)*

5. Quand je joue *au tennis / au basket / ???*, je gagne *toujours / souvent / rarement. (Je n'aime pas faire de sport.)*

6. Je joue *mieux / aussi bien / moins bien* au basket qu'au hockey.

7. Je vais plus souvent au cinéma *seul(e) / avec des amis / avec mon meilleur ami / avec ma meilleure amie / avec ma famille / ???.*

8. Je chante *très bien / assez bien / ???.*

9. Je joue *du piano / de la guitare / de la batterie / ???. (Je ne joue pas d'instrument de musique.)*

👥 À VOUS!

Avec un(e) partenaire, relisez à haute voix la conversation entre David et Léa. Ensuite, adaptez la conversation pour décrire vos activités du week-end et pour inviter votre partenaire à faire quelque chose que vous voudriez faire.

🌐 You can find a list of the new words from this *Compétence* on page 100 and access the audio online.

---

tu fais (faire *to do, to make*) **faire du shopping** *to go shopping* **à la fac** *at the university* **passer** *to pass (by)* **Compétence 2** | *soixante-quinze* **75**

TELLING WHAT YOU DO, HOW OFTEN, AND HOW WELL

Les verbes en -er et les adverbes

Regular verbs are groups of verbs that follow a predictable pattern of conjugation. The largest group of regular verbs have infinitives ending in **-er.** Most verbs ending in **-er** that you have learned, *except* **aller,** are conjugated in the present tense by dropping the **-er** and adding the following endings: **-e, -es, -e, -ons, -ez, -ent.**

PARLER *(to speak, to talk)*	
je parl**e**	nous parl**ons**
tu parl**es**	vous parl**ez**
il/elle parl**e**	ils/elles parl**ent**

The present tense can be expressed in three ways in English. Express all three of the following English structures by a single verb in French.

I work.
I am working. ⎫ Je travaille.
I do work. ⎭

We study.
We are studying. ⎫ Nous étudions.
We do study. ⎭

Here are the regular **-er** verbs that you have seen so far.

aimer	*to like, to love*	jouer	*to play*
bricoler	*to do handiwork*	manger	*to eat*
chanter	*to sing*	nager	*to swim*
commencer	*to begin, to start*	parler	*to speak, to talk*
compter	*to count*	passer	*to pass (by), to spend* (time)
danser	*to dance*	penser	*to think*
dîner	*to have dinner*	préférer	*to prefer*
donner	*to give*	regarder	*to look (at), to watch*
écouter	*to listen (to)*	répéter	*to repeat*
envoyer	*to send*	rester	*to stay, to remain*
étudier	*to study*	réviser	*to review*
fermer	*to close*	surfer	*to surf* (the Internet)
habiter	*to live*	travailler	*to work*
inviter	*to invite*		

Remember that words such as **je, le, que,** and **ne** make elision before a vowel sound.

j'aime / je **n'**aime pas   j'habite / je **n'**habite pas

Adverbs such as **bien, souvent, rarement,** and **beaucoup** tell how well, how often, or how much you do something. In French, these adverbs are generally placed *directly after the conjugated verb.* **D'abord, quelquefois,** and **d'habitude** may also be placed at the beginning or end of the clause.

Thomas regarde **souvent** la télé.   *Thomas **often** watches T.V.*
Quelquefois, je joue **bien** au tennis.   ***Sometimes,** I play tennis **well.***
D'habitude, je travaille le week-end.   ***Usually,** I work weekends.*

Notice that **ne... jamais** *(never)* follows the same placement rule as **ne... pas.**

Je **ne** joue **jamais** au golf.   *I **never** play golf.*

✔ *Pour vérifier*

1. How do you determine the stem of an **-er** verb? What endings do you add to it?

2. When do you drop the final **e** of words like **je, ne,** and **le**?

3. Where do you generally place adverbs such as **bien**?

4. Which **-er** verb endings are silent? Which ones are pronounced?

iLrn Grammar Tutorials

Note *de grammaire*

Verbs whose infinitives do not end in **-er,** and a few irregular verbs whose infinitives do, such as **aller,** do not follow the pattern of conjugation shown here. You will learn how to conjugate such verbs later. You may want to use these forms now to talk about yourself.

I go	**je vais**
I sleep	**je dors**
I do, I make	**je fais**
I read	**je lis**
I write	**j'écris**
I take	**je prends**
I go out	**je sors**

Vocabulaire sans peine!

Most English verbs ending with *-ate* were French **-er** verbs that were borrowed into English.

imiter *to imitate*
décorer *to decorate*

Also notice these cognate patterns among **-er** verbs.

-iser = *-ize*
utiliser *to utilize*
économiser *to economize*

-fier = *-fy*
défier *to defy*
identifier *to identify*

How would you say the following verbs in French?

to manipulate, to calculate
to digitalize, to hypnotize
to notify, to justify

🌐 **Sélection musicale.** Search the Web for the song **"Elle chante pour moi"** by Faudel to enjoy a musical selection using this vocabulary.

PRONONCIATION

Les verbes en -er

All the present tense endings of **-er** verbs, except for the **nous (-ons)** and **vous (-ez)** forms, are silent.

je rest~~e~~	il rest~~e~~	ils rest~~ent~~
tu rest~~es~~	elle rest~~e~~	elles rest~~ent~~

Rely on context to distinguish between **il** and **ils,** or **elle** and **elles.** You will hear a difference only with verbs beginning with a vowel sound.

il travaill~~e~~ — il~~s~~ travaill~~ent~~   il aim~~e~~ — ils ᶻaim~~ent~~

The **-ons** ending of the **nous** form rhymes with **maison** and the **-ez** of the **vous** form rhymes with **café** and sounds like the **-er** ending of the infinitive. There is liaison between the **s** of **nous** and **vous** and verbs beginning with vowel sounds.

nou~~s~~ parlons	nous ᶻétudions
vou~~s~~ parlez	vous ᶻétudiez

A   Prononcez bien!   Écrivez ces phrases sur une feuille de papier. D'abord, complétez chacun des verbes avec la terminaison appropriée. Ensuite, barrez *(cross out)* chaque terminaison qui n'est pas prononcée. Finalement, lisez chaque phrase à haute voix *(aloud)* et dites si elle est vraie en disant **c'est vrai** ou **ce n'est pas vrai.**

EXEMPLE   Le samedi soir, j'aim~~e~~ rester à la maison.
C'est vrai. / Ce n'est pas vrai.

1. Le samedi soir, j'aim__ sortir avec des amis.
2. *[to a classmate]* Et toi, tu aim__ beaucoup sortir, non?
3. *[to a classmate]* Tes amis et toi, vous invit__ souvent des amis à la maison, non?
4. Mes amis et moi, nous préfér__ aller danser.
5. Mais mon meilleur ami préfèr__ rester à la maison.
6. Les étudiants aim__ mieux sortir que de travailler.

B   Opinions.   Comment est le/la colocataire idéal(e)?

EXEMPLE   travailler beaucoup
Il/Elle travaille beaucoup.
Il/Elle ne travaille pas beaucoup.

1. aimer beaucoup aller en boîte
2. parler souvent au téléphone
3. bricoler bien
4. passer toujours le week-end à la maison
5. inviter souvent des amis à la maison
6. regarder toujours la télé le week-end
7. écouter toujours du hip-hop

Comment est le/la colocataire idéal(e)?

C   Et toi?   Interviewez un(e) partenaire en formant des questions avec les verbes de l'exercice précédent.

EXEMPLE   — **Est-ce que tu travailles beaucoup?**
— **Oui, je travaille beaucoup.**
Non, je ne travaille pas beaucoup.

Après, parlez de votre partenaire à la classe.

EXEMPLE   **Il/Elle travaille beaucoup et...**

D **Le samedi.** Est-ce que vous faites toujours, souvent ou rarement ces choses le week-end? N'oubliez pas *(Don't forget)* de conjuguer le verbe!

> (presque) toujours   souvent   quelquefois   rarement   ne... jamais

EXEMPLE le samedi matin: passer la matinée à la maison
> **Le samedi matin, je passe toujours (souvent...) la matinée à la maison.**
> **Je ne passe jamais la matinée à la maison.**

Un restaurant dans le Vieux Nice

1. le samedi matin:
    rester au lit jusqu'à midi
    manger à la maison
    jouer au tennis

2. le samedi après-midi:
    nager
    bricoler
    surfer sur Internet

3. le samedi soir:
    dîner au restaurant
    danser en boîte
    chanter dans un karaoké

4. le dimanche
    passer la matinée avec la famille
    jouer du piano
    manger dans un fast-food

Maintenant, demandez à votre professeur s'il/si elle fait souvent les choses indiquées.

EXEMPLE le samedi matin: passer la matinée à la maison
> **Le samedi matin, est-ce que vous passez souvent la matinée à la maison?**

E **C'est vrai?** Formez des phrases pour décrire *(to describe)* votre classe.

EXEMPLE nous / parler beaucoup en cours
> **Nous parlons beaucoup en cours.**
> **Nous ne parlons pas beaucoup en cours.**

1. le professeur / parler quelquefois anglais en cours
2. les étudiants / commencer à très bien parler français
3. nous / travailler beaucoup en cours
4. je / aimer dormir en cours
5. les étudiants / travailler quelquefois ensemble *(together)*
6. nous / regarder des vidéoclips en cours
7. je / écouter toujours le prof en cours
8. les étudiants / manger quelquefois en cours

F **Talents.** Dites si ces personnes font bien ou mal ces choses.

> très bien   assez bien   assez mal   très mal

EXEMPLE Ma sœur **joue très bien (assez mal) de la guitare.**
> Ma sœur **ne joue pas de guitare.**
> **Je n'ai pas de sœur.** *(I don't have a sister.)*

1. Mon meilleur ami (Ma meilleure amie)...
Mon frère...

2. Mes parents...
Moi, je...

3. Moi, je...
Mon ami _____ *[name a friend]*...

4. Mes ami(e)s _____ et _____
[name two friends]...
Mes amis et moi, nous...

G Entretien. Interviewez votre partenaire.

1. Tu es musicien(ne)? Est-ce que tu danses bien ou mal? Est-ce que tu chantes bien? Tu préfères écouter la radio ou regarder la télé? Est-ce que tu regardes souvent la télé quand tu manges? Tu écoutes de la musique quand tu étudies?

2. Est-ce que tu es sportif (sportive)? Est-ce que tu aimes le sport? Quel sport est-ce que tu préfères, le football américain, le basket, le golf ou le baseball? Est-ce que tu joues au tennis? au golf? au volley? (Est-ce que tu gagnes souvent?)

3. Est-ce que tu restes souvent à la maison le week-end? Est-ce que tu bricoles quelquefois le week-end? Est-ce que tu étudies? Est-ce que tu préfères bricoler ou étudier?

H Qu'est-ce qui se passe? Décrivez la scène chez la famille Li ce week-end. Donnez au moins cinq détails.

Étienne   Monsieur Li   Madame Li
Audrey   Louise   Dominique   Georges   Antoine et le chien

TELLING WHAT YOU DO

✔ Pour vérifier

1. In verbs like **préférer**, which forms have a spelling change in the stem in the present tense? What is the change? Which forms have stems like the infinitive?

2. In verbs that end in **-yer,** like **envoyer,** which forms have a spelling change in the stem in the present tense? What is the change? Which forms have stems like the infinitive?

3. What is special about the **nous** form of a verb with an infinitive ending in **-ger**? in **-cer**?

4. What is the difference in pronunciation between **é** and **è**?

Vocabulaire sans peine!

Note the following cognate patterns with these verbs with spelling changes.

*-nounce = -***noncer**
to pronounce **prononcer**
to denounce **dénoncer**

*-erate = -***érer**
to accelerate **accélérer**
to cooperate **coopérer**

How would you say:
to announce, to renounce
to tolerate, to exasperate

Quelques verbes à changements orthographiques

A few **-er** verbs have spelling changes in their stems in the present tense.

- When the next-to-last syllable of an infinitive has an **e** or **é,** this letter often changes to **è** in all forms except **nous** and **vous.** The stem for the **nous** and **vous** forms is like the infinitive.

PRÉFÉRER *(to prefer)*		RÉPÉTER *(to repeat)*	
je préf**è**re	nous préférons	je rép**è**te	nous répétons
tu préf**è**res	vous préférez	tu rép**è**tes	vous répétez
il/elle préf**è**re	ils/elles préf**è**rent	il/elle rép**è**te	ils/elles rép**è**tent

- In verbs with infinitives ending in **-yer,** the **y** changes to **i** in all forms except **nous** and **vous.**

ENVOYER *(to send)*	
j'envo**i**e	nous envoyons
tu envo**i**es	vous envoyez
il/elle envo**i**e	ils/elles envo**i**ent

- Verbs ending in **-cer** and **-ger** also have spelling changes. With verbs ending in **-ger,** like **manger, nager,** and **voyager,** an **e** is inserted before the **-ons** ending in the **nous** form. With verbs ending in **-cer,** like **commencer,** the **c** changes to a **ç** before the **-ons** ending in the **nous** form.

VOYAGER *(to travel)*		COMMENCER *(to start, to begin)*	
je voyage	nous voyag**e**ons	je commence	nous commen**ç**ons
tu voyages	vous voyagez	tu commences	vous commencez
il/elle voyage	ils/elles voyagent	il/elle commence	ils/elles commencent

iLrn **Prononcez bien!** See Modules 18, 29, and 34.

PRONONCIATION

Les verbes à changements orthographiques
1-36

Spelling changes occur in verbs to reflect pronunciation. The letter **é (e accent aigu)** sounds like the vowel of **les.**

— Vous préf**é**rez passer la matin**é**e à la maison?

— Non, nous préf**é**rons passer la matin**é**e au caf**é.**

The letter **è (e accent grave)** often occurs in the final syllable of words ending in a silent **e (Michèle),** and sounds similar to the *e* in the English word *let.*

Je préf**è**re aller à la biblioth**è**que avec Mich**è**le.

In French, **c** and **g** are pronounced soft (the **c** like an **s** and the **g** like a French **j**) before an **e, i,** or **y.** They are pronounced hard (the **c** like **k** and the **g** similar to the *g* in the English word *go*) before an **a, o, u,** or a consonant.

Soft **g: Ge**orges, **Gé**rard, **Gi**lbert   Hard **g: Ga**brielle, Hu**go, Gu**illaume

Soft **c: Cé**cile, Mauri**ce**   Hard **c: Ca**therine, **Co**lette

The letter **ç** is used to indicate that a **c** is soft before **a, o,** or **u.** In verb endings, use **ç** to keep **c** soft before **o,** and introduce an **e** to keep **g** soft before **o.**

commen**ço**ns   man**geo**ns   voya**geo**ns   na**geo**ns

A Prononcez bien!
Dans les mots suivants, la lettre **c** est prononcée [s]. Lesquels de ces mots requièrent *(require)* une cédille?

1. menace / menacant
2. facade / facile
3. Nice / nicois
4. France / francais
5. provencal / Provence
6. prononciation / prononcons

Maintenant, dites si vous aimez les gens avec les traits de caractère suivants. Faites attention à la prononciation des lettres **c** et **g**.

J'aime bien les gens... / Je n'aime pas les gens...

> créatifs   cultivés   arrogants   vulgaires
> menaçants   superficiels   imaginatifs   généreux
> calmes   courageux   égoïstes   gentils

B Préférences.
Complétez ces questions avec le verbe indiqué et interviewez votre partenaire.

1. Avec qui *(With whom)* est-ce que tu _____ (préférer) sortir?
2. Est-ce que tu _____ (envoyer) souvent des textos à des amis?
3. Quel jour est-ce que tes amis _____ (préférer) sortir?
4. Vous _____ (manger) souvent ensemble *(together)*?
5. Est-ce que vous _____ (préférer) dîner ensemble à la maison ou au restaurant?
6. En général, est-ce que les étudiants _____ (préférer) dîner au restaurant ou étudier à la bibliothèque?
7. Tu _____ (aimer) voyager? Tu _____ (voyager) souvent?
8. Tes amis et toi, vous _____ (voyager) souvent ensemble?

C Posez vos stylos!
Par équipes *(In teams)*, utilisez des verbes en **-er** de la liste à la page 76 pour compléter chaque phrase que votre professeur vous donnera *(will give you)*. Arrêtez d'écrire quand le professeur dira **Posez vos stylos!** *(Stop writing when the professor says **Put down your pens!**)* Chaque groupe gagnera *(will earn)* un point pour chaque phrase correcte et logique.

EXEMPLE En cours de français, le professeur...
En cours de français, le professeur préfère parler français.
Il écoute les étudiants.
Il répète souvent.
Il envoie beaucoup de mails...

Tes amis et toi, est-ce que vous passez beaucoup de temps au café?

Asking about someone's day

LA JOURNÉE

Note *culturelle*

D'après une étude *(According to a study)* de l'Institut national de la statistique et des études économiques (Insee) en France, le Français moyen *(average)* consacre *(dedicates)* 11 heures 45 de sa journée aux besoins *(needs)* physiologiques (dormir, manger, faire sa toilette *[to wash up]*); 4 heures 07 au travail, aux études et au transport; 3 heures 10 aux tâches *(tasks)* domestiques et 4 heures 58 aux loisirs ou aux amis. Combien de temps consacrez-vous à ces activités tous les jours?

Note *de vocabulaire*

1. The adjective **tout** is placed before a noun's article. It means *the whole* or *all* before singular nouns (**toute la journée**) and *all* or *every* before plural nouns (**tous les jours**). It has four forms: **tout** *(masc. sing.)*, **toute** *(fem. sing.)*, **tous** *(masc. plur.)*, and **toutes** *(fem. plur.)*.

2. Use the following pronouns after prepositions such as **avec** or **chez**.

avec moi *with me*
avec toi *with you*
avec lui *with him*
avec elle *with her*
avec nous *with us*
avec vous *with you*
avec eux *with them (m)*
avec elles *with them (f)*

🔊 1-37

— Quand est-ce que vous êtes à l'université?
— Je suis à l'université... le lundi, le mardi... de dix heures à quatre heures.
le matin, l'après-midi, le soir.
tous les jours, **sauf** le week-end.
toute la journée.

— Où est-ce que vous **déjeunez** d'habitude?
— Je déjeune... chez moi / chez des amis / chez...
au restaurant universitaire.
au café Trianon / dans un fast-food...

— Qu'est-ce que vous aimez faire après les cours?
— J'aime... aller au parc / aller à la bibliothèque / aller chez un(e) ami(e).
rentrer à la maison.
dormir...

— **Avec qui** est-ce que vous **aimez mieux** sortir?
— J'aime mieux sortir... avec mon ami(e)...
avec **mon copain (ma copine).**
avec **mon mari (ma femme).**

— Pourquoi est-ce que vous préférez sortir **avec lui / avec elle**?
— Parce qu'il/elle est... amusant(e), riche, intéressant(e), beau (belle)...

— Quand est-ce que vous préférez sortir **ensemble**?
— Nous préférons sortir... le vendredi soir.
le samedi après-midi...

Jean **demande** à Léa comment elle passe une journée typique.

JEAN: Quand est-ce que tu es en cours ce semestre?

LÉA: Je suis en cours tous les jours, sauf le week-end. Le lundi, par exemple, je suis en cours de midi à trois heures. Je passe la matinée à la bibliothèque.

JEAN: Et après les cours, qu'est-ce que tu fais en général?

LÉA: **Après,** je rentre à la maison. Je travaille ou **je dors** un peu.

JEAN: Et le soir?

LÉA: Le soir, je reste à la maison et je révise mes cours ou je surfe sur Internet.

sauf *except* **toute la journée** *all day* **déjeuner** *to eat lunch* **rentrer** *to return, to go back (home)* **Avec qui** *With whom* **aimer mieux** *to like better, to prefer* **mon copain (ma copine)** *my boyfriend (my girlfriend)* **mon mari (ma femme)** *my husband (my wife)* **avec lui (avec elle)** *with him (with her)* **ensemble** *together* **demander** *to ask (for)* **Après** *Afterwards, After* **je dors (dormir** *to sleep)*

A Précisions. Demain, David déjeune avec des amis au café Chez Marie. Quelle est la réponse logique pour chaque question?

1. Quel jour est-ce que nous déjeunons ensemble?
2. À quelle heure?
3. Qui déjeune avec nous?
4. Pourquoi est-ce que tu n'invites pas Thomas?
5. Où est-ce que nous déjeunons?
6. Qu'est-ce que tu voudrais faire après?

a. Au café Chez Marie.
b. Elsa et Cyril.
c. Vendredi.
d. Aller au cinéma.
e. Parce qu'il travaille.
f. À midi et demi.

Chez Marie
Pizzas – Snack – Bar
27, rue de Rennes

euros

Calzone: **6,00**
Tomate, champignons, œuf, crème fraîche

Marguerite: **5,00**
Tomate, fromage

Poivrons: **5,80**
Tomate, fromage, champignons, poivrons

Reine: **5,80**
Tomate, fromage, olives, champignons, jambon

Service continu de midi à 2h du matin.

© Cengage Learning

B C'est vrai? Lisez chaque phrase et dites si **c'est vrai** ou si **ce n'est pas vrai.**

1. Je suis à l'université tous les jours, sauf le dimanche.
2. Nous sommes en cours de français le matin, tous les jours sauf le week-end.
3. Le cours de français est de dix heures à onze heures.
4. Les autres étudiants et moi passons beaucoup de temps ensemble après les cours.
5. Nous déjeunons souvent ensemble.
6. Le samedi, j'étudie le français toute la journée.
7. J'aime mieux aller en cours de français que de sortir avec des amis.

Maintenant, corrigez les phrases qui ne sont pas vraies.

C Entretien. Interviewez votre partenaire.

1. Quels jours est-ce que tu es à l'université? De quelle heure à quelle heure est-ce que tu es en cours? Est-ce que tu restes à l'université toute la journée? À quelle heure est-ce que tu rentres à la maison?
2. Quand est-ce que tu étudies? Où est-ce que tu aimes mieux étudier: chez toi ou à la bibliothèque? Avec qui est-ce que tu préfères étudier?
3. Où est-ce que tu aimes mieux déjeuner? À quelle heure? Est-ce que tu déjeunes souvent chez toi? Où est-ce que tu préfères manger le soir? Est-ce que tu dînes plus souvent chez toi ou au restaurant? Est-ce que tu manges souvent dans un fast-food? Qu'est-ce que tu préfères: les hamburgers, la pizza ou les tacos?
4. Qu'est-ce que tu aimes faire le week-end? Où est-ce que tu aimes mieux aller avec des amis: au cinéma, au café ou en boîte? Avec qui est-ce que tu préfères sortir? Pourquoi est-ce que tu aimes sortir avec lui (elle)? Quand est-ce que vous aimez mieux sortir?

À VOUS!

Avec un(e) partenaire, relisez à haute voix la conversation entre Jean et Léa. Ensuite, adaptez la conversation pour décrire votre situation. Changez de rôles.

iLrn 🌐 You can find a list of the new words from this *Compétence* on page 101 and access the audio online.

ASKING FOR INFORMATION

✔ *Pour vérifier*

1. How do you form an information question?

2. Does **qui** or **que** become **qu'** before a vowel?

3. When are three times you do not use **est-ce que**?

4. How do you say *Who is this? What is this?*

⬆️

iLrn Grammar Tutorials

Les mots interrogatifs

You have learned to ask questions with **est-ce que.** To ask for information such as *what, when,* or *why,* add the appropriate question word before **est-ce que.**

où *where*	**Où est-ce que** vous étudiez?
que (qu') *what*	**Qu'est-ce que** vous étudiez?
pourquoi *why*	**Pourquoi est-ce que** vous étudiez le français?
quand *when*	**Quand est-ce que** vous étudiez?
qui / avec qui *who(m) / with whom*	**Avec qui est-ce que** vous étudiez?
comment *how*	**Comment est-ce que** vous passez la journée?
quel(s) jour(s) *(on) what / which day(s)*	**Quels jours est-ce que** vous êtes en cours?
à quelle heure *at what time*	**À quelle heure est-ce que** vous êtes en cours?

Note that **que** makes elision before a vowel sound, but **qui** does not.

Qu'est-ce que vous aimez faire le soir? Avec **qui** est-ce que vous aimez sortir?

Do not use **est-ce que** with **qui** when it is the subject of the verb, or with **où** or **comment** when they are followed directly by **être.**

qui *who*	**Qui** travaille avec toi?
où *where*	**Où est** la bibliothèque?
comment *how*	**Comment est** l'université?

Use **Qui est-ce?** to ask *who* someone is. Use **Qu'est-ce que c'est?** to ask *what* something is.

— Qui est-ce? — Qu'est-ce que c'est?
— C'est Jean. — C'est un livre.

PRONONCIATION

*Les lettres **qu** et la prononciation du mot **quand** en liaison* 1-38

In French, **qu** is usually pronounced as in the word **quiche.** It is generally only pronounced with the *w* sound heard in the English word *quite* when it is followed by **oi,** as in **pourquoi.**

  qui que quand quelle heure pourquoi

Note that **d** in liaison is pronounced as a **t.**

  Quand ͭ est-ce que tu travailles?

A **Prononcez bien!** Des amis décident de déjeuner ensemble. D'abord, lisez la liste des mots donnés en faisant attention à la prononciation de la combinaison **qu.** Ensuite, complétez les questions avec le mot qui convient et lisez à haute voix la conversation avec votre partenaire.

> Qui   Que (Qu')   Quand   Où
> Pourquoi   À quelle heure

— Tu voudrais déjeuner avec nous?

— __1__?

— Aujourd'hui.

— Oui, d'accord. __2__?

— Vers midi.

— __3__ est-ce que tu voudrais manger?

— Chez moi.

— __4__ est-ce que tu prépares?

— Une pizza.

— __5__ est-ce que tu invites?

— Quentin et toi.

— __6__ est-ce que tu voudrais faire après?

— Aller au cinéma.

— __7__?

— Parce que je voudrais voir le nouveau film avec Marion Cotillard.

B **Beaucoup de questions.** Formez des questions en utilisant l'équivalent français des mots interrogatifs donnés. Ensuite, posez-les à un(e) autre étudiant(e).

1. _____ est-ce que tu étudies? *(What? Where? With whom? When?)*

2. _____ est-ce que tu aimes mieux déjeuner? *(At what time? With whom? Where?)*

3. _____ est-ce que tu dînes d'habitude le samedi soir? *(Where? With whom? At what time?)*

C **Un jeu.** Par équipes *(In teams)*, pensez à une question appropriée pour obtenir chaque réponse, en utilisant un mot interrogatif **(qui, que...)** basé sur les mots en gras *(boldfaced)*. Les équipes sélectionnent tour à tour *(take turns)* un élément. Les équipes gagnent les points indiqués pour chaque bonne réponse.

	A	B	C	D
5 points	Ça va **bien,** merci.	Je m'appelle **Léa Clark.**	Il est **5 heures.**	Aujourd'hui, c'est **lundi.**
10 points	C'est **Lisa.**	C'est **un parc.**	David est **sympa.**	Léa est **à la maison.**
15 points	Lisa aime **la musique.**	Thomas travaille **toute la journée.**	David aime sortir **avec Léa.**	Je rentre **à une heure.**
20 points	**Léa et David** étudient les maths.	Nous aimons mieux **aller au cinéma.**	**Parce que le prof est très intéressant.**	Léa parle **bien** français.

ASKING QUESTIONS

✔ *Pour vérifier*

1. How would you invert the question: **Il est ici?**

2. Do you ever use **est-ce que** and inversion in the same question?

3. When do you insert a **-t-** between a verb and an inverted subject pronoun?

4. Generally, can you invert nouns, or only pronouns? What do you do if the subject of the question is a noun? How would you invert the question: **Marie déjeune à midi?**

5. What is the inverted form of **il y a?** of **c'est?**

6. How would you invert: **Où est-ce que vous déjeunez?**

 Grammar Tutorials

Les questions par inversion

You can ask a question using rising intonation or **est-ce que.** You can also use inversion; that is, you can invert the subject pronoun and the verb. Add a hyphen when the subject and verb are inverted.

> Est-ce que tu travailles le lundi? = **Travailles-tu le lundi?**

- Invert the *conjugated* verb and the *subject pronoun.* Do not invert a following infinitive.

> **Aimes-tu** aller au cinéma?   **Voudriez-vous** aller danser?

- Never use both **est-ce que** and inversion in the same question.

> **Joues-tu** de la guitare?   *OR*   **Est-ce que tu joues** de la guitare?

- Inversion is not normally used with **je.**

- When the subject is **il** or **elle** and *the verb ends in a vowel,* place a **-t-** between the verb and the pronoun. Do not add **-t-** if the verb ends in a consonant.

> Parle-**t**-il anglais?   Est-il d'ici?
> Travaille-**t**-elle ici?   Est-elle d'ici?

- If the subject of the question is a *noun,* rather than a *pronoun,* state the noun first, then supply a matching pronoun for inversion.

> **Le prof** est-**il** français?   **Marie** parle-t-**elle** français?
> **Les cours** sont-**ils** difficiles?   **Ophélie et Juliette** étudient-**elles** ici?

- The inverted form of **il y a** is **y a-t-il. C'est** becomes **est-ce.**

> **Y a-t-il** un café dans le quartier?   **Est-ce** un bon café?

- To ask information questions, place the question word before the inverted verb. **Qu'est-ce que** becomes **que (qu')** when using inversion.

> **Où** voudrais-tu aller? **Que** voudrais-tu faire? **Qu'**aimes-tu faire?

PRONONCIATION

L'inversion et la liaison 1-39

When the subject is **il, elle, ils,** or **elles,** there is liaison between the verb and its pronoun in inversion.

> Lisa est‿elle américaine?
> David et Thomas parlent‿ils anglais?

🔊 1-40 👥 **A** **Prononcez bien!** D'abord, écoutez et répétez ces questions. Ensuite, posez-les à un(e) autre étudiant(e). Faites attention à la prononciation!

Gisèle, où est-elle ce soir? Est-elle seule? Étudie-t-elle? Thomas et Gisèle aiment-ils la musique? Dansent-ils bien? Et toi? Aimes-tu danser? Dansons-nous en cours quelquefois? Tes amis et toi, aimez-vous aller en boîte ensemble? Aimez-vous mieux aller au cinéma? Y a-t-il un bon cinéma dans le quartier universitaire?

Thomas   Gisèle

© Cengage Learning

B **Entretien.** Changez ces phrases pour parler de vous. Après, posez une question logique à un(e) autre étudiant(e). Utilisez l'inversion.

EXEMPLE Je travaille *le matin.* Et toi?...
Je travaille le soir. Et toi? Quand travailles-tu?

1. Je suis en cours *le lundi, le mercredi et le jeudi.* Et toi?...
2. J'étudie *chez moi.* Et toi?...
3. J'étudie *avec des amis.* Et toi?...
4. Je préfère étudier *le français.* Et toi?...
5. Je préfère étudier *le français parce que le cours est intéressant.* Et toi?...

C **Jouons au tennis!** David parle avec Lisa. Posez les mêmes questions à un(e) partenaire en utilisant *l'inversion.*

EXEMPLE Tu es sportive?
Es-tu sportive?

1. Tu aimes jouer au tennis?
2. Tu gagnes souvent?
3. Est-ce que tu voudrais jouer au tennis ce week-end?
4. Quand est-ce que tu préfères jouer?
5. À quelle heure est-ce que tu voudrais commencer?
6. Qu'est-ce que tu voudrais faire après?
7. Tes amis sont sportifs?
8. Est-ce qu'ils jouent au tennis?
9. Ton meilleur ami est sportif aussi?
10. Est-ce qu'il joue bien au tennis?

D **Le samedi.** Voici un samedi typique pour Adrien, l'ami de David. Posez cinq questions à un(e) autre étudiant(e) sur ce qu'Adrien fait *(on what Adrien does)* le samedi. Utilisez un mot interrogatif dans chaque question. Dites **il fait** pour *he does,* si nécessaire.

| qui | que | où | quand | pourquoi | comment |

ses copains *(his friends)*

Going to the café

AU CAFÉ

Vous êtes au café. Qu'est-ce que vous allez prendre?

Je voudrais...   Pour moi...   Je vais prendre...

un expresso   un café au lait   un thé au citron

une eau minérale   un jus de fruit ou un jus d'orange   **un coca (light)**   un Orangina

un verre de vin rouge ou un verre de vin blanc   **un demi**   une bière

un sandwich au jambon   un sandwich au fromage   des frites

1-41

David et Léa **commandent une boisson** au café.

DAVID:	**Je n'ai pas très faim,** mais **j'ai soif.** Je vais prendre un demi. Et toi?
LÉA:	Moi, je voudrais bien un chocolat **chaud.**
DAVID:	Monsieur, s'il vous plaît.
LE SERVEUR:	Bonjour. Vous désirez?
DAVID:	Pour moi, un demi. Et pour mon amie, un chocolat chaud.
LE SERVEUR:	Très bien.

un coca (light) *a (diet) Coke, a (diet) cola*   **un demi** *a draft beer*   **commander** *to order*   **une boisson** *a drink, a beverage*
Je n'ai pas très faim (J'ai faim) *I'm not very hungry (I'm hungry)*   **j'ai soif** *I'm thirsty*   **chaud(e)** *hot*
le serveur (la serveuse) *the server*

Après, David et Léa **paient.**

DAVID:	Ça fait combien, monsieur?
LE SERVEUR:	Ça fait sept euros cinquante.
DAVID:	**Voilà** dix euros.
LE SERVEUR:	Et **voici** votre **monnaie**. Merci bien.

Note *culturelle*

La monnaie d'usage en France est l'euro, comme dans tous les pays membres de l'Union monétaire européenne (UME). L'euro, représenté par le symbole €, est divisé en 100 centimes. Le mot *argent* veut dire *money* en français, mais on entend *(one hears)* aussi des termes d'argot *(slang)* tels que *le fric, un radis (a radish)* ou *une balle (a bullet)* pour parler de l'argent. En anglais, est-ce qu'il y a une expression en argot pour dire *money* ou *a dollar?*

A **Préférences.** Proposez les choses suivantes à un(e) autre étudiant(e).

EXEMPLE   —Tu voudrais une eau minérale ou un coca?
—Je voudrais une eau minérale / un coca.

1.

2.   3.

4.   5.

© Cengage Learning

B **J'aime...** Est-ce que vous aimez les choses indiquées dans l'exercice précédent? Utilisez **le, la, l'** ou **les** pour indiquer ce que vous aimez ou ce que vous n'aimez pas.

EXEMPLE J'aime bien l'eau minérale. Je n'aime pas du tout le coca.

À VOUS!

Avec deux autres étudiants, relisez à haute voix la conversation au café. Ensuite, adaptez la conversation pour commander ce que *(what)* vous voudriez. La troisième personne va jouer le rôle du serveur/de la serveuse. N'oubliez pas *(Don't forget)* de payer. Changez de rôles.

You can find a list of the new words from this *Compétence* on page 101 and access the audio online.

ils paient (payer *to pay)* **Voilà** *There is, There are* **voici** *here is, here are* **la monnaie** *change*

PAYING THE BILL

✔ Pour vérifier

1. How do you say 30? 40? 50? 60? 70? 80? 90?

2. When do you use et with numbers? Do you use et with 81 and 91?

3. How do you say one hundred? Do you translate the word one?

→

Les nombres de trente à cent et l'argent

— Un thé au citron, c'est combien?
— 3,50 € (trois euros cinquante).

30 trente		**70** soixante-dix
31 trente et un		**71** soixante et onze
32 trente-deux		**72** soixante-douze
33 trente-trois...		**73** soixante-treize...
40 quarante		**80** quatre-vingts
41 quarante et un		**81** quatre-vingt-un
42 quarante-deux		**82** quatre-vingt-deux
43 quarante-trois...		**83** quatre-vingt-trois...
50 cinquante		**90** quatre-vingt-dix
51 cinquante et un		**91** quatre-vingt-onze
52 cinquante-deux		**92** quatre-vingt-douze
53 cinquante-trois...		**93** quatre-vingt-treize...
60 soixante		**100** cent
61 soixante et un		
62 soixante-deux		
63 soixante-trois...		

© Oliver Hoffmann/Shutterstock.com

 Prononcez bien! See Module 4.

PRONONCIATION

Les nombres 🔊 1-42

Some French numbers are pronounced differently, depending on what follows them.

deux	deux cafés	deux ^{z} euros
trois	trois cafés	trois ^{z} euros
six^{s}	six cafés	six ^{z} euros
huit^{t}	huit cafés	huit ^{t} euros
dix^{s}	dix cafés	dix ^{z} euros

A **Prononcez bien!** Commandez ces boissons. Faites attention à la prononciation des nombres.

EXEMPLES trois demis   **Trois demis, s'il vous plaît.**
             trois expressos   **Trois expressos, s'il vous plaît.**

deux demis   trois demis   six demis   huit demis   dix demis
deux expressos   trois expressos   six expressos   huit expressos   dix expressos

Maintenant, lisez ces prix *(prices)*. N'oubliez pas *(Don't forget)* de faire la liaison avec le mot **euro** si *(if)* nécessaire.

   1 €   11 €   2 €   12 €   3 €   13 €   6 €   16 €   10 €   20 €
   61 €   71 €   82 €   92 €   63 €   73 €   86 €   96 €   100 €   80 €

B **Prix indicatifs.** Combien coûte chaque chose?

EXEMPLE une baguette   **C'est 90 centimes.**

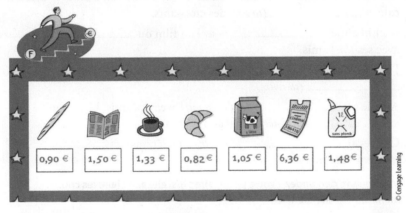

© Cengage Learning

1. un journal   **3.** un croissant   **5.** un billet de cinéma

2. un expresso   **4.** un litre de lait   **6.** un litre d'essence *(gasoline)*

C **Votre monnaie.** Vous êtes au café et vous payez pour vos amis et vous. Suivez l'exemple.

EXEMPLE 6,85 € (10 €)
           — **C'est combien, monsieur?**
           — **Six euros quatre-vingt-cinq, madame.**
           — **Voilà dix euros.**
           — **Et voici votre monnaie.**

1. 12,98 € (15 €)   **4.** 14,88 € (15 €)   **7.** 2,50 € (5 €)

2. 32,45 € (40 €)   **5.** 36,75 € (40 €)   **8.** 16,80 € (20 €)

3. 23,68 € (30 €)   **6.** 7,95 € (10 €)   **9.** 13,25 € (20 €)

D **Ça fait combien?** Écrivez les prix *(prices)* que vous entendez.

1-43

EXEMPLE Vous entendez: C'est dix euros cinquante.
           Vous écrivez: **10,50 €**

VIDÉOREPRISE

Les Stagiaires

© Cengage Learning

Rappel!
So far in the video, Amélie and Rachid, two new interns at the Technovert company, have met and found out a little about their new colleagues, M. Vieilledent (the boss), Camille (M. Vieilledent's assistant), Céline (the sales manager), Matthieu (the company's shy techie), and Christophe (M. Vieilledent's son and the company's gofer).

See the *Résumé de grammaire* section at the end of each chapter for a review of all the grammar presented in the chapter.

In *Épisode 2,* Camille realizes that Matthieu, the company's computer specialist, is interested in Amélie, as he tries to find out from her what kinds of things Amélie likes to do. Before you watch the episode, do these exercises to review what you have learned in *Chapitre 2.*

A Loisirs préférés. Camille parle des loisirs préférés des employés de Technovert. Complétez chaque phrase avec l'expression indiquée.

EXEMPLE Christophe aime <u>lire</u> *(to read)* des mangas.

1. Matthieu aime _____ *(to play)* à des jeux vidéo et _____ *(to work)* sur l'ordinateur.

2. M. Vieilledent aime _____ *(to go)* au café où il aime prendre un café et _____ *(to eat)* des croissants.

3. Rachid aime _____ *(to see)* un film ou _____ *(to dance)* avec ses *(his)* amis.

4. J'aime _____ *(to exercise)*. J'aime surtout *(most of all)* _____ *(to swim)*.

5. Amélie aime _____ *(to go out)* avec des amis. Elle aime _____ *(to have lunch)* au restaurant.

6. Céline aime _____ *(to talk)* au téléphone et _____ *(to write)* des mails.

Maintenant, demandez à votre partenaire s'il/si elle aime faire les choses mentionnées par Camille.

EXEMPLE — Est-ce que tu aimes lire des mangas?
— J'aime lire, mais je n'aime pas les mangas.

B Qu'est-ce qu'ils font? Rachid et Amélie parlent ensemble. Imaginez comment ils complètent les phrases suivantes. Complétez chacune logiquement avec un verbe conjugué et un adverbe.

EXEMPLE mon meilleur ami / jouer au tennis
Mon meilleur ami joue assez bien au tennis.
Mon meilleur ami ne joue jamais au tennis.

toujours	souvent	quelquefois	rarement	ne... jamais
beaucoup	assez	(un) peu	ne... pas du tout	
très bien	assez bien	assez mal	très mal	

1. moi, je / nager
2. ma meilleure amie / aimer le sport
3. mes amis / jouer au golf
4. je / manger à la maison
5. ma famille et moi / dîner ensemble
6. nous / manger au restaurant
7. ma famille et moi / aimer voyager
8. nous / voyager ensemble

Maintenant, utilisez les mêmes éléments pour former des phrases pour parler de vous et de vos connaissances *(acquaintances)*.

C C'est combien? Voilà le menu du café en face de *(across from)* Technovert. Demandez à votre partenaire le prix de cinq ou six choses.

EXEMPLE — Un expresso, c'est combien?
— C'est deux euros quarante-cinq.

L'heure du thé

Prix Service Compris (15 %)

Expresso	2,45	Thé (avec lait ou citron)	3,50
Double expresso	4,10	Thé à la menthe	3,50
Café au lait	3,40	Thé au fruit de la passion	3,50
Infusion	3,50	Thé à la framboise	3,50
(Tilleul, verveine, menthe, tilleul-		Cappuccino	4,30
menthe, verveine-menthe, camomille)		Croissants	1,60
Lait chaud	2,90	Confiture pot	1,40
Café décaféiné	2,60	Tartines beurrées	2,80
Double expresso avec pot de lait. .	3,60	Grog au rhum	6,10
Chocolat	3,50	Vin chaud	3,75
Café ou chocolat viennois	4,30	Irish Coffee	7,80

Source: L'heure du thé

Maintenant, dites ce que vous aimez prendre aux moments donnés.

1. Quand j'ai très soif, j'aime prendre...
2. Le matin, j'aime bien prendre...
3. Maintenant, je voudrais...
4. Avec un hamburger, j'aime prendre...
5. Quand je dîne au restaurant, j'aime prendre... comme *(as a)* boisson.

D Questions. Céline et Amélie décident de sortir ensemble. Complétez leur conversation comme indiqué ci-dessous. Utilisez **est-ce que** pour poser les questions.

— Je voudrais sortir ce soir.
— _____?
   What would you like to do?

— Je voudrais aller voir le film *Star Time*.
— _____?
   Why would you like to see Star Time?

— Parce que c'est un film d'action. Et toi? _____?
   Would you like to see Star Time too?

— Oui, bien sûr!
— _____? _____?
   Are you free this evening? *Would you like to go to the movies with me?*

— D'accord. _____?
   What time does the movie start?

— À 8h30. Je passe chez toi vers 8 heures?
— D'accord. À ce soir, alors.

Maintenant, recommencez la conversation. Utilisez l'inversion pour poser les mêmes questions.

Access the Video *Les Stagiaires* on iLrn.

© Cengage Learning

▶ **Épisode 2: Elle est belle, non?**

AVANT LA VIDÉO

Dans ce clip, Matthieu pose beaucoup de questions à Camille au sujet d'Amélie. Quand Céline et Camille se rendent compte *(realize)* qu'il s'intéresse à Amélie, elles font un pari *(bet)* de dix euros: Aura-t-il *(Will he have)* le courage d'inviter Amélie à sortir ou non? Avant de regarder le clip, imaginez une des questions que Matthieu pose à Camille au sujet d'Amélie.

APRÈS LA VIDÉO

Regardez le clip et notez les questions posées par *(asked by)* Matthieu.

LECTURE ET COMPOSITION

LECTURE

By using cognates and what you already know about cafés, you should be able to make intelligent guesses about what is offered on this Parisian café menu. The following exercise will guide you.

Vous savez déjà... What you already know about cafés and restaurants will help you determine the following information.

1. Under **Buffet chaud,** what would **une omelette jambon** be? **une omelette fromage**? **une omelette nature**?
2. What you see at the bottom of the menu indicates that checks are accepted under one condition. What is the condition?
3. At the bottom of the menu, you see that the management claims it is not responsible for something. For what does management claim not to be responsible?

AUX TROIS OBUS
120, rue Michel-Ange
Paris

NOS SALADES

SALADE VERTE	2,60
SALADE NIÇOISE	7,00
(Tomate, œuf, thon, olives, salade, anchois, riz, poivron)	
SALADE 3 OBUS	7,00
(Salade, choux-fleur, foies de volaille, jambon, œuf dur)	
SALADE POULET	7,00
(Émincé de poulet, maïs, riz, tomates, poivron, salade)	

SALADE MIXTE	5,00
(Tomates, œuf dur, salade)	
SALADE CHEF	7,00
(Tomates, pommes à l'huile, jambon, gruyère, salade, œuf dur)	
SALADE DE CRUDITÉS	6,00
(Concombres, tomates, carottes, choux)	

BUFFET CHAUD

ŒUFS AU PLAT NATURE (3 œufs)	4,00
ŒUFS PLAT JAMBON (3 œufs)	4,50
OMELETTE NATURE	4,00
OMELETTE JAMBON	4,50
OMELETTE FROMAGE	4,50
OMELETTE MIXTE (jambon, fromage)	6,50
OMELETTE PARMENTIER	4,50

CROQUE-MONSIEUR	4,00
CROQUE-MADAME	4,80
HOT-DOG	4,00
FRANCFORTS FRITES	5,00
ASSIETTE DE FRITES	2,60

MOULES MARINIERES	7,00 €
FRISEE AUX LARDONS	7,00 €
ROTI DE BOEUF PUREE	7,50 €
CASSOULET AU CONFIT	11,00 €
ST JACQUES PROVENCALE	14,00 €

NOS SANDWICHES

JAMBON DE PARIS	2,20
SAUCISSON SEC	2,20
SAUCISSON A L'AIL	2,20
RILLETTES	2,20
MIXTE (jambon, gruyère)	3,50
SANDWICH CRUDITÉS	3,50

JAMBON DE PAYS	4,00
PÂTÉ	2,20
TERRINE DU CHEF	4,00
CLUB SANDWICH	6,00
(Pain de mie, poulet, jambon, tomates, œuf, laitue, mayonnaise)	
JAMBON A L'OS	4,00
GRUYÈRE, CAMEMBERT	2,20

Suppl. Pain mie 0,50 Campagne 0,80

FROMAGES

Camembert	2,60
Roquefort	3,00
Brie	3,00
Cantal	3,00
Chèvre	3,00

Gruyère	3,00
Assiette de fromages	5,00

PRIX SERVICE COMPRIS (15%)
Les chèques sont acceptés sur présentation d'une pièce d'identité.

La direction n'est pas responsable des objets oubliés dans l'établissement.

Courtesy of l'abac de la Sorbonne

© Aaron Black/Getty Images

COMPOSITION

POUR MIEUX ÉCRIRE:
Using logical order and standard phrases

When writing about an activity that you have done often, such as ordering at a café or restaurant, it is useful to start by jotting down the usual sequence of events and typical phrases that are used at each step. This will provide you with a basic framework that you can flesh out with details.

Organisez-vous. You are going to prepare a scene in which two friends meet, talk, and order at a café. Before you begin, make sure you remember how to do these things in French.

- How do you greet a friend?
- How do you call the server over and order a drink?
- How do you talk about what you do on the weekend?
- How do you ask what your companion likes to do and say what you like or do not like to do?
- How do you invite a friend to do something?
- How do you pay the bill?
- How do you say good-bye?

Compréhension

A **Mots apparentés.** Read the menu and use cognates to identify:

1. Two kinds of sandwiches.
2. Three or four items used in the salads.
3. Two or three items you could order from the **buffet chaud.**

B **Lisez bien.** Read the menu and answer these questions.

1. C'est combien, une salade verte? une salade niçoise? une salade de crudités? une omelette jambon?
2. Le service est-il compris? À quel pourcentage?

C **Bon appétit!** Make a list of everything you can identify on this menu, then order something in French.

Au café

Using your answers from the preceding activity, write a conversation in which you meet another student at a café. You greet each other, order a drink, and start to chat about what you have in common. Remember to add details, such as when you like to do some things or why you do not like to do other things. You finally make plans to do something later, you get the bill, and you pay.

iLrn Share It!

COMPARAISONS CULTURELLES

LES CAFÉS EN FRANCE

En France, il existe **toute une vie autour des** cafés. **On y va** pour passer du temps avec des amis, discuter, **s'amuser,** prendre un verre ou regarder **les passants!** On ne va pas au café seulement pour boire quelque chose, mais aussi pour le contact social.

Café Le Procope

Fréquenté dans le passé par des **hommes de lettres**, des artistes et des politiciens, comme Voltaire, Victor Hugo, Benjamin Franklin, Napoléon et bien d'autres, Le Procope, créé en 1686, est le café le plus ancien de Paris. Aujourd'hui, c'est un endroit élégant où intellectuels jeunes et moins jeunes **se retrouvent.**

Aller au café du coin est un rituel quotidien pour certains Français.

Le café du coin est un centre social traditionnel pour les populations rurales et il **apporte une âme** à son quartier dans les grandes villes. Les cafés ont aussi une importance touristique en France. Aux cafés, les touristes ont l'impression de voir la France de l'intérieur et de **faire partie de la vie quotidienne** française.

L'accès à Internet est commun dans les cafés fréquentés par les étudiants.

Dans les grandes villes, la connexion Wi-Fi est de plus en plus considérée comme un service de base dans les quartiers d'étudiants et **d'affaires. Cependant,** en France, il est moins commun qu'**aux États-Unis** de voir des gens utiliser un ordinateur ou un téléphone portable en ignorant d'autres personnes **assises** à la même table.

---

toute une vie autour de *a whole lifestyle around*   **On y va** *People go there*   **s'amuser** *to have fun*   **les passants** *the passers-by*   **hommes de lettres** *literary figures*   **se retrouvent** *get together*   **Le café du coin** *The corner café*   **apporte une âme** *gives a soul*   **faire partie de la vie quotidienne** *to be part of daily life*   **d'affaires** *business*   **Cependant** *However*   **aux États-Unis** *in the United States*   **assises** *seated*

Dans les cafés, **les prix** sont généralement **moins élevés** au bar. Si vous préférez être en terrasse, les prix sont souvent **plus élevés**.

Les chaises font face à la rue, parce qu'un des plaisirs du café est de **pouvoir** regarder les passants.

Malgré leur renommée, il y a de moins en moins de cafés traditionnels en France et de plus en plus de fast-foods comme McDonald's (Macdo) et Quick ou de chaînes de *coffee shops* comme Starbucks. Aujourd'hui, avec **des trajets** de plus en plus longs pour aller au travail le matin et des pauses pour déjeuner à midi de plus en plus **courtes,** les établissements qui offrent des boissons et sandwichs **à emporter** sont de plus en plus **nombreux. En outre,** les téléphones portables et les réseaux sociaux sur Internet comme Facebook ou Twitter remplacent les cafés pour certains jeunes Français comme **lieux de rencontre.**

Compréhension

1. Pourquoi les Français aiment-ils aller au café?

2. Quel est le café le plus ancien de Paris? Nommez des hommes célèbres qui ont fréquenté ce café.

3. Dans quels cafés le Wi-Fi est-il commun? Citez une différence entre les habitudes des Français et des Américains dans les cafés avec accès à Internet.

4. Pourquoi y a-t-il de moins en moins de cafés traditionnels en France? Donnez deux raisons.

5. Quels sont deux renseignements utiles pour les touristes dans les cafés en France?

6. À votre avis *(In your opinion)*, le café est-il plus populaire en France qu'ici? Qu'est-ce que vous aimez faire au café?

iLrn Share It!

Visit **www.cengagebrain.com** for additional cultural information and activities.

---

les prix *prices*   **moins élevés** *lower*   **plus élevés** *higher*   **pouvoir** *to be able to*   **Malgré leur renommée** *Despite their fame*
des trajets *routes*   **courtes** *short*   **à emporter** *to go*   **nombreux** *numerous*   **En outre** *Moreover*   **lieux de rencontre**
meeting places

RÉSUMÉ DE GRAMMAIRE

THE INFINITIVE, -ER VERBS, AND ADVERBS

Qu'est-ce que tu aimes **faire** le soir?

J'aime **rester** à la maison et **lire** ou **sortir** pour **aller voir** un film.

Mes amis **aiment** sortir, mais moi j'**aime** rester à la maison.

The first verb in a clause is conjugated. Verbs after the first verb are in the infinitive (the base form of the verb). French infinitives end in **-er, -ir, -oir,** or **-re.**

Here is the pattern of conjugation for verbs ending in **-er,** except **aller.**

PARLER (to speak)	
je parl**e**	nous parl**ons**
tu parl**es**	vous parl**ez**
il/elle parl**e**	ils/elles parl**ent**

Nous voyag**e**ons souvent ensemble.

Nous commen**ç**ons l'examen.

With verbs ending in **-ger,** insert an **e** before the **-ons** ending in the **nous** form.

With verbs ending in **-cer,** the **c** changes to a **ç** before the **-ons** ending in the **nous** form.

If the next-to-last syllable of an **-er** infinitive has an **e** or an **é,** this letter often changes to an **è** in all forms except **nous** and **vous.**

Après les cours, je **préfère** rentrer à la maison. Mais le vendredi après-midi, mes amis et moi **préférons** aller prendre un verre.

PRÉFÉRER (to prefer)	
je préf**è**re	nous préférons
tu préf**è**res	vous préférez
il/elle préf**è**re	ils/elles préf**è**rent

With verbs ending in **-yer,** the **y** changes to an **i** in all forms, except **nous** and **vous.**

J'**envoie** souvent des textos.

Vous **envoyez** rarement des textos.

ENVOYER (to send)	
j'envo**ie**	nous envoyons
tu envo**ies**	vous envoyez
il/elle envo**ie**	ils/elles envo**ie**nt

The present tense in French is the equivalent of three present tenses in English.

Je parle français. $\begin{cases} \textit{I speak French.} \\ \textit{I am speaking French.} \\ \textit{I do speak French.} \end{cases}$

Je danse **souvent** le week-end.

Je joue **bien** au tennis.

Je vais **quelquefois** au cinéma.

D'abord, je révise mes cours.

Je travaille le soir, **d'habitude.**

Je **ne** travaille **jamais** le samedi.

Adverbs that tell how much, how often, or how well you do something are generally placed immediately after the verb. **D'abord, quelquefois,** and **d'habitude** are also placed at the beginning or end of the clause and **ne... jamais** surrounds the conjugated verb.

INFORMATION QUESTIONS AND INVERSION

To ask information questions, place the appropriate question word (**où, qui,** etc.) before **est-ce que.**

Où est-ce que tu travailles?	(Where . . . ?)
Qui est-ce que tu voudrais inviter?	(Who . . . ?)
Avec qui est-ce que tu déjeunes?	(With whom . . . ?)
Pourquoi est-ce que tu es ici?	(Why . . . ?)
Qu'est-ce que tu voudrais?	(What . . . ?)
Quand est-ce que tu déjeunes?	(When . . . ?)
À quelle heure est-ce que tu dînes?	(At what time . . . ?)
Quels jours est-ce que tu es en cours?	(What / Which days . . . ?)
Comment est-ce que tu aimes passer la matinée?	(How . . . ?)

Je suis en cours le mardi et le jeudi. Et toi? **Quand est-ce que** tu es en cours?

Do not use **est-ce que** with **qui** when it is the subject of the verb, or with **où** or **comment** when they are followed by **être.**

You can also form questions by inverting the verb and its subject pronoun. Remember that:

- You do not normally use inversion with **je.**
- If the subject of the verb is a noun, state the noun, then insert the corresponding pronoun to invert with the verb.
- When the inverted subject is **il** or **elle** and the verb ends *in a vowel,* place a **-t-** between the verb and the pronoun.
- The inverted forms of **il y a** and **c'est** are **y a-t-il** and **est-ce.**

Qui travaille ici?
Où est la salle de gym?
Comment sont tes cours?

Où **travaillez-vous?**
À quelle heure **êtes-vous** en cours?
(Est-ce que) je comprends bien?
Les cours **sont-ils** difficiles?
Marie **parle-t-elle** français?
Marie **est-elle** d'ici?
Y a-t-il un café dans le quartier?
Est-ce un bon café?

THE NUMBERS FROM 30 TO 100 AND MONEY

The **euro** is the official currency of France. A euro is composed of 100 **centimes.** Read prices as:

10,10 € = dix euros dix

84,35 € = quatre-vingt-quatre euros trente-cinq

65,75 € = soixante-cinq euros soixante-quinze

100,50 € = cent euros cinquante

The numbers from 30 to 100 are based on:

30 trente

40 quarante

50 cinquante

60 soixante

70 soixante-dix

80 quatre-vingts

90 quatre-vingt-dix

100 cent

— C'est combien, un expresso?
— C'est **deux euros quarante.**

VOCABULAIRE

COMPÉTENCE 1

Saying what you like to do

EXPRESSIONS VERBALES

Allons au cinéma / au café... !	Let's go to the movies / to the café ...!
J'aime...	I like ...
Je préfère...	I prefer ...
Je voudrais...	I would like ...
aller en boîte (de nuit) / au café / au cinéma	to go to a (night)club / to the café / to the movies
bricoler	to do handiwork
danser	to dance
dîner au restaurant	to have dinner at a restaurant
dormir	to sleep
écouter la radio / de la musique	to listen to the radio / music
écrire un mail	to write an e-mail
envoyer un texto	to send a text message
faire	to do, to make
faire de l'exercice	to exercise
faire du jogging	to jog, to go jogging
faire du ski	to ski, to go skiing
faire du sport	to play sports
faire du vélo	to ride a bike
faire quelque chose	to do something
inviter des amis à la maison	to invite friends to the house
jouer à des jeux vidéo	to play video games
jouer au baseball / au basket / au football / au football américain / au golf / au tennis / au volley	to play baseball / basketball / soccer / football / golf / tennis / volleyball
jouer du piano / de la batterie / de la guitare	to play piano / drums / guitar
lire	to read
parler au téléphone	to talk on the phone
prendre un verre	to have a drink
regarder la télé(vision)	to watch TV
regarder une vidéo / un DVD	to watch a video / a DVD
rester à la maison	to stay home
sortir avec des ami(e)s	to go out with friends
surfer sur Internet	to surf the Net
travailler sur l'ordinateur	to work on the computer
voir un film	to see a movie
On va...?	How about we go ... ?, Shall we go ... ?
Qu'est-ce que vous aimez faire?	What do you like to do?
Qu'est-ce que vous voudriez faire?	What would you like to do?
Tu voudrais...?	Would you like ... ?

DIVERS

À ce soir!	See you tonight!, See you this evening!
après les cours	after class
Ça te dit de... ? / Ça vous dit de... ?	Would you feel like ... ?
D'accord!	Okay!
un loisir	a leisure activity, a pastime
Pourquoi pas?	Why not?
quelque chose	something
le temps libre	free time
Tu es libre ce soir?	Are you free this evening / tonight?
vers	about, around, toward
(pas) vraiment	(not) really, truly

COMPÉTENCE 2

Saying how you spend your free time

NOMS MASCULINS

le ciné-club	the cinema club
un classique	a classic

NOMS FÉMININS

une activité	an activity
la fac	the university, the campus

EXPRESSIONS VERBALES

Qu'est-ce que vous faites?	What are you doing?, What do you do?
Qu'est-ce que tu fais?	What are you doing?, What do you do?
chanter	to sing
commencer	to begin, to start
faire de la musique	to play music
faire du shopping	to go shopping
gagner	to win
jouer au hockey	to play hockey
manger	to eat
nager	to swim
passer chez...	to go by ... 's house
passer le week-end / la matinée	to spend the weekend / the morning
préférer	to prefer
répéter	to repeat
rester au lit	to stay in bed
réviser les cours	to review (for) classes
je vais	I am going, I go
voyager	to travel

ADVERBES

(très / assez) bien	(very / fairly) well
d'abord	first
d'habitude	usually
jusqu'à	until
(très / assez) mal	(very / fairly) badly
mieux (que)	better (than)
ne... jamais	never
presque	almost
quand	when
quelquefois	sometimes
rarement	rarely
souvent	often
toujours	always

DIVERS

chez...	to / at / in / by ... 's house
le samedi matin / après-midi / soir	(on) Saturday mornings / afternoons / evenings
le week-end	the weekend, weekends, on the weekend

Asking about someone's day

NOMS MASCULINS

l'après-midi	the afternoon
mon copain	my boyfriend
un fast-food	a fast-food restaurant
un jour	a day
mon mari	my husband
le matin	the morning
un parc	a park
le soir	the evening

NOMS FÉMININS

ma copine	my girlfriend
ma femme	my wife
la journée	the day

EXPRESSIONS VERBALES

aimer mieux	to like better, to prefer
aller au parc	to go to the park
déjeuner	to have lunch, to eat lunch
demander	to ask (for)
je dors	I am sleeping, I sleep
manger dans un fast-food	to eat in a fast-food restaurant
rentrer	to return, to go back (home)

EXPRESSIONS ADVERBIALES

après	afterwards
l'après-midi	in the afternoon, afternoons
de... heures à... heures	from ... o'clock to ... o'clock
ensemble	together
le matin	in the morning, mornings
le soir	in the evening, evenings
tous les jours	every day
toute la journée	all day

EXPRESSIONS INTERROGATIVES

à quelle heure	at what time
avec qui	with whom
comment	how
où	where
pourquoi (parce que)	why (because)
quand	when
quel(s) jour(s)	(on) what / which day(s)
que (qu'est-ce que)	what
Qu'est-ce que c'est?	What is this/that/it?, What are these/those/they?
qui	who(m)
Qui est-ce?	Who is he/she/it/this/that?, Who are they?

DIVERS

avec elle/elles	with her/them (f)
avec lui/eux	with him/them (m or mixed)
en général	in general
par exemple	for example
riche	rich
sauf	except
tout/toute/tous/toutes	all, whole
typique	typical

Going to the café

NOMS MASCULINS

l'argent	money, silver
un café (au lait)	a coffee (with milk)
un centime	a cent
un chocolat (chaud)	a (hot) chocolate
un coca (light)	a (diet) Coke, a (diet) cola
un demi	a draft beer
un euro	a euro
un expresso	an espresso
un jus de fruit / d'orange	a fruit / an orange juice
un Orangina	an Orangina
un sandwich au fromage / au jambon	a cheese / ham sandwich
un serveur	a server
un thé (au citron)	a tea (with lemon)
un verre de vin blanc / rouge	a glass of white / red wine

NOMS FÉMININS

une bière	a beer
une boisson	a drink, a beverage
une eau minérale	a mineral water
des frites	(some) fries
la monnaie	change
une serveuse	a server

NOMBRES

quarante, quarante et un...	forty, forty-one . . .
cinquante, cinquante et un...	fifty, fifty-one . . .
soixante, soixante et un...	sixty, sixty-one . . .
soixante-dix, soixante et onze...	seventy, seventy-one . . .
quatre-vingts, quatre-vingt-un...	eighty, eighty-one . . .
quatre-vingt-dix, quatre-vingt-onze...	ninety, ninety-one . . .
cent	one hundred

DIVERS

Ça fait combien?	How much is it?
Ça fait... euros.	That makes . . . euros.
C'est combien?	How much is it?
chaud(e)	hot
commander	to order (food and drink)
J'ai faim. / Je n'ai pas faim.	I'm hungry. / I'm not hungry.
J'ai soif. / Je n'ai pas soif.	I'm thirsty. / I'm not thirsty.
payer	to pay
Qu'est-ce que vous allez prendre?	What are you going to have?
Vous désirez?	What would you like?
Je vais prendre...	I'm going to have . . .
Je voudrais...	I would like . . .
Pour moi... s'il vous plaît.	For me . . . please.
voici	here is, here are
voilà	there is, there are
votre (vos)	your

INTERLUDE MUSICAL

JE SUIS

🌐 You can find these songs on iTunes. You can also search the Internet for videos to hear them performed and to find the lyrics.

AMEL BENT

Amel Bent Bachir, known as Amel Bent, is a dancer and singer of popular French music and RnB. Born in France of an Algerian father and Moroccan mother, Amel originally intended to study psychology. In the song *Je suis,* Amel's theme is the universality of the human experience, as she compares herself and her experiences to those of everyone else. The following activities will help you better understand the song.

Amel Bent est née *(was born)* **en France.**

A **Je suis.** Dans la chanson *(song) Je suis,* la chanteuse compare ses expériences de jeunesse *(childhood)* avec celles de chaque *(those of every)* jeune personne. Voilà une liste de choses et d'activités similaires à celles *(those)* qu'elle mentionne. Devinez le sens de chaque expression.

1. chaque fille ou garçon
2. chaque rue et quartier
3. les jeux d'enfants
4. des heures de colle
5. les cœurs et les vœux des enfants
6. faire des bêtises
7. plonger dans un rêve
8. jouer au ballon
9. sauter à la corde
10. sécher les cours
11. jouer sur le palier
12. grandir dans le même quartier

a. *every street and neighborhood*
b. *every girl or boy*
c. *to do dumb things*
d. *hours of detention*
e. *to cut class*
f. *to play ball*
g. *to jump rope*
h. *to plunge into a dream*
i. *the hearts and wishes of children*
j. *children's games*
k. *to grow up in the same neighborhood*
l. *to play in the corridor*

B **Je suis toi!** Lisez la deuxième partie de la *Note de vocabulaire* à la page 82. Comment dit-on les choses suivantes? Utilisez les pronoms **moi, toi, lui, elle, nous, vous, eux** ou **elles.**

1. *I am you.*
2. *I am him and her.*
3. *I am them.*
4. *I am you and us.*

CHANTEZ, CHANTEZ

AMADOU ET MARIAM

Amadou Bagayoko and Mariam Doumbia met at Mali's *Institute for the Young Blind* and married in 1980. In 1986, they moved from Mali to Côte d'Ivoire to advance their career. Mixing rock guitar with traditional Malian sounds, their music is known as Afro-blues. Like many francophone Africans, they speak both French and an African language. The song **Chantez, chantez** is mainly in French, with a few lines in Bambara, another language spoken in Mali. The following activity will help you better understand the song.

Amadou et Mariam sont du Mali.

Chérie *(Sweetheart).* Dans la chanson *Chantez, chantez,* Amadou parle de son amour *(love)* pour Mariam et de sa bonne volonté envers tout le monde *(goodwill toward everyone)*. Choisissez *(Choose)* un mot logique pour compléter chaque phrase. Il y a plus d'une possibilité pour certaines phrases.

aime	donne	parle
voix *(voice)*	tiens *(hold)*	jure *(swear)*
adore	guitare	
préfère	chante	

1. Écoutez cette *(this)* _____.
2. _____ -moi ta main *(your hand)* / ton cœur *(your heart)*.
3. _____ -moi dans tes bras *(your arms)*.
4. C'est toi que je (j') _____.
5. Je ne _____ que pour toi. *(I only _____ for you.)*
6. Je ne _____ qu'avec toi. *(I only _____ with you.)*
7. Je ne _____ que par toi. *(I only _____ by you.)*

belle	du bonheur *(happiness)*	perdre *(to lose)*
reste	liberté	jolie
abandonner	jouer	de l'amour *(love)*
sauter *(to jump)*	gentille	
danser	chanter	

8. _____ à côté de *(beside)* moi.
9. Tu es la plus _____.
10. Je ne veux pas te (t') _____. *(I don't want to _____ you.)*
11. Nous allons *(We are going to)* _____ ensemble.
12. _____ pour tout le monde.

Un nouvel appartement

iLrn Heinle Learning Center

www.cengagebrain.com

Horizons Video: Les Stagiaires

Audio

Internet web search

Pair work

Group work

© Pete Ryan/National Geographic/Glow

3

COMPÉTENCE

1 Talking about where you live
Le logement

Giving prices and other numerical information
Les nombres au-dessus de 100 et les nombres ordinaux

Stratégies et Lecture
- **Pour mieux lire:** *Guessing meaning from context*
- **Lecture:** *Un nouvel appartement*

2 Talking about your possessions
Les effets personnels

Saying what you have
Le verbe avoir

Saying where something is
Quelques prépositions

3 Describing your room
Les meubles et les couleurs

Identifying your belongings
La possession et les adjectifs possessifs mon, ton et son

Indicating to whom something belongs
Les adjectifs possessifs notre, votre et leur

4 Giving your address and phone number
Des renseignements

Telling which one
Les adjectifs ce et quel

Vidéoreprise *Les Stagiaires*

Lecture et Composition
- **Pour mieux lire:** *Previewing content*
- **Lecture:** *Les couleurs et leurs effets sur la nature humaine*
- **Pour mieux écrire:** *Brainstorming*
- **Composition:** *Un mail*

Comparaisons culturelles *Le Québec d'aujourd'hui*

Résumé de grammaire

Vocabulaire

Dans quelle province canadienne y a-t-il le plus de francophones? Voudriez-vous visiter cette province?

Plus vaste que l'Alaska, le Québec est la plus grande des provinces canadiennes et plus de 25 % de la population canadienne habite dans cette province.

la plus grande *the largest*

Montréal, grand centre culturel et commercial, est la plus grande ville du Québec.

Le Québec

Visit it live on Google Earth!

NOMBRE D'HABITANTS:
7 886 100

CAPITALE: **Québec**

Le savez-vous?

Lisez le texte qui accompagne les photos. Ensuite, complétez ces phrases. Aimeriez-vous mieux *(Would you prefer)* visiter la ville de Québec ou de Montréal?

1. Le _____ est la plus grande province du Canada et plus de _____ % de la population canadienne y habite *(lives there)*. C'est la province francophone la plus importante du Canada!

2. _____ est la plus grande ville de la province de Québec, mais _____ est sa capitale. Québec est la plus _____ ville du Canada.

La ville de Québec est la capitale de la province de Québec. Fondée en 1608, c'est la plus vieille ville du Canada.

Do you know why there are so many francophones in Quebec? How would you characterize the linguistic situation in Canada today? Research online the history of French in Canada and the current linguistic situation there and report your findings.

Talking about where you live

LE LOGEMENT

In the **Culture Modules** in the video library, see **Housing.**

Sélection musicale. Search the Web for the song "**Le temps de partir**" by Brigitte Boisjoli to enjoy a musical selection related to this vocabulary.

J'habite...	dans une maison
	dans un appartement
	dans un grand **immeuble**
	dans une résidence universitaire
	chez mes parents

Ma maison est...	grand(e) / petit(e)
Mon appartement est...	moderne / vieux (vieille)
Ma chambre est...	joli(e) / laid(e)
	(trop) cher (chère)
	confortable

J'habite...	sur le campus	**en centre-ville**
	tout près de l'université	**en ville**
	(assez) loin de l'université	**en banlieue**
		à la campagne

Le loyer est de...	550 $ (cinq cent cinquante dollars) **par mois**
	600 $ (six cents dollars)
	1 200 $ (mille deux cents dollars)

Je n'ai pas de loyer!

Chez moi, il y a six **pièces** (*f*).

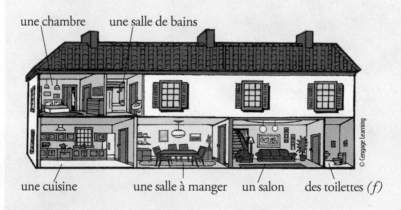

une chambre   une salle de bains

une cuisine   une salle à manger   un salon   des toilettes (*f*)

© Cengage Learning

Le logement *Lodging, Housing*   **un immeuble** *an apartment building*   **trop** *too*   **cher (chère)** *expensive*   **(tout) près (de)** *(very) near*   **(assez) loin (de)** *(rather) far (from)*   **en centre-ville** *downtown*   **en ville** *in town* (**une ville** *a city / town*)   **en banlieue** *in the suburbs*   **à la campagne** *in the country(side)*   **Le loyer** *The rent*   **par mois** *per month*   **Je n'ai pas** *I don't have*   **une pièce** *a room*

Vocabulaire supplémentaire

une caravane *a travel trailer*
une cave *a cellar*
un duplex *a split-level apartment*
un prêt immobilier *a home loan*
un garage *a garage*
un grenier *an attic*
un jardin *a yard, a garden*
un loft
un mobil-home *a mobile home*
une buanderie *a laundry room*
une salle de jeux *a game room*
une salle de séjour *a family room, a den*
un studio *a studio apartment, an efficiency*
des W.-C. *(m) a restroom*

Robert, un jeune Américain, **va** étudier à l'Université Laval, au Québec. Il téléphone à son ami Thomas, avec qui il pense habiter.

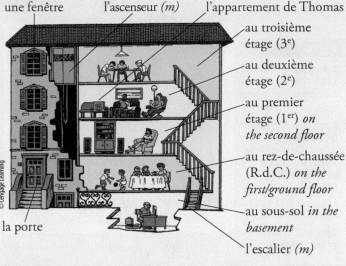

une fenêtre — l'ascenseur *(m)* — l'appartement de Thomas
au troisième étage (3ᵉ)
au deuxième étage (2ᵉ)
au premier étage (1ᵉʳ) *on the second floor*
au rez-de-chaussée (R.d.C.) *on the first/ground floor*
au sous-sol *in the basement*
l'escalier *(m)*
la porte

ROBERT:	Où est-ce que tu habites?
THOMAS:	J'habite dans un immeuble en centre-ville.
ROBERT:	**À quel étage?**
THOMAS:	Mon appartement est au deuxième étage.
ROBERT:	Tu habites seul?
THOMAS:	Non, j'habite avec mon ami Gabriel.
ROBERT:	L'université est loin de chez toi?
THOMAS:	Non, pas très loin. Et il y a **un arrêt de bus** tout près. C'est très **pratique.**
ROBERT:	Et l'appartement est agréable?
THOMAS:	Oui, j'aime beaucoup mon appartement. Il est assez grand et pas trop cher.

A Et vous? Complétez les phrases avec les mots en italique qui correspondent le mieux à votre situation.

1. J'habite dans *un appartement / une maison / une chambre.*
2. *Mon appartement / Ma chambre / Ma maison* est *sur le campus / (tout) près de l'université / (très / assez) loin de l'université.*
3. Il/Elle est *en centre-ville / en ville / en banlieue / à la campagne.*
4. Il/Elle est *joli(e) / grand(e) / moderne / confortable / ???.*
5. Il/Elle *est / n'est pas* trop cher (chère).
6. Le loyer est de *plus / moins* de cinq cents dollars par mois.
7. Chez moi, il y a *une / deux / trois / quatre / ???* chambre(s).
8. Je passe beaucoup de temps dans *la cuisine / le salon / ma chambre / ???.*
9. Ma chambre est *au rez-de-chaussée / au premier étage / ???.*
10. *Il y a un ascenseur / Il n'y a pas d'ascenseur* chez moi.

B Entretien. Interviewez votre partenaire.

1. Est-ce que tu habites chez tes parents? Est-ce que tu habites dans une maison, dans un appartement ou dans une résidence universitaire?
2. Tu habites près de l'université, loin de l'université ou sur le campus? Est-ce que c'est pratique? Est-ce qu'il y a un arrêt de bus tout près?
3. Préfères-tu habiter en centre-ville, en ville, en banlieue ou à la campagne? Préfères-tu habiter au rez-de-chaussée ou au premier étage?
4. Quelles pièces est-ce qu'il y a chez toi? Dans quelle pièce aimes-tu passer beaucoup de temps?

Note *culturelle*

Dans les immeubles au Québec et en France, faites attention: Le premier étage est l'étage au-dessus du *(above the)* rez-de-chaussée. C'est-à-dire *(That is to say)* que le rez-de-chaussée correspond à *the first floor / ground floor* aux USA et le premier étage correspond à *the second floor.* À quel étage est votre chambre/votre appartement?

À VOUS!

Avec un(e) partenaire, relisez à haute voix la conversation entre Robert et Thomas. Ensuite, adaptez la conversation pour décrire votre propre situation.

You can find a list of the new words from this *Compétence* on page 138 and access the audio online.

va (aller *to go***)**   **À quel étage?** *On what floor?* **(un étage** *a floor* [of a building]**)**   **un arrêt de bus** *a bus stop*
pratique *practical, convenient*

GIVING PRICES AND OTHER NUMERICAL INFORMATION

✔ *Pour vérifier*

1. How do you say 100? 1,000? 1,000,000? Before which two of these numbers do you never put **un**?

2. How do you say 1,503? 12,612?

3. In the numbers 200, 2,000, and 2,000,000, which two words would have an **s, cent, mille,** or **million**? Which one of those words would drop the **s** if another number followed it?

4. Do you use a period or a comma to express decimals in French?

5. How do you say *first? fifth?* How do you say *on the* with a floor?

Les nombres au-dessus de 100 et les nombres ordinaux

Here is how to say numbers over 100.

100 cent		**1 000** mille	
101 cent un		**1 001** mille un	
102 cent deux		**1 352** mille trois cent cinquante-deux	
199 cent quatre-vingt-dix-neuf		**2 000** deux mille	
200 deux cents		**1 000 000** un million	
201 deux cent un		**2 234 692** deux millions deux cent	
999 neuf cent quatre-vingt-dix-neuf		trente-quatre mille six cent quatre-vingt-douze	

Note the following about numbers:

- **Cent** means *one hundred,* never say **un cent. Mille** means *one thousand,* never say **un mille.** On the other hand, do say **un million.** Use **de (d')** after the word **million(s)** whenever a noun follows it directly.

  cent habitants   **mille habitants**   **un million d'habitants**

- **Million** takes an **s** in the plural. **Cent** generally only takes an **s** when plural if not followed by another number. Never add an **s** to **mille.**

  deux **cents** habitants   deux **cent** cinquante habitants
  trois **millions** d'habitants   trois **millions** six **mille** habitants

- There is no hyphen between **cent, mille,** or **un million** and another number.

  un million deux cent cinquante-quatre mille habitants

- In France and in Quebec, commas are used to denote decimals, and a space (or a period) is used after thousands, millions, etc. Read a decimal as **virgule (1,5 = un virgule cinq).**

USA	FRANCE / QUÉBEC
1.5	1,5
1,000	1 000 *or* 1.000

Vocabulaire supplémentaire

un milliard *one billion*
deux milliards *two billion*

Use **À quel étage?** to ask *On what floor?* To say *on the* with a floor, use **au.** When counting floors, use the ordinal numbers and remember that in a French-speaking country, the first floor (**le premier étage**) is the floor above the ground floor (**le rez-de-chaussée**).

—**À quel étage habitez-vous?**   *— What floor do you live on?*
—**J'habite au troisième étage.**   *—I live on the third* (= American fourth) *floor.*

In French, to convert cardinal numbers *(two, three, four . . .)* to ordinal numbers *(second, third, fourth . . .)*, add the suffix **-ième.** Drop a final **e** from cardinal numbers before adding **-ième.**

  deux → deuxième   **quatre → quatrième**   **mille → millième**

These ordinal numbers are irregular: **premier (première), cinquième, neuvième.**

A **C'est combien?** De combien est le loyer?

EXEMPLE 900 $ Le loyer est de neuf cents dollars par mois.

1. 865 $ 3. 1 545 $ 5. 670 $ 7. 1 385 $
2. 490 $ 4. 3 110 $ 6. 750 $ 8. 2 235 $

B **Maisons à vendre.** Lisez ces prix.

1. 150 279 $ 3. 399 459 $ 5. 15 999 500 $ 7. 885 700 $
2. 999 999 $ 4. 679 825 $ 6. 1 950 500 $ 8. 248 500 $

C **Ça coûte combien?** Choisissez un prix pour chaque article sur ce prospectus publicitaire *(flyer)*. Ensuite, comparez vos choix à ceux de votre partenaire.

EXEMPLE — Moi, je pense que le téléviseur de 40 pouces coûte... Et toi?
— Moi...

331,88$	349,50$	650,65$
999,99$	1 799,00$	2 499,99$

TÉLÉ À GRAND ÉCRAN | ORDINATEUR PORTABLE ÉCRAN TACTILE | APPAREIL PHOTO NUMÉRIQUE + VIDÉO

40ᵖᵒ 55ᵖᵒ 60ᵖᵒ

15,6ᵖᵒ/2 Go 17,3ᵖᵒ/8 Go

écran 3ᵖᵒ

Photos: Télé © K. Miri Photography/Shutterstock.com; Ordinateur portable © ifong/Shutterstock.com; Appareil photo © Masalski Maksim/Shutterstock.com. Graphic © Cengage Learning

Note *de vocabulaire*

1. Use **un téléviseur** when talking about a *TV set*.

2. In Québec, the size of such things as TV screens is indicated in **pouces** *(inches),* shown as **ᵖᵒ**.

3. **Go** is short for **giga-octet** *(gigabyte).* You can find the words for the latest electronic devices at http://www.fnac.com/.

l'appartement de Thomas

D **Chez Thomas.** Posez les questions suivantes à un(e) partenaire, qui répondra d'après *(will respond according to)* l'illustration.

1. Il y a un ascenseur dans l'immeuble où habite Thomas? Il y a un escalier?
2. À quel étage est le vieux monsieur? Qu'est-ce qu'il fait *(What is he doing)*?
3. À quel étage habitent Thomas et son *(his)* colocataire? Qu'est-ce qu'ils font *(What are they doing)*?
4. À quel étage habite la jeune femme? Elle regarde la télé ou elle écoute de la musique?
5. Où habitent les enfants? Qu'est-ce qu'ils font?

© Cengage Learning

STRATÉGIES ET LECTURE

POUR MIEUX LIRE: Guessing meaning from context

You can often guess the meaning of unknown words from context. Read this passage in its entirety, then guess the meaning of the boldfaced words.

L'immeuble de Thomas **se trouve** en centre-ville. Arrivé **devant** l'immeuble, Robert **entre,** il **monte** l'escalier et il **sonne** à la porte de l'appartement de son ami. Une jeune femme **ouvre** la porte. Après un instant, elle **referme** la porte.

Some words may have different meanings in different contexts. For example, the word **bien** can mean *well* or it can be used for emphasis, meaning *indeed*. It may also be used in place of **très,** to mean *very*. Read the following sentences and use the context to decide if **bien** means *well, indeed,* or *very.*

—Tu comprends bien?
—Oui, mais c'est bien compliqué!

—C'est bien ici que Thomas habite?
—Oui, c'est bien ça.

The word **même** has several meanings, including both *self* and *same.* Read the following sentences and use the context to determine whether **même** means *self* or *same.*

Les prénoms Gabriel et Gabrielle se prononcent de la même manière.

Je travaille pour moi-même.

A **Selon le contexte.** The boldfaced word in each of the following sentences can have a different meaning, depending on the context. Can you guess the different meanings?

Bravo! **Encore! Encore!**
Ça, c'est **encore** plus compliqué.
Je suis au premier étage, alors je monte **encore** un étage pour aller au deuxième?

B **Vous savez déjà...** You already know the boldfaced words in sentence **a.** Guess the meaning of the boldfaced words in sentence **b,** using the context.

1. a. **Ouvrez** votre livre, **lisez** le paragraphe et **fermez** le livre.

b. Robert **ouvre** la lettre de Thomas, **lit** les instructions et **referme** la lettre.

2. a. **Prenez** une feuille de papier.

b. Elle **prend** la lettre.

3. a. **Donnez**-moi un café, s'il vous plaît.

b. Thomas **donne** l'adresse de l'appartement à Robert.

Lecture: *Un nouvel appartement*

1-45

Robert, un jeune Américain de Louisiane, arrive devant l'immeuble où habitent Thomas et son colocataire, Gabriel.

Robert ouvre la lettre de Thomas, consulte les instructions et vérifie l'adresse. Il lit: «Mon appartement se trouve au 38, rue Dauphine. C'est un grand immeuble avec une porte bleue. J'habite au deuxième étage.» «Oui, c'est bien ça», pense-t-il. Il descend de la voiture, entre dans l'immeuble et monte l'escalier.

Il sonne à la porte de l'appartement. Quelques instants après, une jolie jeune femme lui ouvre la porte.
—Euh... Bonjour, je suis Robert. C'est bien ici que Gabriel et Thomas habitent?
—Gabrielle, c'est moi, Mais...
Robert, très surpris, l'interrompt:
—Gabriel, c'est vous? Euh... Mais vous êtes une femme.
—Eh oui, monsieur, comme vous le voyez, je suis une femme!
—Euh, je veux dire... Euh, excusez-moi. Maintenant, je comprends! C'est que je pensais rencontrer Gabriel, un homme et non pas Gabrielle, une femme. Excusez-moi. Alors, vous êtes Gabrielle. Et moi, je suis Robert, Robert Martin. Thomas est ici?
—Thomas? Dit-elle d'un air surpris.
—Eh oui, Thomas, mon ami. Il habite ici avec vous, non?
—Mais certainement pas! dit-elle d'un ton un peu énervé.

Quand elle essaie de fermer la porte, Robert s'exclame:
—Un instant, s'il vous plaît. Regardez! Voici l'adresse que mon ami m'a donnée. Elle prend la lettre, lit les instructions et commence à comprendre.
—En fait oui, c'est bien ici le 38, rue Dauphine, mais vous êtes au *premier* étage et votre ami habite au *deuxième* étage.
—Au premier étage? Ah! Oui, je comprends maintenant. *First floor,* c'est le rez-de-chaussée et *second floor,* c'est le premier étage. Alors, je monte encore un étage pour trouver l'appartement de mon ami?
—Oui, c'est bien ça. Au revoir, et bienvenue au Québec, Robert!
—Au revoir, Gabrielle, et merci.

A Vrai ou faux?

1. Robert arrive au 38, rue Dauphine, l'adresse de son ami Thomas.
2. Il monte directement au deuxième étage.
3. Il sonne et Gabrielle, la jeune femme qui habite avec Thomas, ouvre la porte.
4. Gabriel est un prénom masculin et Gabrielle est son *(its)* équivalent féminin en français.
5. En France et au Québec, le *first floor* est le rez-de-chaussée et le *second floor* est le premier étage.

B Voilà pourquoi. Complétez le paragraphe pour expliquer la confusion de Robert.

> homme   premier   premier   deuxième   deuxième   Thomas   Thomas

Robert entre dans l'immeuble pour trouver l'appartement de __1__. Thomas habite au __2__ étage avec Gabriel, un ami. Robert monte au __3__ étage et sonne. Une jeune femme ouvre la porte. C'est Gabrielle, mais elle n'habite pas avec Thomas. Robert ne comprend pas; il pense que la jeune femme habite avec __4__. Voilà le problème: Robert est au __5__ étage et Thomas et son ami Gabriel habitent au __6__ étage. C'est un autre Gabriel, un jeune __7__, pas une jeune femme, qui habite avec Thomas.

COMPÉTENCE 2

Talking about your possessions

LES EFFETS PERSONNELS

iLrn In the **Culture Modules** in the video library, see **Technology**.

Note *culturelle*

L'accent du français canadien est plus nasal qu'en France. Il y a aussi certaines différences de vocabulaire. Au Canada, on entend *(one hears)*, par exemple, *un copain/une copine de chambre* pour *un(e) camarade de chambre* et *un vivoir* ou *un living* pour *un salon.* Y a-t-il des différences régionales en anglais?

Vocabulaire supplémentaire

une cuisinière *a stove*
un (four à) micro-ondes *a microwave (oven)*
un lave-vaisselle *a dishwasher*
un lave-linge *a washer*
un lecteur MP3 *an MP3 player*
une moto *a motorcycle*
un réfrigérateur (un frigo)
un sèche-linge *a dryer*
une table basse *a coffee table*

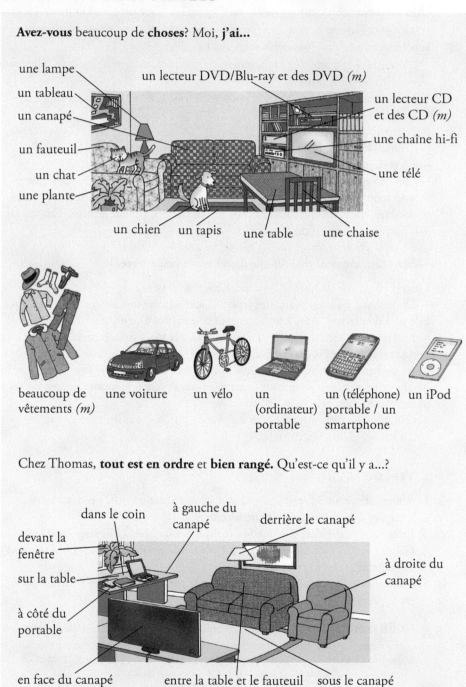

Avez-vous beaucoup de **choses**? Moi, **j'ai...**

une lampe
un tableau
un canapé
un fauteuil
un chat
une plante

un lecteur DVD/Blu-ray et des DVD *(m)*
un lecteur CD et des CD *(m)*
une chaîne hi-fi
une télé

un chien   un tapis   une table   une chaise

beaucoup de vêtements *(m)*   une voiture   un vélo   un (ordinateur) portable   un (téléphone) portable / un smartphone   un iPod

Chez Thomas, **tout est en ordre** et **bien rangé.** Qu'est-ce qu'il y a...?

devant la fenêtre
sur la table
à côté du portable

dans le coin
à gauche du canapé
derrière le canapé
à droite du canapé

en face du canapé   entre la table et le fauteuil   sous le canapé

Line art on this page: © Cengage Learning

Avez-vous (avoir *to have)*   **une chose** *a thing*   **j'ai (avoir** *to have)*   **tout est en ordre** *everything is in order*
bien rangé(e) *neat, put away, straightened up*

🔊 1-46 Avant d'arriver au Québec, Robert **cherche** un appartement. Il téléphone à Thomas.

THOMAS: Tu cherches un appartement ici à Québec? Écoute, tu sais, moi, je **partage** un appartement avec mon ami Gabriel. **Nous avons** trois chambres; tu voudrais habiter avec nous?

ROBERT: **Peut-être.** Comment est **ton** appartement?

THOMAS: Il est assez grand et confortable, mais pas trop cher. Tu aimes les animaux?

ROBERT: Oui, pourquoi? **Tu as** des animaux?

THOMAS: Gabriel **a** un chien et un chat. Ils sont quelquefois **embêtants** et ils aiment dormir **partout.**

ROBERT: Pas de problème. J'aime bien les animaux. Vous **fumez?**

THOMAS: Non, je ne fume pas et Gabriel **non plus.**

ROBERT: Bon, moi non plus. Alors, ça va.

A Cherchez l'intrus! Quel objet de chaque liste ne va pas logiquement à l'endroit *(place)* indiqué?

EXEMPLE sur la table: un portable / un iPod / un vélo / des livres
Sur la table, il y a un portable, un iPod et des livres, mais il n'y a pas de vélo!

1. sur la table: un lecteur DVD / un portable / un fauteuil / un chat / une lampe
2. devant la fenêtre: une table / un tableau / une chaise / une plante
3. dans le salon: un canapé / un lit / un lecteur CD / une chaîne hi-fi / une lampe
4. dans la chambre: des vêtements / un chien / un lecteur DVD / une voiture / une télé

B Qu'est-ce que c'est? Regardez l'illustration du salon de Thomas en bas de *(at the bottom of)* la page précédente. Qu'est-ce qu'il y a à chaque endroit *(place)*?

EXEMPLE sur la table
Il y a des livres et un portable sur la table.

1. devant la fenêtre   4. à droite des livres   7. à gauche du portable
2. en face du canapé   5. à côté du portable   8. entre le fauteuil et la table
3. derrière le canapé   6. dans le coin   9. sous le canapé

C Entretien. Interviewez votre partenaire.

1. Tu as beaucoup de choses chez toi? Qu'est-ce qu'il y a dans le salon? En général, est-ce que tout est en ordre et bien rangé dans ta chambre ou est-ce que ta chambre est souvent en désordre?
2. Est-ce que tu aimes les animaux? Tu as des animaux? Tu préfères les chiens ou les chats?
3. Est-ce que tu fumes?

À VOUS!

Avec un(e) partenaire, relisez à haute voix la conversation entre Thomas et Robert. Ensuite, imaginez que votre partenaire veuille *(wants)* habiter chez vous. Adaptez la conversation pour décrire votre situation.

 You can find a list of the new words from this *Compétence* on page 138 and access the audio online.

---

chercher *to look for*   **partager** *to share*   **Nous avons** *(avoir to have)*   **Peut-être** *Maybe, Perhaps*   **ton/ta/tes** *your (singular familiar)*
Tu as *(avoir to have)*   **a** *(avoir to have)*   **embêtant(e)** *annoying*   **partout** *everywhere*   **fumer** *to smoke*   **non plus** *neither*

SAYING WHAT YOU HAVE

✔ Pour vérifier

1. What does **avoir** mean? What are its forms? Why might one confuse the **tu** and **ils/elles** forms of **avoir** *(to have)* with those of **être** *(to be)*?

2. What does the indefinite article **(un, une, des)** change to after expressions of quantity such as **combien** or **beaucoup**? When else does this change occur?

3. Which of these nouns would have a plural ending with **-x** instead of **-s: un hôpital, un animal, un tableau, un bureau, une table, un canapé**?

 Grammar Tutorials

Vocabulaire sans peine!

Many adjectives ending in *-al* in English have French cognates with masculine plural forms ending in **-aux.**

régional → régionaux

How would you say these words in French? What would their masculine plural forms be?

normal
horizontal
vertical

Le verbe **avoir**

To say what someone has, use the verb **avoir.** Its conjugation is irregular.

AVOIR *(to have)*	
j'**ai**	nous ^z **avons**
tu **as**	vous ^z **avez**
il/elle **a**	ils/elles ^z **ont**

Remember to use **de (d')** rather than **des** after **combien** *(how much, how many)*, as you do after quantity expressions like **beaucoup** and **assez.** Also remember to use **de (d')** instead of **un, une,** or **des** after most negated verbs other than **être.**

AFFIRMATIVE	NEGATIVE	AFTER A QUANTITY EXPRESSION
J'ai **des** chats.	Je n'ai pas **de** chats.	Combien **de** chats as-tu?
BUT:		
C'est **un** chat.	Ce n'est pas **un** chat.	C'est beaucoup **de** chats.

Although the plural of most nouns and adjectives is formed by adding **-s,** words ending in **-eau, -au,** or **-eu** usually form their plural with **-x.** Words ending in **-al** often change this ending to **-aux** in the plural. Acronyms like **DVD** and **CD** do not add **-s** in the plural.

un tableau	un bureau	un animal	un CD	un DVD
des tableau**x**	des bureau**x**	des anim**aux**	des CD	des DVD

PRONONCIATION

Avoir et Être 1-47

Be careful to pronounce the forms of the verbs **avoir** and **être** distinctly. Open your mouth wide to pronounce the **a** in **tu as** and **il/elle a.** Contrast this with the vowel sound in **es** and **est.** Pronounce **ils sont** with an **s** sound, and the liaison in **ils ont** with a **z** sound.

être: Tu es professeur.   avoir: Tu as beaucoup de cours.
      Elle est professeur.   Elle a beaucoup de cours.
      Ils sont professeurs.   Ils ^z ont beaucoup de cours.

👥 A Prononcez bien! Posez ces questions à votre partenaire. Faites attention à la prononciation des verbes **avoir** et **être.**

   EXEMPLE a. — Tu es plutôt extraverti(e)?
                   — Oui, je suis plutôt extraverti(e).
                     Non, je ne suis pas très extraverti(e).
               b. — Tu as beaucoup d'amis?
                   — Oui, j'ai beaucoup d'amis.
                     Non, je n'ai pas beaucoup d'amis.

1. **a.** Tu es d'ici? **b.** Tu as beaucoup de choses chez toi?
2. **a.** Ton meilleur ami est sympa? **b.** Il a beaucoup d'amis?
3. **a.** Tes parents, ils sont sportifs? **b.** Ils ont un vélo?
4. **a.** Ils sont plutôt intellectuels? **b.** Ils ont beaucoup de livres?

B Qu'est-ce qu'ils ont? Dites si ces personnes ont ou n'ont pas les choses suivantes.

EXEMPLE Moi, je (j')... un chat
un chien
Moi, j'ai un chat. Je n'ai pas de chien.

1. Chez moi, je (j')... une chaîne hi-fi
des CD de hip-hop

2. Mon meilleur ami (Ma meilleure amie)... une voiture
beaucoup de vêtements

3. En cours de français, nous... beaucoup de devoirs
un examen aujourd'hui

4. Généralement, les étudiants à l'université... beaucoup de temps libre
beaucoup de devoirs

C Combien? Circulez parmi les étudiants. Demandez à au moins trois étudiants combien ils ont de chaque *(each)* chose illustrée.

EXEMPLE — Combien de chiens est-ce que tu as?
— J'ai un (deux, trois...) chien(s). / J'ai beaucoup de
chiens. / Je n'ai pas de chiens.

EXEMPLE
 1.
 2.
 3.
 4.

D Oui ou non? Vous cherchez un nouveau logement. Lisez ces textos d'autres étudiants qui voudraient partager leur *(their)* appartement / maison. Complétez leurs phrases avec la forme correcte du verbe **avoir**. Ensuite, dites si vous voudriez habiter avec ces personnes. Répondez **oui, non** ou **peut-être**.

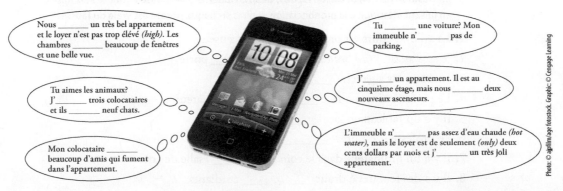

Nous _____ un très bel appartement et le loyer n'est pas trop élévé *(high)*. Les chambres _____ beaucoup de fenêtres et une belle vue.

Tu aimes les animaux? J'_____ trois colocataires et ils _____ neuf chats.

Mon colocataire _____ beaucoup d'amis qui fument dans l'appartement.

Tu _____ une voiture? Mon immeuble n'_____ pas de parking.

J'_____ un appartement. Il est au cinquième étage, mais nous _____ deux nouveaux ascenseurs.

L'immeuble n'_____ pas assez d'eau chaude *(hot water)*, mais le loyer est de seulement *(only)* deux cents dollars par mois et j'_____ un très joli appartement.

SAYING WHERE SOMETHING IS

✔ *Pour vérifier*

1. How do you say *on? under? facing? next to?*

2. What does the preposition **de** mean? With which two forms of the definite article does it combine to form **du** and **des**?

 Grammar Tutorials

Quelques prépositions

You can use the following prepositions to tell where something or someone is.

sur *on*	**près (de)** *near*
sous *under*	**loin (de)** *far (from)*
entre *between*	**à côté (de)** *next to, beside*
dans *in*	**à droite (de)** *to the right (of)*
devant *in front of*	**à gauche (de)** *to the left (of)*
derrière *behind*	**en face (de)** *across (from), facing*
	dans le coin (de) *in the corner (of)*

The preposition **de** *(of, from, about),* which is used as part of some of the prepositions above, contracts with the forms of the definite article **le** and **les,** to become **du** and **des.** It does not change when followed by **la** or **l'.**

CONTRACTIONS WITH *DE*

de + le	→	du	J'habite près **du** centre-ville.
de + la	→	de la	La salle de cours est près **de la** bibliothèque.
de + l'	→	de l'	Mon appartement est près **de l'**université.
de + les	→	des	Il n'y a pas de parking près **des** résidences.

PRONONCIATION

De, du, des 🔊 1-48

Be careful to pronounce **de, du,** and **des** distinctly.

- As you know, the **e** in words like **de, le,** and **ne** is pronounced with the lips slightly puckered. The tongue is held firm in the lower part of the mouth.
- The **u** in **du,** as in **tu,** is pronounced with the tongue arched firmly near the roof of the mouth, like the French vowel **i** in **il,** but with the lips puckered.
- The vowel in **des** is a sharp sound like the **é** in **café,** pronounced with the corners of the lips spread.

A **Prononcez bien!** D'abord, complétez ces phrases avec la forme correcte de la préposition de **(de, d', du, de la, de l', des).** Ensuite, lisez les phases à haute voix *(aloud)* en faisant attention à la prononciation et dites si chaque phrase est vraie ou fausse.

1. La salle de cours est près _____ ascenseur.

2. Je suis assis(e) *(am seated)* à côté _____ porte.

3. La porte est à gauche _____ moi.

4. Le professeur est en face _____ un ordinateur.

5. Il y a un tableau en face _____ étudiants.

6. Le professeur est près _____ tableau.

7. Il y a un ordinateur dans le coin _____ salle de cours.

8. Il y a des fenêtres à droite _____ étudiants.

B **Descriptions.** Faites des phrases pour décrire ce salon.

> **EXEMPLE** les livres / la table
> **Les livres sont sur la table.**

1. le chat / la table
2. la télé / le fauteuil
3. les plantes / la télé
4. le chien / le fauteuil et la télé
5. le chien / le fauteuil
6. la table / le salon
7. la porte / le fauteuil
8. les livres / l'ordinateur
9. l'ordinateur / la table
10. l'escalier / les tableaux

C **Qui est-ce?** Utilisez trois prépositions pour indiquer où un(e) des étudiant(e)s de votre cours est assis(e) *(is seated)* et les autres étudiants devineront *(will guess)* qui est la personne décrite.

> **EXEMPLE** — Elle est assise près de la fenêtre. Elle est à droite de Brent
> et elle est derrière Catherine.
> — C'est Julie?
> — Oui.

D **À vendre.** Avec un(e) partenaire, préparez au moins huit phrases décrivant cette maison.

> **EXEMPLE** Quand vous entrez *(enter)* dans la maison, les toilettes sont
> à gauche de la porte et le bureau est à droite. Derrière les
> toilettes, il y a...

au rez-de-chaussée

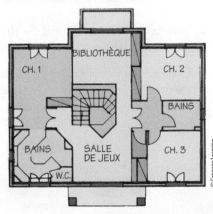

au premier étage

Maintenant, dessinez *(draw)* votre maison idéale. Décrivez cette maison à votre partenaire qui va la dessiner selon votre description *(who will draw it from your description)*.

Describing your room

LES MEUBLES ET LES COULEURS

Thomas **montre** les chambres à Robert.

un poster

un placard

des rideaux *(m)*

une commode

un bureau

un tapis

un lit

une étagère

Voici **ma** chambre. **Les murs** sont beiges et le tapis et les rideaux sont bleus. **La couverture** est bleue, rouge et verte.

Ma chambre est toujours **propre** et en ordre. Tout est **à sa place.**

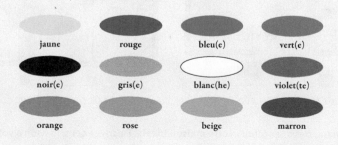

Voici la chambre de Gabriel. **Sa** chambre est souvent un peu **sale** et en désordre. Il **laisse** tout **par terre.**

Et vous? Comment est votre chambre, en ordre ou en désordre?
De quelle couleur *(f)* est votre tapis? De quelle couleur sont vos murs?
Voici des adjectifs pour indiquer la couleur de quelque chose.

jaune	rouge	bleu(e)	vert(e)
noir(e)	gris(e)	blanc(he)	violet(te)
orange	rose	beige	marron

Line art on this page: © Cengage Learning

Les meubles *Furniture, Furnishings*   **montrer** *to show*   **mon/ma/mes** *my*   **un mur** *a wall*   **une couverture** *a (bed)cover, a blanket*   **propre** *clean*   **à sa place** *in its place*   **son/sa/ses** *his/her/its*   **sale** *dirty*   **laisser** *to leave*   **par terre** *on the floor, on the ground*

1-49

Thomas montre les chambres à Robert.

THOMAS: Voici la chambre de Gabriel à côté de la cuisine. Sa chambre est toujours en désordre. Il laisse ses vêtements partout. **Quel bazar!**

ROBERT: C'est ta chambre en face de la chambre de Gabriel?

THOMAS: Oui, **comme tu vois,** je préfère avoir tout bien rangé et **chaque chose** à sa place.

ROBERT: Et ça, c'est ma chambre **au bout du couloir**?

THOMAS: Oui, **viens voir...** Tu as un lit, un bureau et une grande fenêtre avec **une** belle **vue.** J'**espère** que **ça te plaît.**

ROBERT: Oui, merci, **ça a l'air bien**!

THOMAS: Les murs sont blancs. Tu préfères une autre couleur?

ROBERT: Non, **justement,** le blanc, c'est ma couleur **préférée.**

THOMAS: Moi, je préfère le vert.

Sélection musicale. Search the Web for the song **"Y a une fille qui habite chez moi"** by Bénabar to enjoy a musical selection containing related vocabulary.

Note *de vocabulaire*

1. The formal/plural version of **ça te plaît** is **ça vous plaît.** Use **ça me plaît** to say *I like it.*
2. **Espérer** is a spelling-change verb and is conjugated like **préférer.**
3. **Préféré** *(favorite)* is an adjective and must match the noun it describes in gender and number: **Ce sont mes vêtements préférés.**

A **Chez vous?** Décrivez votre chambre en choisissant l'adverbe qui convient.

(presque) toujours   souvent   quelquefois
rarement   ne... (presque) jamais

EXEMPLE Ma chambre est en ordre.
Ma chambre est presque toujours en ordre.
Ma chambre n'est presque jamais en ordre.

1. Ma chambre est propre.
2. Ma chambre est en désordre.
3. Mes livres sont sur l'étagère.
4. Ma chambre est sale.
5. Mes vêtements sont par terre.
6. Mes livres sont sur le lit.
7. Je laisse mes vêtements partout.
8. Mes vêtements sont dans le placard ou dans la commode.

B **Les couleurs.** Complétez les phrases suivantes avec le nom d'une couleur.

1. Ma couleur préférée, c'est le...
2. J'ai beaucoup de vêtements...
3. Les murs de ma chambre sont...
4. La couverture de mon lit est...
5. Les rideaux de ma chambre sont...
6. Ma voiture est...
7. Chez moi, le canapé est...
8. Le tapis de la salle de bains est...

À VOUS!

Avec un(e) partenaire, relisez à haute voix la conversation entre Thomas et Robert. Ensuite, imaginez que votre partenaire va habiter *(is going to live)* chez vous et adaptez la conversation pour décrire votre propre maison / appartement.

You can find a list of the new words from this *Compétence* on page 139 and access the audio online.

Quel bazar! *What a mess!*   **comme tu vois** *as you see*   **chaque chose** *each thing*   **au bout de** *at the end of*   **le couloir** *the hallway, the corridor*   **viens voir** *come see*   **une vue** *a view*   **espérer** *to hope*   **ça te plaît** *you like it*   **ça a l'air bien** *it seems nice*   **justement** *as a matter of fact, precisely, exactly*   **préféré(e)** *favorite*

IDENTIFYING YOUR BELONGINGS

✔ *Pour vérifier*

1. How do you say *John's friend* and *Mary's car* in French?

2. With which two forms of the definite article does **de** combine to form the contractions **du** and **des**?

3. How do you say *my*? How do you say *your* (singular familiar)? What are the forms of each word?

4. When do you use **mon, ton,** and **son,** instead of **ma, ta,** and **sa** before a feminine noun?

5. Does French have different words for *his, her,* and *its*? How do you say *his house* and *her house* in French? How do you say *his dog* and *her dog*?

La possession et les adjectifs possessifs mon, ton et son

In French, use a phrase with **de**, rather than *'s* to indicate possession or relationship.

There is Thomas's room.	Voilà la chambre **de** Thomas.
That's Gabriel's dog.	C'est le chien **de** Gabriel.

Remember that **de** contracts with the articles **le** and **les** to form **du** and **des.** It does not change when followed by **la** or **l'.**

le livre **du** professeur	les livres **des** étudiants
la porte **de l'**appartement	la porte **de la** cuisine

The possessive adjectives **mon/ma/mes** *(my),* **ton/ta/tes** *(your* [singular familiar]), and **son/sa/ses** *(his, her, its)* agree in gender and number with the noun that follows them. However, before feminine singular nouns that begin with a vowel sound, use **mon/ton/son.**

	MASCULINE SINGULAR	FEMININE SINGULAR *(plus consonant sound)*	FEMININE SINGULAR *(plus vowel sound)*	PLURAL
my	**mon** lit	**ma** commode	**mon** étagère	**mes** rideaux
your	**ton** lit	**ta** commode	**ton** étagère	**tes** rideaux
his/her/its	**son** lit	**sa** commode	**son** étagère	**ses** rideaux

—C'est **la couverture de Thomas**?
—Non, ce n'est pas **sa** couverture. C'est **ma** couverture. Et ce sont **mes** rideaux, aussi.

The use of the forms **son/sa/ses** depends on the gender and number of the object possessed, not the person who owns it. **Son/sa/ses** can all mean *his, her,* or *its.*

C'est **son** fauteuil.　　C'est **son** fauteuil.　　Et c'est aussi **son** fauteuil.

A **Compliments.** Une amie vous montre *(is showing you)* sa maison. Formez la phrase la plus logique pour faire des compliments.

> **EXEMPLE** maison (jolie, laide)
> **Ta maison est jolie.**

1. bureau (en désordre, en ordre)
2. tapis (beau, laid)
3. chambre (désagréable, agréable)
4. maison (grande, petite)
5. plantes (jolies, laides)
6. placards (trop petits, immenses)
7. étagère (en désordre, bien rangée)
8. chien (beau, laid)

ii B De quelle couleur? Demandez à votre partenaire de quelle couleur sont ces choses. Utilisez **ton, ta** ou **tes.**

> **EXEMPLE** voiture
> —De quelle couleur est ta voiture?
> —Ma voiture est grise. / Je n'ai pas de voiture.

> chambre   canapé   couverture   tapis   rideaux   vêtements préférés

Maintenant, décrivez les affaires *(belongings)* de votre partenaire à la classe.

> **EXEMPLE** Sa voiture est grise. / Il/Elle n'a pas de voiture.

ii C C'est à moi! Un locataire change d'appartement et il voudrait tout prendre avec lui *(him),* mais l'autre locataire n'est pas d'accord. Jouez les rôles avec un(e) partenaire.

> **EXEMPLE** la plante
> —Bon, je prends *(I'm taking)* ma plante.
> —Ah non, ce n'est pas ta plante. C'est ma plante!

1. le bureau   3. le poster   5. l'étagère
2. les rideaux   4. la commode   6. les chiens

ii D La chambre de qui? Complétez chaque phrase avec **son, sa** ou **ses** pour dire *his.* Après, lisez chaque phrase et choisissez *(choose)* un(e) autre étudiant(e) pour dire si la phrase décrit la chambre de Robert ou la chambre de Gabriel.

> **EXEMPLE** <u>Sa</u> chambre est en ordre.
> **C'est la chambre de Robert.**

1. _____ tapis est jaune.
2. _____ rideaux sont gris.
3. _____ vélo est rouge.
4. _____ couverture est verte.
5. _____ murs sont blancs.
6. Il n'y a pas de posters dans _____ chambre.
7. Beaucoup de _____ affaires *(belongings)* sont par terre.
8. Il y a un livre rouge sous _____ bureau.
9. _____ chambre est propre.
10. _____ chambre est sale.

la chambre de Robert

la chambre de Gabriel

iii E Comparaisons. Regardez bien les illustrations de l'activité *D. La chambre de qui?* Fermez votre livre et travaillez en groupe pour comparer de mémoire les chambres de Robert et de Gabriel. Le groupe qui trouve le plus grand nombre de comparaisons correctes gagne.

> **EXEMPLE** Les murs de Robert sont blancs, mais les murs de Gabriel sont gris. Le bureau de Robert est devant sa fenêtre et...

INDICATING TO WHOM SOMETHING BELONGS

✔ *Pour vérifier*

1. How do you say *our, your* (formal, plural), and *their* in French?

2. Do these words have separate forms for masculine and feminine?

(i)Lrn **Grammar Tutorials**

(i)Lrn *Prononcez bien!* See Module 13.

Les adjectifs possessifs **notre, votre** *et* **leur**

The possessive adjectives for *our, your* (formal or plural), and *their* have only two forms, singular and plural.

	MASCULINE SINGULAR	FEMININE SINGULAR *(plus consonant sound)*	FEMININE SINGULAR *(plus vowel sound)*	PLURAL
my	**mon** lit	**ma** chambre	**mon** amie	**mes** livres
your (sing. fam.)	**ton** lit	**ta** chambre	**ton** amie	**tes** livres
his, her, its	**son** lit	**sa** chambre	**son** amie	**ses** livres
our	**notre** lit	**notre** chambre	**notre** amie	**nos** livres
your (pl./form.)	**votre** lit	**votre** chambre	**votre** amie	**vos** livres
their	**leur** lit	**leur** chambre	**leur** amie	**leurs** livres

PRONONCIATION

La voyelle **o** *de* **notre / votre** *et de* **nos / vos**   1-50

Compare the **o** sounds in **notre / votre** and **nos / vos.** The lips are puckered to make both of these sounds and the tongue is held firm, but the **o** in **nos / vos** is pronounced with the back of the tongue arched higher in the mouth than for the **o** in **notre** and **votre.** The letter **o** is pronounced with the sound of **nos** when it is the last sound in a syllable, when it is followed by an **s,** or when it is written **ô.** Otherwise, it is pronounced with the more open sound of **notre.**

notre chien / nos chiens   votre chat / vos chats

A **Prononcez bien!** Complétez les questions suivantes avec **votre** ou **vos,** puis lisez chacune d'elles. Faites attention à la prononciation de la voyelle **o.**

EXEMPLE <u>Votre</u> quartier est joli?

1. _____ appartement est très cher?

2. _____ chiens sont méchants?

3. _____ cuisine est grande?

4. _____ parents passent beaucoup de temps dans l'appartement?

5. _____ appartement a beaucoup de fenêtres?

 Maintenant, imaginez que deux amis veuillent *(want)* persuader un troisième ami de partager leur appartement. Comment répondent-ils aux questions? Utilisez **notre** ou **nos** dans les réponses.

EXEMPLE —<u>Votre</u> quartier est joli?
—**Oui, notre quartier est très joli.**

B Tu ou vous? Robert passe le week-end chez les parents de ses amis Patrick et Antoine Dupont et il veut savoir à qui chaque chose appartient *(wants to know to whom everything belongs)*. Complétez ce qu'il dit avec **ton/ta/tes** ou **votre/vos**.

EXEMPLES Patrick, c'est ___ vélo?   Mme Dupont, c'est ___ voiture?

Patrick, c'est ton vélo?   Mme Dupont, c'est votre voiture?

1. Patrick et Antoine, c'est _____ maison? Ce sont _____ parents?

2. M. Dupont, c'est _____ garage? Ce sont _____ voitures?

3. M. et Mme Dupont, j'aime bien _____ quartier. Ce sont _____ voisins *(neighbors)*?

4. Patrick, c'est _____ chambre? Tu laisses souvent _____ vêtements par terre ou ils sont toujours dans _____ placard ou dans _____ commode?

5. M. et Mme Dupont, c'est _____ bureau? J'aime bien _____ étagère. Il y a de la place pour tous _____ livres.

6. Patrick et Antoine, c'est _____ salle de jeux? Où sont _____ jeux vidéo? Ah, voilà... ça, Antoine, c'est _____ jeu préféré, non?

C Je préfère notre université. Comparez votre université avec une autre université dans votre région ou avec une université connue *(well-known)*. Formez des phrases avec **notre/nos** ou **leur/leurs**.

EXEMPLE campus / beau

Leur campus est plus beau que notre campus.
Notre campus est plus beau que leur campus.
Leur campus est aussi beau que notre campus.

L'Université Laval

1. campus / grand
2. cours / difficiles
3. étudiants / sympas
4. professeurs / intéressants
5. bâtiments / modernes

D Préférences. Dites si vous aimez ces choses et demandez à un(e) partenaire s'il/si elle aime ces choses aussi. Utilisez **son/sa/ses** ou **leur/leurs**.

EXEMPLES la musique de Jennifer Lopez
— **Moi, j'aime bien la musique de Jennifer Lopez. Et toi, est-ce que tu aimes sa musique?**
— **Oui, j'aime bien sa musique.**
Je ne connais pas sa musique *(I don't know her music).*

la musique du groupe Coldplay
— **Moi, j'aime bien la musique du groupe Coldplay. Et toi, est-ce que tu aimes leur musique?**
— **Oui, j'aime bien leur musique.**
Je ne connais pas leur musique.

la musique des Black Eyed Peas	les vidéos de Lady Gaga	la musique de Beyoncé
les chansons *(songs)* des Beatles	les livres de J. K. Rowling	les films avec Jim Carrey

TELLING WHICH ONE

✔ Pour vérifier

1. How do you say this, that, these, and those? When do you use the alternate masculine form cet?

2. When do you use quel to say what? When do you use qu'est-ce que? What are the four forms of quel?

Les adjectifs ce et quel

To say *this/that* and *these/those*, use **ce (cet, cette, ces)**. Notice that the masculine singular **ce** changes to **cet** before a vowel sound.

	MASCULINE		FEMININE
	(plus consonant sound)	*(plus vowel sound)*	*(plus consonant or vowel sound)*
SINGULAR	**ce** canapé	**cet** appartement	**cette** rue
PLURAL	**ces** canapés	**ces** appartements	**ces** rues

To say *which* and *what,* use **quel (quels, quelle, quelles)**. The form you use depends on the gender and number of the noun it modifies.

	MASCULINE	FEMININE
SINGULAR	**quel** appartement	**quelle** rue
PLURAL	**quels** appartements	**quelles** rues

Quel est ton **nom**?   **Quelle** est ton **adresse**?

Quels meubles as-tu?   **Quelles couleurs** préfères-tu?

Quel and **qu'est-ce que** both mean *what,* but they are not interchangeable. Use:

QUEL	QU'EST-CE QUE (QU')

• directly before a noun
   Tu es de **quel pays**?
	• before a subject and verb
	   Qu'est-ce que tu as chez toi?
	   Qu'est-ce qu'il y a dans ton quartier?

• before **est** or **sont** followed by a noun
   Quel est ton nom?
   Quels sont tes loisirs préférés?	

Note *de vocabulaire*

1. If you need to distinguish *this* from *that,* you can add the suffixes -ci and -là to the noun.

ce livre-ci ou ce livre-là *this book or that book*

ces maisons-ci ou ces maisons-là *these houses or those houses*

2. **Quel** followed by a noun is also used as an exclamation. It is most often the equivalent of *What . . . !* or *What a . . . !* in English.

Quels chiens embêtants! *What annoying dogs!*

Quelle chance! *What luck!*

Quelle belle maison! *What a pretty house!*

🌐 **Sélection musicale.** Search the Web for the song "**Je suis**" by Florent Pagny to enjoy a musical selection illustrating the use and pronunciation of the demonstrative adjective.

PRONONCIATION

Prononcez bien! See Modules 9–10.

La voyelle e de ce/cet/cette/ces 🔊 1-52

You already know that a final **e** is usually not pronounced in French, except in short words like **je.** As you notice in **ce/cet/cette/ces,** unaccented **e** has three different pronunciations, depending on what follows it.

In short words like **ce** and **que,** or when **e** is followed by a single consonant within a word, pronounce it as in:

   je   ne   le   regarde   vendredi

When, as in **ces, e** is followed by an unpronounced consonant at the end of a word, pronounce it as in:

   les   mes   parlez   manger   premier

In words like **cette** and **cet,** where **e** is followed by two consonants within a word, or a single pronounced consonant at the end of a word, pronounce it as in:

   quel   cher   belle   elle   cherche

A **Prononcez bien!** Demandez à votre partenaire s'il/si elle aime ces choses. Faites attention à la prononciation de **ce (cet)/cette/ces**.

EXEMPLE — Tu aimes ce tableau?
— Oui, j'aime bien ce tableau. / Non, je n'aime pas ce tableau.

EXEMPLE tableau   **1.** canapé   **2.** escalier   **3.** lampe

4. tableaux   **5.** étagère   **6.** rideaux   **7.** commode

B **Entretien.** Complétez les questions suivantes avec la forme correcte de **quel** ou avec **qu'est-ce que (qu'est-ce qu')**. Ensuite, posez les questions à votre partenaire.

1. ____ il y a dans ta chambre?
2. Dans ____ pièce est-ce que tu passes le plus de temps?
3. ____ meubles est-ce que tu voudrais acheter *(to buy)* pour ton salon?
4. ____ tu voudrais acheter pour ta chambre?
5. Ta chambre est à ____ étage?
6. De ____ couleurs sont les murs de ta chambre?
7. ____ tu voudrais changer chez toi?

C **Au Canada.** Travaillez en équipes *(teams)*. Complétez les questions suivantes avec la forme correcte de **quel/quelle/quels/quelles** et **ce (cet)/cette/ces** comme dans l'exemple. Ensuite, répondez aux questions. La première équipe qui complète tout correctement et qui répond correctement aux questions gagne.

EXEMPLE **Quelle** est la province canadienne avec le plus de francophones?
Cette province est plus grande que l'Alaska.
C'est le Québec.

1. _____ est la plus grande ville du Québec?
_____ ville n'est pas la capitale de la province.
2. _____ est la plus vieille ville du Canada?
Fondée en 1608, _____ ville est la capitale de la province de Québec.
3. _____ pourcentage *(m)* de la population canadienne habite au Québec?
_____ pourcentage est entre 20 et 30 %.
4. _____ explorateur est le premier Français à explorer le Canada?
_____ explorateur arrive au Canada en 1534.
5. De _____ couleurs est le drapeau *(flag)* canadien?
_____ couleurs sont deux des couleurs du drapeau des États-Unis.

VIDÉOREPRISE

Les Stagiaires

See the **Résumé de grammaire** section at the end of each chapter for a review of all the grammar presented in the chapter.

Rappel!
So far in the video, Amélie and Rachid, two new interns at the Technovert company, have become better acquainted with their new colleagues. Matthieu, the company's shy techie, revealed to Camille a secret interest in Amélie, which led to a bet between Camille and Céline as to whether Matthieu would ever have the courage to ask Amélie out.

In *Épisode 3* of *Les Stagiaires,* Amélie considers rooming with Céline, the Technovert marketing director, who has been looking for someone to share her apartment for a while. Before you watch the episode, review what you learned in *Chapitre 3* by doing these exercises in which Céline discusses her apartment with other prospective apartment mates.

© Cengage Learning

A Quelques questions. Une amie pose des questions à Céline parce qu'elle pense peut-être habiter chez elle. Complétez les questions avec **de, d', du, de la, de l'** ou **des.**

1. Est-ce que tu habites près ou loin _____ centre-ville?

2. Tu habites près _____ université?

3. Y a-t-il un arrêt de bus près _____ appartement?

4. Qu'est-ce qu'il y a en face _____ chez toi, de l'autre côté _____ rue?

5. Est-ce qu'il y a une salle de bains à côté _____ chambres?

 Maintenant, posez ces questions à un(e) partenaire pour parler de sa maison, de son appartement ou de sa résidence.

B L'appartement de Céline.
Céline décrit son appartement. Complétez le paragraphe suivant avec les expressions indiquées.

porte d'entrée

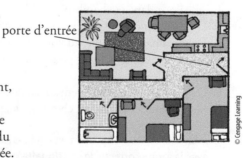
© Cengage Learning

Quand on entre dans mon appartement, la cuisine et le salon sont __1__ *(to the right)* et les deux chambres et la salle de bains sont __2__ *(to the left).* La porte du salon est __3__ *(facing the)* porte d'entrée.
Il faut *(One must)* passer par le salon pour aller à la cuisine et il y a une petite salle à manger __4__ *(between)* les deux pièces. La salle de bains est __5__ *(at the end of the)* couloir, __6__ *(next to the)* deuxième chambre.

C Quelques questions. Une amie voudrait passer chez Céline pour voir son appartement. Quelle question avec **quel/quelle/quels/quelles** est-ce qu'elle pose à Céline pour obtenir les réponses suivantes?

> **EXEMPLE** Le nom de la rue, c'est *rue du Stade.*
> **Quel est le nom de la rue?**

1. L'adresse exacte de l'immeuble, *c'est le 125 rue du Stade.*

2. C'est l'appartement *numéro 12.*

3. Mon numéro de téléphone, c'est *le 06 35 42 89 95.*

4. Je rentre chez moi *vers six heures et demie* ce soir.

D Qu'est-ce que vous avez? Céline parle à une amie. Complétez les phrases suivantes avec le verbe **avoir** dans le premier espace et le bon adjectif possessif dans le deuxième.

EXEMPLE J'**ai** un portable. **Mon** numéro de téléphone, c'est le 06 35 42 89 95.

1. J' _____ un appartement en centre-ville. _____ adresse, c'est le 125 rue du Stade, appartement 12.
2. Le quartier _____ beaucoup de restaurants et de cafés. C'est un quartier très agréable et j'aime beaucoup _____ ambiance.
3. Quelquefois, je passe le week-end chez mes parents. Ils _____ une maison en banlieue. _____ jardin *(yard)* est très joli.
4. Chez moi, j'_____ un petit chien. _____ chien est sympa, mais il aboie *(barks)* toujours quand quelqu'un s'approche de *(someone approaches)* la porte.
5. Le seul inconvénient de mon appartement, c'est que dans le parking de mon immeuble, nous n' _____ pas assez de places pour _____ voitures.

Maintenant, changez les phrases pour décrire votre situation.

E C'est combien? Céline cherche du mobilier *(furnishings)* pour son appartement sur *Craigslist*. Donnez le prix de chaque objet comme dans l'exemple. Utilisez **ce, cet, cette** ou **ces**.

EXEMPLE

> TABLE, 6 CHAISES 450 €
> Tél: 06 96 78 26 65

Cette table et ces chaises coûtent *(cost)* **quatre cent cinquante euros.**

1.
> TABLE, 6 CHAISES
> laquées noires, très propres
> 1 150 €
> Tél: 06 53 44 94 95

2.
> FAUTEUIL, CANAPÉ
> fleuris 550 €
> Tél: 06 31 42 51 15

3.
> TÉLÉ Sony,
> état neuf 700 €
> Tél: 06 12 21 49 14

4.
> LIT «king» complet:
> base, lit en pin, matelas,
> le tout en très bon état 150 €
> Tél: 06 11 09 07 67

5.
> TABLE D'ORDINATEUR
> blanche, 3 tiroirs, en bon
> état 115 €
> Tél: 06 89 85 10 11

6.
> ORDINATEUR Toshiba,
> excellente condition 495 €
> Tél: 06 55 64 69 94

© Cengage Learning

Access the Video *Les Stagiaires* on (iLrn.

© Cengage Learning

▶ **Épisode 3: Un nouvel appartement**

AVANT LA VIDÉO

Dans cet épisode, Céline demande à Amélie si elle voudrait être sa colocataire. Avant de regarder l'épisode, pensez à trois questions qu'on pose souvent à un(e) colocataire potentiel(le).

APRÈS LA VIDÉO

Regardez le clip et notez trois questions qu'Amélie pose à Céline à propos de l'appartement et de ses habitudes.

LECTURE ET COMPOSITION

LECTURE

Looking at the title of an article and thinking about the topic can help you anticipate its content and read it more easily. You are going to read an article by an interior decorator in Quebec about how colors can change your moods. Before you begin to read, look at the title of the article. What is it about? What feelings do you associate with the following colors?

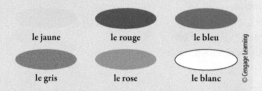

le jaune   le rouge   le bleu

le gris   le rose   le blanc

© Cengage Learning

Associations. Quelle(s) couleur(s) associez-vous le plus aux choses suivantes?

1. la passion
2. la dépression
3. la concentration
4. l'énergie
5. la relaxation
6. la pureté
7. l'appétit
8. l'irritation

© Artazum/Shutterstock.com

Les couleurs et leurs effets sur la nature humaine

Les couleurs changent nos **humeurs** et reflètent notre personnalité. **Pour mieux vous faire connaître** les effets qu'ont les couleurs sur la nature humaine, nous avons préparé un guide qui va vous aider à choisir les couleurs pour votre maison ou appartement.

Les couleurs chaudes: le rouge et le jaune

Le rouge stimule le métabolisme, le rythme cardiaque et la température **corporelle.** Le rouge est une couleur agressive, vitale et passionnante. **Puisque** c'est une couleur qui stimule l'appétit, le rouge est souvent utilisé pour les salles à manger et les restaurants.

Le jaune stimule la mémoire, le mouvement, la coordination et le système digestif. Le jaune et le rouge sont considérés comme «énergiques». Mais **faites attention,** le jaune dans une chambre de bébé **peut rendre** l'enfant irritable.

Les couleurs froides: le bleu et le vert

Le bleu encourage la concentration, **fait ralentir** le rythme cardiaque et la respiration et **fait baisser** la température du **corps.** Cette couleur est très recommandée dans un bureau.

Le vert augmente la relaxation. Le corps et **l'esprit se détendent** dans une atmosphère verte. Il est **donc parfait** pour une chambre à coucher.

---

humeurs *moods*   **Pour mieux vous faire connaître** *To inform you better about*
corporelle *body*   **Puisque** *Since*   **faites attention** *be careful*   **peut**
rendre *can make*   **froides** *cold*   **fait ralentir** *slows down*   **fait baisser** *lowers*
corps *body*   **l'esprit** *the mind*   **se détendent** *relax*   **donc** *therefore*
parfait *perfect*

Les couleurs neutres: le blanc, le gris et le noir

Le blanc stimule les fonctions vitales, par conséquent **le sommeil** n'est pas aussi **bénéfique** dans une chambre blanche. Le blanc est aussi associé à la pureté et à l'honnêteté.

Le gris incite à la dépression et à l'indifférence. Il est préférable de l'utiliser comme accent plutôt que couleur dominante dans votre décor.

Le noir est une couleur distincte, audacieuse et classique. Le noir est un fond idéal **pour faire ressortir** les autres couleurs, mais il peut être **étouffant** en trop grande quantité.

© Kate Macrae

---

le sommeil *sleep* **bénéfique** *beneficial* **pour faire ressortir** *to make stand out* **étouffant** *stifling*

Compréhension

Quelles couleurs? **Complétez les phrases suivantes en indiquant les couleurs appropriées d'après la lecture du texte.**

1. Si vous désirez manger moins, évitez *(avoid)* le _____ pour décorer votre salle à manger.
2. Pour mieux vous concentrer, étudiez dans une pièce _____.
3. Si votre bébé pleure *(cries)* beaucoup, utilisez le _____ dans sa chambre et évitez le _____.
4. Si vous souffrez de dépression, évitez le _____ dans votre décor.
5. Si vous avez souvent froid *(feel cold)* chez vous, utilisez le _____ et évitez le _____.

COMPOSITION

POUR MIEUX ÉCRIRE:
Brainstorming

Brainstorming on a topic before writing about it can help you organize your thoughts. To brainstorm, first think about what general sections you will want to include in your writing, then jot down as many notes for each section as you can. Finally, use these sections to organize your writing.

Organisez-vous. Imagine that you are responding to a roommate ad in Quebec. What would you want to know about the apartment and its occupant? Jot down as many words and phrases in French as you can under each heading in this chart, using a separate piece of paper.

location	rooms and furnishings	roommate's personality/ habits

Un mail

You are moving to Quebec and respond to an ad for a roommate. Write an e-mail in which you introduce yourself and tell the sort of place you are looking for. Then, write three paragraphs asking about the apartment's location, the rooms and furnishings, and what the roommate is like. Begin with **Cher monsieur / Chère madame** and end the e-mail with **En attendant votre réponse.** Don't forget to sign your name.

iLrn Share It!

COMPARAISONS CULTURELLES

LE QUÉBEC D'AUJOURD'HUI

Grâce à son histoire, à sa langue et à **ses coutumes**, le Québec est, **à bien des égards**, une société distincte à l'intérieur du Canada. Dans cette province, la seule où le français est **l'unique** langue officielle, 80 % de la population parle français à la maison, 8 % parle anglais et 12 % parle d'autres langues.

En 1534, Jacques Cartier **découvre** un pays où habitent les Amérindiens et les Inuits. Il **établit** une colonie qu'il appelle la Nouvelle France. Cette colonie se développe rapidement: en 1608, Samuel de Champlain **fonde** la ville de Québec et, en 1642, Paul de Maisonneuve **crée** Montréal.

Malheureusement, les Français et les Anglais **se battent** pour le contrôle du Canada. L'armée anglaise est plus nombreuse, et les Anglais gagnent **la guerre.** En 1763, la France cède ses territoires canadiens aux Anglais et pendant 200 **ans,** les Québécois **vivent** sous la domination anglophone.

Grâce à *Thanks to*   **ses coutumes** *its customs*   **à bien des égards** *in many regards*   **l'unique** *the only*   **découvre** *discovers* **établit** *establishes*   **fonde** *founds*   **crée** *creates*   **Malheureusement** *Unfortunately*   **se battent** *battle*   **la guerre** *the war* **ans** *years*   **vivent** *live*

Dans les années 1960, les Québécois prennent conscience de leur identité et de leur culture francophone et un mouvement pour un Québec francophone se développe. **On appelle ce mouvement** la Révolution tranquille. En 1976, **une loi** pour la défense du français est votée et oblige **les immigrés à apprendre** le français. Aujourd'hui, les immigrés qui arrivent **de partout dans le monde** représentent 11,5 % de la population du Québec.

Le Québec d'aujourd'hui est une société multi-ethnique **qui** s'inspire des contributions **que lui apportent ces immigrés** et ses peuples **indigènes** (les Inuits et les Amérindiens), **aussi bien que de ses racines** françaises et anglaises. **Pourtant,** le Québec **maintient surtout** un attachement profond à son héritage français.

Source: www.gouv.qc.ca

Compréhension

1. Au Québec, 80 % de la population parle _____, 8 % parle _____ et 12 % parle d'_____. Quelle est la situation linguistique dans votre région?

2. Au cours du 17e et du 18e siècles, les _____ et les _____ se battent pour le contrôle du Canada. En 1763, les _____ gagnent la guerre. Comment est-ce que l'histoire de votre région influence sa situation linguistique?

3. Le Québec d'aujourd'hui est une société francophone qui est aussi une société multi-ethnique. Il s'ouvre aux contributions que lui apportent ses peuples _____ et ses _____ venant de toutes les parties du monde. Quelles cultures ont influencé votre société?

iLrn Share It!

Visit **www.cengagebrain.com** for additional cultural information and activities.

Dans les années 1960 *In the sixties*   **On appelle ce mouvement** *This movement is called*   **une loi** *a law*   **les immigrés à apprendre** *immigrants to learn*   **de partout dans le monde** *from throughout the world*   **qui** *that*   **que lui apportent ces immigrés** *that these immigrants bring to it*   **indigènes** *indigenous*   **aussi bien que de ses racines** *as well as by its roots*   **Pourtant** *However*   **maintient surtout** *maintains especially*

RÉSUMÉ DE GRAMMAIRE

cent = *one hundred*
mille = *one thousand*
un million = *one million*
un million d'habitants

300	trois cents
301	trois cent un
3 000	trois mille
3 100 000	trois millions cent mille

Ma rue, c'est la première (deuxième, troisième, quatrième, cinquième, sixième, septième, huitième, neuvième, dixième, onzième...) rue à droite.

—J'**ai** un appartement. Et toi? Tu **as** une maison?
—Ma famille **a** une petite maison. J'habite chez mes parents.

—Tu as **des** chats, non?
—Non, ce ne sont pas **des** chats. J'ai **des** chiens.
—Combien **de** chiens as-tu?
—Quatre.
—Tu n'as pas **de** problèmes avec tes colocataires?
—Non, je n'ai pas **de** colocataire.

un tableau → des tableaux
un bureau → des bureaux
un animal → des animaux

Je rentre **de** l'université à cinq heures.

Ma résidence est **près d'**ici, **derrière** la bibliothèque et **à côté de** la librairie.

NUMBERS ABOVE 100

- Use **un** in **un million**, but not before the words **cent** and **mille**. The word **million(s)** is followed by **de (d')** when followed directly by a noun.
- **Million** takes an **s** when plural. **Cent** generally only takes an **s** when plural if not followed by another number. Never add an **s** to **mille**.
- There is no hyphen between the words **cent, mille,** or **million** and another number.
- Use commas to denote decimals, and spaces or periods to set off numbers in the thousands, millions, etc.

ORDINAL NUMBERS

Use **premier (première)** to say *first*. To form the other ordinal numbers *(second, third, fourth . . .)*, add the suffix **-ième** to the cardinal numbers **(deux, trois, quatre...)**. Drop a final **e** of cardinal numbers before adding **-ième**. Note the spelling changes in **cinquième** *(fifth)* and **neuvième** *(ninth)*.

AVOIR

The verb **avoir** *(to have)* is irregular.

j' **ai**	nous **avons**
tu **as**	vous **avez**
il/elle **a**	ils/elles **ont**

UN, UNE, DES → *DE (D')*

Use **de (d')** rather than **un, une,** or **des** after . . .

- most verbs in the negative form, except **être**.
- quantity expressions like **combien, beaucoup,** and **assez**.

PLURALS ENDING WITH *-X*

In the plural, most words ending in **-eau, -au,** or **-eu** end in **-x** rather than **-s**, and the ending **-al** becomes **-aux**.

PREPOSITIONS

When used alone, the preposition **de** means *of, from,* or *about*. **De** is also used in some of the following prepositions.

sur	*on*	**près (de)**	*near*
sous	*under*	**loin (de)**	*far (from)*
entre	*between*	**à côté (de)**	*next to, beside*
dans	*in*	**à droite / gauche (de)**	*to the right / left (of)*
devant	*in front of*	**en face (de)**	*across (from), facing*
derrière	*behind*	**dans le coin (de)**	*in the corner (of)*

De contracts with the articles **le** and **les,** but not with **la** or **l'.**

CONTRACTION:			NO CONTRACTION:		
de + le	→	du	de + la	→	de la
de + les	→	des	de + l'	→	de l'

POSSESSION

De is used instead of *'s* to indicate possession. Remember the contractions **de + le → du** and **de + les → des.**

le bureau du professeur	*the professor's office*
la voiture de mon frère	*my brother's car*

The possessive adjectives also indicate possession.

	MASCULINE SINGULAR	FEMININE SINGULAR (+ consonant sound)	FEMININE SINGULAR (+ vowel sound)	PLURAL
my	**mon** vélo	**ma** voiture	**mon** adresse	**mes** meubles
your (sing. fam.)	**ton** vélo	**ta** voiture	**ton** adresse	**tes** meubles
his/her/its	**son** vélo	**sa** voiture	**son** adresse	**ses** meubles
our	**notre** vélo	**notre** voiture	**notre** adresse	**nos** meubles
your (form./pl.)	**votre** vélo	**votre** voiture	**votre** adresse	**vos** meubles
their	**leur** vélo	**leur** voiture	**leur** adresse	**leurs** meubles

Use the forms **mon, ton,** and **son** rather than **ma, ta,** and **sa** before feminine nouns beginning with vowel sounds.

The use of the forms **son/sa/ses** (*his, her, its*) depends on the gender and number of the object possessed, not the person who owns it. **Son/sa/ses** can all mean *his, her,* or *its.*

CE (CET)/CETTE/CES AND QUEL/QUELLE/QUELS/QUELLES

Use the demonstrative adjective **ce (cet)/cette/ces** to say both *this/these* and *that/those.* The masculine **ce** becomes **cet** before masculine singular nouns beginning with a vowel sound.

	SINGULAR	PLURAL
MASCULINE (+ consonant sound)	ce chien	ces chiens
MASCULINE (+ vowel sound)	cet animal	ces animaux
FEMININE	cette étagère	ces étagères

Use **quel/quelle/quels/quelles** to say *which* or *what* directly before a noun or the verbs **est** and **sont.** It agrees with the gender and number of the noun it modifies.

	MASCULINE	FEMININE
SINGULAR	quel état	quelle ville
PLURAL	quels états	quelles villes

Je n'aime pas habiter dans la résidence parce qu'elle est loin **du** parking et ma chambre est en face **des** ascenseurs, à côté **de l'**escalier et loin **de la** salle de bains!

—C'est ta voiture?
—Non, c'est la voiture **de** mon amie.

—C'est la porte **de la** salle de bains?
—Non, c'est la porte **du** placard.

—Tu habites encore chez **tes** parents?
—Non, j'habite chez **mon** frère.
—Où est **sa** maison?
—Pas loin de chez **nos** parents.
—Dans quelle rue est la maison de **vos** parents?
—**Leur** adresse est le 435, rue Martin.

Mon amie s'appelle Marion.

son quartier = *his/her/its neighborhood*
sa porte = *his/her/its door*
ses murs = *his/her/its walls*

—Tu habites dans **cette** rue?
—Oui, j'aime beaucoup **ce** quartier. Mon appartement est dans **cet** immeuble.
—Mon appartement est derrière **ces** arbres.

—Dans **quelle** ville habites-tu?
—J'habite à Sherbrooke.
—**Quelle** est ton adresse?
—C'est le 1202, rue Galt.
—**Quel** est ton numéro de téléphone?
—C'est le (819) 569-1208.

VOCABULAIRE

  Audio Flashcards

COMPÉTENCE 1 🔊

Talking about where you live

NOMS MASCULINS

un appartement	an apartment
un arrêt de bus	a bus stop
un ascenseur	an elevator
le centre-ville	downtown
un dollar	a dollar
un escalier	stairs, a staircase
un étage	a floor
un immeuble	an apartment building
le logement	lodging, housing
le loyer	the rent
le rez-de-chaussée	the ground floor
un salon	a living room
un sous-sol	a basement

NOMS FÉMININS

la banlieue	the suburbs
la campagne	the country(side)
une chambre	a bedroom
une cuisine	a kitchen
une fenêtre	a window
une maison	a house
une pièce	a room
une porte	a door
une salle à manger	a dining room
une salle de bains	a bathroom
des toilettes	a restroom, a toilet
une ville	a city

ADJECTIFS

cher (chère)	expensive
confortable	comfortable
pratique	practical, convenient

DIVERS

à la campagne	in the country(side)
À quel étage?	On what floor?
au sous-sol	in the basement
au rez-de-chaussée	on the ground/first floor
au premier (deuxième...) étage	on the second (third ...) floor
cent	a/one hundred
dans une résidence universitaire	in a university dorm
en banlieue	in the suburbs
en centre-ville	downtown
en ville	in town
Je n'ai pas de...	I don't have ...
loin (de)	far (from)
mille	a/one thousand
un million (de)	a/one million
par mois	per month
(tout) près (de)	(very) near
téléphoner (à)	to phone
trop	too (much/many)
il/elle va	he/she is going, he/she goes

Pour les nombres ordinaux, voir la page 110.

COMPÉTENCE 2 🔊

Talking about your possessions

NOMS MASCULINS

un animal (*pl* des animaux)	an animal
un canapé	a couch
un CD	a CD
un chat	a cat
un chien	a dog
un DVD	a DVD
des effets personnels	personal belongings
un fauteuil	an armchair
un iPod	an iPod
un lecteur CD/DVD/Blu-ray	a CD/DVD/Blu-ray player
un ordinateur	a computer
un (ordinateur) portable	a laptop
un (téléphone) portable	a cell phone
un smartphone	a smartphone
un tableau (*pl* des tableaux)	a painting
un tapis	a rug
un vélo	a bicycle
des vêtements	clothes

NOMS FÉMININS

une chaîne hi-fi	an audio system
une chaise	a chair
une chose	a thing
une lampe	a lamp
une plante	a plant
une table	a table
une télé	a TV
une voiture	a car

PRÉPOSITIONS

à côté (de)	next to, beside
à droite (de)	to the right (of)
à gauche (de)	to the left (of)
dans	in
dans le coin (de)	in the corner (of)
de	of, from, about
derrière	behind
devant	in front of
en face (de)	across from, facing
entre	between
sous	under
sur	on

VERBES

arriver	to arrive
avoir	to have
chercher	to look for
fumer	to smoke
partager	to share

DIVERS

combien (de)	how many, how much
embêtant(e)	annoying
en ordre	in order, orderly
non plus	neither
partout	everywhere
Pas de problème.	No problem.
peut-être	maybe, perhaps
(bien) rangé(e)	neat, put away, straightened up
ton/ta/tes	your (sing. fam.)
tout	everything, all

COMPÉTENCE 3

Describing your room

NOMS MASCULINS

un adjectif	*an adjective*
un bureau (*pl* des bureaux)	*a desk*
un couloir	*a hall, a corridor*
un lit	*a bed*
des meubles	*furniture, furnishings*
un mur	*a wall*
un placard	*a closet*
un poster	*a poster*
un rideau (*pl* des rideaux)	*a curtain*

NOMS FÉMININS

une commode	*a dresser, a chest of drawers*
une couleur	*a color*
une couverture	*a (bed)cover, a blanket*
une étagère	*a bookcase, a shelf*
une vue	*a view*

ADJECTIFS POSSESSIFS

mon/ma/mes	*my*
ton/ta/tes	*your*
son/sa/ses	*his, her, its*
notre/nos	*our*
votre/vos	*your*
leur/leurs	*their*

EXPRESSIONS VERBALES

Ça a l'air bien.	*It seems nice.*
Ça te plaît.	*You like it.*
comme tu vois	*as you see*
espérer	*to hope*
indiquer	*to indicate*
laisser	*to leave*
montrer	*to show*
Viens voir!	*Come see!*

LES COULEURS

De quelle couleur est…?	*What color is…?*
De quelle couleur sont…?	*What color are…?*
beige	*beige*
blanc(he)	*white*
bleu(e)	*blue*
gris(e)	*gray*
jaune	*yellow*
marron	*brown*
noir(e)	*black*
orange	*orange*
rose	*pink*
rouge	*red*
vert(e)	*green*
violet(te)	*purple*

DIVERS

à sa place	*in its place*
au bout (de)	*at the end (of)*
chaque	*each*
en désordre	*in disorder, disorderly*
justement	*as a matter of fact, precisely, exactly*
par terre	*on the floor, on the ground*
préféré(e)	*favorite*
propre	*clean*
Quel bazar!	*What a mess!*
sale	*dirty*

COMPÉTENCE 4

Giving your address and phone number

NOMS MASCULINS

un code postal	*a zip code*
un État	*a state*
les États-Unis	*the United States*
un nom (de famille)	*a (sur/last)name, a noun*
un numéro de téléphone	*a telephone number*
un pays	*a country*
un prénom	*a first name*
des renseignements	*information*

NOMS FÉMININS

une adresse (mail)	*an (e-mail) address*
la Louisiane	*Louisiana*
une nationalité	*a nationality*
une province	*a province*
une rue	*a street*

DIVERS

ce (cet)/cette	*this, that*
ces	*these, those*
il/elle doit…	*he/she must…*
partagé(e)	*shared, divided*
poser une question	*to ask a question*
quel/quelle/quels/quelles	*which, what*
s'inscrire	*to register*
suivant(e)	*following*

En Amérique: En Louisiane
En famille

 iLrn Heinle Learning Center   Internet web search

🌐 www.cengagebrain.com   Pair work

▶ *Horizons* Video: Les Stagiaires   Group work

🔊 Audio

4

COMPÉTENCE

1 Describing your family
Ma famille

Describing feelings and appearance
*Les expressions avec **avoir***

Stratégies et Compréhension auditive
- **Pour mieux comprendre:** *Asking for clarification*
- **Compréhension auditive:** *La famille de Robert*

2 Saying where you go in your free time
Le temps libre

Saying where you are going
*Le verbe **aller**, la préposition **à** et le pronom **y***

Suggesting activities and telling people what to do
*Le pronom sujet **on** et l'impératif*

3 Saying what you are going to do
Le week-end prochain

Saying what you are going to do
Le futur immédiat

Saying when you are going to do something
Les dates

4 Planning how to get there
Les moyens de transport

Deciding how to get there and come back
*Les verbes **prendre** et **venir** et les moyens de transport*

Vidéoreprise *Les Stagiaires*

Lecture et Composition
- **Pour mieux lire:** *Using your knowledge of the world*
- **Lecture:** *Deux mots*
- **Pour mieux écrire:** *Visualizing your topic*
- **Composition:** *Ma famille*

Comparaisons culturelles *L'histoire des Cadiens*

Résumé de grammaire

Vocabulaire

EN AMÉRIQUE: EN LOUISIANE

Que savez-vous de la Louisiane francophone et de ses traditions? **Connaissez-vous** la cuisine ou la musique de cette région?

Il y a deux traditions francophones en Louisiane, **les Cadiens** et les Créoles. Les Cadiens sont les descendants des Acadiens déportés du Canada par les Anglais après 1755. Les Créoles sont les descendants des premiers **colons** français et européens, d'**immigrés** des îles caraïbes **ou encore** d'**esclaves échappés** de cette région.

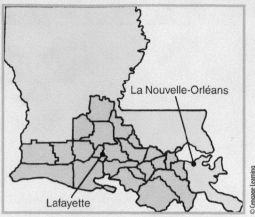

La ville de Lafayette est au cœur de la région cadienne, l'Acadiane, 22 paroisses dans la partie sud de la Louisiane. La Nouvelle-Orléans est au cœur de la région créole.

Les Cadiens et les Créoles sont fiers de leur cuisine.

Les Cadiens et les Créoles aiment bien manger et ils sont **fiers** de leurs cuisines. La cuisine cadienne est une cuisine **campagnarde** des bayous. La cuisine créole **tire ses racines** des familles aristocrates européennes de La Nouvelle-Orléans. Les deux cuisines sont similaires et beaucoup de **plats** sont à base d'une sauce appelée «un roux» (composée de **beurre** et de **farine**), de **riz** et de «la sainte trinité»: l'oignon, **le poivron vert** et le céleri. En général, les plats sont très **épicés** comme **les écrevisses** ou **les crevettes étouffées,** le jambalaya, le gumbo, **l'andouille** et **le boudin**.

Que savez-vous de *What do you know about* **Connaissez-vous** *Are you familiar with* **les Cadiens** *the Cajuns* **colons** *settlers, colonists* **immigrés** *immigrants* **ou encore** *as well as* **esclaves échappés** *escaped slaves* **au cœur de** *in the heart of* **paroisses** *parishes* **la partie sud** *the southern part* **fiers** *proud* **campagnarde** *country style* **tire ses racines** *gets its roots* **plats** *dishes* **beurre** *butter* **farine** *flour* **riz** *rice* **le poivron vert** *green bell pepper* **épicés** *spicy* **les écrevisses** *crawfish* **les crevettes** *shrimp* **étouffées** *stewed* **l'andouille** *andouille (a smoked pork sausage with garlic)* **le boudin** *blood sausage*

Les Cadiens et les Créoles aiment aussi la musique et la danse. Le zydeco et le swamp pop sont deux genres de musique originaires de la Louisiane. Dérivé du blues, de la musique country et du swing, les instruments traditionnels du zydeco sont le violon, l'accordéon, la guitare, l'harmonica et **le frottoir.** Le swamp pop est **un mélange** de zydeco, de rock et de boogie.

© Joe Raedle/Getty Images

Le frottoir et l'accordéon sont deux instruments traditionnels du zydeco.

Un «fais dodo» est une soirée dansante cadienne. Le nom «**fais dodo**» **vient de la berceuse:** *Fais dodo Colas mon p'tit frère.* **On chantait cette chanson pour que les enfants dorment pendant que** les parents dansaient et chantaient **aux bals** avec leurs amis.

© Philip Gould/ZUMAPRESS/Newscom

Un fais dodo est une soirée dansante cadienne.

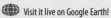

La Louisiane   🌐 Visit it live on Google Earth!

NOMBRE D'HABITANTS: **4 600 000 (les Louisianais) (Un peu moins de 195 000 parlent français, cadien [cajun] ou créole et parmi eux [among them] 180 000 parlent ces langues à la maison.)**

CAPITALE: **Bâton-Rouge**

Le savez-vous?

Que savez-vous de la Louisiane francophone? Avez-vous visité la Louisiane? Quel mot de la liste va avec chaque définition?

> **le zydeco   la sainte trinité   les Créoles
> les Cadiens   Lafayette   La Nouvelle-Orléans
> un fais dodo   un roux   le frottoir   l'Acadiane**

1. les descendants des habitants de la Louisiane avant son annexion par les États-Unis, principalement d'origines européennes et africaines
2. les descendants des Francophones expulsés du Canada par les Anglais au dix-huitième siècle *(century)*
3. la ville au cœur de la région créole
4. la ville au cœur de la région cadienne
5. les 22 paroisses de la région cadienne au sud de la Louisiane
6. un genre de musique influencé par le blues, la musique country et le swing et le plus souvent joué à l'accordéon
7. un instrument du zydeco
8. une sauce qui est la base des cuisines cadienne et créole
9. trois ingrédients de nombreux *(numerous)* plats cadiens et créoles: l'oignon, le poivron vert et le céleri
10. une soirée dansante cadienne

🌐 Search for a video and lyrics of a Zydeco song in French that you like. Also search for Cajun or Creole recipes from Louisiana. Share what you find with the class.

Laissez les bons temps rouler!

---

le frottoir *the rubboard*   **un mélange** *a mix*   **fais dodo** *go to sleep*   **vient de la berceuse** *comes from the lullaby*   **On chantait cette chanson pour que les enfants dorment pendant que** *People used to sing this song so the children would sleep while*   **aux bals** *at dances*   **Laissez les bons temps rouler!** *Let the good times roll!* (regional)

Describing your family

MA FAMILLE

Note *culturelle*

En 1916, l'État de Louisiane exige que la scolarité se fasse *(requires that education be done)* en anglais. L'anglais commence alors à être la langue prédominante chez les jeunes. Plus de 90 % de la population née *(born)* en Acadiane avant cette époque est bilingue français-anglais, mais moins de 10 % de leurs petits-enfants *(grandchildren)* parlent français. Certains Américains voudraient faire de l'anglais la seule langue officielle aux États-Unis. Que pensez-vous de cette idée?

Vocabulaire supplémentaire

adopté(e) *adopted*
un beau-frère *a brother-in-law*
une belle-sœur *a sister-in-law*
l'aîné (l'aînée) *the oldest child*
le cadet (la cadette) *the middle child, the younger child*
le benjamin (la benjamine) *the youngest child (of more than two)*
un demi-frère (une demi-sœur) *a stepbrother, a half-brother (a stepsister, a half-sister)*
un ex-mari (une ex-femme) *an ex-husband (an ex-wife)*
un fils unique (une fille unique) *an only child*
des petits-enfants (un petit-fils, une petite-fille) *grandchildren (a grandson, a granddaughter)*
porter des lentilles *(f) to wear contact lenses*

Note *de vocabulaire*

Use **avoir l'air** (+ *adjective*) to say someone *looks young, happy*…
Il a l'air sympa. *(He looks nice.)*. Use **ressembler à** to say a person *looks like* someone: **Je ressemble à ma mère.** *(I look like my mother.)*

Robert et ses amis **ont l'intention de** passer une semaine de **vacances** *(f)* chez **le père** de Robert à Lafayette. Robert parle de sa famille.

Voici ma famille. Mes parents sont divorcés maintenant. Ils ont quatre **enfants,** trois **garçons** et **une fille.**

(mes grands-parents)

mon grand-père
(Il est **décédé**
maintenant.)

ma grand-mère

(mes parents)

ma mère
mon père
mon oncle   ma tante

moi
mes frères   ma sœur   son mari
mon cousin   ma cousine

le **fils** et la fille de ma sœur
(mon neveu et ma nièce)

Mon père s'appelle Luke.
Il **a (environ) 50 ans** *(m).*
Il est **encore** jeune, mais il **a l'air** plus âgé.
Il est **de taille moyenne.**
Il **a les cheveux courts** et gris.

Il **a les yeux** *(m)* marron.
Il a **une barbe** grise et une moustache.
Il **porte des lunettes** *(f).*

Et vous? Comment êtes-vous?

J'ai les yeux **noirs** / marron / **noisette** / verts / bleus / gris.
J'ai les cheveux courts / **mi-longs** / longs et noirs / **bruns** / **châtains** / auburn / blonds / gris / blancs / **roux.**

avoir l'intention de *to intend to*   **les vacances** *vacation*   **le père** *the father*   **des enfants** *children*   **un garçon** *a boy*   **une fille** *a girl, a daughter*   **décédé(e)** *deceased*   **un fils** *a son*   **avoir… ans** *to be… years old*   **environ** *about*   **encore** *still*   **avoir l'air… to look, to seem…*   **de taille moyenne** *of medium height*   **avoir les cheveux…** *to have… hair*   **court(e)** *short*   **avoir les yeux…** *to have… eyes*   **une barbe** *a beard*   **porter** *to wear*   **des lunettes** *glasses*   **noirs** *(with eyes) very dark brown, almost black*   **noisette** *(inv) hazel*   **mi-longs** *(with hair) shoulder-length*   **bruns** *(with hair) medium to dark brown*   **châtains** *(with hair) light to medium brown*   **roux** *(with hair) red*

🔊
2-2

Robert parle de sa famille avec Thomas.

THOMAS: Vous êtes combien dans ta famille?
ROBERT: Nous sommes sept: mon père, **ma belle-mère,** ma mère, mes deux frères, ma sœur et moi. Ma sœur est mariée et elle habite à La Nouvelle-Orléans.
THOMAS: Elle est plus jeune ou **plus âgée que** toi? Quel âge a-t-elle?
ROBERT: Elle a 28 ans.
THOMAS: Comment s'appelle-t-elle?
ROBERT: Elle s'appelle Sarah.

A **La famille.** Donnez l'équivalent féminin.

EXEMPLE le frère   **la sœur**

1. le père
2. l'oncle
3. le garçon
4. le neveu
5. le beau-père
6. le cousin
7. le fils
8. le grand-père

B **Généalogie.** Complétez les phrases.

EXEMPLE Les parents de mon père, ce sont **mes grands-parents.**

1. Le père de mon père, c'est _____. Sa femme, c'est _____.
2. La sœur de ma mère, c'est _____. Son mari, c'est _____. Leurs enfants sont _____. Leur fils, c'est _____ et leur fille, c'est _____.
3. Le fils de ma sœur, c'est _____. Sa fille, c'est _____.

C **Mon meilleur ami.** Changez les mots en italique pour décrire votre meilleur ami.

1. Il s'appelle *Emmitt / Chuong / ???* et il a *18 / 25 / 38 / 45 / ???* ans.
2. Il est *grand / petit / de taille moyenne.*
3. Il a les cheveux *longs / mi-longs / courts* et *blonds / noirs / ???.*
4. Il a les yeux *marron / gris / ???.*
5. Il a l'air *intellectuel / sportif / jeune / ???.*

D **Entretien.** Posez ces questions à votre partenaire. Ensuite, changez de rôles.

1. Vous êtes combien dans ta famille? Tu as des frères et sœurs? (Ils sont plus âgés ou moins âgés que toi?)
2. Avec quel membre de la famille préfères-tu passer du temps? Comment s'appelle-t-il/elle? Quel âge a-t-il/elle? Il/Elle est grand(e), petit(e) ou de taille moyenne? Il/Elle a les yeux de quelle couleur? Il/Elle a les cheveux longs, mi-longs ou courts? Il/Elle a les cheveux de quelle couleur? Il/Elle a l'air plutôt sportif (sportive) ou plutôt intellectuel(le)? Il/Elle porte des lunettes?

À VOUS!

Avec un(e) partenaire, relisez à haute voix la conversation entre Thomas et Robert. Ensuite, adaptez la conversation pour parler d'un membre de votre famille.

iLrn 🌐 You can find a list of the new words from this **Compétence** on page 174 and access the audio online.

---

une belle-mère (un beau-père, des beaux-parents) *a stepmother / a mother-in-law (a stepfather / a father-in-law, stepparents / in-laws)*   **plus âgé(e) que** *older than*

DESCRIBING FEELINGS AND APPEARANCE

✔ **Pour vérifier**

1. How do you say *I'm hungry? I'm thirsty? I'm hot? I'm cold? I'm sleepy? I'm afraid? I'm right? I'm never wrong? I need to stay home? I feel like staying home? I intend to stay home?*

2. How do you say *How old is he? He's 24? He has short black hair and brown eyes? He seems nice? He has a black beard, a mustache, and glasses?*

Note *de vocabulaire*

1. Use **les** when talking about someone's hair and eyes. **Les cheveux** and **les yeux** are both masculine plural, so follow them with an adjective in the masculine plural form. **Ma sœur a les cheveux bruns et les yeux verts. Auburn, marron,** and **noisette,** however, are invariable.

2. Brown eyes can be **noirs** *(almost black or dark brown)* or **marron** *(light to medium brown)*. Brown hair can be **bruns** *(dark or medium brown)* or **châtains** *(light to medium brown)*. The words **brun, roux, auburn,** and **châtain** are mainly used to describe someone's hair.

3. You can say that someone is *blond* or *a blond, brunette* or *a brunette,* or *red-headed* or *a red-head,* using **blond(e), brun(e),** or **roux (rousse). Elle est rousse, mais sa sœur est blonde.** *She's a red-head, but her sister's a blonde.*

4. To say you are *very hot / cold / hungry . . .* use *très.* **J'ai *très* chaud.**

Vocabulaire supplémentaire

avoir un tatouage / un piercing
avoir un bouc *to have a goatee*
avoir des pattes *(f)* to have sideburns
être chauve *to be bald*
avoir la tête rasée *to have a shaved head*

🌐 **Sélection musicale.** Search the Web for the song **"J'ai besoin d'un chum"** by Céline Dion to enjoy a musical selection containing structures and vocabulary from this *Compétence.*

Les expressions avec **avoir**

Use these expressions with **avoir** to describe people or say how they feel.

avoir (environ)... ans	*to be (around) . . . years old*	avoir faim	*to be hungry*
		avoir soif	*to be thirsty*
avoir l'air...	*to look . . ., to seem . . .*	avoir froid	*to be cold*
avoir une barbe / une moustache / des lunettes	*to have a beard / a mustache / glasses*	avoir chaud	*to be hot*
		avoir raison	*to be right*
		avoir tort	*to be wrong*
avoir les yeux bleus / verts...	*to have blue / green . . . eyes*	avoir peur (de)	*to be afraid (of)*
avoir les cheveux longs / roux...	*to have long / red . . . hair*	avoir sommeil	*to be sleepy*

— Mon fils **a peur** des chiens.
— Quel **âge a**-t-il? Il **a l'air** très jeune.
— Tu **as raison.** Il **a quatre ans.**

— *My son is afraid of dogs.*
— *How old is he? He looks very young.*
— *You're right. He's four.*

Notice these three expressions that also use **avoir** in French.

avoir besoin de (d') + noun or infinitive	*to need* + noun or infinitive
avoir envie de (d') + noun or infinitive	*to feel like* + noun or verb
avoir l'intention de (d') + infinitive	*to intend* + infinitive

J'**ai besoin de** la voiture.
J'**ai envie de** sortir.
J'**ai l'intention de** rentrer à midi.

I need the car.
I feel like going out.
I intend to return at noon.

Tu **as besoin de** manger?
Tu **as envie de manger** un sandwich?

Do you need to eat?
You feel like eating a sandwich?

A **Comment est-il?** Répondez aux questions pour faire une description du meilleur ami de Robert.

1. Comment s'appelle-t-il? Quel âge a-t-il?

2. Il a les cheveux de quelle couleur? Il a les cheveux longs ou courts? Il a les yeux de quelle couleur?

3. Il a une barbe? Il porte des lunettes? Il a l'air sympa?

Maintenant, changez la description précédente d'Antoine pour parler de vous.

Antoine, 20 ans

© Cengage Learning

EXEMPLE Je m'appelle Pat. J'ai 25 ans. J'ai les cheveux...

B **Les activités de Robert.** Quelles sont les activités que Robert a probablement envie de faire? Quelles sont les activités qu'il a probablement besoin de faire?

EXEMPLES faire ses devoirs **Il a besoin de faire ses devoirs.**
regarder la télé **Il a envie de regarder la télé.**

1. aller au cinéma   **3.** aller travailler   **5.** sortir avec des amis
2. aller prendre un verre **4.** étudier   **6.** faire la lessive *(the laundry)*

 Maintenant, circulez dans la classe et trouvez quelqu'un qui a l'intention de faire les activités mentionnées ce week-end.

EXEMPLE faire tes devoirs
— **As-tu l'intention de faire tes devoirs ce week-end?**
— **Oui, j'ai l'intention de faire mes devoirs dimanche soir.**

C **Moi, j'ai...** Utilisez une expression avec **avoir** de la liste à la page précédente. Faites attention au contexte.

EXEMPLE Je voudrais aller prendre un verre.   **J'ai soif.**

1. Brrrr... Fermez la fenêtre.   **4.** J'ai envie de manger quelque chose.
2. Ah! C'est un serpent!   **5.** Je voudrais un coca.
3. Voilà. Ma réponse est correcte.   **6.** J'ai besoin de dormir.

D **Qu'est-ce qu'ils ont?** Aujourd'hui, la fille d'une amie fête ses cinq ans *(is celebrating her fifth birthday)*. Que dit sa mère? Utilisez une expression avec **avoir.**

1. Ma fille... aujourd'hui.   **2.** Ses amis...   **3.** Mon frère...   **4.** Mes cousins...

5. Mon mari et moi, nous...   **6.** Moi, j'...   **7.** Le chien de mon fils...   **8.** Tu... de faire ça au chien!

Line art on this page: © Cengage Learning

E **Entretien.** Interviewez votre partenaire.

1. Qu'est-ce que tu as envie de faire ce week-end? Qu'est-ce que tu as besoin de faire? Qu'est-ce que tu as l'intention de faire dimanche soir?

2. Tu as faim maintenant? Tu as soif? Est-ce que tu as l'intention de manger quelque chose après le cours? As-tu sommeil maintenant? As-tu l'intention de dormir après le cours?

STRATÉGIES ET COMPRÉHENSION AUDITIVE

POUR MIEUX COMPRENDRE: Asking for clarification

When you do not understand something, it is useful to be able to ask for clarification. You already know three ways to do this: by asking for something to be repeated, by asking what a word means, or by asking how a word is spelled.

> Comment? Répétez, s'il vous plaît.
> Je ne comprends pas. Qu'est-ce que ça veut dire, **belle-sœur**?
> Ça s'écrit comment?

A Je ne comprends pas. Listen to three conversations. In each, which method is used to ask for clarification: **a, b,** or **c**?

2-3

a. asking for something to be repeated (**Comment? Répétez, s'il vous plaît.**)

b. asking the meaning of a word (**Qu'est-ce que ça veut dire…?**)

c. asking the spelling of a word (**Ça s'écrit comment?**)

Line art on this page: © Cengage Learning

B Comment? Listen to these three other scenes, in which one of the speakers is having difficulty understanding. In each case, what could he or she say to ask for clarification?

2-4

Compréhension auditive: *La famille de Robert*

🔊
2-5
Robert is describing his family to a friend who is studying French. Use what you know and your ability to guess logically to help you understand what he says. The first time, listen only for the number of times his friend asks for clarification.

A **La famille de Robert.** Écoutez encore une fois *(again)* la description de la famille de Robert et complétez l'arbre généalogique *(family tree)* avec les prénoms des membres de sa famille.

Robert

© Cengage Learning

B **C'est qui?** Écoutez encore une fois la description de la famille de Robert et répondez aux questions.

1. Qui habite à Lafayette?
2. Qui habite à Atlanta?
3. Qui habite à La Nouvelle-Orléans?
4. Qui est marié?
5. Qui est divorcé?
6. Comment dit-on **pédiatre** en anglais?
7. Dans la famille de Robert, qui est pédiatre?
8. Quelle est la profession du père de Robert?

Saying where you go in your free time

LE TEMPS LIBRE

Vocabulaire supplémentaire

à la synagogue
à la mosquée
au temple *to church (Protestant), to temple*
au lac *to the lake*
au bar

Note *de grammaire*

1. Use **pour** before infinitives to say *in order to*. In English, *in order to* may be shortened to just *to: One goes to the bookstore **(in order) to** buy books.* **On va à la librairie** *pour* **acheter des livres.**
2. With the verb **retrouver**, say whom you are meeting: **Je retrouve *mes amis* au café.** To say *We meet (each other) at the café,* use **On *se* retrouve au café.**
3. Notice the accent spelling change in the conjugation of **acheter** *(to buy)*.

j'achète	nous achetons
tu achètes	vous achetez
il/elle achète	ils/elles achètent

4. The name of a place generally follows the type of place. For example, for *Tinseltown Cinema,* say **le cinéma Tinseltown.**

Chez vous, où est-ce qu'**on va** pour passer **son temps libre**?

On aime beaucoup les activités culturelles et **de temps en temps,** on va...

au musée pour voir **une exposition**

au théâtre pour voir **une pièce**

à un concert ou à un festival de musique

On aime aussi **les activités de plein air** et on va souvent...

au parc pour faire du jogging

à la piscine pour nager

à la plage pour **prendre un bain de soleil**

Pour **retrouver des amis,** on va...

à un match de basket

en boîte

à l'église

Pour faire du shopping, on va...

Et pour **acheter** des livres, on va...

au centre commercial

dans les petits magasins

à la librairie

Line art on this page: © Cengage Learning

on va *one goes*   **son temps libre** *one's free time*   **de temps en temps** *from time to time*   **une exposition** *an exhibit*
une pièce *a play*   **les activités de plein air** *outdoor activities*   **prendre un bain de soleil** *to sunbathe*   **retrouver des**
amis *to meet friends*   **acheter** *to buy*

🔊 2-6 Robert et Gabriel parlent de leurs projets *(m)* pour ce soir.

GABRIEL: **On sort** ce soir?

ROBERT: D'accord. On va au cinéma?

GABRIEL: Ah, non, je préfère **connaître** un peu la région. **On dit que** la cuisine **cadienne** est **extra**! Allons **plutôt** au restaurant.

ROBERT: D'accord. Allons dîner au restaurant Préjean. C'est un très bon restaurant où **on sert** les spécialités de la région, et il y a un orchestre cadien. Ça te dit?

GABRIEL: Oui, bonne idée. Allons au restaurant et après, allons écouter de la musique zydeco.

ROBERT: Pas de problème. **On peut** toujours **trouver** des concerts ici!

👫 **A Où va-t-on pour...** Demandez à un(e) partenaire où on va pour faire les choses suivantes.

EXEMPLE lire
— **Où est-ce qu'on va pour lire?**
— **On va à la bibliothèque.**

1. dîner
2. voir une pièce
3. retrouver des amis
4. prendre un verre
5. faire du shopping
6. nager
7. voir une exposition
8. prendre un bain de soleil
9. acheter des livres
10. faire du jogging

au restaurant
au musée
à la piscine
au café
au centre commercial
à l'église
au parc
au théâtre
à la plage
à la librairie
à la bibliothèque

👫 **B Entretien.** Interviewez votre partenaire.

1. Où aimes-tu passer ton temps libre? Qu'est-ce que tu aimes faire après les cours? le week-end?
2. Où aimes-tu retrouver tes amis? Où aimez-vous aller ensemble? Aimez-vous les activités de plein air? Préférez-vous aller à la plage, à la piscine ou au parc? Aimes-tu nager? prendre un bain de soleil?
3. Aimes-tu faire du shopping? Préfères-tu acheter des vêtements, des livres, des DVD ou des CD? Dans quel magasin aimes-tu faire du shopping? Ce magasin est au centre commercial? C'est un magasin cher? Aimes-tu faire des achats en ligne *(buy things online)*?
4. Aimes-tu les activités culturelles? Préfères-tu aller au musée, au théâtre ou à un concert? Préfères-tu aller voir une pièce, une exposition ou un film?

👫 **À VOUS!**

Avec un(e) partenaire, relisez à haute voix la conversation entre Gabriel et Robert. Ensuite, imaginez que vous êtes chez un(e) ami(e) dans une autre ville et que vous parlez de vos projets pour ce soir. Décidez ensemble d'un type de cuisine (mexicaine, italienne, française, japonaise, chinoise...) et d'un genre de musique (du rock, du jazz, du hip-hop...) populaire dans votre région et refaites la conversation pour parler de vos projets.

iLrn 🌐 You can find a list of the new words from this *Compétence* on page 174 and access the audio online.

On sort...? *How about going out...?* **connaître** *to know, to get to know* **On dit que** *They say that* **cadien(ne)** *Cajun* **extra(ordinaire)** *great* **plutôt** *instead, rather* **on sert** *they serve* (**servir** *to serve*) **On peut** *One can* (**pouvoir** *can, may, to be able*) **trouver** *to find*

SAYING WHERE YOU ARE GOING

✔ **Pour vérifier**

1. What are the forms of **aller**?

2. With which forms of the definite article does **à** contract? What are the contracted forms? With which forms does it not contract? How do you say *to the café*? *to the library*? *to the university*? *to the students*?

3. What does the word **y** mean and how do you pronounce it? What happens to words like **je** and **ne** before **y**?

4. Where do you place **y** in a sentence where there is a verb followed by an infinitive? Where do you place it otherwise?

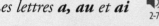 **Grammar Tutorials**

Le verbe *aller,* la préposition *à* et le pronom *y*

To talk about going places, use the irregular verb **aller** *(to go).*

ALLER *(to go)*	
je **vais**	nous ‿z **allons**
tu **vas**	vous ‿z **allez**
il/elle **va**	ils/elles **vont**

Use the preposition **à** *(to, at, in)* to say where you are going. When **à** falls before **le** or **les,** the two words contract to **au** and **aux.**

PREPOSITION À + LE, LA, L', LES	
à + le → au	Je vais **au** cinéma.
à + la → à la	Je vais **à la** librairie.
à + l' → à l'	Gabriel va **à l'**université.
à + les → aux	Robert va **aux** festivals de musique de la région.

The pronoun **y** *(there)* is used to avoid repeating the name of the place where one is going. Pronounce it like the letter **i.** Treat **y** as a vowel sound and use elision and liaison before it.

Je vais **au parc.** J'**y** vais avec mes cousins. Nous ‿z **y** allons à trois heures.

Y is generally placed *immediately* before the verb. It goes before the infinitive if there is one. If not, it goes before the conjugated verb.

— Il voudrait aller **au cinéma**?
— Oui, il voudrait **y** aller.

— Ils vont **au musée**?
— Oui, ils **y** vont.

In the negative, **y** remains *immediately* before the infinitive or the conjugated verb.

— Tu voudrais aller **au parc**?
— Non, je n'ai pas envie d'**y aller.**

— Tu **y** vas aujourd'hui?
— Non, je n'**y vais** pas aujourd'hui.

Whenever you use **aller** to talk about going somewhere and don't name the place you are going, use **y** even when the word *there* would not be stated in English.

On **y** va? *Shall we go (there)?*   J'**y** vais. *I'm going (there).*

PRONONCIATION

ⓘⓛⁿ *Prononcez bien!* See Modules 23 and 16.

Les lettres *a, au et ai* 🔊 2-7

- Pronounce **a** or **à** with the mouth wide open as in the word *father,* but with the tongue slightly higher and closer to the front of the mouth.

  Ton *a*mi v*a* *à* P*a*ris.   Tu v*a*s *à* P*a*ris *a*vec t*a* c*a*mar*a*de?

- Pronounce **au** like the **o** in **nos.**

  Ton beau-père va *au* rest*au*rant?   Les *au*tres y vont *au*ssi?

- Pronounce the **ai** of **je vais** like the **ais** of **français.** Be sure to distinguish this sound from the **a** of **tu vas** or **il va.**

  Je v*ai*s au café.   Tu n'y vas jam*ai*s?

A **Prononcez bien!** D'abord, pratiquez la prononciation des formes de la préposition **à** dans la troisième colonne. Ensuite, formez des phrases logiques en vous servant d'un élément de chaque colonne.

EXEMPLE Mon ami a envie de voir un film. Il va au cinéma.

Mon ami a envie de voir un film. Il...			piscine
Toi, tu as envie de nager. Tu...	allez		arrêt de bus
Nous avons soif. Nous...	vais	au	librairie
Mes amis vont en cours. Ils...	va	à la	café
Vous voudriez acheter un livre. Vous...	allons	à l'	université
Mon frère aime écouter de la musique. Il...	vas	aux	cinéma
Je prends (am taking) le bus ce matin. Je...	vont		concerts de ses artistes préférés

B **On sort.** Robert parle avec Thomas de ses amis et de sa famille. Complétez ses phrases. Utilisez la forme convenable du verbe **aller** et de la préposition **à** (**au, à la, à l', aux**).

EXEMPLE Je vais à la piscine.

la piscine

la piscine
1. Toi et moi, nous...

l'église
2. Mes cousins...

la bibliothèque
3. Toi, tu...

l'université
4. Ma sœur...

le musée
5. Gabriel et son frère...

la librairie
6. Mon père...

le parc
7. Notre chien...

les matchs de basket de l'université
8. Le week-end, mes amis...

Line art on this page: © Cengage Learning

C **Où aiment-ils aller?** Demandez à votre partenaire si ces personnes aiment aller aux endroits indiqués. Il/Elle va utiliser le pronom **y** dans ses réponses et va aussi dire si les personnes y vont souvent, rarement...

EXEMPLE tu: au musée
— **Tu aimes aller au musée?**
— **Oui, j'aime y aller. J'y vais souvent / quelquefois...**
  Non, je n'aime pas y aller. Je n'y vais jamais.

1. tu: à l'opéra, à un match de basket

2. tes amis et toi: en boîte, au centre commercial

3. ton meilleur ami (ta meilleure amie): au parc, à l'église

4. tes parents: à la piscine, à un concert de musique hip-hop

SUGGESTING ACTIVITIES AND TELLING PEOPLE WHAT TO DO

✔ *Pour vérifier*

1. What are the three possible uses of the pronoun **on**? What form of the verb do you always use with **on**?

2. How do you form the imperative (commands)? With which verbs do you drop the final **s** in the **tu** form of the imperative?

3. What are the command forms of **avoir** and **être**? How do you tell a friend: *Be on time! Be good! Let's be calm! Have confidence! Let's have patience!*

(iLrn Grammar Tutorials

🌐 **Sélection musicale.** Search the Web for the song "**Toi plus moi**" by Grégoire to enjoy a musical selection containing these structures.

*Le pronom sujet **on** et l'impératif*

Use **on** as the subject of a sentence when you are referring to people in general *(one, people, they)*. Consider the difference between these sentences.

À Paris, **on** parle français. *In Paris, **they** speak French.* (general group)
Tes amis? **Ils** parlent français? *Your friends? Do **they** speak French?* (specific people)

The pronoun **on** is also often used instead of **nous** to say *we*. **On** takes the same form of the verb as **il** and **elle**, regardless of its translation in English.

Gabriel et moi, **on** aime sortir. *Gabriel and I, we like to go out.*

You can propose doing something with someone *(How about . . . ? Shall we . . . ?)* by asking a question with **on**.

On va au cinéma? *How about going to the movies?*
Qu'est-ce qu'**on** fait ce soir? *What shall we do this evening?*

The imperative (command form) can also be used to make suggestions, as well as to tell someone else to do something. Use the imperative as follows.

- To make suggestions with *Let's . . .*, use the **nous** form of the verb, without the pronoun **nous.**

  Allons au cinéma! *Let's go to the movies!*
  Ne **restons** pas à la maison! *Let's not stay home!*

- To give instructions, or to tell someone to do something, use either the **tu** form of the verb or the **vous** form of the verb, as appropriate, without the pronoun. In **tu** form commands, drop the final **s** of **-er** verbs and of **aller.** However, as you learn other verbs that do not end in **-er,** do not drop the **s** in the commands.

  Va à la bibliothèque! / **Allez** à la bibliothèque! *Go to the library!*
  Ne **mange** pas ça! / Ne **mangez** pas ça! *Don't eat that!*

The verbs **être** and **avoir** have irregular command forms.

ÊTRE (be . . .)		AVOIR (have . . .)	
Sois sage!	*Be good!*	**Aie** confiance!	*Have confidence!*
Soyons calmes!	*Let's be calm!*	**Ayons** de la patience!	*Let's have patience!*
Soyez à l'heure!	*Be on time!*	**Ayez** confiance!	*Have confidence!*

 A **Endroits logiques.** En groupes, pensez à des endroits *(places)* où on fait les choses suivantes. Le groupe qui pense au plus grand nombre d'endroits logiques gagne.

EXEMPLE On y écoute de la musique.
On écoute de la musique à un concert, à un festival de musique, dans sa voiture, sur son iPod, à la radio...

1. On y étudie.
2. On y va pour faire de l'exercice.
3. On y retrouve ses amis.
4. On y achète des livres.
5. On y regarde un film.
6. On y mange.

👥 B Tes amis et toi? Posez ces questions à votre partenaire. Il/Elle va répondre en utilisant le pronom **on**.

EXEMPLE —Tes amis et toi, vous préférez aller à quel restaurant?
—**On préfère aller au restaurant Vermilionville.**

1. Tes amis et toi, quand est-ce que vous aimez sortir ensemble?
2. Est-ce que vous allez souvent au cinéma ensemble?
3. Est-ce que vous regardez souvent des DVD ensemble?
4. Dans quel restaurant est-ce que vous mangez le plus souvent?
5. Est-ce que vous parlez beaucoup au téléphone?

👥 C On... ? Un(e) ami(e) vous invite *(invites you)* à faire ces choses. Répondez à ses suggestions selon vos goûts *(according to your tastes)*.

EXEMPLE —On joue à des jeux vidéo?
—**D'accord. Jouons à des jeux vidéo.**
Non, ne jouons pas à des jeux vidéo.
Regardons plutôt un DVD.

1.
2.
3.
4.

Line art on this page: © Cengage Learning

D Pour réussir. Donnez des conseils à un groupe de nouveaux étudiants. Utilisez l'impératif.

EXEMPLE préparer les examens avec d'autres étudiants
Préparez les examens avec d'autres étudiants.
Ne préparez pas les examens avec d'autres étudiants.

1. aller à tous les cours
2. être à l'heure
3. avoir confiance
4. copier sur un autre étudiant
5. aller en boîte tous les soirs
6. avoir peur de parler au prof

👥 Maintenant, avec un(e) partenaire, préparez cinq autres conseils pour un groupe de nouveaux étudiants.

E Des parents difficiles. Des parents disent à leur fils adolescent qu'il doit faire *(must do)* l'une des choses indiquées et qu'il ne doit pas faire l'autre. Qu'est-ce qu'ils lui disent? Utilisez l'impératif et soyez logique!

EXEMPLE arrêter *(to stop)* de fumer / fumer dans la maison
Arrête de fumer. Ne fume pas dans la maison.

1. être plus propre / laisser tes vêtements partout
2. rester au lit tout le temps / être plus dynamique
3. jouer à des jeux vidéo tout le temps / avoir un peu d'ambition
4. aller au café tous les jours / réviser tes cours
5. manger toujours la même chose / avoir un peu d'imagination

Saying what you are going to do

LE WEEK-END PROCHAIN

Robert va passer le week-end prochain à La Nouvelle-Orléans. Et vous? Qu'est-ce que vous allez faire?

Je vais… / Je ne vais pas…

quitter la maison **tôt**   **partir** pour le week-end   visiter une autre ville

faire un tour de la ville   aller **boire** quelque chose au café   rentrer **tard**

2-8

Robert et Thomas **font des projets** *(m)* pour le week-end prochain.

THOMAS: Qu'est-ce qu'on fait ce week-end?

ROBERT: J'ai beaucoup de projets pour ce week-end. Jeudi matin, on va partir très tôt pour La Nouvelle-Orléans. **D'abord,** on va visiter la ville. **Ensuite,** on va **aller voir** ma sœur. On va **passer la soirée** chez elle. Vendredi, on va faire un tour du **Vieux Carré.** On va rentrer à Lafayette assez tard.

THOMAS: Et samedi?

ROBERT: À midi, on va déjeuner au restaurant Prudhomme. C'est un restaurant célèbre pour sa cuisine régionale. **Et puis,** le soir, on va aller à Eunice, une petite ville pas loin de Lafayette. Il y a une soirée de musique et de folklore cadiens tous les samedis.

THOMAS: **Génial!**

Le week-end prochain *Next weekend*   **quitter** *to leave*   **tôt** *early*   **partir** *to leave*   **boire** *to drink*   **tard** *late*   **faire des projets** *to make plans*   **D'abord** *First*   **Ensuite** *Then, Afterwards*   **aller voir** *to go see, to visit* (a person)   **passer la soirée** *to spend the evening*   **le Vieux Carré** *the French Quarter*   **Et puis** *And then*   **Génial!** *Great!*

A Le week-end prochain. Est-ce que vous allez faire les choses suivantes samedi prochain?

EXEMPLE rester à la maison

Je vais rester à la maison. / Je ne vais pas rester à la maison.

1. quitter la maison tôt
2. partir pour la journée
3. faire un tour de la ville
4. visiter une autre ville
5. aller voir des amis
6. retrouver des amis en ville

7. aller boire quelque chose
8. dîner au restaurant
9. rentrer tard
10. passer la soirée à la maison
11. inviter des amis à la maison
12. regarder des DVD

B Entretien. Interviewez votre partenaire.

1. Quel(s) jour(s) est-ce que tu quittes la maison tôt? D'habitude, à quelle heure est-ce que tu quittes la maison le lundi? le mardi? Est-ce que tu rentres tard quelquefois? Quels jours est-ce que tu rentres tard? À quelle heure est-ce que tu rentres?

2. Est-ce que tu aimes partir quelquefois pour le week-end? Est-ce que tu aimes aller voir des amis qui habitent dans une autre ville? Quelle ville aimes-tu visiter? Qu'est-ce que tu aimes faire dans cette ville?

3. Vas-tu souvent au café? Qu'est-ce que tu aimes boire le matin? Et quand tu as très soif? Et quand tu as froid? Et quand tu as chaud?

4. En général, quel(s) jour(s) est-ce que tu passes la journée à la maison? et la soirée? Est-ce que tu passes toute la journée chez toi de temps en temps?

© Leon Ritter/Shutterstock.com

À VOUS!

Avec un(e) partenaire, relisez à haute voix la conversation entre Thomas et Robert. Ensuite, imaginez qu'un(e) ami(e) passe le week-end chez vous et que vous parlez de vos projets pour vendredi, samedi et dimanche.

iLrn You can find a list of the new words from this *Compétence* on page 175 and access the audio online.

SAYING WHAT YOU ARE GOING TO DO

✔ **Pour vérifier**

1. How do you say what you are going to do? How do you say what you are not going to do? How would you say *I'm going to stay home? I'm not going to study? I'm going to go to the mall?*

2. Where do you place the pronoun **y** in the immediate future?

3. What is the immediate future form of **il y a**? How do you negate it?

4. How do you say *today? tomorrow? this morning? tomorrow morning? this month? next month? this year? next year?*

ⓘ**Lrn Grammar Tutorials**

🌐 **Sélection musicale.** Search the Web for the song "**Je vais changer le monde**" by Jean-François Bastien to enjoy a musical selection containing this structure.

Le futur immédiat

To say what you *are going to do,* use a form of **aller** followed by an infinitive.

je vais étudier	nous allons rentrer
tu vas travailler	vous allez sortir
il/elle/on va lire	ils/elles vont nager

—Qu'est-ce que tu **vas faire** demain?

—Je **vais sortir.**

— *What* ***are you going to do*** *tomorrow?*

— *I'm going to go out.*

In the negative, put the **ne... pas** around the conjugated form of **aller.**

Je **ne vais pas** sortir ce soir.   *I'm not going to go out tonight.*

Place the pronoun **y,** when needed, *immediately before* the infinitive.

Ma sœur va aller en boîte, mais moi, je **ne vais pas y aller.**

Il y a becomes **il va y avoir** when saying *there is/are going to be.*

Il va y avoir un concert demain. **Il ne va pas y avoir** de film.

Use these expressions to tell when you are going to do something.

maintenant *now*	**plus tard** *later*
aujourd'hui *today*	**demain** *tomorrow*
ce matin *this morning*	**demain matin** *tomorrow morning*
cet après-midi *this afternoon*	**demain après-midi** *tomorrow afternoon*
ce soir *tonight / this evening*	**demain soir** *tomorrow night / evening*
lundi *Monday*	**lundi prochain** *next Monday*
ce week-end *this weekend*	**le week-end prochain** *next weekend*
cette semaine *this week*	**la semaine prochaine** *next week*
ce mois-ci *this month*	**le mois prochain** *next month*
cette année *this year*	**l'année prochaine** *next year*

A **Que vont-ils faire?** Dites ou demandez si ces personnes vont faire les choses indiquées aux moments donnés.

> **EXEMPLE** Ce soir, moi, je **vais** travailler.
> Ce soir, moi, je **ne vais pas** travailler.

1. Ce soir, je _____ rentrer tard.

2. Demain matin, je _____ quitter la maison tôt.

3. Samedi prochain, mes amis et moi _____ passer la soirée ensemble.

4. Le week-end prochain, mon meilleur ami (ma meilleure amie) _____ aller voir sa famille.

5. La semaine prochaine, en cours de français, nous _____ avoir un (d')examen.

6. Les cours universitaires _____ se terminer *(to end)* le mois prochain.

7. *[au professeur]* L'année prochaine, vous _____ continuer à travailler ici?

8. *[à un(e) autre étudiant(e)]* L'année prochaine, tu _____ étudier ici?

B Et ensuite? Qu'est-ce que ces personnes vont faire **d'abord** et qu'est-ce qu'elles vont faire **ensuite**?

EXEMPLE   moi, je: manger / préparer le dîner
D'abord, moi, je vais préparer le dîner et ensuite, je vais manger.

1. nous: travailler tout l'après-midi / aller prendre un verre
2. moi, je: dormir / rentrer à la maison
3. mon frère: retrouver sa copine en ville / dîner au restaurant avec elle
4. vous: dîner au restaurant / sortir danser
5. mes amis: préparer le dîner / aller au supermarché *(supermarket)*
6. toi, tu: faire cet exercice / commencer l'exercice suivant

C Projets. Demandez à votre partenaire si ces personnes vont faire les choses indiquées aux moments donnés.

EXEMPLE   tes amis et toi / jouer à des jeux vidéo ce soir
— **Tes amis et toi, vous allez jouer à des jeux vidéo ce soir?**
— **Oui, nous allons jouer à des jeux vidéo ce soir. Non, nous n'allons pas jouer à des jeux vidéo ce soir.**

1. tu / rester au lit demain matin **2.** tu / retrouver des amis au café ce week-end **3.** tes amis et toi / aller en boîte samedi prochain **4.** nous / avoir des devoirs de français ce soir

Line art on this page: © Cengage Learning

D Pourquoi y vont-ils? Robert dit où ces personnes vont aller ce week-end et ce qu'elles vont y faire. Complétez ce qu'il dit.

EXEMPLE   moi, je / musée
Moi, je vais aller au musée ce week-end. Je vais y voir une exposition.

1. moi, je / au centre commercial
2. mes amis / à la piscine
3. nous / au cinéma
4. Gabriel / à la salle de gym
5. mes amis et moi / à la librairie
6. mon père et ma belle-mère / au théâtre

E Entretien. Interviewez un(e) partenaire avec les questions suivantes.

1. Avec qui est-ce que tu vas passer l'après-midi, samedi? (Qu'est-ce que vous allez faire ensemble?)
2. Est-ce que tu vas retrouver des amis en ville samedi soir? (Où? Qu'est-ce que vous allez faire ensemble?)
3. Où est-ce que tu vas passer la journée, dimanche? Qu'est-ce que tu vas faire l'après-midi et le soir?
4. Quand est-ce que tu vas réviser tes cours ce week-end? Avec qui est-ce que tu vas étudier?

SAYING WHEN YOU ARE GOING TO DO SOMETHING

✔ *Pour vérifier*

1. Do you generally use cardinal or ordinal numbers to give dates in French? What is the exception?

2. In what two ways can the year 1789 be expressed in French? How do you say the year 2016?

3. How do you say *in* with months and years? How do you say *in January? in 2017?*

4. What are these dates in French: 15/3/1951 and 11/1/2022?

ⓘLrn In the **Culture Modules** in the video library, see **Celebrations.**

Vocabulaire supplémentaire
LES FÊTES ET LES OBSERVANCES
RELIGIEUSES

un anniversaire de mariage
  a wedding anniversary
la fête des Mères / la fête des Pères
la fête nationale *the national holiday*
Hanoukka *(f)*
le (réveillon du) jour de l'An *New Year's (Eve)*
Noël *(m) Christmas*
Pâques *(f) Easter*
la pâque juive *Passover*
le ramadan
la Saint-Valentin
Yom Kippour
Bon anniversaire! *Happy Birthday!*
Bonne année! *Happy New Year!*
Joyeux Noël! *Merry Christmas!*

Vocabulaire sans peine!

The word **anniversaire** means both *birthday* and *anniversary* in French. Note the cognate pattern *-ary* = **-aire.**

le contraire = *the contrary*
révolutionnaire = *revolutionary*
nécessaire = *necessary*

How would you say the following in French?

commentary
imaginary
ordinary

Les dates

To express the date in French, use **le** and the cardinal numbers (**deux, trois...**), except for *the first* of the month. For *the first,* use the ordinal number: **le premier (1ᵉʳ).**

—Quelle est la date aujourd'hui? / C'est quelle date aujourd'hui?
—C'est **le premier... le deux... le trois... le quatre...**

janvier	avril	juillet	octobre
février	mai	août	novembre
mars	juin	septembre	décembre

—Quelle est la date de la fête *(holiday)* nationale française?
—C'est le 14 (quatorze) juillet.

You can express the years 1100–1999 in French in either of two ways. Years starting at 2000 are only expressed using the word **mille.**

1945: mille neuf cent quarante-cinq / dix-neuf cent quarante-cinq
2015: deux mille quinze

Note that the day goes before the month in French.

14/7/1789 = le quatorze juillet dix-sept cent quatre-vingt-neuf

Use **en** to say *in* what month or year. Use **le** when saying *on* a certain date.

—Ton anniversaire *(birthday)*, c'est quand?
—C'est **en** novembre. C'est **le** 18 novembre *([on] November 18ᵗʰ).* Je vais faire une fête **le** 16 novembre *(I am going to have a party [on] November 16ᵗʰ).*

—**En** quelle année vas-tu finir tes études?
—**En** 2019.

A Quel mois? Regardez la liste de fêtes dans la marge de cette page et complétez ces phrases avec le nom du mois correspondant.

EXEMPLE Le jour de l'An, c'est en **janvier.**

1. Le réveillon du jour de l'An, c'est en...
2. L'année scolaire commence en...   Elle finit en...
3. La fête nationale française, c'est en...   Notre fête nationale, c'est en...
4. La fête des Mères, c'est en...   La fête des Pères, c'est en...
5. Thanksgiving, c'est en...

B Encore des dates. Demandez à votre partenaire la date des jours indiqués.

> aujourd'hui   demain   de lundi   de ton anniversaire
> de notre fête nationale   de Noël   de *Halloween*
> du jour de l'An *(New Year's Day)*   de la Saint-Valentin
> de ta fête préférée

††† **C** **Votre anniversaire.** Les autres étudiants vont essayer de deviner *(will try to guess)* la date de votre anniversaire. Répondez **avant** ou **après** jusqu'à ce qu'ils devinent juste *(guess right)*.

EXEMPLE —Ton anniversaire, c'est en mars?
—Après.
—C'est en mai?
—Oui.
—C'est le quinze mai?
—Avant...

D **Comparaisons culturelles.** Lisez à haute voix ces dates importantes.

EXEMPLE 4/7/1776 (le début de la Révolution américaine)
le quatre juillet mille sept cent soixante-seize
(le quatre juillet dix-sept cent soixante-seize)

1. 1/11/1718 (Bienville fonde La Nouvelle-Orléans.)
2. 14/7/1789 (la prise de la Bastille)
3. 30/4/1812 (La Louisiane devient *[becomes]* un État des États-Unis.)
4. 11/11/1918 (le jour de l'Armistice de la Première Guerre mondiale)
5. 6/6/1944 (le jour du débarquement en Normandie)

E **À quelle date?** Dites si ces personnes vont faire les choses indiquées aux dates données.

EXEMPLE 25/12 je / aller voir mes parents
Le 25 décembre, je vais aller voir mes parents.
Le 25 décembre, je ne vais pas aller voir mes parents.

beaucoup de mes amis / faire un pique-nique
ma famille / aller voir des feux d'artifice *(fireworks)*
mes amis et moi / aller à la plage

1. 4/7

beaucoup de mes amis / dîner au restaurant
je / sortir avec un(e) ami(e) (des amis)
je / acheter des chocolats pour mes amis

2. 14/2

je / passer la soirée avec des amis
mes parents / aller voir des amis
mon meilleur ami (ma meilleure amie) / rentrer tard

3. 31/12

Line art on this page: © Cengage Learning

je / inviter des amis chez moi
mes amis et moi / faire une fête
je / avoir ?? ans

4. la date de votre anniversaire

††† **F** **Entretien.** Interviewez votre partenaire.

1. Quelle est la date aujourd'hui? Quelle est la date de ton anniversaire? Qu'est-ce que tu vas probablement faire ce jour-là *(that day)*? Quelle est la date de ta fête préférée? Qu'est-ce que tu aimes faire ce jour-là?
2. Quelle est la date du dernier *(last)* jour du cours de français? Qu'est-ce que tu vas faire après ton dernier cours ce semestre / trimestre? Est-ce que tu vas continuer à étudier ici l'année prochaine?

Planning how to get there

LES MOYENS DE TRANSPORT

Robert et ses amis vont aller à La Nouvelle-Orléans en voiture. Et vous? Comment préférez-vous voyager?

Pour visiter une autre ville, je préfère y aller...

en avion *(m)*

en train *(m)*

en bateau *(m)*

en car / en autocar *(m)*

Il y a d'autres possibilités pour aller en ville. Comment **venez-vous** en cours?

Je viens en cours...

à pied *(m)*

à vélo *(m)*

en taxi *(m)*

en voiture *(f)*

en métro *(m)*

en bus / en autobus *(m)*

Robert parle à Thomas du voyage à La Nouvelle-Orléans.

ROBERT: Bon, demain matin, on va à La Nouvelle-Orléans. Tout est **prêt**?

THOMAS: Oui. On y va en car?

ROBERT: Non, on va **louer** une voiture, c'est plus pratique.

THOMAS: C'est loin? **Ça prend combien de temps pour y aller?**

ROBERT: Ça prend environ deux heures et demie en voiture, **pas plus.**

THOMAS: Et **on revient** quand?

ROBERT: On revient **après-demain.**

les moyens *(m)* **de transport** *means of transportation*   **vous venez / Je viens (venir** *to come)*   **prêt(e)** *ready*   **louer** *to rent*
Ça prend combien de temps pour y aller? *How long does it take to go there?*   **pas plus** *no more*   **on revient (revenir** *to come back)*   **après-demain** *the day after tomorrow*

A **Moyens de transport.** Complétez les phrases pour parler de vous.

> en avion   en train   en car   en bateau   en voiture
> à pied   à vélo   en taxi   en métro   en bus

1. Pour faire un long voyage, je préfère voyager...
2. Je n'aime pas beaucoup voyager...
3. Je ne voyage presque jamais...
4. Je préfère aller en ville...
5. D'habitude, je viens en cours...
6. Je ne viens presque jamais en cours...

B **On y va comment?** Dites où chacun va et comment.

EXEMPLE Ils **vont à La Nouvelle-Orléans en voiture.**

1. Je...

2. Ils...

3. Vous...

4. Nous...

5. Elle...

Line art on this page: © Cengage Learning

C **Entretien.** Interviewez votre partenaire.

1. Quelle ville est-ce que tu visites souvent? Comment est-ce que tu préfères y aller? (en voiture? en train? en avion?) Ça prend combien de temps pour y aller?
2. Tu voyages souvent en avion? Tu as peur de voyager en avion? Pour aller de chez toi à l'aéroport, ça prend combien de temps? Qu'est-ce que tu aimes faire pendant *(during)* les longs voyages en avion? (dormir? lire? parler?...)
3. Quels jours est-ce que tu viens en cours? Comment préfères-tu venir en cours? Comment viens-tu en cours, d'habitude? Comment est-ce que tu rentres chez toi?

À VOUS!

Avec un(e) partenaire, relisez à haute voix la conversation entre Robert et Thomas. Ensuite, adaptez la conversation pour parler d'un voyage que vous allez faire ensemble pour visiter une autre ville. Parlez de comment vous allez voyager et de combien de temps ça va prendre pour y aller.

iLrn 🌐 You can find a list of the new words from this ***Compétence*** on page 175 and access the audio online.

DECIDING HOW TO GET THERE AND COME BACK

Les verbes *prendre* et *venir* et les moyens de transport

The conjugations of **prendre** *(to take)* and **venir** *(to come)* are irregular.

PRENDRE *(to take)*		VENIR *(to come)*	
je **prends**	nous **prenons**	je **viens**	nous **venons**
tu **prends**	vous **prenez**	tu **viens**	vous **venez**
il/elle/on **prend**	ils/elles **prennent**	il/elle/on **vient**	ils/elles **viennent**

Prendre means *to take.*

> Je **prends** des notes en cours.　　　**Prenez** votre livre.

Use **prendre** to say that you are *taking* a means of transportation. Remember that you can also use **aller, venir,** or **voyager** and the preposition *en* (or *à* with **vélo**) to say that you are *going, coming,* or *traveling **by*** a particular means of transportation. To say *on foot,* use **à pied.**

> Je **prends** mon vélo.　　Je **prends** l'avion.
> J'y **vais à vélo.**　　　　Je **voyage en avion.**　　Je **viens** en cours **à pied.**

Use **prendre** as *to have* when talking about *having* something to eat or drink.

> Je vais **prendre** un sandwich et une eau minérale.

Comprendre *(to understand)* and **apprendre** *(to learn)* are conjugated like **prendre.** When **apprendre** is followed by an infinitive, the infinitive is preceded by **à.**

> **J'apprends à** parler français. Ma sœur **apprend** le français aussi.
> Tu **comprends**?

Use **venir** to say *to come.* **Revenir** *(to come back)* and **devenir** *(to become)* are conjugated like **venir.**

> Vous **revenez** tard et il **devient** impatient.

Pour vérifier

1. What are the forms of **venir**? of **prendre**? What two verbs are conjugated like **venir**? like **prendre**? What verb do you use to say you are *having* something to eat or drink? When is **apprendre** followed by **à**?

2. In what forms of the verbs **venir** and **prendre** are the vowels nasal? **Je viens / tu viens / il vient** rhyme with what word? **Je prends / tu prends / il prend** rhyme with what word? How do you pronounce the **ils/elles viennent** form? the **ils/elles prennent** form?

Note *de vocabulaire*

1. Use **en** with **aller, venir,** or **voyager** to say you are traveling *by* a means of transportation. **Je viens *en* bus, *en* taxi, *en* train...**

2. Use **prendre** to say what means of transportation you are *taking.* In this case, you can generally use the same article with the noun that you would in English: *I take **the** bus, **a** cab, **the** train...* **Je prends *le* bus, *un* taxi, *le* train...**

 Grammar Tutorials

Sélection musicale. Search the Web for the songs "**La liberté de penser**" by Florent Pagny and "**Où aller**" by Kathleen to enjoy musical selections containing these structures.

PRONONCIATION

Les verbes *prendre* et *venir* 🔊 2-10

In the **je, tu,** and **il/elle/on** forms of the verb **venir,** the vowel combination **ie** has the nasal sound [jɛ̃]. The consonants after **ie** are all silent. All three forms rhyme with the word **bien.** In the **ils/elles viennent** form, however, the **ie** is not nasal and the **nn** is pronounced.

> **je viens**　　　**tu viens**　　　**il vient**　　　**ils viennent**　　　**elles viennent**

Similarly, the **e** in the **je, tu,** and **il/elle/on** forms of the verb **prendre** is nasal and the consonants after the vowel are silent. All three forms rhyme with the word **quand.** In the **ils/elles prennent** form, however, the **e** is not nasal. It is pronounced like the **è** in **mère** and the **nn** is pronounced.

> **je prends**　　　**tu prends**　　　**il prend**　　　**ils prennent**　　　**elles prennent**

The **e** in the **nous** and **vous** forms of both verbs is pronounced like the **e** in **je.**

> **nous venons**　　　**vous venez**　　　**nous prenons**　　　**vous prenez**

2-11

ᵢᵢ A Prononcez bien! D'abord, écoutez les phrases et indiquez pour chacune si on parle d'**une personne** ou de **plus d'une personne**. Après, écrivez deux phrases avec le verbe **prendre** et deux phrases avec le verbe **venir**. Lisez-les à un(e) partenaire qui va dire si vous parlez d'**une personne** ou de **plus d'une personne**.

ᵢᵢ B Qu'est-ce qu'on fait? Conjuguez les verbes entre parenthèses et posez les questions à votre partenaire.

1. Quels jours est-ce que tu *(venir)* en cours? Est-ce que tu *(prendre)* le bus pour venir en cours? Est-ce que tu *(venir)* en cours à pied ou à vélo quelquefois?
2. Est-ce que les autres étudiants du cours de français *(venir)* toujours en cours? Est-ce qu'ils *(comprendre)* bien le français? Est-ce que nous *(apprendre)* beaucoup en cours?
3. Est-ce que le cours de français *(devenir)* plus difficile? Est-ce que le (la) prof *(devenir)* impatient(e) quand les étudiants *(ne pas apprendre)* le vocabulaire?
4. Est-ce que tu *(avoir)* l'intention de revenir à cette université l'année prochaine? Est-ce que tu *(avoir)* l'intention de devenir prof après tes études?

C Que font-ils? Faites une phrase logique à partir de chaque sujet donné pour parler de votre cours de français.

EXEMPLE Moi, je ne viens pas en cours en bus.

moi, je le (la) prof nous les étudiants	(ne/n')	prendre apprendre comprendre venir revenir devenir	(pas)	des/de notes en cours bien le professeur beaucoup de verbes beaucoup de vocabulaire à l'université le week-end impatient(e)(s) paresseux (paresseuse[s]) le bus pour venir en cours en cours à pied en cours en bus

D La santé. Votre ami voudrait être en meilleure santé *(health)*. Donnez-lui des conseils. Utilisez l'impératif.

EXEMPLE Je prends un coca ou un jus d'orange?
Prends un jus d'orange! Ne prends pas de coca!

1. Je prends une bière ou une eau minérale?
2. Je viens en cours en voiture ou à vélo?
3. Je prends une salade ou des frites?
4. Je vais au parc ou je reste à la maison?
5. Je vais au parc en voiture ou à pied?
6. Je prends un bain de soleil ou je nage?

Prenons les vélos!

VIDÉOREPRISE

Les Stagiaires

© Cengage Learning

Rappel!
Dans le dernier *(last)* épisode de la vidéo, Amélie et Céline ont décidé d'être colocataires et d'habiter ensemble dans l'appartement de Céline.

See the *Résumé de grammaire* section at the end of each chapter for a review of all the grammar presented in the chapter.

Dans l'*Épisode 4,* Céline et Amélie parlent de la famille d'Amélie et de celle de *(that of)* Christophe. Avant de regarder l'épisode, faites ces exercices pour réviser ce que vous avez appris dans le *Chapitre 4.*

A La famille de Christophe. Rachid parle à Christophe de sa famille. Complétez leur conversation avec les mots logiques.

RACHID: Alors, Christophe, c'est vrai que M. Vieilledent est ton __1__?
CHRISTOPHE: Oui, c'est vrai.
RACHID: Tu as une grande __2__? Tu as des __3__ et sœurs?
CHRISTOPHE: Moi, je suis le seul __4__, mais j'ai deux __5__, Léa et Emma.
RACHID: Elles sont plus __6__ ou plus jeunes que toi?
CHRISTOPHE: Je suis le plus jeune. Elles __7__ vingt-six et vingt-quatre __8__.
RACHID: Et ta __9__, elle s'appelle comment?
CHRISTOPHE: Elle s'appelle Pauline, mais mes parents ne sont plus ensemble. Ils sont __10__.

Maintenant, préparez une conversation avec un(e) partenaire dans laquelle *(in which)* vous parlez de vos familles.

B Aujourd'hui. Utilisez des expressions avec **avoir** pour dire comment l'équipe *(team)* de Technovert se sent *(feels)* aujourd'hui.

EXEMPLE M. Vieilledent voudrait des croissants parce qu'il **a faim.**

1. Camille voudrait boire quelque chose parce qu'elle _____.
2. Matthieu voudrait enlever son pull *(to take off his sweater)* parce qu'il _____.
3. Amélie a besoin d'un pull parce qu'elle _____.
4. Christophe voudrait faire la sieste *(to take a nap)* parce qu'il _____.
5. Rachid _____ d'étudier parce qu'il a un examen demain.

C Les anniversaires. Les résultats du trimestre sont tellement bons que M. Vieilledent pense donner un bonus à chaque employé(e) pour son anniversaire. Donnez la date de l'anniversaire de chacun.

EXEMPLE Camille: 25/1
       L'anniversaire de Camille, c'est le vingt-cinq janvier.

1. Céline: 30/3   3. Matthieu: 21/8   5. Amélie: 14/2
2. Christophe: 16/5   4. Rachid: 1/6

D Pauvre Matthieu. Matthieu voudrait sortir avec Amélie, mais il n'a pas le courage de lui parler *(to talk to her)* parce qu'il est trop timide. Est-ce que Camille dit *(tells)* à Matthieu de faire ou de ne pas faire les choses suivantes pour l'encourager *(to encourage him)*? Utilisez l'impératif des verbes suivants à la forme affirmative ou négative pour former des phrases logiques.

EXEMPLE être timide
       Ne sois pas timide!

1. avoir un peu de courage
2. être ridicule
3. avoir peur de parler à Amélie
4. aller à son bureau sans rien dire *(without saying anything)*
5. regarder Amélie tout le temps sans parler
6. parler avec elle de temps en temps
7. prendre l'initiative de parler à Amélie
8. inviter Amélie au nouveau restaurant du quartier

E **Parlons ensemble.** M. Vieilledent parle aux stagiaires de leur travail. Complétez les phrases suivantes avec l'impératif des verbes entre parenthèses. Mettez l'un des verbes à la forme de **vous** et l'autre à la forme de **nous** pour faire des phrases logiques.

> **EXEMPLE** Rachid et Amélie, **venez** (venir) avec moi, s'il vous plaît.
> **Allons** (aller) dans mon bureau.

1. S'il vous plaît, _____ (entrer) dans mon bureau, tous les deux, et asseyez-vous *(have a seat)*, je vous en prie. Si vous voulez bien, _____ (prendre) un peu de temps pour parler de votre travail à Technovert.

2. _____ (commencer) par vos responsabilités. _____ (ne pas hésiter) à poser des questions si vous ne comprenez pas quelque chose.

3. _____ (venir) me voir *(to see me)* s'il y a un problème et _____ (trouver) une solution ensemble.

4. _____ (partager) vos idées et vos opinions avec moi. _____ (être) toujours ouverts et francs les uns avec les autres.

5. _____ (travailler) tous ensemble! _____ (ne pas avoir) peur de faire des suggestions. Ma porte est toujours ouverte.

F **Le week-end.** Rachid pose des questions à Amélie. Complétez chaque question avec la forme correcte du verbe logique entre parenthèses.

1. (aller, venir) Le week-end, est-ce que tu _____ plus souvent chez tes amis ou est-ce que tes amis _____ plutôt chez toi?

2. (aller, prendre) Qui _____ sa voiture généralement quand tes amis et toi _____ en ville le week-end?

3. (aller, avoir) Est-ce que tu _____ envie de sortir samedi soir ou est-ce que tu _____ rester chez toi?

4. (aller, avoir) Et dimanche, qu'est-ce que tu _____ l'intention de faire? Tu _____ étudier?

5. (avoir, devenir) Est-ce que tu _____ une page sur Facebook? On _____ amis sur Facebook?

 Maintenant, utilisez ces questions pour interviewer un(e) partenaire.

Access the Video *Les Stagiaires* on (iLrn.

© Cengage Learning

▶ **Épisode 4: Vive la famille!**

AVANT LA VIDÉO

Dans cet épisode, Céline parle de la famille de Christophe et pose des questions à Amélie au sujet de sa famille. Avant de regarder l'épisode, imaginez une des questions que Céline pose à Amélie.

APRÈS LA VIDÉO

Regardez l'épisode et notez une chose au sujet de la famille de Christophe et une chose au sujet de la famille d'Amélie.

LECTURE ET COMPOSITION

LECTURE

POUR MIEUX LIRE:
Using your knowledge of the world

You are going to read the poem *Deux mots* by Jean Gentil that appeared in 1878 in *Le Louisianais,* a newspaper published in the town of Convent in the Saint James Parish of Louisiana. In this poem, Jean Gentil expresses the importance of the freedom of religion. Using what you already know about different religions of the world will help you understand as you read. Before reading it, do this activity to make your reading easier.

Associations. À quelle religion de la liste associez-vous les choses ou les personnes suivantes?

le catholicisme	le protestantisme
le judaïsme	l'islamisme

1. Rome et le pape
2. le Pater noster
3. Martin Luther
4. un rabbin
5. le Talmud
6. le Coran

Deux mots

Homme, sois catholique,
Si ça te fait plaisir;
Sois **aristotélique,**
Si c'est là ton désir;
Jure par le pape et Rome,
En disant ton Pater,
Ou bien proteste comme
A protesté Luther;
Suis le Talmud **lui-même,**
En rabbin révérend,
Ou bien, si ton **cœur** l'aime,
Obéis au Coran;
Bien plus, si tu préfères
Les Kings et **le Chou-King,**
Ce sont là **tes affaires,**
Et j'aime assez Péking.
Chacun de nous est libre,
Et **croit comme il l'entend:**
Je prends mon équilibre;
Tu peux en faire autant.
Aussi, petits bonhommes
De trois ou quatre jours,
Étant ce que nous sommes,
Respectons-nous toujours.
Mais si **l'apostasie**
Est une indignité,
Certes, l'hypocrisie
Est **une lâcheté.**

Source: Jean Gentil, "Deux mots" in *Le Louisianais,* June 1878

Si ça te fait plaisir *If that makes you happy*   **aristotélique** (someone who follows the philosophy of Aristotle)   **Jure par** *Swear by*   **En disant** *By saying*   **Suis** *Follow*   **lui-même** *itself*   **cœur** *heart*   **Obéis** *Obey* **le Chou-King** (a Chinese dynasty)   **tes affaires** *your business*   **Chacun** *Each one*   **croit comme il l'entend** *believes as he thinks best*   **Tu peux en faire autant** *You can do the same*   **Étant ce que** *Being what*   **l'apostasie** *apostasy* (abandoning your beliefs)   **Certes** *Certainly*   **une lâcheté** *a cowardly act*

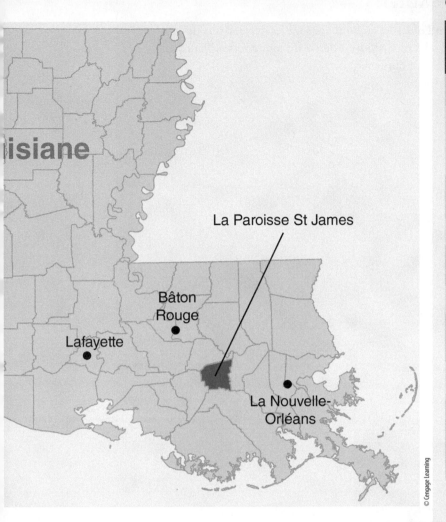

La Paroisse St James

Bâton Rouge

Lafayette

La Nouvelle-Orléans

COMPOSITION

POUR MIEUX ÉCRIRE:
Visualizing your topic

Sometimes it is easier to write a description of people or things if you visualize or look at images of them. An image such as a family tree provides a logical order to a description.

Organisez-vous. Vous allez écrire une description de votre famille. D'abord, dessinez *(draw)* un arbre généalogique de votre famille. À côté de chaque membre de votre famille sur l'arbre généalogique, écrivez tous les mots que vous associez à cette personne: son âge, sa profession, son apparence physique, son caractère et ses activités.

Compréhension

Deux mots. Lisez le poème et répondez aux questions suivantes.

1. De quelles religions ou philosophies est-ce que Jean Gentil parle dans le poème?
2. Dans le poème, il dit «Je prends mon équilibre, Tu peux en faire autant.» Qu'est-ce que ça veut dire?
3. Que pense-t-il de l'hypocrisie?
4. Est-ce que vous trouvez le message de ce poème publié en 1878 tout aussi valable *(just as pertinent)* aujourd'hui?

Ma famille

Faites une description écrite détaillée de votre famille. Basez votre description sur l'arbre généalogique que vous venez de créer *(that you just created)*.

(iLrn Share It!

COMPARAISONS CULTURELLES

L'HISTOIRE DES CADIENS

La majorité des Cadiens en Louisiane aujourd'hui sont les descendants des Acadiens **venus** du Canada. Le mot *cajun* est dérivé du mot *acadien*. Pourquoi ces Acadiens **sont-ils venus** en Louisiane?

En 1604, les Français **fondent** une colonie dans **la partie est** du Canada qu'ils appellent l'Acadie.

L'Acadie

© Cengage Learning

Courtesy of Claude Picard and the Grand-Pré National Historic Site, Nova Scotia

En 1713, les Anglais prennent possession de l'Acadie. Les Acadiens prospèrent et, en 1755, ils sont au nombre de 15 000. Cela **inquiète** les autorités anglaises, qui commencent alors à déporter les Français. Cette expulsion des Acadiens est **appelée** «le Grand Dérangement».

---

venus *who came*   **sont-ils venus** *did they come*   **fondent** *found*   **la partie est** *the eastern part*   **inquiète** *worries*
appelée *called*

Après une période noire **pendant laquelle** beaucoup d'Acadiens **meurent,** certains groupes d'Acadiens viennent **s'établir dans la partie sud** de la Louisiane. **En raison de** l'inaccessibilité de la région, ces Francophones restent **isolés pendant** plus de 200 ans, et leur culture et leur langue restent dominantes dans le sud de la Louisiane.

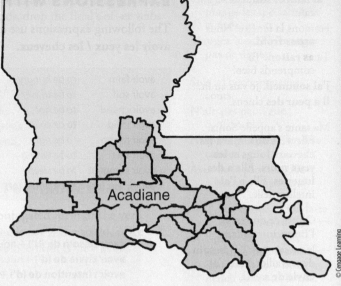

Acadiane

© Cengage Learning

No French to be spoken in school. Oil on canvas © 1984 Georges Rodrigue

Vers la fin du 19ᵉ siècle, des vagues d'Anglophones commencent à arriver dans la région. En 1916, l'État de Louisiane **exige que la scolarité se fasse** en anglais et l'anglais devient de ce **fait** la langue prédominante chez les jeunes. L'usage du français en Louisiane **diminue.**

En 1968, la Louisiane **met** en place le CODOFIL, le Conseil pour le Développement du Français en Louisiane, pour **protéger** la langue et la culture françaises. Et en 1971, l'État crée la région d'Acadiane, **comprenant 22 paroisses** francophones dans la partie sud de l'État.

Compréhension

1. La majorité des Cadiens en Louisiane sont les descendants de quel groupe?

2. Qu'est-ce que «le Grand Dérangement»?

3. Pourquoi est-ce que l'anglais devient la langue prédominante après 1916?

4. Quel est le but *(goal)* du CODOFIL? Que pensez-vous de cette idée de créer une agence pour la défense de la langue et de la culture d'une minorité? Est-ce qu'il y a des organisations publiques dans votre région qui protègent la langue ou la culture d'une minorité?

CODOFIL
AGENCE DES AFFAIRES FRANCOPHONES

www.codofil.org

---

pendant laquelle *during which* **meurent** *die* **s'établir dans la partie sud** *establish themselves in the southern part* **En raison de** *Because of* **isolés pendant** *isolated for* **Vers la fin du 19ᵉ siècle, des vagues** *Towards the end of the 19th century, waves* **exige que la scolarité se fasse** *requires that education be done* **fait** *act, deed, fact* **diminue** *diminishes* **met** *puts* **protéger** *to protect* **comprenant 22 paroisses** *including 22 parishes* (equivalent of counties)

iLrn Share It!

Visit **www.cengagebrain.com** for additional cultural information and activities.

VOCABULAIRE

 iLrn Audio Flashcards

COMPÉTENCE 1 🔊

Describing your family

LA FAMILLE

des beaux-parents /	stepparents, in-laws /
un beau-père /	a stepfather, a father-in-
une belle-mère	law / a stepmother,
	a mother-in-law
un(e) cousin(e)	a cousin
un(e) enfant	a child
un fils / une fille	a son / a daughter
un frère / une sœur	a brother / a sister
un garçon / une fille	a boy / a girl
des grands-parents /	grandparents /
un grand-père /	a grandfather /
une grand-mère	a grandmother
un neveu (pl des neveux) /	a nephew /
une nièce	a niece
un oncle / une tante	an uncle / an aunt
des parents / un père /	parents / a father /
une mère	a mother

NOMS FÉMININS

une barbe	a beard
des lunettes	glasses
une moustache	a mustache
des vacances	vacation

ADJECTIFS

âgé(e)	old
auburn (inv)	auburn
blond(e)	blond(e)
brun(e)	medium / dark brown (with hair)
châtain	light / medium brown (with hair)
court(e)	short
décédé(e)	deceased
long(ue)	long
mi-longs	shoulder-length (with hair)
noir(e)	black, very dark brown (with eyes)
noisette (inv)	hazel (with eyes)
roux (rousse)	red (with hair)

EXPRESSIONS VERBALES

avoir besoin de	to need
avoir chaud / froid	to be hot / cold
avoir envie de	to feel like, to want
avoir faim / soif	to be hungry / thirsty
avoir l'air...	to look ..., to seem ...
avoir les cheveux / les yeux...	to have ... hair / eyes
avoir l'intention de	to intend to
avoir peur (de)	to be afraid (of)
avoir raison / tort	to be right / wrong
avoir sommeil	to be sleepy
Comment s'appelle-t-il/elle?	What is his/her name?
Il/Elle s'appelle...	His/Her name is ...
porter	to wear, to carry
Quel âge a...?	How old is ...?
avoir (environ)... ans	to be (about) ... years old
Vous êtes combien dans votre (ta) famille?	How many people are there in your family?
Nous sommes...	There are ... of us.

DIVERS

de taille moyenne	of medium height
encore	still
environ	about
La Nouvelle-Orléans	New Orleans

COMPÉTENCE 2 🔊

Saying where you go in your free time

NOMS MASCULINS

un centre commercial	a shopping mall
un concert	a concert
un festival	a festival
un magasin	a store
un musée	a museum
un orchestre	an orchestra, a band
un parc	a park
des projets	plans
le temps libre	free time
un théâtre	a theater

NOMS FÉMININS

une activité (de plein air)	an (outdoor) activity
la cuisine	cooking, cuisine
une église	a church
une exposition	an exhibit
une librairie	a bookstore
la musique zydeco	Zydeco music
une pièce (de théâtre)	a play
une piscine	a swimming pool
une plage	a beach
une région	a region
une spécialité	a specialty

EXPRESSIONS VERBALES

acheter	to buy
aie, ayons, ayez	have, let's have, have
aller (à)	to go (to)
avoir confiance	to have confidence
avoir de la patience	to have patience
connaître	to know, to get to know, to be acquainted / familiar with
prendre un bain de soleil	to sunbathe
retrouver	to meet
servir	to serve
sois, soyons, soyez	be, let's be, be
trouver	to find

DIVERS

à l'heure	on time
bonne idée	good idea
cadien(ne)	Cajun
calme	calm
culturel(le)	cultural
de temps en temps	from time to time
extra(ordinaire)	great
on	one, people, they, we
On...?	Shall we ...?, How about ...?
on dit que	they say that
on peut	one can
plutôt	rather, instead
pour	in order to
sage	good, well-behaved
y	there

Saying what you are going to do

NOMS MASCULINS

un anniversaire	*a birthday*
le folklore	*folklore*

NOMS FÉMININS

une fête	*a holiday, a party*
la soirée	*the evening*

EXPRESSIONS VERBALES

aller voir	*to go see, to visit* (a person)
boire	*to drink*
faire une fête	*to have a party*
faire des projets	*to make plans*
faire un tour	*to take a tour, to go for a ride*
il va y avoir	*there is / are going to be*
partir (pour le week-end)	*to go away, to leave (for the weekend)*
quitter	*to leave*
visiter	*to visit* (a place)

LES DATES

En quelle année?	*In what year?*
Quelle est la date?	*What is the date?*
C'est quelle date?	*What is the date?*
C'est le premier (deux, trois...)	*It's the first (second, third . . .) of*
janvier / février / mars / avril / mai / juin / juillet / août / septembre / octobre / novembre / décembre	*January / February / March / April / May / June / July / August / September / October / November / December*

EXPRESSIONS ADVERBIALES

ce matin	*this morning*
ce mois-ci	*this month*
ce soir	*tonight, this evening*
ce week-end	*this weekend*
cet après-midi	*this afternoon*
cette année	*this year*
cette semaine	*this week*
d'abord	*first*
demain matin / après-midi / soir	*tomorrow morning / afternoon / evening*
ensuite	*then, afterwards*
l'année prochaine	*next year*
la semaine prochaine	*next week*
le mois prochain	*next month*
le week-end prochain	*next weekend*
lundi (mardi...) prochain	*next Monday (Tuesday . . .)*
plus tard	*later*
(et) puis	*(and) then*
tard	*late*
tôt	*early*

DIVERS

célèbre	*famous*
génial(e) (*m pl* géniaux)	*great*
national(e) (*m pl* nationaux)	*national*
prochain(e)	*next*
régional(e) (*m pl* régionaux)	*regional*
le Vieux Carré	*the French Quarter*

Planning how to get there

NOMS MASCULINS

un (auto)bus	*a bus* (in a city)
un (auto)car	*a bus* (between cities)
un avion	*a plane*
un bateau	*a boat*
le métro	*the subway*
un moyen de transport	*a means of transportation*
un taxi	*a cab, a taxi*
un train	*a train*
un voyage	*a trip*

NOMS FÉMININS

une possibilité	*a possibility*
des notes	*notes*

EXPRESSIONS VERBALES

aller à pied	*to go on foot*
à vélo	*by bike*
en (auto)bus	*by bus*
en (auto)car	*by bus*
en avion	*by plane*
en bateau	*by boat*
en métro	*by subway*
en taxi	*by taxi*
en train	*by train*
en voiture	*by car*
apprendre	*to learn*
comprendre	*to understand*
devenir	*to become*
louer	*to rent*
prendre	*to take*
revenir	*to come back*
venir	*to come*

DIVERS

après-demain	*the day after tomorrow*
Ça prend combien de temps?	*How long does it take?*
Ça prend...	*It takes . . .*
impatient(e)	*impatient*
pas plus	*no more*
prêt(e)	*ready*

INTERLUDE MUSICAL

FILLE DE VILLE

🌐 You can find these songs on iTunes. You can also search the Internet to hear them performed and to find the lyrics.

MARIE-ÉLAINE THIBERT

Marie-Élaine Thibert has always had a passion for music and dreamed of singing on stage. To fulfill her dream, she had to work hard and overcome her shyness. Her dream finally became a reality when she was selected to sing on *Star Académie* (the Francophone Canadian equivalent of *American Idol)*, which made her a star. The following activity will help you better understand her song *Fille de ville.*

Marie-Élaine Thibert est née *(born)* à La Salle, un arrondissement *(district)* de Montréal.

Fille de ville. Dans cette chanson *(this song),* Marie-Élaine Thibert explique qu'elle n'a rien contre *(has nothing against)* la campagne, mais elle se considère *(considers herself)* clairement une fille de ville. Associez-vous ces choses mentionnées dans la chanson à la campagne ou à la ville?

les champs *(fields)*	l'espace *(space)*
les lumières *(lights)*	les montagnes
le bruit *(noise)*	l'énergie
les bois *(woods)*	les plaines
gronder *(to rumble)*	les odeurs
les lacs et les rivières	les millions de choses à faire
le béton *(concrete)* et la circulation *(traffic)*	les oiseaux *(birds)* et les fleurs

NONC WILLIE

BRUCE DAIGREPONT

Bruce Daigrepont, true to his Cajun heritage, focuses his music around the traditional Cajun instruments, the accordion and fiddle, backed by drums, bass, rubboard, and triangle. His sets are comprised of Cajun waltzes and two-steps, fiddle reels, deep blues, swamp pop, zydeco, and R&B. The following activities will help you better understand his song *Nonc Willie.*

Bruce Daigrepont donne des concerts de musique cadienne partout dans le monde *(world)*.

A **Chez Nonc Willie.** Dans la chanson *(song) Nonc Willie (Uncle Willie)*, le chanteur invite des amis à aller chez Nonc Willie pour s'amuser *(to have fun)*. Voilà les choses à faire chez Nonc Willie. Devinez le sens des mots que vous ne connaissez pas. *(Guess the meaning of the words you don't know.)*

gagner de l'argent	s'amuser	boire de la bière
jouer à des jeux de cartes	acheter des bonbons	se rassembler

B **Dans le passé.** Le chanteur dit «je me souviens» *(I remember)* pour parler de quand il était *(was)* petit. Dans les phrases suivantes, tous les verbes sont au passé. Utilisez le contexte pour deviner leur sens.

Nonc Willie *était* le frère de mon grand-père. Il n'*avait* pas beaucoup d'argent, mais il *s'amusait* bien. Tous ses amis *se rassemblaient* le samedi soir pour jouer aux cartes ensemble. Le gagnant *donnait* un peu d'argent aux enfants qui *observaient* le jeu.

À Paris
Les projets

 iLrn Heinle Learning Center

 www.cengagebrain.com

 Horizons Video: Les Stagiaires

 Audio

 Internet web search

 Pair work

 Group work

5

COMPÉTENCE

1 Saying what you did
Le week-end dernier

Saying what you did
*Le passé composé avec **avoir***

Stratégies et Lecture
- **Pour mieux lire:** *Using the sequence of events to make logical guesses*
- **Lecture:** *Qu'est-ce qu'elle a fait?*

2 Telling where you went
Je suis parti(e) en voyage

Telling where you went
*Le passé composé avec **être***

Telling when you did something
Les expressions qui désignent le passé et reprise du passé composé

3 Discussing the weather and your activities
Le temps et les projets

Talking about the weather and what you do
*Le verbe **faire**, l'expression **ne… rien** et les expressions pour décrire le temps*

Talking about activities
*Les expressions avec **faire***

4 Deciding what to wear and buying clothes
Les vêtements

Avoiding repetition
*Les pronoms **le, la, l'** et **les***

Vidéoreprise *Les Stagiaires*

Lecture et Composition
- **Pour mieux lire:** *Using visuals to make guesses*
- **Lecture:** *Je blogue donc je suis*
- **Pour mieux écrire:** *Using standard organizing techniques*
- **Composition:** *Un voyage en France*

Comparaisons culturelles *Le sport et le temps libre des Français*

Résumé de grammaire

Vocabulaire

© Magdalena Jankowska/iStockphoto.com

LA FRANCE

Voudriez-vous visiter la France? La France vous offre une grande variété de **paysages.** Il y a...

de grandes villes

des plaines

de petits villages ruraux

paysages *(m) landscapes*   **ruraux** *rural*

des plages de sable

des fleuves

des montagnes

La France
(La République française)

Visit it live on Google Earth!

NOMBRE D'HABITANTS:
65 350 000 (les Français)

CAPITALE: **Paris**

Le savez-vous?

Est-ce que vous connaissez *(know)* un peu la France? Regardez la carte *(map)* de la France à la fin du *(at the end of the)* livre. Ensuite, répondez à ces questions. Si vous ne savez pas, devinez! *(If you don't know, guess!)*

1. La France a à peu près la même superficie *(about the same area)* que...

   a. l'Alaska   **b.** le Texas   **c.** la Louisiane

2. Regardez la carte de la France. À cause de *(Because of)* sa forme, on appelle la France...

   a. le Pentagone   **b.** l'Octogone   **c.** l'Hexagone

3. Il y a huit pays qui bordent la France. Lequel *(Which one)* des pays suivants est au nord *(north)* de la France?

   a. la Suisse   **b.** la Belgique   **c.** l'Espagne

4. Quel massif montagneux *(mountain range)* forme une frontière entre la France et l'Espagne?

   a. les Alpes   **b.** les Pyrénées   **c.** le Massif Central

5. Quel fleuve *(river)* français traverse *(crosses)* Paris?

   a. la Seine   **b.** la Loire   **c.** le Rhône

6. Lyon et Marseille sont les deuxième et troisième villes de la France. Où se trouvent-elles?

   a. dans le nord du pays

   b. dans le centre et dans le sud *(south)* du pays

What part of France would you like to visit? Would you like to do a special kind of trip like a bicycle tour or a cooking or wine-tasting tour? Do an online search for various trips to France. Find a trip you would like to take and describe where you are going to go and what you are going to do.

---

des fleuves *rivers*

Saying what you did

LE WEEK-END DERNIER

Alice Pérez, **femme d'affaires** *businesswoman* américaine **travaillant** à Paris, parle de ses activités de **samedi dernier.** Et vous?

Où est-ce que vous êtes allé(e)? *where go?* **Qu'est-ce que vous avez fait?** *what do?*

Samedi matin,...

je ne suis pas sortie,
je suis restée chez moi.

J'ai dormi jusqu'à *(until)* 10 heures.

J'ai **pris** *have* mon **petit déjeuner.**

Samedi après-midi,...

je suis allée en ville.

Je n'ai pas travaillé.

J'ai déjeuné avec une amie et j'ai bien mangé.

Samedi soir,...

je suis sortie.

J'ai vu un film étranger.

J'ai retrouvé un ami au café.

je suis rentrée chez moi.

J'ai lu le journal.

Je **n'ai rien** fait. *I didn't do anything*

Line art on this page: © Cengage Learning

Le week-end dernier *Last weekend*   **une femme d'affaires (un homme d'affaires)** *a businesswoman (a businessman)* **travaillant** *working*   **samedi dernier** *last Saturday*   **Où est-ce que vous êtes allé(e)?** *Where did you go?*   **Qu'est-ce que vous avez fait?** *What did you do?*   **prendre son petit déjeuner** *to have one's breakfast*   **ne... rien** *nothing*

2-12

C'est lundi et Cathy, la fille d'Alice, parle avec un ami des activités du week-end dernier.

CATHY: Tu as passé un bon week-end?

JÉRÉMY: Oui, pas mal. Samedi matin, j'ai révisé mes cours et samedi après-midi, j'ai joué au foot avec des amis.

CATHY: Qu'est-ce que tu as fait samedi soir?

JÉRÉMY: Je suis sorti. Je suis allé en boîte et j'ai beaucoup dansé.

CATHY: Et **hier**?

JÉRÉMY: Hier matin, **j'ai fait une promenade** sur les Champs-Élysées où j'ai fait du shopping. Et **hier soir,** j'ai regardé la télé.

Sélection musicale. Search the Web for the song **"Champs-Élysées"** by Joe Dassin and sung by Soma Riba to enjoy a musical selection related to this theme.

A **Activités logiques.** Formez des phrases logiques. Complétez chaque début de phrase à gauche avec la fin de phrase logique à droite.

Je suis resté(e) au lit et...	j'ai pris un verre.
J'ai retrouvé des amis au café où...	j'ai dormi.
J'ai dîné au restaurant où...	j'ai beaucoup dansé.
Je suis allé(e) au cinéma où...	je n'ai pas gagné. (won)
Je suis allé(e) en boîte où...	j'ai vu un film étranger.
J'ai joué au tennis avec une amie, mais...	j'ai très bien mangé.
Je suis allé(e) au parc où...	j'ai fait une promenade.

B **Et vous?** Complétez les phrases pour indiquer comment vous avez passé la journée d'hier.

1. J'ai dormi jusqu'à *8 heures / 10 heures / ???*.
2. J'ai pris le petit déjeuner *chez moi / au café / chez une amie / ???. (Je n'ai pas pris de petit déjeuner.)*
3. J'ai lu *le journal / un livre / un blog / un article sur Internet / ???. (Je n'ai rien lu.)*
4. J'ai déjeuné *chez moi / chez des amis / au restaurant / ???. (Je n'ai pas déjeuné.)*
5. *J'ai travaillé. / Je n'ai pas travaillé.*
6. J'ai dîné *chez moi / chez mes parents / ???. (Je n'ai pas dîné.)*
7. J'ai *beaucoup / peu* mangé. *(Je n'ai pas mangé.)*
8. Le soir, *je suis resté(e) chez moi / je suis sorti(e).*

Courtesy of Esther Marshall

Hier, j'ai fait une promenade au jardin des Tuileries.

À VOUS!

Avec un(e) partenaire, relisez à haute voix la conversation entre Cathy et Jérémy. Ensuite, adaptez la conversation pour parler de votre week-end passé. *Note: You may not know how to say everything you did. Pick two or three things that you know how to say or ask your instructor for help.*

You can find a list of the new words from this *Compétence* on page 214 and access the audio online.

hier *yesterday*   **faire une promenade** *to take a walk*   **hier soir** *last night, yesterday evening*

SAYING WHAT YOU DID

Le passé composé avec **avoir**

To say what happened in the past, put the verb in the **passé composé.** It is composed of two parts, the auxiliary verb and the past participle. The auxiliary verb, usually **avoir,** is conjugated in the present tense. The past participle of all **-er** verbs ends in **-é,** and that of most **-ir** verbs ends in **-i.**

PARLER		DORMIR	
j'**ai parlé**	nous **avons parlé**	j'**ai dormi**	nous **avons dormi**
tu **as parlé**	vous **avez parlé**	tu **as dormi**	vous **avez dormi**
il/elle/on **a parlé**	ils/elles **ont parlé**	il/elle/on **a dormi**	ils/elles **ont dormi**

Many irregular verbs have irregular past participles that must be memorized.

avoir	j'ai **eu**, tu as **eu...**	être	j'ai **été**, tu as **été...**
il y a	il y a **eu**	faire	j'ai **fait**, tu as **fait...**
boire	j'ai **bu**, tu as **bu...**	écrire	j'ai **écrit**, tu as **écrit...**
lire	j'ai **lu**, tu as **lu...**	prendre	j'ai **pris**, tu as **pris...**
voir	j'ai **vu**, tu as **vu...**	apprendre	j'ai **appris...**
		comprendre	j'ai **compris...**

Adverbs indicating *how often* (**toujours, souvent...**) and *how well* (**bien, mal...**) are usually placed between the two parts of the verb. To put a verb in the negative form, place **ne** directly after the subject, and place **pas, jamais,** or **rien** just after the auxiliary verb.

J'ai **beaucoup** travaillé hier matin. Après, je **n'**ai **rien** fait.

The **passé composé** can be translated in a variety of ways in English.

I took the bus.
I have taken the bus. } J'ai pris le bus.
I did take the bus.

A ## La journée de Cathy. Voici les activités de Cathy hier. Est-ce qu'elle a fait les choses suivantes?

EXEMPLE Hier matin, Cathy... quitter la maison tôt
Hier matin, Cathy n'a pas quitté la maison tôt.

Hier matin, Cathy...
1. dormir
2. passer la matinée chez elle
3. faire une promenade (walk)
4. travailler tôt

Hier soir, Cathy et ses amis...
5. voir un film
6. prendre un café
7. beaucoup parler
8. faire du sport

✓ Pour vérifier

1. The **passé composé** always has two parts. What are they called?

2. What verb is usually used as the auxiliary verb? Do you conjugate it?

3. How do you form the past participle of all **-er** and most **-ir** verbs? Which verbs that you know have irregular past participles? What are their past participles?

4. How is the negative of verbs formed in the **passé composé**? How do you say *I did nothing / I didn't do anything*?

5. In the **passé composé,** where do you place adverbs like **souvent** or **bien**?

6. What are the three possible English translations of **j'ai mangé**?

iLrn Grammar Tutorials

Note *de grammaire*

Some verbs expressing *going, coming,* and *staying,* such as **aller, sortir, rentrer,** and **rester,** have **être,** not **avoir,** as their auxiliary verb. You will learn about them in the next **Compétence.** For now, remember to use **je suis allé(e), je suis sorti(e), je suis resté(e),** and **je suis rentré(e)** if you want to say *I went, I went out, I stayed,* and *I returned.* (If you are a female, add the extra **e** to the past participle of these verbs, just as you do with adjectives. Do not add this feminine **e** to the verbs you are learning to conjugate with the auxiliary **avoir** in this **Compétence.**)

B **Qu'avez-vous fait?** Dites si ces personnes ont fait les choses suivantes la dernière fois que *(the last time)* vous êtes allé(e) en cours de français.

EXEMPLE Moi, je (j') / dormir jusqu'à 10 heures
Moi, j'ai dormi jusqu'à 10 heures.
Moi, je n'ai pas dormi jusqu'à 10 heures.

AVANT LE COURS
Moi, je (j')...
1. être dans un autre cours
2. passer la matinée chez moi
3. lire le journal

Mon (Ma) meilleur(e) ami(e)...
4. boire un café avec moi
5. manger avec moi
6. passer la matinée avec moi

EN COURS
Les étudiants...
7. dormir en cours
8. bien comprendre la leçon
9. beaucoup apprendre

Nous...
10. avoir un examen
11. écrire beaucoup d'exercices
12. voir un film français

 C **Entretien.** Posez ces questions à votre partenaire sur ce qu'il/elle a fait hier.

EXEMPLE — À quelle heure est-ce que tu as quitté la maison hier?
— J'ai quitté la maison vers 9 heures.
Je n'ai pas quitté la maison hier.

1. Jusqu'à quelle heure est-ce que tu as dormi?
2. Quand est-ce que tu as quitté la maison?
3. Où est-ce que tu as pris ton petit déjeuner?
4. Avec qui est-ce que tu as déjeuné?
5. Qu'est-ce que tu as étudié?
6. Qu'est-ce que tu as fait hier soir?

Après, décrivez la journée de votre partenaire à la classe.

EXEMPLE **Rachel a dormi jusqu'à sept heures. Elle a quitté la maison...**

 D **Devinez!** Dites à votre partenaire combien des choses suivantes vous avez faites récemment *(recently)* avec des ami(e)s. Votre partenaire va deviner lesquelles *(guess which ones)*.

> boire un café   parler sur Skype   voir un bon film
> visiter une autre ville   faire une promenade
> prendre un verre   déjeuner
> prendre le petit déjeuner   faire du vélo

EXEMPLE — Mes amis et moi, on a fait cinq choses de la liste récemment.
— Vous avez bu un café ensemble?
— Oui, on a bu un café. / Non, on n'a pas bu de café.
— Vous avez parlé sur Skype?...

On a joué au frisbee à la plage.

STRATÉGIES ET LECTURE

POUR MIEUX LIRE: Using the sequence of events to make logical guesses

You can often guess the meaning of unfamiliar verbs in a narrative by thinking about what actions would occur together and in what order. For example, when taking the bus, you wait for the bus first, get on the bus, then get off at your destination. Learn to read a whole sentence or paragraph, rather than one word at a time.

Notice that the prefix **re-** means that an action in a sequence is done again, as in English (*do* and *redo, read* and *reread*).

You will also notice that prepositions can indicate relationships between actions. **Pour** means *in order to* when it is followed by a verb. **Sans,** meaning *without,* can also be followed by an infinitive.

A **Devinez!** Use the sequence of events in this passage to guess the meaning of the boldfaced words.

Cathy **a ouvert** une enveloppe et elle **a sorti** une feuille de papier. Elle **a lu** les instructions sur la feuille, mais elle n'a pas compris. Alors, elle **a relu** les instructions et elle **a remis** la feuille de papier dans l'enveloppe.

Cathy **a attendu** le bus devant son appartement. Quand il est arrivé, elle **est montée** dedans, et elle **est descendue** quand elle est arrivée à sa destination. Elle **est entrée** dans un café et a commandé un coca. Elle a bu son coca, elle **a payé l'addition** et elle **est repartie.**

Elle est entrée dans une station de métro où elle a acheté un ticket **au guichet,** mais elle n'a pas pris le métro. Elle **a mis** le ticket dans son enveloppe et elle a quitté la station.

Devant un magasin de vélos, Cathy a admiré un vélo rouge dans **la vitrine.** Elle est entrée dans le magasin et a demandé **le prix** du vélo.

B **Dans l'ordre logique.** Mettez les activités suivantes de Cathy dans l'ordre logique. La première et la dernière *(last)* sont indiquées.

_____ Elle est allée vers la porte.
_____ Elle a lu les instructions sur la feuille de papier.
___1___ Cathy a vu une enveloppe sur la table.
_____ Elle a sorti une feuille de papier de l'enveloppe.
_____ Elle a ouvert l'enveloppe.
___7___ Elle a ouvert la porte et elle est sortie.
_____ Elle a remis la feuille dans l'enveloppe.

© Cengage Learning

C **Quel verbe?** Complétez ces phrases logiquement. N'oubliez pas *(Don't forget)* que **pour** veut dire *in order to* et **sans** veut dire *without.*

1. Cathy a quitté l'appartement sans... (boire son café, ouvrir la porte).
2. Elle a pris le bus pour... (rester à la maison, aller en ville).
3. Elle a retrouvé des amis pour... (passer le week-end seule, aller au cinéma).
4. Elle est allée au guichet pour... (acheter des tickets, boire un coca).
5. Elle est rentrée à la maison sans... (quitter le café, prendre le bus).

Lecture: *Qu'est-ce qu'elle a fait?*

🔊
2-13

© Cengage Learning

Seule dans son appartement, Cathy Pérez avait l'air un peu agitée. Elle a pris une enveloppe qui était sur la table et en a sorti une feuille de papier. Elle a lu les instructions et a remis la feuille dans l'enveloppe. Elle a pris l'enveloppe et a quitté son appartement.

Cathy est entrée dans un café où elle a commandé un coca et ensuite, elle a demandé l'addition. Quand l'addition est arrivée, elle a payé. Elle a ouvert l'enveloppe, a relu les instructions, a mis l'addition dans l'enveloppe et a quitté le café sans boire son coca. C'est bien bizarre! Pourquoi avait-elle l'air si agitée?

Ensuite, Cathy est allée à la station de métro. Elle est entrée dans la station et sans regarder le plan, est allée au guichet et a demandé un ticket. Quand on lui a donné son ticket, elle l'a mis dans l'enveloppe, a remonté l'escalier et a quitté la station de métro. Pourquoi a-t-elle acheté un ticket sans prendre le métro? Tout cela est fort bizarre!

Cathy a continué sa route jusqu'à un magasin de vélos. Elle a regardé un vélo rouge qui était dans la vitrine. Elle est entrée dans le magasin et elle a demandé le prix du vélo. Elle a écrit le prix du vélo sur une feuille de papier et elle a mis la feuille de papier dans l'enveloppe. Ensuite, elle est sortie du magasin.

Cathy est allée au coin de la rue pour attendre l'autobus. Quand l'autobus est arrivé, elle l'a pris, et puis elle est descendue à l'université. Elle avait l'air un peu plus calme. Pourquoi a-t-elle fait tout ça? Pourquoi a-t-elle mis ces choses dans l'enveloppe? Pourquoi est-elle plus calme maintenant?

A **Comprenez-vous?** Dites ce que Cathy a fait d'abord et ce qu'elle a fait ensuite.

1. Elle a sorti une feuille de papier de l'enveloppe. / Elle a lu les instructions.
2. Elle a quitté son appartement. / Elle est allée au café.
3. Elle a commandé un coca. / Elle est partie sans boire son coca.
4. Elle a payé le serveur. / Elle a demandé l'addition.
5. Elle a demandé un ticket de métro. / Elle est allée au guichet.

B **Maintenant... c'est à vous!** Est-ce que vous trouvez les actions de Cathy plutôt bizarres? Pourquoi est-ce qu'elle a fait tout ça? Imaginez une explication.

Est-ce qu'elle... est agent de police ou détective privé? souffre d'amnésie? travaille pour la CIA? est espionne comme James Bond? collectionne des souvenirs de Paris? fait un exercice pour son cours de français?

Réponse:
Il y a une explication simple et logique! Cathy suit *(is taking)* un cours de français pour étrangers à Paris. Ses devoirs, dans l'enveloppe, consistent à prouver au professeur qu'elle est capable de commander quelque chose à boire au café, de demander le prix d'un vélo et d'acheter un ticket de métro. Elle doit rapporter *(needs to bring back)* l'addition, le prix du vélo et le ticket de métro à son professeur.

Telling where you went

JE SUIS PARTI(E) EN VOYAGE

La dernière fois que vous êtes parti(e) en voyage, où est-ce que vous êtes allé(e)? Qu'est-ce que vous avez fait?

Je suis allé(e)	à Denver.	**J'y suis allé(e)**	en avion.
	à New York.		en train.
	???		en autocar.
			en voiture
			(de location).
Je suis parti(e)	en mars.	Je suis arrivé(e)	le même jour.
	le matin.		trois heures plus tard.
	vers trois heures.		**le lendemain.**
	???		???
Je suis descendu(e)	à l'hôtel.	Je suis resté(e)	**une nuit.**
			le week-end.
			trois jours.
Je suis allé(e)	dans un camping.		
Je suis resté(e)	chez des amis.		
	chez **des parents.**		
Je suis allé(e)	à la plage.	Je suis rentré(e)	trois jours après.
	à un concert.		la semaine suivante.
	en boîte.		deux semaines plus tard.

2-14

Alice est partie en week-end. Le mardi suivant, elle parle avec son amie Claire du voyage qu'elle a fait le week-end passé.

CLAIRE: Qu'est-ce que tu as fait le week-end dernier?
ALICE: J'ai pris le train pour aller à Deauville.
CLAIRE: Quand est-ce que tu es partie?
ALICE: Je suis partie samedi matin et je suis rentrée hier soir.
CLAIRE: Tu as trouvé un bon hôtel?
ALICE: Je suis descendue dans un petit hôtel confortable, pas trop loin de la plage.
CLAIRE: **Quelle chance!** Moi aussi, j'ai envie de visiter Deauville.

A En week-end. Décrivez la dernière fois que vous êtes parti(e) en voyage.

1. Je suis allé(e) à (Chicago, Houston, ???).
2. J'y suis allé(e) (en avion, en train, ???).
3. Je suis parti(e) (le soir, vers cinq heures, ???).
4. Je suis arrivé(e) (une heure, trois jours, ???) plus tard.
5. Je suis resté(e) (à l'hôtel, chez des amis, ???).
6. Je suis resté(e) (deux jours, une semaine, ???).

La dernière fois *The last time* **J'y suis allé(e)** *I went there* **de location** *rental* **le lendemain** *the next day, the following day*
Je suis descendu(e) (descendre [dans / à / de]) *I stayed (to stay [at]; to descend, to come down, to get off / out [of] [a vehicle])*
une nuit *one night* **des parents** *some relatives* **Quelle chance!** *What luck!*

B **Un tour de Paris.** Alice et sa famille adorent visiter Paris et la région parisienne. Regardez les photos et complétez les phrases avec une expression de la colonne de droite.

1. Son mari, Vincent, est allé à la Sainte-Chapelle pour...
2. Ses enfants sont allés à Versailles pour...
3. Ils sont allés à Notre-Dame pour...
4. Ils sont allés au musée d'Orsay pour...
5. Ils sont allés au café sur les Champs-Élysées pour...

voir une nouvelle exposition.
prendre un café.
voir son architecture gothique.
admirer les vitraux *(stained-glass windows)*.
visiter le château.

les Champs-Élysées

la Sainte-Chapelle

le château de Versailles

Notre-Dame

le musée d'Orsay

À VOUS!

Avec un(e) partenaire, relisez à haute voix la conversation entre Claire et Alice. Ensuite, adaptez la conversation pour parler de la dernière fois que vous êtes parti(e) en week-end.

 You can find a list of the new words from this *Compétence* on page 214 and access the audio online.

TELLING WHERE YOU WENT

✔ **Pour vérifier**

1. Which verbs have **être** as the auxiliary in the **passé composé**? What do you have to remember to do with the past participle of these verbs that you don't do with verbs that have **avoir** as their auxiliary?

2. How do you say *to enter*? What preposition do you use with it? How do you say *to go out*? *to go out of*?

3. What preposition do you use with **partir** to say *to leave from*? What is the difference between **partir** and **quitter**? between **rentrer** and **retourner**?

4. How do you say *to go/come down, to descend*? *to get out of/down from/ off of*? *to stay at*? How do you say *to go up*? *to get on/in*?

(iLrn Grammar Tutorials

Note *de grammaire*

1. When **on** means *we*, its past participle may either be left in the masculine singular form **(On est sorti.)** or it may agree **(On est sorti[e]s).** Either is correct.

2. **Passer** takes **être** in the **passé composé** when it means *to pass by.* **Je suis passé(e) chez toi.** It takes **avoir** when it means *to spend time.* **J'ai passé la soirée avec mes amis.**

3. **Rentrer** means *to return/go back home* (or to the place you are staying). Use **retourner** for *to return* in most other cases.

4. **Partir** and **quitter** both mean *to leave*. **Partir** has **être** as its auxiliary, but **quitter** takes **avoir** and *must* have a direct object: **Elle *est partie* tôt. Elle *a quitté la maison* à 6h.**

Le passé composé avec **être**

The following verbs, many of which have to do with coming and going, have **être** as their auxiliary verb in the **passé composé**. The past participle of these verbs agrees with the subject in number and gender. Do not make this agreement when **avoir** is the auxiliary.

Elle est *partie* hier.   **Elle a *pris* le train.**

ALLER → ALLÉ		SORTIR → SORTI	
je **suis allé(e)**	nous **sommes allé(e)s**	je **suis sorti(e)**	nous **sommes sorti(e)s**
tu **es allé(e)**	vous **êtes allé(e)(s)**	tu **es sorti(e)**	vous **êtes sorti(e)(s)**
il **est allé**	ils **sont allés**	il **est sorti**	ils **sont sortis**
elle **est allée**	elles **sont allées**	elle **est sortie**	elles **sont sorties**
on **est allé(e)(s)**		on **est sorti(e)(s)**	

aller	je suis allé(e)	*I went*
venir / devenir / revenir	je suis venu(e) / devenu(e) / revenu(e)	*I came / became / came back*
arriver	je suis arrivé(e)	*I arrived*
rester	je suis resté(e)	*I stayed, I remained*
entrer (dans)	je suis entré(e) (dans)	*I entered, I went in*
sortir (de)	je suis sorti(e) (de)	*I went out / came out (of)*
partir (de)	je suis parti(e) (de)	*I left*
passer (par/ chez/devant)	je suis passé(e) (par/ chez/devant)	*I passed (by [. . .'s house])*
rentrer	je suis rentré(e)	*I came home, I returned*
retourner	je suis retourné(e)	*I returned, I went back*
monter (dans)	je suis monté(e) (dans)	*I went up, I got on/in*
descendre (de/dans/à)	je suis descendu(e) (de/dans/à)	*I came down, I got out (of) / off (of) (a vehicle), I stayed (at)*
tomber	je suis tombé(e)	*I fell (down)*
naître	je suis né(e)	*I was born*
mourir	il/elle est mort(e)	*he/she died*

In the **passé composé**, place **y** *(there)* immediately before the auxiliary verb.

J'**y** suis allé(e).   Je n'**y** suis pas allé(e).

PRONONCIATION

Les verbes auxiliaires **avoir** et **être** 2-15

As you practice when to use **avoir** and when to use **être** to form the **passé composé**, be careful to pronounce the forms of these auxiliary verbs distinctly.

tu as parlé / tu es parti(e)   il a parlé / il est parti   ils͜ ont parlé / ils sont partis

🔊 2-16 👥 **A** **Prononcez bien!** Écoutez les questions suivantes et écrivez les verbes auxiliaires que vous entendez *(hear)*. Ensuite, posez les questions à un(e) partenaire.

1. Est-ce que tes parents ___sont___ allés à l'université? Est-ce qu'ils ___ont___ étudié le français? Est-ce qu'ils ___ont___ fait du sport?
2. Où est-ce que ta mère ___est___ née? Où est-ce qu'elle ___a___ passé *(has)* sa jeunesse *(youth)*? Dans quelles villes est-ce qu'elle ___a___ habité? *(genese)*

— her youth
— not movement

👥 **B** **Tu es parti(e) en week-end?** Pensez à la dernière fois que vous êtes parti(e) en week-end. Votre partenaire va vous poser des questions au sujet de ce week-end.

EXEMPLE où / aller
— **Où est-ce que tu es allé(e)?**
— **Je suis allé(e) à Deauville.**

1. quand / partir
2. comment / y aller
3. quand / arriver
4. où / descendre
5. combien de temps / rester
6. quand / rentrer

Maintenant, posez ces mêmes questions au professeur.

EXEMPLE — **Où est-ce que vous êtes allé(e)?**
— **Je suis allé(e) à Rome.**

👥 **C** **Qu'est-ce que tu as fait?** Posez ces questions à votre partenaire au sujet de la dernière fois qu'il/qu'elle a mangé au restaurant avec un(e) ami(e) ou avec des amis.

EXEMPLE — **Avec qui est-ce que tu es sorti(e)?**
— **Je suis sorti(e) avec Thomas et Karima.**

1. Avec qui est-ce que tu es sorti(e)?
2. Vous êtes allé(e)s à quel restaurant?
3. Vers quelle heure est-ce que vous êtes arrivé(e)s au restaurant?
4. Combien de temps est-ce que vous êtes resté(e)s au restaurant?
5. Vers quelle heure est-ce que tu es rentré(e)?

D **Le week-end dernier.** Regardez les illustrations et formez des phrases pour dire qui a fait chacune des choses indiquées: **Cathy, Evan** ou **Vincent et Alice**. *Attention!* Certains verbes sont conjugués avec **avoir**, mais d'autres prennent **être**.

EXEMPLE aller à Nice   **Cathy est allée à Nice.**
voir des amis   **Vincent et Alice ont vu des amis.**

Cathy

Evan

Vincent et Alice

© Cengage Learning

✓ 1. sortir en couple
✓ 2. aller ensemble chez des amis
C 3. arriver à l'hôtel du Vieux Nice en taxi
C 4. faire du ski
C 5. descendre à l'hôtel du Vieux Nice
E 6. avoir un accident de ski

E 7. tomber en faisant du ski *(while skiing)*
E 8. aller à l'hôpital
V 9. prendre un verre chez des amis
E 10. rentrer la jambe cassée *(with a broken leg)*

= a
= est

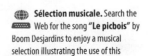
Sélection musicale. Search the Web for the song **"Le picbois"** by Boom Desjardins to enjoy a musical selection illustrating the use of this structure.

TELLING WHEN YOU DID SOMETHING

✔ **Pour vérifier**

1. How do you say *last month? last week? last year? the last time?* How do you say *last?* What is the feminine form? Does it go before or after the noun in most of these expressions? What is the exception? Most of the expressions with **dernier (dernière)** are preceded by **le** or **la.** Which one is not?

2. How do you say that you did something *yesterday? yesterday morning? yesterday evening / last night?*

3. How would you say *for two hours?* How do you say *for* when talking about time in the past?

4. How do you say *ago?* How do you say *a year ago? a long time ago?*

5. What do **déjà** and **ne... pas encore** mean? Where do you place them?

Les expressions qui désignent le passé et reprise du passé composé

The following expressions are useful when talking about the past.

hier (matin, après-midi)	*yesterday (morning, afternoon)*
hier soir	*last night, yesterday evening*
lundi (mardi...) dernier	*last Monday (Tuesday . . .)*
le week-end dernier	*last weekend*
la semaine dernière	*last week*
le mois dernier	*last month*
l'année dernière	*last year*
la dernière fois	*the last time*
récemment	*recently*
Pendant combien de temps?	*For how long?*
pendant deux heures (longtemps)	*for two hours (a long time)*
Il y a combien de temps?	*How long ago?*
il y a trois jours (cinq ans, quelques semaines, deux minutes, trois secondes...)	*three days (five years, a few weeks, two minutes, three seconds . . .) ago*
déjà	*already, ever*
ne... pas encore	*not yet*

Most of these time expressions go at the beginning or end of a clause or sentence. However, **déjà** is placed between the two parts of the verb in the **passé composé.** When using **ne... pas encore,** place **ne** immediately after the subject and **pas encore** between the two parts of the verb.

Note *de vocabulaire*

1. Use **an** *(m)* instead of **année** *(f)* after a number: il y a trois ans.

2. To say *a week ago,* people in France often use **il y a huit jours**; and to say *two weeks ago,* **il y a quinze jours.**

— Tu as **déjà** fait tes devoirs?   — *Have you **already** done your homework?*

— Non, je **n'**ai **pas encore** fait mes devoirs.   — *No, I haven't done my homework **yet**.*

— Moi, j'ai fait mes devoirs **il y a trois heures.**   — *I did my homework **three hours ago**.*

A **Quand?** Voici le calendrier de Cathy. Quand est-ce qu'elle a fait les choses indiquées? Aujourd'hui, c'est le 14 novembre.

EXEMPLE   beaucoup travailler (la semaine dernière, le mois dernier)
Cathy a beaucoup travaillé le mois dernier.

1. dîner chez une amie (il y a trois jours, le mois dernier)
2. aller au Louvre (il y a un mois, il y a deux semaines)
3. préparer un examen (la semaine dernière, hier)
4. passer *(to take)* l'examen (la semaine dernière, hier)
5. faire du shopping (il y a une semaine, le week-end dernier)
6. passer le week-end à Deauville (il y a une semaine, le week-end dernier)

OCTOBRE

L	m	m	J	V	S	D
						1
2	3 Dîner chez Brigitte	4	5 travailler	6	7	8
9	10	11 travailler	12	13	14 Louvre	15
16	17	18 travailler	19	20	21	22
23 / 30	24 / 31 travailler	25	26	27	28	29

NOVEMBRE

L	m	m	J	V	S	D
		1	2	3	4	5
6	7 shopping	8	9 Préparer l'examen	10	11 Deauville	12
13	14 examen	15	16	17	18	19
20	21	22	23	24	25	26
27	28	29	30			

B Déjà? Demandez à un(e) partenaire s'il/si elle a déjà fait ces choses. Utilisez **ne... pas encore** pour les réponses négatives.

EXEMPLE faire ses devoirs aujourd'hui
— **Tu as déjà fait tes devoirs aujourd'hui?**
— **Oui, j'ai déjà fait mes devoirs.**
Non, je n'ai pas encore fait mes devoirs.

1. aller au bureau du prof ce semestre/trimestre
2. apprendre tout le vocabulaire de ce chapitre
3. être absent(e) ce mois
4. travailler en groupes avec tous les autres étudiants

C Et toi? Circulez parmi vos camarades de classe et posez des questions pour trouver quelqu'un qui a fait chacune des choses suivantes récemment. Après, dites à la classe qui a fait chaque chose et quand il/elle l'a faite.

EXEMPLE voir un bon film
— **Sam, tu as vu un bon film récemment?**
— **Non, je n'ai pas vu de bon film récemment.**

— **Lisa, tu as vu un bon film récemment?**
— **Oui, j'ai vu un bon film hier soir.**

Après, à la classe: **Lisa a vu un bon film hier soir...**

> voir un bon film   faire de l'exercice   partir en week-end   être malade *(sick)*
> aller au café avec des amis   sortir avec des amis
> arriver en cours en retard *(late)*   rentrer à la maison après minuit

D Entretien. Posez ces paires de questions à votre partenaire.

EXEMPLE tu / aller au café ce matin
tu / prendre un café ce matin
— **Tu es allé(e) au café ce matin?**
— **Non, je ne suis pas allé(e) au café.**

— **Tu as pris un café?**
— **Oui, j'ai pris un café chez moi.**

1. tu / aller au cinéma récemment
   tu / voir un bon film récemment
2. tu / venir en cours la semaine dernière
   tu / bien comprendre la leçon sur le passé composé
3. tes amis et toi, vous / sortir ensemble le week-end dernier
   vous / prendre un verre ensemble récemment
4. tu / étudier ici l'année dernière
   tu / venir étudier ici à l'université il y a combien de temps
5. tu / dormir jusqu'à quelle heure ce matin
   tu / partir de chez toi à quelle heure ce matin
6. tu / rester chez toi samedi dernier
   tu / réviser tes cours pendant combien de temps samedi dernier

Discussing the weather and your activities

LE TEMPS ET LES PROJETS

Vocabulaire supplémentaire

Il fait bon. *The weather's nice.*
Il fait humide. *It's humid.*
Il y a des nuages. / C'est nuageux. *It's cloudy.*
Il y a du brouillard. *It's foggy.*
Il y a du verglas. *It's icy.*
Il grêle. *It's hailing.*
Il y a un orage. *There's a storm.*
C'est orageux. *It's stormy.*
Le ciel est couvert. *The sky is overcast.*

Quel temps fait-il aujourd'hui?

 Il fait froid.

 Il fait **frais.**

 Il fait chaud.

 Il fait beau.

 Il fait mauvais.

 Il fait (du) soleil.

 Il fait/Il y a du vent.

 Il pleut.

Il neige.

Quelle **saison** préférez-vous? Qu'est-ce que vous faites **pendant** cette saison? Est-ce que vos projets **dépendent du temps qu'il fait**?

J'adore **l'été** *(m)*. En été,...

 je vais à la plage.
je fais du bateau et du ski nautique.

J'aime **l'automne** *(m)*. En automne,...

 je fais du camping.
je **fais du VTT.**

J'aime beaucoup **l'hiver** *(m)*. En hiver,...

 je vais à la montagne.
je fais du ski.

J'adore **le printemps.** Au printemps,...

 je vais au parc.
je fais des randonnées.

Quel temps fait-il? *What is the weather like?* **frais** *cool* **la saison** *the season* **pendant** *during, for* **dépendre de** *to depend on* **le temps qu'il fait** *what the weather is like* **l'été** *summer* **faire du VTT (vélo tout terrain)** *to go all-terrain biking* **l'hiver** *winter* **le printemps** *spring* **faire une randonnée (faire des randonnées)** *to go for a hike (to go hiking, to hike)*

🔊 2-17

C'est vendredi après-midi et Alice et Cathy parlent de leurs projets pour le week-end.

ALICE: **S'il** fait beau demain, je vais faire une promenade au jardin du Luxembourg. J'ai besoin de faire de l'exercice. Et toi, qu'est-ce que tu as l'intention de faire?
CATHY: S'il fait beau, j'ai envie de faire du jogging.
ALICE: Et s'il fait mauvais?
CATHY: S'il fait mauvais, je ne vais rien faire de spécial.

Note *de grammaire*

The use of **si** *(if)* clauses is as common in French as it is in English. As in English, when the verb in the *if* clause is in the present tense, the verb in the second clause is in the present tense, the immediate future, or the imperative.
S'il pleut, j'aime rester chez moi.
S'il pleut demain, je vais rester chez moi.
S'il pleut demain, je reste chez toi.

A Et chez vous? Chez vous, en quelle saison fait-il le temps indiqué?

EXEMPLE Il neige.
Ici, il neige souvent (rarement, quelquefois) en hiver.
Ici, il ne neige jamais.

1. Il fait frais.
2. Il fait du vent.
3. Il fait mauvais.
4. Il fait très beau.
5. Il fait froid.
6. Il fait chaud.
7. Il fait du soleil.
8. Il pleut.
9. Il neige.

B Et vous? Complétez les phrases.

1. Quand il fait beau, j'aime...
2. S'il fait beau ce week-end, j'ai l'intention de...
3. Quand il pleut, je préfère...
4. S'il fait mauvais ce week-end, je vais...
5. À la montagne, j'aime...
6. À la plage, j'aime...

Quel temps fait-il aujourd'hui?

👥 **C Quel temps fait-il?** Demandez à un(e) partenaire quel temps il fait aux moments indiqués. Il/Elle doit répondre en utilisant au moins *deux* expressions pour décrire le temps.

EXEMPLE en automne
— **Quel temps fait-il en automne?**
— **Il fait beau et il fait frais.**

1. en hiver
2. en été
3. en automne
4. au printemps
5. aujourd'hui

👥 **D Entretien.** Posez ces questions à votre partenaire.

1. Aimes-tu l'été? Aimes-tu aller à la plage? Aimes-tu nager? Préfères-tu faire du bateau ou faire du ski nautique?
2. Aimes-tu l'hiver? Aimes-tu aller à la montagne? Préfères-tu faire des randonnées ou faire du ski? Aimes-tu faire du camping? du VTT?
3. Qu'est-ce que tu aimes faire quand il fait chaud? Et quand il fait froid? Et quand il neige?
4. Quelle saison préfères-tu? Quel temps fait-il d'habitude? Qu'est-ce que tu aimes faire pendant cette saison?

👥 **À VOUS!**

Avec un(e) partenaire, relisez à haute voix la conversation entre Alice et Cathy. Ensuite, adaptez la conversation pour parler de vos projets pour le week-end.

iLrn 🌐 You can find a list of the new words from this *Compétence* on page 215 and access the audio online.

S'il *If it* (**si** *if*)

TALKING ABOUT THE WEATHER AND WHAT YOU DO

✔ Pour vérifier

1. What is the present tense of **faire**? How is the **vous** form of this verb different from the usual **vous** form of a verb? What does the verb mean?

2. How do you say that you are doing *nothing*?

3. How do you say *What is the weather like? The weather is nice? It is raining? It is snowing?* How do you say *What is the weather going to be like? It is going to be nice? It is going to rain? It is going to snow?* How do you say *What was the weather like? It was nice? It rained? It snowed?*

4. How do you say *I like snow? I like rain?*

Note *de prononciation*

The **ai** in **fais** and **fait** rhymes with the **ai** in **français**. The **ai** in **faites** rhymes with the **ai** in **française**, but the **ai** in **faisons** rhymes with the **e** in **je**.

iLrn Grammar Tutorials

Le verbe **faire,** *l'expression* **ne... rien** *et les expressions pour décrire le temps*

To say *to make* or *to do,* use the irregular verb **faire.**

FAIRE (to make, to do)	
je **fais**	nous **faisons**
tu **fais**	vous **faites** (fet)
il/elle/on **fait**	ils/elles **font**
PASSÉ COMPOSÉ: **j'ai fait**	

— Qu'est-ce que tu fais ce soir?
— Je reste à la maison. Je fais mes devoirs.

— Qu'est-ce que papa fait dans la cuisine?
— Il fait des sandwichs.

To say that you do *nothing* or you do *not* do *anything,* use **ne... rien.** This expression can be the subject or object of the verb, or the object of a preposition.

Rien n'est prêt.   Je **n'**achète **rien.**   Je **n'**ai besoin de **rien.**

When negating an infinitive, place both parts of the negative expression before it.

Je préfère **ne pas** sortir ce soir.   Je voudrais **ne rien** faire demain soir.

The verb **faire** is used in many, but not all, weather expressions. You will also need the infinitives and past participles **pleuvoir** *(to rain)* → **plu** and **neiger** *(to snow)* → **neigé.** Use **la pluie** to say *(the) rain* and **la neige** to say *(the) snow.*

AUJOURD'HUI	DEMAIN	HIER
Quel temps fait-il?	Quel temps va-t-il faire?	Quel temps a-t-il fait?
Il fait beau / du vent...	Il va faire beau / du vent...	Il a fait beau / du vent...
Il pleut.	Il va pleuvoir.	Il a plu.
Il neige.	Il va neiger.	Il a neigé.

A **Que faites-vous?** Dites ou demandez si ces personnes font les choses indiquées.

1. Moi, je...

faire beaucoup de choses seul(e)
faire beaucoup de choses le soir

2. Mon meilleur ami (Ma meilleure amie)...

faire beaucoup de choses pour moi
faire souvent du VTT

3. En cours, nous...

faire beaucoup d'exercices ensemble
faire les devoirs en ligne

4. Mes parents...

faire beaucoup de choses ensemble
faire souvent du sport

5. *[au professeur]* Est-ce que vous...?

faire souvent du camping
faire souvent du bateau

Aimez-vous faire du camping?

© Jean Louis Bellurget/Getty Images

B **Quel temps va-t-il faire?** Voilà la météo *(weather forecast)* pour certaines régions de France pour demain. Pour chaque région, dites quel temps il va faire. Utilisez deux expressions pour chaque région.

EXEMPLE Demain, en Bretagne, il va faire frais et....

1. Demain, en Bretagne...
2. Demain, dans les Alpes...
3. Demain, sur la Côte d'Azur...

Maintenant, imaginez qu'hier dans ces régions, il a fait le même temps qu'il va faire demain. Dites quel temps il a fait dans chaque région.

EXEMPLE Hier, en Bretagne, il a fait frais et...

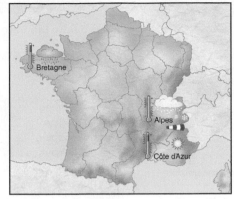

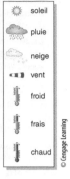

soleil
pluie
neige
vent
froid
frais
chaud

© Cengage Learning

C **Qu'est-ce qu'ils ont fait?** Alice parle des activités récentes de sa famille et du temps qu'il a fait ce jour-là. Complétez ses phrases. Utilisez deux expressions pour décrire le temps.

EXEMPLE Hier, j'**ai lu un livre.** Il **a fait mauvais et il a plu** toute la journée.

EXEMPLE Hier, j'...
Il... toute la journée.

1. À Deauville, nous...
Il...

2. Vendredi dernier, Vincent et moi...
Il...

3. À Chamonix, les enfants... Il...

4. Hier, Vincent...
Il...

5. Ce matin, Vincent et notre fils... Il...

Line art on this page: © Cengage Learning

D **Entretien.** Interviewez votre partenaire.

1. Qu'est-ce que tu aimes faire le vendredi soir? le samedi soir? Qu'est-ce que tu fais d'habitude le dimanche matin?
2. Quel temps va-t-il faire ce week-end? Qu'est-ce que tu as envie de faire s'il fait beau? Qu'est-ce que tu as l'intention de faire s'il fait mauvais? Qu'est-ce que tu vas faire samedi soir? Est-ce que tu préfères ne rien faire quelquefois?

Note *de grammaire*

Questions asked with **faire** are often answered with a different verb.
— **Qu'est-ce que tu fais le samedi matin?**
— **Je regarde la télé.**

TALKING ABOUT ACTIVITIES

✔ **Pour vérifier**

1. How do you say *to go camping?
to take a trip? to do housework? to
do laundry?*

2. In the expressions with **faire**, which
articles change to **de (d')** in a negative
sentence? Which do not?

ilrn Grammar Tutorials

Vocabulaire supplémentaire

aller à la chasse/chasser *to go hunting /
to hunt*

aller à la pêche/pêcher *to go fishing /
to fish*

faire de la muscu(lation) *to do body
building*

faire de la varappe / de l'escalade *to
go rock climbing*

faire du cheval / de l'équitation *to go
horseback riding*

faire du patin (à glace) *to go (ice-)
skating*

faire du roller *to go rollerblading*

faire du snowboard *to go
snowboarding*

faire la fête *to party*

faire de la marche *to go walking*

*Les expressions avec **faire***

The verb **faire** can have a variety of meanings in idiomatic expressions.

LE SPORT ET LES DISTRACTIONS	LE MÉNAGE ET LES COURSES
faire de l'exercice	faire des courses *(to run errands)*
faire du bateau	faire les courses *(to buy groceries)*
faire du camping	faire du jardinage *(to garden)*
faire du jogging	faire la cuisine *(to cook)*
faire du shopping	faire la lessive *(to do laundry)*
faire du ski (nautique)	faire la vaisselle *(to do the dishes)*
faire du sport (du tennis, du hockey,...)	faire le ménage *(to do housework)*
faire du vélo	
faire du VTT	
faire une promenade	
faire une randonnée	
faire un voyage *(to take a trip)*	

The **un, une, des, du, de la,** and **de l'** in the expressions with **faire**
become **de (d')** when the verb is negated. The definite article (**le, la, l',
les**) does not change.

> Je ne fais pas **de** jogging en hiver. Nous ne faisons pas **la** cuisine le matin.

A Un besoin ou une envie? Commencez ces phrases logiquement avec
J'ai envie de... ou **J'ai besoin de...**

> **EXEMPLE** faire des devoirs   **J'ai besoin de faire des devoirs.**
> faire du ski   **J'ai envie de faire du ski.**

1. faire des courses
2. faire du bateau
3. faire la lessive
4. faire du vélo
5. faire le ménage
6. faire la cuisine
7. faire la vaisselle
8. rester à la maison et ne rien faire

Aimez-vous faire du snowboard?

B Préférences. Écrivez les activités suivantes dans l'ordre de vos préférences.
Votre partenaire va vous poser des questions pour déterminer l'ordre des activités
sur votre feuille de papier.

> faire du jogging   faire des randonnées   faire du jardinage
> faire la cuisine   faire du vélo   ne rien faire

> **EXEMPLE** — Préfères-tu faire du jogging ou ne rien faire?
> — Je préfère ne rien faire.
> — Préfères-tu ne rien faire ou faire la cuisine?...

C **Que font-ils?** Éric parle des projets de la famille pour aujourd'hui. Complétez ses phrases avec une expression avec **faire.**

1. Maman... ce matin.

2. Maman et Michel...

3. Papa... cet après-midi.

4. Papa et maman...

5. Cathy et moi, nous...

6. Moi, je...

Line art on this page: © Cengage Learning

D **Activités.** Complétez les phrases avec une expression avec **faire.** Ensuite, dites si c'est vrai pour vos amis et vous. Corrigez les phrases fausses.

1. Je _fais du shopping_ au centre commercial le samedi.
2. Mes amis et moi aimons jouer au tennis et au basket. Nous _faisons du sport_ ensemble tous les week-ends.
3. Mes parents ont un joli jardin. Ils aiment _faire du jardinage_
4. Chez moi, tout est toujours propre parce que je _fais le ménage_ tous les week-ends.
5. Je vais _faire des courses_ aujourd'hui après les cours. J'ai besoin d'aller au bureau de poste et à la banque. _(need to)_

E **Conseils.** Donnez des conseils à un ami. Utilisez une expression avec **faire** et mettez le verbe à l'impératif.

EXEMPLE — La vaisselle est sale.
— **Eh bien, fais la vaisselle!**

1. J'ai faim.
2. Tous mes vêtements sont sales.
3. J'ai envie de faire de l'exercice.
4. J'ai besoin d'acheter de nouveaux vêtements.
5. Mon appartement est très sale.
6. Il n'y a pas de café, de fromage ou de lait à la maison!

| faire la cuisine |
| faire du sport |
| faire du jardinage |
| faire la lessive |
| faire du shopping |
| faire des courses |
| faire une promenade |
| faire le ménage |
| faire la vaisselle |
| faire du vélo |
| faire les courses |

COMPÉTENCE 4

Deciding what to wear and buying clothes

LES VÊTEMENTS

iLrn In the **Culture Modules** in the video library, see **Fashion.**

Vocabulaire supplémentaire

un blouson *a windbreaker, a jacket*
une casquette *a cap*
une ceinture *a belt*
un chapeau *a hat*
des chaussettes *(f) socks*
un col roulé *a turtleneck*
un débardeur *a tank top*
un legging *leggings*
un pyjama *pajamas*
des sous-vêtements *(m) underwear*
un sweat-shirt *a sweatshirt*
un tailleur *a woman's suit*
des hauts talons *(m) high heels*
une tunique *a tunic*
une veste *a sports coat*

Note *de vocabulaire*

Porter means *to carry* or *to wear* and **mettre** *to put, to put on,* or *to wear.* They can both be used to say what one wears in general, although **mettre** is more commonly used in this case and in the **passé composé. Il porte/met souvent un jean. Il a mis un jean hier.** Use **porter** to say what someone is wearing at a particular moment. **Aujourd'hui, il porte un pantalon blanc.**

The forms of **mettre** are:

je **mets**	nous **mettons**
tu **mets**	vous **mettez**
il/elle/on **met**	ils/elles **mettent**

PASSÉ COMPOSÉ: **j'ai mis** (ne)

The verb **essayer** means both *to try* and *to try on.* It is a **-yer** spelling-change verb, like **envoyer.**

The forms of **essayer** are:

j' **essaie**	nous **essayons**
tu **essaies**	vous **essayez**
il/elle/on **essaie**	ils/elles **essaient**

PASSÉ COMPOSÉ: **j'ai essayé**

Sélection musicale. Search the Web for the song **"Je vends des robes"** by Nino Ferrer to enjoy a musical selection related to this vocabulary.

Qu'est-ce que vous **mettez** pour aller en cours? pour sortir le soir?
Qu'est-ce que vous **avez mis** ce matin? hier soir?

Je mets souvent...   Je mets **parfois...**   Ce matin, j'ai mis...

un jean   un short   un pantalon   une jupe

un pull   un polo ou   une chemise et   un chemisier
            un tee-shirt   une cravate

un survêtement   une robe   un costume   des chaussures *(f)*,
                                               des baskets *(f)*, des bottes *(f)*,
                                               des sandales *(f)* ou des tongs *(f)*

un anorak   un imperméable   un manteau   un maillot de bain ou
                                                 un bikini

J'emporte...   Je porte...

un parapluie   un sac ou un   une montre   des lunettes de soleil
                 portefeuille

Line art on this page: © Cengage Learning

---

mettez (mettre *to put, to put on*)   **avez mis (mettre** past participle: **mis) parfois** *sometimes*   **emporter** *to take (along), to carry (away)*

un veste
blazer/jacket

Alice Pérez cherche un nouveau maillot de bain. Elle entre dans un magasin.

2-18

LA VENDEUSE: Bonjour, madame. **Je peux vous aider?**

ALICE: Je cherche un maillot de bain.

LA VENDEUSE: **Quelle taille faites-vous?**

ALICE: **Je fais du** 42.

LA VENDEUSE: Nous avons **ces** maillots**-ci**. Ils sont très jolis et ils sont **en solde**.

ALICE: J'aime bien ce maillot noir. **Je peux l'essayer?**

LA VENDEUSE: **Bien sûr**, madame. **La cabine d'essayage** est **par ici**.

Alice sort de la cabine d'essayage.

LA VENDEUSE: Alors, **qu'en pensez-vous**?

ALICE: **Il me plaît** beaucoup. Il **coûte** combien?

LA VENDEUSE: **Voyons**, c'est 65 euros.

ALICE: C'est bien. Alors, je **le** prends.

Note *culturelle*

Notez que les tailles en France ne sont pas les mêmes qu'aux USA.

Robes et chemisiers		Chemises hommes	
USA	FRANCE	USA	FRANCE
8	38	15	38
10	40	15 ½	39
12	42	16	40
14	44	16 ½	41
16	46	17	42

Chaussures femmes		Chaussures hommes	
USA	FRANCE	USA	FRANCE
5	35	7	39
6	36	8	41
7	37½	9	43
8	38½	10	44
8½	39	11	45
9	40	12	46
9½	41	13	47
10	42	14	48

Avez-vous déjà acheté des vêtements avec la taille française sur l'étiquette *(tag)* ou des chaussures avec la pointure *(shoe size)* française?

A Préférences. Complétez ces phrases pour parler de vos préférences.

1. Quand il fait froid, je préfère mettre *un pantalon et un pull / un survêtement / un manteau ou un anorak*.
2. Quand il fait chaud, je préfère mettre *un jean / un pantalon / un short / un maillot de bain* et *un polo / un tee-shirt / une chemise / un chemisier*.
3. Pour aller à la plage, je mets le plus souvent *un bikini / un maillot de bain / un short*.
4. Quand il fait du soleil, *je mets / je ne mets pas* souvent des/de lunettes de soleil.
5. Quand il pleut, je préfère *emporter un parapluie / mettre un imperméable*.
6. Je porte *souvent / rarement* une montre. *(Je préfère regarder l'heure sur mon téléphone portable.)*
7. Comme chaussures, je préfère mettre *des baskets / des bottes / des sandales / des tongs*.
8. Normalement, je mets mon argent dans *un sac / un portefeuille / ma poche* (pocket).

B Entretien. Interviewez votre partenaire.

1. Tu aimes faire du shopping? Tu préfères acheter des vêtements, des CD, des DVD, des jeux vidéo ou des livres?
2. Tu préfères acheter tes vêtements au centre commercial, dans les petits magasins, dans un magasin d'occasion *(second-hand store)* ou sur Internet?
3. Pour aller à un mariage ou à un entretien *(interview)*, qu'est-ce que tu préfères mettre?

À VOUS!

Avec un(e) partenaire, relisez à haute voix la conversation entre la vendeuse et Alice. Après, adaptez la conversation pour acheter un jean, un anorak ou un manteau. Jouez le rôle d'Alice et votre partenaire va jouer le rôle du vendeur (de la vendeuse). Ensuite, échangez les rôles.

---

une vendeuse (un vendeur) *a salesclerk* **Je peux vous aider?** *Can I help you?* **Quelle taille faites-vous?** *What size do you wear?* **Je fais du...** *I wear size...* **ces... -ci / là** *these / those... over here / over there* **en solde** *on sale* **Je peux l'essayer? (essayer)** *Can I try it on? (to try, to try on)* **Bien sûr** *Of course* **La cabine d'essayage** *The fitting room* **par ici** *this way* **qu'en pensez-vous?** *what do you think about it?* **Il me plaît. (plaire)** *I like it. / It pleases me. (to please)* **coûter** *to cost* **Voyons** *Let's see* **le (l')** *it, him* **(la, l')** *it, her*

You can find a list of the new words from this *Compétence* on page 215 and access the audio online.

AVOIDING REPETITION

✔ *Pour vérifier*

1. How do you say the direct object pronouns *him, her, it,* and *them* in French?

2. Where do you place the direct object pronouns and **y** when there is an infinitive? in the **passé composé**? Where do you place them otherwise? Where do you place them in a negative sentence?

iLrn Grammar Tutorials

Les pronoms **le, la, l'** *et* **les**

Use the direct object pronouns **le, la, l',** and **les** to replace a person, animal, or thing that is the direct object of the verb. Use **le** *(him, it)* to replace masculine singular nouns, **la** *(her, it)* to replace feminine singular nouns, and **les** *(them)* to replace all plural nouns. **Le** and **la** become **l'** when the following word begins with a vowel or silent **h.**

— Tu prends ce maillot?
— Oui, je **le** prends.
— Tu achètes cette chemise?
— Oui, je **l'**achète.

— Tu prends cette robe aussi?
— Oui, je **la** prends.
— Tu achètes ces bottes?
— Oui, je **les** achète.

	BEFORE A CONSONANT SOUND	BEFORE A VOWEL OR SILENT *H*
him, it (masculine)	le	l'
her, it (feminine)	la	l'
them	les	les

- Like **y,** these pronouns are generally placed *immediately before* the verb, even in the negative.

— Tu aimes **cette chemise**?
— Oui, je **l'**aime bien.
　Non, je ne **l'**aime pas.

— Tu vas **au centre commercial**?
— Oui, j'**y** vais.
　Non, je n'**y** vais pas.

- Place them *immediately before* an infinitive, if there is one in the clause.

— Tu vas acheter **cette chemise**?
— Oui, je vais **l'**acheter. / Non, je ne vais pas **l'**acheter.

- In the **passé composé,** direct object pronouns and **y** are placed *immediately before* the auxiliary verb (the conjugated form of **avoir** or **être).**

Je **l'**ai fait.
Je ne **l'**ai pas fait.

J'**y** suis allé(e).
Je n'**y** suis pas allé(e).

Generally, in the **passé composé,** the past participle agrees in gender and number with the subject when the auxiliary verb is **être,** but not when it is **avoir.** However, the past participle used with **avoir** will agree with *direct objects,* but only if they *precede* the verb, as with direct object pronouns.

Éric a acheté **cette chemise.** Il **l'**a achetée hier.

Cathy a acheté **ces pulls.** Elle **les** a achetés ce matin.

A Au magasin de vêtements. Alice et Vincent sont au magasin de vêtements. Complétez ce que chacun dit avec le pronom qui convient (**le, la, l', les**).

1. J'aime ce maillot de bain. Je peux _____ l' _____ essayer?
2. J'aime ces bottes. Je _____ les _____ prends.
3. Je n'aime pas ce bikini. Je ne _____ le _____ prends pas.
4. Comment trouves-tu cette robe? Voudrais-tu _____ l' _____ essayer?
5. Je n'aime pas cet anorak. Je ne vais pas _____ le _____ prendre.
6. Regarde cette belle cravate! Je _____ la _____ trouve super!

B **À Paris.** Dites si vous reconnaissez *(recognize)* ces sites parisiens. Utilisez **Je reconnais...** *(I recognize . . .)* et le pronom qui convient **(le, la, l', les)**.

EXEMPLE Cette avenue?
Oui, je la reconnais. C'est les Champs-Élysées.
Non, je ne la reconnais pas.

EXEMPLE Cette avenue?

1. Cette cathédrale?

2. Ce musée?

3. Cette tour?

4. Cette place?

5. Ce fleuve *(river)*?

C **Le samedi.** Dites si vous faites ou ne faites pas souvent ces choses. Remplacez les mots en italique avec **le, la, l'** ou **les**.

EXEMPLE écouter souvent *la radio* dans la voiture
Oui, je l'écoute souvent dans la voiture.

1. faire souvent *le ménage* le samedi   *Oui, je le fais souvent/Non, je ne le fais pas souvent*
2. passer souvent *le samedi soir* à la maison
3. regarder souvent *la télé* le matin
4. inviter souvent *mon meilleur ami (ma meilleure amie)* chez moi
5. faire souvent *les courses* le week-end
6. prendre souvent *le petit déjeuner* dans un café
7. réviser souvent *mes cours* le samedi soir

D **Intentions.** Un(e) ami(e) voudrait savoir ce que vous allez faire avec les choses suivantes. Répondez en utilisant un pronom **(le, la, l', les)** et un verbe logique. Jouez les deux rôles avec un(e) partenaire.

EXEMPLE ces frites
— **Qu'est-ce que tu vas faire avec ces frites?**
— **Je vais les manger!**

1. ces vêtements
2. ce DVD
3. ce jus de fruit
4. cette chemise
5. ces bottes
6. cette eau minérale
7. ce journal
8. ce CD
9. ce sandwich

E Et vous? Avez-vous fait ces choses le week-end dernier? Répondez en employant le pronom qui convient: **y, le, la, l'** ou **les**.

> **EXEMPLE** Vous avez regardé *la télé* le week-end dernier?
> **Oui, je l'ai regardée.**
> **Non, je ne l'ai pas regardée.**

1. Vous êtes resté(e) *chez vous* tout le week-end? *Oui, j'y suis restée*
2. Vous avez fait *le ménage*? *Oui je l'ai fait*
3. Vous avez fait *la lessive*?
4. Vous avez lu *le livre de français*?
5. Vous avez fait *vos devoirs*?
6. Vous avez dîné *au restaurant*?
7. Vous êtes allé(e) *au cinéma*?

F Le week-end des Pérez. Regardez les explications de ce que les Pérez ont fait le week-end dernier et complétez les réponses. Utilisez **y, le, la, l'** ou **les**.

> **EXEMPLE** Qui est allé *au Quartier latin*?
> Éric et Michèle **y sont allés.**

1. Quand est-ce qu'ils sont allés *au Quartier latin*?
   Ils _____ vendredi après-midi.

2. Qui a commandé *les spaghettis à la carbonara*?
   Éric _____.

3. Qui a acheté *le nouveau livre de Jérôme Ferrari*?
   Michèle _____.

4. Où est-ce qu'ils ont retrouvé *leurs amis*?
   Ils _____ dans un café du quartier.

5. Avec qui est-ce qu'ils ont pris *leur café*?
   Ils _____ avec des amis.

6. Où est-ce qu'Éric et Michèle ont vu *le film avec Jean Reno*?
   Ils _____ au cinéma du Panthéon.

Vendredi après-midi, Éric et sa copine Michèle sont allés au Quartier latin, où ils ont mangé dans un restaurant italien. Michèle a mangé des raviolis et Éric a commandé des spaghettis à la carbonara. Après le repas, ils sont allés dans une librairie où Michèle a acheté un livre de Jérôme Ferrari. Après ça, ils ont retrouvé des amis dans un café du quartier et ils ont pris un café ensemble en terrasse. Plus tard, Éric et Michèle sont allés au cinéma du Panthéon pour voir le nouveau film avec Jean Reno.

© Bill Ross/Corbis

7. Quand est-ce qu'Alice est allée *au musée d'Orsay*?

Elle _____ samedi matin.

8. Où est-ce qu'elle a vu *la nouvelle exposition sur Cézanne*?

Elle _____ au musée d'Orsay.

9. Elle a vu *les autres expositions du musée*?

Non, elle _____.

10. Elle est allée *au cinéma* après le musée?

Non, elle _____.

11. Où est-ce qu'elle a retrouvé *Vincent*?

Elle _____ dans un restaurant du quartier.

Samedi matin, Alice est allée au musée d'Orsay, où elle a vu la nouvelle exposition de Cézanne. Elle n'a pas eu le temps de voir les autres expositions parce qu'elle est allée acheter une jupe dans un magasin de vêtements. Vers une heure et demie, elle a retrouvé Vincent dans un restaurant du quartier.

G Préférences. Répondez aux questions de votre ami(e) en remplaçant les mots en italique par le pronom qui convient. Jouez les rôles avec un(e) partenaire.

EXEMPLE — Je révise *mes leçons* tous les jours. Et toi?
— Moi aussi, je les révise tous les jours.
Moi non, je ne les révise pas tous les jours.

1. Je regarde souvent *la télé* le week-end. Et toi?

2. J'ai envie de regarder *la télé* ce soir. Et toi?

3. J'invite souvent *mes parents* à la maison. Et toi?

4. Ce week-end, j'ai l'intention de voir *mes parents*. Et toi?

5. Je trouve *mes cours* plutôt difficiles. Et toi?

6. Ce soir, je vais préparer *le prochain examen de français*. Et toi?

7. Samedi soir, je vais faire *mes devoirs*. Et toi?

8. Samedi dernier, je suis allé(e) *au cinéma*. Et toi?

9. Dimanche dernier, j'ai fait *mes devoirs*. Et toi?

10. Hier soir, j'ai regardé *la télé*. Et toi?

H Entretien. Interviewez votre partenaire. Utilisez **y** ou un pronom complément d'objet direct pour remplacer les mots en italique dans vos réponses.

1. Est-ce que tu achètes *tes vêtements* au centre commercial? Dans quel magasin est-ce que tu achètes *tes vêtements* le plus souvent? Où est-ce que tu as acheté *les vêtements que tu portes maintenant*?

2. Chez toi, dans quelle pièce préfères-tu regarder *la télé*? Aimes-tu faire tes devoirs *dans cette pièce* aussi? Vas-tu passer beaucoup de temps *dans cette pièce* ce soir?

3. Invites-tu souvent *tes amis* chez toi? Où préfères-tu retrouver *tes amis*? La dernière fois que tu es sorti(e) avec des amis, où est-ce que tu as retrouvé *tes amis*?

4. Où aimes-tu passer *ton temps libre*? Où est-ce que tu as passé *la soirée* hier? Est-ce que tu vas passer la soirée *chez toi* ce soir?

VIDÉOREPRISE

Les Stagiaires

Rappel!

Matthieu, l'informaticien timide à Technovert, est amoureux fou d'Amélie *(crazy about Amélie)* mais trop timide pour le lui dire *(to tell her)*. Il parle aux autres pour découvrir tout ce qu'il peut *(to discover all that he can)* à son sujet.

See the *Résumé de grammaire* section at the end of each chapter for a review of all the grammar presented in the chapter.

Dans l'***Épisode 5,*** Matthieu parle à Christophe d'une soirée que Christophe, Rachid et Amélie ont passée ensemble. Avant de regarder l'épisode, faites ces exercices pour réviser ce que vous avez appris dans le ***Chapitre 5.***

© Cengage Learning

A Samedi dernier. Un ami pose des questions à Christophe sur ce qu'il a fait samedi dernier. Complétez ses questions en mettant les verbes au passé composé.

> **EXEMPLE** Tu **es sorti** (sortir) avec des amis ou ils **sont venus** (venir) chez toi?

1. Avec qui est-ce que tu _____ (sortir)?
2. Tu _____ (retrouver) les autres en ville ou vous y _____ (aller) tous ensemble?
3. Tu _____ (prendre) ta voiture?
4. Quel temps est-ce qu'il _____ (faire)? Il _____ (pleuvoir)?
5. Quels vêtements est-ce que tu _____ (mettre) pour sortir?
6. Qu'est-ce que vous _____ (faire)? Vous _____ (dîner) ensemble? Vous _____ (aller) danser? Vous _____ (voir) un film au cinéma?
7. De quoi *(About what)* est-ce que vous _____ (parler)?
8. Tu _____ (rentrer) vers quelle heure?
9. Vous _____ (partir) tous en même temps ou les autres _____ (rester) plus longtemps?

Maintenant, utilisez les questions précédentes pour interviewer un(e) partenaire sur la dernière fois qu'il/elle est sorti(e) avec des amis.

B Je veux tout savoir. Céline pose des questions à Amélie sur une soirée qu'elle a passée avec Christophe et Rachid. Complétez les réponses d'Amélie en remplaçant les mots en italique par le pronom qui convient: **le, la, l', les** ou **y.** Utilisez le verbe de la question dans la réponse.

> **EXEMPLE** — Alors, Christophe et toi avez passé *la soirée* ensemble l'autre jour?
> — Oui, on **l'a passée** ensemble samedi dernier.

1. — Est-ce que tu as retrouvé *Christophe* en ville ou vous y êtes allés ensemble?
   — Je _____ en ville.
2. — Vous êtes allés *en ville* seuls tous les deux?
   — Non, Rachid _____ avec nous.
3. — Comment est-ce que tu trouves *Rachid*?
   — Je _____ très sympa.
4. — Comment est-ce que tu as trouvé *le restaurant* où vous avez dîné?
   — On a dîné dans le restaurant marocain *(Moroccan)* de la sœur de Rachid et moi, je _____ excellent.
5. — Vous êtes allés *en boîte* aussi?
   — Oui, on _____ après le dîner.
6. — Tu vas voir *Christophe et Rachid* le week-end prochain, aussi?
   — Pour l'instant, je n'ai pas l'intention de _____ le week-end prochain, mais on ne sait jamais *(you never know)*.

C Qui fait quoi? Amélie dîne avec Rachid et Christophe dans le restaurant de la sœur de Rachid. Complétez ses phrases avec une expression logique de la liste. Mettez la forme correcte du verbe **faire** dans le premier espace et le reste de l'expression dans le deuxième espace.

> faire les courses   faire le ménage   faire la vaisselle
> faire la cuisine   faire une promenade

EXEMPLE Ta sœur et toi, vous **faites** toujours **les courses** pour le restaurant très tôt tous les matins, non? Où est-ce que vous trouvez tous les produits pour ces plats marocains *(Moroccan)*?

1. Ta sœur _____ très bien _____. Mon plat *(dish)* est excellent.

2. Céline et moi _____ toujours _____ immédiatement après le dîner parce qu'elle a peur d'avoir des insectes dans la cuisine.

3. Notre appartement est toujours très propre. Céline _____ souvent _____.

4. Je _____ souvent _____ après le dîner si je mange beaucoup pour faciliter la digestion.

D Quel temps fait-il? Au dîner, Rachid parle du temps qu'il fait au Maroc au cours de l'année. Complétez ses phrases.

1.    2.    3.

© Cengage Learning

1. En été, il fait du ___soleil___ et il fait souvent très ___beau___.
2. Quelquefois en hiver, il fait ___froid___, mais il ne ___pleuvoir___ presque jamais.
   almost never
3. Il fait souvent du ___vent___, mais il ne ___chaud___ pas beaucoup.
   often

Access the Video *Les Stagiaires* on iLrn.

© Cengage Learning

▶ Épisode 5: Qu'est-ce que vous avez fait?

AVANT LA VIDÉO

Dans cet épisode, Matthieu parle à Christophe d'une soirée que Christophe et Rachid ont passée avec Amélie. Avant de regarder l'épisode, pensez à des activités qu'on fait quand on passe une soirée en ville avec des amis.

APRÈS LA VIDÉO

Regardez l'épisode et répondez aux questions suivantes.

- Où est-ce que Christophe, Rachid et Amélie sont allés?
- Qu'est-ce qu'ils ont fait?
- De quoi *(About what)* ont-ils parlé?

LECTURE ET COMPOSITION

LECTURE

Before reading a text, scan it and use the title and any accompanying visuals (photos, charts, etc.) to help you anticipate content and read more easily.

Un blog. Regardez le texte et les photos. Quel genre de blog est-ce? Quelle sorte de renseignements est-ce que vous pensez y trouver?

Je blogue donc je suis

Les blogs **font** de plus en plus **partie des** loisirs des Français, et la France est devenue championne du **monde** du nombre de blogs par **internaute.** Bloguer est surtout populaire chez les jeunes, surtout les jeunes politiquement engagés, mais **chacun** a sa **propre** raison de bloguer. Pour certains, c'est le désir de faire partie d'une communauté. Pour d'autres, c'est le besoin de mettre en mots ses sentiments, **promouvoir** ses idées ou **décrire** ses expériences. Les blogs de voyage sont **parmi** les plus populaires. Lisez le blog de voyage **qui suit.**

Mon week-end à Paris

Je suis allé passer un week-end à Paris avec des amis. Arrivés le vendredi vers 18h, on a profité de la première soirée pour visiter Montmartre. J'ai trouvé la vue de Paris de là-haut inoubliable.

Le lendemain, on a fait une promenade le long des Champs-Élysées et ensuite, on a longé les quais de la Seine. Après, on a visité Notre-Dame. J'ai admiré la façade avec toutes ses statues et j'ai pris beaucoup de photos.

Le dimanche matin, on a vu une exposition d'art moderne au Centre Pompidou avant de quitter Paris.

Paris, c'est sans doute la plus belle ville du monde!

---

font partie de *are part of*   **le monde** *the world*   **internaute** *Internet user*
chacun *each one*   **propre** *own*   **promouvoir** *to promote*   **décrire** *to describe*
parmi *among*   **qui suit** *that follows*

COMPOSITION

To write well, you first need to organize your ideas. You can sometimes base your organization on a document you already have or can easily create. For example, to describe a book you have read, you can use the table of contents to organize your thoughts. To talk about a trip you have taken, you can use your itinerary, and when writing a blog, you can look at how other blogs are organized.

Organisez-vous. Vous allez écrire un blog sur une semaine imaginaire en France. D'abord, sur une feuille de papier, créez votre itinéraire.

1.
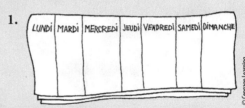

2. Sous chaque jour, écrivez des phrases pour décrire *(describe)* une progression logique de votre séjour *(your stay)*. Dites:

   - quand vous êtes parti(e), et avec qui et comment vous avez voyagé
   - où et à quelle heure vous êtes arrivé(e) en France et dans quelle sorte d'hôtel(s) vous êtes descendu(e)
   - ce que *(what)* vous avez fait chaque jour
   - quand vous avez quitté la France

Compréhension

1. Est-ce que les Français aiment bloguer? Quel groupe blogue le plus?
2. Pourquoi est-ce qu'on blogue?
3. Dans ce blog de voyage, quels endroits à Paris est-ce que le blogueur mentionne?

Un voyage en France

En vous basant sur votre itinéraire, écrivez un blog sur votre voyage imaginaire.

   EXEMPLE L'été dernier, je suis allé(e) en France avec...

iLrn Share It!

COMPARAISONS CULTURELLES

In the **Culture Modules** in the video library, see **Leisure activities.**

LE SPORT ET LE TEMPS LIBRE DES FRANÇAIS

Les Français passent souvent leur temps libre chez eux où ils aiment regarder la télé, écouter de la musique, passer du temps sur Internet et lire.

© Floresco Productions/Getty Images

© graphic design: Isabelle Jégo

Les Français aiment beaucoup les activités culturelles aussi et ils consacrent beaucoup de temps à ces activités, **allant** souvent au cinéma, à des expositions d'art, au théâtre, à des concerts... De nombreux festivals et fêtes qui permettent d'avoir accès à l'art, à la musique, **au monde du septième art** et à leur **patrimoine** montrent **l'engouement** des Français pour la culture.

Pourtant, selon une enquête récente **auprès des Français,** l'activité **dite** la plus satisfaisante (après passer du temps entre amis), est faire du sport, et beaucoup d'entre eux pratiquent une activité sportive **plusieurs** fois par mois.

À l'école, le sport est obligatoire et il est **enseigné** comme les autres **matières.** Pourtant, **les élèves ne peuvent pas** pratiquer de sports à l'école après les cours. Ils **doivent** s'inscrire dans un club. Les clubs de football, de tennis et d'**équitation** sont les plus souvent choisis.

© Chameleons Eye/Shutterstock.com

allant *going*　**au monde du septième art** *to the world of the seventh art (cinema)*　**patrimoine** *heritage*　**l'engouement** *(m) enthusiasm*　**Pourtant, selon une enquête** *However, according to a survey*　**auprès des Français** *with the French*　**dite** *said* **plusieurs** *several*　**À l'école** *At school*　**enseigné** *taught*　**matières** *subjects*　**les élèves** *the students*　**ne peuvent pas** *can't* **doivent** *have to*　**équitation** *(f) horseback riding*

Beaucoup de Français **ne font pas partie de** clubs, mais ils pratiquent une activité sportive seuls. Ils font du jogging, **de la marche, de la natation** ou du cyclisme. À Paris, tous les week-ends, **les berges** de la Seine sont fermées pour permettre aux cyclistes de se promener; et le vendredi soir, **grâce à** l'association sportive «Pari roller», les Parisiens **peuvent traverser la ville en roller** sur un circuit **interdit à la circulation automobile.**

Les sports d'hiver (**le patin à glace,** le ski, le snowboard), les sports d'été (la natation, **la voile, la planche à voile**) aussi bien que les sports «d'aventure» (**l'escalade, le parapente,** le canoë-kayak) sont aussi très appréciés!

Et chez vous, quels sont les sports les plus populaires dans votre région?

© Greer/Photomasi/Camera Press/Redux

Compréhension

1. Qu'est-ce que les Français aiment faire chez eux pendant leur temps libre? Est-ce que ce sont les mêmes activités que celles *(those)* qui sont populaires chez vous?

2. Quelles sont les activités culturelles les plus populaires en France? Et chez vous?

3. Est-ce que le sport fait partie du cursus scolaire *(school curriculum)* d'un(e) élève français(e)? Et des élèves dans votre région? Qu'est-ce que les jeunes doivent faire *(have to do)* pour participer à des activités sportives après les cours? Est-ce que c'est similaire ou différent dans votre région?

4. Quelles activités sportives sont populaires chez les Français? Et chez vous?

iLrn Share It!

Visit **www.cengagebrain.com** for additional cultural information and activities.

ne font pas partie de *don't belong to*   **de la marche** *walking*   **de la natation** *swimming*   **les berges** *the banks* (of a river)
grâce à *thanks to*   **peuvent traverser la ville en roller** *can skate across the city*   **interdit à la circulation automobile** *closed to traffic*   **le patin à glace** *ice-skating*   **la voile** *sailing*   **la planche à voile** *windsurfing*   **l'escalade** *rock climbing*
le parapente *paragliding*

RÉSUMÉ DE GRAMMAIRE

PASSÉ COMPOSÉ

J'ai mangé.
I ate.
I have eaten.
I did eat.

Ils n'ont pas beaucoup dormi.
They didn't sleep much.
They haven't slept much.

To say what happened in the past, put the verb in the **passé composé.** It may be translated in a variety of ways. The **passé composé** is composed of an auxiliary verb and a past participle. For most verbs the auxiliary verb is **avoir,** but for a few verbs it is **être.** All **-er** verbs have past participles with **-é (parler: j'ai parlé)** and most **-ir** verbs with **-i (dormir: j'ai dormi).**

PARLER → PARLÉ	
j'**ai parlé**	nous **avons parlé**
tu **as parlé**	vous **avez parlé**
il/elle/on **a parlé**	ils/elles **ont parlé**

These verbs conjugated with **avoir** have irregular past participles.

avoir:	j'ai eu	mettre:	j'ai mis	être:	j'ai été
il y a:	il y a eu	prendre:	j'ai pris	faire:	j'ai fait
boire:	j'ai bu	apprendre:	j'ai appris	écrire:	j'ai écrit
lire:	j'ai lu	comprendre:	j'ai compris		
pleuvoir:	il a plu				
voir:	j'ai vu				

— Qu'est-ce que tu **as fait** hier soir?
— J'**ai vu** un film avec des amis et après, on **a pris** un verre au café.

A few verbs have **être** as their auxiliary. With these verbs, the past participle agrees with the subject for gender and plurality.

ALLER → ALLÉ	
je **suis allé(e)**	nous **sommes allé(e)s**
tu **es allé(e)**	vous **êtes allé(e)(s)**
il **est allé**	ils **sont allés**
elle **est allée**	elles **sont allées**
on **est allé(e)(s)**	

— Est-ce que ta mère et ta tante **sont allées** à Paris avec toi?
— Oui, elles ont fait le voyage avec moi, mais je **suis restée** plus longtemps. Elles **sont rentrées** une semaine avant moi.

Here are some verbs that have **être** as their auxiliary verb. Use **être** with **passer** only when it means *to pass by* and not when it means *to spend time.*

aller:	je suis allé(e)	monter:	je suis monté(e)
arriver:	je suis arrivé(e)	descendre:	je suis descendu(e)
rester:	je suis resté(e)	venir:	je suis venu(e)
entrer:	je suis entré(e)	revenir:	je suis revenu(e)
sortir:	je suis sorti(e)	devenir:	je suis devenu(e)
partir:	je suis parti(e)	naître:	je suis né(e)
passer:	je suis passé(e)	mourir:	il/elle est mort(e)
rentrer:	je suis rentré(e)	tomber:	je suis tombé(e)
retourner:	je suis retourné(e)		

— Tu as **déjà** dîné?
— Non, je **n'**ai **pas encore** mangé.

— Qu'est-ce que ton mari et toi avez fait l'année dernière pour les vacances?
— On **n'**a **rien** fait.

To negate a verb in the **passé composé,** place **ne** immediately after the subject and **pas, rien** *(nothing),* or **jamais** after the auxiliary verb. Use **ne... pas encore** to say *not yet* and **déjà** to say *already* or *ever.* **Déjà** and adverbs indicating *how often* (**toujours, souvent...**) and *how well* (**bien, mal...**) are usually placed between the auxiliary verb and the past participle.

The following adverbs indicate when something happened in the past. They may be placed at the beginning or end of a clause.

hier (matin, après-midi, soir)	récemment
le week-end (le mois) dernier	pendant deux heures (longtemps)
la semaine (l'année) dernière	il y a quelques secondes (cinq minutes, cinq ans...)
la dernière fois	

FAIRE

The verb **faire** *(to do, to make)* is irregular.

FAIRE *(to do, to make)*	
je **fais**	nous **faisons**
tu **fais**	vous **faites**
il/elle/on **fait**	ils/elles **font**
PASSÉ COMPOSÉ: **j'ai fait**	

Faire is also used in many weather expressions, as well as the expressions listed on page 198.

 The **un, une, des, du, de la,** and **de l'** in the expressions with **faire** become **de (d')** when the verb is negated. The definite article (**le, la, l', les**) does not change.

NE... RIEN

Ne... rien means *nothing* or *not anything*. This expression can be the subject or object of the verb, or the object of a preposition.

When negating an infinitive, place both parts of the negative expression before it.

DIRECT OBJECT PRONOUNS

The direct object pronouns are **le, la, l',** and **les.** Use **le** *(him, it)* to replace masculine singular nouns and **la** *(her, it)* to replace feminine singular nouns. **Les** *(Them)* replaces all plural nouns. **Le** and **la** become **l'** when the following word begins with a vowel or silent **h.**

	BEFORE A CONSONANT	BEFORE A VOWEL OR SILENT *H*
him, it (masculine)	le	l'
her, it (feminine)	la	l'
them	les	les

These pronouns are generally placed *immediately before* the verb. They go before the infinitive if there is one. If not, they go before the conjugated verb. In the negative, the pronoun remains *immediately before* the conjugated verb or the infinitive.

 In the **passé composé,** direct object pronouns are placed just before the auxiliary verb (the conjugated form of **avoir**), and the past participle agrees with them for gender and plurality by adding **-e, -s,** or **-es.**

— Tu es parti en vacances **pendant combien de temps?**
— **Pendant** quinze jours.
— Tu es rentré **il y a combien de temps?**
— Je suis rentré **mardi dernier.**

Je ne **fais** rien ce week-end.
Qu'est-ce que tu **fais?**
On **fait** quelque chose ensemble?
Faisons quelque chose avec mes amis.
Que **faites**-vous généralement?
Mes amis **font** beaucoup de sport.

— Quel temps **fait**-il?
— Il **fait** beau (mauvais, froid, chaud, frais, [du] soleil, du vent).
Ils **font** la cuisine et nous **faisons** la vaisselle.

Je ne fais jamais **d'**exercice.
Mon colocataire ne fait jamais **le** ménage.

Rien n'est en solde?
Tu **n'**achètes **rien?**
Je **n'**ai besoin de **rien.**
Je préfère **ne rien** acheter.

— Tu prends ce sac?
— Oui, je **le** prends.
— Tu aimes cette robe aussi?
— Oui, je **l'**aime bien.
— Tu achètes tes vêtements ici?
— Oui, je **les** achète souvent ici.

Je **les** achète.
Je ne **les** achète pas.
Je vais **les** acheter.
Je ne vais pas **les** acheter.

— A-t-il acheté les chaussures?
— Oui, il **les** a acheté**es.**
Non, il ne **les** a pas acheté**es.**

VOCABULAIRE

COMPÉTENCE 1

Saying what you did

NOMS MASCULINS

un homme d'affaires	*a businessman*
le journal	*the newspaper*
le petit déjeuner	*breakfast*

NOM FÉMININ

une femme d'affaires	*a businesswoman*

EXPRESSIONS ADVERBIALES

hier	*yesterday*
hier soir	*last night, yesterday evening*
samedi dernier	*last Saturday*
le week-end dernier	*last weekend*

DIVERS

dernier (dernière)	*last*
faire une promenade	*to take a walk*
ne... rien	*nothing, not anything*
prendre son petit déjeuner	*to have one's breakfast*
travaillant	*working*

COMPÉTENCE 2

Telling where you went

NOMS MASCULINS

un an	*a year*
un camping	*a campground*
un hôtel	*a hotel*
le lendemain	*the next day, the following day*
des parents	*relatives*

NOMS FÉMININS

la chance	*luck*
une heure	*an hour*
une minute	*a minute*
une nuit	*a night*
une seconde	*a second* (in time)
une voiture de location	*a rental car*

EXPRESSIONS VERBALES

descendre (de/à/dans)	*to descend, to come down, to get off/out (of) (a vehicle), to stay (at)*
entrer (dans)	*to enter*
faire un voyage	*to take a trip*
monter (dans)	*to go up, to get on/in*
mourir (mort[e])	*to die (dead)*
naître (né[e])	*to be born (born)*
partir en voyage	*to leave on a trip*
partir en week-end	*to go away for the weekend*
passer (chez/devant/par)	*to pass (by [. . . 's house])*
retourner	*to return, to go back*
tomber	*to fall*

EXPRESSIONS ADVERBIALES

l'année dernière	*last year*
déjà	*already, ever*
la dernière fois	*the last time*
hier (matin, après-midi)	*yesterday (morning, afternoon)*
hier soir	*last night, yesterday evening*
Il y a combien de temps?	*How long ago?*
il y a quelques secondes	*a few seconds ago*
longtemps	*a long time*
lundi (mardi...) dernier	*last Monday (Tuesday . . .)*
le mois dernier	*last month*
ne... pas encore	*not yet*
Pendant combien de temps?	*For how long?*
pendant deux heures	*for two hours*
récemment	*recently*
la semaine dernière	*last week*
le week-end dernier	*last weekend*
le week-end passé	*the past weekend*

DIVERS

Quelle chance!	*What luck!*
quelques	*some, a few*

last year : l'an dernier
last week : la semaine dernière

jusqu'a   until

Discussing the weather and your activities

NOMS MASCULINS

l'automne (en automne)	autumn/fall (in autumn/in the fall)
l'été (en été)	summer (in summer)
l'hiver (en hiver)	winter (in winter)
un jardin	a garden
le printemps (au printemps)	spring (in spring)
le temps	the weather, time

NOMS FÉMININS

des distractions	entertainment
la neige	snow
la pluie	rain
une saison	a season

EXPRESSIONS VERBALES

adorer	to love, to adore
aller à la montagne	to go to the mountains
dépendre (de)	to depend (on)
faire de l'exercice	to exercise
faire des courses	to run errands
faire du bateau	to go boating
faire du camping	to go camping
faire du jardinage	to garden
faire du jogging	to go jogging
faire du shopping	to go shopping
faire du ski (nautique)	to (water)ski
faire du sport (du tennis, du hockey...)	to play sports (tennis, hockey...)
faire du vélo	to go bike-riding
faire du VTT	to go all-terrain biking
faire la cuisine	to cook
faire la lessive	to do laundry
faire la vaisselle	to do the dishes
faire le ménage	to do housework
faire les courses	to buy groceries
faire une promenade	to take a walk
faire une randonnée (faire des randonnées)	to take a hike, to hike (to go hiking, to hike)
faire un voyage	to take a trip
neiger	to snow
pleuvoir (Il a plu.)	to rain (It rained.)

DIVERS

ne... rien (de spécial)	nothing, not anything (special)
pendant	during, for
Quel temps fait-il?	What's the weather like?
Il fait beau / chaud / frais / froid / mauvais / (du) soleil / du vent.	It's nice / hot / cool / cold / bad / sunny / windy.
Il y a du vent.	It's windy.
Il pleut.	It is raining., It rains.
Il neige.	It is snowing., It snows.
Quel temps va-t-il faire?	What's the weather going to be like?
Il va faire...	It's going to be ...
Il va pleuvoir / neiger.	It's going to rain / to snow.
si	if

Deciding what to wear and buying clothes

NOMS MASCULINS

un anorak	a ski jacket
un bikini	a bikini
un chemisier	a blouse
un costume	a suit (for a man)
un imperméable	a raincoat
un jean	jeans
un maillot de bain	a swimsuit
un manteau	an (over)coat
un pantalon	pants
un parapluie	an umbrella
un polo	a knit shirt
un portefeuille	a wallet
un pull	a pullover sweater
un sac	a purse, a sack, a bag
un short	shorts
un survêtement	a jogging suit
un tee-shirt	a T-shirt
un vendeur	a salesclerk

NOMS FÉMININS

des baskets	tennis shoes, sneakers
des bottes	boots
une cabine d'essayage	a fitting room
des chaussures	shoes
une chemise	a shirt
une cravate	a tie
une jupe	a skirt
des lunettes (de soleil)	(sun)glasses
une montre	a watch
une robe	a dress
des sandales	sandals
des tongs	flip-flops
une vendeuse	a salesclerk

EXPRESSIONS VERBALES

coûter	to cost
emporter	to take (along), to carry (away)
essayer	to try, to try on
Il/Elle me plaît.	I like it.
mettre (je mets, vous mettez) (j'ai mis)	to wear, to put, to put on (I wore, put, put on)
porter	to wear

DIVERS

Bien sûr!	Of course!
ce (cet, cette, ces)...-ci/-là	this/that/these/those... over here/ over there
en solde	on sale
Je peux vous aider?	May I help you?
le (l') / la (l')	him, it / her, it
les	them
parfois	sometimes
par ici	this way
Quelle taille faites-vous? Je fais du...	What size do you wear? I wear size...
Qu'en pensez-vous?	What do you think about it?
voyons	let's see

BIENVENUE EN EUROPE FRANCOPHONE

En Europe, le français est une langue officielle dans quatre pays et **une principauté:** la France, la Belgique, la Suisse, le Luxembourg et Monaco. **Lesquels aimeriez-vous** visiter?

Fondée en 963, la ville de Luxembourg offre la possibilité de voir plus de mille ans d'histoire.

Le **Grand-Duché** du Luxembourg est un des plus petits États d'Europe. Il y a trois langues **officielles** au Luxembourg: le français, le luxembourgeois et l'allemand.

Grâce à sa forte immigration, surtout **venant** des pays de l'Union européenne, le Luxembourg est devenu un microcosme de l'Europe moderne.

Bienvenue *Welcome*   **une principauté** *a principality*   **Lesquels aimeriez-vous** *Which ones would you like*
Grand-Duché *Grand Duchy*   **officielles** *official*   **Grâce à** *Thanks to*   **surtout venant** *especially coming*

La Suisse a quatre langues officielles: l'allemand, le français, l'italien et le romanche, et **chacun de** ces groupes linguistiques a **ses propres coutumes** et traditions. Les Suisses sont très **fiers de** leur culture et de leur diversité multiculturelle.

La Suisse offre de très belles vues.

Qu'aimeriez-vous faire en Suisse: du ski, des randonnées en montagne ou de l'alpinisme?

---

chacun de *each of*   **ses propres coutumes** *its own customs*   **fiers de** *proud of*   **Qu'aimeriez-vous** *What would you like*
de l'alpinisme *mountain climbing*

Les trois régions qui forment la Belgique, la Région **flamande,** la Région **wallonne** et la Région de Bruxelles (la capitale) donnent à la Belgique une riche diversité culturelle. Les Flamands (58 % [pour cent] de la population) parlent **néerlandais.** Les Wallons (32 % de la population) parlent français. **Quant au reste,** 9 % sont bilingues et 1 % parle allemand.

La Belgique est connue pour la variété de son architecture, pour la beauté de ses **paysages** et pour ses **nombreux** châteaux.

On peut aller sur la **Grand-Place à Bruxelles pour admirer son architecture baroque et gothique, prendre un café et faire du shopping.**

Monaco est célèbre pour le tourisme, le luxe et pour ses casinos, **ainsi que** pour son fameux Grand Prix de Formule 1.

Monaco est **une principauté** et une monarchie constitutionnelle. Le français y est la langue officielle, mais on y parle aussi l'anglais et l'italien. Près de 5 000 personnes parlent **monégasque,** un dialecte dérivé de l'italien.

---

flamande *Flemish*   **wallonne** *French-speaking, Walloon*   **néerlandais** *Dutch*   **Quant au reste** *As for the rest*
paysages *landscapes, countryside*   **nombreux** *numerous*   **une principauté** *a principality*   **monégasque** *Monegasque (language native to Monaco)*   **ainsi que** *as well as*

La France **comprend la France métropolitaine** et **plusieurs** départements, régions et collectivités **d'outre-mer, tels que** la Guadeloupe (dans la mer des Caraïbes, près de l'Amérique centrale), Mayotte (près de l'Afrique) et la Polynésie française (dans le Pacifique). Regardez la carte du monde francophone **au début du** livre. Quelle partie de la France **aimeriez-vous** visiter?

Dans les villes françaises, comme ici à Strasbourg, **on peut** visiter les parties historiques de la ville.

En sortant des grandes villes, on trouve de beaux paysages et de petits villages fascinants.

Dans le sud de la France, on peut voir des ruines romaines, comme **celles-ci** à Aix-en-Provence.

Aimeriez-vous mieux visiter un des départements ou territoires d'outre-mer, comme Mayotte?

---

comprend *includes* **la France métropolitaine** *metropolitan France* (the part of France in Europe) **plusieurs** *several* **d'outre-mer** *overseas* **tels que** *such as* **au début du** *at the beginning of the* **aimeriez-vous** *would you like* **on peut** *one can* **En sortant des** *By leaving the* **celles-ci** *these*

À Paris

Les sorties

 iLrn Heinle Learning Center

 www.cengagebrain.com

 Horizons Video: Les Stagiaires

 Audio

 Internet web search

 Pair work

 Group work

© Brigitte Merle/Photononstop/Getty Images

6

COMPÉTENCE

1 Inviting someone to go out
Les invitations

Issuing and accepting invitations
*Les verbes **vouloir**, **pouvoir** et **devoir***

Stratégies et Compréhension auditive
- **Pour mieux comprendre:** *Noting the important information*
- **Compréhension auditive:** *On va au cinéma?*

2 Talking about how you spend and used
to spend your time
Aujourd'hui et dans le passé

Saying how things used to be
L'imparfait

Talking about activities
*Les verbes **sortir**, **partir** et **dormir***

3 Talking about the past
Une sortie

Telling what was going on when something else happened
L'imparfait et le passé composé

Telling what happened and describing the circumstances
Le passé composé et l'imparfait

4 Narrating in the past
Les contes

Narrating what happened
Le passé composé et l'imparfait (reprise)

Vidéoreprise   *Les Stagiaires*

Lecture et Composition
- **Pour mieux lire:** *Using standard formats*
- **Lecture:** *Deux films français*
- **Pour mieux écrire:** *Using standard formats*
- **Composition:** *Un film à voir*

Comparaisons culturelles   *Le cinéma: les préférences
des Français*

Résumé de grammaire

Vocabulaire

PARIS

iLrn In the **Culture Modules** in the video library, see **Architecture**.

© Cengage Learning

Rive droite

La Seine

Île de la Cité

Île Saint-Louis

Rive gauche

© Cengage Learning

© Mark Antman/The Image Works

Paris, la capitale de la France, est une des plus belles villes **du monde.**

La Seine sépare la ville en deux parties, **la rive** gauche et la rive droite. Les deux îles situées **au milieu de** la Seine sont l'île de la Cité et l'île Saint-Louis. C'est sur l'île de la Cité que la ville de Paris est née il y a plus de 2 000 ans.

© Rostislav Glinsky/Shutterstock.com

La célèbre avenue des Champs-Élysées s'étend de la place de la Concorde à l'arc de Triomphe.

© tungtopgun/Shutterstock.com

Le Louvre, l'un des plus grands musées d'art du monde, fait presque un kilomètre de long.

---

du monde *in the world*   **la rive** *the bank* (of a river)   **au milieu de** *in the middle of*   **s'étend** *extends*

Pour avoir une vue panoramique de la ville, on peut monter en haut de la tour Eiffel.

Paris

 Visit it live on Google Earth!

NOMBRE D'HABITANTS: **2 235 000 (avec la région parisienne: plus de 12 089 000) (les Parisiens)**

DÉPARTEMENT: **Paris**

RÉGION: **Île-de-France**

Le savez-vous?

Devinez quel site touristique représenté ici correspond à chaque description.

les Champs-Élysées   le Louvre   la tour Eiffel
Montmartre   le Quartier latin

1. Cet ancien palais royal est devenu un musée en 1791. C'est aujourd'hui un des musées les plus visités du monde.

2. Dans ce quartier, Robert de Sorbon a établi la Sorbonne en 1253, ce qui est aujourd'hui l'Université de Paris. Le latin était la langue officielle dans le quartier jusqu'en 1793.

3. Cette célèbre avenue est longue de presque deux kilomètres et s'étend *(extends)* de l'arc de Triomphe jusqu'à la place de la Concorde.

4. En 1860, la ville de Paris a annexé ce quartier situé sur une colline *(hill)* avec une vue panoramique de la ville. La basilique du Sacré-Cœur, construite entre 1875 et 1914, est le point le plus haut *(highest)* de Paris.

5. L'ingénieur qui a construit ce monument pour l'Exposition universelle de 1889 a aussi travaillé sur la statue de la Liberté à New York. C'est le site touristique le plus visité de France.

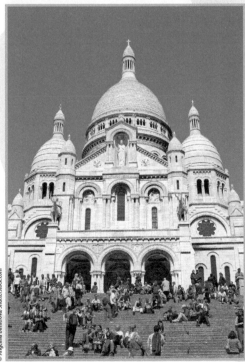

Si vous aimez **la vie** de bohème, visitez le quartier de Montmartre.

Le Quartier latin est un des quartiers les plus sympathiques de Paris.

Sur ces pages, vous voyez quelques-unes des 180 musées et monuments de Paris. Cherchez des visites virtuelles de la ville de Paris sur Internet. Faites des recherches sur un des sites parisiens que vous aimeriez *(would like)* visiter. Découvrez au moins cinq choses au sujet de ce site.

la vie *life*

Inviting someone to go out

LES INVITATIONS

Pour inviter **quelqu'un** à sortir, **vous pouvez dire...**

À UN(E) AMI(E)	À UNE AUTRE PERSONNE OU À UN GROUPE DE PERSONNES
Tu veux...?	**Vous voulez...?**
Tu voudrais...?	Vous voudriez...?
Je t'invite à...	Je voudrais vous inviter à...

Si **quelqu'un vous invite**, vous pouvez répondre...

POUR DIRE OUI	POUR DIRE NON
Oui, je veux bien...	Je regrette mais...
Quelle bonne idée!	je ne suis pas libre.
Avec plaisir!	**je ne peux** vraiment **pas.**
D'accord!	**je dois** travailler.

POUR SUGGÉRER UNE AUTRE ACTIVITÉ

Je préfère...

J'aime mieux...

Allons plutôt à...

Les Français **utilisent** l'heure officielle pour tous **les horaires** (le train, le cinéma, **les heures d'ouverture...**). Pour lire l'heure officielle, on utilise uniquement des nombres. Aux États-Unis, on **appelle** cette **façon** de lire l'heure *military time*.

L'HEURE OFFICIELLE		L'HEURE FAMILIÈRE
0h05	zéro heure cinq	minuit cinq
1h15	une heure quinze	une heure et quart (du matin)
12h20	douze heures vingt	midi vingt
13h30	treize heures trente	une heure et demie (de l'après-midi)
20h40	vingt heures quarante	neuf heures moins vingt (du soir)
20h45	vingt heures quarante-cinq	neuf heures moins le quart (du soir)

THÉÂTRE DE PARIS

CLAUDE BRASSEUR
PATRICK CHESNAIS

LE TARTUFFE
MOLIÈRE

© Théâtre de Paris/EFIL/B. Richebé

Séances: du lundi au samedi à 20h30 | mardi à 17h00 | samedi à 16h00.

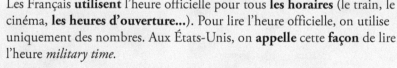

quelqu'un *someone* **vous pouvez** (*pouvoir* *can, may, to be able*) **dire** *to say* **Tu veux/Vous voulez** (*vouloir* *to want*) **quelqu'un vous invite** *someone invites you* **je ne peux pas** (*pouvoir* *can, may, to be able*) **je dois** (*devoir* *must, to have to*) **utiliser** *to use, to utilize* **un horaire** *a schedule* **les heures d'ouverture** *opening times* **appeler** *to call* **une façon** *a way*

Éric téléphone à sa copine Michèle.

MICHÈLE: Allô?

ÉRIC: Salut, Michèle. C'est moi, Éric. Ça va?

MICHÈLE: Oui, très bien. Et toi?

ÉRIC: Moi, ça va. Écoute, tu es libre ce soir? Tu voudrais sortir?

MICHÈLE: Oui, je veux bien. Qu'est-ce que tu as envie de faire?

ÉRIC: **Je pensais** aller voir la nouvelle comédie qu'on **passe** au cinéma Gaumont.

MICHÈLE: Tu sais, moi, je n'aime pas **tellement** les comédies. Je préfère les films d'**amour**. Allons plutôt voir le nouveau film d'amour au cinéma Rex.

ÉRIC: Bon, je veux bien. À quelle heure?

MICHÈLE: Il y a **une séance** à vingt heures quarante-cinq.

ÉRIC: Alors, je passe chez toi vers huit heures?

MICHÈLE: D'accord. Alors, au revoir.

ÉRIC: À tout à l'heure, Michèle.

ᵼᵼᵼ A Invitations. Circulez dans la classe et utilisez différentes expressions pour inviter d'autres étudiants à faire les choses suivantes. Ils vont accepter ou refuser chaque invitation ou proposer une autre activité.

INVITEZ UN(E) AMI(E) À...

1. aller danser samedi soir
2. dîner au restaurant ce soir
3. aller voir une exposition demain
4. aller prendre un verre aujourd'hui après les cours

INVITEZ UN GROUPE D'AMIS À...

5. aller voir un film d'amour demain
6. réviser ensemble ce soir
7. faire du vélo au parc ce week-end
8. aller au match de football américain / de basket ce week-end

ᵼᵼ B Je regrette, mais... Préparez la conversation suivante avec un(e) partenaire.

Un ami téléphone à Éric pour l'inviter à sortir, mais Éric préfère ne rien faire et il refuse. L'ami insiste. Éric est très imaginatif dans ses excuses. Jouez les deux rôles avec un(e) partenaire.

ᵼᵼ C À quelle heure? Regardez la liste des séances de la pièce de théâtre *Le Tartuffe* à la page précédente. Exprimez l'heure de chaque séance de deux façons. Ensuite, préparez une conversation avec un(e) partenaire dans laquelle vous l'invitez à voir la pièce et vous choisissez une séance.

EXEMPLE 20h30
**Du lundi au samedi, il y a une séance à vingt heures trente;
c'est-à-dire *(that is to say)* à huit heures et demie du soir.**

ᵼᵼ À VOUS!

Avec un(e) partenaire, relisez à haute voix la conversation entre Michèle et Éric. Ensuite, adaptez la conversation pour faire des projets pour aller au cinéma ensemble. Servez-vous du *Vocabulaire supplémentaire* et parlez de quel(s) genre(s) de film vous aimez, de quel film vous voudriez voir et de comment et où vous allez vous retrouver *(you are going to meet up)*.

Vocabulaire supplémentaire
LES FILMS

un dessin animé *a cartoon*
un drame
un film d'aventure
un film d'horreur
un film de science-fiction
un film fantastique
un film policier
un film d'animation
une comédie romantique

POUR SE RETROUVER

Je passe chez toi / chez vous. *I'll come by your place.*
Passe / Passez chez moi. *Come by my place.*
Rendez-vous à... *Let's meet at ...*

You can find a list of the new words from this *Compétence* on page 254 and access the audio online.

Je pensais *I was thinking*   **passer (un film)** *to show (a movie)*   **tellement** *so much*   **l'amour** *(m) love*   **une séance** *a showing*

ISSUING AND ACCEPTING INVITATIONS

Les verbes *vouloir*, *pouvoir* et *devoir*

The verbs **vouloir** *(to want)* and **pouvoir** *(can, may, to be able)* are useful when inviting someone to do something. They have similar conjugations.

VOULOIR (to want)	
je **veux**	nous **voulons**
tu **veux**	vous **voulez**
il/elle/on **veut**	ils/elles **veulent**
PASSÉ COMPOSÉ: **j'ai voulu**	

POUVOIR (can, may, to be able)	
je **peux**	nous **pouvons**
tu **peux**	vous **pouvez**
il/elle/on **peut**	ils/elles **peuvent**
PASSÉ COMPOSÉ: **j'ai pu**	

Je **veux** sortir, mais je **ne peux pas**.   *I **want** to go out, but I **can't**.*

Use **devoir** followed by an infinitive to say what you *must* or *have to* do. **Devoir** also means *to owe*.

DEVOIR (must, to have to, to owe)	
je **dois**	nous **devons**
tu **dois**	vous **devez**
il/elle/on **doit**	ils/elles **doivent**
PASSÉ COMPOSÉ: **j'ai dû**	

Je **dois** travailler demain.   *I **have to** work tomorrow.*
Je **dois** 100 dollars à mon frère.   *I **owe** my brother 100 dollars.*

In the **passé composé, devoir** can mean that someone *had to* do something or *must have* done something. Context will clarify the meaning.

Michèle n'est pas chez elle. Elle **a dû** partir.
*Michèle isn't home. She **had to** leave. / She **must have** left.*

Il n'a pas pu sortir parce qu'il **a dû** travailler.
*He wasn't able to go out because he **had to** work.*

✔ Pour vérifier

1. What does **vouloir** mean? What are three meanings of **pouvoir**? What are the meanings of **devoir**? What are the conjugations of these three verbs?

2. The **nous** and **vous** forms have the same vowels in the stem as the infinitive. What vowels do the other forms have?

3. What auxiliary verb do you use to form the **passé composé** of these three verbs? What are their past participles?

🌐 **Sélection musicale.** Search the Web for the songs **"Tu peux compter sur moi"** by Bénabar and **"Je ne veux pas travailler"** by Pink Martini to enjoy musical selections with these verbs.

🄸🄻🅛 **Grammar Tutorials**

A En cours. Dites si ces personnes veulent faire chaque chose indiquée en cours de français.

EXEMPLE Je... manger   **Je ne veux pas manger en cours.**

1. Je...
boire du café
beaucoup parler

2. Nous...
souvent travailler en groupes
souvent partir en avance *(early)*

3. Le prof...
parler français tout le temps
toujours comprendre les étudiants

4. Les étudiants...
toujours comprendre le prof
souvent poser des questions

Maintenant, dites s'ils peuvent faire chaque chose indiquée en cours de français.

EXEMPLE Je... manger   **Je ne peux pas manger en cours.**

B **Qu'est-ce qu'on doit faire?** Pour chaque paire d'activités proposées, indiquez ce que chacun doit et ne doit pas faire en cours de français.

EXEMPLE le prof (être patient / être impatient)
Le prof doit être patient. Il ne doit pas être impatient.

1. le prof (insulter les étudiants / aider les étudiants)
(toujours parler anglais en cours / parler français en cours)
2. les étudiants (dormir en cours / écouter le prof)
(faire leurs devoirs / sortir tous les soirs)
3. moi, je (apprendre le vocabulaire et les verbes / toujours sortir avec des amis)
(dormir en cours / écouter en cours)

C **On veut...** Aujourd'hui, les Pérez ne peuvent pas faire ce qu'ils veulent. Jouez le rôle d'Alice et expliquez ce que chacun veut et doit faire.

EXEMPLE **Moi, je veux dormir, mais je dois sortir le chien.**

Moi...

1. Éric...

2. Éric et Cathy...

3. Vincent...

4. Nos amis...

5. Michel...

Line art on this page: © Cengage Learning

Plus tard, Alice dit que chacun n'a pas pu faire ce qu'il voulait *(wanted)* et elle explique ce qu'ils ont dû faire. Qu'est-ce qu'elle dit? Utilisez le passé composé.

EXEMPLE **Moi, je n'ai pas pu dormir. J'ai dû sortir le chien.**

D **Comparaisons culturelles.** Un lycéen *(high school student)* parle de la vie des jeunes en France. Complétez ce qu'il dit avec la forme correcte des verbes entre parenthèses. Ensuite, comparez la situation en France avec la situation ici.

EXEMPLE Je **peux** (pouvoir) faire ce que *(what)* je **veux** (vouloir) le mercredi après-midi, parce que je n'ai pas cours. Mais, je **dois** (devoir) assister aux *(attend)* cours le samedi matin.

Ici, on doit assister aux cours toute la journée le mercredi, mais on peut faire ce qu'on veut le samedi matin.

1. Je ne _peux_ (pouvoir) pas faire de sport après les cours au lycée *(high school)*, parce qu'il n'y a pas beaucoup d'activités extrascolaires. Si on _veut_ (vouloir) faire du sport, on _doit_ (devoir) aller à un club de sport.
2. Mes amis et moi _devons_ (devoir) prendre le bus pour aller en ville, parce qu'on ne _peut_ (pouvoir) pas avoir de permis de conduire *(driver's license)* avant l'âge de 18 ans.
3. Les jeunes qui _veulent_ (vouloir) apprendre à conduire *(to drive)* _doivent_ (devoir) payer pour aller à une auto-école *(driving school)*. Les lycéens ne _peuvent_ (pouvoir) pas suivre de cours de conduite *(take driver's ed)* au lycée.
4. Quand je _veux_ (vouloir) aller au centre-ville, je _peux_ (pouvoir) y aller facilement en bus. Les transports publics sont excellents ici.

POUR MIEUX COMPRENDRE: Noting the important information

When making plans, we often jot down important information for later reference. If a friend invited you to do something, what sort of information would you want to remember? Look at the following invitation and think about what information is given.

Nous vous attendons

le   samedi 18 novembre

à   19   heures.

Notre adresse:

85 boulevard St Michel

Téléphone: 02-43-29-69-50

R.S.V.P.

© Cengage Learning

🔊 **A** **Prenez des notes.** Trois amis invitent Éric à faire quelque chose. Écoutez
2-20   chaque invitation et prenez des notes en français. Qu'est-ce qu'ils vont faire? Où?
Quel jour? À quelle heure?

👥 **B** **À vous.** Éric demande à Michèle de l'accompagner. Utilisez vos notes de
l'exercice précédent pour jouer les rôles d'Éric et de Michèle avec un(e) partenaire.

EXEMPLE — Je vais jouer au tennis avec Marc demain à... Est-ce que tu
voudrais jouer avec nous?
— Oui, je veux bien!

🔊 Compréhension auditive: *On va au cinéma?*

2-21

Vincent demande à Alice si elle voudrait aller au cinéma. Lisez les questions de l'exercice suivant. Ensuite, écoutez la conversation et notez les détails importants sur une feuille de papier.

A **Quel film?** Répondez aux questions suivantes d'après la conversation entre Alice et son mari.

1. Comment est-ce qu'Alice trouve les films de science-fiction?
2. Quel genre *(type)* de film est-ce qu'ils décident d'aller voir?
3. À quelle séance est-ce qu'ils vont aller?

B **Vos notes.** Utilisez vos notes pour recréer *(to recreate)* la conversation entre Alice et Vincent avec un(e) partenaire.

C **Tu veux sortir?** Invitez votre partenaire à aller voir un film avec vous. Choisissez une séance et décidez à quelle heure vous allez passer chez votre ami(e).

10:35 I 13:20 I 16:05 I 19:00 I 21:45

11:50 I 14:40 I 17:25 I 20:05

12:10 I 13:30 I 15:55 I 18: 45 I 21:20

Talking about how you spend and used to spend your time

AUJOURD'HUI ET DANS LE PASSÉ

Michèle compare sa **vie** quand **elle était** au **lycée** avec sa vie d'aujourd'hui.

Quand j'étais au lycée...

Aujourd'hui...

J'avais 15 ans.
J'étais **lycéenne.**
J'habitais avec ma famille.
J'avais cours du lundi au vendredi et aussi le samedi matin.
Je n'aimais pas beaucoup **l'école** *(f)*.
Je rentrais souvent à la maison pour déjeuner.
Le week-end, j'étais toujours **fatiguée** et **je dormais** beaucoup.
Le vendredi soir, je passais du temps avec ma famille ou **je sortais** avec **des copains.** On allait au cinéma, au café ou à une fête.
Le samedi, je faisais du sport avec des amis: on jouait au foot ou **on faisait du roller.**

J'ai 21 ans.
Je suis étudiante à l'université.
J'habite avec ma famille.
J'ai cours du lundi au vendredi.

J'aime l'université.
En général, je déjeune au **resto U.**

Le week-end, je suis souvent fatiguée et je dors beaucoup.
Le vendredi soir, **je sors** souvent avec des copains. On va au cinéma, en boîte ou à **une soirée.**

Tous les samedis, je joue au tennis avec des amis et je fais aussi souvent du roller.

dans le passé *in the past*   **la vie** *life*   **elle était** *she was*   **le lycée** *high school*   **J'avais 15 ans.** *I was fifteen.*   **un(e) lycéen(ne)** *a high school student*   **J'habitais** *I lived, I used to live*   **J'avais cours** *I had class, I used to have class*   **l'école** *school*   **le resto U** *the university cafeteria*   **fatigué(e)** *tired*   **je dormais** *I slept, I used to sleep*   **je sortais** *I went out, I used to go out*   **un copain (une copine)** *a (boy/girl)friend, a pal*   **je sors (sortir)** *I go out (to go out)*   **une soirée** *a party*   **on faisait du roller** *we went in-line skating, we used to go in-line skating*

🔊 2-22

Michèle demande à Éric **ce qu'**il faisait quand il était au lycée aux États-Unis.

MICHÈLE: Qu'est-ce que tu aimais faire quand tu étais au lycée?
ÉRIC: J'aimais passer mon temps avec des copains. Le vendredi soir, on allait aux matchs de football américain ou de basket au lycée.
MICHÈLE: Et le samedi?
ÉRIC: Le samedi matin, je travaillais. Le samedi après-midi, on faisait du skateboard. Le samedi soir, je sortais avec ma copine. On allait au cinéma.
MICHÈLE: Et qu'est-ce que tu faisais le dimanche?
ÉRIC: Le dimanche, je ne faisais rien de spécial. Je restais à la maison. Je regardais la télé ou une vidéo.

A **Maintenant ou dans le passé?** Est-ce que Michèle parle de sa vie maintenant ou de sa vie quand elle avait 15 ans? Commencez chaque phrase avec **Quand j'avais 15 ans...** ou **Maintenant...**

1. J'étais lycéenne.
2. J'ai cours du lundi au vendredi.
3. Je n'aimais pas beaucoup l'école.
4. Je déjeune souvent au resto U.
5. Je sors beaucoup le week-end.
6. Mes copains et moi, on aimait aller au café.
7. On faisait souvent du sport ensemble.

B **Et vous?** Dites si vous faites ces choses maintenant et si vous faisiez ces choses quand vous aviez 10 ans.

EXEMPLES Maintenant, j'habite avec ma famille.
Maintenant, j'habite avec ma famille.
Maintenant, je n'habite pas avec ma famille.

Quand j'avais 10 ans, j'habitais avec ma famille.
Quand j'avais 10 ans, j'habitais avec ma famille.
Quand j'avais 10 ans, je n'habitais pas avec ma famille.

1. Maintenant, j'ai cours tous les jours.
   Quand j'avais 10 ans, j'avais cours tous les jours.
2. Maintenant, j'aime mes études.
   Quand j'avais 10 ans, j'aimais l'école.
3. Maintenant, mes copains (copines) et moi, on fait souvent du sport ensemble.
   Quand j'avais 10 ans, on faisait souvent du sport ensemble.
4. Maintenant, je sors souvent le samedi soir.
   Quand j'avais 10 ans, je sortais souvent le samedi soir.
5. Maintenant, je suis souvent fatigué(e) le dimanche.
   Quand j'avais 10 ans, j'étais souvent fatigué(e) le dimanche.
6. Maintenant, je dors beaucoup le week-end.
   Quand j'avais 10 ans, je dormais beaucoup le week-end.

👥 **À VOUS!**

Avec un(e) partenaire, relisez à haute voix la conversation entre Michèle et Éric. Ensuite, adaptez la conversation pour parler de ce que vous faisiez *(what you used to do)* quand vous étiez au lycée. Si vous voulez utiliser des verbes que vous n'avez pas encore appris dans cette forme du passé, demandez à votre professeur comment les conjuguer.

iLrn 🌐 You can find a list of the new words from this *Compétence* on page 254 and access the audio online.

ce que *what*

SAYING HOW THINGS USED TO BE

L'imparfait

Use the **passé composé** to talk about what happened on a specific occasion. To tell what things used to be like, or what happened over and over, use the **imparfait** *(imperfect)*. The **imparfait** can be translated in a variety of ways in English.

I was working mornings.
I used to work mornings.   } Je travaillais le matin.
I worked mornings.

All verbs except **être** form this tense by dropping the **-ons** from the present tense **nous** form and adding the endings you see below. The stem for **être** is **ét-**.

	PARLER (nous parl~~ons~~ → parl-)	FAIRE (nous fais~~ons~~ → fais-)	PRENDRE (nous pren~~ons~~ → pren-)	ÊTRE (ét-)
je (j')	parl**ais**	fais**ais**	pren**ais**	ét**ais**
tu	parl**ais**	fais**ais**	pren**ais**	ét**ais**
il/elle/on	parl**ait**	fais**ait**	pren**ait**	ét**ait**
nous	parl**ions**	fais**ions**	pren**ions**	ét**ions**
vous	parl**iez**	fais**iez**	pren**iez**	ét**iez**
ils/elles	parl**aient**	fais**aient**	pren**aient**	ét**aient**

Spelling changes in the present tense **nous** form of verbs like **manger** and **commencer** occur in the **imparfait** *only before endings beginning with an **a**.*

MANGER	COMMENCER
je mang**e**ais	je commen**ç**ais
tu mang**e**ais	tu commen**ç**ais
il/elle/on mang**e**ait	il/elle/on commen**ç**ait
nous mangions	nous commencions
vous mangiez	vous commenciez
ils/elles mang**e**aient	ils/elles commen**ç**aient

Also learn these expressions in the imperfect.

c'est → c'était   il y a → il y avait   il pleut → il pleuvait   il neige → il neigeait

✔ Pour vérifier

1. Which form of the present tense do you use to create the stem for all verbs in the imperfect, except for **être**? What is the stem for **être**?

2. You use the **passé composé** to talk about a specific occurrence in the past. When do you use the **imparfait**?

3. Which imperfect endings are pronounced alike? What single letter distinguishes the **nous** and **vous** forms of the imperfect from the present?

iLrn Grammar Tutorials

Note *de grammaire*

Note that verbs like **étudier** retain the **i** of the stem before the **imparfait** endings.

j'étudiais   nous étudiions
vous étudiiez   ils étudiaient

avoir

J'avais
Tu avais
il avait
Nous avions
Vous aviez
elles avaient

PRONONCIATION

Les terminaisons de l'imparfait 🔊 2-23

The **-ais, -ait,** and **-aient** endings of the imperfect are all pronounced alike. The **nous** and **vous** endings of the imperfect, **-ions** and **-iez,** are distinguished from the present only by the vowel **i** in the ending.

Qu'est-ce que vous faisiez?   *What did you use to do?*
Ils travaillaient pour IBM.   *They worked for IBM.*
Nous allions à la plage.   *We used to go to the beach.*

A **Prononcez bien!** Une amie parle de sa vie maintenant et de sa vie quand elle était au lycée. D'abord, pratiquez la prononciation de chaque phrase. Ensuite, lisez à haute voix une phrase de chaque paire. Votre partenaire va dire si vous parlez du **présent** ou du **passé**.

🌐 **Sélection musicale.** Search the Web for the songs **"Comme toi"** by Jean-Jacques Goldman, **"J'aimais mieux avant"** by Christophe Cerillo, or **"Michèle"** by Gérard Lenorman to enjoy musical selections with this structure.

Maintenant	Quand j'étais au lycée
1. J'ai cours tous les jours.	J'avais cours tous les jours.
2. J'étudie beaucoup.	J'étudiais beaucoup.
3. Mon meilleur ami aime le sport.	Mon meilleur ami aimait le sport.
4. Il joue au basket.	Il jouait au basket.
5. Nous aimons sortir ensemble.	Nous aimions sortir ensemble.
6. Nous allons souvent au cinéma.	Nous allions souvent au cinéma.
7. Mes parents travaillent beaucoup.	Mes parents travaillaient beaucoup.
8. Ils sont souvent fatigués.	Ils étaient souvent fatigués.

Maintenant, changez chaque phrase pour parler de vous.

EXEMPLE Maintenant, j'ai cours le mardi et le jeudi. Quand j'étais au lycée, j'avais cours du lundi au vendredi.

B **La jeunesse.** Interviewez un(e) partenaire pour savoir ce qu'il/elle faisait quand il/elle était au lycée.

EXEMPLE fumer / ne pas aimer ça
— **Tu fumais quand tu étais au lycée ou tu n'aimais pas ça?**
— **Je fumais. / Je n'aimais pas ça.**

1. aller presque toujours en cours / être souvent absent(e)
2. avoir beaucoup de copains / passer beaucoup de temps seul(e)
3. faire souvent du sport / préférer faire autre chose
4. pouvoir sortir tard / devoir rentrer tôt
5. aimer dormir tard le week-end / avoir beaucoup d'énergie le matin

Maintenant, avec votre partenaire, préparez six questions pour votre professeur. Demandez ce qu'il/elle faisait quand il/elle était étudiant(e) à l'université.

Quand j'avais dix ans, j'aimais jouer avec mon chien.

C **Chez nous.** Que faisaient ces personnes quand vous aviez dix ans? Dites au moins trois choses pour chacune.

EXEMPLE Mon père...
Mon père était très patient. Il travaillait souvent le week-end et il rentrait tard. Il n'était pas souvent à la maison.

1. Mes parents...	**3.** Ma mère...	**5.** Dans ma famille, nous...
2. Mes amis…	**4.** Mon père...	**6.** Mes copains et moi...

avoir beaucoup d'amis / un chien	arriver à l'école à... heures
être patient(e)(s) / impatient(e)(s)	rentrer à... heures
travailler le week-end	jouer au golf / à des jeux vidéo...
aimer lire / dormir…	faire souvent du roller / du sport...
être à la maison le week-end	voyager souvent
faire le ménage / du shopping...	aller souvent voir mes cousins...
aimer les maths / les sciences...	aller à la plage / au cinéma...

TALKING ABOUT ACTIVITIES

✔ **Pour vérifier**

1. What are the conjugations of **sortir**, **partir**, and **dormir**? Which auxiliary verb is used with each one in the **passé composé**?

2. How do you say *to go out of*? *to leave from*? *to leave for*?

3. How do you say *to leave for the weekend*? *to leave on vacation*? *to leave on a trip*?

4. What is the difference in pronunciation between **il sort** and **ils sortent**?

Les verbes *sortir, partir* et *dormir*

The verbs **sortir, partir,** and **dormir** have similar patterns of conjugation.

SORTIR *(to go out)*	PARTIR *(to leave)*	DORMIR *(to sleep)*
je **sors**	je **pars**	je **dors**
tu **sors**	tu **pars**	tu **dors**
il/elle/on **sort**	il/elle/on **part**	il/elle/on **dort**
nous **sortons**	nous **partons**	nous **dormons**
vous **sortez**	vous **partez**	vous **dormez**
ils/elles **sortent**	ils/elles **partent**	ils/elles **dorment**
P.C. **je suis sorti(e)**	P.C. **je suis parti(e)**	P.C. **j'ai dormi**
IMP. **je sortais**	IMP. **je partais**	IMP. **je dormais**

Note *de vocabulaire*

Remember that **quitter** means *to leave* a person or a place and is *always* used with a direct object. In the **passé composé**, it is conjugated with **avoir**.

J'ai quitté la maison à midi.

You have already seen that **sortir** can mean *to go out,* in the sense of going out with friends. It can also mean *to go / come out of,* in the sense of going out of a place. It is the opposite of **entrer.** Use **de** to say *of.*

Je suis sorti **de** l'appartement en pyjama pour aller chercher le journal.

Partir means *to leave* in the sense of *to go away.* It is the opposite of **arriver.** Some common expressions with **partir** are: **partir en week-end, partir en vacances, partir en voyage.** To name the place you are leaving, use **partir de.** To say where you are leaving *for,* use **partir pour.**

Il part en vacances aujourd'hui. Il est parti **de** son bureau à trois heures et il est parti **pour** l'aéroport vers cinq heures.

PRONONCIATION

Les verbes *sortir, partir* et *dormir* 2-24

You can distinguish aurally between the **il/elle** singular and **ils/elles** plural forms of verbs like **sortir, partir,** and **dormir.** Compare these sentences.

ALICE	ALICE ET SA FILLE
Elle dort bien.	Elles dorment bien.
Elle sort ce soir.	Elles sortent ce soir.
Elle part demain.	Elles partent demain.

When a word ends with a pronounced consonant sound in French, it must be released. Note that when you pronounce the boldfaced consonants in the following English phrases, your tongue or lips do not have to move back and release them.

What par**t**?   What sor**t**?   In the dor**m**.

Compare how the boldfaced consonants in the following plural verb forms are released.

Ils par**t**ent.   Ils sor**t**ent.   Ils dor**m**ent.

A **Prononcez bien!** Pour chaque phrase que vous entendez, dites si Alice parle d'**Éric** ou d'**Éric et de Cathy.**

B **Entretien.** Complétez ces questions avec la forme correcte des verbes indiqués au présent et interviewez un(e) partenaire.

> **EXEMPLE** —Est-ce que tu **sors** (sortir) souvent en semaine avec tes amis?
> — **Je sors quelquefois le mercredi soir.**

1. Est-ce que ton meilleur ami (ta meilleure amie) ___sort___ (sortir) souvent avec toi le week-end? Est-ce que vous ___sortez___ (sortir) quelquefois en semaine?
2. Quand tu ___sors___ (sortir) avec tes amis le samedi soir, jusqu'à quelle heure est-ce que tu ___dors___ (dormir) le dimanche?
3. Est-ce que tes amis ___sortent___ (sortir) souvent pendant la semaine sans toi? Est-ce qu'ils ___dorment___ (dormir) quelquefois pendant leurs cours?
4. Est-ce que tu ___pars___ (partir) souvent en week-end? Généralement, où vas-tu quand tu ___pars___ (partir) pour quelques jours?

Maintenant, mettez les verbes à l'imparfait pour parler de ce que votre partenaire et ses amis faisaient quand il/elle était lycéen(ne).

> **EXEMPLE** —Quand tu étais au lycée, est-ce que tu **sortais** (sortir) souvent en semaine avec tes amis?
> — **Non, je ne sortais jamais en semaine.**

C **Vos habitudes.** Formez des phrases pour parler de ce que vous faites les jours du cours de français et quand vous sortez avec des amis. Circulez dans la classe et trouvez quelqu'un qui fait la même chose que vous.

> **EXEMPLES** Les jours du cours de français, je / dormir jusqu'à... heures.
> — **Les jours du cours de français, je dors jusqu'à 7 heures.**
> **Et toi? Tu dors jusqu'à 7 heures aussi?**
> — **Non, je dors jusqu'à 8 heures.**

1. Les jours du cours de français, je / dormir jusqu'à... heures.
2. Aujourd'hui, je / sortir de mon dernier cours à... heures.
3. Mes amis et moi / sortir le plus souvent le... soir.
4. D'habitude, je / dormir jusqu'à... le dimanche.
5. Je / partir le plus souvent en vacances au mois de...

Maintenant, dites à la classe qui fait les mêmes choses que vous.

> **EXEMPLES** **Les jours du cours de français, Courtney dort jusqu'à 7 heures, comme moi.**
> **Luis et ses amis sortent le plus souvent le samedi soir, comme mes amis et moi.**

D **Toujours des questions!** Parlez avec votre partenaire de la dernière fois qu'il/elle est sorti(e) avec des amis. Posez les questions indiquées.

> **EXEMPLE** quand / sortir ensemble
> — **Quand est-ce que vous êtes sortis ensemble?**
> — **On est sortis ensemble hier.**

1. quand / sortir ensemble
2. où / aller ensemble
3. qu'est-ce que / faire
4. à quelle heure / partir de la maison
5. jusqu'à quelle heure / dormir le lendemain

TELLING WHAT WAS GOING ON WHEN SOMETHING ELSE HAPPENED

✔ *Pour vérifier*

1. With a sequence of events that happen one after another, are the verbs in the **passé composé** or the **imparfait**?

2. If one action interrupts another one that is already in progress, which one is in the **passé composé** and which one is in the **imparfait**?

 Grammar Tutorials

L'imparfait et le passé composé

In French, the **passé composé** and **imparfait** convey different meanings. In English, the use of different past tenses also changes a message. Is the message the same in these sentences?

> *When her husband came home, they kissed.*
> *When her husband came home, they were kissing.*

Use the **passé composé** for a sequence of events that happened one after another.

> Ce matin, **j'ai quitté** la maison à midi et **je suis arrivé** à l'université à midi vingt.

When saying what was going on when something else occurred, use the **imparfait** for the action in progress and use the **passé composé** to say what happened, interrupting it.

ACTIONS IN PROGRESS	INTERRUPTING ACTIONS
IMPARFAIT	PASSÉ COMPOSÉ
Le professeur parlait...	quand je suis entré(e) dans la salle de cours.
Il pleuvait ce matin...	quand j'ai quitté la maison.

PRONONCIATION

 Prononcez bien! See Module 19.

Le passé composé et l'imparfait 🔊 2-27

Since the use of the **passé composé** or the **imparfait** imparts a different message, it is important that you pronounce each tense distinctly. Listen to these pairs of sentences. Where do you hear a difference?

Je travaillais.	Elle mangeait.	Tu parlais.	Il allait.
J'ai travaillé.	Elle a mangé.	Tu as parlé.	Il est allé.

🔊 2-28 **A** **Prononcez bien!** Indiquez si vous entendez la phrase de la colonne A ou de la colonne B.

A	B
L'IMPARFAIT: *(WHAT WAS GOING ON)*	LE PASSÉ COMPOSÉ: *(WHAT HAPPENED)*
1. Je travaillais.	J'ai travaillé.
2. Mon mari téléphonait.	Mon mari a téléphoné.
3. Mon fils était malade.	Mon fils a été malade.
4. J'allais chez moi.	Je suis allée chez moi.
5. J'entrais.	Je suis entrée.
6. Tous mes amis commençaient à chanter «Bon anniversaire».	Tous mes amis ont commencé à chanter «Bon anniversaire».
7. Ils étaient chez moi pour une surprise-partie.	Ils ont été chez moi pour une surprise-partie.
8. On dansait toute la soirée.	On a dansé toute la soirée.
9. Ils restaient jusqu'à minuit.	Ils sont restés jusqu'à minuit.

B Quand ils sont rentrés... Deux couples ont laissé leurs enfants avec une nouvelle baby-sitter le week-end dernier. Qui faisait les choses suivantes quand ils sont rentrés?

EXEMPLE porter les vêtements de sa mère
Annick portait les vêtements de sa mère quand ils sont rentrés.

1. embrasser *(to kiss)* son copain
2. parler au téléphone
3. fumer
4. jouer dans l'escalier
5. jouer à des jeux vidéo
6. manger quelque chose sur la table
7. dormir sur le canapé
8. être surpris(e)

C Que faisaient-ils? Expliquez ce qui s'est passé.

EXEMPLE Alice (lire un livre) / quand une amie (arriver)
Alice lisait un livre quand une amie est arrivée.

1. Cathy (réviser ses cours) / quand un ami (téléphoner)

2. Vincent (jouer au golf) / quand il (commencer à pleuvoir)

3. Michèle (embrasser *[to kiss]* un copain) / quand Éric (arriver)

4. Quand le chien (entrer) / le chat (dormir)

5. Alice (faire la cuisine) / quand le chat (voir le chien)

6. Quand Vincent (rentrer) / Alice (nettoyer *[to clean]* la cuisine)

Line art on this page: © Cengage Learning

TELLING WHAT HAPPENED AND DESCRIBING THE CIRCUMSTANCES

✔ **Pour vérifier**

1. Do you generally use the **passé composé** or the **imparfait** to say what happened at a specific moment, for a specific duration, or a specific number of times? to describe how things were or used to be or to talk about actions in progress?

2. Which would you use to talk about how you were feeling? to describe a change in a mental or physical state?

3. Which tense do you use to say what was going to happen?

Note *de grammaire*

You generally use the verb **vouloir** in the **imparfait** to say what someone wanted to do.

> **Je *voulais* aller voir un film.**
> *I wanted to go see a movie.*

Use **pouvoir** in the **imparfait** to say what people could do if they might have wanted to, but use it in the **passé composé** to say what they managed to do on an occasion when they tried.

> **Ma copine ne *pouvait* pas sortir.**
> *My girlfriend couldn't go out.*

> **J'*ai pu* persuader un autre ami d'y aller.**
> *I was able to persuade another friend to go.*

Use **devoir** in the **imparfait** to say what one was supposed to do, but in the **passé composé** for what one must have done, or had to do on a specific occasion.

> **Il *devait* déjà être ici.**
> *He was supposed to be here already.*

> **Il *a dû* travailler tard.**
> *He had to work late. / He must have worked late.*

🌐 **Sélection musicale.** Search the Web for the songs "**Il avait les mots**" by Sheryfa Luna or **On savait** by La Grande Sophie to enjoy musical selections with these structures.

Le passé composé et l'imparfait

You know to use the **imparfait** to tell how things used to be or what was going on when something else occurred. The **imparfait** is used to describe continuing actions or states, whereas the **passé composé** is used for actions that happened and were finished.

USE THE *IMPARFAIT* TO SAY:	USE THE PASSÉ *COMPOSÉ* TO SAY:
1. HOW THINGS USED TO BE OR WHAT USED TO HAPPEN • continuing actions, states, or situations • repeated or habitual actions of an unspecified duration	**1. WHAT HAPPENED AT A PRECISE MOMENT OR FOR A SPECIFIC DURATION OR NUMBER OF TIMES** • completed actions • actions that occurred for a specific duration or a specific number of times

Notre amie habitait à côté de chez nous.
Our friend lived next to us.
Elle invitait toujours des amis chez elle.
She always invited friends over.

Elle a fait une soirée le mois dernier.
She had a party last month.
Nous sommes allées à cinq de ses soirées.
We went to five of her parties.

2. WHAT THINGS WERE LIKE OR HOW SOMEONE FELT • physical or mental states	**2. WHAT CHANGED** • changes in states

Tout le monde allait bien, mais moi, j'étais fatiguée.
Everyone was doing fine, but I was tired.

Tout à coup, j'ai eu peur.
All of a sudden, I got frightened.

Watch for words like **tout d'un coup** (*all at once*), **tout à coup** (*all of a sudden*), **soudain** (*suddenly*), **une fois** (*once*), and **un jour** (*one day*) indicating changes in states.

3. WHAT SOMEONE WAS GOING TO DO	**3. WHAT ONE WENT TO DO**

On allait partir.
We were going to leave.

Je suis allée chercher mon sac.
I went to get my purse.

A Pourquoi? Expliquez pourquoi Cathy a fait ou n'a pas fait ces choses. Quel verbe doit être au passé composé et lequel *(which one)* doit être à l'imparfait?

EXEMPLE Cathy **était** (être) malade, alors elle **n'a pas travaillé** (ne pas travailler).

1. Cathy _____ (ne pas sortir) parce qu'elle _____ (être) malade.
2. Elle _____ (être) trop fatiguée, alors elle _____ (ne pas faire) ses devoirs.
3. Elle _____ (faire) du shopping parce qu'elle _____ (vouloir) acheter une nouvelle robe.
4. Elle _____ (mettre) un pull parce qu'elle _____ (avoir) froid.
5. Elle _____ (avoir) besoin de réviser ses cours, alors elle _____ (ne pas sortir) avec ses amis.

B Ce matin chez les Pérez. Alice Pérez décrit la journée de sa famille. Qu'est-ce qu'elle dit? Mettez les verbes au passé composé ou à l'imparfait.

EXEMPLE Moi, j'ai fait du jogging ce matin. Je voulais dormir.

Moi...

faire du jogging ce matin
vouloir dormir
avoir sommeil
ne pas avoir envie de sortir
sortir à sept heures
rentrer une heure plus tard
avoir besoin d'un bain *(bath)*
aller dans la salle de bains
prendre un long bain

Éric et Cathy...

préparer le déjeuner aujourd'hui
vouloir faire du shopping
déjeuner avant de sortir
aller au centre commercial à une heure
avoir l'intention d'acheter des vêtements
rentrer vers cinq heures
avoir faim
retrouver des amis au restaurant
rentrer à neuf heures

C Entretien. Parlez à votre partenaire de la dernière fois qu'il/elle est allé(e) au restaurant avec des amis.

La dernière fois que tu es allé(e) au restaurant avec des amis,...

1. Quel temps faisait-il? Qu'est-ce que tu as mis pour sortir? un jean? une robe?
2. Quelle heure était-il quand tu es arrivé(e) au restaurant?
3. Avais-tu très faim? As-tu mangé tout de suite? Comment était le repas?
4. Qu'est-ce que tu as fait après le repas?
5. Quelle heure était-il quand tu es rentré(e)? Étais-tu fatigué(e)? Est-ce que tu es allé(e) tout de suite au lit? As-tu bien dormi?
6. Le lendemain, jusqu'à quelle heure es-tu resté(e) au lit?

Narrating in the past

LES CONTES (Tales)

Vocabulaire sans peine!

Most nouns referring to people that end with *-tor* in English are similar in French, but end with **-teur** in the masculine and **-trice** in the feminine.

actor = **acteur / actrice**
educator = **éducateur / éducatrice**

How would you say these words in French?

protector
procrastinator

Most English adjectives ending with *-ible* are similar in French.

horrible = **horrible**
terrible = **terrible**

How would you say these words in French?

accessible
compatible

Éric et Michèle sont allés voir le film classique *La Belle et la Bête* de Jean Cocteau. **Connaissez-vous** ce film? Connaissez-vous **le conte de fées** sur **lequel** ce film est basé?

© Hulton Archive/DiscIna/Courtesy of Getty Images

Il était une fois un vieux **marchand** qui avait trois filles. Sa plus jeune fille, Belle, était très jolie, **douce** et **gracieuse.**

Un jour, la Bête a emprisonné le marchand. Belle **a promis** à la Bête de venir prendre la place de son père.

Le monstre était horrible! Il était grand et laid et il avait l'air **féroce. Au début,** Belle avait très peur de lui. Mais elle était toujours gentille et patiente avec lui.

Petit à petit, les choses ont changé. Belle et la Bête ont commencé à **se parler.** La Bête a beaucoup changé et Belle a appris à apprécier le monstre. Finalement, Belle **est tombée amoureuse de** lui! Et la Bête a aussi appris à aimer.

À suivre...

🔊 2-29

Cathy parle à son frère de ses activités du week-end dernier.

CATHY: Tu es sorti ce week-end?
ÉRIC: Oui, je suis allé au cinéclub avec Michèle.
CATHY: Quel film est-ce que vous avez vu?
ÉRIC: Nous avons vu *La Belle et la Bête* de Cocteau.
CATHY: C'est un classique! Il t'a plu?
ÉRIC: Oui, il m'a beaucoup plu. Les acteurs **ont bien joué, les effets spéciaux** étaient excellents **pour l'époque** et il n'y avait pas **trop de** violence.

---

un conte *a story* (for children)   **La Belle et la Bête** *Beauty and the Beast*   **Connaissez-vous...?** *Do you know...?*   **un conte de fées** *a fairy tale*   **lequel (laquelle)** *which*   **Il était une fois...** *Once upon a time there was...*   **un marchand** *a merchant, a shopkeeper*   **doux (douce)** *sweet, soft, gentle*   **gracieux (gracieuse)** *gracious*   **elle a promis (promettre** *to promise* [past participle **promis**])   **féroce** *ferocious*   **Au début** *At the beginning*   **se parler** *to talk to each other*   **tomber amoureux (amoureuse) de** *to fall in love with*   **À suivre** *To be continued*   **bien jouer** *to act well* (in movies and theater)   **les effets spéciaux** *the special effects*   **pour l'époque** *for that time (period)*   **trop de** *too much*

A **C'est qui?** Décidez lequel des personnages les adjectifs suivants décrivent: **le père de Belle, Belle** ou **la Bête**. N'oubliez pas d'utiliser l'imparfait pour faire une description!

EXEMPLE douce   **Belle était douce.**

1. jolie   **2.** grande et laide   **3.** vieux   **4.** gracieuse   **5.** horrible

Maintenant, dites qui a fait les choses suivantes. N'oubliez pas d'utiliser le passé composé pour décrire le déroulement de l'action *(sequence of events)*!

EXEMPLE promettre de venir prendre la place de son père
Belle a promis de venir prendre la place de son père.

1. emprisonner le marchand   **4.** apprendre à apprécier la Bête
2. prendre la place de son père   **5.** tomber amoureuse de Belle
3. commencer à parler avec la Bête **6.** beaucoup changer

B **Contes de fées.** En 1697, l'écrivain *(the writer)* français Charles Perrault a publié les contes de fées suivants dans son livre *Histoires ou contes du temps passé.* Choisissez la forme correcte des verbes entre parenthèses pour compléter les descriptions qui suivent. Ensuite, dites quel titre de la liste correspond à chacune.

Le Chat botté   Le Petit Chaperon rouge   La Belle au bois dormant   Cendrillon

1. Les parents d'une princesse (n'ont pas invité / n'invitaient pas) une vieille fée à la fête pour le baptême de leur fille. Vexée, la vieille fée (a jeté / jetait) un sort *(cast a spell)* à la princesse.
2. Une petite fille qui (a porté / portait) toujours un chaperon *(hood)* rouge (a traversé / traversait) *(was crossing)* la forêt en allant voir sa grand-mère quand elle (a rencontré / rencontrait) un grand méchant loup *(wolf)*.
3. Un homme pauvre (a laissé / laissait) un chat à son fils comme seul héritage *(inheritance)*. Mais le chat (a eu / avait) des pouvoirs magiques *(magical powers)* et, avec son aide, le jeune homme (est devenu / devenait) riche.
4. Après la mort de son père, une belle jeune fille vivait *(lived)* avec sa belle-mère et ses deux demi-sœurs. Sa belle-mère (a été / était) cruelle et ses demi-sœurs (ont été / étaient) laides. Le prince (a invité / invitait) les filles des alentours *(surrounding area)* à un bal magnifique.

C **Une sortie au cinéma.** Alice parle du week-end à une amie. Complétez la conversation en mettant les verbes au passé composé ou à l'imparfait. Ensuite, adaptez la conversation pour parler de votre week-end avec un(e) partenaire.

— Tu __1__ *(as passé)* (passer) un bon week-end?
— Assez bon. Mon amie __2__ *(voulait)* (vouloir) aller voir un film, alors je __3__ *(suis allée)* (aller) au cinéma avec elle et je __4__ (rentrer) tard. *(suis rentrée)*
— Quelle heure __5__ *(était)* (être)-il quand tu __6__ (rentrer)? *(es rentrée)*
— On __7__ *(est restées)* (rester) au cinéma jusqu'à 10h30 et après, on __8__ *(avait)* (avoir) faim, alors on __9__ (aller) manger quelque chose. Il y __10__ (avoir) beaucoup de gens au restaurant et on __11__ (devoir) attendre pour avoir une table. *(est allées)* *(avait)* *(a dû)* Il __12__ (être) environ 1h00 quand on __13__ (partir) du restaurant. *(était)* *(est parties)*

on has s if plural + action

À VOUS!

Avec un(e) partenaire, relisez à haute voix la conversation entre Cathy et Éric. Ensuite, adaptez la conversation pour parler d'un film que vous avez vu récemment.

 You can find a list of the new words from this *Compétence* on page 255 and access the audio online.

NARRATING WHAT HAPPENED

✔ Pour vérifier

If you were describing a play that you saw, would you use the **passé composé** or the **imparfait** to describe the setting and what was happening on stage when the curtain went up? Which tense would you use to explain the actions of the actors that advanced the story?

For a chart summarizing all of the uses of the **passé composé** and the **imparfait**, see the **Résumé de grammaire** on page 253.

🌐 **Sélection musicale.** Search the Web for the songs **"Nathalie"** by Gilbert Bécaud or **"La Rua Madureira"** by Nino Ferrer to enjoy musical selections with these structures.

Le passé composé et l'imparfait (reprise)

When telling a story in the past, you use both the **passé composé** and the **imparfait**.

USE THE *IMPARFAIT* TO SAY:	USE THE *PASSÉ COMPOSÉ* TO SAY:
WHAT WAS ALREADY GOING ON	WHAT HAPPENED NEXT / WHAT CHANGED
• descriptions of the scene / setting • background information about the characters • interrupted actions in progress	• sequence of events that advance the storyline • actions interrupting something in progress

If you were telling the old French tale **Cendrillon (Cinderella)**, you might begin . . .

Il **était** une fois une belle jeune fille qui **s'appelait** Cendrillon. Son père **était** mort et elle **habitait** avec sa belle-mère et ses deux demi-sœurs. Sa belle-mère **était** cruelle et ses demi-sœurs **étaient** laides et très gâtées *(spoiled)*. C'**était** Cendrillon qui **faisait** tout le travail, mais elle **était** toujours belle et gracieuse. Un jour, le prince **a décidé** de donner un bal au palais et un messager **est allé** chez Cendrillon avec une invitation.

There are only two events that occur advancing the story: the prince decided to give a ball and the messenger went to Cinderella's house. These two verbs are in the **passé composé.** All the rest of the paragraph is background information, setting the scene, so the verbs are in the **imparfait.**

When deciding whether to put a verb in the **passé composé** or the **imparfait,** learn to ask yourself whether you are talking about background information or something that was already in progress **(imparfait),** or the next thing that happened in the story **(passé composé).**

 A **La journée d'Alice.** Alice parle de sa journée. Décidez si chaque phrase décrit la scène / la situation ou raconte le déroulement de l'action *(sequence of events)*. Décidez dans quelle colonne va chaque phrase.

Il est sept heures. Il pleut. Je quitte la maison. Il y a beaucoup de voitures sur la route. J'arrive au bureau en retard. Mon patron *(boss)* n'est pas content. Je travaille beaucoup. Je ne déjeune pas. Je rentre à cinq heures. Je suis fatiguée. Il n'y a rien à manger. Nous allons au restaurant. Nous rentrons. Je prends un bain. Il est 11 heures. Je vais au lit.

EXEMPLE

LA SCÈNE / LA SITUATION	LE DÉROULEMENT DE L'ACTION
Il est sept heures.	Je quitte la maison.

Maintenant, réécrivez le paragraphe en mettant les verbes qui présentent le déroulement de l'action au passé composé et les verbes qui décrivent la scène ou la situation à l'imparfait.

B Il était une fois... Réécrivez le début de l'histoire de *La Belle et la Bête* au passé en mettant les verbes en caractères gras à l'imparfait ou au passé composé.

EXEMPLE Il y **avait** un marchand très riche...

Il y (1) **a** un marchand très riche qui (2) **a** trois filles. Ils (3) **habitent** tous ensemble dans une belle maison en ville. Mais un jour, des voleurs *(thieves)* (4) **prennent** toute sa fortune et le marchand et ses filles (5) **doivent** aller habiter dans une petite maison à la campagne.

Ses deux filles aînées (6) **sont** très malheureuses *(unhappy).* Elles (7) **parlent** constamment des choses qu'elles (8) **veulent.** Belle (9) **est** la plus jeune de ses filles. Elle (10) **est** très jolie et aussi très douce. Elle (11) **accepte** sa nouvelle vie et elle (12) **est** heureuse *(happy).*

Un jour, le marchand (13) **part** pour la ville voisine *(neighboring).* Il (14) **neige** et il (15) **fait** très froid et en route, il ne (16) **peut** rien voir dans la forêt. Le marchand (17) **pense** qu'il (18) **va** mourir quand, soudain, il (19) **trouve** un château. La porte du château (20) **est** ouverte et il (21) **décide** d'entrer. Il (22) **remarque** [remarquer *to notice*] une grande table couverte de plats délicieux. Il (23) **mange,** puis il (24) **fait** une sieste *(nap).*

Après sa sieste, il (25) **sort** dans le jardin où il (26) **trouve** une jolie rose qu'il (27) **veut** rapporter *(to bring back)* à Belle. À ce moment-là, un monstre horrible (28) **arrive** et (29) **commence** à crier *(to shout)* qu'il (30) **veut** que Belle vienne habiter chez lui, sinon *(otherwise),* la Bête (31) **va** tuer *(to kill)* le marchand.

C La Belle et la Bête. Continuez l'histoire de *La Belle et la Bête* en mettant les verbes entre parenthèses au passé composé ou à l'imparfait.

Quand le marchand __1__ (rentrer), il __2__ (raconter *[to recount]*) ses aventures à ses filles et Belle __3__ (décider) d'aller habiter chez la Bête. Quand elle __4__ (arriver) au château, elle __5__ (trouver) tout ce dont *(that)* elle __6__ (avoir) besoin. Chaque jour, elle __7__ (avoir) tout ce qu'elle __8__ (vouloir). Mais pendant les cinq premiers jours, elle __9__ (ne pas voir) la Bête.

Un jour, elle le (l') __10__ (voir) pour la première fois pendant *(while)* qu'elle __11__ (faire) une promenade dans le jardin. Elle le (l') __12__ (trouver) horrible et elle __13__ (crier). Belle __14__ (avoir) peur et elle __15__ (ne pas pouvoir) regarder la Bête dans les yeux, mais elle __16__ (aller) faire une promenade avec lui. La conversation __17__ (être) agréable. Quand la Bête __18__ (demander) à Belle de faire une promenade deux jours plus tard, elle __19__ (accepter).

Après ce jour-là, ils __20__ (faire) une promenade chaque après-midi. Ils __21__ (parler) de tout. Au début, Belle __22__ (avoir) très peur de la Bête mais, finalement, Belle __23__ (apprendre) à avoir confiance en lui. Après un certain temps, Belle __24__ (commencer) à aimer le monstre et un jour, elle l' __25__ (embrasser *[to kiss]*). Tout à coup, le visage *(face)* de la Bête __26__ (changer) et il __27__ (devenir) un beau et jeune prince.

VIDÉOREPRISE

Les Stagiaires

Dans *l'Épisode 6*, Matthieu essaie de dominer sa timidité pour inviter Amélie à sortir avec lui. Avant de regarder l'épisode, faites ces activités pour réviser ce que vous avez appris dans le *Chapitre 6*.

Rappel!
Dans l'épisode précédent de la vidéo, Matthieu et Christophe ont parlé d'une soirée que Christophe avait passée avec Amélie et Rachid, et Matthieu lui a posé *(asked him)* beaucoup de questions au sujet d'Amélie et de ce qu'elle aimait faire.

© Cengage Learning

See the *Résumé de grammaire* section at the end of each chapter for a review of all the grammar presented in the chapter.

A **Invitations.** Matthieu voudrait inviter Amélie à sortir avec lui. Comment est-ce qu'on invite un(e) ami(e) à aller quelque part *(to go somewhere)*? Invitez un(e) partenaire à faire les choses suivantes. Il/Elle va accepter une de vos invitations, refuser une de vos invitations et suggérer une autre activité pour la troisième. Utilisez des expressions variées.

EXEMPLE aller au cinéma demain
— **Tu voudrais aller au cinéma demain?**
— **Oui, d'accord.**

1. aller prendre un verre après les cours
2. aller danser samedi soir
3. aller voir une exposition au musée dimanche après-midi

B **On ne peut pas toujours faire ce qu'on veut!** Camille explique ce que ses collègues ont envie de faire et ce qu'ils ont besoin de faire. Répétez ce qu'elle dit, en utilisant les verbes **vouloir**, **pouvoir** et **devoir**.

EXEMPLE Christophe a envie de lire un manga, mais il a besoin de faire des photocopies pour son père.
Christophe veut lire un manga, mais il ne peut pas parce qu'il doit faire des photocopies pour son père.

1. M. Vieilledent a envie de boire du café, mais il a besoin de réduire *(reduce)* sa consommation de caféine.
2. Rachid et Amélie ont envie de partir tôt du bureau aujourd'hui, mais ils ont besoin de finir leur travail.
3. J'ai envie de prendre une longue pause pour le déjeuner *(lunch break)* aujourd'hui pour faire du shopping, mais j'ai besoin de rentrer au bureau.
4. Nous avons tous envie de moins travailler, mais nous avons besoin de terminer *(to finish)* ce projet pour des clients.

C **Au bureau.** Camille décrit les habitudes de ses collègues. Complétez chaque phrase en mettant le verbe donné à la forme correcte du présent. Ensuite, dites si les autres personnes indiquées font la même chose.

EXEMPLE Le lundi matin, M. Vieilledent **part** (partir) pour le travail avant huit heures. Et vous?
Moi aussi, je pars pour le travail avant huit heures le lundi matin.

1. Céline _____ (partir) souvent en week-end. Et vous? Et vos amis?
2. Christophe _____ (dormir) souvent jusqu'à midi le week-end. Et vous? Et vos amis?
3. Rachid et Amélie _____ (sortir) souvent danser le samedi soir. Et vos amis et vous?
4. Amélie _____ (sortir) avec ses amis. Et vous?
5. Amélie ne _____ (dormir) jamais en cours. Et le professeur de français? Et les autres étudiants et vous?

D **Hier soir.** Matthieu parle de ce qu'il a fait hier soir. Complétez ce qu'il dit en mettant les verbes donnés au passé composé ou à l'imparfait.

J'aime beaucoup faire la cuisine et hier, j' __1__ *(ai invité)* (inviter) des amis à dîner chez moi. Vers quatre heures, je __2__ *(suis sorti)* (sortir) pour aller faire les courses. J' __3__ *(ai acheté)* (acheter) tout ce dont *(that)* j' __4__ *(avais)* (avoir) besoin et je __5__ *(suis rentré)* (rentrer). Je/J' __6__ *(commençais)* (commencer) à préparer le repas *(meal)* quand le téléphone __7__ *(a sonné)* (sonner *[to ring]*). C' __8__ *(était)* (être) un de mes amis qui __9__ *(voulait)* (vouloir) me dire *(to tell me)* qu'ils __10__ *(allaient)* (aller) arriver un peu en retard *(late)*. Il __11__ *(était)* (être) déjà huit heures quand ils __12__ *(sont arrivés)* (arriver) et nous __13__ *(avions)* (avoir) tous très faim, alors, nous __14__ *(avons commencé)* (commencer) à manger tout de suite. Après, nous __15__ *(avons joué)* (jouer) à des jeux vidéo jusqu'à minuit. Quand mes amis __16__ *(sont partis)* (partir), j' __17__ *(étais)* (être) fatigué et je/j' __18__ *(suis allé)* (aller) au lit.

E **Quelle soirée!** Amélie est allée à une fête chez des amis, les Fédor. Par petits groupes, regardez l'illustration et racontez *(tell)* ce qui s'est passé à la fête. Utilisez **le voleur** pour *the thief,* **voler** pour *to steal* et **entrer par la fenêtre** pour *to come in through the window.* Avant de commencer, réfléchissez *(think)* aux questions suivantes.

- What night was it?
- What time was it?
- What was the weather like?
- How many people were in the Fédors' living room?

- Why were they there?
- What was each person doing?
- What was in the bedroom?
- What happened?
- What happened next?

le voleur

Les Dupont   Hassan   Amélie   Les Fédor

Access the Video *Les Stagiaires* on iLrn.

▶ **Épisode 6: Je t'invite…**

AVANT LA VIDÉO

Dans cet épisode, Matthieu invite Amélie à sortir avec lui. Avant de regarder l'épisode, faites une liste de trois phrases qu'on peut utiliser pour inviter quelqu'un.

APRÈS LA VIDÉO

Regardez l'épisode pour déterminer quand Matthieu et Amélie vont sortir ensemble et où ils vont aller.

LECTURE ET COMPOSITION

LECTURE

POUR MIEUX LIRE:
Using standard formats

You are going to read summaries of the two French movies that are so far the biggest box-office hits in France. Such summaries generally have similar formats. There is a presentation of the characters; a description of a conflict or a struggle between characters, cultures, or with oneself; and a resolution. Most movie plots can be categorized into one of the following categories: 1) a triumph of good over evil (a villain or a monster), 2) a rags to riches story, 3) a comically awkward attempt to acquire or get rid of something, 4) a quest for an object or a place, 5) a spiritual journey or a rebirth, or 6) a tragic spiral towards death or destruction. Can you think of movies that fit in each of these categories? How would you categorize the last three movies you saw? Keeping these common formats in mind will help you understand better as you watch or read about movies in French.

Intrigues. Lisez les résumés des films français *Bienvenue chez les Ch'tis* et *Intouchables* et décidez si on peut les classer *(categorize)* comme: 1) un triomphe du bien sur le mal, 2) une histoire d'ascension de la pauvreté à la richesse, 3) une comédie où quelqu'un veut obtenir ou se débarrasser de *(to get rid of)* quelque chose, 4) la quête d'un objet ou d'un endroit, 5) une quête spirituelle ou une renaissance ou 6) une spirale tragique vers la mort ou la destruction.

Deux films français

Résumé du film *Bienvenue chez les Ch'tis*

Philippe Abrams est directeur d'un bureau de poste et il veut **se faire muter** sur la Côte d'Azur. **De façon à** être prioritaire pour **la mutation,** il essaie de se faire passer pour un handicapé. **Découvrant sa supercherie,** l'administration l'envoie dans le Nord pour une mutation disciplinaire de deux ans. **Croyant** que le Nord est une région froide et inhospitalière, sa femme, Julie, décide de rester dans le Sud avec leur fils, et Philippe part seul pour son nouveau poste chez les «Ch'tis», les habitants du Nord. **Contre toute attente,** Philippe trouve les «Ch'tis» **chaleureux** et charmants. **En outre,** il considère la séparation temporaire positive pour sa relation avec sa femme et il essaie de **lui faire croire** que la vie dans la petite ville du Nord est **un cauchemar** pour la dissuader de venir le rejoindre. Persuadée que son mari est **déprimé,** Julie annonce finalement qu'elle va aller le voir. Avec la complicité de ses amis, Philippe essaie de faire croire à Julie que tous les clichés qu'elle a sur les gens du Nord sont vrais. Découvrant **les mensonges** de son mari et vexée, Julie retourne dans le Sud. Finalement, Philippe redescend dans le Sud pour lui demander de venir le rejoindre dans le Nord. Deux ans plus tard, Philippe doit quitter les «Ch'tis» parce qu'il est muté dans le Sud.

---

se faire muter *to be transferred* **De façon à** *In order to* **la mutation** *the transfer* **Découvrant sa supercherie** *Discovering his deception* **Croyant** *Believing* **Contre toute attente** *Unexpectedly* **chaleureux** *warm* **En outre** *Moreover* **lui faire croire** *to make her believe* **un cauchemar** *a nightmare* **déprimé** *depressed* **les mensonges** *the lies*

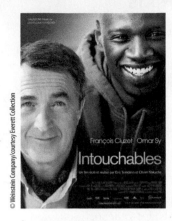

Weinstein Company/courtesy Everett Collection

Résumé du film *Intouchables*

Après six mois de prison, Driss, un jeune homme d'origine sénégalaise de la banlieue parisienne, trouve du travail comme **aide à domicile** chez Philippe, un riche aristocrate devenu **tétraplégique** après un accident de **parapente**. Driss **n'a aucune formation,** mais sa confiance, sa manière franche et spontanée de parler et son énergie impressionnent Philippe, qui est fatigué de la pitié de ses anciens aides. Les différences entre les univers des deux hommes **donnent lieu** à des situations pleines d'humour, et une amitié **inattendue** entre les deux hommes **naît.** Ce film est basé sur une histoire vraie.

aide à domicile *personal assistant, home helper* **tétraplégique** *quadriplegic*
parapente *paragliding* **n'a aucune formation** *has no training*
donnent lieu *give rise* **inattendue** *unexpected* **naît** *is born*

Compréhension

A Répondez aux questions suivantes.

1. Dans quelle catégorie classez-vous ces deux films?

2. Qui sont les personnages *(characters)* du film *Bienvenue chez les Ch'tis*? Quels conflits surgissent *(arise)* dans ce film? Comment est-ce que le film finit?

3. Qui sont les personnages du film *Intouchables*? Quels conflits de culture y a-t-il entre les deux hommes? Est-ce qu'ils deviennent amis? Pourquoi est-ce qu'on pourrait dire *(might you say)* qu'il y a «une renaissance *(a rebirth)*» des personnages?

4. Voudriez-vous plutôt voir *Bienvenue chez les Ch'tis* ou *Intouchables*? Pourquoi?

B On peut résumer un film au présent ou au passé. Changez ces résumés du présent au passé en mettant les verbes au passé composé ou à l'imparfait.

COMPOSITION

POUR MIEUX ÉCRIRE:
Using standard formats

You are going to write a brief summary of one of your favorite films using the **passé composé** and the **imparfait.** Such summaries usually begin with one or two sentences introducing the characters and setting the scene; a few sentences stating the main events that create a conflict or a struggle; and a sentence or two explaining how it is (or is not) resolved. Following this format will help you organize a clear and concise summary.

Organisez-vous. Suivez les étapes *(steps)* suivantes pour organiser votre résumé.

1. Écrivez une ou deux phrases pour présenter les personnages *(characters)* et la situation. Allez-vous utiliser le passé composé ou l'imparfait pour décrire les personnages et la scène?

2. Faites une liste des actions les plus importantes des personnages. Allez-vous utiliser le passé composé ou l'imparfait pour décrire le déroulement de l'action *(the sequence of events)*?

3. Écrivez une ou deux phrases pour expliquer comment le film se termine *(ends)*. Commencez par **À la fin...**

Un film à voir

Utilisez les phrases que vous avez préparées dans la section ***Organisez-vous*** pour écrire un résumé du film que vous avez choisi.

iLrn Share It!

COMPARAISONS CULTURELLES

iLrn In the **Culture Modules** in the video library, see **Film.**

The Artist, un film français, muet en noir et blanc, est un hommage aux films muets hollywoodiens des années 1920. Au Festival de Cannes en 2011, l'acteur Jean Dujardin obtient le Prix d'interprétation masculine *(best leading actor)*. Le film remporte aussi trois Golden Globes, sept BAFTA, six Césars, un Goya et cinq Oscars.

LE CINÉMA: LES PRÉFÉRENCES DES FRANÇAIS

Le cinéma, **que ce soit** les films vus au cinéma, à la télévision ou en DVD, occupe une place centrale dans le temps libre des Français. Avant de lire les renseignements **qui suivent** sur le cinéma en France, essayez de **deviner** comment compléter les phrases. Est-ce que la situation du cinéma en France est comparable à la situation dans votre région?

LES FILMS

Les Français préfèrent...

☑ les films français. ☐ les films étrangers.

Les Français aiment **autant** les films étrangers **que** les films français. En général, les films français représentent à peu près 40% des entrées au cinéma.

Comme films étrangers, ils préfèrent...

☐ les films américains. ☑ les films européens.

Parmi les films étrangers, ce sont les films américains qui sont les plus populaires. Des dix films les plus populaires en France depuis 1945, sept sont des productions américaines.

Comme genre, les Français préfèrent...

☑ les drames. ☐ les films d'aventure.

Ce sont les films qui **attirent** un public jeune qui sont les plus populaires en France: films d'aventure, d'horreur... Les Français aiment aussi les comédies et les films à grand spectacle et on assiste à la popularité **croissante** des films à message social et des films d'amour.

D'après les Français, **les cinéastes** français font les meilleurs...

☑ films à grand spectacle ☐ films comiques et satires sociales

tandis que les Américains font les meilleurs...

☐ films à grand spectacle. ☑ films comiques et satires sociales.

D'après les sondages auprès des Français, les cinéastes français font les meilleures comédies et satires sociales et les Américains sont plus forts pour le grand spectacle.

LES SPECTATEURS

La majorité des spectateurs...

☐ ont plus de 50 ans. ☑ ont entre 25 et 34 ans. ☐ ont moins de 25 ans.

---

que ce soit *whether it be*   **qui suivent** *that follow*   **deviner** *to guess*   **autant que** *as much as*   **attirent** *attract*
croissante *growing*   **D'après** *According to*   **les cinéastes** *film-makers*   **tandis que** *whereas*   **D'après les sondages**
auprès des *According to surveys of the*

Les moins de 25 ans représentent 35 % des spectateurs et deux-tiers (2/3) des gens qui vont au cinéma au moins une fois par mois.

En général, les Français vont au cinéma...

- ❑ pendant la semaine.
- ☑ le week-end.
- ❑ le mercredi, jour de sortie en salle des nouveaux films.

- ☑ en hiver.
- ❑ en été.
- ❑ de façon égale en toute saison.

En France, la saison du cinéma est l'hiver et on y va le plus souvent le week-end.

Source: Gérard Mermet, *Francoscopie 2010*, Éditions Larousse.

Voici une liste des dix films les plus vus au cinéma en France depuis 1945. Qu'est-ce que vous remarquez?

Les plus grands succès du cinéma en France depuis 1945, en millions d'entrées.	
TITANIC (ÉTATS-UNIS)	21,77
BIENVENUE CHEZ LES CH'TIS (FRANCE)	20,49
INTOUCHABLES (FRANCE)	19,44
BLANCHE-NEIGE ET LES SEPT NAINS (ÉTATS-UNIS)	18,32
LA GRANDE VADROUILLE (FRANCE, G.-B.)	17,27
AUTANT EN EMPORTE LE VENT (ÉTATS-UNIS)	16,72
IL ÉTAIT UNE FOIS DANS L'OUEST (ÉTATS-UNIS)	14,86
AVATAR (ÉTATS-UNIS)	14,77
LE LIVRE DE LA JUNGLE (ÉTATS-UNIS)	14,70
LES 101 DALMATIENS (ÉTATS-UNIS)	14,66

Source: www.jpbox-office.com

Compréhension

1. Qu'est-ce que vous pouvez dire au sujet des spectateurs français et de leurs préférences en matière de *(with regards to)* films? Quelles sont les préférences des gens là où vous habitez?

2. Combien de films du tableau ci-dessus *(chart above)* sont américains? français? Certains Français trouvent qu'il y a trop d'influence américaine dans les salles de cinéma en France et que la culture française est menacée *(is threatened)*. Est-ce que ce sentiment est justifié? Quel est le rôle du gouvernement dans la préservation de la culture? Est-ce qu'il doit y avoir une censure? des quotas? des subventions *(subsidies)*?

3. D'après la majorité des Français, quels genres de films est-ce que les cinéastes français font le mieux? Et les cinéastes américains? Est-ce que l'industrie cinématographique d'un pays est un reflet de *(a reflection of)* sa culture? Si oui, quelles comparaisons culturelles peut-on faire entre les Français et les Américains?

(iLrn Share It!

🌐 Visit **www.cengagebrain.com** for additional cultural information and activities.

RÉSUMÉ DE GRAMMAIRE

THE VERBS *VOULOIR, POUVOIR,* AND *DEVOIR*

Je **veux** sortir ce soir, mais je ne **peux** pas. Je **dois** travailler.

Here are the conjugations of **vouloir** *(to want)*, **pouvoir** *(can, may, to be able)*, and **devoir** *(must, to have to, to owe)*.

VOULOIR	POUVOIR	DEVOIR
je **veux**	je **peux**	je **dois**
tu **veux**	tu **peux**	tu **dois**
il/elle/on **veut**	il/elle/on **peut**	il/elle/on **doit**
nous **voulons**	nous **pouvons**	nous **devons**
vous **voulez**	vous **pouvez**	vous **devez**
ils/elles **veulent**	ils/elles **peuvent**	ils/elles **doivent**
P.C. **j'ai voulu**	P.C. **j'ai pu**	P.C. **j'ai dû**
IMP. **je voulais**	IMP. **je pouvais**	IMP. **je devais**

Nous **voulions** partir en vacances, mais nous n'**avons** pas **pu**. Nous **avons dû** travailler.

Elle **a dû** quitter la maison très tôt. Elle **devait** arriver à sept heures.
She must have left / had to leave the house very early. She was supposed to arrive at seven o'clock.

You generally use the verb **vouloir** in the **imparfait** to say what someone wanted to do. Use **pouvoir** in the **imparfait** to say what people could do if they might have wanted to, but use it in the **passé composé** to say what they managed to do on an occasion when they tried. Use **devoir** in the **imparfait** to say what one was supposed to do, but in the **passé composé** for what one must have done, or had to do on a specific occasion.

THE VERBS *SORTIR, PARTIR,* AND *DORMIR*

Je **dors** jusqu'à sept heures et je **pars** pour l'université à huit heures.

Ce matin, j'**ai dormi** jusqu'à sept heures et demie et je **suis partie** pour l'université en retard *(late)*.

Avant, je **sortais** souvent avec des amis, mais nous ne **sommes** pas **sortis** le week-end dernier.

Il **quitte** Paris pour aller travailler à Nice. Il **part** demain.

Je sors **de** la maison à neuf heures.

Je pars **pour** Nice demain.

Je pars **de** chez moi à huit heures.

Here are the conjugations of **sortir** *(to go out)*, **partir** *(to leave)*, and **dormir** *(to sleep)*.

SORTIR	PARTIR	DORMIR
je **sors**	je **pars**	je **dors**
tu **sors**	tu **pars**	tu **dors**
il/elle/on **sort**	il/elle/on **part**	il/elle/on **dort**
nous **sortons**	nous **partons**	nous **dormons**
vous **sortez**	vous **partez**	vous **dormez**
ils/elles **sortent**	ils/elles **partent**	ils/elles **dorment**
P.C. **je suis sorti(e)**	P.C. **je suis parti(e)**	P.C. **j'ai dormi**
IMP. **je sortais**	IMP. **je partais**	IMP. **je dormais**

Sortir means *to go out* both in the sense of going out with friends and going out of a place. Use **partir** to say *to leave* in the sense of *to go away.* **Quitter** means *to leave* a person or a place and *must* be used with a direct object.

Use these prepositions with these verbs:

to go out (of) = **sortir (de)**
to leave (from) = **partir (de)**
to leave (for) = **partir (pour)**

L'IMPARFAIT AND *LE PASSÉ COMPOSÉ*

All verbs except **être** form the **imparfait** by dropping the **-ons** from the present tense **nous** form and adding these endings. The stem for **être** is **ét-.**

	PARLER (nous parl~~ons~~ → parl-)	**FAIRE** (nous fais~~ons~~ → fais-)	**PRENDRE** (nous pren~~ons~~ → pren-)	**ÊTRE** (ét-)
je (j')	parl**ais**	fais**ais**	pren**ais**	ét**ais**
tu	parl**ais**	fais**ais**	pren**ais**	ét**ais**
il/elle/on	parl**ait**	fais**ait**	pren**ait**	ét**ait**
nous	parl**ions**	fais**ions**	pren**ions**	ét**ions**
vous	parl**iez**	fais**iez**	pren**iez**	ét**iez**
ils/elles	parl**aient**	fais**aient**	pren**aient**	ét**aient**

Verbs with spelling changes in the present tense **nous** form, like **manger** and **commencer,** retain the spelling changes in the **imparfait** only before endings beginning with an **a.**

Note these expressions in the **imparfait:**

il y a	→	il y avait
il pleut	→	il pleuvait
il neige	→	il neigeait

When talking about the past, you use both the **passé composé** and the **imparfait.** Note their uses:

USE THE *IMPARFAIT* TO SAY:	USE THE *PASSÉ COMPOSÉ* TO SAY:
1. HOW THINGS USED TO BE OR WHAT USED TO HAPPEN • continuous actions or states • repeated or habitual actions of an unspecified duration	**1. WHAT HAPPENED AT A PRECISE MOMENT, FOR A SPECIFIC DURATION, OR A SPECIFIC NUMBER OF TIMES** • completed actions • actions within a specific duration • actions done a specific number of times
2. WHAT WAS GOING ON • scene or setting • interrupted actions in progress	**2. WHAT HAPPENED NEXT** • sequence of events • actions interrupting something in progress
3. WHAT THINGS WERE LIKE OR HOW SOMEONE FELT • physical or mental states	**3. WHAT CHANGED** • changes in states
4. WHAT SOMEONE WAS GOING TO DO	**4. WHAT SOMEONE WENT TO DO**

(right margin notes)

Quand j'**avais** 16 ans, j'**allais** au lycée. Je **passais** beaucoup de temps avec mes copains. On **aimait** faire du roller.

Nous **mangions** bien, mais je **mangeais** peu.

Vous **commenciez** vos cours à midi, mais moi, je **commençais** mes cours à 11 heures.

Il y avait du vent, il **pleuvait** et **il faisait** froid, mais **il** ne **neigeait** pas.

Cendrillon **pleurait** *(was crying)* quand sa marraine *([fairy] godmother)* **est arrivée.** La marraine **a aidé** Cendrillon et Cendrillon **est allée** au bal du prince. Le prince **est** immédiatement **tombé** amoureux de Cendrillon. Ils **ont dansé** et ils **ont** beaucoup **parlé.** À minuit, Cendrillon **est partie** sans dire au prince qui elle **était,** mais elle **a laissé** tomber *(dropped)* une de ses chaussures.

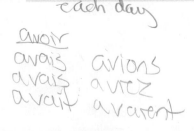

VOCABULAIRE

COMPÉTENCE 1

Inviting someone to go out

NOMS MASCULINS

l'amour	love
un film d'amour	a romantic movie, a love story
un groupe	a group
un horaire	a schedule

NOMS FÉMININS

une comédie	a comedy
une façon	a way
l'heure d'ouverture	opening time
l'heure officielle	official time
une idée	an idea
une invitation	an invitation
une personne	a person
une séance	a showing

EXPRESSIONS VERBALES

appeler	to call
devoir	must, to have to, to owe
dire	to say, to tell
passer un film	to show a movie
pouvoir	can, may, to be able
regretter	to regret, to be sorry
répondre (à)	to answer, to respond (to)
suggérer	to suggest
téléphoner (à)	to phone
utiliser	to use, to utilize
vouloir	to want

DIVERS

allô	hello (on the telephone)
avec plaisir	gladly, with pleasure
Je pensais	I was thinking
Je t'invite...	I'm inviting you . . .
Je voudrais vous inviter...	I'd like to invite you . . .
Quelle bonne idée!	What a good idea!
quelqu'un	someone, somebody
tellement	so much, so
uniquement	uniquely, only
Vous voudriez...?	Would you like . . . ?

COMPÉTENCE 2

Talking about how you spend and used to spend your time

NOMS MASCULINS

un copain	a (boy)friend, a pal
un lycée	a high school
un lycéen	a high school student
un resto U	a university cafeteria

NOMS FÉMININS

une copine	a (girl)friend, a pal
une école	a school
une lycéenne	a high school student
une soirée	a party
la vie	life

EXPRESSIONS VERBALES

avoir cours	to have class
comparer	to compare
dormir	to sleep
faire du roller	to go in-line skating
faire du skateboard	to skateboard
partir (de/pour)	to leave (from/for), to go away (from/to)
partir en vacances	to leave on vacation
partir en voyage	to leave on a trip
partir en week-end	to go away for the weekend
quitter	to leave
sortir (de)	to go out (of)

DIVERS

ce que	what
dans le passé	in the past
fatigué(e)	tired
rien de spécial	nothing special

Talking about the past

NOMS MASCULINS

un bistro	*a pub, a restaurant*
un repas	*a meal*

NOMS FÉMININS

une fois	*once, one time*
une sortie	*an outing*

EXPRESSIONS ADVERBIALES

un jour	*one day*
soudain	*suddenly*
tout à coup	*all of a sudden*
tout de suite	*right away*
tout d'un coup	*all at once*

DIVERS

Ça t'a plu?	*Did you like it?*
délicieux (délicieuse)	*delicious*
Qu'est-ce qui s'est passé?	*What happened?*
rien du tout	*nothing at all*
tout le monde	*everybody, everyone*

Narrating in the past

NOMS MASCULINS

un acteur	*an actor*
un bal	*a ball*
un classique	*a classic*
un conte	*a story* (for children)
un conte de fées	*a fairy tale*
les effets spéciaux	*special effects*
un marchand	*a merchant, a shopkeeper*
un messager	*a messenger*
un monstre	*a monster*
un palais	*a palace*
le travail	*work*

NOMS FÉMININS

une actrice	*an actress*
une bête	*a beast*
une demi-sœur	*a stepsister*
une époque	*a time (period)*
une marchande	*a merchant, a shopkeeper*
une messagère	*a messenger*
la violence	*violence*

EXPRESSIONS VERBALES

apprécier	*to appreciate*
à suivre	*to be continued*
changer	*to change*
Connaissez-vous...?	*Do you know...?*
décider	*to decide*
emprisonner	*to imprison*
jouer	*to act* (in movies and theater)
se parler	*to talk to each other*
prendre la place de	*to take the place of*
promettre (promis)	*to promise (promised)*
tomber amoureux (amoureuse) de	*to fall in love with*

ADJECTIFS

amoureux (amoureuse) (de)	*in love (with)*
basé(e) (sur)	*based (on)*
cruel(le)	*cruel*
doux (douce)	*sweet, soft, gentle*
excellent(e)	*excellent*
féroce	*ferocious*
gâté(e)	*spoiled*
gracieux (gracieuse)	*gracious*
horrible	*horrible*
patient(e)	*patient*

DIVERS

au début (de)	*at the beginning (of)*
finalement	*finally, in the end*
Il était une fois...	*Once upon a time there was...*
il/elle m'a plu	*I liked it*
lequel (laquelle)	*which, which one*
petit à petit	*little by little*
trop de	*too much*

plutôt
(rather/instead)

un conte de fées
(fairy tale)

palais
-palace

horaire -hourly

INTERLUDE MUSICAL

Amélie-les-crayons est connue pour la qualité de son spectacle ainsi que (as well as) pour la qualité de sa musique.

🌐 You can find these songs on iTunes. You can also search the Internet to hear them performed and to find the lyrics.

LA GARDE-ROBE D'ÉLIZABETH

AMÉLIE-LES-CRAYONS

Amélie-les-crayons, la chanteuse (singer) de la troupe du même nom, a fait ses débuts dans les cafés et bars de Lyon. Plus tard, elle s'est jointe aux trois autres musiciens, Heiko, Michel et Laurent, pour former la troupe. Dans leurs chansons, ils parlent de la vie de tous les jours, souvent sur un ton humoristique. Dans *La garde-robe d'Élizabeth,* Élizabeth désespère (becomes exasperated) parce qu'elle n'arrive pas à choisir quels vêtements elle veut mettre. Faites les activités qui suivent pour comprendre plus facilement les paroles (lyrics).

A **Élizabeth devant sa garde-robe.** Voici de nouveaux mots qui se trouvent dans les paroles de *La garde-robe d'Élizabeth.* Organisez ces mots en trois listes: noms de vêtements, verbes et divers. Quels sont les vêtements que vous mettez le plus souvent?

EXEMPLE

VÊTEMENTS	VERBES	DIVERS
un anorak	**s'arracher**	**allumé(e)**
des bas	**attendre**	**à pois**

allumé(e) *turned on*	criser *to panic*	de grandes manches *puffy sleeves*
un anorak *a ski jacket*	croire *to believe*	s'habiller *to dress oneself*
à pois *polka-dotted*	une culotte *panties*	les info(rmation)s *news*
s'arracher *to pull out*	un débardeur *a tank top*	les jambes *legs*
attendre *to wait*	se dérober *to give way*	des jambières *leggings*
attraper *to grab*	désespérer *to despair*	lâcher *to let go, to release*
des bas *hose, stockings*	en boule *in a ball*	laver *to wash*
des baskets *tennis shoes*	en croix *crossed*	louper *to miss*
les bras *the arms*	s'énerver *to get upset*	un maillot *a jersey*
des bretelles *suspenders*	enlever *to take off*	la météo *the weather forecast*
un body *a body suit*	entendre *to hear*	mitigé(e) *mixed, uncertain*
un cadeau *a gift*	en train de *in the process of*	un nu-dos *an open-backed outfit*
un châle *a shawl*	fagoté(e) *done up, dressed*	un pantalon *slacks*
le choix *the choice*	un fer *an iron*	repasser *to iron*
un col roulé *a turtleneck sweater*	fouiller *to dig around*	se ressaisir *to get hold of oneself*
un col V *a V-necked sweater*	un foulard *a scarf*	sentir *to feel*
se coucher *to lie down*	un froc *a frock*	un tablier *an apron*
craquer *to crack*	une garde-robe *a wardrobe*	une tache *a spot*
	un gilet *a vest*	

B **Qu'est-ce qu'elle fait?** Complétez les phrases suivantes avec le choix logique.

1. Élizabeth s'arrache _____ (les jambes / les cheveux). Elle ne sait pas comment s'habiller!
2. Elle se couche par terre devant sa garde-robe, les _____ (bras / cheveux) en croix, le regard en l'air.
3. Élizabeth attrape quelque chose dans sa garde-robe, les _____ (bras / yeux) fermés.
4. Elle se regarde dans le miroir et elle n'en croit pas _____ (ses yeux / ses bras)! Elle voit une tache sur son gilet!

PREMIER AMOUR

TONY PARKER / RICKWEL

Tony Parker, célèbre joueur de basket des San Antonio Spurs, est aussi fana et chanteur de *(fan and singer of)* musique rap et hip-hop. Il est né en Belgique et a grandi *(grew up)* en France. Dans la chanson *Premier amour,* qu'il interprète avec l'artiste martiniquais Rickwel, il parle de son premier amour, un amour qu'il n'oubliera jamais *(he will never forget)*.

Dans la chanson *Premier amour,* c'est Tony Parker qui chante les strophes *(stanzas)* en français et Rickwel qui chante les strophes en anglais.

A **Comment c'était.** Dans la chanson *Premier amour,* le chanteur *(singer)* parle d'une copine de sa jeunesse et de leur relation. Pour mieux comprendre, faites des phrases logiques en utilisant un élément de chaque colonne.

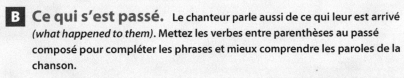

		mon seul amour
		mon porte-bonheur *(lucky charm)*
Tu	étais / était	mon avenir *(future)* et mon chemin *(path)*
On	aimais / aimait	gosses *(kids)*
J'		fous *(crazy)*
		te serrer dans mes bras *(hold you in my arms)*
		toujours ensemble

B **Ce qui s'est passé.** Le chanteur parle aussi de ce qui leur est arrivé *(what happened to them)*. Mettez les verbes entre parenthèses au passé composé pour compléter les phrases et mieux comprendre les paroles de la chanson.

1. On s'est connus *(met)* trop jeunes et on _____ (grandir *[to grow up]*) trop vite.
2. On _____ (évoluer *[to evolve]*) dans la vie et notre amour s'est dissipé *(dissipated)*.
3. On s'est quittés *(We left each other),* les années _____ (passer) et j'ai perdu le fil *(I lost track)*.
4. On _____ (rester) amis et on _____ (garder *[to keep]*) de beaux souvenirs de notre amour.

La Normandie
La vie quotidienne

iLrn iLrn Heinle Learning Center

www.cengagebrain.com

Horizons Video: Les Stagiaires

Audio

Internet web search

Pair work

Group work

© Herve Hughes/hemis/Getty Images

7

COMPÉTENCE

1 Describing your daily routine
La vie de tous les jours

Describing your daily routine
Les verbes réfléchis au présent

Stratégies et Lecture
- **Pour mieux lire:** *Using word families and watching out for* **faux amis**
- **Lecture:** *Il n'est jamais trop tard!*

2 Talking about relationships
La vie sentimentale

Saying what people do for each other
Les verbes réciproques au présent et les verbes réfléchis et réciproques au futur immédiat

Talking about activities
Les verbes en **-re**

3 Talking about what you did and used to do
Les activités d'hier

Saying what people did
Les verbes réfléchis et réciproques au passé composé

Saying what people did and used to do
Les verbes réfléchis et réciproques à l'imparfait et reprise de l'usage du passé composé et de l'imparfait

4 Describing traits and characteristics
Les traits de caractère

Specifying which one
Les pronoms relatifs **qui, que** *et* **dont**

Vidéoreprise *Les Stagiaires*

Lecture et Composition
- **Pour mieux lire:** *Recognizing conversational style*
- **Lecture:** *Conte pour enfants de moins de trois ans*
- **Pour mieux écrire:** *Organizing a paragraph*
- **Composition:** *Le matin chez moi*

Comparaisons culturelles *L'amour et le couple*

Résumé de grammaire

Vocabulaire

LA FRANCE ET SA DIVERSITÉ

In the **Culture Modules** in the video library, see **The Regions of France**.

Existe-t-il une identité française? Quand vous pensez à la culture française et au peuple français, comment est-ce que vous les imaginez?

En réalité, la France n'a pas **une seule** identité ou une seule culture. La France est un pays riche en diversité où chaque région a son **propre** héritage culturel.

Chacune des régions de la France a ses traditions, sa cuisine, sa musique, ses danses et même parfois sa langue.

Pourtant, malgré cette diversité, les Français **se sentent** bien français! Une histoire qui date de plus de 2 000 ans, **un patrimoine** riche en architecture et en culture et une tradition **à la fois laïque** et catholique donnent aux Français leur unité, le sens d'être «français».

---

une seule *a single*   **propre** *own*   **Pourtant, malgré** *However, in spite of*   **se sentent** *feel*   **un patrimoine** *a heritage*
à la fois *at the same time, both*   **laïque** *secular*

Récemment, l'immigration a beaucoup changé le visage de la France. Les nouveaux immigrés cherchent à **maintenir** leurs langues et leurs traditions.

Ainsi, aujourd'hui la France **fait face à** des questions importantes: Comment peut-on préserver l'identité de la culture française **tout en respectant** les divers groupes ethniques qui habitent dans le pays? Est-il possible de combiner l'unité et la diversité?

🌐 Chaque région de la France a sa propre histoire et sa propre culture. Choisissez une région de la France et recherchez des informations sur Internet au sujet de son héritage culturel. Partagez vos renseignements avec la classe.

La Normandie

🌐 Visit it live on Google Earth!

NOMBRE D'HABITANTS:
**3 500 000 habitants
(les Normands)**

CAPITALE: **Rouen**

Le savez-vous?

Qu'est-ce que vous avez appris au sujet de l'identité française? Existe-t-il une seule identité culturelle dans votre région? Complétez ces phrases.

> **breton régions diversité immigration niçois corse laïque catholique unité divers groupes ethniques**

1. La France n'a pas une seule identité ou une seule culture. C'est un pays riche en diversité culturelle, grâce à *(due to)* la variété d'héritages culturels de ses _____ et à l'_____ récente.

2. Dans certaines régions de la France, les gens parlent non seulement *(not only)* français, mais aussi une langue régionale. De ces trois langues régionales – corse, niçois, breton, devinez laquelle *(guess which one)* est parlée dans chacune des régions suivantes.

   En Bretagne, certains parlent _____.

   En Corse, il y a des gens qui parlent _____.

   À Nice et dans sa région, on entend *(hears)* parfois parler _____.

3. Malgré cette diversité, les Français se sentent bien français. La France a un héritage culturel «français» basé surtout sur son histoire, son patrimoine et sa tradition à la fois _____ et _____.

4. À cause de la diversité des cultures qui font aujourd'hui partie de la culture française, les Français cherchent à trouver une réponse à deux questions importantes:

   Est-il possible de combiner l'_____ et la _____?

   Comment peut-on préserver l'identité de la culture française tout en respectant les _____ qui habitent dans le pays?

---

maintenir *to maintain*   **Ainsi** *Thus*   **fait face à** *is facing*   **tout en respectant** *while still respecting*

Describing your daily routine

LA VIE DE TOUS LES JOURS

Quelle est votre **routine quotidienne**?

D'habitude le matin...

Je me réveille vers six heures.

Je me lève tout de suite et je **fais ma toilette.**

Je me lave **la figure** et **les mains** *(f).*

Je prends un bain ou **une douche.**

Je me brosse les cheveux.

Je me brosse les dents.

Je me maquille **avant de m'habiller.**

Je m'habille.

Le soir...

Quelquefois, **je me repose.**

D'autres fois, je m'amuse avec des amis.

Parfois, quand je suis seule, **je m'ennuie.**

Je me déshabille.

Je me couche et **je m'endors** facilement.

la routine quotidienne *the daily routine*   **faire sa toilette** *to wash up*   **la figure** *the face*   **les mains** *(f) the hands*   **une douche** *a shower*   **avant de m'habiller** *before I dress, before dressing*   **je me repose (se reposer** *to rest)*   **D'autres fois** *Other times*   **je m'ennuie (s'ennuyer** *to be bored, to get bored)*   **je m'endors (s'endormir** *to fall asleep)*

2-30

Rosalie Toulouse-Richard, d'origine française, habite à Atlanta **depuis** son mariage avec un Américain. **Veuve** maintenant, elle retourne en France avec sa **petite-fille** Rose qui ne **connaît** pas du tout la France. **Comme** elles partagent une chambre **pendant** leur **séjour,** elles parlent de leurs routines le matin.

ROSALIE: Tu te lèves vers quelle heure d'habitude?

ROSE: Entre six heures et six heures et demie. Je fais **vite** ma toilette, je m'habille et puis je me maquille. Je suis prête en une demi-heure.

ROSALIE: C'est parfait. Moi, je prends quelquefois une douche le matin, mais je préfère prendre mon bain le soir. Je peux très bien **attendre** jusqu'à sept heures pour faire ma toilette.

ROSE: Et moi, je ne quitte jamais la maison avant huit heures et demie. Alors si tu veux, on peut prendre le petit déjeuner ensemble tous les matins.

A **Et ensuite...** Trouvez la suite logique pour compléter chaque phrase.

Je me lève...	avec des amis.
Je me brosse...	je me couche.
Je prends...	vers huit heures.
L'après-midi, je m'amuse...	les dents.
Je me déshabille et puis...	une douche ou un bain.
Je me couche et...	je m'endors.

B **Ma routine.** Complétez les phrases avec une expression de la liste.

EXEMPLE   Je me réveille avant six heures.
              Je me réveille rarement avant six heures.
              Je ne me réveille jamais avant six heures.

toujours (always)
souvent (often)
quelquefois (sometimes)
de temps en temps
rarement

ne... jamais (never) (can put at end)
tous les jours (everyday)
le lundi, le mardi...
le matin, l'après-midi, le soir
une (deux...) fois par jour (semaine...)

1. Je me réveille après neuf heures.
2. Je me lève tout de suite.
3. Je prends une douche ou un bain.
4. Je me lave les mains.
5. Je me lave les cheveux.
6. Je me brosse les dents.

7. Je m'habille vite.
8. Je m'ennuie.
9. Je me repose.
10. Je m'amuse bien.
11. Je me couche tard.
12. Je m'endors sur le canapé.

À VOUS!

Avec un(e) partenaire, relisez à haute voix la conversation entre Rosalie et Rose. Ensuite, imaginez que vous voyagez ensemble et adaptez la conversation pour parler de votre routine le matin.

iLrn 🌐 You can find a list of the new words from this **Compétence** on page 298 and access the audio online.

---

depuis *since*   **Veuve (Veuf)** *Widow (Widower)*   **une petite-fille (un petit-fils)** *a granddaughter (a grandson)*   **elle connaît** **(connaître** *to know)*   **Comme** *Since, As*   **pendant** *during*   **un séjour** *a stay*   **vite** *quickly, fast*   **attendre** *to wait (for)*

DESCRIBING YOUR DAILY ROUTINE

✔ Pour vérifier

1. What is the difference in usage between the reflexive verb **se laver** and the non-reflexive verb **laver**?

2. What are the different reflexive pronouns that are used with each subject pronoun when you conjugate a reflexive verb like **se laver**?

3. Where do you place **ne... pas** when negating reflexive verbs?

4. How is **s'endormir** conjugated?

5. In which forms do verbs like **se lever, s'appeler,** and **s'ennuyer** have spelling changes? What are the changes? Which forms do not have spelling changes?

iLrn Grammar Tutorials

Les verbes réfléchis au présent

You can do something to or for yourself or to or for another person or thing. When someone performs an action on or for himself/herself, a reflexive verb is generally used in French. Compare these sentences.

REFLEXIVE	NON-REFLEXIVE

Je me lave les mains.	Je lave la voiture.

The infinitive of reflexive verbs is preceded by the reflexive pronoun **se.** When you conjugate these verbs, change the reflexive pronoun according to the subject. In the negative, place **ne** directly after the subject and **pas** after the conjugated verb.

SE LAVER *(to wash [oneself])*		NE PAS SE LAVER	
je me lave	nous nous lavons	je ne me lave pas	nous ne nous lavons pas
tu te laves	vous vous lavez	tu ne te laves pas	vous ne vous lavez pas
il/elle/on se lave	ils/elles se lavent	il/elle/on ne se lave pas	ils/elles ne se lavent pas

Me, te, and **se** change to **m', t',** and **s'** before a vowel sound: **je m'habille, tu t'habilles, elle s'habille, ils s'habillent.**

Here are some reflexive verbs you can use to talk about your daily life:

s'amuser	*to have fun*
s'appeler	*to be named*
se brosser (les cheveux, les dents)	*to brush (one's hair, one's teeth)*
se coucher / se recoucher	*to go to bed / to go back to bed*
s'endormir	*to fall asleep*
s'ennuyer	*to be bored, to get bored*
s'habiller / se déshabiller	*to get dressed / to get undressed*
se laver (les mains, la figure)	*to wash (one's hands, one's face)*
se lever	*to get up*
se maquiller	*to put on make-up*
se raser	*to shave*
se reposer	*to rest*
se réveiller	*to wake up*

The verb **s'endormir** is conjugated like **dormir.**

S'ENDORMIR *(to fall asleep)*	
je m'endors	nous nous endormons
tu t'endors	vous vous endormez
il/elle/on s'endort	ils/elles s'endorment

Remember that in verbs ending in **-yer,** such as **s'ennuyer,** the letter **y** changes to **i** in all forms except those of **nous** and **vous.**

S'ENNUYER *(to be bored, to get bored)*	
je m'ennu**i**e	nous nous ennuyons
tu t'ennu**i**es	vous vous ennuyez
il/elle/on s'ennu**i**e	ils/elles s'ennu**i**ent

There is an accent spelling change in the conjugation of **se lever.** Its conjugation is similar to that of **acheter. S'appeler** changes its spelling by doubling the final consonant of the stem in all present tense forms except those of **nous** and **vous.**

SE LEVER *(to get up)*	
je me l**è**ve	nous nous levons
tu te l**è**ves	vous vous levez
il/elle/on se l**è**ve	ils/elles se l**è**vent

(layvez)
(lehv)

S'APPELER *(to be named)*	
je m'appe**ll**e	nous nous appelons
tu t'appe**ll**es	vous vous appelez
il/elle/on s'appe**ll**e	ils/elles s'appe**ll**ent

 A **Équivalents.** Trouvez le verbe réfléchi correspondant à chaque définition.

> s'endormir   s'ennuyer
> se reposer   se lever
> s'habiller   s'amuser
> se coucher   se maquiller

1. aller au lit — se coucher

2. sortir du lit — se lever

3. mettre des vêtements – s'habiller

4. faire quelque chose d'amusant – s'amuser

5. faire quelque chose d'ennuyeux [boring] – s'ennuyer

6. ne rien faire – se reposer (rest)

7. commencer à dormir – s'endormir

8. mettre du mascara – se maquiller

B **D'abord...** Indiquez l'ordre logique des activités données.

EXEMPLE prendre un bain / se lever
D'abord, on se lève et puis on prend un bain.

1. se réveiller / se lever

2. se laver la figure / se maquiller

3. s'habiller / prendre un bain ou une douche

4. quitter la maison / s'habiller

5. se reposer / rentrer à la maison après les cours

6. s'amuser / retrouver des amis

7. se déshabiller / se coucher

8. s'endormir / se coucher

© Javier Larrea/age fotostock

Mes amis et moi, on s'amuse toujours bien le week-end.

C **Un samedi typique.** Voilà la routine de Rose le samedi. Qu'est-ce qu'elle fait?

EXEMPLE Le samedi matin, ... vers neuf heures.
Le samedi matin, **elle se réveille** vers neuf heures.

EXEMPLE 1. 2. 3.

1. ... tout de suite.
2. ... la figure et les mains.
3. ... avant le petit déjeuner.

elle s'habille

4. 5. 6. 7.

4. Après le petit déjeuner, …
5. …. les cheveux juste avant de quitter la maison.
6. Le samedi soir, … avec des amis.
7. … vers deux heures du matin et… facilement.

 D **Et vous?** Regardez les illustrations de **C. *Un samedi typique*.** Est-ce que vous faites les mêmes choses le samedi?

EXEMPLE

… vers 9h
Je me réveille vers 9h.
Je ne me réveille pas vers 9h.
Je me réveille vers 10h.

E **Ma routine.** Complétez ces phrases pour parler de vous.

1. En semaine *(During the week),* je me réveille…
2. Je me lève…
3. Mes amis et moi, nous nous amusons beaucoup quand…
4. Nous nous ennuyons quand…
5. En semaine, je me couche…
6. Je m'endors…

Line art on this page: © Cengage Learning

266 *deux cent soixante-six* | **CHAPITRE 7**

266

††† F Questions. Travaillez en groupes pour préparer autant de questions que possible à poser au professeur au sujet de sa routine quotidienne. Utilisez les éléments donnés ou d'autres expressions logiques. Le groupe avec le plus grand nombre de questions logiques gagne.

> s'amuser   s'ennuyer   se réveiller   se lever
> se coucher   s'endormir   se laver la figure et les mains
> se brosser les dents/les cheveux

> à quelle heure   tôt / tard   facilement   tout de suite
> combien de fois par jour   avant / après le petit déjeuner   quand

EXEMPLE *Est-ce que vous vous couchez tôt d'habitude?*

††† G Beaucoup de questions! Circulez parmi les étudiants. Posez chaque paire de questions à un(e) étudiant(e) différent(e). Notez leurs réponses et ensuite, dites à la classe ce que vous avez appris.

EXEMPLE —Eva, à quelle heure est-ce que tu te réveilles le samedi
          matin?
          —Je me réveille vers 10h.

          Après, à la classe: **Eva se réveille vers 10h.**

> À quelle heure est-ce que tu te réveilles le samedi matin?
> Est-ce que tu te lèves tout de suite?

> Quand est-ce que tu te reposes?
> Tu te couches tôt pendant la semaine?

> Tu t'amuses ou tu t'ennuies quand tu es seul(e) le soir?
> Quand est-ce que tu t'amuses?

> Tu préfères prendre un bain ou une douche?
> Est-ce que tu prends ton bain ou ta douche le matin ou le soir?

> Vers quelle heure est-ce que tu te couches le samedi soir?
> Est-ce que tu t'endors tout de suite?

††† H Vous faites du baby-sitting. Imaginez que vous allez faire du baby-sitting pour les deux enfants d'un(e) ami(e). Demandez ces renseignements à votre ami(e). Votre partenaire va jouer le rôle de votre ami(e) et imaginer ses réponses. Préparez une scène à présenter à la classe.

Find out . . .

EXEMPLE *what time they wake up*
          —**À quelle heure est-ce qu'ils se réveillent?**
          —**Ils se réveillent vers huit heures.**

1. *if they get up right away*
2. *if they take a bath or a shower in the morning or the evening*
3. *if they rest in the afternoon*
4. *at what time they eat dinner*
5. *at what time they go to bed*
6. *if they fall asleep easily*

STRATÉGIES ET LECTURE

POUR MIEUX LIRE: Using word families and watching out for *faux amis*

Recognizing words that belong to the same word family can make reading easier. Can you supply the missing meanings below?

la vie	**vivre**	**se marier**	**le mariage**
life	*to live*	*to marry*	*marriage*
l'arrêt	**s'arrêter**	**espérer**	**l'espoir**
the stop	*???*	*to hope*	*???*

Using cognates and word families can help you understand new texts more easily. However, beware of **faux amis,** words that look like cognates but have different meanings. For example, **rester** does not mean *to rest,* but *to stay.* Use cognates, but if a word does not seem right in the context, look it up.

A **Familles de mots.** Vous allez voir ces mots dans l'histoire qui suit. Servez-vous du sens des mots donnés pour déterminer le sens des autres mots.

rêver	**un rêve**	**dire**	**dit(e)**
to dream	*a dream*	*to say, to tell*	*said, told*
se souvenir de	**des souvenirs**	**connaître**	**connu(e)**
to remember	*???*	*to know*	*???*
saluer	**une salutation**	**reconnaître**	**reconnu(e)**
to greet	*???*	*to recognize*	*???*

B **Faux amis.** Donnez le sens des faux amis en caractères gras selon le contexte.

M. Dupont se repose dans un fauteuil au jardin quand une jolie jeune fille qui passe **attire** son attention. Il la **salue** et lui dit bonjour. Cette fille ressemble à quelqu'un qu'il connaissait dans le passé et il commence à rêver. Il a de beaux **souvenirs** du temps où il était jeune. Il aimait une jeune fille et il **garde** toujours l'espoir de la revoir un jour.

Lecture: *Il n'est jamais trop tard!*

🔊
2-31 *Rosalie Toulouse-Richard, qui habite à Atlanta depuis son mariage avec un Américain, retourne à Rouen avec sa petite-fille Rose. Son vieil ami, André Dupont, ne sait pas encore que Rosalie est à Rouen.*

André Dupont a toujours aimé passer des heures à travailler dans son jardin. Il a une passion pour les roses et depuis des années, il plante des rosiers de toutes les variétés et de toutes les couleurs dans son jardin.

Ses rosiers font l'admiration de tous les gens du quartier et beaucoup d'entre eux passent devant chez lui pour regarder son beau jardin. Aujourd'hui, trois jeunes filles s'arrêtent devant son jardin et lui disent bonjour. Il reconnaît deux d'entre elles, ce sont les petites-filles de son ami Jean Toulouse, mais c'est la troisième qui attire son attention. Il ne l'a jamais vue, et pourtant il a l'impression de la connaître! Elle ressemble à quelqu'un... quelqu'un qu'il a connu il y a très longtemps.

Les souvenirs lui reviennent, comme si c'était hier. C'était il y a longtemps, il avait dix-huit ans et il était amoureux fou d'une jolie jeune fille de son âge. Elle s'appelait Rosalie... ! Il voulait lui dire combien il l'aimait, mais il n'en avait pas le courage. Il était trop timide. Un beau jour, il s'est décidé à tout lui dire. Il a choisi des fleurs de son jardin pour en faire un bouquet, il a pris son vélo et il est allé chez Rosalie. Mais en arrivant, il a trouvé Rosalie en compagnie d'un jeune Américain et elle regardait ce jeune homme d'un regard de femme amoureuse. André, lui, est rentré chez lui sans jamais parler à Rosalie.

Quelques mois après, Rosalie s'est mariée avec le jeune Américain et ils sont partis vivre aux États-Unis. De temps en temps, André avait des nouvelles, car le frère de Rosalie et lui étaient de bons amis. Il savait qu'elle habitait à Atlanta, qu'elle avait eu trois enfants, et il y a trois ans, il a appris que son mari était mort. Il gardait toujours l'espoir de la revoir, mais les années passaient et elle ne revenait toujours pas.

—Vos rosiers sont magnifiques, monsieur!
C'est Rosalie qui parle! En un instant, André Dupont revient au présent et ouvre les yeux. C'est la jeune fille qui parle... celle qu'il ne connaît pas.
—Rosalie???
—Moi, monsieur? Non, je m'appelle Rose. Rosalie, c'est ma grand-mère.
—Ta grand-mère?
—Oui. Vous connaissez ma grand-mère?
—Rosalie Toulouse? Oui, je la connais, mais...
—Eh bien, venez la voir, elle est chez son frère Jean! Je suis sûre qu'elle sera contente de revoir un ami d'ici! Allez, venez donc avec nous!

Line art on this page: © Cengage Learning

Quoi? C'est trop beau! Est-ce qu'il rêve? Rosalie, ici à Rouen! Comme la vie est à la fois belle et bizarre! Va-t-elle le reconnaître? A-t-il le courage de lui dire qu'il l'aime toujours, après toutes ces années? André Dupont choisit les plus belles roses de son jardin et en fait un magnifique bouquet. Il va enfin pouvoir les offrir à la femme pour qui il a planté tous ces rosiers au cours des années.

Qui parle? Qui parle: **André, Rosalie** ou **Rose**?

1. J'adore les fleurs et j'aime faire du jardinage.
2. J'ai eu trois enfants et mon mari est mort il y a trois ans.
3. Je suis passée devant une maison où il y avait des roses splendides.
4. Un monsieur m'a parlé. Il connaît ma grand-mère mais il ne l'a pas vue depuis longtemps.
5. J'ai invité ce monsieur à venir nous voir.
6. Je me suis mariée avec un Américain et je suis allée vivre aux États-Unis.
7. J'étais amoureux de Rosalie mais je n'ai jamais eu le courage de le lui dire.
8. Je garde toujours l'espoir de dire à Rosalie que je l'aime.

Talking about relationships

LA VIE SENTIMENTALE

Note *de grammaire*

Se souvenir de is conjugated like **venir.**

je me souviens
tu te souviens
il/elle/on se souvient
nous nous souvenons
vous vous souvenez
ils/elles se souviennent

André va chez les Toulouse et André et Rosalie **se rencontrent** pour la première fois depuis des années. Voilà **ce qui se passe.**

André et Rosalie se regardent. / Ils s'embrassent. **C'est le coup de foudre!** / Ils se parlent pendant des heures. / Ils **se quittent** vers sept heures.

Pendant les semaines qui **suivent,** André et Rosalie passent beaucoup de temps ensemble. Ils **se souviennent de** leur **jeunesse** ensemble. C'est **le grand amour!**

Ils se retrouvent en ville chaque après-midi. / Quelquefois, ils se disputent. / Mais **la plupart du temps, ils s'entendent** bien.

Enfin, André et Rosalie **prennent une décision.** Ils vont se marier et vont **s'installer à** Rouen. Ils vont être très **heureux.**

Un soir, Rosalie parle à sa petite-fille Rose de sa relation avec André.

2-32

ROSE: Alors, **mamie,** tu as passé une bonne journée?
ROSALIE: Oui. André et moi, nous sommes allés visiter le Mont-Saint-Michel.
ROSE: Alors, vous vous entendez bien?
ROSALIE: Très bien. Nous nous retrouvons tous les jours, nous passons des heures ensemble et nous parlons de tout.
ROSE: **Formidable!** Moi, je **rêve d'une telle** relation.
ROSALIE: Et ton copain et toi, ça va?
ROSE: Pas très bien. On ne s'entend pas très bien. On se dispute souvent.
ROSALIE: **C'est dommage!**

Line art on this page: © Cengage Learning

se rencontrer *to meet each other (by chance), to run into each other*   **ce qui** *what*   **se passer** *to happen*   **le coup de foudre** *love at first sight*   **suivent (suivre** *to follow)*   **se souvenir de** *to remember*   **la jeunesse** *youth*   **le grand amour** *true love* **la plupart du temps** *most of the time*   **s'entendre** *to get along*   **Enfin** *Finally*   **prendre une décision** *to make a decision* **s'installer (à / dans)** *to settle (in), to move (into)*   **heureux (heureuse)** *happy*   **mamie** *grandma*   **Formidable!** *Great!* **rêver (de)** *to dream (of)*   **un(e) tel(le)** *such a*   **C'est dommage!** *That's too bad!*

A **Test.** Faites ce test pour savoir si vous êtes romantique.

Êtes-vous romantique?

I. Indiquez vos opinions sur ces sujets.

1 Pensez-vous que le grand amour...
  a. arrive une fois dans la vie?
  b. n'existe pas?
  c. est sans importance?

2 Pensez-vous qu'un couple peut s'aimer pour toujours?
  a. Certainement.
  b. Je ne sais pas, on peut essayer.
  c. Probablement pas: la vie est trop longue.

3 Au restaurant, **vous voyez** des amoureux qui se regardent dans les yeux pendant tout le dîner. Vous trouvez ça...
  a. assez charmant.
  b. ridicule.
  c. adorable.

II. Comment êtes-vous en couple?

1 Vous vous rencontrez **par hasard** et c'est le coup de foudre. Que pensez-vous?
  a. C'est juste **une attirance** physique.
  b. C'est peut-être l'amour.
  c. **Attention!**

2 Vous vous disputez. Quelle est la meilleure manière de vous réconcilier?
  a. Nous devons nous embrasser.
  b. Nous devons essayer de parler calmement du problème.
  c. Nous devons nous quitter pendant un certain temps.

3 Vous vous adorez. Vous voulez...
  a. essayer de vous voir tous les jours.
  b. vous téléphoner tous les jours et vous voir trois ou quatre fois par semaine.
  c. vous retrouver le week-end, si vous n'avez pas d'autres projets.

SCORE: **Partie I.** 1. a–2 points 2. a–2 points, b–1 point 3. c–2 points, a–1 point
Partie II. 1. b–2 points, a–1 point 2. a–2 points, b–1 point 3. a–2 points, b–1 point

• Si vous avez entre 10 et 12 points, vous êtes une personne très (peut-être même un peu trop?) romantique. Attention! **Ne perdez pas votre temps** à attendre un amour parfait. Essayez d'être un peu plus réaliste, quand même.
• Si vous avez entre 6 et 9 points, vous êtes romantique, mais vous n'exagérez pas. Vous êtes prêt(e) à aimer quand le bon moment arrivera, mais vous ne perdez pas votre temps à chercher l'amour idéal partout.
• Si vous avez entre 0 et 5 points, vous êtes réaliste, cynique même! Ne voulez-vous pas mettre un peu plus de poésie dans votre vie?

© Cengage Learning

B **En couple.** Est-ce qu'on fait ces choses **dans un couple heureux** ou **dans un couple malheureux** (unhappy)?

EXEMPLE On se dispute rarement.
On se dispute rarement **dans un couple heureux.**

1. On se dispute tout le temps.
2. On se parle de tout.
3. On ne s'entend pas bien du tout.
4. On s'amuse ensemble.
5. On s'ennuie ensemble.
6. On s'embrasse tout le temps.

 **À VOUS!**

Avec un(e) partenaire, relisez à haute voix la conversation entre Rose et Rosalie. Ensuite, adaptez la conversation pour parler de votre relation avec votre mari, votre femme, votre copain, votre copine, votre meilleur(e) ami(e) ou votre colocataire.

iLrn You can find a list of the new words from this **Compétence** on page 298 and access the audio online.

---

vous voyez *you see*   **par hasard** *by chance*   **une attirance** *an attraction*   **Attention!** *Watch out!*   **Ne perdez pas votre temps** *Don't waste your time*

SAYING WHAT PEOPLE DO FOR EACH OTHER

✔ Pour vérifier

1. When do you use a reciprocal verb?

2. What verbs can be made into reciprocal verbs? How would you say *to look at each other* or *to listen to each other*?

3. When a reflexive or reciprocal verb is used in the infinitive, does the reflexive pronoun change with the subject? How would you say *I am going to get up at 6:00? I am not going to get up at 6:00?*

iLrn Grammar Tutorials

Note *de grammaire*

Note that although the verbs **se fiancer** and **se marier** are reflexive, **divorcer** is not.

Note *de vocabulaire*

Use **(se) retrouver** to talk about getting together with someone (by plan). Use **(se) rencontrer** to say someone runs into someone else (by accident).

Les verbes réciproques au présent et les verbes réfléchis et réciproques au futur immédiat

You have seen that reflexive verbs are used when someone is doing something to or for himself/herself. You use similar verbs to describe reciprocal actions; that is, to indicate that people are doing something to or for each other. Here are some reflexive and reciprocal verbs commonly used to describe relationships:

s'aimer	*to like each other, to love each other*
se détester	*to hate each other*
se disputer	*to argue*
s'embrasser	*to kiss each other, to embrace each other*
s'entendre (bien / mal)	*to get along (well / badly) with each other*
se fiancer	*to get engaged*
se marier	*to get married*
se quitter	*to leave each other*
se réconcilier	*to make up*
se regarder	*to look at each other*
se rencontrer	*to meet* (for the first time), *to run into each other* (by chance)
se retrouver	*to meet* (by design)
se téléphoner	*to telephone each other*

The verb **s'entendre** *(to get along)* is a regular **-re** verb. You will learn how to conjugate other **-re** verbs in the next section on page 276. The forms of **s'entendre** are:

S'ENTENDRE *(to get along)*	
je m'entends	nous nous entendons
tu t'entends	vous vous entendez
il/elle/on s'entend	ils/elles s'entendent

Most verbs indicating actions done to other people can be used reciprocally.

retrouver quelqu'un *(to meet someone)*   Je retrouve **Jim** au café.

se retrouver *(to meet each other)*   Nous **nous** retrouvons souvent au café.

As with other verbs, use **aller** + an infinitive to form the immediate future of reflexive and reciprocal verbs. When reflexive or reciprocal verbs are used in the infinitive, the pronoun is placed before the infinitive, and it matches the subject. In the negative, place **ne** after the subject and **pas, jamais,** or **rien** after the first verb.

SE LEVER *(to get up)*	
je vais me lever	nous allons nous lever
tu vas te lever	vous allez vous lever
il/elle/on va se lever	ils/elles vont se lever

Je ne vais pas **me** lever tôt.   **Nous** aimons **nous** retrouver au café.

Sélection musicale. Search the Web for the song **"C'est quoi, c'est l'habitude"** by Isabelle Boulay to enjoy a musical selection illustrating the use of this structure.

to settle — s'installer

A Une histoire d'amour. Isabelle, la cousine de Rose, rencontre Luc et ils tombent amoureux. Qu'est-ce qui se passe?

> se regarder se rencontrer au parc se marier
> s'embrasser s'installer dans une maison se fiancer
> se réconcilier se disputer

EXEMPLE  Ils se rencontrent au parc.

1.  2.  3.  4.

5.  6.  7.

Line art on this page: © Cengage Learning

 B Questions. Un(e) ami(e) veut en savoir plus *(to know more)* sur Isabelle et Luc. Avec un(e) partenaire, posez ses questions et imaginez les réponses qu'Isabelle lui donne.

EXEMPLE s'aimer beaucoup
—**Est-ce que vous vous aimez beaucoup?**
—**Oui, nous nous aimons beaucoup.**
Oui, on s'aime beaucoup.

1. se téléphoner tous les jours
2. se disputer souvent
3. se réconcilier facilement
4. s'entendre mal quelquefois
5. s'envoyer des textos plusieurs *(several)* fois par jour

C Isabelle et Luc. Tout va très bien entre Isabelle et Luc. Ils se retrouvent en ville tous les jours. Est-ce qu'ils vont faire les choses suivantes demain?

EXEMPLE se disputer
Non, ils ne vont pas se disputer.

1. se téléphoner
2. se retrouver en ville
3. se parler de tout
4. bien s'entendre
5. s'ennuyer ensemble
6. s'embrasser

D Et demain chez Rose. Dites ce que Rose va faire demain d'après les illustrations.

EXEMPLE

... vers neuf heures.
Elle va se réveiller vers neuf heures.

1. ... tout de suite.

2. ... la figure et les mains.

3. ... les cheveux.

4. ... avant de manger.

5. ... vers deux heures du matin.

E Ce week-end. Dites si ces personnes vont probablement faire ces choses ce week-end.

EXEMPLE Moi, je... (se lever tôt)
Moi, je vais me lever tôt. / Moi, je ne vais pas me lever tôt.

1. Samedi matin, moi, je...
se réveiller tard
se lever tout de suite
rester au lit quelques minutes

2. Samedi matin, mon meilleur ami / ma meilleure amie...
se réveiller tôt
se lever facilement
prendre son petit déjeuner avec moi

3. Ce week-end, cet(te) ami(e) et moi, nous...
se retrouver en ville
s'amuser
s'ennuyer
s'entendre bien

F **Partons en week-end.** Vous allez partir avec un groupe d'amis ce week-end. Travaillez avec un petit groupe d'étudiants et faites des projets. Ensuite, dites à la classe ce que vous allez faire. Dites:

- si vous allez à la campagne, à la montagne ou à la plage
- à quelle heure vous allez partir
- comment vous allez voyager
- si vous allez faire du camping, descendre à l'hôtel ou rester chez des parents/amis
- si vous allez vous lever tôt ou tard tous les jours
- ce que vous allez faire pendant la journée pour vous amuser
- quand vous allez vous reposer
- ce que vous allez faire le soir
- à quelle heure vous allez vous coucher

EXEMPLE **On va aller à la plage. On va partir vers 8h.**

G **Beaucoup de questions!** Circulez parmi les étudiants et posez les questions suivantes pour trouver quelqu'un qui fait la même chose que vous. Après, dites à la classe ce que vous avez en commun avec d'autres étudiants.

EXEMPLE —Eva, à quelle heure est-ce que tu te réveilles en semaine?
—Je me réveille vers 8h.

Après, à la classe:

Eva et moi, nous nous réveillons vers 8h. / Eva et moi, on se réveille vers 8h.

À quelle heure est-ce que tu te réveilles en semaine?	À quelle heure est-ce que tu vas te réveiller demain?	Est-ce que tu préfères te lever tôt ou tard?
Après les cours, est-ce que tu préfères te reposer ou t'amuser avec des amis?	Est-ce que tu vas te reposer aujourd'hui après les cours?	À quelle heure est-ce que tu vas te coucher ce soir?

H **Entretien.** Posez ces questions à votre partenaire au sujet de ses relations avec son meilleur ami (sa meilleure amie).

1. Est-ce que vous vous parlez tous les jours? Est-ce que vous préférez vous téléphoner ou vous envoyer des textos?
2. Combien de fois par semaine est-ce que vous vous retrouvez? Où aimez-vous vous retrouver?
3. Qu'est-ce que vous faites ensemble pour vous amuser? Est-ce que vous vous ennuyez quelquefois ensemble?
4. Est-ce que vous vous entendez toujours bien? Est-ce que vous vous disputez de temps en temps?

TALKING ABOUT ACTIVITIES

✔ Pour vérifier

1. What ending do you add for each subject pronoun after dropping the -re from the infinitive of these verbs? What is the conjugation of perdre?

2. Which of these -re verbs are conjugated with être in the passé composé?

Note de vocabulaire

1. Do not use pour after attendre to say for whom or what you are waiting.

J'attends des amis.
I'm waiting for friends.

2. Notice the difference in meaning between the reflexive and non-reflexive forms of entendre and perdre.

entendre *to hear*
s'entendre *to get along*
perdre *to lose*
se perdre *to get lost*

3. Use **rendre visite à** or **aller voir** to say that you visit a person, but use **visiter** to say that you visit a place.

iLrn Grammar Tutorials

Sélection musicale. Search the Web for the song *"J'attends l'amour"* by Jenifer to enjoy a musical selection related to this vocabulary.

Les verbes en -re

Many verbs that end in **-re** follow a regular pattern of conjugation.

ATTENDRE (to wait for)	
j'attend**s**	nous attend**ons**
tu attend**s**	vous attend**ez**
il/elle/on attend	ils/elles attend**ent**

PASSÉ COMPOSÉ: **j'ai attendu**
IMPARFAIT: **j'attendais**

The following are some common **-re** verbs.

attendre	*to wait (for)*
descendre (de) (à)	*to go down, to get off (of), to stay (at)*
entendre	*to hear*
s'entendre (bien / mal) avec	*to get along (well / badly) with*
perdre	*to lose, to waste*
perdre du temps	*to waste time*
se perdre	*to get lost*
rendre quelque chose à quelqu'un	*to return something to someone, to turn in something to someone*
rendre visite à quelqu'un	*to visit someone*
répondre (à)	*to answer, to respond (to)*
vendre / revendre	*to sell / to sell back, to resell*

In the **passé composé, descendre** and the reflexive verbs are conjugated with **être** as the auxiliary verb. The other verbs in this list are all conjugated with **avoir.**

J'ai rendu visite à une amie à Paris.   Je suis descendu(e) à l'hôtel Étoile.

A   Votre vie. Est-ce que ces personnes font toujours (souvent, quelquefois, rarement, jamais...) les choses suivantes?

EXEMPLE Moi, je... (attendre le bus pour aller en cours)
Moi, je n'attends jamais le bus pour aller en cours.

1. Moi, je...
   rendre visite à mes parents
   attendre le week-end avec impatience
   revendre mes livres à la fin *(end)* du semestre / trimestre

2. Mes amis...
   descendre en ville le week-end
   s'entendre bien
   se rendre visite

3. Mon meilleur ami / Ma meilleure amie...
   perdre patience avec moi
   s'entendre bien avec mes autres amis
   se perdre

4. En cours de français, nous...
   perdre du temps
   répondre correctement aux questions du prof
   rendre les devoirs au professeur à la fin *(end)* du cours

B **La routine de Rose.** En vous servant des illustrations et des phrases proposées, décrivez la routine de Rose quand elle est à Atlanta.

EXEMPLE Rose: attendre le bus le matin / aller en cours à pied *(by foot)*
Rose attend le bus le matin. Elle ne va pas en cours à pied.

1.

2.

3.

4.

1. Rose: perdre patience quand le bus est en retard *(late)* / attendre patiemment
2. Rose: perdre son temps dans le bus / préférer lire
3. Rose: descendre chez un ami / descendre à l'université
4. Rose: s'entendre bien avec ses profs / s'entendre mal avec ses profs

5.

6.

7.

8.

5. Les étudiants: travailler bien en cours / perdre leur temps
6. Les étudiants: perdre leurs devoirs / rendre leurs devoirs au professeur
7. Après les cours, Rose: rentrer chez elle / rendre visite à son ami Daniel
8. Rose et son ami: s'entendre mal / s'entendre bien

Line art on this page: © Cengage Learning

C **Et toi?** Choisissez le verbe logique et complétez les questions. Ensuite, posez les questions à votre partenaire. Utilisez le présent ou le passé composé comme indiqué.

AU PRÉSENT
1. Tu _rends_ souvent visite à tes parents? (rendre, entendre) Ta famille et toi, vous _vous entendez_ bien la plupart du temps? (perdre, s'entendre) Est-ce que tu _perds_ souvent patience avec tes parents? (perdre, répondre) Est-ce qu'ils _perdent_ souvent patience avec toi? (perdre, répondre)
2. Tu _attends_ tes prochaines vacances avec impatience? (attendre, entendre) Tu _te perds_ facilement quand tu es dans une autre ville? (se perdre, vendre) Quand tu voyages avec des amis, vous _descendez_ quelquefois dans un hôtel de luxe? (vendre, descendre)

AU PASSÉ COMPOSÉ
3. Tu _as rendu_ visite à tes parents récemment? (revendre, rendre) La dernière fois que tu as vu tes parents, est-ce qu'ils _ont perdu_ patience avec toi? (perdre, vendre)
4. La dernière fois que vous êtes partis en week-end ensemble, est-ce que vous _êtes descendus_ à l'hôtel? (descendre, entendre)

Talking about what you did and used to do

LES ACTIVITÉS D'HIER

Note *de grammaire*

Se promener is a spelling change verb like **se lever** and **acheter**:

je me promène
tu te promènes
il/elle/on se promène
nous nous promenons
vous vous promenez
ils/elles se promènent

Rose parle de ce qu'elle a fait hier.

Le réveil a sonné et je me suis réveillée.

Je me suis levée.

J'ai pris un bain.

Je me suis brossé les dents.

Je me suis peignée.

Je me suis habillée.

J'ai passé le reste de la journée avec ma cousine et son nouvel ami.

Nous nous sommes promenés.

Nous nous sommes arrêtés au restaurant pour manger.

Nous nous sommes bien amusés.

Nous nous sommes quittés vers 10 heures et je me suis couchée vers 11 heures.

Line art on this page: © Cengage Learning

Le réveil *The alarm clock*   **sonner** *to ring*   **se promener** *to go for a walk*   **s'arrêter** *to stop*

Rose parle à sa cousine, Isabelle, qui **raconte** comment elle a rencontré son ami, Luc.

ROSE: Alors, Luc et toi, vous vous êtes rencontrés où?

ISABELLE: J'étais au parc et Luc était à côté de moi. On s'est vus et on s'est parlé un peu. Quelques jours plus tard, il était dans une librairie où j'achetais un livre et **on s'est reconnus.** Il m'a demandé si je voulais aller prendre un verre et j'ai accepté son invitation. On a passé le reste de la journée ensemble.

ROSE: Vous vous êtes bien entendus, **donc**?

ISABELLE: **Parfaitement** bien. On s'est très bien amusés et on s'est retrouvés le lendemain pour aller au cinéma. Depuis, on s'est téléphoné ou on s'est vus presque tous les jours. _since_

A Récemment. Quand avez-vous fait ces choses?

ce matin	hier soir	il y a deux semaines
cet après-midi	hier matin	il y a un mois
???	lundi dernier	il y a longtemps

1. Le réveil a sonné et je me suis levé(e) tout de suite...
2. J'ai pris un bain / une douche...
3. Je me suis brossé les cheveux / je me suis peigné(e)...
4. Mes amis et moi, nous nous sommes bien amusés ensemble...
5. Nous nous sommes promenés en ville...
6. Je me suis arrêté(e) dans un fast-food pour manger...
7. Je me suis couché(e) après minuit...

B Ils se sont retrouvés. Décrivez la première fois que Rosalie et André se sont revus après toutes ces années en mettant ces phrases dans l'ordre logique.

© Cengage Learning

_____2_____ Ils se sont embrassés.

_____1_____ André et Rosalie se sont vus.

_____4_____ Ils se sont quittés.

___1.5___ Ils se sont reconnus.

_____3_____ Ils se sont parlé pendant plusieurs heures et ils se sont souvenus du passé.

À VOUS!

Avec un(e) partenaire, relisez à haute voix la conversation entre Rose et Isabelle. Ensuite, parlez avec votre partenaire de comment vous avez rencontré votre meilleur(e) ami(e) ou votre copain (copine).

You can find a list of the new words from this **Compétence** on page 299 and access the audio online.

raconter *to tell*   **on s'est reconnus (passé composé** of **se reconnaître** *to recognize each other*)   **donc** *then, thus, so*
Parfaitement *Perfectly*

SAYING WHAT PEOPLE DID

✔ Pour vérifier

1. Do you use **être** or **avoir** as the auxiliary verb with reflexive and reciprocal verbs in the **passé composé**?

2. Where are reflexive pronouns placed with respect to the auxiliary verb? How do you conjugate **s'amuser** in the **passé composé**?

3. Where do you place **ne... pas** in the negative? How do you say *I didn't wake up early*?

4. When does the past participle agree with the reflexive pronoun and subject? When does it not agree? What are three verbs that you know that do not have agreement?

Note *de grammaire*

1. Remember that the past participles of regular **-er** verbs end in **-é** (**je me suis ennuyé[e]**), those of regular **-ir** verbs end in **-i** (**je me suis endormi[e]**), and those of regular **-re** verbs end in **-u** (**nous nous sommes entendu[e]s**).

2. When **on** means *we*, its verb may either be left in the masculine singular form (**on s'est levé**) or it may agree (**on s'est levé[e][s]**). Either form is considered correct.

3. **Se souvenir (de)** is conjugated like **venir**: **je me souviens, je me suis souvenu(e)**.

iLrn Grammar Tutorials

🌐 **Sélection musicale.** To enjoy a musical selection illustrating the use of this structure, search the Web for the song **"Une belle histoire"** by Michel Fugain, which has been sung by numerous artists, including Charles Benevuto.

Les verbes réfléchis et réciproques au passé composé

All reflexive and reciprocal verbs have **être** as the auxiliary verb in the **passé composé.** Always place the reflexive pronoun directly before the auxiliary verb.

SE LEVER	
je me suis levé(e)	nous nous sommes levé(e)s
tu t'es levé(e)	vous vous êtes levé(e)(s)
il s'est levé	ils se sont levés
elle s'est levée	elles se sont levées
on s'est levé(e)(s)	

To negate a reflexive or reciprocal verb in the **passé composé,** place **ne** directly after the subject and **pas** or **jamais** directly after the conjugated form of **être.**

Je me suis réveillé(e) tôt mais je **ne** me suis **pas** levé(e) tout de suite.

In the **passé composé,** the past participle agrees in gender and number with the reflexive pronoun (and the subject) when it is the direct object of the verb.

Rosalie s'est lev**ée** tôt.   André et Rosalie **se** sont mari**és.**

In this chapter, make the past participle agree except in these cases:

- There is no agreement when a reflexive verb is followed by a noun that is the direct object of the verb. Past participles of verbs like **se laver, se maquiller,** or **se brosser** do not agree with the subject when they are followed by the name of a part of the body.

Rose et Rosalie se sont lav**ées.**   BUT   Rose et Rosalie se sont lavé **les mains.**
Rose s'est maquillé**e.**   Rose s'est maquillé **les yeux.**

- With the verbs **se parler, se téléphoner,** and **s'écrire,** there is no agreement because the reflexive pronoun is an *indirect* object, not a *direct* object.

Ils se sont parlé.   Nous nous sommes téléphoné.   Ils se sont écrit.

A **Hier chez Henri et Patricia.** Voilà ce que Patricia, la cousine de Rose, a fait hier. Qu'est-ce qu'elle a fait?

EXEMPLE Patricia **s'est réveillée à six heures.**

EXEMPLE Patricia...   **1.** Elle...   **2.** Son mari Henri et elle...

© Cengage Learning

3. Ils...   **4.** Patricia...   **5.** Patricia et Henri...

B Qu'est-ce qu'ils ont fait? Travaillez avec un groupe d'étudiants pour créer autant de *(create as many)* questions que possible au sujet de ce que Patricia et Henri ont fait hier. Basez vos questions sur les illustrations dans **A. Hier chez Henri et Patricia.** Chaque groupe gagne 1 point pour chaque question bien formée et 1 point chaque fois que les étudiants du groupe répondent correctement à la question d'un autre groupe.

EXEMPLE À quelle heure est-ce que Patricia s'est réveillée?

C Et toi? Demandez à votre partenaire s'il/si elle a fait les choses suivantes hier.

EXEMPLE se lever tôt
—Tu t'es levé(e) tôt hier?
—Oui, je me suis levé(e) tôt hier.
Non, je ne me suis pas levé(e) tôt hier.

1. se réveiller tôt
2. se lever tout de suite
3. prendre un bain ou une douche
4. passer la soirée à la maison

5. se reposer
6. s'ennuyer
7. s'amuser
8. se coucher tard

D Je veux tout savoir. Utilisez les verbes suivants pour poser des questions à votre partenaire sur ses interactions avec son meilleur ami (sa meilleure amie) cette semaine.

EXEMPLE se téléphoner
—Est-ce que vous vous êtes téléphoné cette semaine?
—Oui, on s'est téléphoné hier.
Non, on ne s'est pas téléphoné cette semaine.

se retrouver en ville	se disputer
se promener au parc	s'envoyer des textos
beaucoup se voir	s'amuser ensemble

E Entretien. Posez ces questions à votre partenaire.

1. À quelle heure est-ce que tu t'es couché(e) hier soir? Tu as bien dormi? Tu as dormi jusqu'à quelle heure ce matin? Tu t'es levé(e) facilement?
2. Avec qui est-ce que tu es sorti(e) récemment? Où est-ce que vous vous êtes retrouvé(e)s? Qu'est-ce que vous avez fait? Vous vous êtes bien amusé(e)s?

SAYING WHAT PEOPLE DID AND USED TO DO

✔ Pour vérifier

1. How do you form the **imparfait** of all verbs except **être**? What is the **imparfait** of **je m'amuse**? of **je ne m'amuse pas**?

2. Do you use the **imparfait** or the **passé composé** to say what happened on a specific occasion? to say how things used to be?

Note *de grammaire*

Before doing the exercises in this section, review the specific uses of the **passé composé** and the **imparfait** on page 253.

Les verbes réfléchis et réciproques à l'imparfait et reprise de l'usage du passé composé et de l'imparfait

As with all other verbs (except **être**), the **imparfait** of reflexive verbs is formed by dropping the **-ons** from the present tense **nous** form and adding the endings shown.

SE LEVER	NE PAS SE LEVER
je me lev**ais**	je ne me lev**ais** pas
tu te lev**ais**	tu ne te lev**ais** pas
il/elle/on se lev**ait**	il/elle/on ne se lev**ait** pas
nous nous lev**ions**	nous ne nous lev**ions** pas
vous vous lev**iez**	vous ne vous lev**iez** pas
ils/elles se lev**aient**	ils/elles ne se lev**aient** pas

Remember to use the **imparfait** to tell *what things were like in general* or *what was going on when something else happened* and the **passé composé** to tell *what happened on specific occasions* or to recount *a sequence of events.*

Ce matin, **je me suis levé(e)** à 6h.

Quand j'étais au lycée, **je me levais** à 7h.

A À 16 ans. Parlez de votre routine quotidienne à l'âge de 16 ans.

EXEMPLE se réveiller souvent tôt
À l'âge de 16 ans, je me réveillais souvent tôt.
Je ne me réveillais pas souvent tôt.

1. se réveiller souvent avant 6h

2. se lever facilement

3. prendre un bain / une douche le matin

4. se laver les cheveux tous les jours

5. prendre toujours le petit déjeuner

6. aller toujours en cours

7. sécher mes cours *(to cut class)* quelquefois

8. s'ennuyer quelquefois en cours

B Et hier? Utilisez les verbes de l'exercice précédent pour parler de ce que vous avez fait hier.

EXEMPLE se réveiller tôt
Hier, je me suis réveillé(e) tôt.
Hier, je ne me suis pas réveillé(e) tôt.

C Alors? Rosalie parle de ce qui s'est passé hier. Complétez ses phrases logiquement en mettant les verbes donnés au passé composé ou à l'imparfait.

EXEMPLE Hier matin, j' _étais_ (être) fatiguée, alors je _suis restée_ (rester) au lit.
Hier matin, j'**étais** fatiguée, alors je **suis restée** au lit.

1. Je (J') _voulais_ (vouloir) préparer le petit déjeuner, alors je _me suis lavé_ (se laver) les mains.
2. Vers midi, André et moi, nous _avions_ (avoir) faim, alors on _se s'est préparé_ (se préparer) des sandwichs.
3. Nous _avons bu_ (boire) deux bouteilles d'eau minérale aussi parce que nous _avions_ (avoir) très soif.
4. Après, André _s'est couché_ (se coucher) une demi-heure parce qu'il _était_ (être) fatigué.
5. Il _s'est levé_ (se lever) vers trois heures parce qu'il _voulait_ (vouloir) travailler un peu dans le jardin.
6. Il _faisait_ (faire) très beau, alors nous _nous sommes promenés_ (se promener) dans le quartier.
7. Quand nous _sommes rentrés_ (rentrer), Rose et ses copains _étaient_ (être) à la maison.
8. Nous _nous sommes quittés_ (se quitter) assez tôt parce que nous _voulions_ (vouloir) nous lever tôt le lendemain pour aller au Mont-Saint-Michel.

D Le mariage d'André et de Rosalie. André et Rosalie se sont enfin mariés. Décrivez le jour de leur mariage en mettant les verbes donnés au passé composé ou à l'imparfait.

Le jour de son mariage, Rosalie __1__ _s'est levée_ (se lever) tôt. André __2__ _est arrivé_ (arriver) vers 9h mais, tout de suite après, il __3__ _s'est souvenu_ (se souvenir) d'une course qu'il __4__ _doit_ (devoir) faire et il __5__ _est reparti_ (repartir). Il __6__ _est allé_ (aller) acheter une nouvelle cravate. Il __7__ _était_ (être) 3h quand André __8__ _est revenu_ (revenir). La cérémonie __9__ _a commencé_ (commencer) à 4h. Tous les invités (guests) __10__ _étaient_ (être) dans le jardin. Il __11__ _faisait_ (faire) beau et Rosalie et André __12__ _étaient_ (être) contents. Rosalie __13__ _portait_ (porter) une jolie robe beige et André __14__ _portait_ (porter) un costume noir. Rosalie __15__ _était_ (être) très jolie! Après la cérémonie, les amis __16__ _sont restés_ (rester) et ils __17__ _ont mangé_ (manger) du gâteau (cake). Ils __18__ _s'amusaient_ (s'amuser) bien quand tout d'un coup il __19__ _a commencé_ (commencer) à pleuvoir, alors ils __20__ _sont rentrés_ (rentrer) dans la maison.
André __21__ _est parti_ (partir) et il __22__ _est revenu_ (revenir) avec assez de chaises pour tout le monde. Vers 8h, les invités __23__ _sont partis_ (partir). André et Rosalie __24__ _se sont regardés_ (se regarder) et ils __25__ _ont commencé_ (commencer) à sourire (to smile). Ils __26__ _étaient_ (être) fatigués mais très, très heureux.

E Entretien. Interviewez votre partenaire.

1. Est-ce que tu te réveillais facilement quand tu étais ado (teenager)? À quelle heure est-ce que tu te réveillais pour aller au lycée? Tu prenais l'autocar (schoolbus), une voiture ou tu y allais à pied? Tu y arrivais souvent en retard (late)?
2. Quand tu étais lycéen(ne), tu t'ennuyais ou tu t'amusais la plupart du temps (most of the time)? Qu'est-ce que tu faisais pour t'amuser le week-end? Comment s'appelait ton meilleur ami (ta meilleure amie)? Qu'est-ce que vous aimiez faire ensemble?
3. À quelle heure est-ce que tu t'es réveillé(e) ce matin? Tu t'es levé(e) tout de suite? Qu'est-ce que tu as fait ensuite?
4. La dernière fois que tu es sorti(e) avec des amis, est-ce que tu t'es bien amusé(e) ou est-ce que tu t'es un peu ennuyé(e)? Qu'est-ce que vous avez fait ensemble?

Describing traits and characteristics

LES TRAITS DE CARACTÈRE

Note culturelle

Ridicule ou romantique? 60 % des Français donnent un petit surnom *(nickname)* amoureux à leur partenaire. Parmi *(Among)* les plus utilisés, il y a mon chéri (ma chérie) *(darling)*, mon cœur *(heart)*, mon bébé, mon amour et ma puce *(flea)*, suivi par *(followed by)* mon doudou *(cuddly toy)*, ma biche *(doe)* et mon minou *(kitten)*. Trouvez-vous ces surnoms amoureux romantiques ou ridicules? Quels sont les surnoms les plus populaires dans votre région?

Sélection musicale. Search the Web for the song "**À nos actes manqués**" by M. Pokora to enjoy a musical selection related to this vocabulary.

Vocabulaire sans peine!

English words ending in *-ance*, *-ence*, or *-ion* often have corresponding cognates in French. Such nouns are often feminine.

-ance = **-ance**
tolerance = **la tolérance**
-ence = **-ence**
innocence = **l'innocence**
-ion = **-ion**
comprehension = **la compréhension**

How would you say these words in French?

ignorance
indulgence
assertion

Rencontres en ligne: Test de compatibilité

Rangez chaque groupe de réponses de 1 (la réponse qui **exprime** le mieux vos sentiments) à 4 (la réponse qui exprime le moins bien vos sentiments).

Je préfère partager la vie avec quelqu'un qui **s'intéresse...**

1 2 3 4   à l'art
1 2 3 4   au sport
1 2 3 4   à la politique
1 2 3 4   à la nature

Je préfère quelqu'un qui cultive...

1 2 3 4   sa spiritualité
1 2 3 4   son **corps**
1 2 3 4   son **esprit**
1 2 3 4   sa vie professionnelle

Le trait de caractère que j'apprécie le plus chez un(e) partenaire, c'est...

1 2 3 4   un bon sens de l'humour
1 2 3 4   la passion
1 2 3 4   la beauté
1 2 3 4   **la tolérance**

Un **défaut** que je ne **supporte** pas chez une autre personne, c'est...

1 2 3 4   l'indécision *(f)*
1 2 3 4   l'inflexibilité *(f)*
1 2 3 4   **l'insensibilité** *(f)*
1 2 3 4   la vanité

Ce que je supporte le moins dans une relation, c'est...

1 2 3 4   la jalousie
1 2 3 4   l'indifférence *(f)*
1 2 3 4   l'infidélité *(f)*
1 2 3 4   la violence

Chez un(e) partenaire, ce qui a le moins d'importance pour moi, c'est...

1 2 3 4   son argent
1 2 3 4   sa profession
1 2 3 4   sa religion
1 2 3 4   son **aspect physique**

---

ranger *to arrange, to order*   **exprimer** *to express*   **s'intéresser à** *to be interested in*   **le corps** *the body*   **l'esprit** *(m) the mind, the spirit*   **la tolérance** *tolerance, acceptance*   **un défaut** *a fault*   **supporter** *to bear, to tolerate, to put up with*   **l'insensibilité** *(f) insensitivity*   **l'aspect physique** *(m) physical appearance*

🔊 2-34

Rose parle à sa cousine, Isabelle, de son copain, Luc.

ROSE: Alors, tu as trouvé **le bonheur** avec ton nouvel ami, Luc? Il est comment?

ISABELLE: Il a un bon sens de l'humour et il est sympa. Son seul défaut, c'est qu'il est un peu **jaloux** si je ne passe pas tout mon temps avec lui.

ROSE: Vous vous intéressez aux mêmes choses?

ISABELLE: Oui et non. On aime plus ou moins la même musique et les mêmes films et il s'intéresse à la politique comme moi, mais il est **de droite** et moi, tu sais, je suis plutôt **de gauche.**

A Et vous? Changez les mots en italique pour parler de vous.

1. J'ai beaucoup d'amis qui s'intéressent *au sport / à la nature / à la politique*…
2. Je ne m'intéresse pas du tout *à la politique / au sport / à l'art*…
3. Je préfère cultiver *mon esprit / mon corps et mon aspect physique / ma spiritualité*…
4. Chez un(e) partenaire, ce qui a le plus d'importance pour moi, c'est *sa beauté / son intelligence / sa religion*….
5. Chez un(e) partenaire, je ne supporte pas bien *la vanité / l'indécision / l'inflexibilité*…
6. Dans une relation, je ne supporterai *(will never tolerate)* jamais *la jalousie / la violence / l'infidélité*…

👥 **B Entretien.** Interviewez votre partenaire.

1. Tu t'intéresses au sport? à l'art? au cinéma? à la politique? à la philosophie? Est-ce que tu t'ennuies si quelqu'un parle de ces choses-là?
2. Tu passes plus de temps à cultiver ton corps, ton esprit, ta spiritualité ou ta vie professionnelle? Qu'est-ce que tu fais pour le (la) cultiver?

👥 **C Test de compatibilité.** Travaillez en groupes pour écrire deux questions pour un nouveau test de compatibilité. Ensuite, utilisez les questions de tous les groupes pour créer *(to create)* le nouveau test.

EXEMPLE Quelle activité aimez-vous le moins faire avec une autre personne?

1 2 3 4   **faire la cuisine**
1 2 3 4   **faire de l'exercice**
1 2 3 4   **faire du shopping**
1 2 3 4   **voyager**

👥 **À VOUS!**

Avec un(e) partenaire, relisez à haute voix la conversation entre Rose et Isabelle. Ensuite, adaptez la conversation pour parler d'un(e) ami(e), de votre copain (copine) ou de votre mari ou femme. Commencez la conversation en disant: **Alors, tu passes beaucoup de temps avec…** (au lieu de dire *[instead of saying]*: **Alors, tu as trouvé le bonheur avec…**).

iLrn 🌐 You can find a list of the new words from this *Compétence* on page 299 and access the audio online.

---

le bonheur *happiness*   **jaloux (jalouse)** *jealous*   **de droite** *conservative*   **de gauche** *liberal*

SPECIFYING WHICH ONE

✔ **Pour vérifier**

1. Can **qui, que,** and **dont** all be used for both people and things?

2. Which relative pronoun functions as the subject of a verb? Which one functions as the direct object of a verb? Which one replaces the preposition **de** and its object? Does **qui** or **que** change to **qu'** before a vowel sound?

3. Where are relative clauses placed with respect to the noun they describe?

Note *de grammaire*

Remember that past participles agree with preceding direct objects and therefore agree with the noun that **que** represents: **Je sors avec une femme que j'ai rencontrée pendant mes vacances.**

🌐 **Sélection musicale.** Search the Web for the song **"Quelqu'un que j'aime, quelqu'un qui m'aime"** by Céline Dion to enjoy a musical selection illustrating the use of this structure.

ⒾLⁿ **Grammar Tutorials**

Les pronoms relatifs **qui, que** *et* **dont**

A relative clause gives more information about a person or object you are talking about in a sentence. A relative clause begins with a relative pronoun, a word like *who, that,* or *which* that refers back to the noun being described.

Je sors avec une femme { **qui** est beaucoup plus âgée que moi.
{ **que** j'ai rencontrée pendant mes vacances.
{ **dont** je suis amoureux.

I'm going out with a woman { **who** *is a lot older than I am.*
{ **whom** *I met during my vacation.*
{ **with whom** *I'm in love.*

The relative pronouns **qui, que,** and **dont** are all used for both people and things. The choice depends on how the pronoun functions in the relative clause. Note how relative pronouns are used to combine two sentences talking about the same thing. The relative clause is placed immediately after the noun it describes.

- Use **qui** for both people or things when they are the *subject* of the relative clause. Since **qui** is the subject, it is followed by a verb and it can mean *that, which,* or *who*. Note that **qui** does not make elision before a vowel sound.

  Comment s'appelle ton ami? **Ton ami** habite à New York.
  Comment s'appelle ton ami **qui** habite à New York?

- Use **que (qu')** for people or things when they are the *direct object* in the relative clause. **Que (qu')** can mean *that, which,* or *whom,* or it may be omitted in English. Note that the pronoun **que** makes elision **(qu')** before a vowel sound.

  Comment s'appelle ton ami? Tu as invité **cet ami** hier.
  Comment s'appelle ton ami **que** tu as invité hier?

- Use **dont** to replace the preposition *de + a person or thing* in relative clauses with verbs such as the following. It can mean *whom, of (about, with) whom, whose, that,* or *of (about, with) which*.

avoir besoin de	se souvenir de
avoir envie de	parler de
avoir peur de	rêver de
être amoureux (amoureuse) de	tomber amoureux (amoureuse) de
être jaloux (jalouse) de	faire la connaissance de (*to make the acquaintance of, to meet* [for the first time])

  Comment s'appelle ton ami? Ta sœur parlait **de cet ami** hier.
  Comment s'appelle ton ami **dont** ta sœur parlait hier?

A **Préférences.** Complétez ces phrases comme dans les exemples. Pour chaque section, utilisez le pronom relatif indiqué.

· Utilisez le pronom relatif **qui** et conjuguez le verbe.

EXEMPLE Je préfère les personnes... (avoir un bon sens de l'humour, avoir beaucoup d'argent)
Je préfère les personnes qui ont un bon sens de l'humour.

1. Je préfère un(e) colocataire... (sortir tout le temps, rester souvent à la maison)
2. Je préfère les films... (avoir beaucoup d'action, avoir peu de violence)
3. Je préfère un(e) partenaire... (cultiver son corps, cultiver son esprit)

Utilisez le pronom relatif **que (qu')**.

EXEMPLE Je préfère les personnes... (je rencontre en cours, je rencontre en boîte)
Je préfère les personnes que je rencontre en boîte.

1. Je préfère les personnes... (on rencontre dans une salle de gym, on rencontre à la bibliothèque)
2. Je préfère les activités... (je fais seul[e], je fais en groupe)
3. Je préfère la musique... (on fait maintenant, on faisait il y a vingt ans)

Utilisez le pronom relatif **dont**.

EXEMPLE L'argent est une chose... (j'ai très envie, je n'ai pas très envie)
L'argent est une chose dont je n'ai pas très envie.

1. L'amour est quelque chose... (j'ai très besoin dans ma vie, je n'ai pas vraiment besoin pour le moment)
2. La ville où je suis né(e) est un endroit *(place)*... (je me souviens bien, je ne me souviens pas bien)
3. Ma vie amoureuse, c'est une chose... (j'aime bien parler, je n'aime pas beaucoup parler)

B **Identification.** Complétez les descriptions suivantes avec **qui, que** ou **dont**. Ensuite, donnez les renseignements demandés.

EXEMPLE Un film _____ j'aime beaucoup, c'est...
Un film que j'aime beaucoup, c'est *Le Maître*.

1. Un film ___qui___ a gagné beaucoup d'Oscars, c'est...
2. Un film ___que___ j'ai vu plusieurs fois, c'est...
3. Un film ___dont___ on parle beaucoup en ce moment, c'est...

4. Un acteur (Une actrice) ___que___ je trouve beau (belle), c'est...
5. Un acteur (Une actrice) ___dont___ tout le monde parle souvent, c'est...
6. Un acteur (Une actrice) ___qui___ n'a vraiment pas de talent, c'est...

7. Une émission *(program)* de télévision ___qui___ est à la télé depuis longtemps, c'est...
8. Une émission de télévision de mon enfance *(childhood)* ___dont___ je me souviens, c'est...
9. Une émission de télévision _____ j'aime beaucoup regarder, c'est...

VIDÉOREPRISE

Les Stagiaires

See the *Résumé de grammaire* section at the end of each chapter for a review of all the grammar presented in the chapter.

Dans l'*Épisode 7* de la vidéo *Les Stagiaires,* Amélie et Céline parlent de la soirée qu'Amélie a passée avec Matthieu. Avant de regarder l'épisode, faites ces exercices pour réviser ce que vous avez appris dans le *Chapitre 7.*

Rappel!
Matthieu a enfin dominé sa timidité et a invité Amélie à sortir. Maintenant, Céline, l'amie et la colocataire d'Amélie, veut qu'Amélie lui raconte tout sur *(to tell her everything about)* sa sortie avec Matthieu.

A Au bureau. Amélie parle à une amie de ses collègues et de son travail à Technovert. Complétez chaque phrase avec la forme correcte du verbe logique entre parenthèses.

© Cengage Learning

EXEMPLE Technovert **vend** (perdre / vendre) des produits technologiques verts.

1. Je prends le bus pour aller au travail et je _____ (descendre / entendre) juste en face du bureau.

2. M. Vieilledent est le directeur, mais son assistante Camille _____ (s'entendre / répondre) à toutes nos questions sur le fonctionnement de l'entreprise.

3. Christophe est un peu paresseux et il _____ (rendre / attendre) toujours le dernier moment pour faire son travail.

4. Camille et Céline _____ (perdre / vendre) souvent patience avec Christophe.

5. Je (J') _____ (entendre / s'entendre) souvent Camille parler de ses frustrations concernant le travail de Christophe.

6. Il _____ (perdre / descendre) beaucoup de temps au bureau en lisant *(reading)* des mangas.

7. J'habite avec la responsable des ventes, Céline. Nous _____ (entendre / s'entendre) bien. Il n'y a jamais de problèmes entre nous.

8. Céline _____ (attendre / rendre) souvent visite à ses parents le week-end, alors je suis seule dans l'appartement.

B Chez Christophe. Christophe parle de ses parents. Complétez les phrases suivantes avec la forme correcte du verbe réfléchi ou réciproque indiqué entre parenthèses.

EXEMPLE Je **m'entends** *(get along)* mieux avec mon père qu'avec ma mère.

1. Ma mère et moi, on _____ *(argue)* souvent.

2. Mon père et moi, nous ne _____ *(talk to each other)* pas beaucoup.

3. Le week-end, mon père est toujours très occupé. Il ne _____ *(rests)* jamais.

4. Mon père _____ *(wakes up)* à 6h le samedi.

5. Moi, je _____ *(get up)* vers midi.

6. Le samedi soir, mes amis et moi, on _____ *(meet one another)* presque toujours en ville.

7. Je _____ *(get bored)* si je reste à la maison le week-end.

8. Je _____ *(have fun)* plus avec mes amis qu'avec ma famille.

Maintenant changez les phrases précédentes pour décrire votre situation.

EXEMPLE Je m'entends aussi bien avec mon père qu'avec ma mère. / Je m'entends bien avec ma mère, mais je m'entends moins bien avec mon père.

C Conseils. Matthieu pose des questions à un ami à propos des relations sociales. Complétez ses questions avec le pronom relatif (**qui, que, dont**) approprié.

1. Quand tu sors avec des amis, quels sont les sujets de conversation _____ vous parlez le plus souvent?

2. As-tu plus d'amis _____ s'intéressent à l'art, au sport ou à la politique?

3. Tu penses que c'est une bonne idée de sortir en couple avec quelqu'un _____ on a rencontré au travail?

4. Est-ce que tu as beaucoup d'amis _____ sont mariés?

5. Est-ce qu'on doit se marier avec la première personne _____ on tombe amoureux?

6. Est-ce que le mariage est quelque chose _____ tu trouves important ou _____ n'est pas important pour toi?

Maintenant interviewez un(e) autre étudiant(e) en utilisant les questions précédentes.

D Hier soir. Après sa soirée avec Amélie, Matthieu parle à son ami. Complétez le paragraphe suivant en mettant les verbes entre parenthèses au passé composé ou à l'imparfait.

Amélie et moi, on __1__ (se retrouver) au restaurant. J' __2__ (être) déjà au restaurant quand elle __3__ (arriver). Au début, quand j' __4__ (attendre), j' __5__ (être) nerveux, mais après, on __6__ (commencer) à parler et j'ai découvert *(discovered)* qu'elle aimait les mêmes choses que moi. Après le dîner, on __7__ (se promener) un peu et on __8__ (s'arrêter) dans un café pour prendre un verre. Il __9__ (être) assez tard quand on __10__ (se quitter).

Access the Video *Les Stagiaires* on iLrn.

▶ **Épisode 7: Vous vous êtes amusés?**

AVANT LA VIDÉO

Dans cet épisode, Céline parle à Amélie de son rendez-vous d'hier soir avec Matthieu. Avant de le regarder, imaginez trois choses dont Amélie et Matthieu ont peut-être parlé.

APRÈS LA VIDÉO

Regardez l'épisode et répondez aux questions suivantes:

- De quoi est-ce que Matthieu et Amélie ont parlé?
- Vers quelle heure est-ce qu'ils se sont quittés?

© Cengage Learning

LECTURE ET COMPOSITION

LECTURE

POUR MIEUX LIRE:
Recognizing conversational style

You are going to read a story by Eugène Ionesco (1912–1994), in which a father finds himself alone one morning with his two- or three-year-old daughter.

Sometimes a writer uses language that is not completely "correct" to portray how someone speaks. To appreciate this style and how it tells something about the character who is speaking, you can compare this conversational language with the more "correct" version of the language. In Ionesco's story, the author modifies his language to represent the way a little girl would speak or how someone might speak to a young child.

Du vocabulaire enfantin. Regardez ces phrases. Comment dit-on la même chose d'une façon plus correcte?

1. Tu laves ta figure.
2. Je rase ma barbe.
3. Tu laves ton «dérère» (backside).

Conte pour enfants de moins de trois ans

Ce matin, comme d'habitude, Josette **frappe** à la porte de la chambre à coucher de ses parents. Papa n'a pas très bien dormi. Maman est partie à la campagne pour quelques jours. Alors papa a profité de cette absence pour manger beaucoup de **saucisson,** pour boire de la bière, pour manger du **pâté de cochon** et beaucoup d'autres choses que maman **l'empêche de** manger parce que c'est pas bon pour **la santé.** Alors, voilà, papa **a mal au foie, il a mal à l'estomac, il a mal à la tête,** et ne voudrait pas se réveiller. Mais Josette frappe toujours à la porte. Alors, papa **lui dit** d'entrer. Elle entre, elle va chez son papa. Il n'y a pas maman. Josette demande:

— *Où elle est maman?*

Papa répond: *Ta maman est allée se reposer à la campagne chez sa maman à elle.*

Josette répond: *Chez Mémée?*

Papa répond: *Oui, chez Mémée.*

— *Écris à maman,* dit Josette. *Téléphone à maman,* dit Josette.

Papa dit: **Faut pas** *téléphoner.* Et puis papa dit pour **lui-même:** *Parce qu'elle est peut-être* **autre part...**

Josette dit: **Raconte** *une histoire avec maman et toi, et moi.*

— *Non,* dit papa, *je vais aller au travail. Je me lève, je vais m'habiller.*

---

frappe *knocks*   **saucisson** *salami*   **pâté de cochon** *pork pâté*   **l'empêche de** *keeps him from*   **la santé** *health*
a mal au foie, il a mal à l'estomac, il a mal à la tête *has indigestion, he has a stomachache, he has a headache*
lui dit *tells her*   **Faut pas** *We must not*   **lui-même** *himself*   **autre part** *somewhere else*   **Raconte** *Tell*

Et papa se lève. Il met **sa robe de chambre** rouge, **par dessus** son pyjama, il met les **pieds** dans ses **pantoufles.** Il va dans la salle de bains. Il ferme la porte de la salle de bains. Josette est à la porte de la salle de bains. Elle frappe avec ses petits **poings,** elle **pleure.**

Josette dit: *Ouvre-moi la porte.*

Papa répond: *Je ne peux pas. Je suis* **tout nu,** *je me lave, après je me rase.*

Josette dit: *Et tu fais pipi-caca.*

—*Je me lave,* dit papa.

Josette dit: *Tu laves ta figure, tu laves tes* **épaules,** *tu laves tes* **bras,** *tu laves ton* **dos,** *tu laves ton «dérère», tu laves tes pieds.*

—*Je rase ma barbe,* dit papa.

— *Tu rases ta barbe avec* **du savon,** dit Josette. *Je veux entrer. Je veux voir.*

Papa dit: *Tu ne peux pas me voir, parce que je* **ne** *suis* **plus** *dans la salle de bains.*

Josette dit (derrière la porte): *Alors, où tu es?*

Papa répond: *Je ne sais pas, va voir. Je suis peut-être dans la salle à manger, va me chercher.*

Josette **court** dans la salle à manger, et papa commence sa toilette. Josette court avec ses petites **jambes,** elle va dans la salle à manger. Papa est tranquille, mais pas pour longtemps. Josette arrive **de nouveau** devant la porte de la salle de bains, elle **crie à travers** la porte:

Josette dit: *Je t'ai cherché. Tu n'es pas dans la salle à manger.*

Papa dit: *Tu n'as pas bien cherché. Regarde sous la table.*

Josette retourne dans la salle à manger. Elle revient.

Elle dit: *Tu n'es pas sous la table.*

Papa dit: *Alors va voir dans le salon. Regarde bien si je suis sur le fauteuil, sur le canapé, derrière les livres, à la fenêtre.*

Josette s'en va. Papa est tranquille, mais pas pour longtemps.

Josette revient.

Elle dit: *Non, tu n'es pas dans le fauteuil, tu n'es pas à la fenêtre, tu n'es pas sur le canapé, tu n'es pas derrière les livres, tu n'es pas dans la télévision, tu n'es pas dans le salon.*

Papa dit: *Alors, va voir si je suis dans la cuisine.*

Josette dit: *Je vais te chercher dans la cuisine.*

---

sa robe de chambre *his robe*   **par dessus** *over*   **pieds** *feet*   **pantoufles** *slippers*   **poings** *fists*   **pleure** *cries*
tout nu *completely naked*   **épaules** *shoulders*   **bras** *arms*   **dos** *back*   **du savon** *soap*   **ne... plus** *no longer*   **court** *runs*
jambes *legs*   **de nouveau** *again*   **crie à travers** *yells through*

Josette court à la cuisine. Papa est tranquille, mais pas pour longtemps. Josette revient.

Elle dit: *Tu n'es pas dans la cuisine.*

Papa dit: *Regarde bien, sous la table de la cuisine, regarde bien si je suis dans le buffet, regarde bien si je suis dans **les casseroles**, regarde bien si je suis dans **le four** avec le poulet.*

Josette va et vient. Papa n'est pas dans le four, papa n'est pas dans les casseroles, papa n'est pas dans le buffet, papa n'est pas sous **le paillasson,** papa n'est pas dans **la poche** de son pantalon, dans la poche du pantalon il y a **seulement le mouchoir.**

Josette revient devant la porte de la salle de bains.

Josette dit: *J'ai cherché partout. Je ne t'ai pas trouvé. Où tu es?*

Papa dit: *Je suis là.*

Et papa, qui a eu le temps de faire sa toilette, qui s'est rasé, qui s'est habillé, ouvre la porte.

Il dit: *Je suis là.*

Il prend Josette **dans ses bras,** et voilà aussi la porte de la maison qui s'ouvre, **au fond** du couloir, et c'est maman qui arrive. Josette **saute** des bras de son papa, elle **se jette** dans les bras de sa maman, elle l'embrasse, elle dit:

*Maman, j'ai cherché papa sous la table, dans l'armoire, sous le tapis, derrière **la glace,** dans la cuisine, dans **la poubelle,** il n'était pas là.*

Papa dit à maman: *Je suis content que tu sois revenue. Il faisait beau à la campagne? Comment va ta mère?*

Josette dit: *Et Mémée, elle va bien? On va chez elle?*

Eugène Ionesco, *Conte No 4* © Éditions GALLIMARD, www.gallimard.fr

---

les casseroles *the pans*   **le four** *the oven*   **le paillasson** *the doormat*   **la poche** *the pocket*   **seulement le mouchoir** *only the handkerchief*   **dans ses bras** *in his arms*   **au fond** *at the end*   **saute** *jumps*   **se jette** *throws herself*   **la glace** *the mirror*   **la poubelle** *the trash can*   **Je suis content que tu sois revenue.** *I'm glad you came back.*

Avez-vous des enfants? Si non *(If not)*, voulez-vous avoir des enfants un jour? Pourquoi ou pourquoi pas?

COMPOSITION

You know how to use words like **d'abord, ensuite, alors,** and **et puis** to connect your sentences into a well-ordered paragraph. Another way to link ideas is to use **pour** to say *in order to*. In this case, **pour** is followed by an infinitive.

> **Je pars à 7h pour arriver à 8h.**
> *I leave at 7:00 (in order) to arrive at 8:00.*

To say that you do something *before* you do something else, use **avant de** followed by an infinitive.

> **Avant de m'habiller, je mange.**
> *Before I get dressed (Before getting dressed), I eat.*

Organisez-vous. Vous allez décrire votre routine matinale. Avant de commencer, traduisez les phrases qui suivent.

1. *I'm tired in the morning, so I don't wake up easily.*
2. *First, I eat breakfast. Next, I take a shower. Then, I get dressed. And then, I leave.*
3. *I eat quickly in order to be on time.*
4. *Before I eat, I get dressed.*
5. *I take a bath before I dress.*

Compréhension

1. Pourquoi est-ce que le père de Josette a mal à la tête et à l'estomac?
2. Quel jeu invente-t-il pour pouvoir faire sa toilette?
3. Dans quelles pièces est-ce que la petite fille cherche son papa?
4. Où est-ce qu'elle le cherche dans la cuisine?
5. Qui rentre à la fin du conte? Quelle est la réaction du papa?

Le matin chez moi

Décrivez votre routine du matin. Utilisez des mots comme **d'abord, ensuite** et **avant de** pour indiquer l'ordre de vos actions.

> **EXEMPLE** **Le matin, je me lève vers six heures. D'abord...**
> **iLrn** Share It!

L'AMOUR ET LE COUPLE

Voici les résultats de **sondages** d'opinion des Français sur le couple et les relations entre hommes et femmes. Quelles sont vos opinions?

À quoi croit-on en amour?

Question: Pour chacune des choses suivantes, **diriez-vous que vous y croyez** ou que vous n'y croyez pas?

	Vous y croyez	Vous n'y croyez pas	Sans opinion
À la possibilité d'aimer **plusieurs** fois dans la vie	80	16	4
Au coup de foudre	68	28	4
À l'amour qui **dure** toute la vie	68	29	3
À la possibilité d'être heureux sans être amoureux	56	41	3
À la possibilité de retrouver un amour perdu ou un amour de jeunesse	53	41	6

© TNS Sofres

Jusqu'où va-t-on par amour?

Question: Pour chacune des choses suivantes, lesquelles **seriez-vous prêt(e) à faire par amour**?

	Prêt(e) à le faire	Pas prêt(e) à le faire	Sans opinion
Quitter votre travail pour **suivre** votre **conjoint**	64	29	7
Pratiquer avec lui des activités que vous n'aimez pas	59	37	4
Changer votre manière de vous habiller	49	47	4
Pardonner une infidélité	43	47	10
Vous **soumettre à ses fantasmes** romantiques	39	47	14
Accepter de **vivre** séparément	35	59	6
Renoncer à voir un ami ou une amie	31	64	5
Adopter sa religion	20	75	5
Avoir recours à **la chirurgie esthétique**	11	85	4

© TNS Sofres

sondages *polls*   **À quoi croit-on en amour?** *What does one believe about love?*   **diriez-vous que vous y croyez** *would you say that you believe in it*   **plusieurs** *several*   **dure** *lasts*   **seriez-vous prêt(e) à faire par amour** *would you be ready to do out of love*   **suivre** *to follow*   **conjoint** *partner*   **soumettre** *to submit*   **à ses fantasmes** *to his/her fantasies*   **vivre** *to live*   **la chirurgie esthétique** *plastic surgery*

Ce qui menace le couple

Question: Aujourd'hui, dans votre vie, qu'est-ce qui pourrait mettre en danger votre couple?

	Ensemble	Vivent en couple
L'infidélité	35	42
L'habitude	23	27
Les disputes	18	21
Les difficultés matérielles ou d'argent	14	17
La jalousie	14	15
Le vieillissement	6	8
Le travail	5	6
Le chômage	4	4
Avoir des enfants	2	1
Rien	7	10

© TNS Sofres

Compréhension

A Vrai ou faux. D'abord, complétez les phrases suivantes avec le pronom relatif convenable: **que** ou **qui**. Ensuite, dites si les phrases sont vraies ou fausses et corrigez les phrases fausses.

1. Pour la majorité des Français, c'est le chômage *(unemployment)* _____ menace le plus le couple.

2. Les Français _____ croient au coup de foudre sont peu nombreux.

3. Avoir recours à la chirurgie esthétique est quelque chose _____ la plupart des Français trouvent normal de faire par amour pour l'autre.

4. L'infidélité est quelque chose _____ la majorité des Français acceptent dans un couple.

5. Pour la majorité des Français, l'amour _____ dure toute la vie n'existe pas.

B Comparaisons. Discutez les questions suivantes.

1. Dans les réponses des Français au sondage, qu'est-ce qui vous surprend *(surprises you)*? Qu'est-ce qui ne vous surprend pas? Pourquoi?

2. Dans un sondage sur ce sujet fait dans votre pays, quelles autres questions est-ce qu'on poserait *(would one ask)*? Quelles questions est-ce qu'on ne poserait probablement pas? Voyez-vous des attitudes différentes sur ce sujet?

© Bronwyn Kidd/Photodisc/Getty Images

(iLrn Share It!

Visit **www.cengagebrain.com** for additional cultural information and activities.

menace *threatens*   **Ensemble** *The whole group*   **Vivent en couple** *(Just those who) live as a couple*
le vieillissement *aging*   **le chômage** *unemployment*

RÉSUMÉ DE GRAMMAIRE

REFLEXIVE VERBS

Reflexive verbs are used to say that people do something to or for themselves. In French, the reflexive pronoun corresponding to the subject is placed before the verb.

SE COUCHER (to go to bed)	
je **me** couche	nous **nous** couchons
tu **te** couches	vous **vous** couchez
il/elle/on **se** couche	ils/elles **se** couchent

Je **me** réveille à six heures et puis, je réveille mes enfants à sept heures.
I wake (myself) up at six o'clock, and then I wake up my children at seven.

Mon fils de trois ans **s'**habille tout seul.
My three-year-old son dresses all by himself.

The reflexive pronouns **me, te,** and **se** become **m', t',** and **s'** before vowel sounds. Also note the spelling changes with **s'ennuyer, s'appeler,** and **se lever.** Remember that all verbs ending with **-yer,** such as **envoyer, essayer,** and **payer,** follow the same pattern as **s'ennuyer. Se promener** is conjugated like **se lever.**

S'ENNUYER (to be / get bored)	S'APPELER (to be named)	SE LEVER (to get up)
je m'ennuie	je m'appelle	je me lève
tu t'ennuies	tu t'appelles	tu te lèves
il/elle/on s'ennuie	il/elle/on s'appelle	il/elle/on se lève
nous nous ennuyons	nous nous appelons	nous nous levons
vous vous ennuyez	vous vous appelez	vous vous levez
ils/elles s'ennuient	ils/elles s'appellent	ils/elles se lèvent

—Tu **ne** t'ennuies **pas** dans ce cours?
—Non, mes camarades et moi, nous **ne** nous y ennuyons **jamais!**
—Comment vous appelez-vous?
—Je m'appelle Catherine Faure.
—À quelle heure est-ce que vous vous levez?
—Je me lève très tôt.

To negate reflexive verbs, place **ne** directly after the subject and **pas** or **jamais** directly after the conjugated verb.

Verbs that are reflexive in English, such as *to amuse **oneself*** or *to buy **oneself** something* will generally also be reflexive in French. Many other verbs are reflexive in French that are not in English. Consult the end-of-chapter vocabulary list to find all the reflexive verbs learned in this chapter.

Mon père **s'**achète une nouvelle voiture chaque année.
*My father buys **himself** a new car each year.*

Je me brosse **les** dents trois fois par jour.
*I brush **my** teeth three times a day.*

Verbs indicating that people are doing something to their own body are generally reflexive in French. After such verbs, in French, you generally use the definite article (**le, la, l', les**) with a body part, rather than the possessive adjective *(my, your, his . . .).*

Vous **vous** retrouvez après les cours?
*Do you meet **each other** after class?*

Mes voisins ne **se** parlent pas.
*My neighbors don't talk **to one another.***

RECIPROCAL VERBS

Reciprocal verbs indicate that two or more people do something to or for one another. Most verbs naming something one person might do to another can be made reciprocal by adding a reciprocal pronoun.

aimer	*to love*	s'aimer	*to love each other*
détester	*to hate*	se détester	*to hate each other*
regarder	*to look at*	se regarder	*to look at each other*

—**Vous** voulez **vous** marier?
—Oui, et **nous** allons **nous** installer dans un petit appartement.

When reflexive / reciprocal verbs are used in the infinitive, the reflexive / reciprocal pronoun changes to match the subject of the conjugated verb.

PAST TENSES OF REFLEXIVE AND RECIPROCAL VERBS

All reflexive / reciprocal verbs are conjugated with **être** in the **passé composé.** The past participle agrees in gender and number with the reflexive / reciprocal pronoun (and the subject) when it is the *direct* object of the verb.

S'AMUSER	
je me suis amusé(e)	nous nous sommes amusé(e)s
tu t'es amusé(e)	vous vous êtes amusé(e)(s)
il s'est amusé	ils se sont amusés
elle s'est amusée	elles se sont amusées
on s'est amusé(e)(s)	

—Tous tes amis se sont retrouvé**s** chez toi?
—Oui, et on s'est bien amusé**s** jusqu'à très tard. Mon amie Rose s'est endormi**e** sur le canapé.

With negated verbs, place **ne** directly after the subject and **pas** after the conjugated form of **être.**

—Vous **ne** vous êtes **pas** vus hier?
—Non, mais nous nous sommes téléphoné trois fois.

Past participles do not agree with reflexive / reciprocal pronouns that are *indirect* objects. For this reason, there is no agreement with **se parler, se téléphoner, s'écrire,** or when a reflexive verb is followed directly by a noun that is the direct object of the verb, such as a part of the body.

Ma petite sœur s'est maquillé**e.**
Ma petite sœur s'est maquillé **les yeux.**

As with all verbs except **être,** form the imperfect of reflexive verbs by dropping the **-ons** from the **nous** form of the verb and adding the imperfect endings: **-ais, -ais, -ait, -ions, -iez, -aient.**

—Tu te levais plus tôt l'année dernière?
—Oui, je me levais à six heures.

REGULAR *-RE* VERBS

The following verbs are conjugated like **répondre: descendre, entendre, s'entendre (bien / mal) (avec), perdre, se perdre, rendre visite à quelqu'un, rendre quelque chose à quelqu'un, vendre, revendre.** They all take **avoir** in the **passé composé** except **descendre** and the reflexive verbs.

—Tu ne rends jamais visite à ton ex-copine?
—Non, on a perdu contact. On ne s'entend pas très bien. Si je téléphone chez elle, elle ne répond pas au téléphone.

RÉPONDRE *(to answer)*	
je répond**s**	nous répond**ons**
tu répond**s**	vous répond**ez**
il/elle/on répond	ils/elles répond**ent**

PASSÉ COMPOSÉ: **j'ai répondu**
IMPARFAIT: **je répondais**

RELATIVE PRONOUNS

A relative clause is a phrase that describes a noun. The word that begins the phrase, referring back to the noun described is a relative pronoun. The relative pronouns **qui, que,** and **dont** are all used for both people and things. The choice of relative pronoun depends on the pronoun's function in the relative clause. **Qui** replaces the subject of the relative clause, **que (qu')** replaces the direct object, and **dont** replaces the preposition **de** and its object.

Place relative clauses directly after the noun they describe. When **que** is the object of a verb in the **passé composé,** the past participle agrees in number and gender with the noun it represents.

La femme **qui** habite à côté est française. (= La femme est française. **Cette femme** habite à côté.)
La femme **que** j'ai invité**e** est française. (= La femme est française. J'ai invité **cette femme.**)
La femme **dont** je parle souvent est française. (= La femme est française. Je parle souvent **de cette femme.**)

VOCABULAIRE

 Audio Flashcards

COMPÉTENCE 1

Describing your daily routine

NOMS MASCULINS

un bain	*a bath*
le mariage	*marriage*
un petit-fils	*a grandson*
un séjour	*a stay*
un veuf	*a widower*

NOMS FÉMININS

une demi-heure	*a half hour*
les dents	*the teeth*
une douche	*a shower*
la figure	*the face*
la main	*the hand*
une petite-fille	*a granddaughter*
une routine	*a routine*
une veuve	*a widow*

EXPRESSIONS VERBALES

s'amuser	*to have fun*
s'appeler	*to be named / called*
attendre	*to wait (for)*
se brosser (les cheveux / les dents)	*to brush (one's hair / one's teeth)*
connaître	*to be familiar with, to be acquainted with, to know*
se coucher / se recoucher	*to go to bed / to go back to bed*
s'endormir	*to fall asleep*
s'ennuyer	*to be bored, to get bored*
faire sa toilette	*to wash up*
s'habiller / se déshabiller	*to get dressed / to get undressed*
se laver (la figure / les mains)	*to wash (one's face / one's hands)*
se lever	*to get up*
se maquiller	*to put on makeup*
prendre un bain / une douche	*to take a bath / a shower*
se raser	*to shave*
se reposer	*to rest*
se réveiller	*to wake up*

DIVERS

avant de	*before*
comme	*since, as*
d'autres fois	*other times*
depuis	*since (then), for*
d'origine...	*of . . . origin*
facilement	*easily*
parfait(e)	*perfect*
pendant	*during*
quotidien(ne)	*daily*
vite	*quick(ly), fast*

COMPÉTENCE 2

Talking about relationships

NOMS MASCULINS

le coup de foudre	*love at first sight*
le grand amour	*true love*

NOMS FÉMININS

la jeunesse	*youth*
une relation	*a relationship*

EXPRESSIONS VERBALES

s'aimer	*to like each other, to love each other*
descendre	*to go down, to get off, to stay (at a hotel)*
se détester	*to hate each other*
se disputer	*to argue*
s'embrasser	*to kiss each other, to embrace each other*
entendre	*to hear*
s'entendre (bien / mal) (avec)	*to get along (well / badly) (with)*
se fiancer	*to get engaged*
s'installer (dans / à)	*to move (into), to settle (in)*
se marier (avec)	*to get married (to)*
se parler	*to talk to each other*
se passer	*to happen*
perdre	*to lose*
perdre du temps	*to waste time*
se perdre	*to get lost*
prendre une décision	*to make a decision*
se quitter	*to leave each other*
se réconcilier	*to make up with each other*
se regarder	*to look at each other*
se rencontrer	*to meet each other (by chance, for the first time), to run into each other*
rendre quelque chose à quelqu'un	*to return something to someone*
rendre visite à quelqu'un	*to visit someone*
répondre (à)	*to answer, to respond (to)*
se retrouver	*to meet each other (by design)*
revendre	*to sell back / resell*
rêver (de)	*to dream (of, about)*
se souvenir de	*to remember*
suivre	*to follow*
se téléphoner	*to phone each other*
vendre	*to sell*

DIVERS

ce qui	*what*
C'est dommage!	*That's too bad!*
enfin	*finally*
formidable	*great*
heureux (heureuse)	*happy*
la plupart du temps	*most of the time*
mamie	*grandma*
sentimental(e) (*mpl* sentimentaux)	*sentimental, emotional*
un(e) tel(le)	*such a*

Talking about what you did and used to do

NOMS MASCULINS

le reste (de)	*the rest (of)*
un réveil	*an alarm clock*

EXPRESSIONS VERBALES

accepter	*to accept*
s'arrêter	*to stop*
se peigner	*to comb one's hair*
se promener	*to go walking*
raconter	*to tell*
se reconnaître	*to recognize each other*
sonner	*to ring*
se voir	*to see each other*

DIVERS

ce que	*what*
donc	*then, so, thus, therefore*
parfaitement	*perfectly*

Describing traits and characteristics

NOMS MASCULINS

l'aspect physique	*physical appearance*
le bonheur	*happiness*
le corps	*the body*
un défaut	*a fault*
l'esprit	*the mind, the spirit*
un groupe	*a group*
un partenaire	*a partner*
un sens de l'humour	*a sense of humor*
un sentiment	*a feeling*
un test	*a test*
un trait (de caractère)	*a (character) trait*

NOMS FÉMININS

la beauté	*beauty*
la compatibilité	*compatibility*
l'importance	*the importance*
l'indécision	*indecision*
l'indifférence	*indifference*
l'infidélité	*infidelity*
l'inflexibilité	*inflexibility*
l'insensibilité	*insensitivity*
la jalousie	*jealousy*
la nature	*nature*
une partenaire	*a partner*
la passion	*passion*
la politique	*politics*
la profession	*the profession*
la religion	*religion*
une rencontre	*an encounter*
la spiritualité	*spirituality*
la tolérance	*tolerance, acceptance*
la vanité	*vanity*

VERBES

cultiver	*to cultivate*
exprimer	*to express*
faire la connaissance de	*to make the acquaintance of, to meet (for the first time)*
s'intéresser à	*to be interested in*
ranger	*to arrange, to order*
supporter	*to bear, to tolerate, to put up with*

DIVERS

chez (une personne)	*with, in (a person)*
de droite	*conservative*
de gauche	*liberal*
dont	*whom, of (about, with) whom, whose, that, of (about, with) which*
jaloux (jalouse)	*jealous*
le mieux	*the best*
professionnel(le)	*professional*
que	*that, which, whom*
qui	*that, which, who*

La violence
le coup de foudre

© Romain Cintract/hemis/age fotostock

8

COMPÉTENCE

1 Ordering at a restaurant
Au restaurant

Talking about what you eat
Le partitif

Stratégies et Compréhension auditive
- **Pour mieux comprendre:** *Planning and predicting*
- **Compréhension auditive:** *Au restaurant*

2 Buying food
Les courses

Saying how much
Les expressions de quantité

Talking about foods
L'usage des articles

3 Talking about meals
Les repas

Saying what you eat and drink
*Le pronom **en** et le verbe **boire***

Talking about choices
*Les verbes en -**ir***

4 Choosing a healthy lifestyle
La santé

Saying what you would do
Le conditionnel

Vidéoreprise *Les Stagiaires*

Lecture et Composition
- **Pour mieux lire:** *Reading a poem*
- **Lecture:** *Déjeuner du matin*
- **Pour mieux écrire:** *Finding the right word*
- **Composition:** *Une critique gastronomique*

Comparaisons culturelles: *À table!*

Résumé de grammaire

Vocabulaire

La bonne cuisine

 iLrn iLrn Heinle Learning Center

 www.cengagebrain.com

 Horizons Video: Les Stagiaires

Audio

Internet web search

 Pair work

 Group work

LA NORMANDIE

Que savez-vous de la Normandie? Comment imaginez-vous cette région? Pensez-vous à...

des bateaux de pêche?

des fermes normandes?

des villes anciennes?

de pêche *fishing*   des fermes normandes *Norman farms*

des falaises isolées?

des villes au bord de la mer?

La Normandie, **c'est tout cela! Et encore plus!**

Élargissez vos connaissances *(Broaden your knowledge)* sur l'histoire de la Normandie en recherchant les sujets suivants sur Internet: Guillaume le Conquérant et l'invasion normande de l'Angleterre; Jeanne d'Arc; le Jour J *(D-Day)*.

Rouen

Visit it live on Google Earth!

NOMBRE D'HABITANTS:
**113 000 habitants
(avec ses agglomérations
[*metropolitan region*]:
650 000) (les Rouennais)**

Le savez-vous?

Que savez-vous de *(What do you know about)* l'histoire de la Normandie? Trouvez la date qui correspond à chacun de ces événements historiques.

a. 1066	**c.** 820–911
b. le 6 juin 1944	**d.** 1453

1. le Jour J, jour du débarquement en Normandie des forces alliées (américaines, anglaises, canadiennes et françaises)

2. la conquête de la région par les Vikings (Normandie veut dire «*Land of the Northmen*».)

3. la fin de la guerre de Cent Ans entre la France et l'Angleterre *(England)* (que la France a gagnée grâce surtout aux batailles remportées *[thanks especially to the battles won]* par Jeanne d'Arc)

4. la conquête de l'Angleterre par Guillaume le Conquérant, duc de Normandie

La tapisserie de Bayeux raconte en images la conquête de l'Angleterre par Guillaume le Conquérant, duc de Normandie.

---

des falaises *cliffs*   **au bord de la mer** *at the seaside*   **c'est tout cela! Et encore plus!** *it's all that! And even more!*

Ordering at a restaurant

AU RESTAURANT

iLrn In the **Culture Modules** in the video library, see **Cuisine**.

Note *de grammaire*

1. The article you see in front of many of these nouns is called the partitive. It expresses the idea of *some* or *any*. Why are there four different forms?

du pâté *some pâté*
de la soupe *some soup*
de l'eau *some water*
des œufs *some eggs*

You will learn more about how to use the partitive article in the next section.

2. The irregular verb **servir** *(to serve)* is conjugated like **sortir: je sers, tu sers, il/elle/on sert, nous servons, vous servez, ils/elles servent;** PASSÉ COMPOSÉ: **j'ai servi;** IMPARFAIT: **je servais.**

Les Français aiment bien les grands repas traditionnels.

On commence par **une entrée** ou **un hors-d'œuvre:**

de la soupe à l'oignon

du pâté

des œufs *(m)* durs à la mayonnaise

des crudités *(f)*

de la salade de tomates

des escargots *(m)*

Sur la table, il y a aussi...

du sel et du poivre

du pain

de l'eau minérale

Ensuite, **on sert** le plat principal:

DE LA VIANDE

du rosbif

une côte de porc

un bifteck

DU POISSON

du thon

du saumon

DE LA VOLAILLE

du poulet

du canard

DES FRUITS *(m)* **DE MER**

des moules *(f)*

du homard

des huîtres *(f)*

des crevettes *(f)*

Line art on this page: © Cengage Learning

une entrée *a first course* **un hors-d'œuvre** *an appetizer* **des crudités** *(f) raw vegetables* **on sert (servir** *to serve)* **de la viande** *meat* **du poisson** *fish* **du thon** *tuna* **du saumon** *salmon* **de la volaille** *poultry* **du canard** *duck* **des fruits** *(m)* **de mer** *shellfish* **des moules** *(f) mussels* **du homard** *lobster* **des huîtres** *(f) oysters* **des crevettes** *(f) shrimp*

Le plat principal **comprend** aussi **du riz** et des légumes *(m):*

des haricots verts—

—des pommes de terre *(f)*

—des petits pois

On sert généralement la salade verte après le plat principal. On sert le fromage après ou avec la salade.

une salade

du fromage

On finit le repas avec des fruits – ou un dessert.

de la glace à la vanille

de la tarte aux pommes

du gâteau au chocolat

des fruits *(m)*

un yaourt

Pour finir, on sert le café. Prenez-vous **du sucre,** du lait ou de la crème dans votre café?

du café

Line art on this page: © Cengage Learning

Vocabulaire sans peine!

Most foreign names of food items borrowed into English from other languages will be the same words in French. They tend to be masculine, unless they are borrowed from another romance language such as Spanish and Italian and end with **-a,** or sometimes **-e.** Italian pasta dishes ending with **-i** are plural, as in Italian.

du sushi	**une enchilada**
du curry	**des spaghetti**
un baklava	

How would you say the following in French?
a taco	*tofu*
chow mein	*macaroni*

Vocabulaire supplémentaire

bleu(e) *very rare*
saignant(e) *rare*
à point *medium*
bien cuit(e) *well-done*
végétarien(ne) *vegetarian*
végétalien(ne) *vegan*
D'AUTRES PLATS *(DISHES):*
   de l'agneau *(m) lamb*
   du bifteck haché *ground meat*
   des coquilles St-Jacques *(f) scallops*
   de la dinde *turkey*
   des pâtes *(f) pasta, noodles*
   du rôti de porc *pork roast*
   de la sole *sole*
   de la truite *trout*
   du veau *veal*
POUR METTRE LA TABLE *(TO SET THE TABLE):*
   une assiette *a plate*
   un bol *a bowl*
   un couteau *a knife*
   une cuillère / cuiller *a spoon*
   une fourchette *a fork*
   une nappe *a tablecloth*
   une serviette *a napkin*
   une tasse *a cup*
   un verre *a glass*

Pour une liste de fruits et de légumes, voir la page 315.

PRONONCIATION

Le **h** aspiré 3-2

In French, **h** is never pronounced and there is usually liaison or elision before it.

J'aime les*ᶻ* huîtres.   Il y a beaucoup **d'**huile *(oil)* dans la salade.

Before a few words beginning with **h,** there is no liaison or elision, even though the **h** is silent. These words are said to begin with **h aspiré.** In vocabulary lists, they are indicated by an asterisk (*). English words that begin with *h* often have an **h aspiré** when used in French. The following words have **h aspiré:**

   le homard   les haricots   les hors-d'œuvre   les hot-dogs   les hamburgers

---

comprend (comprendre *to include)*   **du riz** *rice*   **du sucre** *sugar*

André a invité Rosalie au restaurant La Jardinière. Regardez **la carte** de ce restaurant aux pages 308–309.

LE SERVEUR:	Bonsoir, monsieur. Bonsoir, madame. Aimeriez-vous **un apéritif** avant de commander?
ANDRÉ:	Rosalie?
ROSALIE:	Non, merci, pas ce soir.
ANDRÉ:	Pour moi non plus.
LE SERVEUR:	Et pour dîner? Est-ce que vous avez décidé?
ANDRÉ:	Nous allons prendre le menu à 22 euros.
LE SERVEUR:	Très bien, monsieur. Et qu'est-ce que vous désirez **comme** entrée?
ANDRÉ:	Pour madame, le saumon fumé, s'il vous plaît. Et pour moi, les huîtres.
LE SERVEUR:	Et comme plat principal?
ROSALIE:	**La raie** pour moi, s'il vous plaît.
ANDRÉ:	Et pour moi, **le pavé de saumon.**
LE SERVEUR:	Bien, monsieur. Et comme boisson?
ANDRÉ:	Une carafe de vin blanc et **une bouteille d'**eau minérale.
LE SERVEUR:	Évian ou Perrier?
ROSALIE:	Évian, s'il vous plaît.
LE SERVEUR:	Très bien, madame.

A **Prononcez bien!** Demandez à votre partenaire s'il/si elle aime ces choses. Faites attention à la prononciation du **h aspiré** et du **h non-aspiré**.

1. *le homard   2. *les haricots verts   3 *les hamburgers   4. les huîtres

B **Préférences.** Circulez parmi les étudiants et pour chaque question trouvez quelqu'un qui préfère la même chose que vous. Pour répondre *neither . . . nor . . . ,* utilisez **ne... ni... ni...** comme dans l'exemple.

EXEMPLE la viande ou le poisson
— **Est-ce que tu aimes mieux la viande ou le poisson?**
— **J'aime mieux la viande. Et toi?**
— **Moi aussi, je préfère la viande. / Je n'aime ni la viande ni le poisson. / J'aime les deux.**

1. la viande rouge ou la volaille
2. les légumes ou la viande
3. le poisson ou les fruits de mer
4. les crudités ou la salade verte
5. les pommes de terre ou le riz
6. les haricots verts ou les petits pois
7. les escargots ou les œufs durs
8. les crevettes ou le homard

C **Catégories logiques.** Quel mot ne va pas logiquement avec les autres? Pourquoi?

EXEMPLE le thé, le jus de fruit, le sel, le lait, l'eau
Le sel, parce que ce n'est pas une boisson.

1. le pain, les petits pois, les pommes de terre, les haricots verts
2. le gâteau au chocolat, le poivre, la tarte aux pommes, la glace
3. la salade de tomates, le pâté, la soupe à l'oignon, le rosbif
4. le déjeuner, le dîner, le petit déjeuner, le sel
5. le homard, le rosbif, les crevettes, les huîtres, les moules
6. les pommes de terre, les petits pois, les haricots verts, le gâteau

---

la carte *the menu*   **un apéritif** *a before-dinner drink*   **comme** *for, as a(n)*   **la raie** *skate, rayfish*   **le pavé de saumon** *the salmon steak*   **une bouteille de** *a bottle of*

D **Aujourd'hui on sert...** Regardez la liste et indiquez ce qu'il y a par catégorie.

> de l'eau minérale   du vin   du canard   du thon
> du saumon   des crevettes   des huîtres
> des petits pois   des pommes de terre   du gâteau
> de la tarte aux pommes   des côtes de porc
> du bifteck   du pâté   des œufs durs   du poulet

EXEMPLE viande
Comme viande, il y a des côtes de porc et...

1. entrée
2. volaille
3. viande
4. poisson
5. dessert
6. légume
7. boisson
8. fruits de mer

E **Comparaisons culturelles.** Pour chaque catégorie, est-ce que vous préférez la même chose que les Français (indiquée par un X)?

1. Je préfère...
   X le café noir ou avec du sucre.
   __ le café au lait.
   __ le café vanille ou le café noisette (*hazelnut*).

2. Je préfère prendre la salade...
   __ avant le plat principal.
   __ avec le plat principal.
   X après le plat principal.

3. Pour terminer un repas, je préfère...
   __ du gâteau ou de la tarte.
   __ un fruit.
   X un yaourt ou un fromage blanc.

4. Comme glace, je préfère...
   X la glace à la vanille.
   __ la glace au chocolat.
   __ la glace à la fraise (*strawberry*).

F **Un dîner.** Voici ce que Rosalie a mangé hier soir. Qu'est-ce qu'elle a mangé? Dans quel ordre? Utilisez **du** (*m. sing.*), **de la** (*f. sing.*) ou **des** (*pl.*) pour dire *some* ou **un(e)** pour dire *a* avant chaque substantif (*noun*).

© Cengage Learning

À VOUS!

Avec deux autres étudiant(e)s, relisez à haute voix la conversation au restaurant. Ensuite, imaginez que vous dînez au restaurant La Jardinière avec un(e) ami(e). Commandez un repas complet. Le (La) troisième étudiant(e) va jouer le rôle du serveur (de la serveuse).

Sélection musicale. Search the Web for the song **"Les cornichons"** by Nino Ferrer to enjoy a musical selection containing food vocabulary.

You can find a list of the new words from this *Compétence* on page 342 and access the audio online.

BISTROT DE MICHEL

RESTAURANT

LA JARDINIÈRE

Servis Jusqu'à 23 H.

Le Bistrot - 15 €.
Service 15% Compris
*Michel vous propose son petit Menu Bistrot
composé uniquement de produits frais de saison*

Première Assiette
9 Huîtres "Fines de Claires no3" Sur lit de glace
Assiette de Coquillages farcis à l'ail
Cocotte de moules marinières
Salade aux Lardons, Oeuf poché
Terrine de canard maison, au poivre vert
Plateau de fruits de mer "L'écailler" + 10 €

Deuxième Assiette
Brochette de poissons, beurre blanc
Moules de pays, frites
Sardines grillées aux herbes
Langue de bœuf, sauce piquante
Poêlée de Rognon de bœuf, flambée au cognac
Bavette Poêlée à la fondue d'oignons

Troisième Assiette
Crème Caramel
Fraises au vin ou fraises au sucre
Feuillantine aux pommes
Glace et sorbet artisanaux
Île flottante
Coupe normande

**Arrivage Journalier
de Poissons, d'Huîtres et de Fruits de Mer**

LA JARDINIÈRE - 22 €.
Service 15% Compris
*Les plus beaux produits du Terroir Sélectionnés
et cuisinés dans la grande tradition de la Jardinière*

Première Assiette
12 Huîtres "Fines de Claires n°3" Sur lit de glace
Saumon Fumé par nos soins, Toasts chauds
Poêlon de 12 Escargots de Bourgogne à l'ail
Beignets de Langoustines, Sauce tartare
Salade de cervelle d'agneau poêlée
Plateau de fruits de mer "L'écailler" + 10 €

Deuxième Assiette
Aile de Raie capucine
Daurade entière au lard fumé
Pavé de Saumon Rôti, beurre de moules
Filet de Canard à la Rouennaise
Andouillette à la ficelle "du Père Tafournel"
Faux-filet grillé ou Sauce Poivre

Troisième Assiette
Salade de Saison, ou plateau de fromages

Quatrième Assiette
Tarte tatin chaude, crème fraîche
Bavarois ananas coco
Symphonie aux trois chocolats
Feuillantine aux Fraises ou fraises Melba
Glace et Sorbet artisanaux
Crème Brûlée

LA JARDINIÈRE

37 · BISTROT DE MICHEL · 37
RESTAURANT

La Carte
Service 15% Compris

Servie Jusqu'à Minuit

Nos Huîtres et Fruits de Mer (Arrivage Journalier)

12 Huîtres "Fines de Claires" Sur lit de glace n°3 "14€" n°2 "16€"
12 Huîtres "Spéciales St Vaast" Sur lit de glace n°3 "15€" n°2 "17€"
Plateau de fruits de mer "L'Écailler" 18€ "le marayeur" 30€ "le Royal" 60€ 1 ou 2 personnes avec 1 Homard frais

Fraîcheur du Marché & Préparations Maison

Soupe de poissons maison, sa rouille et ses croûtons, 6€   Assiette de coquillages farcis 6€
Moules à la crème 7€ – Salade aux lardons, œuf poché 6€   Terrine de canard maison au poivre 6€
Salade de cervelle d'agneau poêlée 8€   Beignets de langoustines, Sauce Tartare 10€
Saumon fumé par nos soins toasts chauds 10€   Poêlon de 12 Escargots de Bourgogne à l'ail 10€

Poissons Frais d'Arrivage

– Brochette de poissons frais, beurre Blanc 7,50€ Moules de pays frites 7,50€
– Sardines grillées aux herbes 7,50€ Pavé de Saumon Rôti, Beurre de Noues 10,50€
– Aile de Raie capucine 10,50€ Daurade entière au lard fumé 10,50€
– Sole Meunière ou Sole Normande 19€

Traditionnels & Spécialités

Langue de Bœuf, sauce piquante 7,50€   Tête de veau ravigote 7,50€ Bavette poêlée
à la fondue d'oignons 7,50€ Poêlée de Rognon de bœuf Flambée au cognac 7,50€ Faux Filet
Grillé ou Sauce Poivre 10,50€ Filet de canard à la Rouennaise 10,50€ Andouillette à la Ficelle 10,50€
Cœur de Filet au Poivre Flambé au calvados 15€ Chateaubriand Grillé Beurre Persillé 14,50€

Desserts
Plateau de Fromages 5,50€

Île Flottante au caramel 4€   Crème au Caramel 4€   Baiser de vierge 5€   Glace et Sorbet
artisanaux 5€   Fraises au vin ou sucrées 5€   After eight 5€   Coupe normande 5€   Feuillantine aux
pommes 5,50€ Tarte Tatin crème fraîche 5,50€ Crème Brûlée 5,50€ Bavarois ananas coco 5,50€
Feuillantine aux fraises 6€   Fraises Melba 6€   Symphonie aux trois chocolats 6,50€

TALKING ABOUT WHAT YOU EAT

✔ *Pour vérifier*

1. How do you express the idea of *some* in French? What are the forms of the partitive and when do you use each? Can you drop the word for *some* or *any* in French, as you can in English?

2. In what two circumstances do you use **de** instead of the partitive?

Le partitif

To express the idea of *some* or *any*, use the partitive article (**du, de la, de l', des**).

MASCULINE SINGULAR BEFORE A CONSONANT SOUND	FEMININE SINGULAR BEFORE A CONSONANT SOUND	SINGULAR BEFORE A VOWEL SOUND	PLURAL
du pain	de la glace	de l'eau	des fruits

The words *some* or *any* may be left out in English, but the partitive article must be used in French.

| Je voudrais **du café.** | *I'd like **(some) coffee.*** |
| Tu as **du temps libre?** | *Do you have **(some) free time?*** |

The partitive article becomes **de (d'):**

* after negated verbs (except after the verb **être**).

| Tu **ne** veux **pas de café?** | *Don't you want **(any) coffee?*** |
| Je n'ai **pas de temps libre.** | *I don't have **(any) free time.*** |

* after expressions of quantity like **beaucoup, combien,** and **trop.**

| J'ai acheté **trop de café.** | *I bought **too much coffee.*** |
| J'ai **peu de temps libre.** | *I have **little free time.*** |

A **Je prends...** Complétez les espaces avec la forme correcte de l'article partitif. Ensuite, demandez à un(e) partenaire s'il/si elle prend souvent ces choses le soir.

EXEMPLE <u>du</u> vin
— Est-ce que tu prends souvent du vin le soir?
— Oui, je prends souvent du vin.
Je prends du vin quelquefois.
Non, je ne prends jamais de vin.

1. ___ pain
2. ___ œufs
3. ___ eau minérale
4. ___ viande rouge
5. ___ crevettes
6. ___ poisson
7. ___ volaille
8. ___ soupe

B **Comparaisons culturelles.** Indiquez si les Français prennent souvent ces choses **comme entrée, comme plat principal, comme boisson, comme dessert** ou **comme légume.** Ensuite, dites si vous faites souvent la même chose.

EXEMPLE pâté
Les Français prennent souvent du pâté comme entrée.
Moi aussi, je prends souvent du pâté comme entrée.
Moi, je ne prends jamais de pâté comme entrée.

1. salade de tomates
2. eau minérale
3. petits pois
4. saumon
5. canard
6. tarte
7. gâteau
8. vin
9. pâté

C **Sur la table.** Rose est invitée à une fête où il y a beaucoup à manger et à boire. Voici la table de la salle à manger et la table de la cuisine. Travaillez en groupes pour faire des comparaisons entre les deux.

EXEMPLE Il y a des chips dans la cuisine et dans la salle à manger.
Il y a de l'eau minérale dans la salle à manger mais il n'y a pas d'eau minérale dans la cuisine.

© Cengage Learning

la salle à manger   la cuisine

D **Entretien.** Complétez les questions avec l'article qui convient: **du, de la, de l', des** ou **de**. Ensuite, utilisez ces questions pour interviewer un(e) partenaire.

1. Qu'est-ce que tu préfères faire quand tu as ___du___ temps libre: faire ___du___ sport, écouter ___de la___ musique, faire ___du___ shopping, faire ___du___ jardinage ou jouer à ___des___ jeux vidéo? Est-ce que tu as beaucoup ___de___ temps libre ou est-ce que tu as beaucoup ___de___ travail? Tu invites souvent ___des___ amis à dîner chez toi?

2. Est-ce que tu prends beaucoup ___de___ repas au restaurant avec tes amis? Quand tu vas au restaurant, tu commandes plus souvent ___de la___ viande, ___du___ poisson, ___des___ légumes ou ___des___ fruits de mer? Tu prends ___du___ vin quelquefois avec tes repas? Tu manges beaucoup ___des___ légumes? Est-ce que tu prends plus souvent ___de la___ glace, ___de la___ tarte ou ___du___ gâteau comme dessert?

E **Préparatifs.** Vous allez inviter des amis pour un grand repas traditionnel à la française. Avec un(e) partenaire, faites des projets pour ce dîner.

Parlez de:

- quand et où vous allez faire ce dîner et qui vous allez inviter.
- ce que vous allez servir. (Imaginez que tout le monde n'aime pas les mêmes choses et proposez au moins trois possibilités pour l'entrée, le plat principal, le dessert et la boisson.)

STRATÉGIES ET COMPRÉHENSION AUDITIVE

POUR MIEUX COMPRENDRE: Planning and predicting

Since no two cultures are identical, you may sometimes find yourself lacking the cultural knowledge to understand what you hear in French. For example, if the waiter asks «**Évian ou Perrier?**», you will not be able to answer unless you recognize that these are brand names of French mineral waters. In such situations, try to infer what is being asked from the context. Also, when possible, prepare and predict from previous experiences what might be asked or said. For example, before ordering mineral water, glance at the menu to see what kinds are sold.

🔊 **A Pendant le repas.** Vous êtes au restaurant. Est-ce qu'on vous dit les choses
3-4 que vous entendez **avant le repas** ou **à la fin du repas**?

B Questions. Faites une liste de trois questions qu'un(e) client(e) pose souvent au serveur ou à la serveuse dans un restaurant.

Compréhension auditive: *Au restaurant*

🔊 Deux touristes sont dans un restaurant français. Écoutez leur conversation.
3-5 Qu'est-ce qu'ils commandent? Nommez au moins quatre choses.

Que demandent-ils? Écoutez encore une fois la conversation au restaurant et écrivez deux questions que les clients posent à la serveuse.

© Markus Kirchgessner/laif/Redux

Buying food

LES COURSES

Vocabulaire supplémentaire

la confiserie *the candy shop, the confectioner's shop*
la fromagerie *the cheese shop*
le marchand de fruits et légumes *the fruit and vegetable market*
le traiteur *the caterer*

De plus en plus de Français font leurs courses dans les supermarchés et **les grandes surfaces** où on vend de tout. Mais beaucoup préfèrent aller chez les petits **commerçants** du quartier où le service est plus personnalisé.

À la boulangerie-pâtisserie, on peut acheter du pain et **des pâtisseries** *(f)*:

une baguette   un pain au chocolat   **un pain complet**   une tarte aux **cerises**   une tartelette aux **fraises**

À la boucherie, on achète de la viande:

du poulet   du bœuf   du porc

À la charcuterie, on achète **de la charcuterie** et **des plats préparés:**

du saucisson   du jambon   des saucisses *(f)*   des plats préparés

On achète du poisson et des fruits de mer à la poissonnerie.

Et on va à l'épicerie pour acheter des fruits, des légumes, **des conserves** *(f)* et des produits **surgelés.**

Line art on this page: © Cengage Learning

une grande surface *a superstore*   **un(e) commerçant(e)** *a shopkeeper*   **une pâtisserie** *a pastry*   **un pain complet** *a loaf of whole-grain bread*   **une cerise** *a cherry*   **une fraise** *a strawberry*   **de la charcuterie** *deli meats, cold cuts*   **un plat préparé** *a ready-to-serve dish*   **des conserves** *(f) canned goods*   **surgelé(e)** *frozen*

Beaucoup de Français **disent** que pour avoir un bon **choix** de légumes et de fruits vraiment **frais, il faut** aller au marché.

Au marché, on peut acheter:

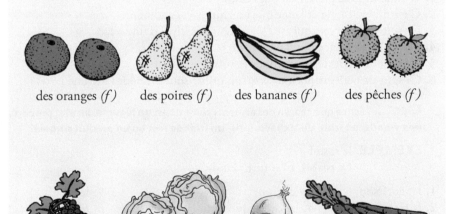

des oranges *(f)*   des poires *(f)*   des bananes *(f)*   des pêches *(f)*

du raisin   **des laitues** *(f)*   des oignons *(m)*   des carottes *(f)*

Line art on this page: © Cengage Learning

Vocabulaire supplémentaire

LÉGUMES
un artichaut *an artichoke*
des asperges (f) *asparagus*
une aubergine *an eggplant*
du brocoli
des champignons (m) *mushrooms*
du chou *cabbage*
du chou-fleur *cauliflower*
des choux de Bruxelles (m) *Brussels sprouts*
un concombre *a cucumber*
une courgette *a zucchini*
des épinards (m) *spinach*
du maïs *corn*
un radis *a radish*

FRUITS
un abricot *an apricot*
un ananas *a pineapple*
des bleuets (m) *blueberries* (Canada)
un citron vert *a lime*
des framboises (f) *raspberries*
un kiwi
une mandarine *a tangerine*
un melon
des myrtilles (f) *blueberries* (France)
une nectarine
un pamplemousse *a grapefruit*
une pastèque *a watermelon*
une prune *a plum*
un pruneau *a prune*
des raisins secs (m) *raisins*

---

disent (dire *to say, to tell*)   **un choix** *a choice*   **frais** (fraîche) *fresh*   **il faut** *it is necessary, one needs, one must*
une laitue *a head of lettuce*

Rosalie fait ses courses au marché.

ROSALIE:	Bonjour, monsieur.
LE MARCHAND:	Bonjour, madame. **Qu'est-ce qu'il vous faut aujourd'hui?**
ROSALIE:	Euh... voyons... un kilo de pommes de terre, **une livre** de tomates... Vous avez des haricots verts?
LE MARCHAND:	Non, madame, pas aujourd'hui. Mais j'ai des petits pois. Regardez comme ils sont beaux.
ROSALIE:	Non, merci, pas de petits pois aujourd'hui.
LE MARCHAND:	Alors, qu'est-ce que je peux vous proposer d'autre?
ROSALIE:	Donnez-moi aussi 500 grammes de fraises.
LE MARCHAND:	Et voilà, 500 grammes. Et avec ça?
ROSALIE:	C'est tout, merci. Ça fait combien?
LE MARCHAND:	Voilà... Alors, un kilo de pommes de terre – 1,20 €, une livre de tomates – 1,36 € et 500 grammes de fraises – 1,50 €. Ça fait 4,06 €.
ROSALIE:	Voici 5 euros.
LE MARCHAND:	Et voici votre monnaie. Merci, madame, et à bientôt!
ROSALIE:	Merci. Au revoir, monsieur.

A Devinettes. Qu'est-ce que c'est?

EXEMPLE C'est un fruit rond, orange et plein de vitamine C.
C'est une orange.

1. C'est le légume préféré de Bugs Bunny.
2. C'est un fruit long et jaune que les chimpanzés adorent.
3. C'est le légume vert qui est l'ingrédient principal d'une salade.
4. On utilise ce fruit pour faire du vin.
5. Ce sont de petits légumes ronds et verts.
6. Ce sont de petits fruits rouges qu'on utilise souvent pour faire une tarte.

B C'est... Est-ce que chacun des aliments suivants est **un légume, un plat préparé, une viande, un fruit, de la charcuterie, un fruit de mer** ou **un produit surgelé?**

EXEMPLE le rosbif
Le rosbif, c'est une viande.

1. le saucisson	3. le raisin	5. le porc	7. le bœuf
2. la glace	4. le pâté	6. la laitue	8. le homard

C Cuisine française. Voici des spécialités françaises mondialement connues *(French specialties known worldwide)*. Travaillez en groupes pour trouver le mot qui manque à chacune. Choisissez dans la liste suivante.

EXEMPLE un **pain** au chocolat

> bœuf   canard   chocolat   crème   oignon   pain   quiche   salade   vin

1. de la mousse au _____
2. du coq au _____
3. de la _____ lorraine
4. de la _____ brûlée
5. une _____ niçoise
6. du _____ à l'orange
7. de la soupe à l'_____
8. du _____ bourguignon

Qu'est-ce qu'il vous faut aujourd'hui? *What do you need today?*   **une livre** *half a kilo (≈ a pound)*

D **Un dîner.** Votre classe va préparer un dîner. Qu'est-ce que vous allez servir? Chaque étudiant doit répéter de mémoire les choses déjà mentionnées et ajouter *(add)* quelque chose.

EXEMPLE Étudiant 1: **On va servir du pain.**
Étudiant 2: **On va servir du pain et du pâté.**
Étudiant 3: **On va servir du pain, du pâté et du bifteck...**

Maintenant travaillez en groupes pour dire ce que vous allez acheter de cette liste dans chaque magasin. Vous allez faire les courses chez les petits commerçants au lieu d'aller au supermarché. Le premier groupe à compléter la liste de courses gagnera.

EXEMPLE À la boulangerie-pâtisserie, on va acheter du pain...

À la charcuterie

E **Entretien.** Interviewez votre partenaire.

1. Aimes-tu faire les courses? Combien de fois par semaine est-ce que tu fais les courses? Où est-ce que tu fais tes courses d'habitude? Est-ce que tu achètes quelquefois des choses chez les petits commerçants?

2. Aimes-tu les fruits? les légumes? Préfères-tu les fruits ou les légumes? Quels légumes préfères-tu? Quels légumes est-ce que tu n'aimes pas? Quels fruits préfères-tu? Quels fruits est-ce que tu n'aimes pas?

À VOUS!

Avec un(e) partenaire, relisez à haute voix la conversation entre Rosalie et le marchand. Ensuite, imaginez que vous êtes à la boulangerie-pâtisserie. Achetez au moins trois choses.

iLrn You can find a list of the new words from this *Compétence* on page 342 and access the audio online.

SAYING HOW MUCH

✔ **Pour vérifier**

What word follows quantity expressions before nouns? Do you use **de** or **des** after a quantity expression followed by a plural noun?

Les expressions de quantité

Use these expressions to specify how much you want at the market or in a restaurant.

un verre de	*a glass of*	une boîte de	*a box of, a can of*
un litre de	*a liter of*	un pot de	*a jar of*
une carafe de	*a carafe of*	un paquet de	*a bag of, a sack of*
une bouteille de	*a bottle of*	une douzaine de	*a dozen*
une tranche de	*a slice of*	300 grammes de	*300 grams of*
un morceau de	*a piece of*	un kilo (et demi) de	*a kilo (and a half) of*
		une livre de	*a half a kilo (1.1 pounds) of*

After quantity expressions like those above, use **de (d')** before a noun instead of **du, de la, de l',** or **des.** This is also true for less specific quantities such as:

combien de	*how much, how many*
(un) peu de	*(a) little*
assez de	*enough*
beaucoup de	*a lot of*
trop de	*too much, too many*
beaucoup trop de	*much too much, much too many*
plus de	*more*
moins de	*less*

J'ai acheté une bouteille **de** vin rouge, un kilo **de** viande et beaucoup **de** légumes!

A **C'est assez?** Dans chaque situation, est-ce que la quantité indiquée est suffisante?

EXEMPLE Vous prenez le petit déjeuner seul(e) le matin et il y a un verre de lait dans le réfrigérateur.

Il y a trop de lait. / Il y a assez de lait. / Il y a trop peu de lait.

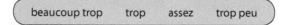

beaucoup trop   trop   assez   trop peu

1. Vous êtes quatre au restaurant et il y a une demi-bouteille d'eau.
2. Vous allez préparer une salade de tomates pour deux personnes. Vous avez un kilo de tomates.
3. Vous allez faire une omelette pour deux personnes et vous avez un seul œuf.
4. C'est le matin et il y a un verre de lait dans le réfrigérateur chez vous.
5. Vous dînez seul(e) au restaurant et il y a trois carafes d'eau.
6. Vous voulez préparer des carottes pour six personnes et vous avez deux carottes.

B **Je voudrais...** Complétez de façon logique chaque quantité proposée.

> thon cerises jambon vin tomates fromage
> jus de fruit rosbif lait sel sucre riz

Je voudrais...

1. une bouteille de
2. un paquet de
3. une boîte de
4. une livre de
5. deux kilos de
6. un morceau de
7. un litre de
8. dix tranches de

Je voudrais six tranches de jambon, s'il vous plaît.

C **Donnez-moi...** Demandez les quantités indiquées des produits suivants.

EXEMPLE Une bouteille de vin, s'il vous plaît.

1. 2. 3. 4.

5. 6. 7. 8.

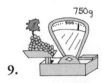

9. 10. 11.

Line art on this page: © Cengage Learning

D **Ces courses.** Avec un(e) partenaire, faites une liste de choses qu'on achète dans les endroits suivants. Utilisez une expression de quantité logique avec chacune.

EXEMPLE à la charcuterie
une tranche de pâté, une livre de jambon, trois cents grammes de saucisson, un kilo de saucisses

1. à la boucherie
2. au marché de fruits et légumes

Maintenant, préparez une conversation avec un(e) commerçant(e) dans laquelle vous achetez trois choses d'une de ces listes.

TALKING ABOUT FOODS

✔ Pour vérifier

1. Which article do you use to say *a* in French? Which articles do you use to express the idea of *some* or *any*?

2. Which article do you use to say *the*? to talk about likes, dislikes, and preferences? to make statements about entire categories?

3. Which articles change to **de**? When do they make this change? Which articles do not change to **de**?

Note *de grammaire*

Note that **je voudrais** expresses a want or desire, not a preference, and is often followed by a partitive article: **Je voudrais *du* jambon et *des* légumes.**

L'usage des articles

Each article you use with a noun conveys a different meaning.

Vous voulez **de la** tarte?
*Do you want **(some)** pie?*
(This refers to a portion.)

Vous voulez **une** tarte?
*Do you want **a** pie?*
(This refers to a whole pie.)

- To say *a* or talk about a whole, use **un** or **une**. To say *some* or *any*, use **du, de la, de l'**, or **des**.

  J'ai acheté **un croissant** et **du thé**.   *I bought **a croissant** and **(some) tea**.*

- Remember that after a negative or an expression of quantity, **un, une, du, de la, de l'**, and **des** all change to **de (d')**.

  Elle ne mange jamais **de viande**.   *She never eats **meat**.*
  Elle mange beaucoup **de légumes**.   *She eats a lot **of vegetables**.*

- To say *the* or refer to a specific item, such as on a menu, use **le, la, l'**, or **les**. Also use these articles to talk about likes and dislikes, and to talk about something as a general category.

  Comme entrée, je voudrais **le pâté**.   *As an appetizer, I'd like **the pâté**.*
  Le pâté qu'ils servent ici est bon.   ***The pâté** that they serve here is good.*
  J'aime **la viande** mais je n'aime pas **le poisson**.   *I like **meat,** but I don't like **fish**.*
  Mais **le poisson** a moins de calories que **la viande**.   *But **fish** has fewer calories than **meat**.*

- Remember that **le, la, l'**, and **les** do *not* change to **de** after a negative or an expression of quantity.

  Je n'aime pas **le poisson**, mais j'aime beaucoup **les fruits de mer**.   *I don't like **fish,** but I like **shellfish** a lot.*

	IN AFFIRMATIVE STATEMENTS, USE:	IN NEGATIVE STATEMENTS AND AFTER QUANTITY EXPRESSIONS, USE:
To say *a* or to talk about a whole:	**un, une** (J'achète **une** tarte.)	**de (d')** (Je n'achète pas **de** tarte.) (Je mange trop **de** tarte.)
To say *some* or *any*:	**du, de la, de l', des** (J'achète **du** lait.)	**de (d')** (Je n'achète pas **de** lait.) (J'achète beaucoup **de** lait.)
To say *the,* to talk about likes and dislikes, or to make generalizations about categories:	**le, la, l', les** (**Le** thon est bon.) (J'aime **le** thon.) (**Le** thon est un poisson.)	**le, la, l', les** (**Le** thon n'est pas bon.) (Je n'aime pas **le** thon.) (**Le** thon n'est pas une viande.) (Je n'aime pas trop **le** thon.)

A Manges-tu bien? Demandez à votre partenaire s'il/si elle mange souvent les choses suivantes.

EXEMPLE pâté
— **Manges-tu souvent du pâté?**
— **Je mange rarement du pâté. / Je ne mange jamais de pâté.**

1. escargots
2. tarte
3. légumes
4. viande rouge
5. poulet
6. crudités
7. glace
8. tarte aux pommes
9. carottes

Maintenant, demandez à votre partenaire s'il/si elle aime ces mêmes choses.

EXEMPLE pâté
— **Aimes-tu le pâté?**
— **J'aime assez le pâté. / Je n'aime pas le pâté.**

B Vos préférences. Dites si vous achetez souvent les choses suivantes et expliquez pourquoi.

EXEMPLE café
J'achète souvent du café parce que j'aime le café.
Je n'achète jamais de café parce que je n'aime pas le café.

1. fromage
2. bananes
3. viande rouge
4. raisin
5. eau minérale
6. jambon
7. huîtres
8. jus de fruit
9. crevettes

C Vos goûts. Complétez les phrases suivantes avec le nom d'un aliment (food) ou d'une boisson logique. Utilisez les articles appropriés.

1. Moi, j'adore...
2. J'aime bien...
3. Comme viande, je mange souvent...
4. Chez moi, il n'y a jamais...
5. Pour le déjeuner, je prends souvent...

D Ce soir. Rosalie parle du dîner qu'elle va préparer ce soir. Complétez ses phrases avec l'article qui convient: **un, une, du, de la, de l', des, le, la, l', les** ou **de (d')**.

Ce soir, je vais servir __1__ soupe de légumes, __2__ poulet, __3__ riz et __4__ petits pois. Et comme dessert, je pense préparer __5__ tarte aux cerises. Moi, je préfère __6__ gâteau, mais André aime beaucoup __7__ tarte! Cet après-midi, je dois aller acheter __8__ sucre, 500 grammes __9__ cerises et beaucoup __10__ légumes. Il y a un marché tout près où __11__ légumes sont toujours très frais! Je ne mets pas __12__ oignons dans la soupe parce qu'André n'aime pas __13__ oignons. C'est dommage parce que __14__ oignons sont bons pour la santé (health).

E Entretien. Interviewez votre partenaire.

1. Quels fruits de mer aimes-tu? Quelles viandes? Est-ce que tu manges plus de fruits de mer ou plus de viande?
2. Manges-tu plus souvent des fruits ou des légumes? Quel fruit préfères-tu? Quel légume préfères-tu? Quels fruits et légumes est-ce que tu n'aimes pas? Est-ce que tu achètes plus de légumes surgelés, frais ou en conserve?

Talking about meals

LES REPAS

Note *culturelle*

La grande majorité des Français prennent le petit déjeuner tous les matins et généralement chez eux. La plupart *(Most)* des adultes boivent une boisson chaude (café, café au lait, thé ou chocolat) accompagnée d'une tartine (de beurre, confiture ou miel *[honey]*) ou d'une viennoiserie *(pastry)* (croissant, pain au chocolat). Un jeune sur quatre préfère manger des céréales avec du lait ou un yaourt. Les fruits et les jus de fruit ne sont pas très présents au petit déjeuner des Français! Dans votre région, qu'est-ce que les gens prennent le matin?

En France, le petit déjeuner est généralement un repas **léger**. On prend:

du café au lait   du thé

des tartines *(f)* ou des croissants *(m)*

du chocolat   du beurre   de la confiture

De plus en plus de Français, **surtout** les jeunes, prennent aussi des céréales le matin.

Les Américains et les Canadiens prennent souvent un petit déjeuner plus **copieux.** Ils prennent:

des œufs au bacon   des céréales *(f)*   du pain grillé   des fruits

À midi, certains Français prennent un déjeuner complet. D'autres prennent un repas rapide. Dans les cafés, les fast-foods et les self-services, on peut manger:

une soupe	une salade	une pizza
une omelette	un hamburger	un sandwich
un steak-frites		

Les gens qui prennent un repas rapide à midi mangent souvent un repas plus complet le soir. **Ceux** qui mangent un repas plus copieux à midi mangent **seulement** de la soupe, des légumes, de la charcuterie, une salade, du fromage ou une omelette comme dîner.

Line art on this page: © Cengage Learning

---

léger (légère) *light*   **une tartine** *bread with butter and jelly*   **surtout** *especially*   **copieux (copieuse)** *copious, large*
un steak-frites *steak and fries*   **Ceux (Celles)** *Those*   **seulement** *only*

Rose prépare le petit déjeuner avec sa cousine Lucie.

3-7

LUCIE: Tu as faim? Je peux te faire des œufs au bacon si tu veux – un vrai petit déjeuner à l'américaine.

ROSE: Merci, c'est gentil, mais je mange très peu le matin. **Pourtant, je prendrais bien** des céréales et du thé si tu **en** as.

LUCIE: Ah, je suis **désolée**... il **n'**y a **plus** de thé. Mais il y a du café. Tu en veux?

ROSE: Oui, je veux bien. Et toi? Qu'est-ce que tu vas prendre?

LUCIE: Le matin, **je bois** toujours du chocolat chaud et quelquefois je prends des tartines.

ROSE: Oh, regarde! **Il n'y a presque plus** de pain.

LUCIE: Mais **si**! Il y a **encore** une baguette, **là**.

Vocabulaire supplémentaire

des gaufres (f) waffles
des muffins (m) anglais
des pancakes (m)
des petites saucisses breakfast sausages
du sirop d'érable maple syrup
du porridge d'avoine oatmeal
une barre de céréales a granola bar
du pain perdu French toast

A Vrai ou faux? Est-ce que ces phrases sont vraies ou fausses?

1. En France, on prend plus souvent des œufs le soir ou à midi que le matin.
2. Les Français prennent un repas copieux le matin.
3. Beaucoup de Français prennent seulement du pain et du café le matin.
4. Certains, surtout les jeunes, aiment prendre des céréales.

B Chez nous. Aux États-Unis et au Canada, à quel(s) repas mange-t-on le plus souvent ces choses: **au petit déjeuner, au déjeuner** ou **au dîner**?

EXEMPLE une omelette
On mange plus souvent une omelette au petit déjeuner.

1. des croissants
2. des céréales
3. du poisson
4. un hamburger
5. de la soupe
6. du pain grillé
7. du saumon
8. des œufs au bacon
9. des légumes

C Comparaisons culturelles. Avec d'autres étudiant(e)s, devinez comment le plus grand nombre de Français ont répondu aux questions suivantes dans des sondages (polls). Après, faites un sondage parmi (among) les étudiants de votre classe.

1. Combien de temps prenez-vous pour le petit déjeuner tous les matins? (moins de 10 minutes / de 10 à 15 minutes / plus de 15 minutes / Je ne prends pas de petit déjeuner.)
2. Que mangez-vous au petit déjeuner? (des céréales / du pain ou des biscottes [melba toast] / des viennoiseries [pastries] / des œufs / rien)
3. Quelle est votre confiture préférée? (cerises / oranges / fraises / abricots / framboises [raspberry])
4. Qu'est-ce que vous aimez manger quand vous avez un peu faim entre les repas? (un fruit / des chips / du fromage / des biscuits [cookies, crackers] / du yaourt)

À VOUS!

Avec un(e) partenaire, relisez à haute voix la conversation entre Rose et Lucie. Ensuite, imaginez que vous passez des vacances avec un(e) ami(e) français(e). Parlez de ce que vous mangez d'habitude le matin.

iLrn You can find a list of the new words from this **Compétence** on page 343 and access the audio online.

Pourtant However   **je prendrais bien** I would gladly have   **en** some, any   **désolé(e)** sorry   **ne... plus** no more, no longer   **je bois (boire** to drink)   **Il n'y a presque plus** There is almost no more   **si** yes (in response to a question / statement in the negative)   **encore** still, again, more   **là** there

SAYING WHAT YOU EAT AND DRINK

✔ *Pour vérifier*

1. In what three instances do you use the pronoun **en**? How is **en** usually translated in English? Can you omit **en** in French as you often can its equivalent in English?

2. How do you say *to drink* in French? What is the conjugation of this verb? How do you say *I drank some coffee this morning*? *I used to drink a lot of coffee*?

Le pronom **en** *et le verbe* **boire**

Use the pronoun **en** *(some, any, of it, of them)* to replace a noun preceded by a partitive article, an expression of quantity, **un, une, des,** or a number. Although the equivalent expression may be omitted in English, **en** is always used in French.

— Tu veux un croissant?	— *Do you want a croissant?*
— Oui, j'**en** veux un.	— *Yes, I want one (of them).*

En is placed *immediately* before the verb. It goes before the infinitive if there is one. If not, it goes before the conjugated verb. In the **passé composé,** it is placed before the auxiliary verb.

— Tu prends du gâteau?
— Oui, je vais **en** prendre. / Oui, j'**en** prends. / Non, merci, j'**en** ai déjà pris.

Use **en** to replace:

* a noun preceded by **du, de la, de l', des,** or **de (d').**

— Tu veux **du café**?	— *Do you want **some coffee**?*
— Non merci, je n'**en** veux pas.	— *No thanks, I don't want **any**.*

* a noun preceded by an expression of quantity. (In this case, repeat the expression of quantity in the sentence containing **en,** unless it is negative.)

— Vous voulez un kilo **de cerises**?	— *Do you want a kilo **of cherries**?*
— Oui, j'**en** veux un kilo.	— *Yes, I want a kilo **(of them)**.*
Non, je n'**en** veux pas.	*No, I don't want **any**.*

* a noun preceded by **un, une,** or a number. (In this case, include **un, une,** or the number in the sentence containing **en,** unless it is negative.)

— Tu as mangé **une tartelette**?	— *You ate **a tart**?*
— Oui, j'**en** ai mangé une.	— *Yes, I ate one **(of them)**.*
Non, je n'**en** ai pas mangé.	*No, I didn't eat **any (of them)**.*

Here is the conjugation of **boire** *(to drink).*

BOIRE *(to drink)*	
je **bois**	nous **buvons**
tu **bois**	vous **buvez**
il/elle/on **boit**	ils/elles **boivent**

PASSÉ COMPOSÉ: j'**ai bu**
IMPARFAIT: je **buvais**

Vous avez bu du vin hier soir?	Je buvais du lait quand j'étais petit.

 A **À table.** Un(e) ami(e) vous propose les choses suivantes au petit déjeuner. Comment répondez-vous? Utilisez le pronom **en** dans vos réponses.

EXEMPLE du café
— **Tu veux du café?**
— **Non merci, je n'en veux pas. / Oui, j'en veux bien.**

🌐 **Sélection musicale.** Search the Web for the song **"Bois ton café"** by L'Affaire Louis' trio to enjoy a musical selection containing the verb **boire**.

1. du café	3. des œufs	5. des tartines
2. du thé	4. de l'eau	6. des céréales

B **Des courses.** Voici la liste de Rosalie pour les courses. Combien va-t-elle acheter de chaque chose? Utilisez le pronom **en** dans vos réponses.

EXEMPLE du sucre
Elle va en acheter un paquet.

1. des pommes
2. du bœuf
3. du lait
4. des œufs

5. du vin rouge
6. des cerises
7. du pâté
8. des céréales

un paquet de sucre
6 pommes
un kilo de bœuf
2 litres de lait
une douzaine d'œufs
une bouteille de vin rouge
500 grammes de cerises
300 grammes de pâté
une boîte de céréales

© Cengage Learning

C **Et toi?** Posez ces questions à un(e) partenaire pour savoir s'il/si elle fait attention à sa santé. Il/Elle va répondre avec le pronom **en**.

EXEMPLE —Tu manges des œufs?
—Oui, j'en mange trop / beaucoup / assez / peu.
Oui, mais je n'en mange pas assez.
Non, je n'en mange pas.

1. Tu bois de l'eau?
2. Tu manges des desserts?
3. Tu fais de l'exercice?
4. Tu manges des fruits?

5. Tu manges du poisson?
6. Tu fumes des cigarettes?
7. Tu manges des légumes?
8. Tu manges de la viande?

D **Boissons.** Complétez les phrases logiquement en utilisant le verbe **boire**.

EXEMPLE Le matin, je **bois du lait.**

1. Au petit déjeuner, les Français...
2. Au petit déjeuner, les Américains / Canadiens...
3. Le matin, je...
4. Quand j'étais jeune, le matin, je...
5. Ce matin, j'...
6. Avec un hamburger, on...
7. Dans cette région, quand il fait chaud, nous...
8. Quand j'ai très soif, je...
9. *[À un(e) autre étudiant(e)]* À une fête, qu'est-ce que tu... ?
10. *[Au professeur]* Est-ce que vous... beaucoup de café?

E **Entretien.** Interviewez votre partenaire. Utilisez le pronom **en** dans les réponses.

1. Manges-tu souvent des légumes? Est-ce que tu en as déjà mangé aujourd'hui? Manges-tu souvent de la viande rouge? En manges-tu tous les jours? Est-ce que tu vas en manger aujourd'hui ou demain?

2. Fais-tu souvent de l'exercice? Combien de fois par semaine est-ce que tu en fais?

3. Est-ce que tu bois du café? En bois-tu trop? Quand est-ce que tu en bois? Et tes amis, est-ce qu'ils en boivent souvent?

TALKING ABOUT CHOICES

<table>
<tr><td>

✔ *Pour vérifier*

1. How do you find the stem of a regular **-ir** verb? What are the endings? What is the conjugation of **grandir**? of **grossir**?

2. What auxiliary verb do you use in the **passé composé** with the verbs listed here, except with the reflexive verb **se nourrir**? How do you form the past participle? How do you say *I finished*? What is the conjugation of **-ir** verbs in the imperfect?

3. How do you pronounce an initial **s**? a single **s** between vowels? How do you pronounce double **ss**? How can you hear the difference between the singular and plural forms of **-ir** verbs in the present tense?

</td></tr>
</table>

 Grammar Tutorials

Prononcez bien! See **Module 26.**

Note *de vocabulaire*

Notice that some **-ir** verbs are based on a related adjective: (**gros →
grossir, grand → grandir**).

Les verbes en *-ir*

To conjugate regular **-ir** verbs in the present tense, drop the **-ir** and add the following endings. All **-ir** verbs presented here form the **passé composé** with **avoir,** except the reflexive verb **se nourrir.**

CHOISIR *(to choose)*	
je chois**is**	nous chois**issons**
tu chois**is**	vous chois**issez**
il/elle/on chois**it**	ils/elles chois**issent**

PASSÉ COMPOSÉ: j'**ai choisi**
IMPARFAIT: je **choisissais**

Here are some common **-ir** verbs.

choisir (de faire)	*to choose (to do)*
finir (de faire)	*to finish (doing)*
grandir	*to grow (up), to grow taller*
grossir	*to get fatter*
maigrir	*to get thinner, to slim down*
(se) nourrir	*to feed, to nourish, to nurture (oneself)*
obéir (à quelqu'un / à quelque chose)	*to obey (somebody / something)*
réfléchir (à)	*to think (about)*
réussir (à)	*to succeed (at), to pass [a test]*

PRONONCIATION

La lettre *s* et les verbes en *-ir* 🔊 3-8

To remember whether to spell words like **choisir** and **réussir** with one **s** or two, it is helpful to know the rules for pronouncing the letter **s**.

Pronounce an **s** as [s] when it is the first letter of the word, it is followed by a consonant, or it appears as a double **s** between two vowels, as in **réussir.**

$\overset{s}{s}$alade $\overset{s}{s}$eulement $\overset{s}{s}$urtout $\overset{s}{s}$teak   re$\overset{s}{s}$taurant $\overset{s}{s}$port   de$\overset{s}{s}$sert   réu$\overset{s}{s}$sir   gro$\overset{s}{s}$sir

Pronounce an **s** as [z] when it appears in liaison or as a single **s** between two vowels, as in **choisir.**

le$\overset{z}{s}$ apéritifs   me$\overset{z}{s}$ enfants   le$\overset{z}{s}$ entrées   serveu$\overset{z}{s}$e   choi$\overset{z}{s}$ir   copieu$\overset{z}{s}$e

Notice that in the present tense, an **s** sound in the ending of **-ir** verbs indicates that you are talking about more than one person.

il grandit / ils grandissent   elle finit / elles finissent   il choisit / ils choisissent

 A   Prononcez bien! D'abord, prononcez chaque paire de mots en faisant attention à la prononciation de la lettre **s.** Ensuite, prononcez un seul mot de chaque paire. Votre partenaire va dire si vous prononcez **le premier mot** ou **le deuxième mot.**

1. basse / base
2. coussin / cousin
3. croissant / croisant
4. poisson / poison

5. dessert / désert
6. il grossit / ils grossissent
7. il réussit / ils réussissent
8. il choisit / ils choisissent

Maintenant, écoutez les phrases et dites si on parle **du professeur** ou **des étudiants**.

EXEMPLE Ils réussissent toujours à comprendre.
On parle des étudiants.

B **Une histoire d'amour.** Complétez cette description de la relation de Rosalie et d'André avec la forme correcte des verbes indiqués au présent.

Rosalie est réaliste et elle répète toujours qu'on ne __1__ (se nourrir) pas d'amour et d'eau fraîche. Cependant *(However)*, elle __2__ (réfléchir) beaucoup à sa vie sentimentale et elle __3__ (réussir) à trouver le grand amour avec André. Leur amour __4__ (se nourrir) des plus petites choses, une caresse ou un mot doux *(sweet)*, et André __5__ (choisir) toujours de petits cadeaux *(gifts)* parfaits pour Rosalie. Cet amour __6__ (grandir) de jour en jour et ils __7__ (finir) par se marier. Ils ne __8__ (réfléchir) pas trop aux défauts de l'autre et ils __9__ (réussir) toujours à garder *(to keep)* leur sens de l'humour. Ils __10__ (finir) leur vie ensemble à l'âge de presque cent ans et tous les matins pendant toutes ces années, André __11__ (choisir) des roses de son jardin pour en faire un bouquet pour Rosalie.

C **Il y a cinq ans.** Demandez à votre partenaire s'il/si elle fait les choses suivantes maintenant ou s'il/si elle les faisait plutôt il y a cinq ans.

EXEMPLE réfléchir plus à ton avenir *(future)*
— **Tu réfléchis plus à ton avenir maintenant ou est-ce que tu réfléchissais plus à ton avenir il y a cinq ans?**
— **Je réfléchis plus à mon avenir maintenant.**
Je réfléchissais plus à mon avenir il y a cinq ans.

1. réfléchir plus à tes problèmes
2. réussir mieux à contrôler le stress
3. finir la journée plus tôt
4. choisir mieux tes priorités
5. te nourrir mieux
6. obéir plus aux autres

D **Un repas.** Interviewez votre partenaire avec les questions suivantes.

1. Quand tu sors dîner avec ton meilleur ami (ta meilleure amie), qui choisit le restaurant en général? Quel genre de cuisine choisissez-vous le plus souvent? Si vous buvez du vin au restaurant, choisissez-vous quelquefois un vin français?
2. Quand tu choisis un plat principal au restaurant, est-ce que tu réfléchis aux calories? Est-ce que tu finis le repas par un dessert? Et ton meilleur ami (ta meilleure amie)? Qu'est-ce que tu choisis le plus souvent comme dessert?
3. Si tu ne réussis pas à tout manger est-ce que tu demandes à emporter les restes chez toi *(ask for a doggy bag)*?

Maintenant, adaptez les questions précédentes en mettant les verbes au passé composé pour interviewer votre partenaire sur la dernière fois qu'il/elle a dîné avec son meilleur ami (sa meilleure amie) au restaurant.

VIDÉOREPRISE

Les Stagiaires

Rappel!
Amélie a tout raconté *(told)* à Céline sur sa sortie avec Matthieu. Maintenant tout le monde semble *(seems)* être au courant *(aware)* de cette sortie.

Dans l'*Épisode 8,* Amélie parle à Rachid du restaurant où elle a dîné avec Matthieu. Avant de regarder la vidéo, faites ces activités pour réviser ce que vous avez appris dans le *Chapitre 8.*

A Un grand dîner. Matthieu va préparer un grand dîner avec un groupe d'amis. Qu'est-ce qu'ils pourraient servir? Travaillez avec un(e) partenaire pour nommer autant de choses que possible pour chaque catégorie.

EXEMPLE Comme entrée, **ils pourraient servir du pâté...**

Comme entrée...   Comme légumes...   Comme boisson...

Comme plat principal...   Comme dessert...

Matthieu fait les courses pour le dîner. Dites où il va aller pour acheter chacune des choses indiquées.

EXEMPLE Il va aller à l'épicerie pour acheter un pot de confiture.

1.  2.   3.  4.

B La bonne santé. Camille fait très attention à sa santé, mais elle n'arrive pas à convaincre *(she's not able to convince)* Monsieur Vieilledent de boire moins de café et de manger moins de croissants. Répondez à ces questions en employant le pronom **en**.

EXEMPLE Camille mange beaucoup *de pâtisseries?*
Non, elle n'en mange pas beaucoup.

1. Camille mange *de la viande rouge* tous les soirs?
2. Elle fait *de l'exercice* tous les jours?
3. Elle a bu beaucoup *de vin* hier soir?
4. Monsieur Vieilledent va boire moins *de café?*
5. Il va prendre *des croissants* ce matin?

C Comparaisons culturelles. Monsieur Vieilledent dîne avec un client américain. Son client parle des différences entre les habitudes alimentaires des Américains et les habitudes alimentaires des Français. Nommez autant de choses que possible pour chaque repas ou situation.

EXEMPLE au petit déjeuner
En France, au petit déjeuner, vous mangez des tartines ou des croissants et vous buvez du café. Chez nous, on mange...

1. au petit déjeuner
2. dans un fast-food
3. pour un dîner léger
4. pour un repas traditionnel

D **À table!** Continuez à faire des comparaisons culturelles en complétant ces phrases avec la forme correcte de l'article qui convient.

Ce qu'on mange varie d'une culture à l'autre. Aux États-Unis, par exemple, on prend __1__ petit déjeuner copieux. On mange souvent __2__ œufs au bacon et __3__ pain grillé. En France, __4__ petit déjeuner est un repas léger. On boit __5__ café au lait, __6__ thé ou __7__ chocolat chaud et on mange __8__ tartines.

À midi, on peut manger dans un café où on peut prendre __9__ omelette, __10__ salade ou __11__ sandwich avec __12__ vin ou __13__ eau minérale. __14__ vins français sont très bons, mais __15__ eau minérale est très populaire aussi. On peut finir son repas avec __16__ café avec un peu __17__ sucre ou un peu __18__ lait.

E **Qu'est-ce qu'ils font?** Amélie parle à Rachid des habitudes alimentaires des gens à Technovert. Complétez ses phrases de façon logique.

    EXEMPLE Je ne veux pas grossir. Alors, je (finir) tous mes repas par un dessert.
                Je ne veux pas grossir. Alors, je **ne finis pas** tous mes repas par un dessert.

1. Céline et moi faisons attention à notre santé. Alors, nous (choisir) des plats sains.
2. Céline et son chien (maigrir) parce qu'ils marchent tous les jours.
3. Toi, tu n'aimes pas les boissons alcoolisées. Alors, tu (boire) beaucoup de bière.
4. Camille et Céline veulent rester en bonne forme. Alors, elles (boire) très rarement de la bière.
5. Monsieur Vieilledent ne fait pas attention à sa santé. Il (boire) beaucoup de café et il (choisir) toujours des croissants au petit déjeuner.
6. Tes amis et toi, vous voulez rester en forme. Alors, vous (choisir) de bien manger et vous (boire) trop de café.

F **Si…** Amélie dit ce que tous les gens de Technovert feraient s'ils avaient plus de temps libre. Qu'est-ce qu'elle dit?

    EXEMPLE Monsieur Vieilledent (voyager plus, passer plus de temps avec ses enfants)
                Si Monsieur Vieilledent avait plus de temps libre, il voyagerait plus et il passerait plus de temps avec ses enfants.

1. Matthieu (inventer des jeux vidéo, apprendre à danser)
2. Moi, je (réfléchir plus à mon avenir, sortir plus souvent)
3. Camille et Céline (faire de l'exercice, se reposer plus)
4. Christophe (dormir plus, lire plus de mangas, aller plus souvent au cinéma)
5. Rachid et moi (réussir mieux à nos cours, être moins stressés)

Access the Video *Les Stagiaires* on (iLrn).

© Cengage Learning

▶ **Épisode 8: Qu'est-ce qu'ils servent?**

AVANT LA VIDÉO

Dans cet épisode, Amélie parle du restaurant où elle est allée avec Matthieu. Avant de le regarder, citez au moins trois choses qu'on sert dans un restaurant que vous aimez bien.

APRÈS LA VIDÉO

Regardez la vidéo et déterminez ce que Matthieu et Amélie ont commandé au restaurant.

LECTURE ET COMPOSITION

LECTURE

POUR MIEUX LIRE:
Reading a poem

To appreciate a poem, it is important to read it with the right rhythm. Traditionally, French poems have verses with an even number of syllables, with regular pauses in the middle. Modern poets such as Jacques Prévert often use more irregular rhythms to create different moods. Prévert's poem *Déjeuner du matin* can be read in more than one way, creating different impressions. Do the following activity to help you read it.

Sentiments. Jacques Prévert (1900–1977), l'un des poètes les plus célèbres du vingtième siècle *(century)*, aimait parler de la vie de tous les jours dans sa poésie. Lisez les phrases suivantes du poème *Déjeuner du matin* en faisant une pause à la fin de chaque vers *(line)*. Ensuite, relisez les phrases sans pause. Pour vous, quels sentiments sont évoqués par les différentes manières de lire les vers?

l'hésitation	l'angoisse	le calme
la patience	la confusion	le désaccord
la décision	l'accord	???
l'indifférence	l'indécision	
l'impatience	la réflexion	

Il a mis
Son chapeau *(hat)* sur sa tête *(head)*

Il a fait des ronds *(rings)*
Avec la fumée *(smoke)*

Et moi, j'ai pris
Ma tête *(head)* dans ma main
Et j'ai pleuré *(cried)*

Déjeuner du matin

Jacques Prévert

Il a mis le café
Dans **la tasse**
Il a mis le lait
Dans la tasse de café
Il a mis le sucre
Dans le café au lait
Avec la petite **cuiller**
Il a tourné
Il a bu le café au lait
Et il a reposé la tasse
Sans me parler
Il a allumé
Une cigarette
Il a fait des ronds
Avec la fumée
Il a mis **les cendres**
Dans **le cendrier**
Sans me parler
Sans me regarder
Il s'est levé
Il a mis
Son **chapeau** sur sa **tête**
Il a mis
Son manteau de pluie
Parce qu'il pleuvait
Et il est parti
Sous la pluie
Sans **une parole**
Sans me regarder
Et moi j'ai pris
Ma tête dans ma main
Et **j'ai pleuré.**

© James Leynse/Corbis

Jacques Prévert, "Déjeuner du matin" in *Paroles* © Éditions GALLIMARD
© Fatras / succession Jacques Prévert pour les droits électroniques réservés.

---

la tasse *the cup*   **cuiller** *spoon*   **les cendres** *the ashes*   **le cendrier** *the ashtray*
chapeau *hat*   **tête** *head*   **une parole** *a word*   **j'ai pleuré** *I cried*

Compréhension

Qu'est-ce qui s'est passé? Qu'est-ce qui s'est passé dans le poème?

1. Faites une liste des choses qu'il a faites.
2. Nommez deux choses qu'il n'a pas faites.
3. Quelle a été la réaction de l'autre personne?
4. Qui sont ces personnages? Sont-ils amis? parents? Sont-ils mariés, divorcés... ?
5. Pourquoi est-ce qu'ils ne se parlent pas? Qu'est-ce qui s'est passé?

COMPOSITION

POUR MIEUX ÉCRIRE:
Finding the right word

You are going to write a review of a restaurant. When you write, try to use the most precise word possible to get your message across. Note how, in the following sentence, the word *small* can convey different messages.

It is a *small* restaurant with only fifteen tables.
Positive: It is a *cozy (intimate)* restaurant with only fifteen tables.
Negative: It is a *cramped (crowded)* restaurant with only fifteen tables.

To find the right word to express your meaning in French, you may need to use a synonym dictionary. Once you select a French word from an English-French dictionary, double check that you understand its use by looking it up in a French-English or French-French dictionary, or search for it on the Internet in the context in which you wish to use it.

Organisez-vous. Dans les phrases suivantes, voici quelques mots qu'on pourrait utiliser au lieu des mots en italique pour décrire un restaurant. Trouvez un mot supplémentaire pour chaque liste en cherchant dans un dictionnaire de synonymes sur Internet ou à la bibliothèque.

Le décor est *joli* (beau, charmant, harmonieux, pittoresque, ???).
Le décor est *laid* (atroce, hideux, grotesque, vulgaire, ???).
Le menu est *intéressant* (exotique, varié, extraordinaire, sensationnel, phénoménal, ???).
Le menu est *ennuyeux* (médiocre, ordinaire, limité, commun, insuffisant, banal, ???).
La cuisine est *bonne* (délicieuse, appétissante, savoureuse, délectable, exquise, succulente, ???).
La cuisine est *mauvaise* (insipide, déplorable, révoltante, fade, désastreuse, ???).
L'ambiance est *agréable* (sympathique, chaleureuse, intime, charmante, confortable, ???).
L'ambiance est *désagréable* (déplaisante, inhospitalière, froide, ???).
Le service est *bon* (rapide, animé, enthousiaste, immédiat, plaisant, gracieux, ???).
Le service est *mauvais* (lent, impoli, hostile, inconsistant, honteux, exaspérant, ???).

Une critique gastronomique

Écrivez une critique gastronomique d'un restaurant de votre ville. Parlez du décor, du menu, de la cuisine, de l'ambiance et du service.

iLrn Share It!

À TABLE!

Ce qui est considéré «normal» ou **«poli»** diffère souvent d'une culture à l'autre. Chaque société a ses **propres coutumes,** ses plats préférés, et même sa propre **façon** de manger.

Par exemple, lorsqu'on est invité chez des Français, pour **éviter de venir les mains vides,** on offre généralement un bouquet de fleurs (mais pas de chrysanthèmes, qui sont des fleurs de cimetières en France) ou des chocolats. Il est préférable d'éviter d'**apporter** un dessert ou une bouteille de vin, **car** cela voudrait dire que votre hôte ou hôtesse a oublié ou les a peut-être mal choisis!

À table, **on garde** toujours les deux mains sur la table, mais on ne met pas **les coudes** sur la table. **Après avoir coupé** la viande, on garde sa **fourchette** dans la main gauche. On ne boit jamais de lait avec les repas comme le font certains Américains et le café est servi à la fin du repas, après le dessert. De nombreux restaurants et cafés acceptent que leurs clients viennent en compagnie de leur chien, du moment qu'il **se comporte** correctement.

Regardez ces photos. Qu'est-ce que vous **remarquez**?

---

poli *polite*   **propres coutumes** *own customs*   **façon** *way, manner*   **éviter de venir les mains vides** *to avoid coming empty-handed*   **apporter** *to bring, bringing*   **car** *because*   **on garde** *one keeps*   **les coudes** *elbows*   **Après avoir coupé** *After cutting*   **fourchette** *fork*   **se comporte** *behaves*   **remarquez** *notice*

Lisez ces phrases concernant les coutumes et les bonnes manières. Lesquelles sont vraies dans votre région? Et en France?

	CHEZ NOUS	EN FRANCE
1. On boit quelquefois du lait aux repas.	☐	☐
2. On mange souvent des œufs le matin.	☐	☐
3. On mange plus souvent des œufs le soir ou à midi.	☐	☐
4. On mange assez souvent dans des fast-foods.	☐	☐
5. La présentation est presque aussi importante que la saveur *(taste)* d'un plat.	☐	☐
6. Le pain est presque indispensable à tous les repas.	☐	☐
7. Le pain se mange généralement sans beurre, sauf le matin.	☐	☐
8. On fait assez souvent les courses chez les petits commerçants.	☐	☐
9. On mange beaucoup de choses avec les mains.	☐	☐
10. On mange très peu de choses avec les mains et certains mangent même les fruits avec un couteau et une fourchette.	☐	☐
11. Quand on mange, on garde toujours les deux mains sur la table.	☐	☐
12. On met le pain directement sur la table, pas sur l'assiette *(plate)*.	☐	☐
13. Au restaurant, on peut commander à la carte ou on peut choisir un menu à prix fixe.	☐	☐
14. La carte est toujours affichée *(posted)* à l'extérieur d'un restaurant.	☐	☐

Pour la France – Vrai: 3, 4, 5, 6, 7, 8, 10, 11, 12, 13, 14

Compréhension

1. Quelles différences est-ce qu'il y a entre ce qu'on fait chez vous et ce qu'on fait en France? Quelles ressemblances?
2. Les opinions des Français ne sont pas toujours reflétées *(reflected)* dans leur vie de tous les jours. Comment pouvez-vous expliquer ce contraste entre ce que les Français pensent et ce qu'ils font?

iLrn Share It!

Visit **www.cengagebrain.com** for additional cultural information and activities.

Opinions	Actions
Manger, c'est un art et un plaisir et les qualités esthétiques d'un plat *(dish)* (son apparence, sa présentation, sa fraîcheur,…) sont presque aussi importantes que sa saveur *(taste)*.	Aujourd'hui, les Français se contentent de menus plus simples et passent moins de temps à table. On passe de moins en moins de temps à préparer les repas en se servant *(using)* de produits tout prêts, de produits surgelés et du four à micro-ondes *(microwave)*.
Les repas sont un moment pour se retrouver en famille ou entre amis et pour apprécier la bonne cuisine.	Les repas sont pris moins souvent en famille et plus souvent devant la télé.
Le service et la qualité sont meilleurs chez les petits commerçants que dans les grandes surfaces.	On fait de plus en plus souvent les courses dans les grandes surfaces.

RÉSUMÉ DE GRAMMAIRE

Je vais acheter **de l'**eau, **du** pain, **de la** crème et **des** légumes.

I'm going to buy (some) water, (some) bread, (some) cream and (some) vegetables.

— Je vais prendre **un** sandwich et **des** frites.
— Je **ne** prends **pas de** frites parce qu'elles ont **trop de** calories.

— Tu **n'**aimes **pas les** frites?
— Mais si, j'aime **beaucoup les** frites, mais **le** riz est meilleur pour **la** santé.
— Mais **les** frites qu'ils servent ici sont délicieuses.

Le matin, je **bois** du thé mais mon mari **boit** du café. À midi, nous **buvons** de l'eau.
Qu'est-ce que tu **as bu** ce matin?
Qu'est-ce qu tu **buvais** quand tu étais petit?

Les étudiants **réussissent** bien au cours. Tu **réussis** à tes cours?
J'**ai fini** mes devoirs.
Je ne **réfléchissais** pas beaucoup à mon avenir *(future)* quand j'étais jeune.

— Tu veux **de l'**eau?
— Oui, j'**en** veux bien.
Non merci, je n'**en** veux pas.

— Tu prends un **sandwich**?
— Oui, j'**en** prends **un**.
Non, j'**en** prends **deux**.
Non, je n'**en** prends pas.

— Tu as acheté un kilo **de carottes**?
— Oui, j'**en** ai acheté **un kilo**.
Non, j'**en** ai acheté **une livre**.
Non, je n'**en** ai pas acheté.

THE PARTITIVE AND REVIEW OF ARTICLE USE

In French, use the partitive to convey the idea of *some* or *any*, even when *some* or *any* can be omitted in English.

MASCULINE SINGULAR BEFORE A CONSONANT SOUND	FEMININE SINGULAR BEFORE A CONSONANT SOUND	SINGULAR BEFORE A VOWEL SOUND	PLURAL
du pain	de la glace	de l'eau	des fruits

Un and **une** mean *a* and **du, de la, de l'**, and **des** express the idea of *some* or *any*. All of these forms change to **de (d')** after most negated verbs and after expressions of quantity. (See page 318 for a list of quantity expressions.)

Use the definite article (**le, la, l', les**) to say *the,* to express likes, dislikes, and preferences, or to make statements about entire categories. The definite article does *not* change to **de** after a negative or quantity expression.

THE VERB *BOIRE* AND REGULAR *-IR* VERBS

The verb **boire** *(to drink)* is irregular.

BOIRE *(to drink)*	
je **bois**	nous **buvons**
tu **bois**	vous **buvez**
il/elle/on **boit**	ils/elles **boivent**

PASSÉ COMPOSÉ: **j'ai bu**
IMPARFAIT: **je buvais**

The stem for the present tense of regular **-ir** verbs is obtained by dropping the **-ir.** Add the following endings for the present tense.

RÉUSSIR *(to succeed)*	
je réuss**is**	nous réuss**issons**
tu réuss**is**	vous réuss**issez**
il/elle/on réuss**it**	ils/elles réuss**issent**

PASSÉ COMPOSÉ: **j'ai réussi**
IMPARFAIT: **je réussissais**

See page 326 for a list of common **-ir** verbs. All **-ir** verbs presented in this chapter form the **passé composé** with **avoir**, except the reflexive verb **se nourrir**.

THE PRONOUN *EN*

En replaces a noun preceded by a partitive article, an expression of quantity, **un, une,** or a number. When replacing a noun preceded by **un, une,** a number, or an expression of quantity, repeat the **un, une,** number, or expression of quantity in the sentence containing **en**, unless it's negative. In English, **en** is usually translated by *some, any, of it,* or *of them.* Although the equivalent expression may be omitted in English, **en** is always used in French.

VOCABULAIRE

 Audio Flashcards

COMPÉTENCE 1

Ordering at a restaurant

NOMS MASCULINS

un apéritif	a before-dinner drink
un dessert	a dessert
un fruit	a fruit
des fruits de mer	shellfish, crustaceans
*des haricots (verts)	(green) beans
*un hors-d'œuvre	an hors d'œuvre, an appetizer
du lait	milk
des légumes	vegetables
un menu à prix fixe	a set-price menu
du pain	bread
un pavé (de)	a thick slice (of)
des petits pois	peas
le plat (principal)	the (main) dish
du poisson (fumé)	(smoked) fish
du poivre	pepper
un repas	a meal
du riz	rice
du sel	salt
du sucre	sugar

NOMS FÉMININS

une bouteille (de)	a bottle (of)
une carafe (de)	a carafe (of)
la carte	the menu
de la crème	cream
une entrée	a first course
une pomme	an apple
une pomme de terre	a potato
de la raie	rayfish, skate
une salade	a salad
de la viande	meat
de la volaille	poultry

DIVERS

Aimeriez-vous... ?	Would you like ... ?
comme	for, as (a)
comprendre	to include
décider	to decide
du, de la, de l', des	some, any
finir	to finish
fumé(e)	smoked
généralement	generally
servir	to serve
traditionnel(le)	traditional

Pour les noms des différentes sortes d'entrées, voir la page 304.
Pour les noms des différentes sortes de viandes, de volailles, de poissons et de fruits de mer, voir la page 304.
Pour voir les différentes possibilités pour finir un repas, voir la page 305.

COMPÉTENCE 2

Buying food

NOMS MASCULINS

du bœuf	beef
un choix	a choice
un commerçant	a shopkeeper
un marché	a market
un oignon	an onion
un pain au chocolat	a chocolate-filled croissant
un pain complet	a loaf of whole-grain bread
un plat préparé	a ready-to-serve dish
du porc	pork
un produit	a product
du raisin	grapes
du saucisson	salami
le service personnalisé	personal service
un supermarché	a supermarket

NOMS FÉMININS

une baguette	a loaf of French bread
une banane	a banana
la boucherie	the butcher's shop
la boulangerie-pâtisserie	the bakery-pastry shop
une calorie	a calorie
une carotte	a carrot
une cerise	a cherry
la charcuterie	the deli
de la charcuterie	deli meats, cold cuts
une commerçante	a shopkeeper
des conserves	canned goods
l'épicerie	the grocery store
une fraise	a strawberry
une grande surface	a superstore
une laitue	a head of lettuce
une orange	an orange
une pâtisserie	a pastry
une pêche	a peach
une poire	a pear
la poissonnerie	the fish market
des saucisses	sausages
une tartelette (aux fraises / aux cerises)	a (strawberry / cherry) tart

DIVERS

C'est tout.	That's all.
de plus en plus (de)	more and more (of)
dire	to say, to tell
frais (fraîche)	fresh
il faut	it is necessary, one needs, one must
Qu'est-ce que je peux vous proposer d'autre?	What else can I get you?
Qu'est-ce qu'il vous faut?	What do you need?
surgelé(e)	frozen

Pour les expressions de quantité, voir la page 318.

Talking about meals

NOMS MASCULINS

du bacon	*bacon*
du beurre	*butter*
du chocolat	*chocolate*
un croissant	*a croissant*
le déjeuner	*lunch*
le dîner	*dinner*
*un hamburger	*a hamburger*
du pain grillé	*toast*
un self-service	*a self-service restaurant*
un steak-frites	*a steak and fries*

NOMS FÉMININS

des céréales	*cereal*
de la confiture	*jelly*
une omelette	*an omelet*
une pizza	*a pizza*
une tartine	*bread with butter and jelly*

EXPRESSIONS VERBALES

boire	*to drink*
choisir (de faire)	*to choose (to do)*
finir (de faire)	*to finish (doing)*
grandir	*to grow, to grow up, to get taller*
grossir	*to get fatter*
maigrir	*to get thinner, to slim down*
(se) nourrir	*to feed, to nourish, to nurture (oneself)*
obéir (à)	*to obey*
réfléchir (à)	*to think (about)*
réussir (à)	*to succeed (at, in), to pass [a test]*

DIVERS

à l'américaine	*American-style*
certains	*some (people)*
ceux (celles)	*those*
complet (complète)	*complete*
copieux (copieuse)	*copious, large*
désolé(e)	*sorry*
en	*some, any, of it, of them*
encore	*still, again, more*
grillé(e)	*toasted, grilled*
je prendrais	*I would have, I would take*
là	*there*
léger (légère)	*light*
ne... plus	*no more, no longer*
pourtant	*however*
rapide	*rapid, fast, quick*
seulement	*only*
si	*yes (in response to a question or statement in the negative)*
surtout	*especially*
vrai(e)	*true*

Choosing a healthy lifestyle

NOMS MASCULINS

l'alcool	*alcohol*
des conseils	*advice*
des produits bio	*organic products*
le stress	*stress*
le tabac	*tobacco*

NOMS FÉMININS

des matières grasses	*fats*
la santé	*health*
des vitamines	*vitamins*

EXPRESSIONS VERBALES

contrôler	*to control*
éviter	*to avoid*
faire attention (à)	*to pay attention (to), to watch out (for)*
faire de l'aérobic	*to do aerobics*
faire de la méditation	*to meditate*
faire de la muscu(lation)	*to do weight training, to do bodybuilding*
faire du yoga	*to do yoga*
faire mieux (de)	*to do better (to)*
marcher	*to walk*
on devrait	*one should*
oublier	*to forget*
se sentir	*to feel*

DIVERS

à votre avis	*in your opinion*
content(e)	*content, happy*
en forme	*in shape*
fort(e)	*strong*
lentement	*slowly*
plusieurs	*several*
régulièrement	*regularly*
sain(e)	*healthy*
sans doute	*without doubt, doubtlessly*

Née en banlieue parisienne, Chimène Badi a grandi en Aquitaine, dans le sud-ouest *(southwest)* de la France.

🌐 You can find these songs on iTunes. You can also search the Internet for videos to hear them performed and to find the lyrics.

RETOMBER AMOUREUX

CHIMÈNE BADI

Chimène Badi chante du *rhythm and blues.* Elle est connue pour sa voix puissante *(known for her powerful voice).* Dans ***Retomber amoureux,*** elle chante la joie de retomber amoureux de quelqu'un qu'on avait cessé *(had ceased)* d'aimer. Faites l'activité qui suit pour comprendre plus facilement les paroles *(lyrics).*

Retomber amoureux. Pour mieux comprendre cette chanson, lisez les phrases suivantes. Indiquez si chacune d'elles s'applique à...

a. quand ils ne s'aimaient plus

ou

b. quand ils sont retombés amoureux

_____ On ne se parlait plus.

_____ On ne se faisait plus de dîners aux chandelles *(candlelight).*

_____ On était heureux d'être heureux.

_____ On ne se plaisait *(didn't please each other)* plus.

_____ On ne se parlait plus des prénoms possibles pour les enfants.

_____ Tout a recommencé.

_____ On ne se prenait pas pour Adam et Ève.

_____ On ne croquait *(didn't bite into)* plus dans le même pain.

_____ On s'est dit «on se quitte».

_____ On s'est dit de nouveau «je t'aime».

_____ On ne s'est plus jamais quittés.

_____ On était heureux d'être deux, différents mais toujours les mêmes.

POUR TOI

PRINCESS SARAH

Dans la chanson ***Pour toi,*** Princess Sarah regrette *(misses)* un amour perdu. Elle parle de ce qu'elle aurait dû faire *(what she should have done)* pour garder *(to keep)* cet amour et de ce qu'elle ferait si son amour revenait. Faites l'activité qui suit pour comprendre plus facilement les paroles *(lyrics).*

Princess Sarah s'est fait connaître d'abord *(first made herself known)* par Internet.

Pour toi. Imaginez que vous voulez qu'un ancien amour *(a former love)* revienne. Est-ce que vous feriez ou ne feriez pas les choses suivantes? Faites des phrases au conditionnel.

Si tu revenais, je...
rester à tes côtés *(by your side)*
prendre le temps de te comprendre
être prêt(e) à aimer
gâcher *(to spoil)* notre amour
te donner la terre entière *(give you the whole world)*
t'oublier *(forget you)*
faire tout pour toi

Aux Antilles
En vacances

iLrn iLrn Heinle Learning Center

www.cengagebrain.com

▶ *Horizons* Video: Les Stagiaires

🔊 Audio

Internet web search

Pair work

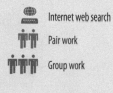

Group work

© Franck Guéziou/Getty Images

9

COMPÉTENCE

1 Talking about vacation
Les vacances

Talking about how things will be
Le futur

Stratégies et Lecture
- **Pour mieux lire:** *Recognizing compound tenses*
- **Lecture:** *Quelle aventure!*

2 Preparing for a trip
Les préparatifs

Communicating with people
*Les verbes **dire**, **lire** et **écrire***

Avoiding repetition
*Les pronoms compléments d'objet indirect **(lui, leur)** et reprise des pronoms compléments d'objet direct **(le, la, l', les)***

3 Buying your ticket
À l'agence de voyages

Saying what people know
*Les verbes **savoir** et **connaître***

Indicating who does what to whom
*Les pronoms **me, te, nous** et **vous***

4 Deciding where to go on a trip
Un voyage

Saying where you are going
Les expressions géographiques

Vidéoreprise *Les Stagiaires*

Lecture et Composition
- **Pour mieux lire:** *Understanding words with multiple meanings*
- **Lecture:** *Ma grand-mère m'a appris à ne pas compter sur les yeux des autres pour dormir*
- **Pour mieux écrire:** *Revising what you write*
- **Composition:** *Un itinéraire*

Comparaisons culturelles *La culture créole aux Antilles*

Résumé de grammaire

Vocabulaire

LA FRANCE D'OUTRE-MER

Saviez-vous qu'on peut visiter la France **sans jamais** aller en Europe? que la France partage **une frontière** avec le Brésil? que la France **possède** une partie du continent antarctique?

En effet, la République française **comprend:**

- la France métropolitaine (la France en Europe plus l'île de Corse)
- cinq départements d'outre-mer (les DOM)
- plusieurs collectivités d'outre-mer (les COM)

La Guadeloupe et la Martinique sont les deux plus grandes îles françaises aux Caraïbes. Leur beauté naturelle **attire un grand nombre** de touristes.

- la Nouvelle-Calédonie
- les **Terres australes** et antarctiques françaises et l'île de Clipperton

Les cinq DOM – la Guadeloupe, la Martinique, la Guyane, La Réunion et Mayotte – **font partie de** la France **tout comme** Hawaii fait partie des États-Unis.

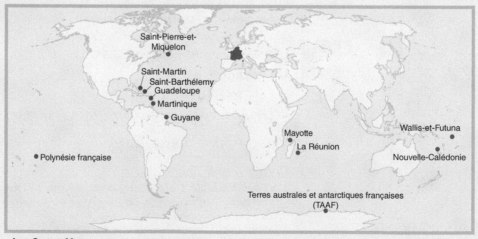

Les Outre-Mer

---

d'outre-mer *overseas*   **Saviez-vous** *Did you know*   **sans jamais** *without ever*   **une frontière** *a border*   **possède** *possesses*
En effet *In fact*   **comprend** *includes*   **Terres australes** *Southern Lands*   **font partie de** *are part of*
tout comme *just as*   **attire** *attracts*

La Guyane est caractérisée par sa biodiversité. Le tourisme vert s'y développe, mais l'économie se base surtout sur l'industrie spatiale.

Les collectivités d'outre-mer – la Polynésie française, Wallis-et-Futuna, Saint-Pierre-et-Miquelon, Saint-Barthélemy et Saint-Martin – sont comparables aux territoires américains de Puerto Rico et Guam.

L'ancien territoire de la Nouvelle-Calédonie est maintenant une collectivité presque **autonome** et ses **citoyens** vont bientôt voter sur l'indépendance.

La Réunion est le département français d'outre-mer **le plus peuplé**, avec une société multiethnique.

La Guadeloupe

Visit it live on Google Earth!

NOMBRE D'HABITANTS:
466 000 (les Guadeloupéens)

CHEF-LIEU *(ADMINISTRATIVE CENTER)*: **Basse-Terre**

La Martinique

NOMBRE D'HABITANTS:
409 000 (les Martiniquais)

CHEF-LIEU: **Fort-de-France**

Le savez-vous?

Quelles régions de la République française voudriez-vous visiter? Servez-vous de la carte *(map)*, des photos et des renseignements donnés sur ces pages pour compléter les phrases qui suivent.

> **Nouvelle-Calédonie   Guyane   Réunion collectivités d'outre-mer   Guadeloupe départements d'outre-mer   Martinique**

1. Les _____ font partie de la France, tout comme Hawaii fait partie des États-Unis. Les _____ sont comparables aux territoires américains de Puerto Rico et Guam.

2. La _____ et la _____ sont deux îles dans la mer des Caraïbes. La majorité des habitants de ces deux départements sont des descendants d'esclaves africains amenés *(African slaves brought)* dans ces îles pour travailler dans les plantations.

3. La _____, en Amérique du Sud, est connue *(known)* pour sa beauté naturelle et pour sa base du programme spatial français.

4. La _____ est située dans l'océan Indien près de Madagascar. C'est le département d'outre-mer le plus peuplé, avec une société multiethnique: des Africains, des Européens, des Indiens, des Chinois et des Malgaches *(inhabitants of Madagascar)*.

5. Les habitants de la _____ vont bientôt voter sur l'indépendance.

Connaissez-vous bien la France d'outre-mer? Regardez la liste des départements d'outre-mer et des collectivités d'outre-mer de la France. Choisissez une des régions nommées et faites des recherches sur Internet pour trouver des informations à son sujet. Préparez une présentation sur un aspect de cette région que vous trouvez intéressant.

---

se base surtout sur *is largely based on*   **L'ancien** *The former*   **autonome** *autonomous*   **citoyens** *citizens*
le plus peuplé *the most populous*

Talking about vacation

LES VACANCES

Note *culturelle*

En vacances, les Français aiment le plus souvent visiter d'autres régions de France où ils préfèrent aller (par ordre de préférence) à la mer, à la campagne, en ville ou à la montagne. Et vous? Où aimez-vous partir en vacances?

In the **Culture Modules** in the video library, see **Work**.

Note *de grammaire*

The verb **courir** is irregular: **je cours, tu cours, il/elle/on court, nous courons, vous courez, ils/elles courent.** Passé composé: **j'ai couru;** Imparfait: **je courais;** Conditionnel: **je courrais.**

Vocabulaire supplémentaire

faire de la plongée avec masque et tuba *to go snorkeling*
faire de la plongée sous-marine *to go scuba diving*
faire de la planche à voile *to go windsurfing*
faire du wakeboard *to go wakeboarding*

Sélection musicale. Search the Web for the song "**Tes vacances avec moi**" by Sonia Dersion from Martinique to enjoy a musical selection related to this vocabulary.

Lucas, un jeune Parisien, va passer ses vacances en Guadeloupe. Et vous? Où aimez-vous passer vos vacances?

dans un pays (payse) étranger ou exotique

sur une île tropicale ou **à la mer**

dans une grande ville

à la montagne

Qu'est-ce qu'on peut faire dans chaque **endroit**?

admirer **les paysage**s *(m)*

visiter des sites *(m)* historiques et touristiques (touristy)

profiter des activités culturelles (aller à l'opéra, au ballet...)

bronzer ou **courir** sur la plage

goûter la cuisine locale **assis** à la terrasse d'un restaurant

faire des randonnées

Lucas parle à son ami Alex de ses prochaines vacances en Guadeloupe.

3-12

LUCAS: Je vais bientôt partir en vacances.
ALEX: Et tu vas où?
LUCAS: Je vais en Guadeloupe.
ALEX: En Guadeloupe? Quelle chance! Tu pars quand?
LUCAS: Je pars le 20 juillet et je **compte** y passer trois semaines.
ALEX: Génial! J'espère que **ça te plaira**!

à la mer *at the coast, by the sea*   **un endroit** *a place*   **les paysages** *(m) the scenery, the landscape*   **bronzer** *to tan*
courir *to run*   **goûter** *to taste*   **assis(e)** *seated*   **compter** *to plan on, to count on*   **ça te plaira** *you'll like it*

A **Activités.** Lesquelles des activités nommées fait-on normalement à l'endroit indiqué?

EXEMPLE dans une grande ville: faire du shopping / faire des randonnées / profiter des activités culturelles
Dans une grande ville, on fait du shopping et on profite des activités culturelles. On ne fait pas de randonnées.

1. sur une île tropicale: manger beaucoup de fruits de mer / courir sur la plage / faire du snowboard
2. à la montagne: profiter des activités culturelles / faire des randonnées / admirer les paysages
3. dans un pays étranger: visiter des sites historiques et touristiques / goûter la cuisine locale / voyager sans passeport
4. à la mer: faire du ski / bronzer / nager

B **Que feriez-vous?** Imaginez où vous iriez et ce que vous feriez si vous aviez assez d'argent pour faire un beau voyage. Choisissez une des destinations données et indiquez trois choses que vous y feriez.

> à la montagne   à la campagne   dans un pays étranger
> sur une île tropicale   dans une grande ville   chez moi

EXEMPLE Si j'avais assez d'argent, je passerais mes vacances **sur une île tropicale** où **je bronzerais, je nagerais et je prendrais beaucoup de photos.**

Au parc national de la Guadeloupe, on peut profiter de tous les loisirs de la nature: randonnées, promenades, VTT...

Maintenant, circulez dans la classe et demandez à plusieurs personnes où elles iraient et ce qu'elles feraient si elles pouvaient faire un beau voyage.

EXEMPLE —**Si tu pouvais faire un beau voyage, où passerais-tu tes vacances et qu'est-ce que tu ferais?**
—**Je passerais mes vacances sur une île tropicale où je bronzerais, je nagerais et je prendrais beaucoup de photos. Et toi?**
—**Moi, je...**

Après, dites à la classe ce que vous avez appris.

EXEMPLE **Clarence passerait ses vacances sur une île tropicale où il...**

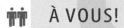 **C** **Entretien.** Interviewez votre partenaire.

1. Préférerais-tu visiter une île tropicale ou visiter une grande ville? aller à la mer ou à la montagne? faire une randonnée ou faire du ski? faire de l'exercice à l'hôtel ou courir sur la plage? bronzer ou nager?
2. Où est-ce que tu aimerais passer tes prochaines vacances? Qu'est-ce qu'on peut faire dans cette région? Où est-ce que tu as passé tes meilleures vacances? Pourquoi as-tu trouvé ces vacances agréables? Qu'est-ce que tu as fait?

À VOUS!

Avec un(e) partenaire, relisez à haute voix la conversation entre Lucas et Alex. Ensuite, imaginez que vous allez faire le voyage de vos rêves *(dreams)* et changez la conversation pour dire où vous allez, avec qui, quand et combien de temps vous comptez rester.

iLrn You can find a list of the new words from this *Compétence* on page 380 and access the audio online.

TALKING ABOUT HOW THINGS WILL BE

Le futur

You have used **aller** + *infinitive* to say what someone *is going* to do. You can use the future tense to say what someone *will* do. Form the future tense by adding the boldfaced endings below to the same stem you use for the conditional.

PARLER	ÊTRE	VENIR
je parler**ai**	je ser**ai**	je viendr**ai**
tu parler**as**	tu ser**as**	tu viendr**as**
il/elle/on parler**a**	il/elle/on ser**a**	il/elle/on viendr**a**
nous parler**ons**	nous ser**ons**	nous viendr**ons**
vous parler**ez**	vous ser**ez**	vous viendr**ez**
ils/elles parler**ont**	ils/elles ser**ont**	ils/elles viendr**ont**

The future is generally used in French as it is in English. However, one difference is its use in clauses with **quand** referring to the future. English has the present in such clauses.

> **quand** + future → future

Quand j'**arriverai** en Guadeloupe, je **prendrai** un taxi à l'hôtel.
*When I **arrive** in Guadeloupe, I'll take a taxi to the hotel.*

As in English, use the future tense to say what will happen if another event occurs. Use the present tense in the clause with **si.**

> **si** + present → future

Si je **peux** visiter la Martinique, je **serai** vraiment content!
*If I **can** visit Martinique, I **will be** really happy!*

✔ **Pour vérifier**

1. What do most verbs have as the stem in the future tense? Which verbs have irregular stems? What other verb form has the same stem as the future?

2. What endings do you use to form the future tense in French?

3. In French, what verb tense is used in clauses with **quand** referring to the future? How do you say *When I finish, I'll go home?*

ⓘⓛⓡⓝ **Grammar Tutorials**

Note *de grammaire*

The future/conditional stem always ends with **-r.** Do you remember these irregular ones?

aller	ir-
avoir	aur-
être	ser-
faire	fer-
devoir	devr-
vouloir	voudr-
venir	viendr-
revenir	reviendr-
devenir	deviendr-
voir	verr-
envoyer	enverr-
pouvoir	pourr-
mourir	mourr-
courir	courr-

Note these forms in the future:

il y a	il y aura
il faut	il faudra
il pleut	il pleuvra
c'est	ce sera

As in the conditional, verbs like **se lever, payer,** and **appeler** have spelling changes in *all* forms of the future (**je me lèverai, je paierai, j'appellerai**). Those like **préférer** do not (**je préférerai**).

Note *de prononciation*

As in the conditional forms, an unaccented **e** is usually not pronounced in future tense forms if you can drop it without bringing together three pronounced consonants (**j'habiterai, nous inviterons**).

🌐 **Sélection musicale.** Search the Web for the song **"Mon île"** by Sonia Dersion to enjoy a musical selection illustrating the use of this structure.

A **Boule de cristal.** **Vous pouvez voir l'avenir** *(the future)* **dans une boule de cristal. Comment sera la vie des personnes suivantes dans cinq ans?**

EXEMPLE Moi, je... (être riche)
Je serai riche. / Je ne serai pas riche.

1. Moi, je (j')...
   habiter ici
   avoir mon diplôme
   devoir travailler
   aller souvent en France

2. Mon meilleur ami
   (Ma meilleure amie)...
   venir souvent me voir
   réussir dans la vie
   sortir souvent avec moi
   faire souvent des voyages

3. La personne de mes rêves
et moi, nous...
se marier
avoir des enfants
acheter une maison
faire beaucoup de voyages
ensemble

4. Tous les membres de ma famille...
s'entendre bien
se rendre souvent visite
se voir souvent
voyager souvent ensemble

5. *[à un(e) autre étudiant(e)]*
Toi, tu...
finir tes études
trouver un bon travail
apprendre beaucoup
avoir beaucoup de problèmes

6. *[au professeur]*
avoir toujours cours à 7 heures du matin
pouvoir prendre votre retraite *(retirement)*
Vous... travailler toujours *(still)* ici
être heureux (heureuse)

B **Je... quand...** Lucas parle à un ami avant de partir en Guadeloupe. Complétez la phrase suivante en mettant les deux actions dans l'ordre logique. Mettez les deux verbes au futur.

Je... quand...

EXEMPLE partir en vacances / pouvoir se reposer
Je pourrai me reposer quand je partirai en vacances.

1. aller en Guadeloupe / être dans l'avion pendant onze heures
2. arriver / envoyer des textos à mes amis
3. s'amuser / être en Guadeloupe
4. faire des excursions / ne pas être à la plage
5. visiter les sites touristiques / voir des choses intéressantes
6. aller voir le volcan la Soufrière / prendre beaucoup de photos
7. écrire un blog de voyage sur ma page Internet / rentrer à l'hôtel chaque soir
8. faire le blog / mettre mes photos sur Facebook

C **Si...** Complétez logiquement ces phrases.

EXEMPLE S'il pleut ce week-end, je **resterai à la maison.**

1. S'il fait beau ce week-end, je (j')...
2. S'il fait mauvais ce week-end, je (j')...
3. Si je sors avec des amis ce week-end, on...
4. Si je peux partir en vacances cette année, je (j')...
5. Si un jour je peux visiter la France, je (j')...
6. Si mes amis et moi décidons de visiter une autre ville, nous...

D **Entretien.** Pensez à un voyage (réel ou imaginaire) que vous ferez pendant les prochaines vacances. Votre partenaire vous posera des questions au sujet de ce voyage. Après, changez de rôles.

1. Où iras-tu? Comment est-ce que tu voyageras?
2. Quand est-ce que tu partiras? Quand est-ce que tu reviendras?
3. Qui fera le voyage avec toi? Quels vêtements est-ce que vous devrez emporter?
4. Où descendrez-vous?
5. Qu'est-ce que vous ferez pendant le voyage? Qu'est-ce que vous verrez d'intéressant? Quels sites touristiques est-ce que vous visiterez?

Visiterez-vous la Martinique ou la Guadeloupe un jour?

© Frank Heuer/laif/Redux

POUR MIEUX LIRE: Recognizing compound tenses

French has other compound tenses, like the **passé composé,** which are formed with the auxiliary verb **avoir** or **être** and a past participle (**dansé, mangé, vu,** etc.). To translate these tenses, change the auxiliary verb *have* in English to the same tense as in French (imperfect, future, conditional): *They had (will have, would have) arrived.*

In the **passé composé,** where the auxiliary verb is in the *present* tense, translate it as the simple past or as *has/have + past participle.*

J'**ai** commencé.   Elle **est** rentrée.
*I began. / I **have** begun.*   *She returned. / She **has** returned.*

If the auxiliary verb is in the *imperfect,* translate it as *had + past participle.*

J'**avais** déjà commencé.   Il **n'était pas** encore rentré.
*I **had** already begun.*   *He **hadn't** returned yet.*

If the auxiliary verb is in the *conditional,* translate it as *would have + past participle.*

J'**aurais** déjà commencé.   Nous **ne serions pas** encore rentrés.
*I **would have** already begun.*   *We **wouldn't have** returned yet.*

If it is in the *future,* translate it as *will have + past participle.*

J'**aurai** déjà commencé.   Tu **ne seras pas** encore rentré(e).
*I **will have** already begun.*   *You **will not have** returned yet.*

Note *de grammaire*

Note the names of these compound tenses.

plus-que-parfait: auxiliary verb in the *imperfect* + past participle
J'avais fini. *I had finished.*

conditionnel passé: auxiliary verb in the *conditional* + past participle
J'aurais fini. *I would have finished.*

futur antérieur: auxiliary verb in the *future* + past participle
J'aurai fini. *I will have finished.*

A **Et vous?** Traduisez les phrases suivantes en anglais.

1. J'ai déjà visité la Guadeloupe.
2. L'année dernière, j'y suis resté un mois.
3. Avant de partir en vacances, j'avais réservé une chambre d'hôtel.
4. J'ai visité la Martinique aussi. J'y étais déjà allé(e) deux fois avant.
5. Si j'avais eu assez d'argent, j'aurais passé mes vacances en Europe.
6. Mes vacances auraient été plus agréables s'il n'avait pas plu tout le temps.
7. Après ce voyage, j'aurai visité la Martinique trois fois.
8. J'aurai fini quatre semestres de français avant d'y aller.

B **Le temps des verbes.** Dans le texte qui suit, traduisez tous les verbes *en italique.*

Lecture: *Quelle aventure!*

🔊
3-13
Lucas, un jeune Parisien qui passe ses vacances en Guadeloupe, raconte ses aventures dans un mail à son ami Alex.

Salut Alex,

Je passe des vacances formidables ici en Guadeloupe! *Je t'aurais écrit* plus tôt si *je n'avais pas été* si occupé. Ici, tout est à mon goût… la cuisine, le paysage, les femmes! En fait, j'ai rencontré une jeune Guadeloupéenne très sympa. Elle s'appelle Anaïs et nous passons beaucoup de temps ensemble depuis notre rencontre assez comique au parc naturel.

J'étais allé au parc pour faire l'escalade de la Soufrière, un énorme volcan en repos… mais comme j'allais bientôt le comprendre, pas si «en repos» que ça! En montant vers le volcan, *j'avais remarqué* qu'il y avait un peu de vapeur qui sortait du cratère, mais *je n'avais pas fait trop attention.* Quand j'étais presque au sommet du volcan, je me suis assis par terre pour me reposer un peu et c'est là que la scène comique a commencé. Là où j'étais assis, la terre était toute chaude, mais vraiment chaude, et je voyais des jets de vapeur qui sortaient du sommet! J'ai pensé que le volcan allait exploser!

La Soufrière

J'ai commencé à crier aux autres touristes: «Attention! Attention! Le volcan entre en éruption, il va exploser!» Heureusement, Anaïs était parmi le groupe et elle nous a expliqué calmement: «Mais non, mais non… calmez-vous! C'est tout à fait normal. Le volcan est en repos, il n'y a pas de danger!» Si *elle n'avait pas été* avec nous, *on aurait* tous *commencé* à courir, paniqués.

Sur le moment, j'ai eu l'impression d'être complètement ridicule! Mais cette impression n'a pas duré. On a commencé à parler et nous avons continué l'escalade du volcan ensemble. Arrivés au sommet, nous avons découvert une vue impressionnante… la lave…, les fissures…, l'odeur… C'était un paysage presque irréel. Pendant un instant, j'ai eu l'impression d'être sur une autre planète!

Alors, tout est bien qui finit bien. Si *je n'avais pas fait* cette bêtise, *Anaïs et moi n'aurions jamais commencé à parler* et *je n'aurais pas fait la connaissance* de cette femme extraordinaire. Elle est super sympa et nous passons presque tous les soirs ensemble!

À bientôt,
Lucas

Compréhension. Répondez aux questions suivantes d'après la lecture.

1. Quel site touristique est-ce que Lucas visitait quand il a rencontré Anaïs?
2. Qu'est-ce que Lucas avait vu avant de commencer à crier que le volcan allait exploser?
3. Qu'est-ce que tous les touristes auraient fait si Anaïs n'avait pas été là pour les calmer?
4. Pourquoi est-ce que Lucas dit que «tout est bien qui finit bien»?

Preparing for a trip

LES PRÉPARATIFS

Note *culturelle*

Succès de l'e-tourisme! La majorité des Français vont sur Internet pour préparer leurs vacances et ils font leurs réservations en ligne. La possibilité de se connecter quand on veut, de comparer les prestations *(services)*, de trouver les promotions *(deals)* et des tarifs compétitifs sont des avantages importants. Comment est-ce que les gens dans votre région préparent leurs vacances?

Note *de grammaire*

Obtenir is conjugated like **venir**: j'obtiens, tu obtiens, il/elle/on obtient, nous obtenons, vous obtenez, ils/elles obtiennent. PASSÉ COMPOSÉ: j'ai obtenu; IMPARFAIT: j'obtenais; FUTUR/CONDITIONNEL: j'obtiendrai/j'obtiendrais.

Leur *(them, to them)* is an indirect object pronoun. Like direct object pronouns, it is placed before a verb. You will learn more about these pronouns in this chapter.

Je ***leur*** *envoie des textos.*
I send ***them*** *text messages.*

Avant de faire un voyage **à l'étranger,** il faut faire beaucoup de préparatifs *(m)*.

Avant **le départ,** il faut...

obtenir votre passeport *(m)* (bien à l'avance!) et acheter votre **billet** *(m)* **d'avion.**

vous informer sur la région sur Internet ou lire **un guide.**

réserver une chambre d'hôtel.

dire à votre famille où vous allez.

demander à **vos voisins** de **donner à manger à** votre chien.

faire vos valises *(f)*.

À votre **arrivée** *(f)*, vous devez...

montrer votre passeport.

passer **la douane.**

changer de l'argent.

Pour rester en contact pendant le voyage, vous pouvez...

envoyer des textos ou téléphoner à vos amis par Skype.

leur écrire des cartes postales.

mettre vos photos sur Facebook ou écrire un blog.

Line art on this page: © Cengage Learning

---

les préparatifs *(m) preparations*   **à l'étranger** *in another country, abroad*   **le départ** *the departure*   **obtenir** *to obtain*   **un billet d'avion** *a plane ticket*   **s'informer** *to find out information*   **un guide** *a guidebook, a guide*   **dire** *to say, to tell*   **un(e) voisin(e)** *a neighbor*   **donner à manger à** *to feed*   **faire une valise** *to pack a suitcase*   **l'arrivée** *(f) the arrival*   **la douane** *customs*   **leur** *them, to them*

Alex parle à sa femme d'un mail qu'**il a reçu** de son ami Lucas.

CATHERINE: Qu'est-ce que **tu lis?**

ALEX: C'est un mail que j'ai reçu de Lucas. Il **m'**écrit de la Guadeloupe où il passe ses vacances.

CATHERINE: Et **ça lui plaît,** la Guadeloupe?

ALEX: Ça lui plaît beaucoup.

CATHERINE: La Guadeloupe, ça doit être beau. J'aimerais bien voir les plages et les paysages tropicaux.

ALEX: Lucas dit qu'il aime beaucoup le paysage, la cuisine et le climat. Il me parle aussi d'une «jeune femme extraordinaire» qu'il a rencontrée là-bas.

A **Avant le départ ou après l'arrivée?** Quand on voyage à l'étranger, est-ce qu'il faut faire les choses suivantes **avant le départ** ou **après l'arrivée?**

EXEMPLE acheter un billet d'avion
Il faut acheter un billet d'avion avant le départ.

1. passer la douane
2. obtenir un passeport
3. s'informer sur Internet
4. réserver une chambre
5. montrer son passeport
6. lire des guides
7. faire ses valises
8. mettre des photos sur Facebook
9. demander à un ami de donner à manger à son chien

B **Et vous?** Quelle sorte de voyageur (voyageuse) êtes-vous? Dites ce que vous feriez si vous voyagiez à l'étranger.

1. J'achèterais mon billet d'avion *sur Internet / dans une agence de voyages*.
2. Pour préparer le voyage, *je m'informerais sur Internet / je lirais un guide / je ne m'informerais pas beaucoup avant de partir*.
3. J'obtiendrais mon passeport *bien à l'avance / au dernier moment*.
4. Je réserverais ma chambre *par téléphone / sur Internet*.
5. *Je dirais / Je ne dirais pas* à ma famille où j'allais.
6. Je ferais ma valise *bien à l'avance / au dernier moment*.
7. Je changerais de l'argent *avant mon départ / à l'arrivée*.
8. Pour rester en contact avec mes amis, *j'écrirais un blog / je leur enverrais des textos / je leur téléphonerais / je leur parlerais par Skype*.
9. Je mettrais les photos du voyage sur Facebook *pendant le voyage / après mon retour* (return). *(Je ne mettrais pas mes photos sur Facebook.)*

À VOUS!

Avec un(e) partenaire, relisez à haute voix la conversation entre Alex et Catherine. Ensuite, imaginez que vous recevez un mail d'un(e) ami(e) qui visite une autre région francophone. Parlez avec votre partenaire de vos impressions de cette région et dites pourquoi vous voudriez ou ne voudriez pas y aller.

iLrn 🌐 You can find a list of the new words from this *Compétence* on page 380 and access the audio online.

---

il a reçu (recevoir *to receive*)   **tu lis (lire** *to read*)   **me (m')** *me, to me*   **ça lui plaît? (plaire** *to please*) *does he like it?*

COMMUNICATING WITH PEOPLE

Les verbes *dire, lire* et *écrire*

iLrn Grammar Tutorials

You have already seen the verbs **dire** *(to say, to tell)*, **lire** *(to read)*, and **écrire** *(to write)*. Here are their full conjugations. The verb **décrire** *(to describe)* is conjugated like **écrire**.

DIRE *(to say, to tell)*	LIRE *(to read)*	ÉCRIRE *(to write)*
je **dis**	je **lis**	j' **écris**
tu **dis**	tu **lis**	tu **écris**
il/elle/on **dit**	il/elle/on **lit**	il/elle/on **écrit**
nous **disons**	nous **lisons**	nous **écrivons**
vous **dites**	vous **lisez**	vous **écrivez**
ils/elles **disent**	ils/elles **lisent**	ils/elles **écrivent**

PASSÉ COMPOSÉ: j'**ai dit**	PASSÉ COMPOSÉ: j'**ai lu**	PASSÉ COMPOSÉ: j'**ai écrit**
IMPARFAIT: je **disais**	IMPARFAIT: je **lisais**	IMPARFAIT: j'**écrivais**
CONDITIONNEL: je **dirais**	CONDITIONNEL: je **lirais**	CONDITIONNEL: j'**écrirais**
FUTUR: je **dirai**	FUTUR: je **lirai**	FUTUR: j'**écrirai**

Here are some things you might want to read or write.

un article *an article*
une carte postale *a postcard*
un mail *an e-mail*
une histoire *a story*
un journal *(pl* **des journaux***)* *a newspaper*

une lettre *a letter*
un magazine *a magazine*
un poème *a poem*
une rédaction *a composition*
un roman *a novel*

A En cours de français. Est-ce que ces personnes font souvent les choses indiquées en cours de français?

> souvent   quelquefois   rarement   ne… jamais

EXEMPLE je / écrire des poèmes
> **Je n'écris jamais de poèmes en cours de français.**

1. le professeur / écrire au tableau
2. les étudiants / écrire au tableau
3. je / écrire quelque chose dans mon cahier
4. les autres étudiants et moi / s'écrire des mails après le cours
5. je / lire le journal
6. le professeur / lire des poèmes à la classe
7. nous / lire des phrases à haute voix *(aloud)*
8. les étudiants / lire des romans en français

Maintenant, dites si ces personnes ont fait ces choses en cours la semaine dernière.

EXEMPLE je / écrire des poèmes
> **Je n'ai pas écrit de poèmes en cours de français la semaine dernière.**

B **Qu'est-ce qu'on dit?** Dites si ces personnes font les choses indiquées.

EXEMPLE je / dire «merci» quand le professeur me rend mes devoirs
Je (ne) dis (pas) «merci» quand le professeur me rend mes devoirs.

1. le prof / dire «bonjour» quand il arrive en cours
2. les autres étudiants et moi / se dire «bonjour» en cours
3. les étudiants / dire la vérité *(the truth)* au prof
4. nous / se dire «au revoir» quand nous quittons la classe
5. je / dire «merci» au prof

Maintenant, dites si ces personnes ont dit les choses indiquées pendant le dernier cours.

EXEMPLE je / dire «merci» quand le professeur me rend mes devoirs
J'ai dit (Je n'ai pas dit) «merci» quand le professeur m'a rendu mes devoirs.

C **En vacances.** Vous faites le voyage de vos rêves avec un(e) ami(e). Avec un(e) partenaire, faites des phrases logiques en utilisant un élément de chaque colonne. Faites au moins deux phrases pour chaque sujet.

EXEMPLE **Je lis des guides.**

| Je...
Nous...
L'agent de voyages *(The travel agent)*... | dire
écrire
lire | un blog sur le voyage
des mails
un mail pour réserver une chambre
des guides
à des voisins de donner à manger aux animaux
«au revoir» à nos amis
le nom de notre hôtel à ma famille
le prix *(price)* du voyage |

D **Entretien.** Interviewez votre partenaire.

1. Est-ce que tu écris plus de textos ou plus de mails? Est-ce que tu as écrit un mail ce matin? À qui? Quand tu voyages, est-ce que tu écris des cartes postales? un blog? Est-ce que tu envoies des textos ou des mails? Tu mets tes photos sur Facebook?

2. Lis-tu le journal tous les jours? Est-ce que tu lis un journal en ligne? Quel journal préfères-tu lire? Le liras-tu ce soir? Est-ce que tu l'as lu ce matin? Quel magazine lis-tu le plus souvent? Est-ce que tu l'as lu ce mois-ci?

3. Lis-tu beaucoup de romans? Quel est le dernier roman que tu as lu? Quand est-ce que tu l'as lu?

AVOIDING REPETITION

✔ Pour vérifier

1. What are the French direct object pronouns for *him, her, it, them*? What are the indirect object pronouns for *(to) him, (to) her, (to) them*?

2. How can you often recognize a noun that is an indirect object in French? What types of verbs are frequently followed by indirect objects?

3. Where do you place the object pronoun when there is an infinitive in the same clause? Where does it go otherwise?

4. Where do you place the object pronoun in the **passé composé**? When does the past participle agree with an object pronoun?

iLrn Grammar Tutorials

Note *de grammaire*

In French, a noun that is a direct object generally follows the verb directly, whereas a noun that is an indirect object is preceded by a preposition, usually **à**.

J'invite **mes amis** chez moi. (direct object)

Je **les** invite chez moi.

Je téléphone **à mes amis**. (indirect object)

Je **leur** téléphone.

Les pronoms compléments d'objet indirect **(lui, leur)** *et reprise des pronoms compléments d'objet direct* **(le, la, l', les)**

In **Chapitre 5,** you learned that you can replace the direct object of the verb with the direct object pronouns **le, la, l',** and **les.**

—Tu fais **ta valise** maintenant? —Tu as acheté **ton billet**?
—Oui, je **la** fais. —Oui, je **l'**ai acheté.

Replace the indirect object of the verb with the indirect object pronouns **lui** *([to] him, [to] her)* and **leur** *([to] them)*. Generally, indirect objects in French can only be people or animals, not places or things. You can recognize a noun that is an indirect object because it is usually preceded by the preposition **à (à, au, à la, à l', aux).**

Verbs indicating communication or exchanges, such as **parler à, téléphoner à, dire à, écrire à, demander à, rendre visite à,** and **donner à,** are often followed by indirect objects.

—Tu écris **à ta mère**? —Tu vas rendre visite **à tes parents**?
—Oui, je **lui** écris un mail. —Oui, je vais **leur** rendre visite ce week-end.

DIRECT OBJECT PRONOUNS		INDIRECT OBJECT PRONOUNS	
le (l')	*him, it* (m)	**lui**	*(to) him*
la (l')	*her, it* (f)	**lui**	*(to) her*
les	*them*	**leur**	*(to) them*

Indirect object pronouns follow the same placement rules as direct object pronouns. Generally, place them *immediately* before the verb. They go before the infinitive if there is one in the same clause. If not, they go before the conjugated verb. In the **passé composé,** they go before the auxiliary verb.

—Lucas va téléphoner **à Anaïs**? —*Is Lucas going to call Anaïs?*
—Oui, il va **lui** téléphoner. —*Yes, he's going to call **her.***

—Il écrit **à son ami**? —*Is he writing **to his friend**?*
—Oui, il **lui** écrit. —*Yes, he is writing **(to) him.***

—Il a parlé **à ses parents**? —*Has he talked **to his parents**?*
—Non, il ne **leur** a pas parlé. —*No, he hasn't talked **to them.***

In negated sentences, place **ne** immediately after the subject and **pas, rien,** or **jamais** immediately after the first verb.

Je **ne** veux **pas lui** écrire.
Je **ne lui** écris **jamais.**
Je **ne lui** ai **pas** écrit.

In the **passé composé,** the past participle agrees with direct object pronouns, but not with indirect objects.

Lucas a invité Anaïs. Lucas **l'**a invité**e.**
Lucas a téléphoné à Anaïs. Lucas **lui** a téléphoné.

A **En voyage.** Quel genre de voyageur (voyageuse) êtes-vous? Formez des phrases pour parler de vos habitudes en voyage. Utilisez les pronoms **le, la, l', les.**

> **EXEMPLE** Je réserve *ma chambre* (sur Internet / par téléphone).
> **Je la réserve sur Internet.**

1. J'achète *mon billet* (dans une agence de voyages *[travel agency]* / sur Internet).
2. Je fais *ma valise* (au dernier moment / à l'avance).
3. Je lis *mon guide* (avant de partir / à l'hôtel au dernier moment).
4. Je visite *les sites touristiques* (avec un guide / sans guide).

Maintenant, utilisez les pronoms **lui** et **leur** pour remplacer les noms compléments d'objet indirect.

5. Je dis (toujours / quelquefois / rarement) *à mes parents* où je vais.
6. J'écris (souvent / quelquefois / rarement) des mails *à mes amis.*
7. (Je téléphone / Je ne téléphone pas) *à mon meilleur ami (à ma meilleure amie).*
8. (J'envoie / Je n'envoie pas) mes photos *à mon meilleur ami (à ma meilleure amie).*

Aimez-vous faire de l'écotourisme?

B **La prochaine fois.** Refaites les phrases de *A. En voyage* pour parler de ce que vous allez probablement faire la prochaine fois que vous partirez en voyage.

> **EXEMPLE** Je réserve *ma chambre* (sur Internet / par téléphone).
> **La prochaine fois, je vais la réserver sur Internet.**

Maintenant, refaites ces mêmes phrases au passé composé pour dire ce que vous avez fait la dernière fois que vous êtes parti(e) en voyage.

> **EXEMPLE** Je réserve *ma chambre* (sur Internet / par téléphone).
> **La dernière fois, je l'ai réservée sur Internet.**

C **Habitudes de voyage.** Parlez de vos voyages en répondant à ces questions. Utilisez **le, la, l', les, lui** ou **leur.**

> **EXEMPLE** Vous demandez de l'argent *à vos parents*?
> **Non, je ne leur demande pas d'argent.**

En général...

1. Vous réservez *votre chambre d'hôtel* sur Internet?
2. Vous achetez *votre billet* sur Internet ou dans une agence de voyages *(travel agency)*?
3. Vous proposez *à vos parents* de partir en vacances avec vous?
4. Vous demandez *à votre meilleur(e) ami(e)* de donner à manger à votre chien ou à votre chat?
5. Vous lisez *le magazine de la compagnie aérienne* dans l'avion?

Et la dernière fois que vous êtes parti(e) en voyage...

6. Vous avez téléphoné *à votre mère* pendant le voyage?
7. Vous avez envoyé des textos *à votre meilleur(e) ami(e)*?
8. Vous avez passé *vos soirées* à l'hôtel?
9. À votre retour *(return)*, vous avez parlé du voyage *à vos parents*?
10. Vous avez mis *vos photos* sur Facebook?

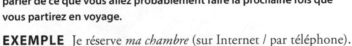

Deciding where to go on a trip

UN VOYAGE

Note *culturelle*

La grande majorité des Français passent leurs vacances en France. Mais pour les séjours *(stays)* à l'étranger, 70 % ont lieu en Europe et l'Espagne est leur première destination. Quels pays voudriez-vous visiter?

Vocabulaire sans peine!

Most countries, states, or regions ending with *-ia* in English end with **-ie** in French, and are feminine (except *India* [**l'Inde**]). Also, the words for the nationalities of the people from these countries end with **-ien(ne)** (except *Russian* [**russe**]).

Australia = **l'Australie**
Australian = **australien(ne)**

How would you say the following in French?

Tunisia / Tunisian

Vocabulaire supplémentaire

EN AFRIQUE	l'Afrique *(f)* du Sud
	la Tunisie
EN ASIE	la Corée (du Nord / du Sud)
	l'Inde *(f)*
	l'Iran *(m)*
	l'Irak *(m)*
EN EUROPE	le Danemark
	la Pologne
	le Portugal
	la République tchèque

Lucas visite la Guadeloupe. Et vous? Quels continents et pays aimeriez-vous visiter?

Moi, j'aimerais visiter...

l'Afrique *(f)*: **le Maroc,** l'Algérie *(f)*, l'Égypte *(f)*, le Sénégal, la Côte d'Ivoire

L'oasis Kerzaz, Algérie

l'Asie *(f)* et **le Moyen-Orient:** la Chine, Israël *(m)*, le Japon, le Viêt Nam

l'Amérique *(f)* du Nord ou l'Amérique centrale: **les Antilles** *(f)*, le Canada, les États-Unis *(m)*, le Mexique

La Guadeloupe

l'Amérique *(f)* du Sud: l'Argentine *(f)*, le Brésil, le Chili, la Colombie, la Guyane, le Pérou

l'Océanie *(f)*: l'Australie *(f)*, la Nouvelle-Calédonie, la Polynésie française

Le Parlement européen, Bruxelles

l'Europe *(f)*: l'Allemagne *(f)*, la Belgique, la Croatie, l'Espagne *(f)*, la France, la Grèce, l'Irlande *(f)*, l'Italie *(f)*, **le Royaume-Uni,** la Russie, la Suisse

Line art on this page: © Cengage Learning

---

le Maroc *Morocco*   **le Moyen-Orient** *the Middle East*   **les Antilles** *(f pl) the West Indies*   **le Royaume-Uni** *the United Kingdom*

Lucas et Anaïs parlent des voyages qu'ils ont faits.

🔊 3-16

ANAÏS: Pourquoi es-tu venu tout seul en Guadeloupe? Tu aimes voyager?

LUCAS: Oui, j'adore ça!

ANAÏS: Quels pays as-tu visités?

LUCAS: J'ai visité les États-Unis, la Chine et le Canada. Et toi? Tu aimes voyager?

ANAÏS: Je n'ai jamais quitté la Guadeloupe, mais j'aimerais bien visiter l'Afrique un jour.

LUCAS: Où aimerais-tu aller en Afrique?

ANAÏS: Moi, j'aimerais surtout visiter le Sénégal et la Côte d'Ivoire.

In the **Culture Modules** in the video library, see **Vacations.**

A **Quel continent?** Où se trouvent *(are located)* ces pays?

> en Amérique du Nord   en Afrique   en Amérique du Sud
> en Océanie   en Asie   en Europe

EXEMPLE la Chine
La Chine se trouve en Asie.

1. les États-Unis   3. le Japon   5. l'Allemagne   7. la Guyane
2. l'Algérie   4. l'Australie   6. le Sénégal   8. le Maroc

B **Quels pays?** Dites quels pays vous aimeriez visiter dans la région indiquée.

EXEMPLE en Europe
En Europe, j'aimerais visiter la France, l'Espagne...

1. en Asie et au Moyen-Orient
2. en Amérique du Nord et centrale
3. en Amérique du Sud
4. en Afrique
5. en Europe
6. en Océanie

C **Associations.** Travaillez avec un(e) partenaire pour trouver quel pays de chaque groupe ne va pas avec les autres. Expliquez pourquoi.

EXEMPLE l'Allemagne, les États-Unis, la France, la Suisse
les États-Unis: Tous les autres sont en Europe.

1. le Canada, l'Argentine, l'Espagne, le Pérou, le Mexique
2. l'Australie, la Polynésie française, la Martinique, le Sénégal
3. la France, les États-Unis, l'Australie, le Royaume-Uni
4. le Sénégal, l'Égypte, le Brésil, l'Algérie, le Maroc
5. la France, la Belgique, le Sénégal, la Suisse, le Mexique

À VOUS!

Avec un(e) partenaire, relisez à haute voix la conversation entre Anaïs et Lucas. Ensuite, changez la conversation pour parler des régions et pays que vous avez visités et de ceux que vous aimeriez visiter.

You can find a list of the new words from this *Compétence* on page 381 and access the audio online.

SAYING WHERE YOU ARE GOING

✔ Pour vérifier

1. With which one of the following do you generally not use a definite article when it is the subject or direct object of a verb: cities, states, provinces, countries, or continents? Would you use **le, la, l',** or **les** before the following place names:

_____ Italie, _____ Antilles, _____ Ohio, _____ Japon, _____ France?

2. Which countries, states, or provinces are generally feminine? masculine?

3. How do you say *to* or *in* with a city? with a feminine country? with a masculine country beginning with a vowel sound? with a masculine country beginning with a consonant? with plural countries?

Note de grammaire

1. The following places are exceptions to the rule that countries and states ending in -e are feminine: **le Royaume-Uni, le Mexique, le Delaware, le Maine, le New Hampshire, le Nouveau-Mexique, le Rhode Island, le Tennessee.**

2. You also say **dans le** with masculine states (**dans le Vermont**).

3. You say **(dans) l'état de New York** and **(dans) l'état de Washington** to clarify that you are talking about the states rather than the cities with the same names.

Les expressions géographiques

When a place name is used as the subject or object of a verb, you generally need to use the definite article with continents, countries, states, and provinces, but not with cities. Most continents, countries, states, and provinces ending in **-e** are feminine, whereas most others are masculine. **Le Mexique** and **le Royaume-Uni** are exceptions.

J'adore l'Europe. **La** France est très belle. Nous allons visiter Londres, Paris et Nice. J'aimerais aussi voir **les** États-Unis: **la** Californie, **le** Texas et **la** Floride.

To say *to* or *in* with a geographical location, the preposition you use varies.

to / in		
à	with cities	**à** Paris
aux	with any plural country or region	**aux** États-Unis
en	with any feminine country or region and with any masculine one beginning with a vowel	**en** France **en** Ontario
au	with any masculine country or region beginning with a consonant	**au** Canada

A C'est connu!
D'abord, mettez la forme convenable de l'article défini devant le nom de chaque pays. Ensuite, demandez à votre partenaire quel pays est connu *(known)* pour les choses indiquées.

_____ Royaume-Uni _____ Égypte _____ Suisse
_____ Colombie _____ États-Unis _____ France
_____ Mexique _____ Italie _____ Brésil

EXEMPLE —Quel pays est connu pour le café?
—La Colombie.

Quel pays est connu pour... ?

1. le fromage et le vin **3.** le chocolat **5.** les spaghetti **7.** la musique rock
2. le carnaval **4.** le thé **6.** les pyramides **8.** le sphinx

B Leçon de géographie.
Votre ami(e) n'est pas très fort(e) en géographie et il/elle vous pose des questions. Répondez-lui. D'abord, donnez la préposition convenable pour dire *to / in* avec chaque pays. Ensuite, jouez les deux rôles avec votre partenaire.

EXEMPLE Londres (_____ Royaume-Uni, _____ Canada)
—Londres se trouve *(is located)* au Royaume-Uni ou au Canada?
—Londres se trouve au Royaume-Uni.

1. Tokyo (__en__ Chine, __au__ Japon)
2. Mexico (__au__ Mexique, __au__ Pérou)
3. Moscou (__en__ Italie, __en__ Russie)
4. Berlin (__en__ Croatie, __en__ Allemagne)
5. Hanoi (__au__ Viêt Nam, __en__ Chine)
6. Alger (__en__ Algérie, __au__ Maroc)

🌐 **Sélection musicale.** Search the Web for the song **"Sénégal fast-food"** by Amadou & Mariam to enjoy a musical selection illustrating the use of this structure.

7. Le Caire (__au__ Maroc, __en__ Égypte)
8. Dakar (__au__ Sénégal, __en__ Côte d'Ivoire)
9. La Nouvelle-Orléans (__aux__ États-Unis, __en__ Irlande)
10. Abidjan (__en__ Côte d'Ivoire, __au__ Sénégal)

C **C'est où?** Devinez où dans le monde francophone se trouvent *(are located)* ces sites touristiques.

EXEMPLE Le château de Versailles
Le château de Versailles se trouve à Versailles en France.

Dakar (Sénégal)	Versailles (France)
Bruxelles (Belgique)	Fès (Maroc)
Québec (Canada)	Papeete (Polynésie française)

Le château de Versailles

1.

La Grand-Place

4.

Le marché de Papeete

2.

Le Château Frontenac

3.

La Médina

5.

La Grande Mosquée

VIDÉOREPRISE

Les Stagiaires

See the **Résumé de grammaire** section at the end of each chapter for a review of all the grammar of the chapter.

Rappel!

Dans l'épisode précédent de la vidéo, Amélie a parlé avec Rachid du restaurant où elle a dîné avec Matthieu.

Dans l'**Épisode 9** de la vidéo **Les Stagiaires,** M. Vieilledent fait des projets pour des vacances en Martinique. Avant de regarder l'épisode, faites ces exercices pour réviser ce que vous avez appris dans le **Chapitre 9.**

© Cengage Learning

A Qu'est-ce qu'on fait? Avant de décider où aller en vacances, M. Vieilledent parle à ses amis de ce qu'il pourrait faire dans les différents endroits où il pense peut-être aller. Avec un(e) partenaire, faites une liste de ce qu'il pourrait faire dans les endroits suivants: **dans une grande ville, à la mer, à la montagne.**

> **EXEMPLE** dans une grande ville
> **Dans une grande ville, il pourrait profiter des activités culturelles...**

B Destinations. Tout le monde à Technovert parle des vacances. Complétez chaque espace avec la préposition appropriée (**en, au, aux**).

> **EXEMPLE** Christophe veut aller **au** Japon parce qu'il adore les mangas.

1. Matthieu veut aller _____ États-Unis pour pratiquer son anglais.
2. Rachid est marocain. Il est né _____ Maroc. Il a déjà voyagé _____ Algérie et _____ Égypte.
3. Amélie aime passer les vacances d'hiver _____ Suisse.
4. M. Vieilledent va bientôt partir pour la Martinique, _____ Antilles.

C En Martinique. M. Vieilledent dit à Camille qu'il va partir en vacances. Complétez les phrases suivantes en mettant les verbes au futur dans l'espace le plus logique.

> **EXEMPLE** (être, prendre) Je **prendrai** des vacances à la fin de ce mois, alors je ne **serai** pas au bureau.

1. (partir, rentrer) Je _____ pour la Martinique le quinze et je _____ le vingt-neuf.
2. (arriver, décider, visiter) Je _____ peut-être la Guadeloupe aussi, mais je _____ ça quand j'_____ en Martinique.
3. (être, faire) Céline _____ mon travail et elle _____ responsable du bureau pendant mon absence.
4. (pouvoir, lire) Je _____ mes mails pendant les vacances et vous _____ aussi me téléphoner.

D Renseignements. M. Vieilledent parle à Camille de son voyage en Martinique. Complétez chaque phrase avec la forme correcte du verbe **savoir** ou **connaître.**

1. Vous _____ à quel hôtel je vais descendre en Martinique?
2. _____-vous un bon site Web où on peut comparer des hôtels?
3. Je ne _____ pas la région. Ce sera mon premier voyage aux Antilles.
4. Je _____ qu'il y a des plantations de café que je voudrais voir.
5. _____-vous combien d'heures dure (lasts) le vol d'ici en Martinique?

E **Un mail.** Lisez la conversation suivante entre Céline et Amélie et complétez-la avec la forme correcte du verbe indiqué entre parenthèses.

CÉLINE: Qu'est-ce que tu _1_ (lire)?

AMÉLIE: C'est un mail de Matthieu.

CÉLINE: Vous _2_ (s'écrire) beaucoup de mails, on dirait, non?

AMÉLIE: Oui, Matthieu m' _3_ (écrire) souvent. Il est un peu timide quand on est face à face et il _4_ (dire) plus facilement ce qu'il pense dans un mail.

CÉLINE: Alors, ça devient sérieux entre vous deux si vous _5_ (se dire) tous vos secrets.

AMÉLIE: Je ne lui _6_ (dire) pas encore tous mes secrets,... mais je le trouve sympa.

F **Interactions.** Matthieu pense souvent à Amélie et rêve de leur relation. Décrivez tout ce que Matthieu fait dans ses rêves en faisant des phrases avec les verbes suivants et le pronom convenable, **la (l')** ou **lui.**

EXEMPLES écouter avec attention quand elle parle
Il l'écoute avec attention quand elle parle.
envoyer beaucoup de textos
Il lui envoie beaucoup de textos.

1. parler de tout
2. téléphoner tous les jours
3. inviter à sortir le week-end
4. retrouver en ville
5. acheter des fleurs (*flowers*)
6. dire tous ses secrets

 Maintenant parlez à un(e) autre étudiant(e) de sa relation avec son meilleur ami (sa meilleure amie). Posez des questions avec les verbes précédents et le pronom **te (t')** comme dans les exemples.

EXEMPLES écouter avec attention quand elle parle
—**Est-ce que ton meilleur ami (ta meilleure amie) t'écoute avec attention quand tu parles?**
—**Il/Elle m'écoute en général.**

Access the Video *Les Stagiaires* on **iLrn**.

© Cengage Learning

▶ **Épisode 9: J'ai acheté vos billets**

AVANT LA VIDÉO

Dans ce clip, Camille aide M. Vielledent à choisir un hôtel pour son voyage en Martinique et elle lui donne les renseignements sur les réservations pour son billet d'avion. Avant de regarder l'épisode, imaginez quel genre d'hôtel M. Vielledent pourrait préférer et les services qu'il aimerait y trouver.

APRÈS LA VIDÉO

Regardez le clip et répondez aux questions suivantes:

- Quel genre d'hôtel est-ce que M. Vielledent a choisi?
- À quelle heure partira son vol pour la Martinique et à quelle heure arrivera-t-il?

Vidéoreprise | *trois cent soixante-treize* **373**

LECTURE ET COMPOSITION

LECTURE

You are going to read an extract from a work by Dany Bébel-Gisler (1935–2003), whose stories depict the culture of the Antilles. As you will find in this reading, words often have more than one meaning. Learning to be flexible about the meanings of words will help you read more easily. Consider the multiple meanings of these words.

apprendre	*to learn*	*to teach*
la terre	*the ground*	*the earth*
serrer	*to squeeze*	*to wrap around*
une berceuse	*a lullaby*	*a rocking chair*
soigner	*to care for*	*to treat*
frais (fraîche)	*cool*	*fresh*
finir	*to finish*	**finir par** *to end up*
compter	*to count, to plan*	**compter sur** *to depend on, to count on*

Quel sens? Traduisez les phrases suivantes. Choisissez selon le contexte le sens le plus logique pour les mots en italique. Voir la liste ci-dessus. *(See the above list.)*

1. Ma grand-mère *m'a appris* à ne pas trop *compter sur* les autres.
2. Elle m'a appris le travail de *la terre,* à reconnaître les plantes qui *soignent* les maladies.
3. Je *serre* ma tête *(head)* avec ce madras [a type of Caribbean scarf].
4. Quand ma grand-mère avait la tête *fraîche,* elle s'asseyait *(used to sit)* dans sa *berceuse.*
5. Ils *finissaient par* devenir riches.

Ma grand-mère m'a appris à ne pas compter sur les yeux des autres pour dormir

Je suis restée avec grand-mère moins longtemps qu'avec maman. Maman était en meilleure santé, elle ne buvait pas, mais grand-mère a plus fait pour moi que maman. Elle m'a beaucoup appris. Et surtout à ne pas compter sur les yeux des autres pour dormir.

Elle m'**a enseigné** le travail de la terre, à organiser un jardin, à planter des légumes. À reconnaître aussi les plantes qui soignent, celles qui sont bonnes pour **le ventre,** pour **la toux,** pour **les blessures.**

[Quand **j'ai très mal,** ma grand-mère m'avait donné **un mouchoir.** Alors je prends ce mouchoir – ce que l'on appelle un madras chez nous ici – et je serre **ma tête** avec ce madras et **je me sens très forte.**]

La nuit venue, quand grand-mère **était d'attaque, debout** sur ses deux pieds, la tête bien fraîche, elle s'asseyait dans sa berceuse et me lançait: *Yékrik!* Je répondais: *Yékrak!* et allais m'installer **sur ses genoux.** Ma petite main dans **la sienne, j'enfouissais** ma tête entre ses deux **seins.** Alors grand-mère me faisait voyager dans **un monde étrange, celui** des contes... J'aimais beaucoup les contes où les **enfants orphelins, pauvres, à force de lutter contre la misère,** de marcher, de marcher, de marcher, **d'employer la ruse comme Compère Lapin,** finissaient, une fois grands, par devenir riches et respectés par tous.

iLrn In the **Culture Modules** in the video library, see **Francophone Literature.**

Dany Bébel-Gisler, À la recherche d'une odeur de grand-mère © Éditions Jasor, 2000.

a enseigné *taught*   **le ventre** *the belly*   **la toux** *coughing*   **les blessures** *injuries*   **j'ai très mal** *I hurt very badly*   **un mouchoir** *a handkerchief*   **ma tête** *my head*
je me sens très forte *I feel very strong*   **était d'attaque, debout** *was feeling fit, standing*   **Yékrik! Yékrak!** *a cry used to begin a story*   **sur ses genoux** *on her lap*
la sienne *hers*   **j'enfouissais** *I buried*   **seins** *breasts*   **un monde étrange, celui** *a strange world, the one*   **enfants orphelins, pauvres** *orphaned children, poor*
à force de lutter contre la misère *by fighting poverty*   **d'employer la ruse comme Compère Lapin** *using trickery like Compère Lapin (equivalent of Brer Rabbit)*

Compréhension

1. Avec qui est-ce que la petite fille aimait passer son temps? Pourquoi?
2. Qu'est-ce qu'elle a appris de sa grand-mère?
3. Quelle sorte de contes est-ce qu'elle aimait?

COMPOSITION

POUR MIEUX ÉCRIRE:
Revising what you write

Editing and revising what you write is an important final step in the writing process. Once you finish a composition, reread it and make sure you have an introductory and a concluding sentence and that your sentences and paragraphs are clear and well organized. Then, check each sentence against this checklist:

- Are the verbs in the proper form for the subject and the tense?
- Do all of your adjectives agree (masculine, feminine, singular, plural) with the nouns they modify?
- Are all the words spelled correctly (including accents) and do the nouns have the correct article (**un, une, le, du, de,...**), possessive adjective (**mon, ton, ses,...**),...?
- Did you use the correct forms of the prepositions **de (du, de la,...)** and **à (au, à la,...)**?

Révisons! Lisez ce paragraphe. D'abord, trouvez une phrase pour commencer le paragraphe et une autre pour le terminer. Ensuite, corrigez les 16 erreurs *(errors)* (marqués en italique) dans le paragraphe.

Philippe préfère *voyagé* à l'étranger, mais Marie préfère *reste* dans son propre *(own)* pays. Quand ils *voyage* ensemble, Philippe passe très peu *du* temps *au* hôtel mais Marie aime passer toutes les soirées dans *son* chambre. Philippe préfère visiter une *grand* ville et profiter *de les* activités culturelles. Marie préfère les activités de plein air et elle aime passer *sa* vacances à la *montange* ou à la *mère*. L'année *prochain*, ils visiteront Nice *ou* Philippe *iront au* musées et Marie passera *sa* temps à la plage.

Un itinéraire

Imaginez que votre classe de français va faire un voyage d'une semaine dans un pays francophone. Écrivez une description détaillée du voyage que la classe fera ensemble. Dans la description, donnez les renseignements suivants:

- où vous irez, quand vous partirez et quand vous reviendrez
- comment vous voyagerez et combien coûtera le voyage par personne
- où vous descendrez et où vous prendrez les repas
- ce que vous ferez chaque jour de la semaine

N'oubliez pas de relire votre composition et de la réviser si nécessaire.

(iLrn) Share It!

© Chad Ehlers/Glow

LA CULTURE CRÉOLE AUX ANTILLES

La culture **antillaise** est une culture créole qui reflète l'histoire de ces îles et la diversité de leurs peuples. La majorité des habitants sont les descendants d'**esclaves africains amenés** dans ces îles pour travailler dans les plantations. Il y a aussi des Amérindiens, des Indiens, des Chinois, des békés (les descendants des premiers **colons** français), des métros (les Français plus récemment arrivés d'Europe) et bien d'autres.

Le français est la langue officielle des Antilles françaises mais la population locale parle aussi créole. Le créole antillais est **un mélange de** français, de langues **indigènes** et africaines, d'espagnol, de portugais, d'anglais et de hindi. D'origine une langue orale, il y a de nos jours un fort mouvement littéraire créole et un mouvement de **créolité** pour encourager et protéger la langue et la culture créoles.

Aux Antilles, les fêtes traditionnelles sont nombreuses. Le Tour des Yoles Rondes au mois d'août est une fête très populaire en Martinique: une semaine de compétition avec les bateaux typiques de l'île. C'est aussi l'occasion de **déguster** des plats antillais accompagnés de rhum dans une ambiance de musique et de fête.

La cuisine créole antillaise est un mélange délicieux de fruits tropicaux, de poissons et fruits de mer, de rhum et d'**épices d'Inde,** avec des influences africaines et françaises.

La Fête des **Cusinières** est une grande tradition guadeloupéenne. Au mois d'août, à l'occasion de la St Laurent, **patron** des cuisinières, 200 cuisinières **vêtues** de leurs plus belles robes et **parées** de leurs plus beaux **bijoux,** se rendent en procession à la cathédrale de Pointe-à-Pitre. Elles portent des **paniers remplis de** plats typiquement créoles (**écrevisses, boudin…**) pour **les faire bénir.** Après **la messe, elles défilent** dans les rues, puis passent à table. La fête se termine le soir avec le Bal des Cuisinières.

---

antillaise of the Antilles   **esclaves africains amenés** African slaves brought   **des colons** colonists   **un mélange de** a mixture of   **indigènes** indigenous
créolité "Creoleness"   **déguster** to savor   **épices d'Inde** Indian spices   **Cuisinières** Cooks   **patron** patron saint   **vêtues** dressed   **parées** adorned
bijoux jewels   **paniers remplis de** baskets filled with   **écrevisses** crawfish   **boudin** blood sausage   **les faire bénir** to have them blessed   **la messe** the mass
elles défilent they parade

Le créole, c'est plus qu'une langue, c'est «également **une façon de vivre**, et l'histoire d'un peuple, **évoquant à la fois** l'Afrique, **l'esclavage**, mais aussi la danse, la musique, les îles, la fête... »[1]

La musique et la danse antillaises, **dérivées d'**un mélange de **sons** et de rythmes européens, américains et africains, reflètent l'histoire des îles caraïbes et sont connues partout dans le monde: le zouk, le zouk-love, la biguine, la Cadence-lypso et d'autres. **Parmi** les artistes antillais les plus connus sont Expérience 7, Zouk Machine et Kassav'.

Compréhension

1. La majorité des habitants des Antilles sont de quelle origine?

2. Quelle est la langue officielle des Antilles françaises? Quelle autre langue est-ce que la population locale parle?

3. Par définition une langue créole est une langue formée d'une combinaison de plusieurs langues. Le créole antillais est un mélange de quelles langues?

4. Comment s'appelle le mouvement qui a pour but *(goal)* la préservation et le développement de la culture créole?

5. Aimeriez-vous mieux participer au Tour des Yoles Rondes ou à la Fête des Cuisinières? Pourquoi?

6. Comment est la cuisine créole?

7. La musique et la danse antillaises sont dérivées d'un mélange de sons et de rythmes de quelles origines?

8. Quelles sont les cultures importantes dans votre région? Est-ce qu'il y a des traditions, des fêtes, de la musique ou une cuisine que vous associez à chacune?

[1] http://www.webcaraibes.com/guadeloupe/culture.htm

une façon *a way*   **évoquant à la fois** *evoking at the same time*   **l'esclavage** *slavery*   **dérivées de** *derived from*
sons *sounds*   **Parmi** *Among*

RÉSUMÉ DE GRAMMAIRE

THE FUTURE TENSE *(LE FUTUR)*

Use the future tense to say what someone *will* do. Form it by adding the bold-faced endings below to the same stem that you used for the conditional. For most verbs, it is the infinitive, but drop the final **e** of infinitives ending with **-re.**

Je **prendrai** des vacances en été.

Tu resteras ici?

Tu partiras tout seul?

Mes parents voyageront avec moi.

VISITER	CONNAÎTRE	FINIR
je visiter**ai**	je connaîtr**ai**	je finir**ai**
tu visiter**as**	tu connaîtr**as**	tu finir**as**
il/elle/on visiter**a**	il/elle/on connaîtr**a**	il/elle/on finir**a**
nous visiter**ons**	nous connaîtr**ons**	nous finir**ons**
vous visiter**ez**	vous connaîtr**ez**	vous finir**ez**
ils/elles visiter**ont**	ils/elles connaîtr**ont**	ils/elles finir**ont**

The following verbs have irregular stems.

J'irai en Europe.

Combien de temps **serez-vous** en Europe?

On reviendra après trois semaines.

-r-		-vr- / -dr-		-rr-	
aller:	ir-	devoir:	devr-	voir:	verr-
être:	ser-	pleuvoir:	pleuvr-	pouvoir:	pourr-
faire:	fer-	vouloir:	voudr-	mourir:	mourr-
avoir:	aur-	venir:	viendr-	courir:	courr-
savoir:	saur-	devenir:	deviendr-	envoyer:	enverr-
		revenir:	reviendr-		
		obtenir	obtiendr-		

[handwritten note: acheter accent irreg]

S'**il peut**, mon frère **ira** en vacances avec nous.

Il décidera quand **on saura** la date exacte de notre départ.

As in English, use the future tense in *if / then* sentences to say what will happen if something else occurs. Use the present tense in the clause with **si.** Unlike English, use the future in French in clauses with **quand** referring to the future. English has the present tense in such clauses.

THE VERBS *DIRE, LIRE,* AND *ÉCRIRE*

The verbs **dire, lire,** and **écrire** are irregular in the present tense and the **passé composé (j'ai dit, j'ai lu, j'ai écrit).** As with other verbs, use the stem for **nous** in the present tense to form the imperfect (**je disais, je lisais, j'écrivais**). Obtain the future / conditional stem by dropping the final **e** of the infinitive (**je dirai, je lirai, j'écrirai**).

Est-ce que **tu lis** tes mails quand tu voyages?

J'écris à mes amis et je leur montre des photos de mon voyage.

Mes parents disent que la Méditerranée est très jolie.

DIRE	LIRE	ÉCRIRE
je **dis**	je **lis**	j' **écris**
tu **dis**	tu **lis**	tu **écris**
il/elle/on **dit**	il/elle/on **lit**	il/elle/on **écrit**
nous **disons**	nous **lisons**	nous **écrivons**
vous **dites**	vous **lisez**	vous **écrivez**
ils/elles **disent**	ils/elles **lisent**	ils/elles **écrivent**

THE VERBS *SAVOIR* AND *CONNAÎTRE*

Savoir and **connaître** both mean *to know*. Use **savoir** when *to know* is followed by a verb, a question word (**qui, où...**), or by **si, que,** or **ce que,** or to say that one knows a language. When *to know* is followed by a noun, use **savoir** to say one *knows a fact or information*, and **connaître** to say one is *familiar with a person, place, or thing*.

SAVOIR	CONNAÎTRE
je **sais**	je **connais**
tu **sais**	tu **connais**
il/elle/on **sait**	il/elle/on **connaît**
nous **savons**	nous **connaissons**
vous **savez**	vous **connaissez**
ils/elles **savent**	ils/elles **connaissent**

PASSÉ COMPOSÉ:	j'**ai su** *(I found out)*	j'**ai connu** *(I met)*
IMPARFAIT:	je **savais** *(I knew)*	je **connaissais** *(I knew)*
CONDITIONNEL:	je **saurais**	je **connaîtrais**
FUTUR:	je **saurai**	je **connaîtrai**

Quelles langues **sais-tu**?

Je sais parler français et **mes parents savent** l'allemand.

Savez-vous si vous allez visiter l'Allemagne?

On ira à Berlin, où **mes parents connaissent** beaucoup de gens.

Je ne connais pas du tout l'Europe. Est-ce que **tu connais** bien l'histoire de la région?

DIRECT AND INDIRECT OBJECT PRONOUNS

Direct object pronouns replace nouns that are the direct object of the verb. Indirect object pronouns replace nouns that are the indirect object of the verb. Generally, indirect objects are people or animals, not things, and they follow the preposition **à**. They often are used with verbs indicating communication or exchanges (**parler à, téléphoner à, dire à, écrire à, demander à, rendre visite à, donner à**).

DIRECT OBJECT PRONOUNS				INDIRECT OBJECT PRONOUNS			
me (m')	*me*	**nous**	*us*	**me (m')**	*(to) me*	**nous**	*(to) us*
te (t')	*you*	**vous**	*you*	**te (t')**	*(to) you*	**vous**	*(to) you*
le (l')	*him, it* (m)	**les**	*them*	**lui**	*(to) him*	**leur**	*(to) them*
la (l')	*her, it* (f)			**lui**	*(to) her*		

Both direct and indirect object pronouns have the same placement rules. They go immediately before the infinitive if there is one in the same clause. If not, they go before the conjugated verb. In the **passé composé,** they go before the auxiliary verb. The past participle agrees with direct object pronouns, but not with indirect objects.

Est-ce que tu **m'**écriras si je **te** donne mon adresse mail?

Mon frère habite à Paris. Je vais **te** donner son numéro de téléphone et tu pourras **lui** téléphoner quand tu seras en France.

GEOGRAPHICAL EXPRESSIONS

Use the definite article with names of continents, countries, states, and provinces used as the subject or object of a verb, but not with cities. Most continents, countries, states, and provinces ending in **e** are feminine, whereas most others are masculine.

To say *to* or *in* with a geographical location, use...

à	with cities
aux	with any plural country or region
en	with any feminine country or region and with any masculine one beginning with a vowel sound
au	with any masculine country or region beginning with a consonant

Les amis de mes parents **nous** ont demandé de **leur** rendre visite. Mes parents ne **les** ont pas vus depuis vingt ans, la dernière fois qu'ils **leur** ont rendu visite.

Je voudrais visiter **les** États-Unis, **le** Canada et **la** Colombie.

Pendant notre voyage, on ira à Berlin **en** Allemagne, à Copenhague **au** Danemark, à Amsterdam **aux** Pays-Bas et à Paris et à Nice **en** France.

VOCABULAIRE

COMPÉTENCE 1

Talking about vacation

NOMS MASCULINS

le ballet	*the ballet*
un endroit	*a place*
l'opéra	*the opera*
un Parisien	*a Parisian*
le paysage	*the landscape, the scenery*
un site	*a site, a spot*

NOMS FÉMININS

une île	*an island*
la mer	*the sea*
une Parisienne	*a Parisian*
une terrasse	*a terrace*

EXPRESSIONS VERBALES

admirer	*to admire*
bronzer	*to tan*
compter	*to count on, to plan on*
courir	*to run*
goûter	*to taste*
profiter de	*to take advantage of*

ADJECTIFS

assis(e)	*seated*
exotique	*exotic*
historique	*historic*
local(e) (*mpl* locaux)	*local*
touristique	*touristic*
tropical(e) (*mpl* tropicaux)	*tropical*

DIVERS

Ça te plaira.	*You'll like it.*

COMPÉTENCE 2

Preparing for a trip

NOMS MASCULINS

un article	*an article*
un billet (d'avion)	*a (plane) ticket*
un blog	*a blog*
le climat	*the climate*
le départ	*the departure*
un guide	*a guidebook, a guide*
un magazine	*a magazine*
un passeport	*a passport*
un poème	*a poem*
des préparatifs	*preparations*
un roman	*a novel*
un voisin	*a neighbor*

NOMS FÉMININS

une arrivée	*an arrival*
une carte postale	*a postcard*
la douane	*customs*
une histoire	*a story*
une lettre	*a letter*
une rédaction	*a composition*
une région	*a region, an area*
une valise	*a suitcase*
une voisine	*a neighbor*

EXPRESSIONS VERBALES

changer	*to change, to exchange*
décrire	*to describe*
dire	*to say, to tell*
donner à manger à	*to feed*
écrire	*to write*
faire sa valise	*to pack one's bag*
s'informer	*to find out information*
lire	*to read*
obtenir	*to obtain*
passer	*to pass (through)*
recevoir	*to receive*
réserver	*to reserve*

DIVERS

(bien) à l'avance	*(well) in advance*
à l'étranger	*in another country, abroad*
Ça lui plaît?	*Does he/she like it?*
en contact	*in contact*
extraordinaire	*extraordinary, great*
leur	*(to) them*
lui	*(to) him, (to) her*
me (m')	*(to) me*

Buying your ticket

NOMS MASCULINS

un agent de voyages	*a travel agent*
un aller simple	*a one-way ticket*
un billet aller-retour	*a round-trip ticket*
un réseau	*a network*
le retour	*the return*
les transports en commun	*public transportation*
un vol	*a flight*

NOMS FÉMININS

une agence de voyages	*a travel agency*
une carte bancaire	*a bank card, a debit card*
une carte de crédit (une carte bleue)	*a credit card*
la classe économique	*economy class, coach*
la culture	*the culture*
la géographie	*the geography*
l'heure d'arrivée	*the arrival time*
l'heure de départ	*the departure time*
l'heure locale	*local time*
des infos	*info*
la première classe	*first class*

EXPRESSIONS VERBALES

connaître	*to know, to be familiar with, to be acquainted with*
faire une réservation	*to make a reservation*
reconnaître	*to recognize*
savoir	*to know*

DIVERS

Ça te/vous convient?	*Does that work for you?*
il me (te/nous/vous/lui/leur) faut	*I (you/we/you/he [she]/they) need*
me	*(to) me*
nous	*(to) us*
te	*(to) you*
vous	*(to) you*

Deciding where to go on a trip

NOMS MASCULINS

le Brésil	*Brazil*
le Canada	*Canada*
le Chili	*Chile*
un continent	*a continent*
les États-Unis	*the United States*
Israël	*Israel*
le Japon	*Japan*
le Maroc	*Morocco*
le Mexique	*Mexico*
le Moyen-Orient	*the Middle East*
l'Ontario	*Ontario*
le Pérou	*Peru*
le Royaume-Uni	*the United Kingdom*
le Sénégal	*Senegal*
le Texas	*Texas*
le Viêt Nam	*Vietnam*

NOMS FÉMININS

l'Afrique	*Africa*
l'Algérie	*Algeria*
l'Allemagne	*Germany*
l'Amérique centrale	*Central America*
l'Amérique du Nord	*North America*
l'Amérique du Sud	*South America*
les Antilles	*the West Indies*
l'Argentine	*Argentina*
l'Asie	*Asia*
l'Australie	*Australia*
la Belgique	*Belgium*
la Californie	*California*
la Chine	*China*
la Colombie	*Colombia*
la Côte d'Ivoire	*Ivory Coast*
la Croatie	*Croatia*
l'Égypte	*Egypt*
l'Espagne	*Spain*
l'Europe	*Europe*
la Floride	*Florida*
la France	*France*
la Grèce	*Greece*
la Guyane	*French Guiana*
l'Irlande	*Ireland*
l'Italie	*Italy*
la Nouvelle-Calédonie	*New Caledonia*
l'Océanie	*Oceania*
la Polynésie française	*French Polynesia*
la Russie	*Russia*
la Suisse	*Switzerland*

DIVERS

adorer	*to adore, to love*

Tableaux des verbes

VERBES AUXILIAIRES

VERBE INFINITIF	PRÉSENT	PASSÉ COMPOSÉ	IMPARFAIT	FUTUR	CONDITIONNEL PRÉSENT	SUBJONCTIF PRÉSENT	IMPÉRATIF
avoir	ai	ai eu	avais	aurai	aurais	aie	
to have	as	as eu	avais	auras	aurais	aies	aie
	a	a eu	avait	aura	aurait	ait	
	avons	avons eu	avions	aurons	aurions	ayons	ayons
	avez	avez eu	aviez	aurez	auriez	ayez	ayez
	ont	ont eu	avaient	auront	auraient	aient	
être	suis	ai été	étais	serai	serais	sois	
to be	es	as été	étais	seras	serais	sois	sois
	est	a été	était	sera	serait	soit	
	sommes	avons été	étions	serons	serions	soyons	soyons
	êtes	avez été	étiez	serez	seriez	soyez	soyez
	sont	ont été	étaient	seront	seraient	soient	

VERBES RÉGULIERS

VERBE INFINITIF	PRÉSENT	PASSÉ COMPOSÉ	IMPARFAIT	FUTUR	CONDITIONNEL PRÉSENT	SUBJONCTIF PRÉSENT	IMPÉRATIF
-er verbs							
parler	parle	ai parlé	parlais	parlerai	parlerais	parle	
to talk,	parles	as parlé	parlais	parleras	parlerais	parles	parle
to speak	parle	a parlé	parlait	parlera	parlerait	parle	
	parlons	avons parlé	parlions	parlerons	parlerions	parlions	parlons
	parlez	avez parlé	parliez	parlerez	parleriez	parliez	parlez
	parlent	ont parlé	parlaient	parleront	parleraient	parlent	
-ir verbs							
finir	finis	ai fini	finissais	finirai	finirais	finisse	
to finish	finis	as fini	finissais	finiras	finirais	finisses	finis
	finit	a fini	finissait	finira	finirait	finisse	
	finissons	avons fini	finissions	finirons	finirions	finissions	finissons
	finissez	avez fini	finissiez	finirez	finiriez	finissiez	finissez
	finissent	ont fini	finissaient	finiront	finiraient	finissent	
-re verbs							
vendre	vends	ai vendu	vendais	vendrai	vendrais	vende	
to sell	vends	as vendu	vendais	vendras	vendrais	vendes	vends
	vend	a vendu	vendait	vendra	vendrait	vende	
	vendons	avons vendu	vendions	vendrons	vendrions	vendions	vendons
	vendez	avez vendu	vendiez	vendrez	vendriez	vendiez	vendez
	vendent	ont vendu	vendaient	vendront	vendraient	vendent	

VERBES RÉFLÉCHIS

VERBE INFINITIF	INDICATIF PRÉSENT	INDICATIF PASSÉ COMPOSÉ	INDICATIF IMPARFAIT	INDICATIF FUTUR	CONDITIONNEL PRÉSENT	SUBJONCTIF PRÉSENT	IMPÉRATIF
se laver *to wash oneself*	me lave	me suis lavé(e)	me lavais	me laverai	me laverais	me lave	
	te laves	t'es lavé(e)	te lavais	te laveras	te laverais	te laves	lave-toi
	se lave	s'est lavé(e)	se lavait	se lavera	se laverait	se lave	
	nous lavons	nous sommes lavé(e)s	nous lavions	nous laverons	nous laverions	nous lavions	lavons-nous
	vous lavez	vous êtes lavé(e)(s)	vous laviez	vous laverez	vous laveriez	vous laviez	lavez-vous
	se lavent	se sont lavé(e)s	se lavaient	se laveront	se laveraient	se lavent	

VERBES À CHANGEMENTS ORTHOGRAPHIQUES

VERBE INFINITIF	INDICATIF PRÉSENT	INDICATIF PASSÉ COMPOSÉ	INDICATIF IMPARFAIT	INDICATIF FUTUR	CONDITIONNEL PRÉSENT	SUBJONCTIF PRÉSENT	IMPÉRATIF
préférer *to prefer*	préfère	ai préféré	préférais	préférerai	préférerais	préfère	
	préfères	as préféré	préférais	préféreras	préférerais	préfères	préfère
	préfère	a préféré	préférait	préférera	préférerait	préfère	
	préférons	avons préféré	préférions	préférerons	préférerions	préférions	préférons
	préférez	avez préféré	préfériez	préférerez	préféreriez	préfériez	préférez
	préfèrent	ont préféré	préféraient	préféreront	préféreraient	préfèrent	
acheter *to buy*	achète	ai acheté	achetais	achèterai	achèterais	achète	
	achètes	as acheté	achetais	achèteras	achèterais	achètes	achète
	achète	a acheté	achetait	achètera	achèterait	achète	
	achetons	avons acheté	achetions	achèterons	achèterions	achetions	achetons
	achetez	avez acheté	achetiez	achèterez	achèteriez	achetiez	achetez
	achètent	ont acheté	achetaient	achèteront	achèteraient	achètent	
appeler *to call*	appelle	ai appelé	appelais	appellerai	appellerais	appelle	
	appelles	as appelé	appelais	appelleras	appellerais	appelles	appelle
	appelle	a appelé	appelait	appellera	appellerait	appelle	
	appelons	avons appelé	appelions	appellerons	appellerions	appelions	appelons
	appelez	avez appelé	appeliez	appellerez	appelleriez	appeliez	appelez
	appellent	ont appelé	appelaient	appelleront	appelleraient	appellent	
essayer *to try*	essaie	ai essayé	essayais	essaierai	essaierais	essaie	
	essaies	as essayé	essayais	essaieras	essaierais	essaies	essaie
	essaie	a essayé	essayait	essaiera	essaierait	essaie	
	essayons	avons essayé	essayions	essaierons	essaierions	essayions	essayons
	essayez	avez essayé	essayiez	essaierez	essaieriez	essayiez	essayez
	essaient	ont essayé	essayaient	essaieront	essaieraient	essaient	
manger *to eat*	mange	ai mangé	mangeais	mangerai	mangerais	mange	
	manges	as mangé	mangeais	mangeras	mangerais	manges	mange
	mange	a mangé	mangeait	mangera	mangerait	mange	
	mangeons	avons mangé	mangions	mangerons	mangerions	mangions	mangeons
	mangez	avez mangé	mangiez	mangerez	mangeriez	mangiez	mangez
	mangent	ont mangé	mangeaient	mangeront	mangeraient	mangent	
commencer *to begin*	commence	ai commencé	commençais	commencerai	commencerais	commence	
	commences	as commencé	commençais	commenceras	commencerais	commences	commence
	commence	a commencé	commençait	commencera	commencerait	commence	
	commençons	avons commencé	commencions	commencerons	commencerions	commencions	commençons
	commencez	avez commencé	commenciez	commencerez	commenceriez	commenciez	commencez
	commencent	ont commencé	commençaient	commenceront	commenceraient	commencent	

VERBES IRRÉGULIERS

VERBE INFINITIF	INDICATIF PRÉSENT	PASSÉ COMPOSÉ	IMPARFAIT	FUTUR	CONDITIONNEL PRÉSENT	SUBJONCTIF PRÉSENT	IMPÉRATIF
aller *to go*	vais	suis allé(e)	allais	irai	irais	aille	
	vas	es allé(e)	allais	iras	irais	ailles	va
	va	est allé(e)	allait	ira	irait	aille	
	allons	sommes allé(e)s	allions	irons	irions	allions	allons
	allez	êtes allé(e)(s)	alliez	irez	iriez	alliez	allez
	vont	sont allé(e)s	allaient	iront	iraient	aillent	
s'asseoir *to sit* *(down)*	m'assieds	me suis assis(e)	m'asseyais	m'assiérai	m'assiérais	m'asseye	
	t'assieds	t'es assis(e)	t'asseyais	t'assiéras	t'assiérais	t'asseyes	assieds-toi
	s'assied	s'est assis(e)	s'asseyait	s'assiéra	s'assiérait	s'asseye	
	nous asseyons	nous sommes assis(es)	nous asseyions	nous assiérons	nous assiérions	nous asseyions	asseyons-nous
	vous asseyez	vous êtes assis(e)(s)	vous asseyiez	vous assiérez	vous assiériez	vous asseyiez	asseyez-vous
	s'asseyent	se sont assis(es)	s'asseyaient	s'assiéront	s'assiéraient	s'asseyent	
battre *to beat*	bats	ai battu	battais	battrai	battrais	batte	
	bats	as battu	battais	battras	battrais	battes	bats
	bat	a battu	battait	battra	battrait	batte	
	battons	avons battu	battions	battrons	battrions	battions	battons
	battez	avez battu	battiez	battrez	battriez	battiez	battez
	battent	ont battu	battaient	battront	battraient	battent	
boire *to drink*	bois	ai bu	buvais	boirai	boirais	boive	
	bois	as bu	buvais	boiras	boirais	boives	bois
	boit	a bu	buvait	boira	boirait	boive	
	buvons	avons bu	buvions	boirons	boirions	buvions	buvons
	buvez	avez bu	buviez	boirez	boiriez	buviez	buvez
	boivent	ont bu	buvaient	boiront	boiraient	boivent	
conduire *to drive*	conduis	ai conduit	conduisais	conduirai	conduirais	conduise	
	conduis	as conduit	conduisais	conduiras	conduirais	conduises	conduis
	conduit	a conduit	conduisait	conduira	conduirait	conduise	
	conduisons	avons conduit	conduisions	conduirons	conduirions	conduisions	conduisons
	conduisez	avez conduit	conduisiez	conduirez	conduiriez	conduisiez	conduisez
	conduisent	ont conduit	conduisaient	conduiront	conduiraient	conduisent	
connaître *to be* *acquainted* *with,* *to know*	connais	ai connu	connaissais	connaîtrai	connaîtrais	connaisse	
	connais	as connu	connaissais	connaîtras	connaîtrais	connaisses	connais
	connaît	a connu	connaissait	connaîtra	connaîtrait	connaisse	
	connaissons	avons connu	connaissions	connaîtrons	connaîtrions	connaissions	connaissons
	connaissez	avez connu	connaissiez	connaîtrez	connaîtriez	connaissiez	connaissez
	connaissent	ont connu	connaissaient	connaîtront	connaîtraient	connaissent	
courir *to run*	cours	ai couru	courais	courrai	courrais	coure	
	cours	as couru	courais	courras	courrais	coures	cours
	court	a couru	courait	courra	courrait	coure	
	courons	avons couru	courions	courrons	courrions	courions	courons
	courez	avez couru	couriez	courrez	courriez	couriez	courez
	courent	ont couru	couraient	courront	courraient	courent	
croire *to believe*	crois	ai cru	croyais	croirai	croirais	croie	
	crois	as cru	croyais	croiras	croirais	croies	crois
	croit	a cru	croyait	croira	croirait	croie	
	croyons	avons cru	croyions	croirons	croirions	croyions	croyons
	croyez	avez cru	croyiez	croirez	croiriez	croyiez	croyez
	croient	ont cru	croyaient	croiront	croiraient	croient	

VERBES IRRÉGULIERS (SUITE)

VERBE INFINITIF	INDICATIF PRÉSENT	PASSÉ COMPOSÉ	IMPARFAIT	FUTUR	CONDITIONNEL PRÉSENT	SUBJONCTIF PRÉSENT	IMPÉRATIF
devoir	dois	ai dû	devais	devrai	devrais	doive	
must,	dois	as dû	devais	devras	devrais	doives	
to have to,	doit	a dû	devait	devra	devrait	doive	
to owe	devons	avons dû	devions	devrons	devrions	devions	
	devez	avez dû	deviez	devrez	devriez	deviez	
	doivent	ont dû	devaient	devront	devraient	doivent	
dire	dis	ai dit	disais	dirai	dirais	dise	
to say,	dis	as dit	disais	diras	dirais	dises	dis
to tell	dit	a dit	disait	dira	dirait	dise	
	disons	avons dit	disions	dirons	dirions	disions	disons
	dites	avez dit	disiez	direz	diriez	disiez	dites
	disent	ont dit	disaient	diront	diraient	disent	
dormir	dors	ai dormi	dormais	dormirai	dormirais	dorme	
to sleep	dors	as dormi	dormais	dormiras	dormirais	dormes	dors
	dort	a dormi	dormait	dormira	dormirait	dorme	
	dormons	avons dormi	dormions	dormirons	dormirions	dormions	dormons
	dormez	avez dormi	dormiez	dormirez	dormiriez	dormiez	dormez
	dorment	ont dormi	dormaient	dormiront	dormiraient	dorment	
écrire	écris	ai écrit	écrivais	écrirai	écrirais	écrive	
to write	écris	as écrit	écrivais	écriras	écrirais	écrives	écris
	écrit	a écrit	écrivait	écrira	écrirait	écrive	
	écrivons	avons écrit	écrivions	écrirons	écririons	écrivions	écrivons
	écrivez	avez écrit	écriviez	écrirez	écririez	écriviez	écrivez
	écrivent	ont écrit	écrivaient	écriront	écriraient	écrivent	
envoyer	envoie	ai envoyé	envoyais	enverrai	enverrais	envoie	
to send	envoies	as envoyé	envoyais	enverras	enverrais	envoies	envoie
	envoie	a envoyé	envoyait	enverra	enverrait	envoie	
	envoyons	avons envoyé	envoyions	enverrons	enverrions	envoyions	envoyons
	envoyez	avez envoyé	envoyiez	enverrez	enverriez	envoyiez	envoyez
	envoient	ont envoyé	envoyaient	enverront	enverraient	envoient	
faire	fais	ai fait	faisais	ferai	ferais	fasse	
to do,	fais	as fait	faisais	feras	ferais	fasses	fais
to make	fait	a fait	faisait	fera	ferait	fasse	
	faisons	avons fait	faisions	ferons	ferions	fassions	faisons
	faites	avez fait	faisiez	ferez	feriez	fassiez	faites
	font	ont fait	faisaient	feront	feraient	fassent	
falloir	faut	a fallu	fallait	faudra	faudrait	faille	
to be necessary							
lire	lis	ai lu	lisais	lirai	lirais	lise	
to read	lis	as lu	lisais	liras	lirais	lises	lis
	lit	a lu	lisait	lira	lirait	lise	
	lisons	avons lu	lisions	lirons	lirions	lisions	lisons
	lisez	avez lu	lisiez	lirez	liriez	lisiez	lisez
	lisent	ont lu	lisaient	liront	liraient	lisent	
mettre	mets	ai mis	mettais	mettrai	mettrais	mette	
to put (on),	mets	as mis	mettais	mettras	mettrais	mettes	mets
to place,	met	a mis	mettait	mettra	mettrait	mette	
to set	mettons	avons mis	mettions	mettrons	mettrions	mettions	mettons
	mettez	avez mis	mettiez	mettrez	mettriez	mettiez	mettez
	mettent	ont mis	mettaient	mettront	mettraient	mettent	

VERBES IRRÉGULIERS (SUITE)

VERBE INFINITIF	INDICATIF PRÉSENT	PASSÉ COMPOSÉ	IMPARFAIT	FUTUR	CONDITIONNEL PRÉSENT	SUBJONCTIF PRÉSENT	IMPÉRATIF
obtenir *to obtain*	obtiens	ai obtenu	obtenais	obtiendrai	obtiendrais	obtienne	
	obtiens	as obtenu	obtenais	obtiendras	obtiendrais	obtiennes	obtiens
	obtient	a obtenu	obtenait	obtiendra	obtiendrait	obtienne	
	obtenons	avons obtenu	obtenions	obtiendrons	obtiendrions	obtenions	obtenons
	obtenez	avez obtenu	obteniez	obtiendrez	obtiendriez	obteniez	obtenez
	obtiennent	ont obtenu	obtenaient	obtiendront	obtiendraient	obtiennent	
ouvrir *to open*	ouvre	ai ouvert	ouvrais	ouvrirai	ouvrirais	ouvre	
	ouvres	as ouvert	ouvrais	ouvriras	ouvrirais	ouvres	ouvre
	ouvre	a ouvert	ouvrait	ouvrira	ouvrirait	ouvre	
	ouvrons	avons ouvert	ouvrions	ouvrirons	ouvririons	ouvrions	ouvrons
	ouvrez	avez ouvert	ouvriez	ouvrirez	ouvririez	ouvriez	ouvrez
	ouvrent	ont ouvert	ouvraient	ouvriront	ouvriraient	ouvrent	
partir *to leave*	pars	suis parti(e)	partais	partirai	partirais	parte	
	pars	es parti(e)	partais	partiras	partirais	partes	pars
	part	est parti(e)	partait	partira	partirait	parte	
	partons	sommes parti(e)s	partions	partirons	partirions	partions	partons
	partez	êtes parti(e)(s)	partiez	partirez	partiriez	partiez	partez
	partent	sont parti(e)s	partaient	partiront	partiraient	partent	
pleuvoir *to rain*	pleut	a plu	pleuvait	pleuvra	pleuvrait	pleuve	
pouvoir *to be able, can*	peux	ai pu	pouvais	pourrai	pourrais	puisse	
	peux	as pu	pouvais	pourras	pourrais	puisses	
	peut	a pu	pouvait	pourra	pourrait	puisse	
	pouvons	avons pu	pouvions	pourrons	pourrions	puissions	
	pouvez	avez pu	pouviez	pourrez	pourriez	puissiez	
	peuvent	ont pu	pouvaient	pourront	pourraient	puissent	
prendre *to take*	prends	ai pris	prenais	prendrai	prendrais	prenne	
	prends	as pris	prenais	prendras	prendrais	prennes	prends
	prend	a pris	prenait	prendra	prendrait	prenne	
	prenons	avons pris	prenions	prendrons	prendrions	prenions	prenons
	prenez	avez pris	preniez	prendrez	prendriez	preniez	prenez
	prennent	ont pris	prenaient	prendront	prendraient	prennent	
recevoir *to receive*	reçois	ai reçu	recevais	recevrai	recevrais	reçoive	
	reçois	as reçu	recevais	recevras	recevrais	reçoives	reçois
	reçoit	a reçu	recevait	recevra	recevrait	reçoive	
	recevons	avons reçu	recevions	recevrons	recevrions	recevions	recevons
	recevez	avez reçu	receviez	recevrez	recevriez	receviez	recevez
	reçoivent	ont reçu	recevaient	recevront	recevraient	reçoivent	
rire *to laugh*	ris	ai ri	riais	rirai	rirais	rie	
	ris	as ri	riais	riras	rirais	ries	ris
	rit	a ri	riait	rira	rirait	rie	
	rions	avons ri	riions	rirons	ririons	riions	rions
	riez	avez ri	riiez	rirez	ririez	riiez	riez
	rient	ont ri	riaient	riront	riraient	rient	
savoir *to know*	sais	ai su	savais	saurai	saurais	sache	
	sais	as su	savais	sauras	saurais	saches	sache
	sait	a su	savait	saura	saurait	sache	
	savons	avons su	savions	saurons	saurions	sachions	sachons
	savez	avez su	saviez	saurez	sauriez	sachiez	sachez
	savent	ont su	savaient	sauront	sauraient	sachent	

VERBES IRRÉGULIERS (SUITE)

VERBE INFINITIF	INDICATIF PRÉSENT	INDICATIF PASSÉ COMPOSÉ	INDICATIF IMPARFAIT	INDICATIF FUTUR	CONDITIONNEL PRÉSENT	SUBJONCTIF PRÉSENT	IMPÉRATIF
sortir *to go out*	sors	suis sorti(e)	sortais	sortirai	sortirais	sorte	
	sors	es sorti(e)	sortais	sortiras	sortirais	sortes	sors
	sort	est sorti(e)	sortait	sortira	sortirait	sorte	
	sortons	sommes sorti(e)s	sortions	sortirons	sortirions	sortions	sortons
	sortez	êtes sorti(e)(s)	sortiez	sortirez	sortiriez	sortiez	sortez
	sortent	sont sorti(e)s	sortaient	sortiront	sortiraient	sortent	
suivre *to follow*	suis	ai suivi	suivais	suivrai	suivrais	suive	
	suis	as suivi	suivais	suivras	suivrais	suives	suis
	suit	a suivi	suivait	suivra	suivrait	suive	
	suivons	avons suivi	suivions	suivrons	suivrions	suivions	suivons
	suivez	avez suivi	suiviez	suivrez	suivriez	suiviez	suivez
	suivent	ont suivi	suivaient	suivront	suivraient	suivent	
venir *to come*	viens	suis venu(e)	venais	viendrai	viendrais	vienne	
	viens	es venu(e)	venais	viendras	viendrais	viennes	viens
	vient	est venu(e)	venait	viendra	viendrait	vienne	
	venons	sommes venu(e)s	venions	viendrons	viendrions	venions	venons
	venez	êtes venu(e)(s)	veniez	viendrez	viendriez	veniez	venez
	viennent	sont venu(e)s	venaient	viendront	viendraient	viennent	
vivre *to live*	vis	ai vécu	vivais	vivrai	vivrais	vive	
	vis	as vécu	vivais	vivras	vivrais	vives	vis
	vit	a vécu	vivait	vivra	vivrait	vive	
	vivons	avons vécu	vivions	vivrons	vivrions	vivions	vivons
	vivez	avez vécu	viviez	vivrez	vivriez	viviez	vivez
	vivent	ont vécu	vivaient	vivront	vivraient	vivent	
voir *to see*	vois	ai vu	voyais	verrai	verrais	voie	
	vois	as vu	voyais	verras	verrais	voies	vois
	voit	a vu	voyait	verra	verrait	voie	
	voyons	avons vu	voyions	verrons	verrions	voyions	voyons
	voyez	avez vu	voyiez	verrez	verriez	voyiez	voyez
	voient	ont vu	voyaient	verront	verraient	voient	
vouloir *to want, to wish*	veux	ai voulu	voulais	voudrai	voudrais	veuille	
	veux	as voulu	voulais	voudras	voudrais	veuilles	veuille
	veut	a voulu	voulait	voudra	voudrait	veuille	
	voulons	avons voulu	voulions	voudrons	voudrions	voulions	veuillons
	voulez	avez voulu	vouliez	voudrez	voudriez	vouliez	veuillez
	veulent	ont voulu	voulaient	voudront	voudraient	veuillent	

This list contains words appearing in *Horizons,* except for absolute cognates. The definitions of active vocabulary words are followed by the number of the chapter where they are first presented. A (P) refers to the *Chapitre préliminaire.* When several translations, separated by commas, are listed before a chapter number, they are all considered active. Since verbs are sometimes introduced lexically in the infinitive before the conjugation of the present indicative is presented, consult the *Index* to find out the chapter where a conjugation is introduced. An *(m)*, *(f)*, or *(pl)* following a noun indicates that it is masculine, feminine, or plural. *Inv* means that a word is invariable. An asterisk before a word beginning with an **h** indicates that the **h** is aspirate.

A

à to, at, in (P); **À bientôt.** See you soon. (P); **à cause de** due to, because of; **À ce soir.** See you tonight/this evening. (2); **à côté (de)** next to (3); **À demain.** See you tomorrow. (P); **à... heure(s)** at . . . o'clock (P); **à la campagne** in the country (3); **à la française** French-style; **à la maison** at home (P); **à la page...** on page . . . (P); **à l'avance** in advance (9); **à l'étranger** abroad (9); **à l'heure** on time (4); **à l'université** at the university (P); **à peu près** about; **à pied** on foot (4); **À plus (tard)!** See you later! (P); **À quelle heure?** At what time? (P); **à suivre** to be continued (6); **À tout à l'heure.** See you in a little while. (P); **au café** at the café (P); **au coin de** on the corner of (10); **au cours de** in the course of, during, while on (10); **au-dessus de** above; **au premier étage** on the second floor (3); **Au revoir.** Good-bye. (P); **à votre avis** in your opinion (8); **café** *(m)* **au lait** coffee with milk (2); **du lundi au vendredi** from Monday to Friday *(every week)* (P); **j'habite à** *(+ city)* I live in *(+ city)* (P)
abandonner to abandon, to leave
abolir to abolish
abonnement *(m)* subscription
abonner: s'abonner à to subscribe to
abord: d'abord first (2)
abricot *(m)* apricot
abriter to shelter
absolument absolutely
Acadie *(f)* Acadia
accent *(m)* accent (P); **accent aigu / circonflexe / grave** acute / circumflex / grave accent (P); **Ça s'écrit avec ou sans accent?** That's written with or without an accent? (P)
accepter to accept (7)
accès *(m)* access (10); **accès Wi-Fi** *(m)* Wi-Fi access (10)
accessoire *(m)* accessory
accidentellement accidentally
accompagner to accompany
accomplir to accomplish
accord *(m)* agreement; **D'accord!** Okay! (2), Agreed!; **se mettre d'accord** to come to an agreement
accorder to give; **s'accorder** to grant each other
achat *(m)* purchase
acheter to buy (4)
acide gras (trans) *(m)* (trans) fatty acid
acteur *(m)* actor (6)
actif (active) active, working
activité *(f)* activity (2)
actrice *(f)* actress (6)
actuellement currently
adapter: s'adapter to adapt

addition *(f)* check, bill
adjectif *(m)* adjective (3)
administratif(-ive): centre administratif *(m)* administration building
admirer to admire (9)
adorer to adore, to love (5)
adresse *(f)* address (3); **adresse** *(f)* **mail** e-mail address (3)
aérien(ne) aerial
aérobic *(f)* aerobics: **faire de l'aérobic** to do aerobics (8)
aéroport *(m)* airport (10)
affaire *(f)* thing, belonging, business; **femme d'affaires** businesswoman (5); **homme d'affaires** businessman (5)
affiché(e) posted
africain(e) African
Afrique *(f)* Africa (9); **Afrique** *(f)* **du Sud** South Africa
âge *(m)* age (4); **Quel âge a... ?** How old is . . . ? (4)
âgé(e) old (4)
agence *(f)* **de voyages** travel agency (9)
agent *(m)* agent; **agent** *(m)* **de police** police officer; **agent** *(m)* **de voyages** travel agent (9)
agir to act, to take action
agité(e) agitated
agneau *(m)* lamb
agréable pleasant (1)
aider to help (5); **Je peux vous aider?** May I help you? (5)
aïe ouch
aigu(ë) acute (P), shrill
ail *(m)* garlic
aile *(f)* wing
ailleurs elsewhere; **par ailleurs** furthermore
aimable kind, amiable
aimer to like, to love (2); **Aimeriez-vous... ?** Would you like . . . ? (8); **aimer mieux** to like better, to prefer (2); **Est-ce que tu aimes/ vous aimez... ?** Do you like . . . ? (1); **J'aime/ Je n'aime pas...** I like/I don't like . . . (1); **J'aimerais...** I would like . . . (8); **J'aimerais autant...** I would just as soon . . . (10); **s'aimer** to love each other (7)
aîné(e) oldest *(child)*
ainsi thus; **ainsi que** as well as
air *(m)* air, look, appearance; **avoir l'air** *(+ adjective)* to look / to seem *(+ adjective)* (4); **Ça a l'air bien.** It/That seems nice. (3); **de plein air** outdoor (4)
aise *(f)* ease; **mal à l'aise** ill at ease
aisé(e): classe aisée *(f)* upper class
ajouter to add
alcool *(m)* alcohol (8)
alcoolisé(e) alcoholic
Algérie *(f)* Algeria (9)
algérien(ne) Algerian
aliment *(m)* food

alimentaire food
Allemagne *(f)* Germany (9)
allemand *(m)* German (1)
allemand(e) German
aller (à) to go (to) (2); **aller à la chasse** to go hunting; **aller à la pêche** to go fishing; **aller à pied** to walk, to go on foot (4); **aller simple** *(m)* one-way ticket (9); **aller très bien à quelqu'un** to look very good on someone; **aller voir** to go see, to visit *(a person)* (4); **Allez au tableau.** Go to the board. (P); **Allons...!** Let's go...! (2); **billet aller-retour** *(m)* round-trip ticket (9); **Ça va?** How's it going? *(familiar)* (P); **Ça va.** It's going fine. (P); **Comment allez-vous?** How are you? *(formal)* (P); **Comment ça va?**, How's it going? *(familiar)* (P); **Comment vas-tu?** How are you? *(informal)* (P); **je vais** I go, I am going (2); **Je vais très bien** I'm doing very well. (P); **On va... ?** Shall we go . . . ? (2); **Qu'est-ce que vous allez prendre?** What are you going to have? (2); **Qu'est-ce qui ne va pas?** What's wrong? (10); **s'en aller** to go away
allergie *(f)* allergy (10)
allié(e) allied
allô hello *(on the telephone)* (6)
allumer to light
alors so, then, therefore (1); **alors que** whereas
alpinisme *(m)* mountain climbing; **faire de l'alpinisme** to go mountain climbing
amande *(f)* almond
amant(e) *(mf)* lover
améliorer to improve
amener to take, to bring
américain(e) American (P); **à l'américaine** American-style (8)
Amérindien(ne) *(mf)* Native American
Amérique *(f)* America (9); **Amérique centrale** *(f)* Central America (9); **Amérique** *(f)* **du Nord** North America (9); **Amérique** *(f)* **du Sud** South America (9)
ami(e) *(mf)* friend (P)
amitié *(f)* friendship
amour *(m)* love (6); **film** *(m)* **d'amour** romantic movie (6); **le grand amour** *(m)* true love (7)
amoureux(-euse) (de) in love (with) (6); **tomber amoureux(-euse) de** to fall in love with (6); **vie amoureuse** *(f)* love life
amphithéâtre *(m)* lecture hall (1)
ampoule *(f)* light bulb
amusant(e) fun (1)
amuser to amuse; **s'amuser** to have fun (7)
an *(m)* year (5); **avoir... ans** to be . . . years old (4); **jour** *(m)* **de l'An** *(m)* New Year's Day
ananas *(m)* pineapple
anchois *(m)* anchovy
ancien(ne) former, old, ancient

andouillette *(f)* small sausage of chitterlings
ange *(m)* angel
anglais *(m)* English (P)
anglais(e) English
Angleterre *(f)* England; **Nouvelle-Angleterre**
(f) New England
anglophone English-speaking
angoisse *(f)* anguish
animal *(m)* *(pl* **animaux)** animal (3)
animé(e) animated; **dessin animé** *(m)* cartoon
année *(f)* year (4); **les années** *(fpl)* **trente** the
thirties
annexion *(f)* annexation
anniversaire *(m)* birthday (4); **anniversaire** *(m)*
de mariage wedding anniversary
annonce *(f)* advertisement, announcement
anorak *(m)* ski jacket, anorak (5)
antillais(e) West Indian
Antilles *(fpl)* West Indies (9)
antimicrobien(ne) antimicrobial
antipathique disagreeable, unpleasant (1)
antique ancient
août *(m)* August (4)
apéritif (apéro) *(m)* (before-dinner) drink (8)
appareil *(m)* device, apparatus, appliance
apparence *(f)* appearance
apparenté(e) related
appartement *(m)* apartment (3)
appartenir (à) to belong (to)
appeler to call; **appelé(e)** called; **Comment
s'appelle... ?** What is . . .'s name? (4);
Comment t'appelles-tu? What's your
name? *(informal);* **Comment vous appelez-
vous?** What's your name? *(formal)* (P); **Il/
Elle s'appelle...** His/Her name is . . . (4); **Je
m'appelle...** My name is . . . (P); **s'appeler**
to be named (7), to be called; **Tu t'appelles
comment?** What's your name? *(informal)*
(P)
appétit *(m)* appetite
apporter to bring
apprécier to appreciate (6), to like
apprendre to learn (4); **Apprenez les mots de
vocabulaire.** Learn the vocabulary words.
(P)
apprentissage *(m)* apprenticeship
approcher: s'approcher (de) to approach
approprié(e) appropriate
approximatif(-ive) approximate
après after (P), afterwards (2); **après les cours**
after class (2); **d'après** according to
après-demain the day after tomorrow (4)
après-midi *(m)* afternoon (P); **cet
après-midi** this afternoon (4); **Il est une
heure de l'après-midi.** It's one o'clock in
the afternoon. (P); **l'après-midi** in the
afternoon, afternoons (P)
arabe *(m)* Arabic
arbre *(m)* tree (1)
arc *(m)* arch, bow
archéologique archeological
archipel *(m)* archipelago
argent *(m)* money, silver (2)
Argentine *(f)* Argentina (9)
armée *(f)* army
arracher: s'arracher les cheveux to pull out
your hair
arrêt *(m)* stop; **arrêt** *(m)* **de bus** bus stop (3)
arrêter to arrest, to stop; **s'arrêter** to stop (7)
arrivée *(f)* arrival (9)
arriver to arrive (3), to happen
art *(m)* art (1); **les arts** the arts (1); **les beaux-
arts** the fine arts
article *(m)* article (9)

artisanal(e) *(mpl* **artisanaux)** handcrafted
artiste *(mf)* artist, performer
ascenseur *(m)* elevator (3)
Asie *(f)* Asia (9)
aspect physique *(m)* physical appearance (7)
asperge *(f)* asparagus
aspirine *(f)* aspirin (10)
assassiner to murder, to assassinate
asseoir: Asseyez-vous. Sit down.; **s'asseoir** to
sit (down)
assez fairly, rather (P); **assez (de)** enough (of)
(1)
assiette *(f)* plate
assis(e) seated (9)
assister à to attend
association caritative *(f)* charitable
organization
associer to associate; **associé(e)** associated
assurance *(f)* insurance
Atlantique *(m)* Atlantic
atroce atrocious, dreadful
attaque *(f)* attack; **attaque** *(f)* **d'apoplexie**
stroke; **être d'attaque** to feel fit
attendre to wait (for) (7); **s'attendre à** to
expect to
attente *(f)* waiting
attention: faire attention (à) to pay attention
(to), to watch out (for) (8)
attirant(e) attractive
attirer to attract
attraper to catch, to get hold of
aube *(f)* dawn
auberge *(f)* inn; **auberge** *(f)* **de jeunesse** youth
hostel (10)
aubergine *(f)* eggplant
auburn *(inv)* auburn (4)
aucun(e): ne... aucun(e) no, none, not one
audacieux(-euse) audacious, bold
au-dessus above
auditif(-ive) auditory
augmenter to augment, to raise
aujourd'hui today (P)
auparavant beforehand
auprès de among
auquel (à laquelle, auxquels, auxquelles) to
which
aussi too, also (P); **aussi... que** as . . . as (1)
austral(e) *(mpl* **austraux)** southern
Australie *(f)* Australia (9)
autant (de)... (que) as much . . . (as), as many
. . . (as); **J'aimerais autant...** I would just as
soon . . . (10)
autobus *(m)* bus (4); **arrêt** *(m)* **d'autobus** bus
stop (3); **en autobus** by bus (4)
autocar *(m)* bus (4); **en autocar** by bus (4)
automne *(m)* autumn, fall (5); **en automne** in
autumn (5)
autoportrait *(m)* self-portrait (P)
autour de around
autre other (P); **dans un autre cours** in another
class (P); **quelquefois... d'autres fois**
sometimes . . . other times (7); **Qu'est-ce
que je peux vous proposer d'autre?**
What else can I get you? (8); **autre part**
somewhere else
autrefois formerly, in the past
Autriche *(f)* Austria
auxiliaire *(m)* auxiliary
avance *(f)* advance; **à l'avance** in advance (9);
en avance early
avancer to advance
avant before (P); **avant de (faire)** before
(doing) (7); **avant tout** above all
avantage *(m)* advantage

avec with (P); **avec elle / lui / elles / eux**
with her / him / them *(f)* / them *(m)* (2);
avec ma famille with my family (P); **Avec
plaisir!** With pleasure! (6)
avenir *(m)* future
aventure *(f)* adventure; **film** *(m)* **d'aventure**
adventure movie
avenue *(f)* avenue (10)
avion *(m)* airplane (4); **en avion** by airplane (4)
avis *(m)* opinion; **à votre avis** in your opinion
(8)
avoir to have (3); **avoir... ans** to be . . . years
old (4); **avoir besoin de** to need (4); **avoir
chaud** to be hot (4); **avoir cours** to have
class (6); **avoir de la fièvre** to have fever;
avoir du mal à... to have difficulty . . . ,
to have a hard time . . . ; **avoir envie de**
to feel like, to want (4); **avoir faim** to be
hungry (4); **avoir froid** to be cold (4); **avoir
l'air (+** *adjective)* to look / to seem
(+ *adjective)* (4); **avoir le nez bouché**
to have a stopped-up nose; **avoir le nez
qui coule** to have a runny nose; **avoir
les cheveux/les yeux...** to have . . . hair/
eyes (4); **avoir lieu** to take place; **avoir
l'intention de** to plan on, to intend to (4);
avoir mal (à) one's . . . hurts (10), to ache;
avoir peur (de) to be afraid (of), to fear
(4); **avoir pitié (de)** to have pity (on / for)
(10); **avoir raison** to be right (4); **avoir soif**
to be thirsty (4); **avoir sommeil** to be sleepy
(4); **avoir tort** to be wrong (4); **j'ai faim** I'm
hungry (2); **j'ai soif** I'm thirsty (2); **il y a...**
there is/there are . . . (1), ago (5); **Quel âge
a... ?** How old is . . . ? (4)
avril *(m)* April (4)
ayant having

B

baccalauréat (bac) *(m) a comprehensive
examination at the end of secondary school*
bacon *(m)* bacon (8)
bagages *(mpl)* baggage
baguette *(f)* loaf of French bread (8)
baie *(f)* bay
bain *(m)* bath (7); **maillot** *(m)* **de bain**
swimsuit (5); **prendre un bain** *(m)* **de soleil**
to sunbathe (4); **salle** *(f)* **de bains** bathroom
(3)
baiser *(m)* kiss
baisser to lower
bal *(m)* ball, dance (6)
balcon *(m)* balcony (10)
baleine *(f)* whale
ballet *(m)* ballet (9)
ballon *(m)* ball
banal(e) *(mpl* **banaux)** commonplace, banal
banane *(f)* banana (8)
bancaire banking; **carte** *(f)* **bancaire** bank card,
debit card (9)
bande-annonce *(f)* movie trailer
bande déssinée *(f)* comic strip, comic book
banlieue *(f)* suburbs (3); **en banlieue** in the
suburbs (3)
banque *(f)* bank (10)
banquier *(m)* banker
barbe *(f)* beard (4)
barrer to cross out
bas *(m)* bottom
bas(se) low; **table basse** *(f)* coffee table
basant: en vous basant sur based on
basé(e) sur based on (6)
baseball *(m)* baseball (2)
basilique *(f)* basilica

basket *(m)* basketball (1)

baskets *(fpl)* tennis shoes (5)

bataille *(f)* battle

bateau *(m)* boat (4); **en bateau** by boat (4); **faire du bateau** to go boating (5)

bâtiment *(m)* building (1)

batterie *(f)* drums (2)

battre to beat; **se battre** to fight

bavarois *(m)* Bavarian cream

bavette *(f)* flank steak

bazar: Quel bazar! *(familiar)* What a mess! (3)

BD (bande déssinée) *(f)* comic strip, comic book

beau (bel, belle, *pl* **beaux, belles)** beautiful, handsome (1); **beau-frère** *(m)* brother-in-law; **beau-père** *(m)* father-in-law (4); **beaux-arts** *(mpl)* fine arts; **beaux-parents** *(mpl)* stepparents, in-laws (4); **belle-mère** *(f)* mother-in-law (4); **belle-sœur** *(f)* sister-in-law; **Il fait beau.** The weather's nice. (5)

beaucoup a lot (P); **beaucoup (de)** a lot (of) (1)

beauté *(f)* beauty (7)

bébé *(m)* baby

beige beige (3)

beignet *(m)* fritter

belge Belgian

Belgique *(f)* Belgium (9)

bénéfique beneficial

bénévole benevolent, volunteer

berbère Berber

berceuse *(f)* lullaby

besoin *(m)* need; **avoir besoin de** to need (4)

bête *(f)* beast (6), animal

bête stupid, dumb (1)

bêtise *(f)* foolish thing, stupidity

beurre *(m)* butter (8); **beurre** *(m)* **de cacahuète** peanut butter

beurré(e) buttered

bibliothèque *(f)* library (1), bookcase

bien *(m)* good; **biens** *(mpl)* goods

bien well (P), very; **à bien des égards** in many regards; **bien d'autres** many others; **bien que** although; **Bien sûr!** Of course! (5); **Ça a l'air bien.** It/That seems nice. (3); **c'est bien de...** it's good to . . . (10)

bien-être *(m)* well-being

bienfait *(m)* benefit

bienfaiteur *(m)*, **bienfaitrice** *(f)* benefactor

bientôt soon (P); **À bientôt.** See you soon. (P)

bienvenu(e) welcome

bière *(f)* beer (2)

bifteck *(m)* steak (8); **bifteck hâché** *(m)* ground meat

bikini *(m)* bikini (5)

bilan *(m)* assessment

bilingue bilingual

billet *(m)* ticket (9), bill; **billet** *(m)* **d'avion** plane ticket (9); **distributeur** *(m)* **de billets** ATM machine (10)

bio organic; **produits bio** *(mpl)* organic products (8)

biologie *(f)* biology (1)

biscotte *(f)* melba toast

bise *(f)* kiss

bistro(t) *(m)* restaurant, pub (6)

blanc(he) white (3); **vin blanc** *(m)* white wine (2)

blanquette *(f)* stew *(usually veal)*

blessure *(f)* injury

bleu(e) blue (3); **carte** *(f)* **bleue** credit card (9)

blog *(m)* blog (9)

bloguer to blog

blond(e) blond (4)

blouson *(m)* windbreaker, jacket

Blu-ray: lecteur *(m)* **Blu-ray** Blu-ray player (3)

bœuf *(m)* beef (8); **bœuf bourguignon** *(m)* beef burgundy

bohème bohemian

boire to drink (4)

boisson *(f)* drink (2)

boîte *(f)* box, can (8); **boîte** *(f)* **de nuit** nightclub (1)

bol *(m)* bowl

bon (ne) good (1); **Bon anniversaire!** Happy birthday!; **Bonne année!** Happy New Year!; **Bonne idée!** Good idea! (4); **Bonne journée!** Have a good day!; **Bon séjour!** Enjoy your stay! (10); **Bon week-end!** Have a good weekend!

bonbon *(m)* candy

bonheur *(m)* happiness (7)

bonhomme *(m)* man, guy, fellow

Bonjour. Hello., Good morning. (P)

bonne *(f)* maid, nanny

Bonsoir. Good evening. (P)

bord *(m)* edge; **à bord** on board; **au bord de** at the edge of; **bord** *(m)* **de la mer** seaside

border to border

botanique botanical

botte *(f)* boot (5)

bouche *(f)* mouth (10)

bouché(e) stopped-up; **cidre bouché** *(m)* bottled cider

boucherie *(f)* butcher's shop (8)

boudin *(m)* blood sausage

bouillabaisse *(f)* fish soup

bouillir to boil

bouillon *(m)* broth

boulangerie *(f)* bakery (8); **boulangerie-pâtisserie** bakery-pastry shop (8)

boule *(f)* ball

boulevard *(m)* boulevard (10)

bouleversant(e) overwhelming, very touching

boulot *(m)* *(familiar)* work

bouquiniste *(mf)* secondhand bookseller

bourg *(m)* town

bout *(m)* end (3); **au bout (de)** at the end (of) (3)

bouteille (de) *(f)* bottle (of) (8)

boutique *(f)* shop (10); **boutique** *(f)* **de cadeaux** gift shop (10)

bras *(m)* arm (10)

bref (brève) short, brief; **Bref,...** In short, . . ., To be brief, . . .

Brésil *(m)* Brazil (9)

Bretagne *(f)* Brittany

breton *(m)* Breton *(language)*

brevet *(m)* certificate, diploma

bricoler to do handiwork (2)

brioche *(f)* brioche *(a type of soft bread)*

brique *(f)* brick

britannique British

brochette *(f)* skewer

brocoli *(m)* broccoli

bronzer to tan (9)

brosser to brush; **se brosser (les cheveux / les dents)** to brush (one's hair / one's teeth) (7)

brouillard *(m)* fog, mist, haze

bruit *(m)* noise (3)

brûler to burn; **se brûler la main** to burn your hand

brun(e) *(with hair)* medium/dark brown (4), brunette, darkhaired

Bruxelles Brussels

bruyant(e) noisy

bulletin *(m)* **d'abonnement** subscription form

bureau *(m)* desk (3), office (1); **bureau** *(m)* **de change** currency exchange (10); **bureau** *(m)* **de poste** post office (10); **bureau** *(m)* **de tabac** tobacco shop

bus *(m)* bus (3); **arrêt** *(m)* **de bus** bus stop (3); **en bus** by bus (4)

but *(m)* goal

C

ça that (P); **Ça fait combien?** How much is it? (2); **Ça fait... euros.** That's . . . euros. (2); **Ça lui plaît?** Does he/she like it? (9); **Ça s'écrit comment?** How is that written? (P); **Ça s'écrit...** That's written . . . (P); **Ça te/vous dit?** How does that sound to you? (2); **Ça te plaît.** You like it. (3); **Ça va?** How's it going? *(familiar)* (P); **Ça va.** It's going fine. (P); **C'est ça!** That's right! (1); **comme ci comme ça** so-so (P); **Comment ça va?** How's it going? *(familiar)* (P); **Qu'est-ce que ça veut dire?** What does that mean? (P)

cabine *(f)* **d'essayage** fitting room (5); **cabine** *(f)* **téléphonique** telephone booth

cacahuète *(f)* peanut; **beurre** *(m)* **de cacahuète** peanut butter

cacher to hide; **se cacher** to hide oneself, to be hidden

cadeau *(m)* gift, present (10); **boutique** *(f)* **de cadeaux** gift shop (10)

cadien(ne) Cajun (4)

cadre *(m)* frame, surroundings

café *(m)* café (1), coffee (2); **café** *(m)* **au lait** coffee with milk (2)

cahier *(m)* workbook (P), notebook; **Faites les devoirs dans le cahier.** Do the homework in the workbook. (P)

calcul *(m)* calculation, calculus

calculer to calculate

Californie *(f)* California (9)

calme calm (4)

calmement calmly

calmer: se calmer to calm down

calorie *(f)* calorie (8)

calorique high in calories

camarade *(mf)* pal; **camarade** *(mf)* **de chambre** roommate (P); **camarade** *(mf)* **de classe** classmate

camerounais(e) Cameroonian

campagne *(f)* country (3), campaign; **à la campagne** in the country (3)

camping *(m)* camping, campground (5); **faire du camping** to go camping (5)

campus *(m)* campus (1)

Canada *(m)* Canada (9)

canadien(ne) Canadian (P)

canapé *(m)* couch (3), open-faced sandwich

canard *(m)* duck (8)

candidat(e) *(mf)* candidate, applicant

canne à sucre *(f)* sugar cane

canoë *(m)* canoeing

caprice *(m)* whim

car *(m)* bus (4); **en car** by bus (4)

car because

caractère *(m)* character; **en caractères gras** boldfaced; **trait** *(m)* **de caractère** character trait (7)

carafe (de) *(f)* carafe (of) *(a decanter)* (8)

caraïbe Caribbean; **mer** *(f)* **des Caraïbes** Caribbean Sea

caritatif(-ive) charitable

carotte *(f)* carrot (8)

carré *(m)* square; **Vieux Carré** *(m)* French Quarter (4)

carrière *(f)* career

carte *(f)* menu (8), card, map; **carte** *(f)* **bancaire** bank card, debit card (9); **carte** *(f)* **bleue** credit card (9); **carte** *(f)* **de crédit** credit card (9); **carte** *(f)* **d'identité** identity card; **carte** *(f)* **postale** postcard (9); **carte** *(f)* **téléphonique** telephone card (10)

cas *(m)* case; **dans tous les cas** in any case

cascade *(f)* waterfall

casquette *(f)* cap

casser to break; **se casser la jambe** to break one's leg

casserole *(f)* pan

catégorie *(f)* category

cathédrale *(f)* cathedral

catholique *(mf)* Catholic (1)

cauchemar *(m)* nightmare

cause *(f)* cause; **à cause de** because of

CD *(m)* CD (3); **lecteur** *(m)* **CD** CD player (3)

ce (cet, cette) this, that (3); **ce (cet, cette)... ci** this . . . over here (3); **ce (cet, cette)... là** that . . . over there (3); **ce que** what, that which (7); **ce qui** what, that which (7); **ces** these, those (3); **ce semestre** this semester (P); **ce soir** tonight, this evening (2); **Ce sont...** They are . . ., These are . . ., Those are . . . (1); **C'est...** It's . . . (P), He / She / This / That is . . . (1); **c'est-à-dire** in other words, that is to say; **Qu'est-ce que c'est?** What is it? (2); **Qui est-ce?** Who is it? (2)

céder to give up

ceinture *(f)* belt

cela that; **depuis cela** since then

célèbre famous (4)

célébrer to celebrate

céleri *(m)* celery

célibataire single, unmarried (1)

celtique Celtic

celui (celle) the one

cendre *(f)* ash

cendrier *(m)* ashtray

censé(e) supposed

censure *(f)* censorship

cent *(m)* one hundred (3)

centime *(m)* centime *(one hundredth part of a euro)* (2)

central(e) *(mpl* **centraux)** central; **Amérique** *(f)* **centrale** Central America (9)

centre *(m)* center; **centre administratif** *(m)* administration building; **centre commercial** *(m)* shopping center, mall (4); **centre** *(m)* **d'étudiants** student center

centre-ville *(m)* downtown (3)

cependant however

céréales *(fpl)* cereal (8)

cerise *(f)* cherry (8)

certain(e) certain; **certains** some, certain people (8)

certainement certainly

cervelle *(f)* brain

cesser to cease

ceux (celles) those (ones) (8)

chacun(e) each one

chagrin *(m)* sorrow

chaîne *(f)* chain; **chaîne de télévision** television channel; **chaîne hi-fi** *(f)* stereo (3)

chaise *(f)* chair (3)

chalet *(m)* **à la montagne** ski lodge (10)

chaleur *(f)* warmth

chaleureux(-euse) warm

chambre *(f)* bedroom (3); **camarade** *(mf)* **de chambre** roommate (P); **chambre** *(f)* **d'hôte** bed and breakfast; **chambre double**
(f) double room (10); **chambre simple** single room *(f)* (10)

champ *(m)* field; **champ** *(m)* **de bataille** battlefield

champignon *(m)* mushroom

chance *(f)* luck (5); **Quelle chance!** What luck! (5)

change: bureau *(m)* **de change** currency exchange (10)

changement *(m)* change

changer to change (6); **changer de l'argent** to exchange money (9)

chanson *(f)* song

chanter to sing (2)

chanteur(-euse) *(mf)* singer

chapeau *(m)* hat

chapelle *(f)* chapel

chapitre *(m)* chapter

chaque each, every (3)

charcuterie *(f)* delicatessen, deli meats, cold cuts (8)

charger to charge, to load; **chargé(e) (de)** busy *(schedule)*, in charge (of); **se charger de** to take charge of

charmant(e) charming

chasse *(f)* hunt, hunting; **aller à la chasse** to go hunting

chasser to hunt, to make go away

chasseur *(m)* hunter

chat *(m)* cat (3)

châtain light/medium brown *(with hair)* (4)

château *(m)* castle

chaud(e) hot (2); **avoir chaud** to be hot (4); **chocolat chaud** *(m)* hot chocolate (2); **Il fait chaud.** It's hot. (5)

chauffeur *(m)* driver

chaussette *(f)* sock

chausson *(m)* **aux pommes** apple turnover

chaussure *(f)* shoe (5)

chef *(m)* head, boss, chief

chef-d'œuvre *(m)* masterpiece

chef-lieu *(m)* administrative center

chemin *(m)* road; **chemin** *(m)* **de fer** railroad; **indiquer le chemin** to give directions, to show the way (10)

chemise *(f)* shirt (5); **chemise** *(f)* **de nuit** nightgown

chemisier *(m)* blouse (5)

chèque *(m)* check (9); **chèque** *(m)* **de voyage** traveler's check

cher(-ère) expensive (3), dear

chercher to look for (3), to seek; **aller / venir chercher quelqu'un** to go / come pick up someone (10)

chéri(e) *(mf)* honey, darling

cheval *(m)* *(pl* **chevaux)** horse; **faire du cheval** to go horseback riding

cheveux *(mpl)* hair (4)

cheville *(f)* ankle; **se fouler la cheville** to sprain one's ankle

chèvre *(m)* goat cheese

chez... at / in / to / by . . . 's house/place (2); in *(a person)* (7)

chien *(m)* dog (3)

chiffre *(m)* number, numeral

Chili *(m)* Chile (9)

chimie *(f)* chemistry (1)

Chine *(f)* China (9)

chinois *(m)* Chinese

chirurgie *(f)* surgery

chocolat *(m)* chocolate (2); **gâteau** *(m)* **au chocolat** chocolate cake (8); **pain au chocolat** *(m)* chocolate-filled croissant (8)
choisir (de faire) to choose (to do) (8)

choix *(m)* choice (8)

chose *(f)* thing (3); **quelque chose** something (2)

chou *(m)* cabbage; **choux** *(mpl)* **de Bruxelles** Brussels sprouts

chou-fleur *(m)* cauliflower

chrysanthème *(m)* chrysanthemum

chute *(f)* waterfall

ci: ce (cet, cette)...-ci this . . . (5); **ce mois-ci** this month (4); **ces...-ci** these . . . (5); **ci-dessous** below; **ci-dessus** above; **comme ci comme ça** so-so (P)

ciao bye *(informal)*

ciel *(m)* sky

cimetière *(m)* cemetery

cinéaste *(mf)* filmmaker

ciné-club *(m)* cinema club (2)

cinéma *(m)* movie theater (1); **aller au cinéma** to go to the movies (2)

cinématographique film

cinq five (P)

cinquante fifty (2); **cinquante et un** fifty-one (2)

cinquième fifth (3)

circonstance *(f)* circumstance

circuler to circulate

cithare *(f)* zither

citoyen(ne) *(mf)* citizen

citron *(m)* lemon (2); **citron vert** *(m)* lime; **thé** *(m)* **au citron** tea with lemon (2)

civilisé(e) civilized

clair(e) light, clear; **bleu clair** light blue

claire *(f)* oyster bed

clairement clearly

classe *(f)* class (1); **classe** *(f)* **économique** economy class, coach (9); **première classe** *(f)* first class (9)

classé(e) ranked

classement *(m)* ranking

classique classical (1), classic (2)

clavier *(m)* keyboard

clé *(f)* key (10)

client(e) *(mf)* customer

climat *(m)* climate (9)

climatisation *(f)* air conditioning

climatisé(e) air-conditioned

coca *(m)* cola (2); **coca** *(m)* **light** diet cola (2)

coco *(m)* coconut

cocotier *(m)* coconut tree, palm tree

cocotte *(f)* casserole, primper

code *(m)* code; **code postal** *(m)* zip code (3)

cœur *(m)* heart; **au cœur de** in the heart of

coin *(m)* corner (3); **au coin de** on the corner of (10); **café** *(m)* **du coin** neighborhood café; **dans le coin (de)** in the corner (of) (3)

collation *(f)* snack

colle *(f)* glue, detention

collectionner to collect

collectivité *(f)* community

collège *(m)* middle school

collègue *(mf)* colleague

colline *(f)* hill

colocataire *(mf)* housemate (P)

Colombie *(f)* Colombia (9)

colon *(m)* colonist

colonne *(f)* column

combien (de) how much, how many (3); **Ça fait combien! / C'est combien?** How much is it? (2); **Combien font... et / moins... ?** How much is . . . plus / minus . . . ? (P); **Pendant combien de temps?** For how long? (5); **Vous êtes combien dans votre (ta) famille?** How many are there in your family? (4)

combinaison (f) slip, combination
comédie (f) comedy (6); comédie musicale (f) musical
comique comical
commander to order (2), to command
comme like, as, for (1), since (7); comme ci comme ça so-so (P); comme tu vois as you see (3); tout comme just as
commencer (à) to begin (to), to start (2); Le cours de français commence à... French class starts at . . . (P)
comment how (P); Ça s'écrit comment? How is that written? (P); Comment allez-vous? How are you? (formal) (P); Comment ça va? How's it going? (familiar) (P); Comment dit-on... en français/en anglais? How does one say . . . in French/in English? (P); Comment est-il/elle (sont-ils/ elles)? What is he/she (are they) like? (1); Comment? Répétez, s'il vous plaît. What? Please repeat. (P); Comment s'appelle... ? What is . . . 's name? (4); Comment vas-tu? How are you? (informal); Comment vous appelez-vous? What's your name? (formal) (P); Tu t'appelles comment? What's your name? (informal) (P)
commentaire (m) commentary
commerçant(e) (mf) shopkeeper (8), merchant
commerce (m) business (1)
commercial: centre commercial (m) shopping center, mall (4)
commettre to commit
commode (f) dresser, chest of drawers (3)
commode convenient
commodité (f) convenience, comfort
commun(e) common
communauté (f) community
communiquer to communicate (10)
compagnie (f) company; en compagnie de accompanied by
comparaison (f) comparison
comparer to compare (6); comparé(e) compared
compatibilité (f) compatibility (7)
compétence (f) skill, competency
complément d'objet direct / indirect (m) direct / indirect object
complet(-ète) complete (8); avec une phrase complète (f) with a complete sentence (P); pain complet (m) (loaf of) whole-grain bread (8)
complètement completely
complicité (f) bonding
comporter: se comporter to behave
composer to compose; composé(e) de composed of; se composer de to be made up of
compréhension (f) understanding
comprenant including
comprendre to understand (4), to include (8); compris(e) included (10); Oui, je comprends. / Non, je ne comprends pas. Yes, I understand. / No, I don't understand. (P); Vous comprenez? Do you understand? (P)
comptabilité (f) accounting (1)
comptable (m) accountant
compte (m) en banque bank account
compter to count, to plan on (9); Comptez de... à... Count from . . . to . . . (P)
concentrer: se concentrer sur to concentrate on
concerner to concern; concernant concerning
concert (m) concert (1); de concert avec along with

concombre (m) cucumber
concours (m) competition, competitive entrance examination
confiance (f) confidence; avoir confiance to have confidence (4); faire confiance à to trust
confirmer to confirm (10)
confit (m) de canard conserve of duck
confiture (f) jam, jelly (8)
confort (m) comfort
confortable comfortable (3)
conforter to comfort
confus(e) confused
congé (m) day off
conjuguer to conjugate
connaissance (f) acquaintance, knowledge; faire la connaissance de to meet (for the first time) (7)
connaître to know, to get to know, to be familiar / acquainted with (4); Connaissez-vous...? Do you know . . . ? (6); faire connaître to inform
connecter to connect; se connecter à Internet to log on to Internet
connu(e) known
conquérant(e) (mf) conqueror
conquête (f) conquest
consacrer to devote; consacré(e) à devoted to
conseil (m) piece of advice (8), council, committee
conseiller(-ère) (mf) counselor, adviser
conséquent: par conséquent consequently
conserver to keep
conserves (fpl) canned goods (8)
considérer to consider; se considérer to consider oneself
consommation (f) consumption, drink
consommer to consume
consonne (f) consonant
constamment constantly
construire to construct, to build; construit(e) built
consulat (m) consulate
contact (m) contact; en contact in contact (9)
conte (m) story (6); conte (m) de fées fairy tale (6)
contempler to contemplate
contenir to contain
content(e) happy, glad (8)
contenter: se contenter de to be happy to / with
continent (m) continent (9)
continu(e) continuous
continuer (tout droit) to continue (straight ahead) (10)
contraire (m) contrary; au contraire on the contrary
contrat (m) contract, agreement
contre against; par contre on the other hand
contrôle (m) control
contrôler to control (8); contrôlé(e) controlled, supervised
convenable appropriate, suitable
convenir to be suitable; Ça te/vous convient? Does that work for you? (9)
cool: assez cool pretty cool (P)
copain (m) boyfriend (2), (male) friend, pal (6)
copier sur to copy from
copieux(-euse) copious, large (8)
copine (f) girlfriend (2), (female) friend, pal (6)
coquelicot (m) poppy
coquillage (m) shellfish

coquilles St-Jacques (fpl) scallops
corde (f) rope, cord
corporel(le) of the body
corps (m) body (7)
correctement correctly
correspondant(e) corresponding
correspondre (à) to correspond (to)
Corse (f) Corsica
corse (m) Corsican (language)
costume (m) suit (for a man) (5)
côte (f) coast; Côte d'Azur (f) Riviera; côte (f) de porc pork chop (8); Côte d'Ivoire (f) Ivory Coast (9)
côté (m) side (3); à côté (de) next to (3); côté cour on the courtyard side (10); d'à côté next-door
cou (m) neck
couchant setting
coucher: se coucher to go to bed (7); chambre à coucher (f) bedroom
couler to run (liquids)
couleur (f) color (3); De quelle couleur est/sont... ? What color is/are . . . ? (3)
coulis (m) purée
couloir (m) hall, corridor (3)
coup (m) stroke, blow; coup (m) de foudre love at first sight (7); coup (m) de téléphone telephone call; tout à coup all of a sudden (6); tout d'un coup all at once (6)
coupe (f) dessert dish
couper to cut; se couper le doigt to cut one's finger
cour (f) court, courtyard; côté cour on the courtyard side (10)
couramment fluently
courant(e) present, current, common; au courant de aware of
courgette (f) zucchini
courir to run (9)
courrier (m) mail; courrier électronique (m) e-mail
cours (m) class, course (P); au cours de in the course of, during, while on (10); avoir cours to have class (6); cours (m) de français French class (P); cours (m) en ligne online course (1); dans un autre cours in another class (P); en cours in class (P); salle (f) de cours classroom (1); suivre un cours to take a course
course (f) errand (5), race; faire des courses to run errands (5); faire les courses to go grocery shopping (5)
court(e) short (4)
cousin(e) (mf) cousin (4)
coûter to cost (5)
coutume (f) custom
couvert(e) de covered with
couverture (f) blanket, cover (3)
covoiturage (m) carpooling
cravate (f) tie (5)
crayon (m) pencil (P); Prenez une feuille de papier et un crayon ou un stylo. Take out a piece of paper and a pencil or a pen. (P)
créancier(-ière) (mf) creditor
créatif(-ive) creative
crèche (f) (government-sponsored) day care
crédit: carte (f) de crédit credit card (9)
créer to create
crème (f) cream (8)
créole Creole
crevette (f) shrimp (8)
crier to shout
crise (f) crisis

critique *(f)* criticism
Croatie *(f)* Croatia (9)
croire (à) (que) to believe (in) (that); **je crois** I think
croiser to run across, to bump into
croisière *(f)* cruise
croissant *(m)* croissant (8)
croissant(e) growing
croix *(f)* cross; **en croix** crossed
croque-madame *(m)* toasted ham-and-cheese sandwich with an egg on top
croque-monsieur *(m)* toasted ham-and-cheese sandwich
cru(e) raw
crudités *(fpl)* raw vegetables (8)
cruel(le) cruel (6)
crustacé *(m)* shellfish
cuiller (cuillère) *(f)* spoon
cuir *(m)* leather
cuisine *(f)* kitchen (3), cuisine, cooking (4); **faire la cuisine** to cook (5)
cuisinier(-ère) *(mf)* cook
cuisinière *(f)* stove
cuivre *(m)* copper
cultiver to cultivate (7); **cultivé(e)** cultivated
culture *(f)* culture (9), cultivation
culturel(le) cultural (4)
curieux(-euse) curious, odd
cyclisme *(m)* cycling

D

dame *(f)* lady
Danemark *(m)* Denmark
dans in (P); **dans la rue...** on . . . Street (10)
dansant(e) dancing
danse *(f)* dance
danser to dance (2)
danseur(-euse) *(mf)* dancer
date *(f)* date (4); **C'est quelle date?** What is the date? (4); **Quelle est la date?** What is the date? (4)
dater de to date from
daurade *(f)* sea bream
de of, from, about (P); **de la, de l', du** some, any (8); **de luxe** deluxe (10); **De rien.** You're welcome. (P); **du lundi au vendredi** from Monday to Friday *(every week)* (P); **parler de** to talk about
débarquement *(m)* landing
déboussolé(e) disoriented
debout standing
début *(m)* beginning (6); **au début (de)** at the beginning (of) (6)
décédé(e) dead; deceased (4)
décembre *(m)* December (4)
décidément decidedly, for sure
décider to decide (6); **se décider** to make up one's mind
décision *(f)* decision (7); **prendre une décision** to make a decision (7)
décorer to decorate
découper to cut out
découverte *(f)* discovery
découvrir to discover; **découvrant** discovering
décret *(m)* decree
décrire to describe (9); **décrit(e)** described
dedans inside
défaut *(m)* fault (7)
défini(e) definite
définir to define
degré *(m)* degree
déguster to sample
dehors outside; **en dehors de** outside of

déjà already (5)
déjeuner *(m)* lunch; **petit déjeuner** *(m)* breakfast (5)
déjeuner to have/eat lunch (2)
délicieux(-euse) delicious (6)
délirer: faire délirer to crack up
demain tomorrow (P); **À demain!** See you tomorrow! (P)
demande *(f)* request
demander to ask (for) (2); **se demander** to wonder
demi *(m)* draft beer (2)
demi(e) half (P); **demi-heure** *(f)* half hour (7); **Il est deux heures et demie.** It's half past two. (P); **un kilo et demi de** a kilo and a half of (8)
dénoncer to denounce, to turn in
dent *(f)* tooth (7)
dentaire dental
départ *(m)* departure (9)
département *(m)* department *(a French administrative region)*
dépassement *(m)* **de soi** surpassing oneself
dépendre (de) to depend (on) (5); **Ça dépend.** That depends.
dépense *(f)* expense
dépenser to spend
déplaisant(e) unpleasant
depuis since, for (7), from; **depuis cela** since then; **depuis que** since
dérivé(e) derived
dernier(-ère) last (5)
derrière behind (3)
des some (1)
dès since, right after; **dès que** as soon as
désaccord *(m)* disagreement
désagréable unpleasant (1)
désastreux(-euse) disastrous
descendre (de) to go down, to get off (5); **descendre dans / à** to stay at *(a hotel)* (5)
déshabiller to undress; **se déshabiller** to get undressed (7)
désigner to designate, to indicate
désirer to desire; **Vous désirez?** What would you like?, May I help you? (2)
désolé(e) sorry (8); **être désolé(e) que...** to be sorry that . . . (10)
désordre: en désordre in disorder (3)
dessert *(m)* dessert (8)
dessin *(m)* drawing; **dessin animé** *(m)* cartoon
dessiner to draw
dessous: ci-dessous below
dessus: au dessus de above; **par dessus** over
destin *(m)* destiny
détaillé(e) detailed
détendre: se détendre to relax
détenir to hold, to possess
détester to hate; **se détester** to hate each other (7)
détruit(e) destroyed
dette *(f)* debt
deux two (P); **deux-tiers** two-thirds
deuxième second (5)
devant in front of (3)
développement *(m)* development
développer to develop; **se développer** to be developed.; **développé(e)** developed
devenir to become (4)
deviner to guess
devinette *(f)* riddle
devoir must, to have to, to owe (6); **il/elle doit** he/she must (3)
devoirs *(mpl)* homework (P); **Faites les devoirs dans le cahier.** Do the homework in the workbook. (P)

diabète *(m)* diabetes
diable *(m)* devil
diamant *(m)* diamond
dictée *(f)* dictation
dictionnaire *(m)* dictionary
dieu *(m)* god
différemment differently
différer to differ
difficile difficult (P)
dimanche *(m)* Sunday (P)
diminuer to diminish
dinde *(f)* turkey
dîner *(m)* dinner (8)
dîner to have dinner (2), to dine
diplôme *(m)* diploma, degree
dire to say, to tell (6); **Ça te/vous dit?** How does that sound to you? (2); **Ça veut dire...** That means . . . (P); **Comment dit-on... en français/en anglais?** How do you say . . . in French/in English? (P); **On dit...** One says . . . (P); **On dit que...** They say that . . . (4); **Qu'est-ce que ça veut dire?** What does that mean? (P)
directement directly
directeur(-trice) *(mf)* director
direction *(f)* direction, management
disciplinaire disciplinary
discothèque *(f)* dance club
discrètement discreetly
discuter to discuss
disparaître to disappear; **disparu(e)** having disappeared
disposer de to have available
disputer to dispute; **se disputer (avec)** to argue (with) (7)
disque *(m)* record; **disque compact** *(m)* compact disc
dissiper to dissipate
distraction *(f)* entertainment (5)
distributeur *(m)* **de billets** ATM machine (10)
divers(e) diverse, different
divisé(e) divided
divorcer to divorce; **divorcé(e)** divorced (1)
dix ten (P); **dix-huit** eighteen (P); **dix-huitième** eighteenth (3); **dix-neuf** nineteen (P); **dix-sept** seventeen (P)
dixième tenth (3)
doctorat *(m)* doctorate
dodo: faire dodo *(m)* to go beddy-bye *(familiar)*
doigt *(m)* finger (10); **doigt** *(m)* **de pied** toe (10)
dollar *(m)* dollar (3)
domestique *(mf)* servant
domestique domestic, household
domicile *(m)* place of residence
dominer to dominate
dommage: C'est dommage! It's a shame!, It's a pity!, That's too bad! (7)
donc so, therefore, thus, then (7)
données *(fpl)* information, data
donner to give (2); **donner à manger à** to feed (9); **donner lieu à** to give rise to; **Donnez-moi votre feuille de papier.** Give me your piece of paper. (P)
dont of which, (among) which, whose (7)
dormir to sleep (2); **je dors** I'm sleeping, I sleep (2)
dos *(m)* back (10); **sac** *(m)* **à dos** backpack
dossier *(m)* file
doté(e) endowed
douane *(f)* customs (9)
double double; **chambre double** *(f)* double room (10)

douche *(f)* shower (7)

doute *(m)* doubt; **sans doute** without doubt, doubtlessly, probably (8)

douter to doubt (10)

douteux(-euse) doubtful

doux (douce) sweet, soft, gentle (6)

douzaine (de) *(f)* dozen (8)

douze twelve (P)

drame *(m)* drama

drap *(m)* sheet

droit *(m)* law *(field of study)*, right *(legal)*; **droits** *(mpl)* **de l'homme** human rights; **tout droit** straight (ahead) (10)

droite *(f)* right *(direction);* **à droite (de)** to the right (of) (3); **de droite** conservative (7)

drôle funny, odd

du (de la, de l', des) some, any (8)

dû (due, dus, dues) à due to

duc *(m)* duke

duché *(m)* dukedom, duchy

dur(e) hard; **œuf dur** *(m)* hard-boiled egg (8)

durant during

durer to last

DVD *(m)* DVD (2); **lecteur** *(m)* **DVD** DVD player (3)

dynamique active (1)

E

eau *(f)* water (2)

écailler to open *(shellfish)*

échange *(m)* exchange

échanger to exchange

échapper to escape; **s'échapper** to escape

échouer to fail

école *(f)* school (6); **école** *(f)* **secondaire** secondary school

économie *(f)* economy; **faire des économies** to save money

économique economic; **classe** *(f)* **économique** economy class, coach (9); **sciences économiques** *(fpl)* economics

écossais(e) plaid

écossé(e) shelled

écouter to listen (to) (2); **Écoutez la question.** Listen to the question. (P)

écran *(m)* screen

écrevisse *(f)* crawfish

écrire to write (2); **Ça s'écrit…** That's written . . . (P); **Ça s'écrit avec un accent ou sans accent?** That's written with or without an accent? (P); **Ça s'écrit comment?** How is that written? (P); **écrit(e)** written; **Écrivez la réponse avec une phrase complète.** Write the answer with a complete sentence. (P)

écrivain *(m)* writer

éducateur *(m),* **éducatrice** *(f)* educator

éduquer to educate

effectuer to carry out

effet *(m)* effect; **effets personnels** personal belongings (3); **effets spéciaux** special effects (6); **en effet** in fact

égal(e) *(mpl* **égaux)** equal; **Ça m'est égal.** It's all the same to me.; **sans égal** unequaled

également also, as well, equally, likewise

égalité *(f)* equality

égard *(m)* respect

église *(f)* church (4)

égoïste selfish

Égypte *(f)* Egypt (9)

électrique electrical

électronique electronic; **billet** *(m)* **électronique** e-ticket; **courrier** *(m)* **électronique** e-mail

élève *(mf)* pupil, student

élevé(e) high, elevated, raised

elle she, it (1); **avec elle** with her (2); **elles** they (1); **avec elles** with them (2); **elle-même** herself

embarquement *(m)* boarding; **porte** *(f)* **d'embarquement** departure gate

embêtant(e) annoying (3)

embrasser to kiss; **s'embrasser** to kiss each other, to embrace each other (7)

émission *(f)* broadcast, show

emmener to take

empêcher (quelqu'un de faire quelque chose) to prevent (somebody from doing something)

emplacement *(m)* location

emploi *(m)* employment, use; **emploi** *(m)* **du temps** schedule

employé(e) *(mf)* employee (10)

employer to use; **s'employer** to be used

emporter to take (along), to carry (away) (5)

emprisonner to imprison (6)

emprunter (à) to borrow (from)

en some, any, of it/them (8), about it/them; **Je vous/t'en prie.** You're welcome. (2); **s'en aller** to go away

en in (P); **de temps en temps** from time to time (4); **en avance** early; **en avion** by plane (4); **en centre-ville** downtown (3); **en désordre** in disorder (3); **en espèces** in cash (10); **en face (de)** across from, facing (3); **en ligne** online (1); **en même temps** at the same time; **en ordre** in order (3); **en outre** in addition; **en retard** late (10); **en solde** on sale (5); **en vacances** on vacation (4); **être en train de…** to be in the process of . . . ; **partir en voyage** to leave on a trip (5); **partir en week-end** to go away for the weekend (5)

enceinte pregnant (10)

enchanter to enchant; **enchanté(e)** enchanted

encore still (4), again, more (8); **ne… pas encore** not . . . yet (5)

endormir: s'endormir to fall asleep (7)

endroit *(m)* place (9)

énergique energetic

énerver to irritate

enfance *(f)* childhood

enfant *(mf)* child (4)

enfin finally (7)

enflé(e) swollen

enfouir to bury

engagé(e) involved

enlever to take off, to remove

ennui *(m)* trouble

ennuyer to bore; **s'ennuyer (de)** to get bored (with), to be bored (with) (7)

ennuyeux(-euse) boring (1)

énorme enormous

enquête *(f)* investigation, survey

enregistrer to record

enseignement *(m)* teaching, education; **enseignement supérieur** higher education

enseigner to teach

ensemble *(m)* whole group

ensemble together (2)

ensuite then, afterwards (4)

entendre to hear (7); **Entendu!** Understood!; **s'entendre bien/mal (avec)** to get along well/badly (with) (7)

enthousiaste enthusiastic

entier(-ère) entire, whole; **à part entière** complete

entièrement entirely, completely

entre between (3), among

entrée *(f)* appetizer, first course (8), entry ticket, entrance, entry; **entrée** *(f)* **au cinéma** cinema attendance

entreprise *(f)* firm, enterprise

entrer (dans) to enter (5), to go in

entretien *(m)* conversation, interview, maintenance

envahir to invade

envers towards

envie: avoir envie de to feel like, to want (4)

environ around, about (4)

envisager to consider, to imagine

envoyer to send (2); **envoyer un texto** to send a text message (2)

épaule *(f)* shoulder

épice *(f)* spice

épicerie *(f)* grocer's shop (8)

épinards *(mpl)* spinach

époque *(f)* time period (6); **à cette époque-là** at that time, in those days

épouser to marry; **s'épouser** to get married

épouvante: film *(m)* **d'épouvante** horror movie

équilibre *(m)* equilibrium, balance

équipe *(f)* team

équipé(e) equipped

escalade *(f)* (rock) climbing

escalier *(m)* stairs, staircase (3)

escargot *(m)* snail (8)

escarpé(e) steep

esclavage *(m)* slavery

esclave *(mf)* slave

Espagne *(f)* Spain (9)

espagnol *(m)* Spanish (P)

espagnol(e) Spanish

espèce: en espèces in cash (10)

espérer to hope (3)

espion(ne) *(mf)* spy

espoir *(m)* hope

esprit *(m)* mind, spirit (7)

essayage: cabine *(f)* **d'essayage** fitting room (5)

essayer to try on (5); **essayer (de faire)** to try (to do)

essentiel(le) essential; **Il est essentiel de…** It's essential to . . . (10)

est *(m)* east; **la partie est** the eastern part

est-ce que *(particle used in questions)* (1)

estomac *(m)* stomach

et and (P); **et quart/et demi(e)** a quarter past/ half past (P); **Combien font… et… ?** How much is . . . plus . . . ? (P)

établir to establish; **s'établir** to establish oneself, to settle

établissement *(m)* establishment

étage *(m)* floor (3); **à l'étage** on the same floor, down the hall; **À quel étage?** On what floor? (3); **au premier étage** on the second floor (3)

étagère *(f)* shelf, bookcase (3)

étape *(f)* stopping place, step

état *(m)* condition; **État** *(m)* state (3), government; **États-Unis** *(mpl)* United States (3)

été *(m)* summer (5); **en été** in summer (5)

étendre: s'étendre to extend; **étendu(e)** stretched out

éternuer to sneeze (10)

étoile *(f)* star

étonner to amaze, to astonish; **être étonné(e) que…** to be astonished that . . . (10)

étouffant(e) stifling

étrange strange

étranger(-ère) foreign (1); **à l'étranger** abroad (9)

être to be (1); **c'est** it's (P), he is, she is, it is, this is, that is (1); **C'est ça!** That's right! (1); **C'est quel jour aujourd'hui?** What day is today? (P); **Comment est / sont... ?** What is / are ... like? (1); **être à** to belong to; **Je suis...** I'm ... (P) **Je ne suis pas...** I'm not ... (P); **le français est...** French is ... (P); **Nous sommes....** There are ... of us. (4); **Quelle est la date?** What is the date? (4); **tu es/vous êtes** you are (P)

étroit(e) tight, narrow

études (fpl) studies, going to school (1)

étudiant(e) (mf) student (P)

étudier to study (1); **J'étudie/Je n'étudie pas...** I study/I don't study ... (1); **Qu'est-ce que vous étudiez/tu étudies?** What are you studying?, What do you study? (1)

euro (m) euro (2)

Europe (f) Europe (9)

européen(ne) European

eux them, they; **eux-mêmes** themselves

évader: s'évader to escape

événement (m) event

éviter to avoid (8)

exact(e) accurate

exactement exactly (10)

examen (m) test, exam (P); **Préparez l'examen pour le prochain cours.** Prepare for the exam for the next class. (P)

excessivement excessively

exclamer: s'exclamer to exclaim, to cry out

excuser to excuse, to forgive; **Excusez-moi.** Excuse me. (P)

exemple (m) example; **par exemple** for example (2)

exercice (m) exercise (P); **faire de l'exercice** to exercise (2); **Faites l'exercice A à la page 21.** Do exercise A on page 21. (P)

exiger to require

exotique exotic (9)

expérience (f) experience, experiment

explication (f) explanation

expliquer to explain (10)

explorateur(-trice) (mf) explorer

exploser to explode

exposition (f) exhibit (4)

expression (f) expression (10)

expresso (m) espresso (2)

exprimer to express

expulser to throw out

exquis(e) exquisite

extérieur (m) outside, exterior

extra(ordinaire) great, terrific (4)

extrascolaire extracurricular

extraterrestre (mf) extraterrestrial

extraverti(e) outgoing, extroverted (1)

F

fac (f) university, campus (2)

face (f) face; **en face (de)** across from, facing (3); **face à** across from, confronted with; **faire face à** to face

facile easy (P)

facilement easily (7)

faciliter to facilitate, to make easy

façon (f) way

faculté (f) university, campus, school, faculty; **la fac** the university, the campus (2)

fade tasteless

faillir: il a failli avoir he almost had

faim (f) hunger; **avoir faim** to be hungry (4); **j'ai faim** I'm hungry (2)

faire to do, to make (2); **Ça fait... euros.** That's ... euros. (2); **Ça ne se fait pas!** That is not done!; **Combien font... et / moins...?** How much is ... plus / minus ... ? (P); **faire attention (à)** to pay attention (to), to watch out (for) (8); **faire connaître** to inform; **faire de l'aérobic** to do aerobics (8); **faire de l'alpinisme** to go mountain climbing; **faire de la méditation** to meditate (8); **faire de la musculation** to do weight training, to do bodybuilding (8); **faire de la musique** to play music (2); **faire de la planche à voile** to go windsurfing; **faire de la plongée sous-marine** to go scuba diving; **faire de la varappe** to go rock climbing; **faire de l'exercice** to exercise (2); **faire des courses** to run errands (5); **faire des économies** to save up (money); **faire des projets** to make plans (4); **faire des randonnées** to go hiking (5); **faire du bateau** to go boating (5); **faire du camping** to go camping (5); **faire du cheval** to go horseback riding; **faire du jardinage** to garden (5); **faire du jogging** to jog (2); **faire du patin (à glace)** to go (ice-)skating; **faire du roller** to go in-line skating (6); **faire du shopping** to go shopping (2); **faire du skateboard(ing)** to skateboard (6); **faire du ski** to go skiing (2); **faire du sport** to play sports (2); **faire du vélo** to go bike-riding (2); **faire du VTT** to go all-terrain biking (5); **faire du yoga** to do yoga (8); **faire face à** to face; **faire la connaissance de** to meet (*for the first time*) (7); **faire la cuisine** to cook (5); **faire la fête** to party; **faire la lessive** to do laundry (5); **faire la vaisselle** to do the dishes (5); **faire le ménage** to do housework (5); **faire les courses** to go grocery shopping (5); **faire mal** to hurt; **faire mieux (de)** to do better (to) (8); **faire noir** to be dark; **faire partie de** to be a part of; **faire quelque chose** to do something (2); **faire sa toilette** to wash up (7); **faire sa valise** to pack your bag (9); **faire une promenade** to go for a walk (5); **faire une réservation** to make a reservation (9); **faire un tour** to take a tour, to go for a ride (4); **faire un voyage** to take a trip (5); **Faites les devoirs dans le cahier.** Do the homework in the workbook. (P); **Faites l'exercice A à la page 21.** Do exercise A on page 21. (P); **Il fait beau / chaud / (du) soleil / du vent / frais / froid / mauvais.** It's nice / hot / sunny / windy / cool / cold / bad. (5); **Il fait bon / du brouillard.** It's nice / foggy.; **Il va faire...** It's going to be ... (5); **Je fais du...** I wear size.... (5); **Quelle taille faites-vous?** What size do you wear? (5); **Quel temps fait-il?** What's the weather like? (5); **Quel temps va-t-il faire?** What's the weather going to be like? (5); **Qu'est-ce que vous aimez faire?** What do you like to do? (2); **Qu'est-ce que vous faites/tu fais?** What are you doing? What do you do? (2); **se faire passer pour** to pass as

fait: en fait in fact

falaise (f) cliff

falloir: il faut... it is necessary ... , one must ... , one needs ... (8); **il me/te/nous/vous/lui/leur faut** I/you/we/you/he (she)/they need(s) (9); **il ne faut pas** one shouldn't, one must not ... (10); **Qu'est-ce qu'il vous faut?** What do you need? (8)

fameux(-euse) famous

familial(e) (mpl **familiaux**) family

familier(-ère) familiar, informal

famille (f) family (P); **nom** (m) **de famille** family name, surname (3)

fantastique fantastic; **film fantastique** (m) fantasy movie

farci(e) stuffed

fascinant(e) fascinating

fast-food (m) fast-food restaurant (1)

fatigué(e) tired (6)

faut *See* **falloir.**

fauteuil (m) armchair (3)

faux (fausse) false

faux-filet (m) sirloin

favoriser to favor, to further

fée (f) fairy; **conte** (m) **de fées** fairy tale (6)

femme (f) woman (1), wife (2); **ex-femme** (f) ex-wife; **femme** (f) **d'affaires** business woman (5)

fenêtre (f) window (3)

fer (m) iron; **chemin** (m) **de fer** railroad

férié(e): jour férié (m) holiday

ferme (f) farm

fermer to close (2); **Fermez votre livre.** Close your book. (P)

féroce ferocious (6)

festival (m) festival (4)

fête (f) holiday, celebration (4), party (1); **faire la fête** (f) to party; **fête** (f) **des Mères** Mother's Day; **fête** (f) **des Pères** Father's Day; **fête** (f) **du travail** Labor Day; **fête nationale** (f) national holiday

fêter to celebrate

feu (m) fire, traffic light

feuille (f) **de papier** sheet of paper (P); **Prenez une feuille de papier et un crayon ou un stylo.** Take out a piece of paper and a pencil or a pen. (P)

feuilleté(e) flaky (pastry)

février (m) February (4)

fiancé(e) engaged (1)

fiancer: se fiancer to get engaged (7)

ficelle (f) string

fidélité (f) faithfulness

fier(-ère) proud

fièvre (f) fever; **avoir de la fièvre** to have fever

figure (f) face (7)

fille (f) girl; daughter (4); **fille unique** (f) only child

film (m) movie, film (1); **film** (m) **à grand spectacle** epic film

fils (m) son (4); **fils unique** (m) only child

fin (f) end

fin(e) fine

finalement finally (6)

financier(-ère) financial

finir (de faire) to finish (doing) (8); **finir par faire** to end up doing; **Le cours de français finit à...** French class finishes at ... (P)

fissure (f) crack, fissure

fixe fixed; **menu à prix fixe** set-price menu (8)

fixer to set, to fix

flamand (m) Flemish (*language*)

fleur (f) flower

fleuri(e) with a floral pattern

fleuve (m) river

flic (m) cop

Floride (f) Florida (9)

flottant(e) floating

foie (m) liver

fois *(f)* time (5), occasion; **à la fois** at the same time; **d'autres fois** other times (7); **Il était une fois...** Once upon a time there was . . . (6)
folique: acide *(m)* **folique** folic acid
folklore *(m)* folklore (4)
foncé(e) dark; **bleu foncé** dark blue
fonction *(f)* function; **en fonction de** according to
fonctionnement *(m)* functioning, operation, running
fond *(m)* bottom, back, background; **au fond de** at the end of; **dans le fond** really, basically
fondateur: père *(m)* **fondateur** founding father
fonder to found; **fondé(e)** founded
fontaine *(f)* fountain
football *(m)* soccer (1); **football américain** *(m)* football (1); **match** *(m)* **de football américain** football game (1)
force *(f)* force, strength; **à force de** as a result of
forcément necessarily, inevitably
forêt *(f)* forest
forme *(f)* shape; **en forme** in shape (8); **en forme de** in the shape of
former to form, to educate
formidable great (7)
formulaire *(m)* form
formule *(f)* formula, expression
fort(e) strong (8)
fort very
fou (folle) crazy
foudre *(f)* lightning, thunderbolt; **coup** *(m)* **de foudre** love at first sight (7)
foulard *(m)* dress scarf
fouler: se fouler la cheville to sprain one's ankle
four (à micro-ondes) *(m)* (microwave) oven
fourchette *(f)* fork
frais (fraîche) fresh (8); **Il fait frais.** It's cool. (5)
fraise *(f)* strawberry (8)
framboise *(f)* raspberry
franc (franche) frank, honest
français *(m)* French (P); **cours** *(m)* **de français** French class (P)
français(e) French (1); **à la française** French style
France *(f)* France (1)
franciscain(e) Franciscan
francophone French-speaking
francophonie *(f)* French-speaking world
frapper to strike; **frapper à la porte** to knock on the door
fréquenté(e) visited, frequented
frère *(m)* brother (1); **beau-frère** *(m)* brother-in-law; **demi-frère** *(m)* stepbrother, half-brother
frigo *(m)* refrigerator
frire to fry
frisson *(m)* shiver (10); **avoir des frissons** to have the shivers (10)
frit(e) fried
frites *(fpl)* French fries (2); **steak-frites** *(m)* steak and fries (8)
frivole frivolous
froid(e) cold (4); **avoir froid** to be cold (4); **Il fait froid.** It's cold. (5)
fromage *(m)* cheese (2)
frontière *(f)* border
fruit *(m)* fruit (8); **fruits** *(mpl)* **de mer** shellfish (8); **jus** *(m)* **de fruit** fruit juice (2)
fuir to flee, to run away
fumé(e) smoked (8)

fumée *(f)* smoke
fumer to smoke (3)
fumeur(-euse) *(mf)* smoker; **fumeur/ non-fumeur** smoking/non-smoking
furieux(-euse) furious (10)
fusée *(f)* rocket
fusiller to shoot down
futur *(m)* future (tense)

G

gagner to win (2), to gain; **gagner de l'argent** to earn money, to make money
gai(e) gay, lively
gamin(e) *(mf)* kid
garçon *(m)* boy (4)
garder to keep
garde-robe *(f)* wardrobe
gare *(f)* train station; **gare routière** bus station
gaspiller to waste
gâté(e) spoiled (6)
gâteau *(m)* cake (8)
gauche *(f)* left; **à gauche (de)** to the left (of) (3); **de gauche** liberal (7)
général(e) *(mpl* **généraux)** general; **en général** in general (2)
généralement generally (8)
génial(e) *(mpl* **géniaux)** great (4)
génie *(m)* genius, engineering
genou *(m)* knee; **sur ses genoux** on one's lap
genre *(m)* gender, kind, type, genre
gens *(mpl)* people (1)
gentil(le) nice (1)
géographie *(f)* geography (9)
géographique geographical
germanique Germanic
geste *(m)* gesture
gilet *(m)* vest
glace *(f)* ice cream (8), ice; **glace à la vanille** vanilla ice cream (8)
glace *(m)* mirror
glacier *(m)* ice cream shop
golf *(m)* golf (2)
gommage *(m)* rubbing out, scrub
gorge *(f)* throat (10); **soutien-gorge** *(m)* bra
gosse *(mf)* kid
goût *(m)* taste
goûter to taste (9)
gouvernement *(m)* government
grâce *(f)* grace; **grâce à** thanks to, due to; **jour** *(m)* **d'Action de Grâce** Thanksgiving
gracieux(-euse) gracious (6)
graisse *(f)* fat, grease
grammaire *(f)* grammar
gramme *(m)* gram (8)
grand(e) big, tall (1); **grande surface** *(f)* superstore (8); **le grand amour** *(m)* true love (7)
grand-chose: ne... pas grand-chose not much, not a lot
grandir to grow, to grow up, to get taller (8)
grand-mère *(f)* grandmother (4)
grand-père *(m)* grandfather (4)
grands-parents *(mpl)* grandparents (4)
gras(se) fatty; **en caractères gras** boldfaced; **matière grasse** *(f)* fat (8)
gratuit(e) free (of charge) (10)
grave serious, grave
Grèce *(f)* Greece (9)
grillé(e) grilled, toasted (8); **pain grillé(e)** toast (8)
grippe *(f)* flu (10)
gris(e) gray (3)
grog *(m)* **au rhum** rum toddy

gros(se) fat (1)
grossesse *(f)* pregnancy
grossir to get fatter (8)
groupe *(m)* group (6); **en groupe** in a group
gruyère *(m)* Swiss cheese
guerre *(f)* war
guichet *(m)* ticket window
guide *(m)* guide, guidebook (9)
guitare *(f)* guitar (2)
Guyane *(f)* French Guiana (9)
gym: salle *(f)* **de gym** gym, fitness club (1)
gymnase *(m)* gym

H

habiller to dress; **s'habiller** to get dressed (7)
habitant(e) *(mf)* inhabitant
habiter to live; **j'habite à** (+ *city*) I live in (+ *city*) (P); **Vous habitez... ?** Do you live . . . ? (P)
habitude *(f)* habit; **comme d'habitude** as usual; **d'habitude** usually (2)
habitué(e) à used to, accustomed to
haché(e) chopped (up)
hamburger *(m)* hamburger (8)
haricots verts *(mpl)* green beans (8)
harmonieux(-euse) harmonious
hasard: par hasard by chance
haut(e) high; **en haut** on top; **là-haut** up there
hein? huh?
héritage *(m)* inheritance, heritage
hériter to inherit
hésiter to hesitate
heure *(f)* hour, time (P); **à l'heure** on time (4); **À tout à l'heure.** See you in a little while. (P); **heure d'ouverture** opening time (6); **heure locale** local time (9); **heure officielle** official time (6), 24-hour clock; **Il est... heure(s).** It's . . . o'clock. (P); **Quelle heure est-il?** What time is it? (P); **tout à l'heure** a little while ago
heureusement luckily
heureux(-euse) happy (7)
hideux(-euse) hideous
hier yesterday (5); **hier soir** last night, yesterday evening (5)
hi-fi: chaîne *(f)* **hi-fi** stereo (3)
histoire *(f)* history (1); story (9)
historique historic (9)
hiver *(m)* winter (5); **en hiver** in winter (5)
hockey *(m)* hockey (2)
homard *(m)* lobster (8)
homme *(m)* man (1); **homme** *(m)* **d'affaires** businessman (5)
honnête honest
honnêteté *(f)* honesty
honteux (-euse) shameful
hôpital *(m)* (pl **hôpitaux)** hospital
horaire *(m)* schedule (6)
horreur *(f)* horror
horrible horrible (6)
hors de outside of
hors-d'œuvre *(m)* (inv) hors d'œuvre, appetizer (8)
hôte *(m)* host; **chambre** *(f)* **d'hôte** bed and breakfast
hôtel *(m)* hotel (5)
hôtelier(-ère) *(mf)* hotel manager (10)
hôtesse *(f)* hostess
huile *(f)* oil
huit eight (P); **huit jours** one week
huitième eighth (3)
huître *(f)* oyster (8)

humain(e) human; **sciences humaines** *(fpl)* social sciences (1)

humeur *(f)* mood; **de bonne humeur** in a good mood

humour *(m)* humor; **sens** *(m)* **de l'humour** sense of humor (7)

hurlement *(m)* howl

hypermarché *(m)* superstore

I

ici here (P); **d'ici** from here (P); **par ici** this way (5)

idéaliste idealistic (1)

idée *(f)* idea (4)

identité *(f)* identity; **carte** *(f)* **/ pièce** *(f)* **d'identité** identity card

ignorer to ignore; **en ignorant** while ignoring

il he (1), it (P); **il faut...** it is necessary . . . , one must . . . (8); **il ne faut pas...** one shouldn't . . . , one must not . . . (10); **ils** they (1); **il y a...** there is . . . , there are . . . (1), ago (5); **Quelle heure est-il?** What time is it? (P); **Qu'est-ce qu'il y a?** What is there? (1), What's the matter?; **s'il vous plaît** please (P)

île *(f)* island (9)

illustré(e) illustrated

image *(f)* picture

imaginaire imaginary

imaginer to imagine

immédiatement immediately

immeuble *(m)* apartment building (3)

immigré(e) *(mf)* immigrant

imparfait *(m)* imperfect

impatient(e) impatient (4)

impératif *(m)* imperative

imperméable *(m)* raincoat (5)

impoli(e) impolite

importance *(f)* importance (7)

important(e) important (10)

importer to be important; **n'importe où** (just) anywhere; **n'importe quoi** (just) anything

impressionnant(e) impressive

impressionner to impress

imprimé(e) printed

inattendu(e) unexpected

inciter à to encourage

inclure to include; **inclus(e)** included

inconnu(e) *(mf)* stranger

inconvénient *(m)* disadvantage, inconvenience

incroyable incredible

Inde *(f)* India

indécision *(f)* indecision (7)

indéfini(e) indefinite

indicatif *(m)* indicative

indications *(fpl)* directions (10)

indifférence *(f)* indifference (7)

indigène native

indigestion *(f)* indigestion (10)

indiquer to show, to indicate (3); **indiqué(e)** indicated; **indiquer le chemin** to give directions, to show the way (10)

indiscret(-ète) indiscreet

industrialisé(e) industrialized

industrie *(f)* industry

inégalé(e) unequaled

infidélité *(f)* unfaithfulness (7)

infinitif *(m)* infinitive

infirmerie *(f)* health center

inflexibilité *(f)* inflexibility

influencer to influence; **s'influencer** to influence each other

informatique *(f)* computer science (1); **salle** *(f)* **d'informatique** computer lab (1)

informer to inform; **s'informer** to find out information (9)

infos *(fpl)* info (9)

infusion *(f)* herbal tea

ingénieur *(m)* engineer

inhospitalier(-ière) inhospitable

inoubliable unforgettable

insaturé(e) unsaturated

inscrire to register; **s'inscrire** to register (3)

insensibilité *(f)* insensitivity (7)

insipide tasteless, insipid

insister to insist (10)

inspecteur *(m)* inspector

inspirer to inspire; **s'inspirer de** to draw inspiration from

installations *(fpl)* facilities

installer: s'installer (à / dans) to settle (in), to move (into) (7), to set up business

instant *(m)* instant; **Un instant!** Just a moment!

institut *(m)* institute

instrument *(m)* **de musique** musical instrument

insuffisant insufficient

intellectuel(le) intellectual (1)

intelligent(e) intelligent (1)

intention: avoir l'intention de to plan on, to intend to (4)

intéressant(e) interesting (P)

intéresser to interest; **s'intéresser à** to be interested in (7)

intérêt *(m)* interest

intérieur *(m)* inside

internaute *(mf)* Internet surfer

Internet *(m)* Internet (2); **surfer sur Internet** to surf the Internet (2); **sur Internet** on the Internet (2)

interrogatif(-ive) interrogative, question

interroger to question

interrompre to interrupt

intime intimate; **ami(e) intime** *(mf)* close friend

intrigue *(f)* plot

investir to invest

invitation *(f)* invitation (6)

invité(e) *(mf)* guest

inviter (à) to invite (to) (2)

iPod *(m)* iPod (3)

Irlande *(f)* Ireland *(9)*

irréel(le) unreal

irresponsable irresponsible

irriter to irritate

isolé(e) isolated

Israël *(m)* Israel (9)

Italie *(f)* Italy (9)

italien(ne) Italian

italique: en italique in italics

itinéraire *(m)* itinerary

ivoirien(ne) from Côte d'Ivoire

J

jalousie *(f)* jealousy (7)

jaloux(-ouse) jealous (7)

jamais: ne... jamais never (2)

jambe *(f)* leg (10); **se casser la jambe** to break your leg

jambon *(m)* ham (2); **sandwich** *(m)* **au jambon** ham sandwich (2)

janvier *(m)* January (4)

Japon *(m)* Japan (9)

japonais *(m)* Japanese

jardin *(m)* garden (5), yard

jardinage *(m)* gardening; **faire du jardinage** to garden (5)

jaune yellow (3)

jazz *(m)* jazz (1)

je (j') I (P)

jean *(m)* jeans (5)

jet *(m)* stream

jeter to throw

jeu *(m)* game; **jeu** *(m)* **vidéo** video game (2)

jeudi *(m)* Thursday (P)

jeune young (1); **jeunes** *(pl)* young people

jeunesse *(f)* youth (7); **auberge** *(f)* **de jeunesse** youth hostel (10)

jogging: faire du jogging to jog (2)

joie *(f)* joy

joindre: se joindre à to join

joli(e) pretty (1)

jouer to play (2), to act *(in movies and theater)* (6); **jouer à** to play *(a sport or game)* (2); **jouer de** to play *(an instrument)* (2)

jour *(m)* day (P); **C'est quel jour aujourd'hui?** What day is today? (P); **jour** *(m)* **de l'An** New Year's Day; **jour J** *(m)* D-day; **tous les jours** every day (P)

journal *(m)* *(pl* **journaux)** newspaper (5), journal; **journal** *(m)* **télévisé** news broadcast

journée *(f)* day (2), daytime; **Bonne journée!** Have a good day!; **journée continue** nine-to-five schedule; **toute la journée** the whole day (2)

joyeux(-euse) happy, joyful; **Joyeux Noël!** Merry Christmas!

juger to judge

juif(-ive) *(mf)* Jew

juillet *(m)* July (4)

juin *(m)* June (4)

jumeau (jumelle) twin (1)

jupe *(f)* skirt (5)

jus *(m)* **(de fruit)** (fruit) juice (2)

jusqu'à until, up to (2)

juste just (10), fair; **juste là** right there

justement precisely, exactly, as a matter of fact (3)

K

kilo (de) *(m)* kilo(gram) (of) *(2.2 pounds)* (8)

kilomètre *(m)* kilometer *(.6 mile)*

kiosque *(m)* kiosk (10)

L

la the (1), her, it (5)

là there (1); **à ce moment-là** at that time; **ce (cet, cette, ces) ...-là** that/those . . . over there (5); **là-bas** over there (1); **là-haut** up there

laboratoire *(m)* **de langues** language laboratory (1)

lac *(m)* lake

laid(e) ugly (1)

laïque lay, secular, civil

laisser to leave (behind) (3), to let; **laisser tomber** to drop

lait *(m)* milk (2); **café** *(m)* **au lait** coffee with milk (2)

laitue *(f)* lettuce (8)

lampe *(f)* lamp (3)

lancer to throw, to fire

langouste *(f)* spiny lobster

langue *(f)* language (1); tongue

lapin *(m)* rabbit

laqué(e) lacquered, with a gloss finish

lard *(m)* bacon

lardon *(m)* piece of bacon

large wide

largement widely

lavabo *(m)* washbasin, sink (10)

lave *(f)* lava
laver to wash; **se laver la figure/les mains** to wash one's face/one's hands (7)
lave-vaisselle *(m)* dishwasher
le the (1), him, it (5); **le lundi** on Mondays (P); **le matin** in the morning, mornings (P); **le week-end** on the weekend, weekends (P)
leçon *(f)* lesson
lecteur (lectrice) *(mf)* reader; **lecteur** *(m)* **CD / DVD / Blu-ray** CD / DVD / Blu-ray player (3); **lecteur** *(m)* **MP3** MP3 player
lecture *(f)* reading
léger(-ère) light (8)
légume *(m)* vegetable (8)
lendemain *(m)* the next day (5)
lent(e) slow
lentement slowly (8)
lequel (laquelle, lesquels, lesquelles) which, which one(s) (6)
les the (1); them (5)
lessive *(f)* laundry (5)
lettre *(f)* letter (9); **lettres** *(fpl)* study of literature
leur (to, for) them (9)
leur their (1)
lever: se lever to get up (7)
liaison *(f)* linking, link
liberté *(f)* freedom
librairie *(f)* bookstore (1)
libre free (2); **temps libre** *(m)* free time (2); **Tu es libre ce soir?** Are you free this evening? (2)
licence *(f)* *three-year university degree*
lien *(m)* link, tie
lier to connect, to link; **lié(e)** linked
lieu *(m)* place; **au lieu de** instead of; **avoir lieu** to take place
light: coca *(m)* **light** diet cola (2)
ligne *(f)* figure; line; **en ligne** online (1)
limande *(f)* dab
limiter to limit, to border; **limité(e)** limited; **se limiter à** to limit oneself to
linguistique linguistic
liquide *(m)* liquid (10)
lire to read (2); **Lisez la page 17.** Read page 17. (P)
liste *(f)* list
lit *(m)* bed (3); **rester au lit** to stay in bed (2)
litre *(m)* liter *(approximately one quart)* (8)
littéraire literary
littérature *(f)* literature (1)
livre *(m)* book (P); **Fermez votre livre.** Close your book. (P); **Ouvrez votre livre à la page 23.** Open your book to page 23. (P)
livre (de) *(f)* pound (of), half-kilo (of) (8)
livrer: se livrer à to participate in
local(e) *(mpl* **locaux)** local (9)
locataire *(mf)* renter
location *(f)* rental; **voiture** *(f)* **de location** rental car (5)
logement *(m)* lodging (3)
logique logical
logiquement logically
loi *(f)* law
loin (de) far (from) (3); **au loin** in the distance; **de loin** by far
loisir *(m)* leisure activity, pastime (2)
Londres London
long: le long de along; **de long** in length
long(ue) long (4)
longer to go alongside
longtemps a long time (5)
longueur *(f)* length

lors de at the time of
lorsque when
louer to rent (4)
Louisiane *(f)* Louisiana (3)
loyer *(m)* rent (3)
lui him (2), (to, for) him/her (9); **lui-même** himself
lumière *(f)* light
lundi *(m)* Monday (P)
lune *(f)* moon; **lune** *(f)* **de miel** honeymoon
lunettes *(fpl)* glasses (4); **lunettes** *(fpl)* **de soleil** sunglasses (5)
luth *(m)* lute
lutter to struggle, to fight
luxe *(m)* luxury; **de luxe** deluxe (10)
luxembourgeois *(m)* Luxembourgish *(native language of Luxembourg)*
lycée *(m)* high school (6)
lycéen(ne) *(mf)* high school student (6)

M

madame (Mme) *(f)* Mrs., madam (P)
mademoiselle (Mlle) *(f)* Miss (P)
magasin *(m)* store (4), shop
magazine *(m)* magazine (9)
magnifique magnificent
mai *(m)* May (4)
maigre skinny
maigrir to get thinner, to slim down (8)
mail *(m)* e-mail (2)
maillon *(m)* link
maillot *(m)* **de bain** swimsuit (5)
main *(f)* hand (7)
maintenant now (P)
maintenir to maintain
mais but (P)
maïs *(m)* corn
maison *(f)* house (1); **à la maison** (at) home (P)
maître *(m)* master
maîtrise *(f)* master's degree
majorité *(f)* majority
mal *(m)* bad, evil; **avoir mal à...** one's ... hurt(s) (10); **faire mal (à...)** to hurt (one's ...)
mal badly (P); **mal à l'aise** ill at ease; **pas mal** not bad(ly) (P)
malade *(mf)* sick person
malade ill, sick; **tomber malade** to get sick (10)
maladie *(f)* illness
malaise *(f)* discomfort
Malgache *(mf)* Madagascan
malgré in spite of
malheureux(-euse) unhappy
malhonnête dishonest
maman *(f)* mama, mom
mamie *(f)* granny, grandma (7)
Manche *(f)* English Channel
mandarine *(f)* tangerine
mandat *(m)* money order, mandate
manger to eat (2); **donner à manger à** to feed (9); **salle** *(f)* **à manger** dining room (3)
manière *(f)* manner, way
manifestation *(f)* demonstration; **manifestation sportive** *(f)* sports event
manquer to miss, to lack
manteau *(m)* overcoat (5)
maquiller: se maquiller to put on make-up (7)
marais *(m)* swamp
marbre *(m)* marble
marchand(e) *(mf)* merchant, shopkeeper (6)
marché *(m)* market (8)

marcher to walk (8), to work
mardi *(m)* Tuesday (P); **Mardi gras** *(m)* Fat Tuesday
marge *(f)* margin
mari *(m)* husband (2); **ex-mari** *(m)* ex-husband
mariage *(m)* marriage (7)
marié(e) married (1)
marier: se marier (avec) to get married (to) (7)
marinier(-ère): moules marinières *(f)* mussels cooked with onions and white wine
marionnettiste *(mf)* puppeteer
marketing *(m)* marketing (1)
Maroc *(m)* Morocco (9)
marocain(e) Moroccan
marquer to mark
marrant(e) funny (1)
marron *(inv)* brown (3)
mars *(m)* March (4)
martiniquais(e) from Martinique
masque *(m)* mask, face pack
massif *(m)* group of mountains, clump
match *(m)* match, game (1)
matelas *(m)* mattress
matérialiste materialistic
maternel(le) maternal; **école maternelle** *(f)* kindergarten
mathématiques (maths) *(fpl)* mathematics (math) (1)
matière *(f)* matter; **matières grasses** *(fpl)* fats (8)
matin *(m)* morning (P); **À huit heures du matin.** At eight o'clock in the morning. (P); **le matin** mornings, in the morning (P)
matinée *(f)* morning (2)
mauvais(e) bad (1); **Il est mauvais de...** It's bad to ... (10); **Il fait mauvais.** The weather's bad. (5)
maxidiscompte *(m)* discount supercenter
me (to, for) me (9), myself (7); **il me faut...** I need ... (9)
mec *(m)* *(familiar)* guy
méchant(e) mean (1)
mécontent(e) displeased
médecin *(m)* doctor (10), physician
médicament *(m)* medication, medicine (10), drugs
Méditerranée: (mer) Méditerranée *(f)* Mediterranean (Sea)
méditerranéen(ne) Mediterranean
méfiance *(f)* mistrust
meilleur(e) best (1), better
mélange *(m)* mixture
membre *(m)* member
même same (1), even; **moi-même** myself; **quand même** all the same
mémoire *(f)* memory
menacer to threaten
ménage *(m)* housework (5), household; **femme** *(f)* **de ménage** cleaning lady
mendiant(e) *(mf)* beggar
menthe *(f)* mint
mentir to lie
menu *(m)* menu; **menu à prix fixe** set-price menu (8)
mer *(f)* sea (9); **bord** *(m)* **de la mer** seaside; **fruits** *(mpl)* **de mer** shellfish (8)
merci thank you, thanks (P)
mercredi *(m)* Wednesday (P)
mère *(f)* mother (4)
mérité(e) deserved, earned
messager(-ère) *(mf)* messenger (6)
messieurs (MM.) gentlemen, sirs
mètre *(m)* meter
métrique metric

métro *(m)* subway (4); **en métro** by subway (4)

mettre to wear, to put (on) (5), to place; **mettre en place** to put in place; **mettre en scène** to stage, to present; **mettre la table** to set the table; **se mettre à** to start, to set out; **se mettre d'accord** to come to an agreement

meubles *(mpl)* furniture, furnishings (3)

meurtre *(m)* murder

Mexico Mexico City

Mexique *(m)* Mexico (9)

mi- mid-, half-; **cheveux mi-longs** *(mpl)* shoulder-length hair (4)

micronutriment *(m)* micronutrient

micro-ondes *(m)* microwave oven

midi *(m)* noon (P)

mie: pain *(m)* **de mie** soft sandwich bread

mien(ne): le/la mien(ne) mine

mieux (que) better (than) (2); **aimer mieux** to prefer (2); **il vaut mieux…** it's better … (10); **le mieux** the best (7)

milieu *(m)* middle, milieu, environment; **au milieu (de)** in the middle (of)

mille one thousand (3)

mille-feuille *(m)* mille-feuille *(a layered pastry)*

million: un million (de) *(m)* one million (3)

mince thin (1)

minéral(e) *(mpl* **minéraux): eau minérale** *(f)* mineral water (2)

mini-bar *(m)* mini-bar (10)

minuit *(m)* midnight (P)

minute *(f)* minute (5)

miroir *(m)* mirror

miser: en misant sur relying on

misère *(f)* misery

mobile *(m)* motive

mobilier *(m)* furnishings

mode *(f)* fashion; **mode** *(m)* **de vie** lifestyle

modèle *(m)* model

moderne modern (1)

moi me (P); **Donnez-moi votre feuille de papier.** Give me your piece of paper. (P); **Excusez-moi.** Excuse me. (P); **moi-même** myself; **Pour moi… s'il vous plaît.** For me … please. (2)

moindre: le moindre the least

moins minus (P), less (1); **au moins** at least; **Combien font… moins… ?** How much is … minus … ? (P); **de moins en moins** fewer and fewer, less and less; **le moins** the least; **moins de** fewer, less (8); **moins le quart** a quarter until (P); **moins… que** less … than (1)

mois *(m)* month (3); **ce mois-ci** this month (4); **par mois** per month (3)

moitié *(f)* half

moment *(m)* moment; **à ce moment-là** at that time; **au dernier moment** at the last minute

mon (ma, mes) my (3); **ma famille** my family (P); **mes amis** my friends (1)

monarchie *(f)* monarchy

monastère *(m)* monastery

monde *(m)* world, crowd; **faire le tour du monde** to take a trip around the world; **tout le monde** everybody, everyone (6)

mondial(e) *(mpl* **mondiaux)** world(-wide)

monétaire monetary

monnaie *(f)* change (2), currency

monotonie *(f)* monotony

monsieur (M.) *(m)* Mr., sir (P)

monstre *(m)* monster (6)

mont *(m)* mount

montagne *(f)* mountain (5); **aller à la montagne** to go to the mountains (5); **chalet** *(m)* **à la montagne** ski lodge (10)

montagneux(-euse) mountainous

monter (dans) to go up; to get on/in (5), to set up, to climb, to raise

montre *(f)* watch (5)

montrer to show (3)

morceau de *(m)* piece of (8)

mort *(f)* death

mort(e) dead (5)

mosquée *(f)* mosque

mot *(m)* word (P); **Apprenez les mots de vocabulaire.** Learn the vocabulary words. (P)

motif *(m)* reason, motive

mouchoir *(m)* handkerchief

moule *(f)* mussel (8)

moulin *(m)* mill

mourir to die (5)

moustache *(f)* mustache (4)

mouton *(m)* sheep

moyen *(m)* means; **moyen** *(m)* **de transport** means of transportation (4)

moyen(ne) medium, average; **de taille moyenne** medium-sized (4); **Moyen-Orient** *(m)* Middle East (9)

moyenne *(f)* average; **en moyenne** on average

muet(te) silent

mur *(m)* wall (3)

musculation: faire de la musculation to do weight training, to do bodybuilding (8)

musée *(m)* museum (1)

musical(e) *(mpl* **musicaux): comédie musicale** *(f)* musical

musicien(ne) *(mf)* musician

musicien(ne) musical

musique *(f)* music (1); **musique zydeco** zydeco music (4)

mutation *(f)* transfer

muter to transfer

myrtille *(f)* blueberry

mystère *(m)* mystery

mystérieusement mysteriously

N

nager to swim (2)

nain(e) *(mf)* dwarf

naissance *(f)* birth

naître to be born (5); **être né(e)** to be born (5)

natation *(f)* swimming

national(e) *(mpl* **nationaux)** national (4)

nationalité *(f)* nationality (3)

nature *(f)* nature (7); **omelette nature** *(f)* plain omelet

naturel(le) natural

naturellement naturally

nautique: faire du ski nautique *(m)* to go water-skiing (5)

navette *(f)* shuttle (10)

ne: je ne travaille pas I don't work (P); **ne… aucun(e)** none, not one; **ne… jamais** never (2); **ne… ni… ni…** neither … nor … ; **ne… nulle part** nowhere; **ne… pas (du tout)** not (at all) (1); **ne… pas encore** not yet (5); **ne… personne** nobody, no one; **ne… plus** no more, no longer (8); **ne… que** only; **ne… rien** nothing (5); **ne… rien que** nothing but; **n'est-ce pas?** right? (1); **n'importe où** (just) anywhere

né(e) born (5); **être né(e)** to be born (5)

nécessaire necessary (10)

néerlandais(e) Dutch

négliger to neglect

négocier to negotiate

neige *(f)* snow (5)

neiger to snow (5)

nerveux(-euse) nervous

n'est-ce pas? right? (1)

neuf nine (P)

neuf (neuve) brand-new

neutre neutral

neuvième ninth (3)

neveu *(m)* *(pl* **neveux)** nephew (4)

nez *(m)* nose (10); **avoir le nez bouché** to have a stopped-up nose

ni: ne… ni… ni… neither … nor …

niçois(e) from Nice

nièce *(f)* niece (4)

niveau *(m)* level

Noël *(m)* Christmas

noir(e) black (3); **Il faisait noir.** It was dark.

noisette *(inv)* hazel *(with eyes)* (4)

nom *(m)* name, noun (3); **au nom de** in the name of; **nom de famille** family name, last name (3)

nombre *(m)* number (P)

nombreux(-euse) numerous

nommer to name; **nommé(e)** named

non no (P); **non?** right? (1); **non plus** neither (3)

nord *(m)* north; **Amérique** *(f)* **du Nord** North America (9)

normalement normally

normand(e) from Normandy

Normandie *(f)* Normandy

Norvège *(f)* Norway

note *(f)* note (4), grade; **régler la note** to pay the bill (10)

noter to note, to notice

notre *(pl* **nos)** our (3)

nourrir to feed, to nourish, to nurture (8); **se nourrir** to feed oneself, to nourish oneself, to nurture oneself (8)

nourrissant(e) nourishing

nourriture *(f)* food, nourishment

nous we (1), us (2), (to, for) us (9), ourselves (7); **Nous sommes…** There are … of us. (4)

nouveau (nouvel, nouvelle) new (1); **de nouveau** again, anew; **Nouvelle-Angleterre** *(f)* New England; **Nouvelle-Calédonie** *(f)* New Caledonia (9); **La Nouvelle-Orléans** *(f)* New Orleans (4)

novembre *(m)* November (4)

nu(e) naked; **pieds nus** barefoot

nuage *(m)* cloud

nuit *(f)* night (5); **boîte** *(f)* **de nuit** nightclub (1)

nuitée *(f)* overnight stay

nul(le) (en) no good (at), really bad (at); **ne… nulle part** nowhere

numéro *(m)* number (3), issue

nutritif(-ive) nutritional

O

obéir (à) to obey (8)

objectif *(m)* objective

objet *(m)* object

obligatoire required, obligatory

obliger to force, to make; **obligé(e)** obliged, forced

observer to observe

obtenir to get, to obtain (9)

occasion *(f)* occasion; **vêtements** *(mpl)* **d'occasion** second-hand clothes

occasionnellement occasionally

occidental(e) *(mpl* **occidentaux)** western

occupé(e) busy

occuper to occupy; **s'occuper de** to take care of

Océanie *(f)* Oceania (9)
octobre *(m)* October (4)
odeur *(f)* odor, smell
œil *(pl* **yeux)** *(m)* eye (10); **avoir les yeux...** to have . . . eyes (4)
œuf *(m)* egg (8); **œuf dur** *(m)* hard-boiled egg (8)
œuvre *(f)* work
office *(m)* **de tourisme** tourist office (10)
offrir to offer; **offert(e)** offered; **offrant** offering
oignon *(m)* onion (8); **soupe** *(f)* **à l'oignon** onion soup (8)
oiseau *(m)* bird
omelette *(f)* omelet (8)
omniprésent(e) ever-present
on one, they, we, people, you (4); **Comment dit-on... en français/en anglais?** How does one say . . . in French/in English? (P); **On...?** Shall we . . . ?, How about we. . . ? (4); **On dit…** One says . . .(P); **On dit que...** They say that . . . (4); **On va... ?** Shall we go . . . ? (2)
oncle *(m)* uncle (4)
Ontario *(m)* Ontario (9)
onze eleven (P)
opéra *(m)* opera (9)
optimiste optimistic (1)
or *(m)* gold
orage *(m)* storm
orange *(f)* orange (8); **jus** *(m)* **d'orange** orange juice (2)
orange *(inv)* orange (3)
Orangina *(m)* Orangina *(an orange drink)* (2)
orchestre *(m)* orchestra, band (4)
ordinateur *(m)* computer (2)
ordonnance *(f)* prescription (10)
ordre *(m)* order; **en ordre** in order (3)
oreille *(f)* ear (10)
organiser to organize; **s'organiser** to get organized
origine *(f)* origin; **d'origine...** of . . . origin (7)
orné(e) (de) decorated with, adorned with
orphelin(e) orphan
orthographique spelling
os *(m)* bone
OTAN (Organisation du Traité de l'Atlantique Nord) NATO
ou or (P)
où where (1); **d'où** from where (1); **n'importe où** (just) anywhere
oublier to forget (8)
ouest *(m)* west
oui yes (P)
outre-mer overseas
ouvert(e) open
ouverture *(f)* opening; **heure** *(f)* **d'ouverture** opening time (6)
ouvrable: jour ouvrable *(m)* workday
ouvrir to open; **Ouvrez votre livre à la page 23.** Open your book to page 23. (P)

P

pacifique pacific, peaceful
page *(f)* page (P)
paiement *(m)* payment
paillasson *(m)* doormat
pain *(m)* bread (8); **pain au chocolat** *(m)* chocolate-filled croissant (8); **pain complet** *(m)* loaf of whole-grain bread (8); **pain grillé** *(m)* toast (8)
palais *(m)* palace (6)

pâle pale
palier *(m)* (floor) landing
pamplemousse *(m)* grapefruit
panique *(f)* panic
paniqué(e) panicked
panoramique panoramic
pantalon *(m)* pants (5)
pantoufles *(fpl)* slippers
papa *(m)* dad, papa
pape *(m)* pope
papier *(m)* paper; **feuille** *(f)* **de papier** sheet of paper (P)
papillon *(m)* butterfly
pâque juive *(f)* Passover
Pâques *(fpl)* Easter
paquet *(m)* package, bag (8)
par per (3), by (5); **par ailleurs** furthermore; **par conséquent** consequently; **par contre** on the other hand; **par exemple** for example (2); **par *hasard** by chance; **par ici** this way (5); **par la fenêtre** through the window; **par mois** per month (3); **par terre** on the ground / floor (2)
paradis *(m)* paradise, heaven
paraître to appear
parapluie *(m)* umbrella (5)
parc *(m)* park (1); **parc naturel** *(m)* natural park, nature reserve
parce que because (P)
parcourir to scan
Pardon. Excuse me. (P)
pardonner to forgive, to pardon
pareil(le) (à) similar (to)
parent *(m)* parent (4), relative (5); **chez mes parents** at my parents' house (3)
paresseux(-euse) lazy (1)
parfait(e) perfect (7)
parfaitement perfectly (7)
parfois sometimes (5)
parfum *(m)* perfume
Parisien(ne) *(mf)* Parisian (9)
parking *(m)* parking lot (1), parking garage
parler to talk, to speak (2); **Je parle/Je ne parle pas...** I speak/I don't speak . . . (P); **parler au téléphone** to talk on the phone (2); **se parler** to talk to each other (7); **Vous parlez... ?** Do you speak . . . ? (P)
parmi among
paroisse *(f)* parish
parole *(f)* word, lyric
part: à part... besides . . . ; **mettre à part** to set aside; **ne... nulle part** not . . . anywhere; **quelque part** somewhere
part *(f)* share
partager to share (3), to divide up; **partagé(e)** shared, divided (3)
partenaire *(mf)* partner (7)
participer (à) to participate (in)
particulier(-ère) particular, private; **en particulier** especially
partie part *(f)*; **en grande partie** mostly, in large part; **en partie** partially; **faire partie de** to be a part of
partir (de... pour...) to leave (from . . . for . . .), to go away (4); **à partir de** starting from; **partir en voyage** to leave on a trip (5)
partout everywhere (3)
pas not (P); **je ne comprends pas** I don't understand (P); **ne... pas (du tout)** not (at all) (1); **ne... pas encore** not . . . yet (5); **Pas de problème!** No problem! (3); **Pas mal.** Not badly. (P); **pas plus** no more (4); **pas tellement** not so much (1); **Pas très bien.** Not very well. (P)

passant(e) *(mf)* passer-by
passé *(m)* past (6); **dans le passé** in the past (6)
passé(e) past (5)
passeport *(m)* passport (9)
passer to spend, to pass (2); **passer chez** to go by . . .'s house (2); **passer le week-end / la matinée** to spend the weekend / the morning (2); **passer un film** to show a movie (6); **s'en passer** to do without; **se faire passer pour** to pass as; **se passer** to happen (7)
passion *(f)* passion (7)
passionnant(e) fascinating
passionné(e) (de) passionate about, fascinated by
pastèque *(f)* watermelon
patate *(f)* *(familiar)* idiot
pâte *(f)* paste, dough; **pâtes** *(fpl)* pasta
pâté *(m)* pâté, meat spread (8); **pâté de cochon** pork pâté
patience *(f)* patience; **avoir de la patience** to have patience (4)
patient(e) patient (6)
patin *(m)* skate; **patin** *(m)* **à glace** ice-skate, ice-skating
pâtisserie *(f)* pastry shop, pastry (8)
patrimoine *(m)* patrimony, heritage
patron(ne) *(mf)* owner, boss
pauvre poor
pauvreté *(f)* poverty
pavé (de) *(m)* thick slice (of) (8)
payer to pay (2)
pays *(m)* country (3)
paysage *(m)* landscape (9)
Pays-Bas *(mpl)* Netherlands
Pays-de-la-Loire *(mpl)* Loire Valley
pêche *(f)* peach (8), fishing; **aller à la pêche** to go fishing
peigner: se peigner to comb one's hair (7)
peine: à peine barely
peintre *(m)* painter
peinture *(f)* painting (1)
pendant during (1), for (5); **pendant que** while
penser to think (2); **je pense que le français est...** I think that French is . . . (P); **penser à** to think about; **Qu'en pensez-vous?** What do you think about it? (5)
penseur (penseuse) *(mf)* thinker
perçu(e) perceived
perdre to lose (7); **perdre du temps** to waste time (7); **perdu(e)** lost; **se perdre** to get lost (7)
père *(m)* father (4)
période *(f)* period; **à cette période** at that time
permettre (de) to permit, to allow; **permis(e)** permitted, allowed
Pérou *(m)* Peru (9)
Perse *(f)* Persia
personnage *(m)* character
personnalisé(e) personalized; **service personnalisé** personal service (8)
personnalité *(f)* personality (1)
personne *(f)* person (6); **ne... personne** nobody, no one, not . . . anyone
personnel(le) personal; **effets personnels** *(mpl)* personal belongings (3)
pessimiste pessimistic (1)
pétanque *(f)* lawn bowling, petanque
petit(e) small, short (1); **petit à petit** little by little (6); **petit déjeuner** *(m)* breakfast (5); **petite annonce** *(f)* classified ad; **petits pois** *(mpl)* peas (8)
petite-fille *(f)* granddaughter (7)

petit-fils *(m)* grandson (7)

petits-enfants *(mpl)* grandchildren

peu little (P); **à peu près** approximately, about; **un peu difficile** a little difficult/hard (P)

peuple *(m)* people

peuplé(e) populated

peur *(f)* fear; **avoir peur (de)** to be afraid (of) (4), to fear; **faire peur à** to frighten

peut-être perhaps, maybe (3)

pharmacie *(f)* pharmacy (10)

pharmacien(ne) *(mf)* pharmacist

philosophie *(f)* philosophy (1)

phrase *(f)* sentence (P); **Écrivez la réponse en phrases complètes.** Write the answer in complete sentences. (P)

physiologique physiological

physique *(f)* physics (1)

physique physical; **aspect physique** *(m)* physical appearance (7)

piano *(m)* piano (2)

pièce *(f)* room (3); **pièce** *(f)* **de monnaie** coin; **pièce** *(f)* **de théâtre** play (4); **pièce** *(f)* **d'identité** identity card

pied *(m)* foot (10); **aller à pied** to walk, to go on foot (4); **doigt** *(m)* **de pied** toe (10); **pieds nus** barefoot

pin *(m)* pine

pique-nique *(m)* picnic

pire worse

piscine *(f)* swimming pool (4)

pistache *(f)* pistachio

pitié *(f)* pity; **avoir pitié (de)** to have pity (on / for) (10)

pittoresque picturesque

pizza *(f)* pizza (8)

placard *(m)* closet (3)

place *(f)* place (3), square, plaza (10); **à sa place** in its place (3)

plage *(f)* beach (4)

plaindre: se plaindre to complain

plaine *(f)* plain

plaire to please; **Ça t'a plu?** Did you like it? (6); **Ça te plaira!** You'll like it! (9); **Ça te plaît!** You like it! (3); **Il/Elle m'a plu!** I liked it! (6); **Il/Elle me plaît.** I like it. (5); **s'il vous plaît** please (P)

plaisant(e) pleasant

plaisir *(m)* pleasure; **Avec plaisir!** With pleasure! (6); **faire plaisir à** to please

plan *(m)* map (10), level; **plan** *(m)* **d'eau** stretch of water

planche *(f)* **à voile** windsurfing; **faire de la planche à voile** to windsurf

plante *(f)* plant (3)

plastique *(m)* plastic

plat *(m)* dish (8); **plat préparé** *(m)* ready-to-serve dish (8); **plat principal** main dish (8)

plat(e) flat; **œuf** *(m)* **au plat** fried egg

plateau *(m)* tray

plein(e) full; **de plein air** outdoor (4); **plein de** full of, a lot of

pleurer to cry

pleuvoir to rain (5)

plongée sous-marine *(f)* scuba diving

pluie *(f)* rain (5)

plupart: la plupart *(f)* the most part; **la plupart de** *(f)* the majority of; **la plupart du temps** most of the time (7)

plus plus; **À plus (tard)!** See you later! (P); **de plus** in addition; **de plus en plus de** more and more of (8); **en plus** besides, furthermore; **ne... plus** no more, no longer (8); **non plus** neither (3); **pas plus** no more

(4); **plus de** more (8); **plus... que** more . . . than (1); **plus tard** later (4)

plusieurs several (1)

plutôt rather (1); instead (4); **plutôt que** rather than

poche *(f)* pocket

poché(e) poached

poêlée (de) *(f)* frying pan full (of)

poêlon *(m)* cast iron pan

poème *(m)* poem (9)

poésie *(f)* poetry

poing *(m)* fist

point *(m)* point; **au point de** to be about to; **point** *(m)* **de vue** viewpoint

poire *(f)* pear (8)

pois: petits pois *(mpl)* peas (8)

poisson *(m)* fish (8); **poisson fumé** smoked fish (8); **poissons** *(mpl)* **d'avril** April Fool's Day

poissonnerie *(f)* fish market (8)

poivre *(m)* pepper (8)

poli(e) polite

police *(f)* police, policy

policier(-ère) detective, police (4)

politesse *(f)* politeness

politique *(f)* politics (7), policy; **sciences** *(fpl)* **politques** political science (1)

politique political; **homme politique** *(m)* politician

politiquement politically

polo *(m)* knit shirt (5)

Pologne *(f)* Poland

Polynésie française *(f)* French Polynesia (9)

pomme *(f)* apple (8); **pomme** *(f)* **de terre** potato (8)

populaire popular, pop (1)

porc *(m)* pork (8); **côte** *(f)* **de porc** pork chop (8)

portable: (ordinateur) portable *(m)* laptop (3); **(téléphone) portable** *(m)* cell phone (1)

porte *(f)* door (3); **porte** *(f)* **d'arrivée** arrival gate; **porte** *(f)* **d'embarquement** departure gate

portefeuille *(m)* wallet (5)

porter to wear, to carry (4)

portugais *(m)* Portuguese

poser to place; **poser une question** to ask a question (3)

posséder to possess, to own

possibilité *(f)* possibility (4)

possible possible (10); **il est possible que** it is possible that (10); **Pas possible!** I don't believe it!

postal(e) *(mpl* **postaux): carte postale** *(f)* postcard (9); **code postal** *(m)* zip code (3)

poste *(f)* post office; **bureau** *(m)* **de poste** post office (10)

poster *(m)* poster (3)

pot (de) *(m)* jar (of) (8)

pote *(m)* *(familiar)* buddy, pal

poubelle *(f)* trash can

poudre *(f)* powder

poulet *(m)* chicken (8)

poumon *(m)* lung

pour for (P), in order to (1); **pour cent** percent; **pour que** so that

pourboire *(m)* tip

pourcentage *(m)* percentage

pourquoi why (2); **Pourquoi pas?** Why not? (2)

pourtant however, yet (8)

pouvoir *(m)* power

pouvoir to be able, can, may (6); **Je peux vous aider?** May I help you? (5); **on peut** one can (4)

pratique *(f)* practice

pratique practical, convenient (3)

pratiquer to practice, to play *(a sport)*, to do

précédent(e) preceding

prêcher to preach

préciser to specify

préférable preferable (10); **il est préférable que** it's preferable that (10)

préféré(e) favorite (3)

préférence *(f)* preference

préférer to prefer (2); **je préfère** I prefer (1)

premier(-ère) first (1)

prendre to take (4); **Ça prend combien de temps?** How long does it take? (4); **Je vais prendre...** I'm going to have . . . (2); **prendre possession de** to take possession of; **prendre son petit déjeuner** to have one's breakfast (5); **prendre un bain** to take a bath (7); **prendre un bain de soleil** to sunbathe (4); **prendre une décision** to make a decision (7); **prendre un verre** to have a drink (2); **Prenez une feuille de papier et un crayon ou un stylo.** Take out a piece of paper and a pencil or a pen. (P); **Qu'est-ce que vous allez prendre?** What are you going to have? (2)

prénom *(m)* first name (3)

préoccuper to worry; **se préoccuper (de)** to worry (about)

préparatifs *(mpl)* preparations (9)

préparer to prepare (2); **plat préparé** ready-to-serve dish (8); **Préparez l'examen pour le prochain cours.** Prepare for the exam for the next class. (P)

près (de) near (1), nearly; **à peu près** approximately, about

présentation *(f)* introduction, presentation

présenter to introduce, to present; **Je vous/te présente...** I would like to introduce . . . to you.; **se présenter** to arise, to introduce oneself

presque almost, nearly (2)

prêt(e) ready (4)

prêter to loan, to lend

prier to beg, to request, to pray; **Je vous/t'en prie.** You're welcome (2).

prière *(f)* prayer

primaire: école primaire *(f)* elementary school

principal(e) *(mpl* **principaux)** main (8)

principalement mainly

principauté *(f)* principality

printemps *(m)* spring (5); **au printemps** in spring (5)

prioritaire having priority

priorité *(f)* priority

prisonnier(-ère) *(mf)* prisoner

privatif(-ive) private

privé(e) private (10)

privilégié(e) privileged, favored

prix *(m)* price; **menu** *(m)* **à prix fixe** set-price menu (8)

probablement probably

problème *(m)* problem; **pas de problème** no problem (3)

prochain(e) next (4); **le prochain cours** the next class (P)

producteur(-trice) producer

produit *(m)* product (8); **produits bio** *(mpl)* organic products (8)

professeur *(m)* professor (P); **Le professeur dit aux étudiants...** The professor says to the students . . . (P)
profession *(f)* profession (7)
professionnel(le) professional (7)
profil *(m)* profile
profiter de to take advantage of (9)
profond(e) deep
programme *(m)* program
projet *(m)* plan (4); **faire des projets** to make plans (4)
promenade *(f)* walk (5); **faire une promenade** to take a walk (5)
promener: se promener to go walking (7)
promettre (de...) to promise (to . . .) (6)
promouvoir to promote
pronom *(m)* pronoun
prononcer to pronounce
prononciation *(f)* pronunciation
propos: à propos de about
proposer to offer, to suggest, to propose; **Qu'est-ce que je peux vous proposer d'autre?** What else can I get you? (8)
propre clean (3), own
propreté *(f)* cleanliness
protéger to protect; **protégé(e) par** protected by
provençal *(m)* Provençal
Provence *(f)* Provence
provenir de to come from
province *(f)* province (3)
proviseur *(m)* principal
provoquer to cause
prune *(f)* plum
pruneau *(m)* prune
psychologie *(f)* psychology (1)
public: le grand public the public at large
publicité *(f)* advertising, advertisement
puis then (4)
puisque since
puissant(e) powerful
pull *(m)* pullover sweater (5)
pureté *(f)* purity
pyjama *(m)* pajamas

Q

quai *(m)* quay, wharf
quand when (2); **quand même** all the same
quantité *(f)* quantity
quarante forty (2); **quarante et un** forty-one (2)
quart *(m)* quarter; **Il est deux heures et quart.** It's a quarter past two. (P)
quartier *(m)* neighborhood (1)
quatorze fourteen (P)
quatre four (P)
quatre-vingts eighty (2); **quatre-vingt-un** eighty-one (2); **quatre-vingt-dix** ninety (2); **quatre-vingt-onze** ninety-one (2)
quatrième fourth (3)
que that (P), than, as (1), what (2), which, whom (7); **ce que** what, that which (7); **Je pense que...** I think that . . . (P); **ne... que** only; **ne... rien que** nothing but; **que ce soit** whether it be; **qu'est-ce que** what (1); **Qu'est-ce que ça veut dire?** What does that mean? (P); **Qu'est-ce que c'est?** What is it? (2)
quel(le) which, what (3); **À quelle heure?** At what time? (P); **C'est quel jour aujourd'hui?** What day is today? (P); **n'importe quel(le)...** (just) any . . . ; **Quel âge a... ?** How old is . . . ? (4)

quelque some; **quelque chose** something (2); **quelque part** somewhere; **quelques** a few (5); **quelques-un(e)s** *(mf)* a few; **quelqu'un** someone, somebody (6)
quelquefois sometimes (2)
quelques-un(e)s *(mf)* a few
question *(f)* question (P); **Écoutez la question.** Listen to the question. (P); **Répondez à la question.** Answer the question. (P)
quête *(f)* quest
qui who (2), that, which, who (7); **ce qui** what (7); **Qu'est-ce qui ne va pas?** What's wrong? (10); **Qu'est-ce qui s'est passé?** What happened? (6); **Qui est-ce?** Who is it? (2)
quinze fifteen (P)
quinzième fifteenth (3)
quitter to leave (4); **se quitter** to leave each other (7)
quoi what; **n'importe quoi** (just) anything; **à quoi bon** what's the point
quotidien(ne) daily (7)

R

rabbin *(m)* rabbi
raccompagner to (re)accompany
racine *(f)* root
raconter to tell (7), to recount
radio *(f)* radio (2), X-ray
raffiné(e) refined
raie *(f)* skate (fish), rayfish (8)
raisin *(m)* grape(s) (8); **raisins secs** *(mpl)* raisins
raison *(f)* reason; **avoir raison** to be right (4), **en raison de** because of
raisonnable reasonable
rajouter to add
ralentir to slow down
randonnée *(f)* hike (5); **faire une randonnée** to go for a hike (5)
rangé(e) orderly, put away, in its place (3)
ranger to arrange, to order (7)
rapide rapid (8)
rapport *(m)* relationship, report
rapporter to bring back; **se rapporter à** to be related to
rarement rarely (2)
raser: se raser to shave (7)
rassembler: se rassembler to gather
rater to miss
ravigote *(f)* a seasoned sauce
rayé(e) striped
réagir (à) to react (to)
réaliste realistic (1)
récemment recently (5)
réception *(f)* front desk (10), receiving
recevoir to receive (9)
recherche *(f)* research, search
rechercher to seek; **recherché(e)** sought
réciproque reciprocal
recoins *(mpl)* the nooks and corners
recommander to recommend (10); **recommandé(e)** recommended
réconcilier: se réconcilier to make up with each other (7)
reconnaître to recognize (9); **se reconnaître** to recognize each other (7)
recoucher: se recoucher to go back to bed (7)
recours: avoir recours à to resort to
recouvert(e) covered
recréer to recreate
récrire to rewrite
récupéré(e) recuperated, salvaged
rédaction *(f)* composition (9)

redéfinir to redefine
réduire to reduce
réel(le) real
réfléchi(e) reflexive
réfléchir (à) to think (about) (8), to reflect (on)
refléter to reflect
réflexion *(f)* reflection, thought
réfrigérateur *(m)* refrigerator
réfugié(e) *(mf)* refugee
regard *(m)* look
regarder to look at, to watch (2); **se regarder** to look at each other (7)
régime *(m)* diet; regime; **être au régime** to be on a diet
région *(f)* region (4); region, area (9)
régional(e) *(mpl* **régionaux)** regional (4)
réglable adjustable
règlement *(m)* payment
réglementé(e) regulated
régler to adjust; **régler la note** to pay the bill (10)
regretter to regret (6)
régulier(-ière) regular
régulièrement regularly (8)
rejoindre to join
relation *(f)* relationship (7)
relativement relatively
relaxant(e) relaxing
religieux(-euse) religious
religion *(f)* religion (7)
relire to reread
remarquable remarkable
remarquer to notice
rembourser to reimburse
remercier (de) to thank (for) (10)
remettre to put back
remonter to go back (up)
remplacer to replace
remplir to fill up
remporter to win
renaissance *(f)* revival, renaissance
rencontre *(f)* meeting, encounter (7)
rencontrer to meet for the first time or by chance, to run into (1); **se rencontrer** to run into each other (7)
rendez-vous *(m)* date, appointment; **Rendez-vous à...** Let's meet at . . .
rendre (quelque chose à quelqu'un), to return (something to someone) (7); **rendre (+ adjective)** to make (+ adjective); **rendre visite à quelqu'un** to visit someone (7); **se rendre (à / chez)** to go (to)
renommé(e) renowned
renommée *(f)* fame
renoncer renounce, give up
renouvelable renewable
rénover to renovate
renseignement *(m)* piece of information (3)
renseigner: se renseigner to inquire, to get information (10)
rentrer to return, to come / go back (home) (2); **rentré(e)** having returned
réparti(e) distributed
repartir to start again, to leave again
répartition *(f)* distribution
repas *(m)* meal (6)
répéter to repeat (2); **Répétez, s'il vous plaît.** Repeat, please. (P); **se répéter** to be repeated
répondre (à) to answer (6); **Répondez à la question.** Answer the question. (P)
réponse *(f)* answer (P); **Écrivez la réponse avec une phrase complète.** Write the answer with a complete sentence. (P)

reposer to set down; **se reposer** to rest (7)
reprendre to catch again
représenter to represent
république (f) republic
réseau (m) network (9)
réservation (f) reservation (9); **faire une réservation** to make a reservation (9)
réserver to reserve (9); **réservé(e)** reserved
résidence (f) dormitory (1), residence hall
résoudre to solve
respecter to respect; **se respecter** to respect one another
respiration (f) breathing
responsable responsible
ressemblance (f) similarity
ressembler à to look like, to resemble
ressortir: faire ressortir to make stand out
restaurant (m) restaurant (1); **dîner au restaurant** to have dinner in a restaurant (2)
reste (m) rest (7); **le reste (de)** the rest (of) (7)
rester to stay (2); **rester au lit** to stay in bed (2)
resto-U (m) university cafeteria (6)
résultat (m) result
résumé (m) summary
resvératrol (m) resveratrol
retard (m) delay; **en retard** late (10)
retirer (de l'argent) to take out, to withdraw (money) (10); **se retirer** to retire
retour (m) return (9); **billet aller-retour** (m) round-trip ticket (9)
retourner to return (5); **se retourner** to turn around
retrouver to meet (4), to find (again); **se retrouver** to meet each other (by design) (7)
réunion (f) meeting
réunir: se réunir to meet
réussir (à) to succeed (at/in), to pass (a test) (8)
revanche: en revanche on the other hand
rêve (m) dream
réveil (m) alarm clock (7), awakening
réveiller to wake up; **se réveiller** to wake up (7)
réveillon (m) **du jour de l'An** New Year's Eve
révélateur(-trice) revealing
révéler to reveal; **se révéler** to be revealed
revendre to resell, to sell back (7)
revenir to come back (4)
revenu (m) income
rêver (de) to dream (about, of) (7)
réviser to review (2)
révision (f) review, revision
revoir to see again; **Au revoir.** Good-bye. (P)
revue (f) magazine
rez-de-chaussée (m) ground floor (3)
rhum (m) rum
rhume (m) cold (10)
riche rich (2)
richesse (f) wealth
rideau (m) curtain (3)
ridicule ridiculous
rien nothing; **de rien** you're welcome (P); **ne... rien** nothing, not . . . anything (5); **ne... rien de spécial** nothing special (5); **ne... rien que** nothing but; **rien à voir avec** nothing to do with; **rien du tout** nothing at all (6)
rillettes (fpl) potted pork or goose
ringard(e) old-fashioned
rire to laugh
rive (f) bank

rivière (f) river
riz (m) rice (8)
robe (f) dress (5); **robe** (f) **de chambre** robe
rock (m) rock music (1)
rockeur(-euse) (mf) rock singer
rôle (m) role; **à tour de rôle** taking turns
roller: faire du roller to go in-line skating (6)
romain(e) Roman
roman (m) novel (9)
romanche (m) Romansh
romantique romantic
rompre to break (up)
rond (m) circle
rosbif (m) roast beef (8)
rose pink (3)
rosier (m) rosebush
rôti(e) roasted; **rôti** (m) **de porc** pork roast
rouennais(e) from Rouen
rouge red (3); **vin rouge** (m) red wine (2)
route (f) route, way
routine (f) routine (7)
roux (rousse) red (with hair) (4)
royaume (m) kingdom; **Royaume-Uni** (m) United Kingdom (9)
rue (f) street (3); **dans la rue...** on . . . Street (10)
ruine (f) ruin
rural(e) (mpl **ruraux**) rural
ruse (f) trick
russe (m) Russian
Russie (f) Russia (9)
rythme (m) rhythm

S

sable (m) sand
sac (m) purse (5); **sac** (m) **à dos** backpack
sage good, well-behaved (4)
sain(e) healthy (8)
saint(e) holy
Saint-Valentin (f) Valentine's Day
saison (f) season (5)
salade (f) salad (8); **salade** (f) **de tomates** tomato salad (8)
salarié(e) (mf) wage earner
sale dirty (3)
salé(e) salted
salle (f) room; **salle** (f) **à manger** dining room (3); **salle** (f) **de bains** bathroom (3); **salle** (f) **de cours** classroom (1); **salle** (f) **de gym** gym, fitness club (1); **salle** (f) **d'informatique** computer lab (1)
salon (m) living room (3)
saluer to greet
Salut! Hi! (P)
salutation (f) greeting
samedi (m) Saturday (P)
sandale (f) sandal (5)
sandwich (m) sandwich (2)
sang (m) blood
sans without (P); **Ça s'écrit avec ou sans accent?** That's written with or without an accent? (P); **sans égal** unequaled
santé (f) health (8)
satisfaisant(e) satisfying
satisfait(e) satisfied
saucisse (f) sausage (8)
saucisson (m) salami (8)
sauf except (2)
saumon (m) salmon (8)
sauter to jump; **faire sauter** to blow up
sauver to save; **sauvé(e)** saved
savane (f) savanna
saveur (f) flavor, taste

savoir to know (how) (9); **Je ne sais pas.** I don't know. (P)
savon (m) soap
savoureux(-euse) tasty
science (f) science (1); **sciences humaines** (fpl) social sciences (1); **sciences politiques** (fpl) political science, government (1)
scientifique scientific
scolaire school; **extra-scolaire** extracurricular
scolarité (f) education
se herself, himself, itself, oneself, themselves (7); **Il/Elle s'appelle...** His/Her name is . . . (4); **Il/Elle se trouve...** It is located . . .
séance (f) showing (6)
sec (sèche) dry
sécher to dry, to skip (class)
secondaire secondary
seconde (f) second (5)
sécurité (f) security, safety
séducteur(-trice) seductive
séduire to seduce
séduisant(e) attractive
sein (m) breast; **au sein de** within
seize sixteen (P)
seizième sixteenth (3)
séjour (m) stay (7)
sel (m) salt (8)
self-service (m) self-service restaurant (8)
selon according to
semaine (f) week (P); **en semaine** weekdays; **les jours de la semaine** the days of the week (P)
semblable similar
sembler to seem
semestre (m) semester (P)
Sénégal (m) Senegal (9)
sénégalais(e) Senegalese
sens (m) meaning, sense; **sens** (m) **de l'humour** sense of humor (7)
sensible sensitive
sentiment (m) feeling (7)
sentimental(e) (mpl **sentimentaux**) sentimental, emotional (7)
sentir: se sentir to feel (8)
séparément separately
séparer to separate; **séparé(e)** separated
sept seven (P)
septembre (m) September (4)
septième seventh (3)
sérieux(-euse) serious
serrer to squeeze
serveur (m) waiter, server (2)
serveuse (f) waitress, server (2)
serviable helpful, obliging
service (m) service (8)
serviette (f) napkin, towel
servir to serve (4); **servi(e)** served (10); **se servir de** to use
seul(e) alone (P), only (1), single, lonely; **le/la seul(e)** the only one
seulement only (8)
shopping: faire du shopping to go shopping (2)
short (m) shorts (5)
si if (5), yes (in response to a question in the negative) (8); **s'il vous plaît** please (P)
siècle (m) century
siège (m) seat
sieste (f) nap
signaler to point out, to draw attention to
similaire (à) similar (to)
simple simple; **aller simple** (m) one-way ticket (9); **chambre simple** single room (f) (10)

simplement simply (10); **tout simplement** quite simply (10)
sinon if not, otherwise
sirène *(f)* mermaid, siren
site *(m)* site (9)
situé(e) situated
six six (P)
sixième sixth (3)
skateboard(ing): faire du skateboard(ing) to skateboard (6)
ski *(m)* skiing (2); **faire du ski** to go skiing (2); **faire du ski nautique** to go water-skiing (5)
smartphone *(m)* smartphone (3)
social(e) *(mpl* **sociaux)** social
société *(f)* company, society
sœur *(f)* sister (1); **belle-sœur** *(f)* sister-in-law; **demi-sœur** *(f)* stepsister (6), half-sister
soi oneself
soif *(f)* thirst; **avoir soif** to be thirsty (4); **j'ai soif** I'm thirsty (2)
soigner to treat, to cure
soin *(m)* care
soir *(m)* evening (P); **à huit heures du soir** at eight in the evening (P); **ce soir** tonight, this evening (2); **le soir** in the evening, evenings (P)
soirée *(f)* evening (4), party (6)
soixante sixty (2); **les années soixante** the sixties; **soixante-dix** seventy (2); **soixante et onze** seventy-one (2); **soixante et un** sixty-one (2)
sol *(m)* ground
solaire solar
soldat *(m)* soldier
solde: en solde on sale (5)
sole *(f)* sole (fish)
soleil *(m)* sun; **Il fait (du) soleil.** It's sunny. (5); **lunettes** *(fpl)* **de soleil** sunglasses (5); **prendre un bain de soleil** to sunbathe (4)
sombre dark, gloomy
sommeil *(m)* sleep; **avoir sommeil** to be sleepy (4)
sommet *(m)* summit
son *(m)* sound
son (sa, ses) her, his, its (3)
sondage *(m)* poll
sonder to poll
sonner to ring (7)
sorte *(f)* kind, sort; **en sorte que** so that
sortie *(f)* outing (6), exit
sortir to go out (2); to take out
soudain suddenly (6)
soudain(e) sudden
soudainement suddenly
souhaiter to wish (10)
soupçonner to suspect
soupe *(f)* soup (8); **soupe** *(f)* **à l'oignon** onion soup (8)
sourire to smile
sous under (3); **sous réserve de** subject to
sous-marin(e) underwater; **plongée sous-marine** *(f)* scuba diving
sous-sol *(m)* basement (3)
sous-vêtements *(mpl)* underwear
souterrain(e) underground
soutien *(m)* support
souvenir *(m)* memory
souvenir: se souvenir (de) to remember (7)
souvent often (2)
spatial(e) *(mpl* **spatiaux): industrie** *(f)* **spatiale** space industry
spécial(e) *(mpl* **spéciaux)** special; **effets spéciaux** *(mpl)* special effects (6); **ne... rien de spécial** nothing special (5)

spécialisé(e) specialized
spécialité *(f)* specialty (4)
spectacle *(m)* show
spectateur(-trice) *(mf)* spectator, viewer
spiritualité *(f)* spirituality (7)
spontané(e) spontaneous
sport *(m)* sports (1); **faire du sport** to play sports (2)
sportif *(m)* athlete
sportif(-ive) athletic (1)
stade *(m)* stadium (1)
stage *(m)* internship
stagiaire *(mf)* intern
station *(f)* station; **station-service** *(f)* service station
statistique *(f)* statistics
statut *(m)* statute, status
steak-frites *(m)* steak and fries (8)
stimuler to stimulate
stratégie *(f)* strategy
stress *(m)* stress (8)
stressé(e) stressed (out)
stylo *(m)* pen (P); **Prenez une feuille de papier et un crayon ou un stylo.** Take out a piece of paper and a pencil or a pen. (P)
subventions *(fpl)* subsidies
sucre *(m)* sugar (8)
sucré(e) sweet, sugary
sud *(m)* south; **Amérique** *(f)* **du Sud** South America (9)
Suède *(f)* Sweden
suffire to suffice; **Suffit!** That's enough!
suffisant(e) sufficient
suggérer to suggest (6)
Suisse *(f)* Switzerland (9)
suisse Swiss
suite: tout de suite right away (6)
suivant(e) following (3)
suivre to follow (7); **à suivre** to be continued (6); **suivi(e) de** followed by; **suivre un cours** to take a course
sujet *(m)* subject; **au sujet de** about
sulfureux(-euse) sulferous
super great (P)
superficie *(f)* area
supérieur(e) superior, higher
supermarché *(m)* supermarket (8)
supplément *(m)* extra charge (10)
supporter to bear, to tolerate, to put up with (7)
sur on (1); **sept jours sur sept** seven days out of seven
sûr(e) sure; **Bien sûr!** Of course! (5)
suranné(e) old-fashioned
surface: grande surface *(f)* superstore (8)
surfer sur Internet to surf the Net (2)
surgelé(e) frozen (8)
surgir to arise, to come up, to appear suddenly
surnom *(m)* nickname
surprenant(e) surprising
surprendre to surprise; **surpris(e)** surprised (10)
sursauter to jump
surtout especially (8), above all
survêtement *(m)* jogging suit (5)
survivre to survive
sympathique (sympa) nice (1)
symptôme *(m)* symptom (10)
synonyme synonymous

T

tabac *(m)* tobacco (8); **bureau** *(m)* **de tabac** tobacco shop
table *(f)* table (3); **à table** at the table; **table basse** *(f)* coffee table

tableau *(m)* board (P), painting, picture (3), scene, chart; **Allez au tableau.** Go to the board. (P); **tableau** *(m)* **d'affichage** bulletin board
tache *(f)* spot
taille *(f)* size (4); **de taille moyenne** medium-sized, of medium height (4); **Quelle taille faites-vous?** What size do you wear? (5)
tailleur *(m)* woman's suit
talon *(m)* heel; *****haut talon** *(m)* high heel
tambour *(m)* drum
tandis que whereas, while
tant (de) so much, so many; **tant que** as long as
tante *(f)* aunt (4)
tapis *(m)* rug (3)
tapisserie *(f)* tapestry
tard late (4); **À plus tard!** See you later! (P); **plus tard** later (4)
tarif *(m)* rate, fare
tarte *(f)* pie (8); **tarte** *(f)* **aux pommes** apple pie (8)
tartelette *(f)* **(aux fraises/aux cerises)** (strawberry/cherry) tart (8)
tartine *(f)* bread with butter and jelly (8)
tas *(m)* pile; **un tas de** a bunch of
tasse *(f)* cup
taxi *(m)* taxi (4); **en taxi** by taxi (4)
te (to, for) you (9), yourself (7); **Ça te dit?** How does that sound to you? (2); **Ça te plaît?** Do you like it? (3); **Je te présente...** I would like to introduce . . . to you.; **s'il te plaît** please; **Te voilà!** There you are!
technologie *(f)* technology (1); **technologies** *(fpl)* technical courses (1)
technologique technological
tee-shirt *(m)* T-shirt (5)
tel(le): tel(le) que such as; **un(e) tel(le)** such a (7)
télé *(f)* TV (2)
téléchargement *(m)* downloading
téléphone *(m)* telephone (2); **au téléphone** on the telephone (2); **numéro** *(m)* **de téléphone** telephone number (3)
téléphoner (à) to phone (3); **se téléphoner** to phone each other (7)
téléphonique: carte *(f)* **téléphonique** telephone card (10)
télévisé(e) televised
télévision (télé) *(f)* television (2)
tellement so much (1), so (6); **pas tellement** not so much (1)
temple *(m)* temple, Protestant church
temporaire temporary
temps *(m)* time (2), weather (5); **Ça prend combien de temps?** How long does it take? (4); **de temps en temps** from time to time (2); **emploi** *(m)* **du temps** schedule; **en même temps** at the same time; **en tout temps** at all times, at any time; **passer du temps** to spend time; **Pendant combien de temps?** For how long? (5); **Quel temps fait-il?** What's the weather like? (5); **temps libre** *(m)* free time (2); **temps verbal** *(m)* tense
tendance *(f)* tendency
tendre tender
tenir to hold, to keep; **Ah tiens!** Hey!; **tenir à** to value, to be keen on; **tenir la maison** to keep house
tennis *(m)* tennis (1); **court** *(m)* **de tennis** tennis court
terme *(m)* term; **mettre terme à** to put an end to
terminaison *(f)* ending

terminer to finish

terrasse *(f)* terrace (9)

terre *(f)* earth; **par terre** on the ground / floor (3); **pomme** *(f)* **de terre** potato (8)

terrine *(f)* earthenware bowl, terrine

territoire *(m)* territory

test *(m)* test (7)

tête *(f)* head (10); **prendre la tête** to take charge

Texas *(m)* Texas (9)

texto *(m)* text message (2)

thé *(m)* tea (2)

théâtre *(m)* theater, drama (1)

thon *(m)* tuna (8)

tiers *(m)* third

timbre *(m)* stamp (10)

timide shy, timid (1)

tiroir *(m)* drawer

toi you (P); **Et toi?** And you? *(familiar)* (P)

toilette: toilettes *(fpl)* toilet, restroom (3); **faire sa toilette** to wash up (7)

tolérance *(f)* tolerance, acceptance (7)

tomate *(f)* tomato (8)

tomber to fall (5); **tomber amoureux(-euse) (de)** to fall in love (with) (6); **tomber malade** to get sick (10)

ton *(m)* tone

ton (ta, tes) your (3); **tes amis** your friends (1)

tongs *(fpl)* flip-flops (5)

tort: avoir tort to be wrong (4)

tôt early (4)

touche *(f)* key

toucher to touch

toujours always (2), still

tour *(m)* tour, ride (4); **à tour de rôle** taking turns; **faire un tour** to take a tour, to go for a ride (4)

tour *(f)* tower

tourisme *(m)* tourism; **office** *(m)* **de tourisme** tourist office (10)

touriste *(mf)* tourist

touristique touristic (9)

tourner (à droite/à gauche) to turn (right/left) (10), to stir, to film; **se tourner (vers)** to turn (toward); **tourné(e)** filmed

tousser to cough (10)

tout (toute, tous, toutes) everything, all (2), whole (2); **(À) tout à l'heure** (See you) in a little while (P), a while ago; **C'est tout.** That's all. (8); **ne... pas du tout** not at all (1); **rien du tout** nothing at all (6); **tous (toutes) les deux** both; **tous les jours** every day (P); **tous les soirs** every evening; **tout à coup** all of a sudden (6); **tout à fait** completely; **tout de suite** right away (6); **tout droit** straight (10); **tout d'un coup** all at once (6); **tout en** while; **toute la journée** the whole day (2); **tout le monde** everybody, everyone (6); **tout près (de)** right by, very near (3); **tout simplement** quite simply (10)

toutefois however

toux *(f)* cough

traditionnel(le) traditional (8)

traduire to translate

train *(m)* train (4); **en train** by train (4); **être en train de...** to be in the process of . . .

trait *(m)* trait (7); **trait** *(m)* **de caractère** character trait (7)

tranche *(f)* slice (8)

tranquille tranquil, calm

transformer: se transformer en to change into

transmettre to transmit; to pass on

transport *(m)* transportation (4); **moyen** *(m)* **de transport** means of transportation (4); **réseau** *(m)* **de transports en commun** public transportation system (9)

travail *(m)* *(pl* **travaux)** work (6); **fête** *(f)* **du travail** Labor Day

travailler to work (2); **Je travaille...** I work . . . (P); **Je ne travaille pas...** I do not work . . . (P); **Tu travailles?/Vous travaillez?** Do you work? (P)

travers: à travers across

traverser to cross, to go across (10)

treize thirteen (P)

trekking *(m)* backpacking

trente thirty (P)

très very (P); **Je vais très bien.** I'm doing very well. (P)

tribu *(f)* tribe

trinité *(f)* trinity

triomphe *(m)* triumph

triste sad (10)

trois three (P)

troisième third (3)

trompe *(f)* horn

trompette *(f)* trumpet

trop too, too much (3); **trop de** too much, too many (6)

tropical(e) *(mpl* **tropicaux)** tropical (9)

trou *(m)* hole

trouver to find (4); **Il/Elle se trouve...** It is located . . ., He/She/It finds himself/herself/ itself

truc *(m)* thing (1); **Ce n'est pas mon truc.** That's not my thing. (1)

truite *(f)* trout

tu you (P)

tuer to kill

Tunisie *(f)* Tunisia

Turquie *(f)* Turkey

typique typical (2)

typiquement typically

tyran *(m)* tyrant

U

un(e) one, a (P)

uni(e) (à) close (to), united, solid-colored; **Royaume-Uni** *(m)* United Kingdom (9)

union: Union *(f)* **européenne** European Union

unique only, single, unique

uniquement only (6)

unité *(f)* unity, unit

universel(le) universal

universitaire university (1); **résidence** *(f)* **universitaire** university dorm (3)

université *(f)* university (P); **à l'université** at the university (P)

urbain(e) urban

urgence *(f)* emergency

usage *(m)* use

usine *(f)* factory

utile useful (10)

utiliser to use, to utilize

V

vacances *(fpl)* vacation (4); **partir en vacances** to leave on vacation (4)

vacancier(-ière) *(mf)* vacationer

vachement really *(slang)*

vadrouille *(f)* stroll

vague *(f)* wave

vaisselle *(f)* dishes; **faire la vaisselle** to wash dishes (5); **lave-vaisselle** *(m)* dishwasher

valeur *(f)* value

valise *(f)* suitcase (9); **faire sa valise** to pack your bag (9)

vallée *(f)* valley; **la Vallée de la Loire** the Loire Valley

valoir to be worth; **il vaut mieux (que)...** it's better (that) . . . (10)

valse *(f)* waltz

vanille *(f)* vanilla (8)

vanité *(f)* vanity (7)

vaniteux(-euse) vain

varié(e) varied

varier to vary

vaut See **valoir**

veau *(m)* veal

végétal(e) *(mpl* **végétaux)** **huile végétale** *(f)* vegetable oil

végétarien(ne) vegetarian

vélo *(m)* bicycle (2); **à vélo** by bike (4); **faire du vélo** to go bike-riding (2)

vendeur(-euse) *(mf)* salesperson (5)

vendre to sell (7)

vendredi *(m)* Friday (P)

venir to come (4); **venir de** (+ *infinitive*) to have just (+ *past participle*); **Viens voir!** Come see! (3)

vent *(m)* wind; **Il fait du vent.** It's windy. (5); **Il y a du vent.** It's windy. (5)

vente *(f)* sale

ventre *(m)* stomach (10), belly

verbe *(m)* verb

verdoyant(e) green, verdant

verdure *(f)* greenery

verglas: Il y a du verglas. It's icy.

vérifier to check, to verify (10)

vérité *(f)* truth

verre *(m)* glass (2); **prendre un verre** to have a drink (2)

vers *(m)* verse

vers toward(s), about, around (2)

verser to pour, to pay

vert(e) green (3)

vêtements *(mpl)* clothes (3); **sous-vêtements** *(mpl)* underwear

veuf *(m)* widower (7)

veuve *(f)* widow (7)

vexé(e) offended

viande *(f)* meat (8)

victime *(f)* victim

vidéo *(f)* video (2); **jeu** *(m)* **vidéo** video game (2)

vie *(f)* life (6)

vieillir to age, to get old

vieillot(te) outdated, old-fashioned

viennois(e) Viennese

viennoiserie *(f) baked goods sold at a bakery*

vierge *(f)* virgin

Viêt Nam *(m)* Vietnam (9)

vieux (vieil, vieille) old (1); **Vieux Carré** *(m)* French Quarter (4)

vif(-ive) lively, bright; **bleu vif** bright blue

village *(m)* village, town

villageois(e) *(mf)* villager

ville *(f)* city (3); **en ville** in town (3)

vin *(m)* wine (2)

vingt twenty (P)

vingtième twentieth

violence *(f)* violence (6)

violet(te) violet (3)

virus *(m)* virus (10)

visage *(m)* face

visite *(f)* visit; **rendre visite à quelqu'un** to visit someone (7)

visiter to visit *(a place)* (1)

visiteur(-euse) *(mf)* visitor
vitamine *(f)* vitamin (8)
vite quick(ly), fast (7)
vitesse *(f)* speed
vivoir *(m)* living room
vivre to live; **Vive… !** Long live… !, Hurray for… !
vocabulaire *(m)* vocabulary (P); **Apprenez les mots de vocabulaire.** Learn the vocabulary words. (P)
vœu *(m)* wish
voici here is, here are (2)
voilà there is, there are (2); **Te/Vous voilà!** There you are!
voile *(f)* sailing; **faire de la planche à voile** *(f)* to go windsurfing
voir to see (1); **aller voir** to go see, to visit (4); **comme tu vois** as you see (3); **rien à voir avec** nothing to do with; **se voir** to see each other (7); **Voyons!** Let's see! (5)
voisin(e) *(mf)* neighbor (9)
voiture *(f)* car (3); **en voiture** by car (4); **voiture** *(f)* **de location** rental car (5)
voix *(f)* voice
vol *(m)* flight (9)
volaille *(f)* poultry (8)
volcan *(m)* volcano
voleur *(m)* thief

volley *(m)* volleyball (2)
volonté *(f)* will, wish
volontiers gladly, willingly
volupté *(f)* voluptuousness
vomir to vomit (10)
voter to vote
votre *(pl* **vos)** your (2); **Ouvrez votre livre à la page 23.** Open your book to page 23. (P)
vouloir to want (6); **Ça veut dire…** That means . . . (P); **Je voudrais (bien)…** I would like . . . (2); **Qu'est-ce que ça veut dire?** What does that mean? (P); **Qu'est-ce que vous voudriez faire?** What would you like to do? (2); **Tu voudrais… ?** Would you like . . . ? (2)
vous you (P), (to, for) you (9), yourself(-selves) (7); **Ça vous dit?** How does that sound to you? (2); **Et vous?** And you? *(formal)* (P); **Je vous présente…** I would like to introduce . . . to you.; **s'il vous plaît** please (P); **vous-même** yourself; **Vous voilà!** There you are!
voyage *(m)* trip (4); **agence** *(f)* **de voyages** travel agency (9); **agent** *(m)* **de voyages** travel agent (9); **chèque** *(m)* **de voyage** traveler's check; **faire un voyage** to take a trip (5); **partir en voyage** to leave on a trip (5); **voyage** *(m)* **de noces** honeymoon
voyager to travel (2)

voyageur(-euse) *(mf)* traveler
voyelle *(f)* vowel
vrai(e) true (8)
vraiment really, truly (2)
VTT (vélo *[m]* **tout-terrain): faire du VTT** to go all-terrain biking (5)
vue *(f)* view (3); **point** *(m)* **de vue** viewpoint

W

wallon(ne) Walloon
W.-C. *(m)* toilet, restroom (10)
week-end *(m)* weekend (P); **Bon week-end!** Have a good weekend!; **le week-end** on the weekend, weekends (P)
Wi-Fi *(m)* Wi-Fi (1); **accès Wi-Fi** *(m)* Wi-Fi access (10)

Y

y there (4); **il y a** there is, there are (1), ago (5)
yaourt *(m)* yogurt (8)
yeux *(mpl)* *(sing* **œil)** eyes (4)

Z

zéro *(m)* zero (P)
zydeco: musique *(f)* **zydeco** zydeco music (4)

VOCABULAIRE anglais–français

The *Vocabulaire anglais-français* includes all words presented in *Horizons* for active use, as well as others that students may need for more personalized expression. The definitions of active vocabulary words are followed by the number of the chapter where they are first presented. A (P) refers to the *Chapitre préliminaire.* When several translations separated by commas are listed before a chapter number, they are all considered active. Since verbs are sometimes introduced lexically in the infinitive before the conjugation of the present indicative is presented, consult the *Index* to find out the chapter where a conjugation is introduced. An *(m)*, *(f)*, or *(pl)* following a noun indicates that it is masculine, feminine, or plural. *Inv* means that a word is invariable. An asterisk before a word beginning with an **h** indicates that the **h** is aspirate.

A

a un(e) (P); **a few** quelques (5); **a lot** beaucoup (P)

able: be able pouvoir (6)

about vers (2), environ (4); **about it/them** en (8); **About what?** À propos de quoi?; **talk about** parler de (1); **think about** penser à

above au-dessus de; **above all** surtout (8)

abroad à l'étranger (9)

absolutely absolument

accent accent *(m)* (P); **Is that written with or without an accent?** Ça s'écrit avec ou sans accent? (P)

accept accepter (7)

acceptance tolérance *(f)* (7)

access accès *(m)* (10); **Wi-Fi access** accès Wi-Fi *(m)* (10)

accident accident *(m)*

accompany accompagner

according to selon

account compte *(m)*

accountant comptable *(mf)*

accounting comptabilité *(f)* (1)

ache avoir mal (à) (10)

acquaintance: make the acquaintance of faire la connaissance de (7)

acquainted: be / get acquainted with connaître (4)

across from en face (de) (3); **go across** traverser (10)

act jouer *(in movies and theater)* (6); agir

active dynamique (1)

activity activité *(f)* (2)

actor acteur *(m)* (6)

actress actrice *(f)* (6)

actually en fait, réellement

adapt s'adapter

add ajouter

address adresse *(f)* (3); **e-mail address** adresse *(f)* mail (3)

adjective adjectif *(m)* (3)

administration office service administratif *(m)*

admire admirer (9)

adopted adopté(e)

adore adorer

adult adulte *(mf)*

advance avance *(f)*; **in advance** à l'avance (9)

advantage avantage *(m)*; **take advantage of** profiter de (9)

adventure aventure *(f)*; **adventure movie** film *(m)* d'aventure

advertisement publicité *(f)*; **classified ad** petite annonce *(f)*

advertising publicité *(f)*

advice conseils *(mpl)* (8); **give a piece of advice** donner un conseil

aerobics: do aerobics faire de l'aérobic (8)

afraid: be afraid (of) avoir peur (de) (4)

Africa Afrique *(f)* (9)

African africain(e)

after après (P); **after having done . . .** après avoir fait... ; **day after tomorrow** après-demain (4)

afternoon après-midi *(m)* (P); **in the afternoon, afternoons** l'après-midi (P); **It's one o'clock in the afternoon.** Il est une heure de l'après-midi. (P); **this afternoon** cet après-midi (4)

afterwards après (2), ensuite (4)

again encore (8), de nouveau

against contre (10)

age âge *(m)* (4)

agency: travel agency agence *(f)* de voyages (9)

agent agent *(m)*; **travel agent** agent *(m)* de voyages (9)

ago il y a (5); **How long ago?** Il y a combien de temps? (5)

agree être d'accord; **Agreed!** D'accord! (2)

ahead: straight ahead tout droit (10)

air air *(m)*

airplane avion *(m)* (4); **by airplane** en avion (4)

airport aéroport *(m)* (10)

alarm: alarm clock réveil *(m)* (7)

alcohol alcool *(m)* (8)

alcoholic drink boisson alcoolisée *(f)*

algebra algèbre *(f)*

Algeria Algérie *(f)* (9)

alive vivant(e)

all tout (toute, tous, toutes) (2); **above all** surtout (8); **all at once** tout à coup (6); **all day** toute la journée (2); **all of the sudden** tout d'un coup (6); **all of the time** tout le temps; **all sorts of** toutes sortes de; **all the better** tant mieux; **not . . . at all** ne... pas du tout (1); **nothing at all** rien du tout (6); **That's all.** C'est tout. (8)

allergy allergie *(f)* (10)

allow permettre (de); **allowed** permis(e)

almost presque (2)

alone seul(e) (P)

along le long de; **get along well / badly** s'entendre bien / mal (7)

already déjà (5)

also aussi (P)

although bien que, quoique

always toujours (2)

A.M. du matin (P)

amaze étonner; **amazed** étonné(e) (10)

America Amérique *(f)* (9)

American américain(e) (P); **American-style** à l'américaine (8)

among parmi

amusing amusant(e) (1)

an un(e) (1)

and et (P)

angry fâché(e); **get angry** se fâcher

animal animal *(m)* *(pl* animaux*)* (3)

animated animé(e)

anniversary *(wedding)* anniversaire *(m)* de mariage

annoying embêtant(e) (3)

another un(e) autre (P); **another glass of . . .** encore un verre de...; **another thing** autre chose; **one another** se, nous, vous (7)

answer réponse *(f)* (P)

answer répondre (à) (6); **Answer the question.** Répondez à la question. (P)

anthropology anthropologie *(f)*

antibiotic antibiotique *(m)*

any du, de la, de l', de, des, en (8)

anymore: not . . . anymore ne... plus (8)

anyone quelqu'un (6); **(just) anyone** n'importe qui; **not . . . anyone** ne... personne

anything quelque chose (2); **(just) anything** n'importe quoi; **not . . . anything** ne... rien (5)

anyway quand même

anywhere: (just) anywhere n'importe où; **not . . . anywhere** ne... nulle part

apartment appartement *(m)* (3); **apartment building** immeuble *(m)* (3)

appear paraître

appearance: physical appearance aspect physique *(m)* (7)

appetite appétit *(m)*

appetizer *hors-d'œuvre *(m)* (8)

apple pomme *(f)* (8); **apple pie** tarte *(f)* aux pommes (8)

appointment rendez-vous *(m)*

appreciate apprécier (6)

appropriate approprié(e), convenable

April avril *(m)* (4); **April Fool's Day** les poissons *(mpl)* d'avril

Arabic arabe *(m)*

architect architecte *(mf)*

architecture architecture *(f)*

Argentina Argentine *(f)* (9)

argue (with) se disputer (avec) (7)

arm bras *(m)* (10)

armchair fauteuil *(m)* (3)

around vers (2), environ (4), autour de

arrange ranger (7)

arranged rangé(e) (3)

arrival arrivée *(f)* (9)

arrive arriver (3)

art art *(m)* (1); **fine arts** beaux-arts *(mpl)*; **the arts** les arts (1)

article article *(m)* (9)

artist artiste *(mf)*

as comme (1); **as . . . as** aussi... que (1); **as long as** tant que; **as many . . . (as)** autant de... (que); **as much . . . (as)** autant (de)... (que); **as soon as** aussitôt que; **as you see** comme tu vois (3)

ashamed: be ashamed avoir *honte

Asia Asie *(f)* (9)

ask (for) demander (2); **ask a question** poser une question (3)

asleep: fall asleep s'endormir (7)

asparagus asperge *(f)*

aspirin aspirine *(f)* (10)

associate associer
astronomy astronomie (f)
at à (P); at home à la maison (P); at . . . 's house / place chez... (2)
athletic sportif(-ive) (1)
ATM machine distributeur de billets (m) (10)
attend assister à
attention attention (f); pay attention (to) faire attention (à) (8)
attract attirer
auburn auburn (inv) (4)
August août (m) (4)
aunt tante (f) (4)
Australia Australie (f) (9)
automatic automatique; automatic teller machine distributeur (m) de billets (10)
autumn automne (m) (5); in autumn en automne (5)
available disponible
avenue avenue (f) (10)
average moyen(ne) (4)
avoid éviter (8)
away: go away partir (4), s'en aller; put away bien rangé(e) (3); right away tout de suite (6)

B

baby bébé (m)
back dos (m) (10)
back: bring back rapporter; come back revenir (4); give back rendre (7); go back rentrer (2), retourner (5); go back to bed se recoucher (7); in the back of au fond de; sell back revendre (7)
bacon bacon (m) (8)
bad mauvais(e) (1); really bad nul(le); That's too bad! C'est dommage (7); The weather's bad. Il fait mauvais. (5)
badly mal (P); not badly pas mal (P)
bag sac (m) (5), paquet (m) (8); pack your bag faire sa valise (9)
baggage bagages (mpl)
bakery boulangerie (f) (8); bakery-pastry shop boulangerie-pâtisserie (8)
balcony balcon (m)
bald chauve
ball balle (f), (inflated) ballon (m)
ballet ballet (m) (9)
banana banane (f) (8)
band orchestre (m) (4), groupe (m)
bank banque (f) (10); bank card carte bancaire (f) (9)
banker banquier (m)
bar bar (m)
baseball baseball (m) (2)
based: based on basé(e) sur (6)
basement sous-sol (m) (3)
basketball basket (m) (1)
bath bain (m) (7); take a bath prendre un bain (7)
bathe prendre un bain (7), se baigner
bathroom salle (f) de bains (3)
be être (1); be able pouvoir (6); be afraid (of) avoir peur (de) (4); be ashamed avoir *honte; be bored s'ennuyer (7); be born naître, (être) né(e) (5); be cold avoir froid (4); be familiar with connaître (4); be hot avoir chaud (4); be hungry avoir faim (4); be interested in s'intéresser à (7); be named s'appeler (7); be right avoir raison (4); be sleepy avoir sommeil (4); be thirsty avoir soif (4); be wrong avoir tort (4); be . . . years old avoir... ans (4); here is/are voici (2); How are you? Comment allez-vous? (P); How is it going? Comment ça va? (P); I am . . . Je suis... (P); I'm hungry. J'ai faim.

(2); I'm thirsty. J'ai soif. (2); isn't it? n'est-ce pas?, non? (1); It is located... Il/Elle se trouve... ; It's Monday. C'est lundi. (P); It's windy. Il fait du vent., Il y a du vent. (5); My name is . . . Je m'appelle... (P); There are . . . of us. Nous sommes.... (4); there is/ are il y a (1), voilà (2); The weather's nice / bad / cold / cool / hot / sunny / windy. Il fait beau / mauvais / froid / frais / chaud / (du) soleil / du vent. (5); to be continued à suivre (6); you are tu es/vous êtes (P)
beach plage (f) (4)
beans: green beans *haricots verts (mpl) (8)
bear supporter
beard barbe (f) (4)
beast bête (f) (6)
beat battre
beautiful beau (bel, belle, pl beaux, belles) (1)
beauty beauté (7)
because parce que (P); because of à cause de
become devenir (4)
bed lit (m) (2); bed and breakfast chambre (f) d'hôte; go back to bed se recoucher (7); go to bed se coucher (7); stay in bed rester au lit (2)
bedroom chambre (f) (3)
beef bœuf (m) (8); roast beef rosbif (m) (8)
beer bière (f) (2); draft beer demi (m) (2)
before avant (P); before (doing) avant de (faire) (7); before-dinner drink apéritif (m) (8)
beforehand auparavant
begin commencer (2); French class begins at . . . Le cours de français commence à... (P)
beginning début (m); at the beginning (of) au début (de) (6)
behaved: well-behaved sage (4)
behind derrière (3)
beige beige (3)
Belgium Belgique (f) (9)
believe (in) croire (à)
belong to appartenir à, être à
belongings effets personnels (mpl) (3), affaires (fpl)
belt ceinture (f)
beside à côté de (3)
besides de plus, d'ailleurs
best (le/la) meilleur(e) (adjective) (1), (le) mieux (adverb)
better meilleur(e) (adjective), mieux (adverb) (2); do better (to) . . . faire mieux (de)... (8); it's better . . . il vaut mieux... (10)
between entre (3)
beverage boisson (f) (2)
bicycle vélo (m) (3)
bicycle-riding: go bicycle-riding faire du vélo (2)
big grand(e) (1), gros(se) (1)
bike vélo (m) (2); by bike à vélo (4); ride a bike faire du vélo (2)
bikini bikini (m) (5)
bilingual bilingue
bill (restaurant) addition (f), (utilities) facture (f); pay the bill (at a hotel) régler la note (10)
billiards billard (m)
biology biologie (f) (1)
bird oiseau (m)
birth naissance (f); date of birth date (f) de naissance
birthday anniversaire (m) (4)
bizarre bizarre
black noir(e) (3)
blackboard tableau (m) (P)
blanket couverture (f) (3)
blog blog (m) (9)
blond blond(e) (4)
blood sang (m)

blouse chemisier (m) (5)
blue bleu(e) (3)
blueberry myrtille (f)
blues (music) blues (m)
Blu-ray player lecteur (m) Blu-ray (3)
board tableau (m) (P)
boat bateau (m) (4); by boat en bateau (4)
boating: go boating faire du bateau (5)
body corps (m) (7)
bodybuilding: to do bodybuilding faire de la musculation (8)
book livre (m) (P)
bookcase étagère (f) (3)
bookstore librairie (f) (1)
boot botte (f) (5)
border frontière (f)
bored: be/get bored s'ennuyer (7)
boring ennuyeux(-euse) (1)
born né(e) (5); be born naître (5); He/She was born . . . Il/Elle est né(e)... (5)
borrow emprunter
boss patron(ne) (mf)
both les deux
bottle (of) bouteille (de) (f) (8)
boulevard boulevard (m) (10)
bowl bol (m)
box (of) boîte (de) (f) (8)
boy garçon (m) (4)
boyfriend copain (m) (2), petit ami (m)
bracelet bracelet (m)
brave courageux(-euse)
Brazil Brésil (m) (9)
bread pain (m) (8); bread with butter and jelly tartine (f) (8); loaf of French bread baguette (f) (8); (loaf of) whole-grain bread pain complet (m) (8)
break casser; break down (machine) tomber en panne; break one's arm se casser le bras
breakfast petit déjeuner (m) (5); bed and breakfast chambre (f) d'hôte; to have one's breakfast prendre son petit déjeuner (5)
breathe respirer
brief bref (brève)
briefly brièvement
briefs slip (m)
bright (colors) vif(-ive)
bring (a thing) apporter, (a person) amener; bring back rapporter
Britain: Great Britain Grande-Bretagne (f)
broccoli brocoli (m)
brother frère (m) (1); brother-in-law beau-frère (m)
brown marron (inv) (3), brun(e) (4), medium/ dark brown (with hair) châtain (4)
brunette brun(e)
brush (one's hair/one's teeth) se brosser (les cheveux/les dents) (7)
Brussels sprouts choux (mpl) de Bruxelles
build construire
building bâtiment (m) (1); administration building centre administratif (m); apartment building immeuble (m) (3)
burn (oneself) (se) brûler
bus (in city) (auto)bus (m) (3), (between cities) (auto)car (m) (4); bus stop arrêt (m) de bus (3)
business commerce (1); affaires (fpl) (5)
businessman homme (m) d'affaires (5)
businesswoman femme (f) d'affaires (5)
busy chargé(e) (schedule), occupé(e) (person)
but mais (P); nothing but ne... rien que
butcher's shop boucherie (f) (8)
butter beurre (m) (8); bread with butter and jelly tartine (f) (8)

buy acheter (4)

by par (5); **by bike / boat / bus / car / plane / taxi** à vélo / en bateau / en (auto)bus ([auto]car) / en voiture / en avion / en taxi (4); **by chance** par *hasard; **by the way** à propos; **go by . . .'s house** passer chez… (2); **right by** tout près (de) (3)

Bye! Salut! (P), Ciao!

C

cab taxi (m) (4)
cabbage chou (m)
café café (m) (1)
cafeteria cafétéria (f); **university cafeteria** resto-U (m) (6)
Cajun cadien(ne) (4)
cake gâteau (m) (8); **chocolate cake** gâteau au chocolat (8)
calculator calculatrice (f)
Caledonia: New Caledonia Nouvelle-Calédonie (f) (9)
California Californie (f) (9)
call communication (f); appel (m)
call téléphoner (3), appeler (6); **Who's calling?** Qui est à l'appareil?
calm calme (4), tranquille
calm down se calmer
calorie calorie (f)
camera appareil photo (m)
campground camping (m) (5)
camping camping (m) (5); **go camping** faire du camping (5)
campus campus (m) (1); fac(ulté) (f) (2)
can (of) boîte (de) (f) (8)
can (be able) pouvoir (6); **one can** on peut (4)
Canada Canada (m) (9)
Canadian canadien(ne) (P)
canceled annulé(e)
candy bonbon (m)
canned goods conserves (fpl) (8)
cap casquette (f)
capital capitale (f)
car voiture (f) (3); **by car** en voiture (4); **rental car** voiture (f) de location (5)
carafe (of) carafe (de) (f) (8)
card carte (f); **bank card** carte bancaire (f) (9); **credit card** carte (f) de crédit, carte bleue (f) (9); **debit card** carte bancaire (f) (9); **identity card** carte (f) d'identité; **play cards** jouer aux cartes; **telephone card** carte téléphonique (f) (10)
care: I don't care. Ça m'est égal.; **take care of** s'occuper de, (health) (se) soigner
career carrière (f)
careful soigneux(-euse); **be careful** faire attention (à)
carefully soigneusement, attentivement
carpenter charpentier (m)
carrot carotte (f) (8)
carry porter (4); **carry (away)** emporter (5)
cartoon dessin animé (m)
cash: in cash en espèces (10)
cashier caissier(-ère) (mf)
cassette cassette (f); **video cassette** vidéocassette (f); **video cassette player** magnétoscope (m)
castle château (m)
cat chat (m) (3)
cathedral cathédrale (f)
Catholic catholique (1)
cauliflower chou-fleur (m)
cause cause (f)
cause causer
CD CD (m) (3), disque compact (m); **CD player** lecteur (m) CD (3)

celebrate célébrer, fêter
cell phone (téléphone) portable (m) (3)
cent centime (m) (2)
center centre (m); **shopping center** centre commercial (m) (4)
centime centime (m) (2)
central central(e) (mpl centraux); **Central America** Amérique centrale (f) (9)
century siècle (m)
cereal céréales (fpl) (8)
certain certain(e), sûr(e)
certainly certainement
certificate certificat (m)
chair chaise (f)
chance: by chance par *hasard; **have the chance to** avoir l'occasion de
change monnaie (f) (2)
change changer (de) (6); **change one's mind** changer d'avis
character (disposition) caractère (m) (7), (from a story) personnage (m); **character trait** trait (m) de caractère (7)
charge: extra charge supplément (m) (10); **in charge of** responsable de
cheap bon marché
check chèque (m), (restaurant) addition (f); **traveler's check** chèque (m) de voyage
check vérifier (10)
cheese fromage (m) (2); **cheese sandwich** sandwich (m) au fromage (2)
chemistry chimie (f) (1)
cherry cerise (f) (8)
chest poitrine (f); **chest of drawers** commode (f) (3)
chicken poulet (m) (8)
child enfant (mf) (4)
childhood enfance (f)
Chile Chili (m) (9)
chill frisson (m) (10)
China Chine (f) (9)
Chinese chinois(e)
chips chips (fpl)
chocolate chocolat (m) (2); **chocolate cake** gâteau (m) au chocolat (8); **chocolate-filled croissant** pain (m) au chocolat (8)
choice choix (m) (8)
choose (to do) choisir (de faire) (8)
chore: household chore tâche domestique (f)
Christian chrétien(ne)
Christmas Noël (m); **Merry Christmas!** Joyeux Noël!
church église (f) (4), (Protestant) temple (m)
cinema cinéma (m) (1); **cinema club** ciné-club (m) (2)
circumstance circonstance (f)
city ville (f) (3)
clarinet clarinette (f)
class cours (m) (P), classe (f) (1); **economy class** classe économique (f) (9); **first class** première classe (f) (9); **French class** cours (m) de français (P); **have class** avoir cours (6); **online class** cours (m) en ligne (1); **Prepare the exam for the next class.** Préparez l'examen pour le prochain cours. (P)
classic classique (m) (2)
classical classique (1)
classmate camarade (mf) de classe
classroom salle (f) de cours (1)
clean propre (3)
climate climat (m) (9)
climb (tree) grimper, (rocks) escalader
climbing: go mountain climbing faire de l'alpinisme; **go rock climbing** faire de l'escalade
clinic clinique (f)

clock horloge (f); **alarm clock** réveil (m) (7)
close fermer (2); **Close your book.** Fermez votre livre. (P)
close (to) (location) près (de) (1); (a friend) proche
closet placard (m) (3)
clothes vêtements (mpl) (3)
cloud nuage (m)
cloudy nuageux(-euse); **It's cloudy.** Il y a des nuages.
club club (m); **cinema club** ciné-club (m) (2); **fitness club** salle (f) de gym (1); **nightclub** boîte (f) de nuit (1)
coach classe économique (f) (9)
coast côte (f)
coat manteau (m) (5), pardessus (m)
code: zip code code postal (m) (3)
coffee (with milk) café (m) (au lait) (2); **coffee table** table basse (f)
coin pièce (f) de monnaie
Coke coca (m) (2)
cola coca (m) (2); **diet cola** coca light (m) (2)
cold froid(e); **be cold** avoir froid (4); **cold cuts** charcuterie (f) (8); **It's cold.** Il fait froid. (5)
cold rhume (m) (10)
colleague collègue (mf)
collect collectionner
college: go to college étudier à l'université
Colombia Colombie (f) (9)
color couleur (f) (3); **What color is/are . . . ?** De quelle couleur est/sont... ? (3)
comb one's hair se peigner (7)
come venir (4); **come back** revenir (4); **come down (from)** descendre (de) (5); **come get someone** venir chercher quelqu'un (10); **Come see!** Viens voir! (4)
comedy comédie (f) (6)
comfortable confortable (3)
commercial publicité (f)
communicate communiquer (10)
communication communication (f)
compact disc CD (m) (3), disque compact (m)
company société (f), compagnie (f), entreprise (f)
compare comparer (6)
compatibility compatibilité (f) (7)
complain se plaindre
complete complet(-ète) (8); **with a complete sentence** avec une phrase complète (P)
completely tout à fait
complicated compliqué(e)
composition rédaction (f) (9), composition (f)
computer ordinateur (m) (2); **computer lab** salle (f) d'informatique (1)
computer science informatique (f) (1)
concern concerner
concert concert (m) (1)
condition condition (f)
confidence confiance (f); **have confidence** avoir confiance (4)
confirm confirmer (10)
confused confus(e)
congratulations félicitations (fpl)
conservative de droite (7)
conserve conserver
constantly constamment
contact contact (m); **contact lenses** lentilles (fpl); **in contact** en contact (9)
content content(e) (8)
continent continent (m) (9)
continue (straight ahead) continuer (tout droit) (10); **to be continued** à suivre (6)
contrary: on the contrary par contre; au contraire
control contrôler (8)

convenient pratique (3), commode
cook faire la cuisine (5); (faire) cuire
cooking cuisine (f) (4)
cool frais (fraîche); pretty cool assez cool (P);
   The weather's cool. Il fait frais. (5)
copious copieux(-euse) (8)
corn maïs (m)
corner coin (m) (3); in the corner (of) dans
   le coin (de) (3); on the corner of au coin
   (de) (10)
cost coûter (5)
cotton coton (m)
couch canapé (m) (3)
cough tousser (10)
count compter (2); Count from . . . to . . .
   Comptez de... à... (P)
country campagne (f) (3), pays (m) (3);
   country music musique country (f); in the
   country à la campagne (3)
couple couple (m)
course cours (m) (1); first course (of a
   meal) entrée (f) (8); in the course of au
   cours de (10); Of course! Bien sûr! (5),
   Évidemment!; take a course suivre un cours
court: tennis court court (m) de tennis
courtyard cour (f); on the courtyard side côté
   cour (10)
cousin cousin(e) (mf) (4)
cover couverture (f) (3)
cover couvrir
crab crabe (m)
crazy fou (folle)
cream crème (f) (8); ice cream glace (f) (8)
create créer
credit card carte (f) de crédit, carte bleue (f)
   (9)
crime crime (m), criminalité (f)
criminal criminel(le) (mf)
criticize critiquer
Croatia Croatie (f) (9)
croissant croissant (m) (8); chocolate-filled
   croissant pain (m) au chocolat (8)
cross traverser (10)
cruel cruel(le) (6)
crustaceans fruits (mpl) de mer (8)
cry pleurer
cucumber concombre (m)
cuisine cuisine (f) (4)
cultiver to cultivate (7)
cultural culturel(le) (4)
culture culture (f) (9)
cup tasse (f)
cure guérir
curly frisé(e)
currency exchange bureau (m) de
   change (10)
current actuel(le)
currently actuellement
curtain rideau (m) (pl rideaux) (3)
custom coutume (f)
customs (border) douane (f) (9)
cut: cold cuts charcuterie (f) (8)
cut (one's finger) (se) couper (le doigt); cut
   class sécher un cours
cycling cyclisme (m)

D

dad(dy) papa (m)
daily quotidien(ne) (7)
dairy product produit laitier (m)
dance danse (f); bal (m) (6)
dance danser (2)
dancer danseur(-euse) (mf)
danger danger (m)
dangerous dangereux(-euse)

dark foncé(e); dark brown (with hair) brun(e)
   (4); to be dark (outside) faire noir
darling chéri(e) (mf)
date date (f) (4); rendez-vous (m); What is
   the date? Quelle est la date?, C'est quelle
   date? (4)
date sortir avec
daughter fille (f) (4)
day jour (m) (P), journée (f) (2); day after
   tomorrow après-demain (4); day before
   yesterday avant-hier; every day tous les
   jours (P); Father's Day fête (f) des Pères;
   the following day le lendemain (m)
   (5); Have a good day! Bonne journée!;
   Mother's Day fête (f) des Mères; the next
   day le lendemain (m) (5); the whole day
   toute la journée (2); What day is today?
   C'est quel jour, aujourd'hui? (P)
daycare crèche (f)
daytime journée (f)
dead mort(e) (5)
death mort (f)
debit: debit card carte bancaire (f) (9)
deceased décédé(e) (4)
December décembre (m) (4)
decide décider (de) (6)
decision décision (f); make a decision prendre
   une décision (7)
degree (temperature) degré (m), (university)
   diplôme (m)
delay retard (m)
deli(catessen) charcuterie (f) (8); deli meats
   charcuterie (f) (8)
delicious délicieux(-euse) (6)
delighted ravi(e); Delighted to meet you.
   Enchanté(e).
deluxe de luxe (10)
demand exiger
democratic démocratique
den salle (f) de séjour
dentist dentiste (mf)
department département (m); department
   store grand magasin (m)
departure départ (m) (9); departure gate porte
   (f) d'embarquement
depend (on) dépendre (de) (5); That depends.
   Ça dépend.
deposit déposer
depressed déprimé(e)
depressing déprimant(e)
depression déprime (f)
descend descendre (5)
describe décrire (9)
description description (f)
desire désirer (2)
desk bureau (m) (3); front desk réception (f)
   (10)
despite malgré
dessert dessert (m) (8)
destroy détruire
detective movie film policier (m)
detest (each other) (se) détester (7)
develop (se) développer
dictionary dictionnaire (m)
die mourir (5)
diet régime (m); be on a diet être au régime;
   diet cola coca (m) light (2)
different différent(e)
differently différemment
difficult difficile (P)
difficulty difficulté (f)
dine (out) dîner (au restaurant) (2)
dining room salle à manger (f) (3)
dinner dîner (m) (8); before-dinner drink
   apéritif (m) (8); have dinner dîner (2)

diploma diplôme (m)
direct diriger
direct direct(e)
directions indications (fpl) (10); give
   directions indiquer le chemin (10)
directly directement
dirty sale (3)
disadvantage inconvénient (m)
disagreeable désagréable, antipathique (1)
disappointed déçu(e)
disc: compact disc CD (m) (3), disque
   compact (m); compact disc player lecteur
   (m) CD (3)
discover découvrir
discuss discuter (de)
disguise (oneself) (se) déguiser
dish plat (m) (8); do the dishes faire la vaisselle
   (5); main dish plat principal (8); ready-to-
   serve dish plat préparé (m) (8)
dishwasher lave-vaisselle (m)
disorder désordre (m) (3); in disorder en
   désordre (3)
diversity diversité (f)
divided partagé(e) (3)
diving: scuba diving plongée sous-
   marine (f)
divorce divorcer
divorced divorcé(e) (1)
do faire (2); do aerobics faire de l'aérobic
   (8); do better (to) . . . faire mieux (de)...
   (8); do handiwork bricoler (2); Do the
   homework. Faites les devoirs. (P); do
   weight training faire de la musculation (8);
   Do you . . . ? Est-ce que vous... ? (1); I do
   not . . . Je ne... pas (P)
doctor médecin (m) (10)
doctorate doctorat (m)
dog chien (m) (3)
dollar dollar (m) (3)
domestic domestique
door porte (f) (3); next door à côté
dormitory résidence universitaire (f) (1)
double room chambre double (f) (10)
doubt doute (m); without doubt sans doute
   (8)
doubt that . . . douter que...(10)
doubtlessly sans doute (8)
down: go / come down descendre (5)
downtown en centre-ville (m) (3)
dozen (of) douzaine (de) (f) (8)
draft beer demi (m) (2)
drama drame (m); drama course cours (m) de
   théâtre (1)
dramatic dramatique
draw dessiner
drawer tiroir (m); chest of drawers commode
   (f) (3)
drawing dessin (m)
dream rêve (m)
dream (about, of) rêver (de) (7)
dress robe (f) (5)
dress habiller; get dressed s'habiller (7)
dresser commode (f) (3)
drink boisson (f) (2); before-dinner drink
   apéritif (m) (8); have a drink prendre un
   verre (2)
drink boire (4)
drive conduire; go for a drive faire un tour en
   voiture
drop laisser tomber
drums batterie (f) (2)
dry sécher; dry cleaner's teinturerie (f)
duck canard (m) (8)
due to à cause de
dumb bête (1)

during pendant (1), au cours de (10)
DVD DVD *(m)* (2); **DVD player** lecteur *(m)* DVD (3)

E

each chaque (3); **each one** chacun(e); **each other** se, vous, nous (7), l'un(e) l'autre
ear oreille *(f)* (10)
early tôt (4), en avance
earn gagner
earring boucle *(f)* d'oreille
earth terre *(f)*
easily facilement (7)
east est *(m)*; **Middle East** Moyen-Orient *(m)* (9)
Easter Pâques *(fpl)*
easy facile (P)
eat manger (2); **eat dinner (out)** dîner (au restaurant) (2); **eat lunch** déjeuner (2); **eat one's breakfast** prendre son petit déjeuner (5); **eat dinner** dîner (2)
eccentric excentrique
ecological écologique
economics sciences économiques *(fpl)*
economy économie *(f)*; **economy class** classe économique *(f)* (9)
editor rédacteur(-trice) *(mf)*
educate éduquer
education éducation *(f)*
effect effet *(m)* (6); **special effects** effets spéciaux *(mpl)* (6)
egg œuf *(m)* (8); **hard-boiled egg** œuf dur *(m)* (8)
Egypt Égypte *(f)* (9)
eight *huit (P)
eighteen dix-huit (P)
eighth *huitième (3)
eighty quatre-vingts (2); **eighty-one** quatre-vingt-un (2)
either . . . or . . . soit... soit...
election élection *(f)*
element élément *(m)*
elementary school école primaire/élémentaire *(f)*
elevator ascenseur *(m)* (3)
eleven onze (P)
else: What else? Quoi d'autre?; **What else can I get you?** Qu'est-ce que je peux vous proposer d'autre? (8)
elsewhere ailleurs
e-mail mail *(m)* (2), courrier électronique *(m)*; **e-mail address** adresse *(f)* mail (3)
embarrassed gêné(e)
embassy ambassade *(f)*
embrace (each other) (s')embrasser (7)
employee employé(e) *(mf)* (10); **government employee** fonctionnaire *(mf)*
encounter rencontre *(f)* (7)
end fin *(f)*; **at the end (of)** au bout (de) (3)
end finir (8), (se) terminer; **end up doing** finir par faire; **French class ends . . .** Le cours de français finit... (P)
energetic énergique
energy énergie *(f)*
engaged fiancé(e) (1); **get engaged** se fiancer (7)
engineer ingénieur *(m)*
engineering études *(fpl)* d'ingénieur, génie *(m)*
English anglais *(m)* (P)
English anglais(e)
enjoy: Enjoy your stay! Bon séjour! (10)
enough assez (de) (1)
enter entrer (dans) (5)
enterprise entreprise *(f)*
entertainment distractions *(fpl)* (5)
enthusiastic enthousiaste

entire entier(-ère)
environment environnement *(m)*
equality égalité *(f)*
equals: . . . plus . . . equals . . . ... et... font... (P)
errand course *(f)* (5); **run errands** faire des courses (5)
especially surtout (8)
espresso expresso *(m)* (2)
essential essentiel(le)
establish établir
euro euro *(m)* (2)
Europe Europe *(f)* (9)
European européen(ne)
eve: New Year's Eve le réveillon *(m)* du jour de l'An
even même; **even though** bien que
evening soir *(m)* (P), soirée *(f)* (4); **At ten o'clock in the evening.** À dix heures du soir. (P); **Good evening.** Bonsoir. (P); **in the evening, evenings** le soir (P); **See you this evening.** À ce soir. (2)
every chaque (3), tout (toute, tous, toutes) (2); **every day** tous les jours (P)
everybody tout le monde (6)
everyone tout le monde (6)
everything tout (6)
everywhere partout (3)
exactly justement (3), exactement (10)
exam examen *(m)* (P)
example exemple *(m)*; **for example** par exemple (2)
excellent excellent(e) (6)
except sauf (2)
exception exception *(f)*; **with the exception of** à l'exception de
exchange: currency exchange bureau *(m)* de change (10)
exchange money changer de l'argent (9)
exciting passionnant(e)
excuse excuser; **Excuse me.** Excusez-moi, Pardon. (P)
executive cadre *(m)*
exercise exercice *(m)* (P)
exercise faire de l'exercice (2)
exhausted épuisé(e)
exhibit exposition *(f)* (4)
ex-husband ex-mari *(m)*
exotic exotique (9)
expensive cher (chère) (3)
experience expérience *(f)*
explain expliquer
express exprimer
expression expression *(f)* (10)
extra charge supplément *(m)* (10)
extracurricular extrascolaire
extraordinary extra(ordinaire) (4)
extroverted extraverti(e) (1)
ex-wife ex-femme *(f)*
eye œil *(m)* (*pl* yeux) (10); **to have . . . eyes** avoir les yeux... (4)

F

face figure *(f)* (7), visage *(m)*
facing en face (de) (3)
fact fait *(m)*; **in fact** en fait
fail échouer (à)
fair juste
fairly assez (P)
fairy tale conte *(m)* de fées (6)
fall automne *(m)* (5); **in (the) fall** en automne (5)
fall tomber (5); **fall asleep** s'endormir (7); **fall in love (with)** tomber amoureux(-euse) (de) (6)

false faux (fausse)
familiar: be familiar with connaître (4)
family famille *(f)* (P); **family name** nom *(m)* de famille (3); **family room** salle *(f)* de séjour
famous célèbre (4), fameux(-euse)
far (from) loin (de) (3); **as far as** jusqu'à (10)
farm ferme *(f)*
fashion mode *(f)*; **designer fashion** *haute couture *(f)*
fast vite (7), rapide (8)
fast food restaurant fast-food *(m)* (1)
fat gros(se) (1); **get fatter** grossir (8)
father père *(m)* (4); **father-in-law** beau-père *(m)* (4); **Father's Day** fête *(f)* des Pères
fats matières grasses *(fpl)* (8)
fault défaut *(m)* (7)
favorite préféré(e) (3)
fear avoir peur (de) (4)
February février *(m)* (4)
feed nourrir (8), donner à manger à (9); **to feed oneself** se nourrir (8)
feel (se) sentir (8); **feel like** avoir envie de (4)
feeling sentiment *(m)* (7)
ferocious féroce (6)
festival festival *(m)* (4)
fever fièvre *(f)*; **have fever** avoir de la fièvre
few: a few quelques (5), quelques-un(e)s
fewer moins de (8); **fewer . . . than** moins de... que
fiancé fiancé *(m)*
fiancée fiancée *(f)*
field champ *(m)*
fifteen quinze (P)
fifth cinquième (3)
fifty cinquante (2); **fifty-one** cinquante et un (2)
fight combattre, se battre; **fight (against)** lutter (contre)
fill (in) remplir
film film *(m)* (1)
finally finalement (6), enfin (7)
find trouver (4); **find out information** s'informer (9), se renseigner (10)
fine: fine arts beaux-arts *(mpl)*; **It's going fine.** Ça va. (P)
finger doigt *(m)* (10)
finish (doing) finir (de faire) (8), terminer
first premier(-ère) (1), d'abord (4); **at first** au début; **first course** *(of a meal)* entrée *(f)* (8); **first floor** rez-de-chaussée *(m)* (3); **first name** prénom *(m)* (3); **in first class** en première classe (9); **love at first sight** coup *(m)* de foudre (7)
fish poisson *(m)* (8); **fish market** poissonnerie *(f)* (8)
fishing pêche *(f)*; **go fishing** aller à la pêche (5)
fitness club salle *(f)* de gym (1)
fitting room cabine *(f)* d'essayage (5)
five cinq (P)
fixed: at a fixed price à prix fixe (8)
flight vol *(m)* (9)
flip-flops tongs *(fpl)* (5)
floor étage *(m)* (3); **ground floor** rez-de-chaussée *(m)* (3); **on the floor** par terre (3); **on the second floor** au premier étage (3)
Florida Floride *(f)* (9)
flower fleur *(f)*
flu grippe *(f)* (10)
fluently couramment
flute flûte *(f)*
foggy: It's foggy. Il fait du brouillard.
folk music folk *(m)*
folklore folklore *(m)* (4)
follow suivre (7)
following suivant(e) (3)

food aliments *(mpl)*, nourriture *(f)*
foot pied *(m)* (10); **go on foot** aller à pied (4)
football football américain *(m)* (1)
for pour (P), pendant (5), depuis (7), comme (8); **for example** par exemple (2); **For how long?** Pendant combien de temps? (5); **for the last three days** depuis les trois derniers jours; **go away for the weekend** partir en week-end (5); **look for** chercher (3); **watch out for** faire attention à (8)
forbidden: It's forbidden to . . . Il est inderdit de...
foreign étranger(-ère) (1)
foreseen prévu(e)
forest forêt *(f)*
forget oublier (8)
forgive pardonner
fork fourchette *(f)*
former ancien(ne)
formerly autrefois, jadis
forty quarante (2); **forty-one** quarante et un (2)
four quatre (P)
fourteen quatorze (P)
fourth quatrième (3)
France France *(f)* (1)
frankly franchement
free libre (2), *(price)* gratuit(e) (10); **Are you free this evening?** Tu es libre ce soir? (2); **free time** temps libre *(m)* (2)
freedom liberté *(f)*
French français *(m)* (P); **French class** cours *(m)* de français (P); **French-speaking** francophone; **How do you say . . . in French?** Comment dit-on... en français? (P)
French français(e) (1); **French fries** frites *(fpl)* (8); **French Guiana** Guyane *(f)* (9); **French Polynesia** Polynésie française *(f)* (9); **French Quarter** Vieux Carré *(m)* (4); **loaf of French bread** baguette *(f)* (8)
frequently fréquemment
fresh frais (fraîche) (8)
Friday vendredi *(m)* (P)
friend ami(e) *(mf)* (P), copain *(m)*, copine *(f)* (6)
friendly amical(e) *(mpl* amicaux)
fries frites *(fpl)* (2); **steak and fries** steak-frites *(m)* (8)
frisbee: to play frisbee jouer au frisbee
from de (P), depuis; **from Monday to Friday** *(every week)* du lundi au vendredi (P)
front: front desk réception *(f)* (10); **in front of** devant (3)
frozen surgelé(e) (8)
fruit fruit *(m)* (8); **fruit juice** jus *(m)* de fruit (2)
full plein(e)
fun amusant(e) (1); **have fun** s'amuser (7); **make fun of** se moquer de
funny marrant(e) (1), drôle
furious furieux(-euse); **to be furious that . . .** être furieux (furieuse) que... (10)
furnishings meubles *(mpl)* (3)
furniture meubles *(mpl)* (3)
furthermore en plus
futon futon *(m)*
future avenir *(m)*

G

gain gagner; **gain weight** prendre du poids
game match *(m)* (1), jeu *(m)* (2); **video game** jeu vidéo *(m)* (2)
garage garage *(m)*
garden jardin *(m)* (5)
garden faire du jardinage (5), jardiner

gardening jardinage *(m)*
gate: arrival gate porte *(f)* d'arrivée; **departure gate** porte *(f)* d'embarquement
general: in general en général (2)
generally généralement (8)
generous généreux(-euse)
gentle doux(-ce) (6)
gentleman monsieur *(m)*; **ladies and gentlemen** messieurs-dames
geography géographie *(f)* (9)
geology géologie *(f)*
German allemand *(m)* (1)
German allemand(e)
Germany Allemagne *(f)* (9)
get obtenir (9), recevoir; **get along** s'entendre (7); **get bored** s'ennuyer (7); **get dressed** s'habiller (7); **get engaged** se fiancer (7); **get fatter** grossir (8); **get information** s'informer (9), se renseigner (10); **get lost** se perdre (7); **get married (to)** se marier (avec) (7); **get off** descendre (de) (5); **get older** vieillir; **get on** monter (dans) (5); **get ready** se préparer; **get sick** tomber malade (10); **get taller** grandir (8); **get thinner** maigrir (8); **get to know** connaître (4); **get undressed** se déshabiller (7); **get up** se lever (7); **get well** guérir; **go/come get someone** aller/venir chercher quelqu'un (10)
gift cadeau *(m)* (10); **gift shop** boutique *(f)* de cadeaux (10)
girl (jeune) fille *(f)* (4)
girlfriend copine *(f)* (2), petite amie *(f)*
give donner (2); **give (something) back (to someone)** rendre (quelque chose à quelqu'un) (7); **give directions** indiquer le chemin (10); **Give me your sheet of paper.** Donnez-moi votre feuille de papier. (P)
glad content(e) (8)
gladly avec plaisir (6), volontiers
glass verre *(m)* (2); **a glass of** un verre de (2)
glasses lunettes *(fpl)* (4)
global global(e) *(mpl* globaux)
glove gant *(m)*
go aller (2), se rendre (à / chez); **go across** traverser (10); **go all-terrain biking** faire du VTT (5); **go away** partir (4), s'en aller; **go back** rentrer (2), retourner (5); **go bike-riding** faire du vélo (5); **go boating** faire du bateau (5); **go by / past** passer (2); **go camping** faire du camping (5); **go down** descendre (5); **go for a ride** faire un tour (4); **go for a walk** faire une promenade (5); **go in-line skating** faire du roller (5); **go grocery shopping** faire les courses (5); **go hiking** faire des randonnées (5); **go in** entrer (dans) (5); **going to school** les études (1); **go jogging** faire du jogging (2); **go on foot** aller à pied (4); **go out** sortir (2); **go pick up someone** aller chercher quelqu'un (10); **go scuba diving** faire de la plongée sous-marine; **go see** aller voir (4); **go shopping** faire du shopping (2); **go skiing** faire du ski (2); **go to bed** se coucher (7); **Go to the board!** Allez au tableau! (P); **go to the movies** aller au cinéma (2); **go up** monter (5); **go walking** se promener (7); **go water-skiing** faire du ski nautique (5); **go windsurfing** faire de la planche à voile; **How's it going?** Comment ça va? (P); **It's going fine.** Ça va. (P); **Let's go . . . !** Allons... ! (2)
goal but *(m)*
god dieu *(m)*
golf golf *(m)* (2)
good: canned goods conserves *(fpl)* (8)

good bon(ne) (1), sage (4); **Good evening.** Bonsoir. (P); **Good idea!** Bonne idée! (4); **good in/at** fort(e) en; **Good morning.** Bonjour. (P); **Have a good day!** Bonne journée!; **Have a good weekend!** Bon week-end!; **It's good to . . .** C'est bien de..., Il est bon de... (10); **One has a good time!** On s'amuse bien!
good-bye au revoir (P)
government gouvernement *(m)*, sciences politiques (1); **government worker** fonctionnaire *(mf)*
gracious gracieux(-euse) (6)
grade note *(f)*
gram (of) gramme (de) *(m)* (8)
grammar grammaire *(f)*
grandchildren petits-enfants *(mpl)*
granddaughter petite-fille *(f)* (7)
grandfather grand-père *(m)* (4)
grandma mamie *(f)* (7)
grandmother grand-mère *(f)* (4)
grandparents grands-parents *(mpl)* (4)
grandson petit-fils *(m)* (7)
grape(s) raisin *(m)* (8)
grapefruit pamplemousse *(m)*
graphic artist dessinateur(-trice) *(mf)* (de publicité)
gray gris(e) (3)
great super (P), extra(ordinaire) (4), génial(e) *(mpl* géniaux) (4), formidable (7), magnifique; **Great Britain** Grande-Bretagne *(f)*
Greece Grèce *(f)* (9)
green vert(e) (3); **green beans** *haricots verts *(mpl)* (8)
greet saluer
grilled grillé(e) (8)
grocery: go buy groceries faire les courses (5); **grocery store** épicerie *(f)* (8)
ground terre *(f)*; **ground floor** rez-de-chaussée *(m)* (3); **on the ground** par terre (3)
ground meat bifteck *haché *(m)*
group groupe *(m)* (6)
grow (up) grandir (8)
guess deviner
Guiana: French Guiana Guyane *(f)* (9)
guide guide *(m)* (9)
guidebook guide *(m)* (9)
guilty coupable
guitar guitare *(f)* (2)
gym salle *(f)* de gym (1), gymnase *(m)*

H

hair cheveux *(mpl)* (4); **comb one's hair** se peigner (7); **hair stylist** coiffeur(-euse) *(mf)*
half moitié *(f)*
half demi-e (P); **a kilo and a half (of)** un kilo et demi (de) (8); **half-brother** demi-frère *(m)*; **half hour** demi-heure *(f)* (7); **half-sister** demi-sœur *(f)*; **It's half past two.** Il est deux heures et demie. (P)
hall couloir *(m)* (3); **lecture hall** amphithéâtre *(m)* (1); **residence hall** résidence universitaire *(f)* (1)
ham jambon *(m)* (2); **ham sandwich** sandwich au jambon *(m)* (2)
hamburger *hamburger *(m)* (8)
hand main *(f)* (7); **on the other hand** par contre
handiwork: do handiwork bricoler (2)
handsome beau/bel (belle) (1)
hang up raccrocher
Hanukkah *Hanoukka *(f)*
happen se passer (7), arriver; **What happened?** Qu'est-ce qui s'est passé? (7)

happiness bonheur (m) (7)
happy content(e) (8), heureux(-euse) (7);
   Happy Birthday! Bon anniversaire!
hard dur(e); **have a hard time** avoir du mal à
hard-boiled egg œuf dur (m) (8)
hardly ne... guère
hard-working travailleur(-euse)
hat chapeau (m)
hate (each other) (se) détester (7)
hatred *haine (f)
have avoir (3); **have a drink** prendre un
   verre (2); **have breakfast** prendre le petit
   déjeuner (5); **have class** avoir cours (6); **have**
   difficulty doing avoir du mal à faire; **have**
   dinner dîner (2); **have fun** s'amuser (7);
   have just (done) venir de (faire); **have lunch**
   déjeuner (2); **have to** devoir (6)
hazel (with eyes) noisette (inv) (4)
he il (1); **he is** . . . c'est..., il est... (1)
head tête (f)
health santé (f) (8); **health center** centre
   médical (m)
healthy sain(e) (8)
hear entendre (7)
heart cœur (m)
heavy lourd(e)
Hebrew hébreu (m)
heels: high heels *hauts talons (mpl)
height *hauteur (f), taille (f); **of medium**
   height de taille moyenne (4)
hello bonjour (P), (on the telephone) allô (6)
help aider (5); **May I help you?** Je peux vous
   aider? (5)
henceforth désormais
her la (5); **to her** lui (9); **with her** avec elle (2)
her son (sa, ses) (3)
here ici (P); **here is/are** voici (2); **this/these** . . .
   over here ce (cet, cette, ces) ...-ci (3)
herself se (7), elle-même
Hi! Salut! (P)
high *haut(e), élevé(e); **high fashion** *haute
   couture (f); **high heels** *hauts talons (mpl);
   high school lycée (m) (6); **high school**
   student lycéen(ne) (mf) (6)
hike: to go for a hike faire une randonnée (5)
hiking: to go hiking faire des randonnées (5)
him le (5); **to him** lui (9); **with him** avec lui (2)
himself se (7), lui-même
his son (sa, ses) (3)
historic historique (9)
history histoire (f) (1)
hobby passe-temps (m)
hockey *hockey (m) (2)
hold tenir
holiday fête (f) (4); **national holiday** fête
   nationale (f)
home: at home à la maison (P); **come / go**
   back home rentrer (2)
homework devoirs (mpl) (P); **Do the**
   homework. Faites les devoirs. (P)
honest honnête
honey miel (m), (endearment) chéri(e)
honeymoon lune (f) de miel, voyage (m) de
   noces
hope espérer (3)
horrible horrible (6), affreux(-euse)
horror movie film (m) d'horreur
hors d'œuvre *hors-d'œuvre (m) (inv) (8),
   entrée (f)
horse cheval (m) (pl chevaux); **ride a horse**
   monter à cheval
horseback: go horseback riding faire du
   cheval
hose: panty hose collant (m)
hospital hôpital (m) (pl hôpitaux)

hostel: youth hostel auberge (f) de jeunesse
   (10)
hot chaud(e) (2); **be hot** avoir chaud (4); **hot**
   chocolate chocolat chaud (m) (2); **The**
   weather's hot. Il fait chaud. (5)
hotel hôtel (m) (5); **hotel manager**
   hôtelier(-ère) (mf) (10)
hour heure (f) (2); **half hour** demi-heure (f) (7)
house maison (f) (1); **at / to / in my house**
   chez moi (2); **pass by the house of . . .**
   passer chez... (2)
household ménage (m); **household chore**
   tâche domestique (f)
housemate colocataire (mf) (P)
housework ménage (m) (5)
housing logement (m) (3)
how comment (P); **How are you?** Comment
   allez-vous? (P); **How does that sound?**
   Ça te/vous dit? (2); **How do you say** . . . ?
   Comment dit-on... ? (P); **How long does**
   it take? Ça prend combien de temps? (4);
   how many combien (de) (3); **How many**
   people are there in your family? Vous êtes
   combien dans votre (ta) famille? (4); **how**
   much combien (de) (3); **How much is it?**
   C'est combien?, Ça fait combien? (2); **How**
   much is . . . plus / minus . . . ? Combien
   font... et / moins... ? (P); **How old is . . . ?**
   Quel âge a... ? (4); **How's it going?**
   Comment ça va? (P); **How's the weather?**
   Quel temps fait-il? (5)
however pourtant (8)
human humain(e)
humid: It's humid. Il fait humide.
humor: sense of humor sens (m) de l'humour
   (7)
hundred: one hundred cent (2)
hunger faim (f)
hungry: be hungry avoir faim (4); **I'm hungry.**
   J'ai faim. (2)
hunter chasseur (m)
hunting chasse (f); **go hunting** aller à la chasse
hurry se dépêcher (de); **hurried** pressé(e)
hurt: hurt (someone) faire mal (à quelqu'un);
   one's... hurt(s) avoir mal (à)... (10)
husband mari (m) (2)

I

I je, j' (P)
ice glace (f); **ice cream** glace (f) (8)
ice-skating patin (m) à glace; **go ice-skating**
   faire du patin à glace
icy: It's icy. Il y a du verglas.
idea idée (f) (4)
idealistic idéaliste (1)
identify identifier
identity card carte (f) d'identité
if si (1)
ill malade (10)
illness maladie (f)
image image (f)
immediately immédiatement, tout de suite (6)
impatient impatient(e) (4)
importance importance (f) (7)
important important(e)
imprison emprisonner (6)
improve améliorer
impulsive impulsif(-ive)
in dans (P), en (P), chez (+ a person) (7); **go in**
   entrer (dans) (5); **I live in** (+ city) J'habite
   à (+ city) (P); **in advance** à l'avance (9); **in**
   bed au lit (2); **in front of** devant (3); **in love**
   amoureux(-euse); **in order to** pour (1); **in the**
   country à la campagne (3); **in the morning** le
   matin (P); **in your opinion** à votre avis (8)

include comprendre (8); **included** compris(e) (10)
indecision indécision (f) (7)
indefinite indéfini(e)
independent indépendant(e)
India Inde (f)
Indies: West Indies Antilles (fpl) (9)
indifference indifférence (f) (7)
indigestion indigestion (f) (10)
inequality inégalité (f)
inexpensive pas cher(-ère)
infidelity infidélité (f) (7)
inflexibility inflexibilité (f) (7)
influence influencer
inform (oneself) (s')informer (9)**;** se renseigner
   (10)
information renseignements (mpl) (3); infos
   (fpl) (9); **find out information**
   s'informer (9)
in-laws beaux-parents (mpl)
inquire se renseigner (10)
insensitivity insensibilité (f) (7)
inside à l'intérieur, dedans
insist insister (10)
instant instant (m)
instead plutôt (4)
instructions instructions (fpl)
intellectual intellectuel(le) (1)
intelligent intelligent(e) (1)
intend (to) avoir l'intention de (4)
interested: be interested in s'intéresser à (7)
interesting intéressant(e) (P)
international international(e) (mpl
   internationaux)
Internet Internet (m) (2); **on the Internet** sur
   Internet (2); **to surf the Internet** surfer sur
   Internet (2)
interpret interpréter
interpreter interprète (mf)
introduce présenter; **Let me introduce . . . to**
   you. Je vous/te présente...
introverted introverti(e)
investigation enquête (f)
invitation invitation (f) (6)
invite inviter (à) (2)
iPod iPod (m) (3)
Irak Iraq (m)
Iran Iran (m)
Ireland Irlande (f) (9)
island île (f) (9)
Israel Israël (m) (9)
it ce (P), il (P), elle (1), le, la (5); **How's it**
   going? Comment ça va? (P); **it's . . .** c'est...
   (P); **It's going fine.** Ça va. (P); **of it** en (8)
Italian italien (m)
Italian italien(ne)
Italy Italie (f) (9)
its son (sa, ses) (3)
Ivory Coast Côte d'Ivoire (f) (9); **from/of the**
   Ivory Coast ivoirien(ne)

J

jacket veste (f), blouson (m); **ski jacket** anorak
   (m) (5); **windbreaker jacket** blouson (m)
jam confiture (f) (8)
January janvier (m) (4)
Japan Japon (m) (9)
Japanese japonais (m)
Japanese japonais(e)
jar (of) pot (de) (m) (8)
jazz jazz (m) (1)
jealous jaloux(-ouse) (7)
jealousy jalousie (f) (7)
jeans jean (m) (5)
jelly confiture (f) (8)
jewelry bijoux (mpl)

job poste *(m)*, travail *(m)* (6)
jog faire du jogging (2)
jogging jogging *(m)* (2); **go jogging** faire du jogging (2); **jogging suit** survêtement *(m)* (5)
join rejoindre
journal journal *(m)* *(pl* journaux*)*
journalism journalisme *(m)*
journalist journaliste *(mf)*
juice jus *(m)* (2)
July juillet *(m)* (4)
June juin *(m)* (4)
just seulement (8), juste (10); **have just (done)** venir de (faire); **I would just as soon . . .** J'aimerais autant... (10); **just anything** n'importe quoi

K

keep garder
key clé *(f)* (10)
keyboard clavier *(m)*
kidney rein *(m)*
kilo (of) J'kilo (de) *(m)* (8)
kilometer kilomètre *(m)*
kind genre *(m)*; **all kinds of . . .** toutes sortes de...
kindergarten école maternelle *(f)*
kingdom royaume *(m)*; **United Kingdom** Royaume-Uni *(m)* (9)
kiosk kiosque *(m)* (10)
kiss baiser *(m)*, bise *(f)*
kiss (each other) (s')embrasser (7)
kitchen cuisine *(f)* (3)
knee genou *(m)*
knife couteau *(m)*
knit shirt polo *(m)* (5)
know *(person, place)* connaître (4), *(how, answers)* savoir (9); **Do you know how to . . . ?** Savez-vous...? (9); **get to know** connaître (4); **I don't know.** Je ne sais pas. (P); **known** connu(e); **What do you know about . . . ?** Que savez-vous de…?
knowledge connaissance *(f)*

L

laboratory laboratoire *(m)* (1); **computer lab** salle *(f)* d'informatique (1); **language lab** laboratoire *(m)* de langues (1)
lack of manque de *(m)*
lady dame *(f)*; **ladies and gentlemen** messieurs-dames; **lady's suit** tailleur *(m)*
lake lac *(m)*
lamb agneau *(m)*
lamp lampe *(f)* (3)
landscape paysage *(m)* (9)
language langue *(f)* (1); **language lab** laboratoire *(m)* de langues (1)
laptop (ordinateur) portable *(m)* (3)
large grand(e) (1); copieux(-euse) (8)
last durer
last dernier(-ère) (5)
late tard (4), en retard (10); **later** plus tard (4); **See you later.** À tout à l'heure., À plus tard!, À plus! (P)
laugh rire
laundry linge *(m)*; **do laundry** faire la lessive (5)
law loi *(f)*; *(field)* droit *(m)*
lawyer avocat(e) *(mf)*
lazy paresseux(-euse) (1)
learn apprendre (à) (4); **Learn . . .** Apprenez... (P)
leave quitter (4), partir (de) (4), sortir (de) (6), *(something behind)* laisser (3), s'en aller; **leave each other** se quitter (7)
lecture hall amphithéâtre *(m)* (1)

left gauche *(f)* (3); **to the left (of)** à gauche (de) (3)
leg jambe *(f)* (10)
leisure activity loisir *(m)* (2)
lemon citron *(m)* (2); **tea with lemon** thé *(m)* au citron (2)
lend prêter
lense: contact lenses lentilles *(fpl)*
less moins de (8); **less . . . than** moins... que (1)
let laisser; **Let's go . . . !** Allons... ! (2); **Let's see!** Voyons! (5)
letter lettre *(f)* (9)
lettuce laitue *(f)* (8)
level niveau *(m)*
liberal de gauche (7)
library bibliothèque *(f)* (1)
life vie *(f)* (6)
lift weights faire des haltères
light *(weight)* léger(-ère) (8), *(color)* clair(e)
like aimer (2); **Did you like it?** Ça t'a plu? (6); **Does he/she like it?** Ça lui plaît? (9); **Do you like . . . ?** Est-ce que vous aimez... ? (1); **I like . . .** J'aime... (1); **I like it!** Il/Elle me plaît! (5); **I liked it!** Il/Elle m'a plu! (6); **I would like . . .** Je voudrais (bien)... (2); **like each other** s'aimer (7); **What would you like?** Vous désirez? (2); **You like it.** Ça te plaît. (3); **You'll like it!** Ça te/vous plaira! (9); **You would like . . .** Tu voudrais…, Vous voudriez... (2)
like comme (1); **What is / are . . . like?** Comment est/sont... ? (1)
lime citron vert *(m)*
line ligne *(f)*; **online** en ligne (1)
lip lèvre *(f)*
liquid liquide *(m)* (10)
listen (to) écouter (2); **Listen to the question.** Écoutez la question. (P)
liter (of) litre (de) *(m)* (8)
literature littérature *(f)* (1); **classical literature** littérature classique (1); **literature class** cours *(m)* de littérature (1)
little (of) peu (de) (8); **a little** un peu (P); **little by little** petit à petit (6)
little petit(e) (1)
live habiter (2); **Do you live . . . ?** Vous habitez…? (P); **I live in . . .** *(+ city)* J'habite à... *(+ city)* (P)
liver foie *(m)*
living room salon *(m)* (3)
loaf of French bread baguette *(f)* (8)
loafers mocassins *(mpl)*
loan prêter
lobster *homard *(m)* (8)
local local(e) *(mpl* locaux) (9)
located situé(e); **It is located . . .** Il/Elle se trouve…
lock fermer à clé
lodge: ski lodge chalet *(m)* à la montagne (10)
lodging logement *(m)* (3)
lonely seul(e)
long long(ue) (4); **a long time** longtemps (5); **as long as** tant que; **How long does it take?** Combien de temps est-ce que ça prend? (4); **no longer** ne... plus (8)
look (at) regarder (2); **look (+ *adjective*)** avoir l'air (+ *adjectif*) (4); **look at each other** se regarder (7); **look for** chercher (3); **look like** ressembler à; **look very good on someone** aller très bien à quelqu'un
lose perdre (7); **get lost** se perdre (7); **lose weight** perdre du poids
lot: a lot beaucoup (P), **a lot of** beaucoup de (1); **not a lot** pas grand-chose

love amour *(m)* (6); **fall in love (with)** tomber amoureux(-euse) (de) (6); **love at first sight** coup *(m)* de foudre (7); **love story** film *(m)* d'amour (6); **true love** le grand amour (7)
love aimer (2), adorer (5); **love each other** s'aimer (7)
luck chance *(f)* (5); **What luck!** Quelle chance! (5)
lucky: be lucky avoir de la chance
luggage bagages *(mpl)*
lunch déjeuner *(m)* (8); **have lunch** déjeuner (2)
lung poumon *(m)*
luxury luxe *(m)*
lyrics paroles *(fpl)*

M

machine machine *(f)*; **automatic teller machine** distributeur de billets *(m)* (10)
madam (Mrs.) madame (Mme) (P)
magazine magazine *(m)* (9)
magnificent magnifique
mail courrier *(m)*; **e-mail** mail *(m)* (2), courrier électronique *(m)*; **mail carrier** facteur *(m)*, factrice *(f)*
main principal(e) *(mpl* principaux); **main dish** plat *(m)* principal (8)
major in se spécialiser en
majority: the majority of the time la plupart du temps (7)
make faire (2); **make (+ *adjective*)** rendre (+ *adjectif*); **make a decision** prendre une décision (7); **make money** gagner de l'argent; **make up with each other** se réconcilier (7); **made up of** composé(e) de
make-up maquillage *(m)*; **put on make-up** se maquiller (7)
mall: shopping mall centre commercial *(m)* (4)
mama maman *(f)*
man homme *(m)* (1); monsieur *(m)*
management gestion *(f)*
manual worker ouvrier(-ère) *(mf)*
many beaucoup (de) (1); **how many** combien (de) (1); **How many people are there in your family?** Vous êtes combien dans votre (ta) famille? (4); **so many** tant (de); **too many** trop (de) (8)
map plan *(m)* (10), carte *(f)*
March mars *(m)* (4)
market marché *(m)* (8)
marketing marketing *(m)* (1)
marriage mariage *(m)* (7)
married marié(e) (1); **get married (to)** se marier (avec) (7)
marvelous merveilleux(-euse)
mathematics mathématiques (maths) *(fpl)* (1)
matter: It doesn't matter to me. Ça m'est égal.; **What's the matter?** Qu'est-ce qu'il y a?
May mai *(m)* (3)
may pouvoir (6); **May I help you?** Je peux vous aider? (5)
maybe peut-être (3)
me moi (P), me (9); **with me** avec moi (2); **Give me . . .** Donnez-moi... (P)
meal repas *(m)* (6)
mean: What does that mean? Qu'est-ce que ça veut dire? (P)
mean méchant(e) (1)
means moyen *(m)*; **means of transportation** moyen *(m)* de transport (4)
meat viande *(f)* (8); **ground meat** bifteck *hâché *(m)*; **meat spread** pâté *(m)* (8)
medical médical(e) *(mpl* médicaux)
medication médicament *(m)* (10)

medicine (studies) médecine (f), (medication) médicament (m) (10)

medium moyen(ne); **medium brown** (with hair) châtain (4); **medium-height** de taille moyenne (4)

meet (by design) retrouver (4), (by chance, for the first time) rencontrer (1), (for the first time) faire la connaissance de (7), se réunir; **Let's meet at . . .** Rendez-vous à...; **meet each other** (by chance, for the first time) se rencontrer, (by design) se retrouver (7)

meeting réunion (f)

melon melon (m)

member membre (m)

memory souvenir (m), mémoire (f)

menu (set-price) menu (m) (à prix fixe), carte (f) (8)

merchant marchand(e) (mf) (6)

Merry Christmas! Joyeux Noël!

mess: What a mess! Quel bazar! (familiar) (3)

message message (m)

messenger messager(-ère) (mf) (6)

Mexico Mexique (m) (9)

microwave oven four (m) à micro-ondes

middle milieu (m); **in the middle of** au milieu de

Middle East Moyen-Orient (m) (9)

midnight minuit (P)

milk lait (m) (8); **coffee with milk** café (m) au lait (2)

million: one million un million (de) (3)

mind esprit (m) (7)

mine le mien (la mienne, les miens, les miennes)

mineral water eau minérale (f) (2)

minus: How much is . . . minus . . . ? Combien font... moins... ? (P)

minute minute (f) (5); **at the last minute** au dernier moment

mirror miroir (m)

mischievous espiègle

miss mademoiselle (Mlle) (P)

mistake erreur (f); **make a mistake** se tromper

mister (Mr.) monsieur (M.) (P)

mistrust se méfier de

modern moderne (1)

mom maman (f)

moment instant (m), moment (m)

Monday lundi (m) (P)

money argent (m) (2)

monster monstre (m) (6)

month mois (m) (3); **per month** par mois (3); **this month** ce mois-ci (4)

mood: in a good/bad mood de bonne/ mauvaise humeur

more plus (1), encore (8), plus de (8); **more and more of** de plus en plus de (8); **more . . . than** plus... que (1); **no more** ne... plus (8), pas plus (4)

morning matin (m) (P); **at eight o'clock in the morning** à huit heures du matin (P); **Good morning.** Bonjour. (P); **in the morning, mornings** le matin (P); **morning hours** matinée (f) (2)

Morocco Maroc (m) (9)

mosque mosquée (f)

most: most of the time la plupart du temps (7), **the most** le (la) plus

mother mère (f) (4); **mother-in-law** belle-mère (f) (4); **Mother's Day** fête (f) des Mères

motorcycle moto (f)

mountain montagne (f) (5); **go mountain climbing** faire de l'alpinisme; **go to the mountains** aller à la montagne (5)

mouth bouche (f) (10)

move (into) s'installer (à/dans) (7)

movement mouvement (m)

movie film (m) (1); **go to the movies** aller au cinéma (2); **movie theater** cinéma (m) (1); **romantic movie** film (m) d'amour (6); **show a movie** passer un film (6)

MP3 player lecteur (m) MP3

Mr. monsieur (M.) (P)

Mrs. madame (Mme) (P)

much beaucoup (de) (1); **as much . . . (as)** autant de... (que); **how much** combien (de) (1); **How much is it?** C'est combien?, Ça fait combien? (2); **not much** ne... pas grand-chose; **so much** tellement (1), tant; **too much** trop (1)

muscular musclé(e)

museum musée (m) (4)

mushroom champignon (m)

music musique (f) (1); **listen to music** écouter de la musique (2)

musical (movie) comédie musicale (f)

musical musicien(ne)

musician musicien(ne) (mf)

mussel moule (f) (8)

must devoir (6); **he/she must** il/elle doit (3); **one must . . .** il faut... (8)

mustache moustache (f) (4)

my mon (ma, mes) (3); **at / in / to my house** chez moi (2); **my best friend** mon meilleur ami (m), ma meilleure amie (f); **my friends** mes amis (1); **My name is . . .** Je m'appelle... (P); **with my family** avec ma famille (P)

myself me (7), moi-même

N

naive naïf(-ïve)

name nom (m) (3); **family name** nom (m) de famille (3); **first name** prénom (m) (3); **His/Her name is . . .** Il/Elle s'appelle... (4); **last name** nom (m) de famille (3); **My name is . . .** Je m'appelle... (P); **What is his/ her name?** Comment s'appelle-t-il/elle? (4); **What's your name?** Tu t'appelles comment? (familiar) (P), Comment vous appelez-vous? (formal) (P)

named nommé(e); **be named** s'appeler (7)

nap sieste (f); **take a nap** faire la sieste

napkin serviette (f)

nationality nationalité (f) (3)

natural naturel(le)

nature nature (f) (7)

near près (de) (1)

nearly presque (2)

necessary nécessaire (10); **it is necessary to . . .** il faut... (8), il est nécessaire (de)... (10)

neck cou (m)

necklace collier (m)

necktie cravate (f) (5)

nectarine nectarine (f)

need avoir besoin de (4); **I/you/we/you/he/ she/they need(s)** Il me/te/nous/vous/lui/lui/ leur faut (9); **one needs . . .** il faut... (8)

needy nécessiteux (mpl)

neighbor voisin(e) (mf) (9)

neighborhood quartier (m) (1)

neither non plus (3); **neither . . . nor** ne... ni... ni...

nephew neveu (pl neveux) (m) (4)

nervous nerveux(-euse); **feel nervous** se sentir mal à l'aise

Net: surf the Net surfer sur Internet (2)

network réseau (m) (9)

never ne... jamais (2)

new nouveau / nouvel (nouvelle) (1); neuf (neuve); **Happy New Year!** Bonne année!; **New Caledonia** Nouvelle-Calédonie (f) (9); **New Orleans** La Nouvelle-Orléans (4); **New Year's Eve** le réveillon (m) du jour de l'An

news nouvelles (fpl), (television program) informations (fpl)

newspaper journal (m) (5)

next prochain(e) (4), ensuite (4); **next to** à côté (de) (3); **the next class** le prochain cours (P); **the next day** le lendemain (m) (5)

nice sympathique (sympa) (1), gentil(le) (1); **It/ That seems nice.** Ça a l'air bien. (3); **The weather's nice.** Il fait beau. (5)

niece nièce (f) (4)

night nuit (f) (5); **night stand** table (f) de chevet

nightclub boîte (f) de nuit (1); **to go to a club** aller en boîte (de nuit) (2)

nightgown chemise (f) de nuit

nine neuf (P)

nineteen dix-neuf (P)

ninety quatre-vingt-dix (2); **ninety-one** quatre-vingt-onze (2)

ninth neuvième (3)

no non (P); **no longer** ne... plus (8); **no more** ne... plus (8), pas plus (4); **no one** ne... personne; **No problem!** Pas de problème! (3)

nobody ne... personne

noise bruit (m) (10)

none ne... aucun(e)

non-smoking section section non-fumeur (f)

noon midi (m) (P)

nor: neither . . . nor . . . ne... ni... ni...

normal normal(e) (mpl normaux)

normally normalement

north nord (m); **North America** Amérique (f) du Nord (9)

nose nez (m) (10)

not ne... pas (P); **I do not work.** Je ne travaille pas. (P); **not . . . at all** ne... pas du tout (1); **not badly** pas mal (P); **not . . . one** ne... aucun(e); **not . . . so much** pas tellement (1); **not yet** ne... pas encore (5); **Why not?** Pourquoi pas? (2)

notebook cahier (m)

nothing ne... rien (5); **nothing at all** rien du tout (6); **nothing but** ne... rien que; **nothing special** ne... rien de spécial (5)

notice remarquer

noun nom (m) (3)

nourish nourrir (8); **nourish oneself** se nourrir (8)

nourishment nourriture (f)

novel roman (m) (9)

November novembre (m) (4)

now maintenant (P)

nowadays de nos jours

nowhere ne... nulle part

number nombre (m) (P), numéro (m) (3), chiffre (m); **telephone number** numéro (m) de téléphone (3)

numeral chiffre (m) (P)

numerous nombreux(-euse)

nurse infirmier(-ière) (mf)

nurture nourrir (8); **nurture oneself** se nourrir (8)

O

obey obéir (à) (8)

object objet (m)

observe observer

obtain obtenir (9)

obvious évident(e)
obviously évidemment
ocean océan *(m)*
Oceania Océanie *(f)* (9)
o'clock: It's . . . o'clock. Il est... heure(s). (P)
October octobre *(m)* (4)
of de (1); **Of course!** Bien sûr! (5); Évidemment!; **of it/them** en (8)
off: get off descendre (de) (5)
offer proposer (8), offrir
office bureau *(m)* (1); **post office** bureau *(m)* de poste (10); **tourist office** office *(m)* de tourisme (10)
official time l'heure officielle *(f)* (6)
often souvent (2)
oil huile *(f)*
okay d'accord (2); **It's going okay.** Ça va.
old vieux/vieil (vieille) (1), âgé(e) (4); **be . . . years old** avoir... ans (4); **get older** vieillir; **How old is . . . ?** Quel âge a... ? (4); **oldest** aîné(e)
omelet omelette *(f)* (8)
on sur (1); **get on** monter dans (5); **on foot** à pied (4); **on Mondays** le lundi (P); **on page . . .** à la page... (P); **on sale** en solde (5); **on . . . Street** dans la rue... (10); **on the corner (of)** au coin (de) (10); **on the courtyard side** côté cour (10); **on the ground/floor** par terre (3); **on the weekend** le week-end (P); **on time** à l'heure (4); **On what floor?** À quel étage? (3); **put on** mettre (5); **try on** essayer (5)
once une fois (6); **all at once** tout d'un coup (6); **once more** encore une fois; **Once upon a time there was . . .** Il était une fois... (6)
one un(e) (P); on (4); **no one** ne... personne; **not one** ne... aucun(e); **one another** se, nous, vous (7)
oneself se (7)
one-way ticket aller simple *(m)* (9)
onion oignon *(m)* (8); **onion soup** soupe *(f)* à l'oignon (8)
online en ligne (1)
only uniquement (6); seul(e) (1), seulement (8), ne... que; **only child** fille unique *(f)*, fils unique *(m)*
Ontario Ontario *(m)* (9)
open ouvrir; **Open your book.** Ouvrez votre livre. (P)
opening time l'heure *(f)* d'ouverture (6)
opera opéra *(m)* (9)
opinion avis *(m)*; **in your opinion** à votre avis (8)
opportunity: have the opportunity to avoir l'occasion de
opposite contraire *(m)*
optimistic optimiste (1)
or ou (P)
orange orange *(f)* (8); **orange juice** jus *(m)* d'orange (2)
orange orange (3)
Orangina Orangina *(m)* (2)
orchestra orchestre *(m)* (4)
order *(food and drink)* commander (2), ranger (7)
order ordre *(m)*; **in order** en ordre (3); **in order to** pour (1)
orderly bien rangé(e) (3)
organic products produits bio *(mpl)* (8)
organization organisation *(f)*
organized organisé(e)
origin origine *(f)*; **of . . . origin** d'origine... (7)
Orleans: New Orleans La Nouvelle-Orléans (4)
other autre (1); **each other** se, nous, vous (7); **on the other hand** par contre; **on the other side (of)** de l'autre côté (de); **sometimes . . . other times** quelquefois... d'autres fois (7)

ought to devoir (6)
our notre (nos) (3)
ourselves nous (7); nous-mêmes
out: dine out dîner au restaurant (2); **go out** sortir (2); **Take out a sheet of paper.** Prenez une feuille de papier. (P); **watch out (for)** faire attention (à) (8)
outdoor de plein air (4)
outdoors en plein air
outgoing extraverti(e) (1)
outing sortie *(f)* (6)
outside à l'extérieur, dehors, en plein air; **outside of** *hors de
oven four *(m)*; **microwave oven** four *(m)* à micro-ondes
over (par-)dessus, plus de; **over there** là-bas (1); **start over** recommencer; **this/these . . . over here** ce (cet, cette, ces) ...-ci (3); **that/those . . . over there** ce (cet, cette, ces) ...-là (3)
overcast: The sky is overcast. Le ciel est couvert.
overcoat manteau *(m)* (5), pardessus *(m)*
owe devoir (6)
own propre
oyster huître *(f)* (8)

P

pack your bag faire sa valise *(f)* (9)
package (of) paquet (de) *(m)* (8), colis *(m)*
page page *(f)* (P)
pain douleur *(f)*
paint peindre
painter peintre *(mf)*
painting tableau *(m)* (3), peinture *(f)* (1)
pajamas pyjama *(m)*
pal copain *(m)*, copine *(f)* (6)
palace palais *(m)* (6)
pale pâle
panties slip *(m)*; **panty hose** collant *(m)*
pants pantalon *(m)* (5)
papa papa *(m)*
paper papier *(m)*; **sheet of paper** feuille *(f)* de papier (P)
parade défilé *(m)*
pardon me pardon (P)
parents parents *(mpl)* (4)
Parisian Parisien(ne) *(mf)* (9)
park parc *(m)* (1)
parking lot parking *(m)* (1)
part partie *(f)*
participate (in) participer (à)
particular: in particular en particulier
partner partenaire *(mf)* (7)
part-time à temps partiel
party *(social)* fête *(f)* (1), soirée *(f)* (6), *(political)* parti *(m)*
party faire la fête
pass passer (2), *(test)* réussir à (8); **pass by the house of . . .** passer chez... (2)
passenger passager(-ère) *(mf)*
passion passion *(f)* (7)
Passover la pâque juive *(f)*
passport passeport *(m)* (9)
past passé *(m)*; **in the past** dans le passé (6), autrefois
past passé(e) (5); **It's a quarter past two.** Il est deux heures et quart. (P)
pasta pâtes *(fpl)*
pastime loisir *(m)* (2)
pastry pâtisserie *(f)* (8); **bakery-pastry shop** boulangerie-pâtisserie *(f)* (8)
pâté pâté *(m)* (8)
patience patience *(f)* (4); **have patience** avoir de la patience (4)
patient patient(e) *(mf)*

patient patient(e) (6)
pay (for) payer (2); **pay attention (to)** faire attention (à) (8); **pay the bill** régler la note (10)
peace paix *(f)*
peaceful tranquille
peach pêche *(f)* (8)
peanut cacahuète *(f)*
pear poire *(f)* (8)
peas petits pois *(mpl)* (8)
pen stylo *(m)* (P)
pencil crayon *(m)* (P)
people gens *(mpl)* (1), on (4); **poor people** les pauvres *(mpl)*; **some people** certains *(mpl)* (8); **young people** les jeunes (gens) *(mpl)*
pepper poivre *(m)* (8)
per par (3)
percent pour cent
perfect perfectionner
perfect parfait(e) (7)
perfectly parfaitement (7)
performer artiste *(mf)*
perhaps peut-être (3)
period époque *(f)* (6), période *(f)*
permit permettre (de); **permitted** permis(e)
person personne *(f)* (6)
personal personnel(le) (3); **personal belongings** effets personnels *(mpl)* (3); **personal service** service personnalisé *(m)* (8)
personality personnalité *(f)* (1)
personally personnellement
Peru Pérou *(m)* (9)
pessimistic pessimiste (1)
pharmacist pharmacien(ne) *(mf)*
pharmacy pharmacie *(f)* (10)
philosophy philosophie *(f)* (1)
phone téléphone *(m)* (2); **on the phone** au téléphone (2)
phone téléphoner (à) (3); **phone each other** se téléphoner (7)
photo photo *(f)*
physical appearance aspect physique *(m)* (7)
physics physique *(f)* (1)
piano piano *(m)* (2)
picnic pique-nique *(m)*
picture tableau *(m)* (3), photo *(f)*
pie tarte *(f)* (8); **apple pie** tarte *(f)* aux pommes (8)
piece (of) morceau (de) *(m)* (8); **piece of advice** conseil *(m)* (8)
pierced percé(e)
pineapple ananas *(m)*
pink rose (3)
pity pitié *(f)*; **have pity (for / on)** avoir pitié (de) (10); **what a pity** c'est dommage (7)
pizza pizza *(f)* (8)
place endroit *(m)* (9), place *(f)* (3); **at/to/in . . . 's place** chez... (2); **in it's place** à sa place (3); **take place** avoir lieu
place mettre
plaid écossais(e)
plan projet *(m)* (4); **make plans** faire des projets (4)
plan organiser; **plan on doing** avoir l'intention de faire (4), compter faire (9); **planned** prévu(e)
plane avion *(m)* (4); **by plane** en avion (4)
plant plante *(f)* (3)
plastic plastique *(m)*; **plastic bag** sac *(m)* en plastique
plate assiette *(f)*
play *(theater)* pièce *(f)* (de théâtre) (4)
play (a sport) jouer (à un sport) (2), faire (du sport) (2); **play music** faire de la musique (2); **play the piano** jouer du piano (2)

player: CD / DVD / Blu-ray player lecteur *(m)* CD / DVD / Blu-ray (3); **MP3 player** lecteur *(m)* MP3

plaza place *(f)* (10)

pleasant agréable (1)

please plaire à

please s'il vous plaît *(formal)* (P), s'il te plaît *(familiar)*

pleasure plaisir *(m)*; **With pleasure!** Avec plaisir! (6)

plum prune *(f)*

plumber plombier *(m)*

plus: **How much is . . . plus . . . ?** Combien font... et... ? (P)

P.M. de l'après-midi, du soir (P)

poem poème *(m)* (9)

point out signaler

police police *(f)*

policeman agent *(m)* de police

polite poli(e)

political politique (1); **political science** sciences politiques *(fpl)* (1)

politics politique *(f)* (7)

poll sondage *(m)*

pollution pollution *(f)*

Polynesia: **French Polynesia** Polynésie française *(f)* (9)

pool: **play pool** jouer au billard; **swimming pool** piscine *(f)* (4)

poor pauvre

pop music musique populaire *(f)* (1)

popular populaire (1)

population population *(f)*

pork porc *(m)* (8); **pork chop** côte *(f)* de porc (8); **pork roast** rôti *(m)* de porc

portrait: **self-portrait** autoportrait *(m)* (P)

Portuguese portugais *(m)*

possibility possibilité *(f)* (4)

possible possible (10); **it is possible that** il est possible que (10)

post office bureau *(m)* de poste (10)

postcard carte postale *(f)* (9)

poster poster *(m)* (3)

potato pomme *(f)* de terre (8)

poultry volaille *(f)* (8)

pound (of) livre (de) *(f)* (8)

poverty pauvreté *(f)*

powerful puissant(e)

practical pratique (3)

preach prêcher

precisely justement (3)

prefer préférer (2), aimer mieux (2); **I prefer . . .** Je préfère... (1)

preferable préférable (10); **it's preferable that** il est préférable que (10)

pregnant enceinte (10)

preparations préparatifs *(mpl)* (9)

prepare préparer (2); **Prepare for the exam.** Préparez l'examen. (P); **prepared dish** plat préparé *(m)* (8)

preschool école maternelle *(f)*

prescription ordonnance *(f)* (10)

present cadeau *(m)* (10)

pretty joli(e) (1), beau/bel (belle) (1); **pretty cool** assez cool (P)

prevent empêcher

price prix *(m)*; **set-price menu** menu à prix fixe (8)

principal principal(e) *(mpl* principaux) (10)

private privé(e) (10)

probable probable

probably sans doute (8); probablement

problem problème *(m)*; **No problem!** Pas de problème! (3)

process: **be in the process of doing** être en train de faire

product produit *(m)* (8); **organic products** produits bio *(mpl)* (8)

profession profession *(f)* (7), métier *(m)*

professional professionnel(le) (7)

professor professeur *(m)* (P)

program programme *(m)*

programmer programmeur(-euse) *(mf)*

progress progrès *(m)*; **make progress** faire des progrès

promise promettre (de) (6)

pronunciation prononciation *(f)*

protect (oneself) (against) (se) protéger (contre)

proud fier(-ère)

province province *(f)* (3)

prune pruneau *(m)*

psychology psychologie *(f)* (1)

public: **public transportation** transports en commun *(mpl)* (9)

pullover (sweater) pull *(m)* (5)

punish punir

purple violet(te) (3)

purpose: **on purpose** exprès

purse sac *(m)* (5)

put (on) mettre (5); **put away** bien rangé(e) (3); **put on make-up** se maquiller (7); **put on weight** prendre du poids; **put up with** supporter (7)

Q

qualify qualifier

quarter quart *(m)* (P); **It's a quarter past two.** Il est deux heures et quart. (P)

question question *(f)* (P); **ask a question** poser une question (3)

quick rapide (8)

quickly vite (7)

quiet tranquille; **be quiet** se taire

quite assez, plutôt; **quite a bit of** pas mal de; **quite simply** tout simplement (10)

R

rabbit lapin *(m)*

radio radio *(f)* (2)

rain pluie *(f)* (5)

rain pleuvoir (5); **It's raining., It rains.** Il pleut. (5)

raincoat imperméable *(m)* (5)

raisin raisin sec *(m)*

Ramadan ramadan *(m)*

rapid rapide (8)

rarely rarement (2)

raspberry framboise *(f)*

rather plutôt (1), assez (1)

raw vegetables crudités *(fpl)* (8)

rayfish raie *(f)* (8)

reach atteindre

react (to) réagir (à)

read lire (2); **Read . . .** Lisez... (P)

ready (to) prêt(e) (à) (4); **get ready** se préparer; **ready-to-serve dish** plat préparé *(m)* (8)

real réel(le), véritable

realistic réaliste (1)

realize se rendre compte

really vraiment (2)

reason raison *(f)*

reasonable raisonnable

receive recevoir (9)

recent récent(e)

recently récemment (5)

recognize (each other) (se) reconnaître (7)

recommend recommander (10)

record disque *(m)*, *(sports)* record *(m)*

record enregistrer

recorder: **video cassette recorder** magnétoscope *(m)*

recount raconter (7)

recycle recycler

red rouge (3), *(with hair)* roux (rousse) (4); **red wine** vin rouge *(m)* (2); **turn red** rougir

reflect (on) réfléchir (à) (8)

refrigerator réfrigérateur *(m)*

refuse refuser (de)

region région *(f)* (4)

regional régional(e) *(mpl* régionaux) (4)

register s'inscrire (3)

regret regretter (6)

regularly régulièrement (8)

relationship relation *(f)* (7), rapport *(m)*

relatives parents *(mpl)* (5)

relax se reposer (7), se détendre; **relaxed** décontracté(e)

religion religion *(f)* (7)

religious religieux(-euse)

remain rester

remarried remarié(e)

remember se souvenir (de) (7)

rent loyer *(m)* (3)

rent louer (4)

rental car voiture *(f)* de location (5)

repeat répéter (2); **Please repeat.** Répétez, s'il vous plaît. (P)

replace remplacer

require exiger, demander; **required** requis(e), obligatoire

research recherche *(f)*; **do research** faire des recherches

resemble ressembler à

reservation réservation *(f)* (9); **make a reservation** faire une réservation (9)

reserve: **nature reserve** parc naturel *(m)*

reserve réserver (9)

residence hall résidence universitaire *(f)* (1)

resources ressources *(fpl)*

respond (to) répondre (à) (6)

rest: **the rest (of)** le reste (de) (7)

rest se reposer (7); **rested** reposé(e)

restaurant restaurant *(m)* (1); **fast food restaurant** fast-food *(m)* (1); **university restaurant** resto-U *(m)* (6)

restful reposant(e)

restroom toilettes *(fpl)* (3), W.-C. *(mpl)* (10)

retired retraité(e)

return retour *(m)* (9)

return rentrer (2), retourner (5); **return something to someone** rendre quelque chose à quelqu'un (7)

review *(for a test)* réviser (2)

rice riz *(m)* (8)

rich riche (2)

ride: **go for a ride** faire un tour (4)

right *(direction)* droite *(f)*, (3) *(legal)* droit *(m)*; **to the right (of)** à droite (de) (3)

right correct(e); **be right** avoir raison (4); **right away** tout de suite (6); **right by** tout près (de) (3); **right there** juste là; **right?** n'est-ce pas?, non? (1); **That's right!** C'est ça! (1)

ring bague *(f)*

ring sonner (7)

river fleuve *(m)*, rivière *(f)*

road chemin *(m)*, route *(f)*

roast: **pork roast** rôti *(m)* de porc; **roast beef** rosbif *(m)* (8)

rock: **rock music** rock *(m)* (1); **go rock climbing** faire de l'escalade; **hard rock** *hard rock (m)*

rollerblade faire du roller (6)

rollerblading roller *(m)*; **go rollerblading** faire du roller (6)
romantic romantique; **romantic movie** film *(m)* d'amour (6)
room pièce *(f)* (3), salle *(f)*; **classroom** salle *(f)* de cours (1); **dining room** salle à manger *(f)* (3); **double room** chambre double *(f)* (10); **fitting room** cabine *(f)* d'essayage (5); **living room** salon *(m)* (3); **single room** chambre simple *(f)* (10)
roommate camarade *(mf)* de chambre (P)
round-trip ticket billet aller-retour *(m)* (9)
routine routine *(f)* (7)
row rang *(m)*
rug tapis *(m)* (3)
run courir (9); **run errands** faire des courses (5); **run into (each other)** (se) rencontrer (1)
runny: have a runny nose avoir le nez qui coule
Russia Russie *(f)* (9)
Russian russe *(m)*

S

sack sac *(m)* (5), paquet *(m)* (8)
sad triste
safety sécurité *(f)*
sailing: go sailing faire de la voile
salad salade *(f)* (8)
salami saucisson *(m)* (8)
sale: on sale en solde (5)
salesclerk vendeur(-euse) *(mf)* (5)
salmon saumon *(m)* (8)
salt sel *(m)* (8)
same même (1); **all the same** quand même
sandal sandale *(f)* (5)
sandwich sandwich *(m)* (2); **bread-and-butter sandwich** tartine *(f)* (8); **cheese sandwich** sandwich au fromage *(m)* (2)
Santa Claus le père Noël
satisfied satisfait(e)
Saturday samedi *(m)* (P)
sauce sauce *(f)*
sausage saucisse *(f)* (8)
save sauver; **save up money** faire des économies
saxophone saxophone *(m)*
say dire (6); **How do you say . . . in French?** Comment dit-on... en français? (P); **They say that . . .** On dit que... (4)
scallops coquilles St-Jacques *(fpl)*
scarf *(winter)* écharpe *(f)*, *(dressy)* foulard *(m)*
scenery paysage *(m)* (9)
schedule *(classes)* emploi *(m)* du temps, *(train)* horaire *(m)*
school école *(f)* (6); **high school** lycée *(m)* (6)
science science *(f)* (1); **computer science** informatique *(f)* (1); **political science** sciences politiques *(fpl)*; **science fiction** science-fiction *(f)*; **social sciences** sciences humaines *(fpl)* (1)
scientist scientifique *(mf)*; **computer scientist** informaticien(ne) *(mf)*
scuba diving plongée sous-marine *(f)*
sculpture sculpture *(f)*
sea mer *(f)* (9)
season saison *(f)* (5)
seat place *(f)*, siège *(m)*
seated assis(e) (9)
second *(in time)* seconde *(f)* (5)
second deuxième (3), second(e); **in second class** en classe économique (9)
secretary secrétaire *(mf)*
section section *(f)*
security sécurité *(f)*

see voir (1); **as you see** comme tu vois (3); **Let's see!** Voyons! (5); **see each other** se voir (7); **See you in a little while.** À tout à l'heure. (P); **See you later!** À plus tard!, À plus! (P); **See you soon.** À bientôt. (P); **See you tomorrow.** À demain. (P)
seem avoir l'air... (4), sembler; **It/That seems nice.** Ça a l'air bien. (3); **It seems to me that . . .** Il me semble que...
self: myself moi-même; **self-portrait** autoportrait *(m)* (P); **self-service restaurant** self-service *(m)* (8)
sell vendre (7); **sell back** revendre (7)
semester semestre *(m)* (P)
send envoyer (2)
Senegal Sénégal *(m)* (9)
sense of humor sens *(m)* de l'humour (7)
sensitive sensible
sentence phrase *(f)* (P); **with a complete sentence** avec une phrase complète (P)
sentimental sentimental(e) *(mpl* sentimentaux) (7)
separate séparer; **separated** séparé(e)
separately séparément
September septembre *(m)* (4)
serious sérieux(-euse), grave
serve servir (4); **served** servi(e) (10)
server serveur *(m)*, serveuse *(f)* (2)
service service *(m)* (8); **service station** station-service *(f)*
set mettre; **set-price menu** menu à prix fixe (8); **set the table** mettre la table
settle (in) s'installer (à/dans) (7)
seven sept (P)
seventeen dix-sept (P)
seventh septième (3)
seventy soixante-dix (2); **seventy-one** soixante et onze (2)
several plusieurs (8)
shall: What shall we do? Qu'est-ce qu'on fait?; **Shall we go . . . ?** On va... ? (2)
shame *honte *(f)*; **It's a shame!** C'est dommage! (7)
shape forme *(f)*; **in shape** en forme (8)
share partager (3); **shared** partagé(e) (3)
shave se raser (7); **have a shaved head** avoir la tête rasée
she elle (1); **she is . . .** c'est..., elle est... (1)
sheet of paper feuille *(f)* de papier (P)
shelf étagère *(f)* (3)
shellfish fruits *(mpl)* de mer (8)
shirt chemise *(f)* (5); **knit shirt** polo *(m)* (5)
shiver frisson *(m)* (10)
shock choquer
shoe chaussure *(f)* (5); **tennis shoes** baskets *(fpl)* (5)
shop magasin *(m)* (4); **bakery-pastry shop** boulangerie-pâtisserie *(f)* (8); **butcher's shop** boucherie *(f)* (8); **fish shop** poissonnerie *(f)* (8); **gift shop** boutique *(f)* de cadeaux (10); **tobacco shop** bureau *(m)* de tabac
shopkeeper marchand(e) *(mf)* (6), commerçant(e) *(mf)* (8)
shopping: go grocery shopping faire les courses; **go shopping** faire du shopping (2); **shopping mall** centre commercial *(m)* (4)
short petit(e) (1), court(e) (4)
shorts short *(m)* (5)
shot piqûre *(f)*; **give a shot** faire une piqûre
should devoir (6); **one shouldn't . . .** il ne faut pas... (10)
shoulder épaule *(f)*; **shoulder-length** *(with hair)* mi-longs (4)
show montrer (3), indiquer (3); **show a movie** passer un film (6)

shower douche *(f)* (7); **take a shower** prendre une douche (7)
showing séance *(f)* (6)
showtime séance *(f)* (6)
shrimp crevette *(f)* (8)
shuttle navette *(f)* (10)
shy timide (1)
sick malade (10); **get sick** tomber malade (10)
side côté *(m)*; **on the courtyard side** côté cour (10); **on the other side (of)** de l'autre côté (de)
sight vue *(f)*; **love at first sight** coup *(m)* de foudre (7)
silver argent *(m)* (2)
similar to semblable à, pareil(le) à
simply simplement (10); **quite simply** tout simplement (10)
since depuis, comme (7), depuis que; **since then** depuis cela
sincere sincère
sing chanter (2)
singer chanteur(-euse) *(mf)*
single célibataire (1), seul(e); **single room** chambre simple *(f)* (10)
sink *(bathroom)* lavabo *(m)* (10), *(kitchen)* évier *(m)*
sir monsieur (M.) (P)
sister sœur *(f)* (1); **sister-in-law** belle-sœur *(f)*
sit (down) s'asseoir; **Sit down!** Asseyez-vous!
site site *(m)* (9)
situation situation *(f)*
six six (P)
sixteen seize (P)
sixth sixième (3)
sixty soixante (2); **sixty-one** soixante et un (2)
size taille *(f)* (4); **medium-sized** de taille moyenne (4)
skate *(fish)* raie *(f)* (8); patin *(m)*
skateboard faire du skateboard (6)
skating patinage *(m)*; **go (ice-)skating** faire du patin (à glace)
skeptical sceptique
ski ski *(m)* (2); **ski jacket** anorak *(m)* (5); **ski lodge** chalet *(m)* à la montagne (10)
ski faire du ski (2); **water-ski** faire du ski nautique (5)
skin peau *(f)*
skinny maigre
skirt jupe *(f)* (5)
sleep dormir (2)
sleepy: be sleepy avoir sommeil (4)
slice (of) tranche (de) *(f)*, pavé (de) *(m)* (8)
slightly légèrement
slim down maigrir (8)
slip combinaison *(f)*
slow lent(e); **slow motion** ralenti *(m)*
slowly lentement (8)
small petit(e) (1)
smart intelligent(e) (1)
smartphone smartphone *(m)* (3)
smell sentir
smoke fumer (3); **smoked** fumé(e) (8)
smoking section section fumeur *(f)*
snack collation *(f)*
snail escargot *(m)* (8)
sneeze éternuer (10)
snob snob
snorkeling: go snorkeling faire de la plongée avec masque et tuba
snow neige *(f)* (5)
snow neiger (5)
so alors (1), tellement (6), donc (7); **not so much** pas tellement (1); **so many, so much** tant (de); tellement (de); **so-so** comme ci comme ça (P); **so that** afin que

soap savon (m)
soccer football (m) (1)
social social(e) (mpl sociaux); **social sciences** sciences humaines (fpl) (1); **social worker** assistant(e) social(e) (mf)
society société (f)
sociology sociologie (f)
sock chaussette (f)
sofa canapé (m) (3)
soft doux(-ce) (6)
software logiciel (m)
sole sole (f)
solid-colored uni(e)
solution solution (f)
some des (1), du, de la, de l', en (8), quelques (5), certain(e)s (8)
somebody quelqu'un (6)
someone quelqu'un (6)
something quelque chose (2)
sometimes quelquefois (2), parfois (5)
somewhere quelque part
son fils (m) (4)
song chanson (f)
soon bientôt (P); **as soon as** aussitôt que; **I would just as soon . . .** j'aimerais autant… (10); **See you soon.** À bientôt. (P)
sorry désolé(e) (8); **be sorry that . . .** être désolé(e) que… (10), regretter que… (6)
sort: all sorts of toutes sortes de
sound: How does that sound? Ça te/vous dit? (2)
soup soupe (f) (8); **onion soup** soupe (f) à l'oignon (8)
south sud (m); **South Africa** Afrique (f) du Sud; **South America** Amérique (f) du Sud (9)
space espace (m)
Spain Espagne (f) (9)
Spanish espagnol (m) (P)
Spanish espagnol(e)
speak parler (2); **Do you speak . . . ?** Vous parlez…? (P); **I speak . . .** Je parle… (P)
special spécial(e) (mpl spéciaux) (6); **nothing special** rien de spécial (6)
specialty spécialité (f) (4)
speech discours (m)
speed vitesse (f)
spend (time) passer (2), (money) dépenser
spider araignée (f)
spinach épinards (mpl)
spirituality spiritualité (f) (7)
spite: in spite of malgré
split partagé(e) (3)
spoiled gâté(e) (6)
spoon cuillère (f)
sport sport (m) (1); **play sports** faire du sport (2); **sports coat** veste (f); **sports field** terrain (m) de sport
spot site (m) (9)
sprain one's ankle se fouler la cheville
spring printemps (m) (5); **in spring** au printemps (5)
square (town) place (f) (10)
stadium stade (m) (1)
stairs escalier (m) (3)
stamp timbre (m) (10)
stand: I can't stand . . . Je ne supporte pas… (7), J'ai horreur de…
star étoile (f)
start commencer (2); **French class starts . . .** Le cours de français commence… (P)
state État (m) (3); **United States** États-Unis (3) (mpl)
station: radio station station (f) de radio; **service station** station-service (f); **subway**

station station (f) de métro; **train station** gare (f)
stay séjour (m) (7); **Enjoy your stay!** Bon séjour! (10)
stay rester (2), (at a hotel) descendre (à) (5)
steak bifteck (m) (8); **steak and fries** steak-frites (m) (8)
steal voler
stepbrother demi-frère (m)
stepfather beau-père (m) (4)
stepmother belle-mère (f) (4)
stepparents beaux-parents (mpl)
stepsister demi-sœur (f) (6)
stereo chaîne hi-fi (f) (3)
still encore (4), toujours
stomach ventre (m) (10); estomac
stop: bus stop arrêt (m) de bus (3)
stop (s')arrêter (7); **stop by the house of . . .** passer chez… (2); **stopped up** bouché(e)
store magasin (m) (4); **bookstore** librairie (f) (1)
storm orage (m)
story histoire (f) (9); conte (m) (6)
stove cuisinière (f)
straight tout droit (10)
straightened up bien rangé(e) (3)
strange bizarre
strawberry fraise (f) (8)
street rue (f) (3); **on . . . Street** dans la rue… (10)
strength force (f)
stress stress (m) (8)
stressed (out) stressé(e)
strict sévère
striped rayé(e)
strong fort(e) (8)
struggle (against) lutter (contre)
stubborn têtu(e)
student étudiant(e) (mf) (P); **high school student** lycéen(ne) (mf) (6); **student center** centre (m) d'étudiants
studies études (fpl) (1)
study étudier (1), réviser les cours (2); **I study . . .** J'étudie… (1); **What are you studying?** Qu'est-ce que vous étudiez? (1)
stupid bête (1), stupide
style style (m); **American-style** à l'américaine (8)
stylist: hair stylist coiffeur(-euse) (mf)
suburbs banlieue (f) (3); **in the suburbs** en banlieue (3)
subway métro (m) (4); **by subway** en métro (4)
succeed (in) réussir (à) (8)
such a un(e) tel(le) (7)
sudden: all of a sudden tout à coup (6)
suddenly soudain, tout à coup (6), soudainement
suffer souffrir
sufficiently suffisamment
sugar sucre (m) (8)
suggest suggérer (6)
suggestion suggestion (f)
suit (for a man) costume (m) (5), (for a woman) tailleur (m); **jogging suit** survêtement (m) (5)
suitcase valise (f) (9)
summer été (m) (5); **in summer** en été (5)
sun soleil (m)
sunbathe prendre un bain de soleil (4)
Sunday dimanche (m) (P)
sunglasses lunettes (f) de soleil (5)
sunny: It's sunny. Il fait (du) soleil. (5)
superior supérieur(e)

supermarket supermarché (m) (8)
superstore grande surface (f) (8)
supplement supplément (m) (10)
supplies provisions (fpl)
sure sûr(e), certain(e)
surely sûrement
surf (Internet) surfer (2), (water) faire du surf; **surf the Net** surfer sur Internet (2)
surprise étonner, surprendre; **be surprised that . . .** être surpris(e) que… (10)
surrounded (by) entouré(e) (de)
swallow avaler
sweater: pullover sweater pull (m) (5)
sweatshirt sweat (m)
sweatsuit survêtement (m) (5)
Sweden Suède (f)
sweet doux(-ce) (6)
sweets bonbons (mpl)
swim nager (2), se baigner
swimming pool piscine (f) (4)
swimsuit maillot (m) de bain (5)
Switzerland Suisse (f) (9)
swollen enflé(e)
symptom symptôme (m) (10)
synagogue synagogue (f)
syrup sirop (m)
system système (m); **public transporation system** réseau (m) de transports en commun (9)

T

table table (f) (3)
take prendre (4); **take (along)** (a thing) emporter (5); (a person) emmener; **take a course** suivre un cours; **take advantage of** profiter de (9); **take a tour** faire un tour (4); **take a trip** faire un voyage (5); **take a walk** faire une promenade (5); **Take out a sheet of paper.** Prenez une feuille de papier. (P); **take place** avoir lieu
tale: fairy tale conte (m) de fées (6)
talent talent (m)
talented doué(e)
talk parler (2); **talk to each other** se parler (7)
tall grand(e) (1)
tan bronzer (9); **tanned** bronzé(e)
tangerine mandarine (f)
tart tartelette (f) (8); **strawberry/cherry tart** tartelette aux fraises/aux cerises (8)
taste goûter (9)
taxi taxi (m) (4); **by taxi** en taxi (4)
tea (with lemon) thé (m) (au citron) (2)
teacher (elementary school) instituteur(-trice) (mf); (secondary school) professeur (m)
team équipe (f)
technical technique; **technical courses** technologies (fpl) (1)
technician technicien(ne) (mf)
technology technologie (f) (1)
tee-shirt tee-shirt (m) (5)
telephone téléphone (m) (2); **talk on the telephone** parler au téléphone (2); **telephone card** carte (f) téléphonique (10); **telephone number** numéro (m) de téléphone (3)
telephone téléphoner (à) (2); **telephone each other** se téléphoner (7)
television télévision (télé) (f) (2)
tell dire (6), raconter (7)
teller: automatic teller machine distributeur de billets (m) (10)
temperature température (f)
temple temple (m)

ten dix (P)
tennis tennis *(m)* (1); **tennis court** court *(m)* de tennis; **tennis shoes** baskets *(fpl)* (5)
tenth dixième (3)
terrace terrasse *(f)* (9)
test examen *(m)* (P), test *(m)* (7), contrôle *(m)*
Texas Texas *(m)* (9)
than: more . . . than plus... que (1)
thank (for) remercier (de) (10); **thank you** merci (bien) (P)
thanks merci (bien) (P)
Thanksgiving jour *(m)* d'Action de Grâce
that ça (P), ce (cet, cette) (...-là) (3), que (P), qui (7), cela; **I think that . . .** je pense que... (P); **that is . . .** c'est... (1); **that/those . . . over there** ce (cet, cette, ces)... là (3)
the le, la, l', les (1)
theater théâtre *(for live performances) (m)* (1); **movie theater** cinéma *(m)* (1)
theft vol *(m)*
their leur(s) (1)
them les (5); **of them** en (8); **to them** leur (9); **with them** avec eux *(m)*, avec elles *(f)* (2)
themselves se (7), eux-mêmes *(mpl)*, elles-mêmes *(fpl)*
then alors (1), ensuite (4), puis, donc (7)
there là (1), y (4); **over there** là-bas (1); **right there** juste là; **that/those . . . over there** ce (cet, cette, ces)... là (3); **there is, there are** il y a (1), voilà (2); **There are . . . of us.** Nous sommes.... (4); **There you are!** Te/ Vous voilà!
therefore donc (7)
these ces (...-ci) (3); **these are . . .** ce sont... (1)
they ils, elles, ce (1), on (4)
thick gros(se)
thief voleur *(m)*
thin mince (1); **get thinner** maigrir (8)
thing chose *(f)* (3), truc *(m)* (1); **my things** mes affaires *(fpl)*; **That's not my thing.** Ce n'est pas mon truc. (1)
think (about) penser (à) (2), réfléchir (à) (8); **I think that . . .** Je pense que... (P); **What do you think (about it)?** Qu'en penses-tu?, Qu'en pensez-vous? (5)
third troisième (3); **two-thirds** deux tiers
thirsty: be thirsty avoir soif (4); **I'm thirsty.** J'ai soif. (2)
thirteen treize (P)
thirty trente (P)
this ce (cet, cette) (3); **this . . . over here** ce (cet, cette)... ci; **this evening** ce soir (2); **this is . . .** c'est... (1); **this month** ce mois-ci (4); **this semester** ce semestre (P); **this way** par ici (5)
those ces (...-là) (3); **those are . . .** ce sont... (1); **those (ones)** ceux (celles) (8)
thousand: one thousand mille (3)
three trois (P)
throat gorge *(f)* (10); **have a sore throat** avoir mal à la gorge
through par; **through the window** par la fenêtre
throw jeter; **throw up** vomir (10)
Thursday jeudi *(m)* (P)
thus donc (7)
ticket billet *(m)* (9), ticket *(m)*; **e-ticket** billet électronique (9); **one-way ticket** aller simple (9); **plane ticket** billet *(m)* d'avion (9); **round-trip ticket** billet aller-retour *(m)* (9); **ticket window** guichet *(m)*
tie cravate *(f)* (5)
tight étroit(e)
till: a quarter till moins le quart (P)

time *(clock)* heure *(f)* (P), temps *(m)* (2), *(occasion)* fois *(f)* (5); **a long time** longtemps (5); **at that time** à ce moment-là; **At what time?** À quelle heure? (P); **free time** temps libre *(m)* (2); **from time to time** de temps en temps (4); **have a hard time** avoir du mal à; **local time** heure locale *(f)* (9); **most of the time** la plupart du temps (7); **official time** heure officielle *(f)* (6); **Once upon a time there was . . .** Il était une fois... (6); **One has a good time.** On s'amuse bien.; **on time** à l'heure (4); **opening time** heure *(f)* d'ouverture (6); **show time** séance *(f)* (6); **sometimes . . . other times** parfois... d'autres fois (7); **the last time** la dernière fois (5); **time period** époque *(f)* (6); **What time is it?** Quelle heure est-il? (P)
timid timide (1)
tip pourboire *(m)*
tired fatigué(e) (6)
tiring fatiguant(e)
title titre *(m)*
to à (P); **from Monday to Friday** *(every week)* du lundi au vendredi (P); **to go to a club** aller en boîte (de nuit) (2); **to . . . 's house/ place** chez... (2)
toast pain grillé *(m)* (8)
toasted grillé(e) (8)
tobacco tabac *(m)* (8); **tobacco shop** bureau *(m)* de tabac
today aujourd'hui (P)
toe doigt *(m)* de pied (10)
together ensemble (2)
toilet toilettes *(fpl)* (3), W.-C. *(mpl)* (10)
tolerance tolérance *(f)* (7)
tolerate supporter (7)
tomato tomate *(f)* (8)
tomorrow demain (P); **day after tomorrow** après-demain (4); **tomorrow morning** demain matin (4)
tonight ce soir (2); **See you tonight.** À ce soir. (2)
too aussi (P), trop (3); **That's too bad!** C'est dommage! (7); **too many** trop (de) (8); **too much** trop (de) (6)
tooth dent *(f)* (7)
tour tour *(m)*; **take a tour** faire un tour (4)
tourism tourisme *(m)*
tourist touriste *(mf)*; **tourist office** office *(m)* de tourisme (10)
touristic touristique (9)
toward(s) vers (2)
towel serviette *(f)*
town ville *(f)* (3); **in town** en ville (3)
toy jouet *(m)*
traditional traditionnel(le) (8)
traffic circulation *(f)*
train train *(m)* (4); **by train** en train (4); **train station** gare *(f)*
training: do weight training faire de la muscu(lation) (8); faire des haltères
trait trait *(m)* (7)
translate traduire
translation traduction *(f)*
transportation transport *(m)*; **means of transportation** moyen *(m)* de transport (4); **public transportation** transports *(mpl)* en commun (9)
travel: travel agency agence *(f)* de voyages (9); **travel agent** agent *(m)* de voyages (9)
travel voyager (2)
traveler's check chèque *(m)* de voyage
treatment traitement *(m)*

tree arbre *(m)* (1)
trimester trimestre *(m)*
trip voyage *(m)* (4); **take a trip** faire un voyage (5)
tropical tropical(e) *(mpl* tropicaux) (9)
trouble difficulté *(f)*; **have trouble** avoir des difficultés, avoir du mal (à)
truck camion *(m)*, *(pick-up)* camionnette *(f)*
true vrai(e) (8); **true love** le grand amour (7)
truly vraiment (2)
trumpet trompette *(f)*
truth vérité *(f)*
try (on) essayer (5)
T-shirt tee-shirt *(m)* (5)
Tuesday mardi *(m)* (P)
tuna thon *(m)* (8)
Tunisia Tunisie *(f)*
Turkey Turquie *(f)*
turkey dinde *(f)*
turn (right/left) tourner (à droite/à gauche) (10); **turn in (something to someone)** rendre (quelque chose à quelqu'un) (7); **turn on** mettre; **turn red** rougir
turnover: apple turnover chausson *(m)* aux pommes
TV télé *(f)* (2)
twelve douze (P)
twenty vingt (P)
twin jumeau (jumelle) (1)
two deux (P)
type genre *(m)*
typical typique (2)
typically typiquement

U

ugly laid(e) (1)
umbrella parapluie *(m)* (5)
unbearable insupportable
unbelievable incroyable
uncle oncle *(m)* (4)
under sous (3)
understand comprendre (4); **Do you understand?** Vous comprenez? (P); **I understand.** Je comprends. (P); **No, I don't understand.** Non, je ne comprends pas. (P)
understanding compréhension *(f)*
underwear sous-vêtements *(mpl)*
undressed: get undressed se déshabiller (7)
unfaithfulness infidélité *(f)* (7)
unfortunately malheureusement
unhappy malheureux(-euse)
uniquely uniquement (6)
united uni(e); **United Kingdom** Royaume-Uni *(m)* (9); **United States** États-Unis *(mpl)* (3)
university université *(f)* (P), fac(ulté) *(f)* (2); **university cafeteria** resto-U *(m)* (6)
university universitaire (1)
unless à moins que
unlikely peu probable
unmarried célibataire (1)
unpack défaire sa valise
unpleasant désagréable, antipathique (1)
until jusqu'à (2)
up: get up se lever (7); **go up** monter (5); **straightened up** rangé(e) (3); **up to** jusqu'à (2); **wake up** se réveiller (7); **wash up** faire sa toilette (7)
us nous (9); **with us** avec nous (2)
use utiliser (6), employer
used to habitué(e) à
useful utile (10)
usually d'habitude (2)
utilize utiliser (6)

V

vacation vacances *(fpl)* (4); **on vacation** en vacances (6)
Valentine's Day Saint-Valentin *(f)*
vanilla ice cream glace *(f)* à la vanille (8)
vanity vanité *(f)* (7)
variety variété *(f)*
VCR magnétoscope *(m)*
veal veau *(m)*
vegetable légume *(m)* (8); **raw vegetables** crudités *(fpl)* (8); **vegetable soup** soupe *(f)* de légumes
vegetarian végétarien(ne)
verify vérifier (10)
very très (P); **very near** tout près (de) (3)
vest gilet *(m)*
veterinarian vétérinaire *(mf)*
video vidéo *(f)*; **video cassette** vidéocassette *(f)*; **video cassette recorder** magnétoscope *(m)*; **video game** jeu vidéo *(m)* (2)
Vietnam Viêt Nam *(m)* (9)
view vue *(f)* (3)
vinegar vinaigre *(m)*
violence violence *(f)* (6)
violent violent(e)
violet violet(te) (3)
violin violon *(m)*
virus virus *(m)* (10)
visa visa *(m)*
visit visite *(f)*; **medical visit** consultation *(f)*
visit *(place)* visiter (1), *(someone)* aller voir (4), rendre visite à (7)
vitamin vitamine *(f)* (8)
vocabulary vocabulaire *(m)* (P)
voice voix *(f)*
volleyball volley *(m)* (2)
vomit vomir (10)
vote voter

W

wait (for) attendre (7)
waiter serveur *(m)* (2)
waitress serveuse *(f)* (2)
wake up (se) réveiller (7)
walk promenade *(f)* (5); **take a walk** faire une promenade (5)
walk aller à pied (4), marcher (8); **walk the dog** promener le chien
walking marche *(f)* à pied; **go walking** se promener (7), faire de la marche à pied
wall mur *(m)* (3)
wallet portefeuille *(m)* (5)
want vouloir (6), avoir envie de (4)
war guerre *(f)*
warmth chaleur *(f)*
wash (one's face/one's hands) se laver (la figure/les mains) (7); **wash clothes** faire la lessive (5); **wash the dishes** faire la vaisselle (5); **wash up** faire sa toilette (7)
washbasin lavabo *(m)* (10)
waste gaspiller; **waste time** perdre du temps (7)
watch montre *(f)* (5)
watch regarder (2); **watch out (for)** faire attention (à) (8)
water eau *(f)* (2)
watermelon pastèque *(f)*
water-skiing ski nautique *(m)* (5)
way façon *(f)* (6); **show the way** indiquer le chemin (10); **this way** par ici (5)
we nous (1), on (4); **Shall we go . . . ?** On va... ? (2); **What shall we do?** Qu'est-ce qu'on fait?

weak faible
weakness faiblesse *(f)*
wear porter (4); **I wear size . . .** Je fais du.... (5); **What size do you wear?** Quelle taille faites-vous? (5)
weather temps *(m)* (5); **The weather's bad / cold / cool / hot / nice / sunny / windy.** Il fait mauvais / froid / frais / chaud / beau / (du) soleil / du vent. (5); **What's the weather like?** Quel temps fait-il? (5)
Website site *(m)* Web
wedding mariage *(m)*; **wedding anniversary** anniversaire *(m)* de mariage
Wednesday mercredi *(m)* (P)
week semaine *(f)* (P); **in one/two week(s)** dans huit/quinze jours
weekend week-end *(m)* (P); **Have a good weekend!** Bon week-end!; **on weekends** le weekend (P)
weigh peser
weight poids *(m)*; **do weight training** faire de la musculation (8), faire des haltères; **gain weight** prendre du poids; **lose weight** perdre du poids; **put on weight** prendre du poids
welcome bienvenue *(f)*, **You're welcome.** De rien. (P); Je vous en prie., Je t'en prie. (2)
well bien (P); **get well** guérir; **well-behaved** sage (4)
west ouest *(m)*; **West Indies** Antilles *(fpl)* (9)
what qu'est-ce que (1), que (2), comment (P), quel(le) (3), ce que (7), ce qui (7), quoi; **What a mess!** Quel bazar! *(familiar)* (3); **What day is today?** C'est quel jour, aujourd'hui? (P); **What does that mean in English?** Qu'est-ce que ça veut dire en anglais? (P); **What is/are . . . like?** Comment est/sont... ? (1); **What is his/her name?** Comment s'appelle-t-il/elle? (4); **What is your name?** Tu t'appelles comment? *(familiar)* (P); Comment vous appelez-vous? *(formal)* (P); **What luck!** Quelle chance! (5); **What's the weather like?** Quel temps fait-il? (5); **What time is it?** Quelle heure est-il? (P)
when quand (2)
where où (1); **from where** d'où (1)
whereas tandis que
which quel(le) (3); que, qui (7); **about/of which** dont (7); **which one** lequel (laquelle) (6)
while tandis que, pendant que; **See you in a little while.** À tout à l'heure. (P); **while on** au cours de (10)
white blanc(he) (3); **white wine** vin blanc *(m)* (2)
who qui (2)
whole tout (toute) (2); **(loaf of) whole-grain bread** pain complet *(m)* (8); **the whole day** toute la journée (2)
whom qui (2), que (7)
whose dont (7)
why pourquoi (2)
widespread répandu(e)
widow veuve *(f)* (7)
widower veuf *(m)* (7)
wife femme *(f)* (2)
Wi-Fi Wi-Fi *(m)* (1); **Wi-Fi access** accès *(m)* Wi-Fi (10)
win gagner (2)
wind vent *(m)*
windbreaker blouson *(m)*

window fenêtre *(f)* (3); **ticket window** guichet *(m)*
windsurfing: go windsurfing faire de la planche à voile
windy: It's windy. Il fait du vent., Il y a du vent. (5)
wine vin *(m)* (2)
winter hiver *(m)* (5); **in winter** en hiver (5)
wish souhaiter (10)
with avec (P); chez (+ *person*) (7); **coffee with milk** café au lait *(m)* (2)
withdraw money retirer de l'argent (10)
without sans (P); **without doing it** sans le faire
woman femme *(f)* (1); **woman's suit** tailleur *(m)*
wonder se demander
wonderful merveilleux(-euse)
word mot *(m)* (P); **words** *(lyrics)* paroles *(fpl)*
work travail *(m)*
work travailler (2); **Does that work for you?** Ça te/vous convient? (9); **I work . . .** Je travaille... (P)
workbook cahier *(m)* (P)
worker *(manual)* ouvrier(-ère) *(mf)*
world monde *(m)*
world-(wide) mondial(e) *(mpl* mondiaux)
worry (about) (se) préoccuper (de)
worse pire
would: I would like to . . . Je voudrais (bien)... (2); **What would you like to do?** Qu'est-ce que vous voudriez faire... ? (2)
write écrire (2); **How is that written?** Ça s'écrit comment? (P); **Write the answer.** Écrivez la réponse. (P)
writer écrivain *(m)*
wrong: be wrong avoir tort (4); **What's wrong?** Qu'est-ce qui ne va pas? (10)

Y

yard jardin *(m)*
year année *(f)* (4), an *(m)* (4); **be . . . years old** avoir... ans (4); **Happy New Year!** Bonne année!; **New Year's Eve** le réveillon *(m)* du jour de l'An
yellow jaune (3)
yes oui (P), si *(in response to a question or a statement in the negative)* (8)
yesterday hier (5)
yet pourtant (8), déjà; **not yet** (ne...) pas encore (5)
yogurt yaourt *(m)* (8)
you tu, vous (P), te (9); **And you?** Et toi?, Et vous? (P); **See you tomorrow!** À demain! (P); **Thank you!** Merci! (P); **There you are!** Te / Vous voilà!; **with you** avec toi, avec vous (2)
young jeune (1)
your ton (ta, tes) (3); votre (vos) (3); **Open your book.** Ouvrez votre livre. (P); **What is your name?** Tu t'appelles comment? *(familiar)* (P), Comment vous appelez-vous? *(formal)* (P); **your friends** tes amis (1)
yourself te, vous (7); toi-même, vous-même(s)
youth jeunesse *(f)* (7); **youth hostel** auberge *(f)* de jeunesse (10)

Z

zero zéro (P), nul(le)
zip code code postal *(m)* (3)
zucchini courgette *(f)*
zydeco music musique *(f)* zydeco (4)

INDEX

A

à,
    contractions with, 152
    with geographical names, 370
    with indirect objects, 360
Accent marks, 22
    spelling-change verbs with, 80, 265, 330, 352
Adjectives,
    agreement, 34–35, 40, 48
    of color, 120
    common irregular, 34–35, 40, 48
    comparative forms of, 38
    demonstrative, 128
    interrogative, 128
    placement, 48
    plural, 34–35, 40
    possessive, 122, 124
Adverbs,
    placement, 76, 184
    time expressions, 158, 192
Agreement,
    adjectives, 34–35, 40, 48
    past participle, 184, 190, 202, 360
    possessive adjectives, 122, 124
aller,
    conditional, 330
    future, 352
    imperative, 154, 408
    passé composé, 190
    present, 152
    subjunctive, 396
    used with infinitives to express the
      future, 158
Alphabet, 22
appeler, verbs like, 265, 330, 352
Articles,
    definite, 52, 118, 122, 152, 320, 370
    indefinite, 46, 116, 320
    omission, 48
    partitive, 310, 320
avoir,
    conditional, 330
    expressions with, 88, 146
    future, 352
    imperative, 154, 408
    passé composé, 184
    passé composé with, 184
    present, 116
    subjunctive, 396

B

beau, 32, 34, 40, 48
bien, 6, 74, 76, 112, 184
boire,
    imperfect, 324
    passé composé, 184, 324
    present, 324
    subjunctive, 395

C

Cardinal numbers, 10, 90, 110
ce,
    -ci, -là 128
    demonstrative adjective, 128
    vs. **il/elle,** 34, 48
Cinema, 68, 248–251
Classroom, useful expressions, 20–22
Clothing, vocabulary for, 200–201
Cognates, 36
Colors, vocabulary for, 120
Commands, 154, 408
commencer, verbs like, 80, 232
Comparison of adjectives, 38
Conditional, 330–331

connaître,
    conditional, 364
    future, 364
    imperfect, 364
    passé composé, 364
    present, 364
    subjunctive, 394
    vs. **savoir,** 364
Consonants, final,
    pronunciation of, 6
Contractions, 118, 122, 152
Countries,
    names of, 368
    prepositions with, 370
Culture
    Africa, 422–425
    America, 106–107, 142–143
    Antilles, 348–349, 376–377, 384–385
    Belgium, 218
    cafés, 88, 96–97
    Canada, 106–107, 134–135
    cinema, 68, 248–251
    clothing sizes, 201
    Côte d'Azur, 64, 66–67
    Côte d'Ivoire, 423
    counting, 10, 90, 110
    Creole culture,
      Louisiana, 142–143
      Antilles, 376–377
    daily life, 16, 262
    départements d'outre-mer, 348–349, 350, 356, 382, 384–385
    eating habits, 96–97, 236, 304–306, 314, 322, 338–339
    education, 20, 32, 38, 44–45, 50, 58–59, 126
    Europe, 216–219
    family, 270, 284
    France, 30–31, 66–67, 180–181, 219, 222–223, 260–261, 302–303, 348–349, 384–385
    francophone music, 412, 414–415
    francophone world, overview, 4–5
    French regions and provinces, 30–31, 219, 222–223, 302–303, 348–349, 384–385
    French West Indies, 348–349, 376–377, 384–385
    friendship, 230
    greetings, 6, 8
    Guadeloupe, 348–349, 350, 356, 376–377, 384–385
    health, 328, 392
    holidays, 160
    hotels, 386
    invitations, 120, 224
    lifestyles, 270
    Louisiana, 142–143, 150, 162, 170–171
    Luxembourg, 216
    Martinique, 348–349, 350, 356, 376–377, 384–385
    metric system, 316
    Monaco, 218
    money, 89, 90
    Montreal, 107, 126
    Morocco, 425
    Nice, 66–67
    Normandy, 302–303
    Paris, 208, 222–223
    pastimes, 68, 74, 182, 210–211
    Quebec, 106–107, 109, 126, 129, 134–135
    relationships, 270, 284, 294–295
    restaurants, 306, 338–339
    Réunion, La, 424
    shopping, 201, 314
    sizes, 201

    Switzerland, 217
    temperatures in centigrade, 194
    twenty-four hour clock, 24–25
    universities in France, 20, 32, 44, 58–59
    vacation, 350, 362

D

Dates, 160–161, 173
Days of the week, 12
de,
    contractions with, 118, 122
    with quantity expressions, 46, 116, 310, 318, 320
    used after a negative, 46, 116, 310, 320
    used to denote possession, 122
Definite articles, 52, 118, 122, 152, 320, 370
Demonstrative adjectives, 128
devoir,
    conditional, 330
    future, 352
    passé composé, 226
    present, 226
    subjunctive, 395
dire,
    conditional, 358
    future, 358
    imperfect, 358
    passé composé, 358
    present, 358
    subjunctive, 394
Direct object pronouns, 202, 360, 366, 408
Directions, 406
dont, 286
dormir,
    passé composé, 184, 234
    present, 234
    subjunctive, 394
    verbs like, 234, 264

E

écrire,
    conditional, 358
    future, 358
    imperfect, 358
    passé composé, 184, 358
    present, 358
    subjunctive, 394
Education, 20, 32, 38, 44–45, 50, 58–59, 126
Elision, 14, 40, 42, 76, 305
Emotion, expressions of, 400, 404
en,
    as a pronoun, 324, 408
    with dates, 160
    with geographical names, 370
    with seasons, 194
ennuyer, verbs like, 265
-er verbs,
    conditional, 330
    future, 352
    imperative, 154, 408
    imperfect, 232
    passé composé, 184, 190
    present, 76
    subjunctive, 394
est-ce que, 42
être,
    after **quel,** 128
    conditional, 330
    future, 352
    imperative, 154, 408
    imperfect, 232
    passé composé, 184
    passé composé with, 184, 190
    present, 40
    subjunctive, 396

F

faire,
  conditional, 330
  expressions with, 198
  future, 352
  imperfect, 232
  passé composé, 184
  present, 196
  subjunctive, 396
Fairy tales, vocabulary for, 242
Family members, vocabulary for,
  144–145
Food, vocabulary for, 88, 304–305, 314–316,
  322–323
Francophone world, 4–5
Future,
  formation and use, 352
  expressed using **aller,** 158

G

Gender of nouns, 46
Geographical names,
  prepositions with, 370
  vocabulary for, 368, 370
Greetings, vocabulary for, 6, 8

H

h, aspirate vs. silent, 305
Holidays, 160
Household chores, vocabulary for,
  198–199
Housing, vocabulary for, 108–109

I

il/elle, vs. **ce,** 34–35, 48
il faut, 330, 352, 366, 388, 394, 404
il y a,
  meaning *ago,* 192
  meaning *there is / there are,* 46, 158
Immediate future, 158
imparfait,
  formation of, 232
  vs. the **passé composé,** 238, 240,
    244, 282
Imperative,
  formation, 154, 408
  with object pronouns, 408
Impersonal expressions, 388, 394
Indefinite article, 46, 116, 320
  omission of, 48
Indirect object pronouns, 360, 366, 408
  after the imperative, 408
Infinitive, 70
  after **savoir,** 364
  vs. the subjunctive, 404
Information questions, 84, 86, 128
Interlude musical, 102–103, 176–177,
  256–257, 344–345, 420–421
Interrogative adjective, 128
Interrogative words, 84
Intonation, 42
Introductions, vocabulary for, 6, 8
Inversion, 86
Invitations, 69, 224
-ir verbs,
  conditional, 330
  future, 352
  imperfect, 326
  passé composé, 326
  present, 326
  subjunctive, 394

J

jouer,
  followed by **à** + *sport,* 70
  followed by **de** + *musical instrument,* 70

L

-là, 128
Learning strategies,
  Anticipating a response, 390
  Asking for clarification, 148
  Brainstorming, 133
  Finding the right word, 337
  Guessing meaning from context, 112
  How to learn a language, xvii
  Listening for specific information, 72
  Making intelligent guesses, 94
  Making suggestions, 413
  Noting the important information, 228
  Organizing a paragraph, 293
  Planning and predicting, 312
  Previewing content, 132
  Reading a poem, 336
  Reading for the gist, 36
  Recognizing compound tenses, 354
  Recognizing conversational style, 290
  Revising what you write, 375
  Scanning and previewing a text, 56
  Understanding words with multiple
    meanings, 374
  Using and combining what you know, 57
  Using cognates and familiar words to read
    for the gist, 36
  Using logical order and standard phrases, 95
  Using standard formats, 248–249
  Using standard organizing techniques,
    209
  Using the sequence of events to make
    logical guesses, 186
  Using visuals to make guesses, 208
  Using word families and watching out for
    faux amis, 268
  Using word families, 412
  Using your knowledge of the world, 168
  Visualizing your topic, 169
Leisure activities, vocabulary for, 68–69,
  74–75, 150, 156, 182, 198
Liaison, 6, 18, 46, 52, 77, 86, 116, 305
lire,
  passé composé, 184, 358
  present, conditional, future, imperfect, 358
  subjunctive, 394

M

manger, verbs like, 80, 232
Meals, vocabulary for, 304–306, 322–323
mettre, 200
  passé composé, 200
Money, 89, 90
Months, vocabulary for, 160
Mood, 394
mourir,
  conditional, 330
  future, 352
  passé composé, 190
Movies, vocabulary for, 225

N

Nasal vowels, 10
Necessity, expressions of, 388, 394
Negation, 40
  ne... jamais, 76
  ne... ni... ni..., 71
  ne... pas, 40
  ne... pas encore, 192
  ne... rien, 196
  with **futur immédiat,** 158
  with imperative, 408
  with indefinite article, 46, 116, 320
  with infinitives, 196
  with pronouns, 152, 202, 264, 324, 360, 408
  with partitive, 310, 320
  with **passé composé,** 184

n'est-ce pas, 42
Nouns,
  gender, 46
  plural, 46, 116
nouveau, 40, 48
Numbers,
  zero to thirty, 10
  thirty to one hundred, 90
  above one hundred, 110
  ordinal, 110

O

Object pronouns,
  with commands, 408
  direct, 202, 360, 366, 408
  indirect, 360, 366, 408
on, 154
Ordinal numbers, 110

P

Participle, past, 184, 190
  agreement of, 190, 202, 280
partir,
  passé composé, 234
  present, 234
  subjunctive, 394
Partitive article, 310, 320
Passé composé,
  formation with **avoir,** 184
  formation with **être,** 190
  of pronominal verbs, 280
  time expressions used with, 192
  vs. the **imparfait,** 238, 240,
    244, 282
Past participle, 184, 190
  agreement of, 190, 202, 280
Plural,
  of adjectives, 34, 40
  of nouns, 46, 116
Possessions, vocabulary for, 114, 120
Possessive adjectives, 122, 124
pouvoir,
  conditional, 330
  future, 352
  passé composé, 226
  present, 226
  subjunctive, 396
préférer, verbs like, 80, 330, 352
prendre,
  imperfect, 232
  passé composé, 184
  present, 164
  subjunctive, 395
  verbs like, 164, 184
Prepositions, 114, 118, 152
  contractions with, 118, 122, 152
  pronouns after, 82
  with geographical names, 370
Present subjunctive, formation, use,
  394–395, 396, 400, 404
Pronominal verbs,
  immediate future, 272
  imperative, 408
  imperfect, 282
  infinitive, 264, 272
  passé composé, 280
  present, 264–265, 272
  reciprocal, 272
  reflexive, 264–265
Pronouns,
  after prepositions, 82
  direct object, 202, 360, 366, 408
  en, 324, 408
  indirect object, 360, 366, 408
  on, 154
  reflexive, 264–265
  relative, 286
  subject, 40
  y, 152, 408

Pronunciation
a, au, ai, 152
adjectives, 35
avoir, 116, 190
c vs. **ç,** 80
conditional, 331
consonants, final, 6
de, du, des, 118
definite articles, 52
dormir, verbs like, 234
e, in forms of **ce,** 128
e, unaccented, 52, 128
é vs. **è,** 80
-er verbs, 77
être, 116, 190
final consonants, 6
g, 80
h, 6, 305
il vs. **elle,** 35
imperfect, 232, 238
indefinite article, 46
infinitive endings, 70
inversion, 86
-ir verbs, 326
liaison, 6, 18, 46, 52, 77, 86, 116, 305
nasal vowels, 10
numbers, 10, 90
o, 124
partir, verbs like, 234
passé composé, 190, 238
prendre, 164
qu, 84
r, 70, 331
s, 326
sortir, verbs like, 234
spelling change verbs, 80
time, 16
venir, 164
vowels, 8, 10, 21

Q
Quantity, expressions of, 46, 116, 310, 318, 320
que,
in questions, 84, 86, 128
as a relative pronoun, 286
quel, 128
qu'est-ce que, 84, 128
Questions,
information, 84, 86, 128
using **est-ce que,** 42, 84
using intonation, 42
using inversion, 86
using **n'est-ce pas,** 42
words used in, 84
yes/no, 42
qui,
as an interrogative pronoun, 84
as a relative pronoun, 286

R
Reading selections,
Ànous2, 428
Aux trois obus, 94–95
Avis de l'hôtel, 412–413
Bébel-Gisler, Dany: *Ma grand-mère m'a appris à ne pas compter sur les yeux des autres pour dormir,* 374–375
Deux films français, 248–249
Gentil, Jean: *Deux mots,* 168–169
Gomez, Lucille: *Le destin d'une lycéenne,* 439
Ionesco, Eugène: *Conte pour enfants de moins de trois ans,* 290–292
Je blogue donc je suis, 208–209
Le beurre de cacahuète, c'est pour les sportifs!, 440
Lucile Gomez auteur de BD et de blog, 436
Macrae, Kate: Les *couleurs et leurs effets sur la nature humaine,* 132

Prévert, Jacques: *L'accent grave,* 56–57; *Déjeuner du matin,* 336–337
Tours Guadeloupe Nature, 444
Vivre vert, 432
-re verbs,
conditional, 330
future, 352
passé composé, 276
present, 276
subjunctive, 394
Reciprocal verbs, *See pronominal verbs.*
Reflexive verbs, *See pronominal verbs.*
Relationships, vocabulary about, 270, 284
Relative pronouns, 286
Restaurants, vocabulary for, 304–306, 308–309

S
savoir,
conditional, 364
future, 364
imperfect, 364
passé composé, 364
present, 364
subjunctive, 396
vs. **connaître,** 364
School, vocabulary related to, 20, 22, 44, 50
Seasons, vocabulary for, 194
Sélection musicale, 40, 48, 52, 76, 88, 108, 121, 128, 146, 154, 158, 164, 183, 191, 194, 200, 226, 233, 240, 244, 262, 270, 272, 276, 280, 284, 286, 307, 314, 324, 330, 350, 352, 358, 364, 366, 370, 388, 396, 400, 408
Shopping, vocabulary for, 201, 314–316
sortir,
passé composé, 190, 234
present, 234
subjunctive, 394
Spelling-change verbs, 80, 265, 330, 352
Sports, vocabulary for, 38, 68, 70, 198
Stagiaires, Les, 54–55, 92–93, 130–131, 166–167, 206–207, 246–247, 288–289, 334–335, 372–373, 410–411
Subject pronouns, 40
Subjunctive,
formation, 394–396
used after expressions of emotion, 400, 404
used after impersonal expressions, 394, 404
with expressions of desire, 400, 404
with irregular verbs, 395, 396
vs. the infinitive, 404
Suggestions, making, 154

T
Time,
expressions, 12, 16–17, 24, 158, 192
official, 24
telling, 16–17
Transportation, vocabulary for, 162
tu vs. **vous,** 40

U
University, vocabulary related to, 20, 22, 44–45, 50

V
Vacation, vocabulary related to, 350, 362
venir,
conditional, 330
future, 352
passé composé, 190
present, 164
subjunctive, 395
Verbs,
-er, 76
-ir, 326
-re, 276

vieux, 34, 48
Vocabulary
addresses, 126
age, expressing, 144, 146
alphabet, 22
body, parts of, 392
café and restaurant, 88, 304–306
classroom expressions, 20, 22
clothes, 200–201
colors, 120
countries, 368
courses, 50
daily activities, 68, 74, 82, 150, 156, 198, 230, 236, 262, 278
dates, 160
days of the week, 12
describing oneself and other people, 14, 32, 34, 38, 40, 144, 146
directions, 406
errands, 398
fairy tales, 242
family members, 144–145
food, 88, 304–305, 314–316, 322–323
French first names, 22
furnishings, 114, 120
geography, 368, 370
greetings, 6, 8
health, 328, 392
holidays, 160, 188
hotel, 386–387
household chores, 198
housing, 108–109
invitations, 68–69, 224
languages, 14, 50
leisure activities, 68–69, 74–75, 150, 156, 182, 198
months, 160
movies, 225
neighborhood places, 44–45, 398
numbers, 10, 90, 110
pastimes, 68–69, 74–75, 150, 156, 182, 198
possessions, 114, 120
quantities, 46, 116, 310, 318, 320
question words, 84
school, 20, 22, 44, 50
seasons, 194
shopping, 201, 314–316
sports, 38, 68, 70, 198
time, expressions of, 12, 16–17, 158
time, telling, 16–17
transportation, 162
travel, 350, 356, 362
university, 20, 22, 44–45, 50
vacation, 188, 350, 356, 362
weather, 194, 196
voir,
conditional, 330
future, 352
vouloir,
conditional, 330
future, 352
passé composé, 226
present, 226
subjunctive, 396
vous vs. **tu,** 40
Vowel sounds, 8, 10, 21
bel, nouvel, and **vieil** before, 48
cet before, 128
liaison before, 6, 16, 46, 52, 77, 86, 116
nasal, 10
voyager, verbs like, 80, 232

W
Weather, vocabulary for, 194, 196
Week, days of the, 12

Y
y, 152, 190, 408